PRAISE FOR *Successful Direct Marketing Methods*

SEVENTH EDITION

BY BOB STONE AND RON JACOBS

"The new edition of *Successful Direct Marketing Methods* is the only reference I could imagine replacing my trusted and now dog-eared sixth edition. With all this new material, it is another major contribution to the industry."

> Peter J. Rosenwald
> VP Direct Marketing Group Abril, Brazil
> Creator and author of ACPO computer
> model and book: *Successful Economic
> Planning for Direct and Data Driven
> Marketing and CRM*

"Rarely does a new edition of a book meet our expectations. This one does and then some! Bob Stone and Ron Jacobs have given all of us—from novice to seasoned practitioner—the single most comprehensive and contemporary tool in direct marketing. It is rich in its coverage of the expanded direct marketing landscape. The examples are great and topical. I can't imagine anyone in direct marketing not finding it indispensible."

> Jerry I. Reitman
> Executive Vice President (retired)
> The Leo Burnett Company
> Author of *Beyond 2000: The Future of
> Direct Marketing*

"Once again, Bob Stone has re-invented direct marketing. His seventh edition of *Successful Direct Marketing Methods*, now with Ron Jacobs, has successfully identified the convergence of direct, database, and the new electronic communication systems. It's the cutting edge and beyond for all marketers who have an interest in dealing directly with their customers and prospects no matter what the medium. Bravo for Bob and Ron."

> Don E. Schultz, Ph.D
> Professor, Integrated Marketing
> Communications
> Northwestern University
> Evanston, IL

"For over twenty years in this business, I have kept the latest edition of *Successful Direct Marketing Methods* near my desk. This new edition is essential to me now that I've become CEO of an on-line direct marketing company, because Bob Stone and Ron Jacobs have done such a good job of laying out the essentials for the new era of one to one marketing on-line."

George S. Wiedemann
President, and CEO
Responsys.com

"If you want to be the best in direct marketing, please read, re-read and read again the new version of *Successful Direct Marketing Methods* by Bob Stone and Ron Jacobs. Written in plain English, this classic text combines the wisdom of years in the business illustrated by great case studies, with the latest thinking on everything that is 'E.'"

Wendy Riches
President, Marketing
Communications Group
D'Arcy

"*Successful Direct Marketing Methods* is without a doubt the most thorough, straightforward, and informative book available on direct marketing. The insight, knowledge, and experience shared by Bob Stone in the seventh edition of *Successful Direct Marketing Methods* is matched only by the progressive outlook of his coauthor Ron Jacobs. As the direct marketing industry continues to grow at such a rapid pace, it is essential we have one central resource to fall back upon which clearly states the defining principles, practices, and applications of the direct marketing discipline. This book represents that one key resource for clients, agencies, and students of direct marketing."

John R. Goodman
Senior Vice President
Helzberg Diamonds (a Berkshire
Hathaway company)

"Bob Stone and Ron Jacobs have done an extraordinary job in updating and expanding this seventh edition of *Successful Direct Marketing Methods*. The result is a totally current, comprehensive, and authoritative marketing corpus for students and executives alike. In this new edition, Stone and Jacobs present a compelling guide to understanding and profiting from the shockwaves of change that have shattered the mass market into pieces as small as a single customer, driving relevancy in marketing and rewriting all the rules."

Daniel Morel
Chairman and CEO Worldwide
impiric

SUCCESSFUL DIRECT MARKETING METHODS

Seventh Edition

SUCCESSFUL DIRECT MARKETING METHODS

Seventh Edition

BOB STONE and Ron Jacobs

McGraw-Hill

Chicago   New York   San Francisco   Lisbon   London   Madrid   Mexico City
Milan   New Delhi   San Juan   Seoul   Singapore   Sydney   Toronto

Library of Congress Cataloging-in-Publication Data

Stone, Bob, 1918–
      Successful direct marketing methods / Bob Stone and Ron Jacobs. — 7th ed.
         p.   cm.
      Includes index.
      ISBN 0-658-00145-0
      1. Direct Marketing.   I. Jacobs, Ron, 1948–   II. Title.

HF5415.126 .S757   2001
658.8'4—dc21   00-67572

   5 6 7 8 9 0   LBM/LBM   0 9 8 7 6 5 4

ISBN 0-658-00145-0

Cover design by Nick Panos

McGraw-Hill books are available at special quantity discounts to use as premiums and
sales promotions, or for use in corporate training programs. For more information, please
write to the Director of Special Sales, Professional Publishing, McGraw-Hill, Two Penn
Plaza, New York, NY 10121-2298. Or contact your local bookstore.

This book is printed on acid-free paper.

CONTENTS

SECTION ONE
Direct Marketing Essentials

SECTION TWO
Media of Direct Marketing

SECTION THREE
Internet Direct Marketing

SECTION FOUR
Managing the Creative Process

SECTION FIVE
Marketing to Businesses

SECTION SIX
Marketing Intelligence

ABOUT THE AUTHORS

Bob Stone

Chairman Emeritus, Stone & Adler, Inc.
President, Bob Stone, Inc.

Member of Direct Marketing Hall of Fame. Eight-time winner of the Direct Marketing Association's Best of Industry Award. Recipient of the Charles S. Downes Award for direct marketing contributions. Recipient of the Edward N. Mayer, Jr. Award for contributions to direct marketing education and two Gold Echo Awards, as well as the John Caples Award for copy excellence.

Bob Stone was a feature columnist in *Advertising Age* for 12 years, writing more than 200 articles on the subject of direct marketing. He is the author of *Successful Direct Marketing Methods*, now in its seventh edition (over 200,000 copies in print, including foreign editions). He has also authored *Direct Marketing Success Stories* and coauthored *Successful Telemarketing*. NTC Business Books of Lincolnwood, Illinois, is the publisher of Stone's books.

Stone has taught degree programs at Northwestern University and the University of Missouri. He has lectured extensively in the United States, Europe, Asia, and Australia. He is a Former Director, Direct Marketing Association; Former President, Chicago Association of Direct Marketing; Former President, Associated Third Class Mail Users; and Former Trustee, Direct Marketing Educational Foundation.

Ron Jacobs

President, Jacobs & Clevenger, Inc.

Founder of an integrated marketing and professional services agency with a focus on customer relationship marketing, Jacobs is also Senior Lecturer in the

Medill/Integrated Marketing Communications Program, Northwestern University, where he teaches interactive marketing and E-commerce. He was Program Coordinator for the Certificate of Direct Marketing Program at DePaul University from 1991 to 1995. Ron is a 1994 recipient of the Direct Marketing Educational Foundation's Outstanding Direct Marketing Educator Award.

A frequent speaker in the United States and internationally, Jacobs is the author of articles on such direct marketing issues as customer acquisition, database development, interactive/new media, business-to-business campaigns, integrated marketing communications, privacy, and customer relationship management.

Jacobs is on the DMA Information and Interactive Tech Council and served as Vice Chair 1997–99 and E-commerce Chair 1998–99. He has served as an expert witness on the uses of consumer data and privacy. He is on the Advisory Board for the DMA Political Action Committee.

A past president of the Chicago Association of Direct Marketing, Ron has served as a Trustee of the Chicago Association of Direct Marketing Educational Foundation and is past General Chairman of CADM's Educational Foundation Campaign Committee. He was CADM's 1998 Direct Marketer of the Year. Prior to beginning his direct marketing career, Ron spent 10 years with Trans World Airlines, where he worked in customer service, operations, and agency sales.

FOREWORD

Since the sixth edition of *Successful Direct Marketing Methods* in 1997, the direct marketing business has experienced some of the most rapid and radical changes to occur in decades—if not in its entire history, which dates back to shortly after Johann Gutenberg's printing press. Bob Stone and Ron Jacobs recognize and understand these changes, and this book offers all a chance to share those insights.

Of course, the changes I refer to, in large part, involve the Internet and related technologies, which are having a powerful, revolutionary impact on the industry.

The Internet is collapsing marketplace borders, giving rise to a true "Global Village" . . . and the best is yet to come!

The historic seller-focused marketing paradigm is shifting rapidly toward one that is customer-centric. Certainly, the marketing aphorism "the Customer Is King" has never been truer than it is today, in an environment where the customer is increasingly in control.

The solid walls of trade built in the Industrial Age are tumbling in the Information Age. In other words, the days of circuitously moving a product from the manufacturer to the end-user are giving way to a sleek, fast, direct-to-purchaser model.

Obviously, the Web presents a new—and very powerful—medium with which to market to people. Interestingly, direct marketers are ahead of the E-commerce curve, with many showing profitable websites in an environment where profits have been, to date, hard to find.

While sales are the most obvious means of measuring a website's "success," direct marketers are keenly aware of other "nonmonetary" benefits of a site. For example, they are finding that a website is a useful way of branding their products and company, facilitating customer service, and contributing in other ways that will turn the casual on-line visitor into a "lifetime customer."

How is it that the direct marketing industry has employed the new media as effectively—and as profitably—as they have in these early days of E-commerce?

The primary answer, I believe, is that the direct marketing industry possesses the expertise and the processes that are at the foundation of the Internet's commercial applications. For example, direct marketers' order-taking and fulfillment processes, database capabilities, and sophisticated customer service systems are vital to E-commerce.

Clearly, direct marketers are well poised for the digital business environment. This, however, by no way means that the more traditional direct marketing methods are being left by the wayside in deference to the Internet. On the contrary, as we move forward we are not so much abandoning our roots as *returning* to them.

The Internet and its technology are allowing us to return to the days of true one-to-one relationships, allowing us to replicate the personal relationship that took place between merchant and customer across the counter of the general store. The highly personalized and direct nature of the Web provides marketers the opportunity to develop closer relationships and build on some of direct marketing's earliest traditions.

In addition, as this new technology has emerged we have experienced a melding of the "old" and "new." The result has been a potent combination that far exceeds the sum of its parts. In fact, this marriage has contributed to ever-increasing direct marketing revenues, which are quickly approaching $2 trillion annually in the United States alone.

I am pleased to say that this complex mix of old and new is fully appreciated and clearly explained in the seventh edition of this book. In short, extensively revised from cover to cover, this edition of *Successful Direct Marketing Methods* is a remarkably clear and accurate representation of the state of direct marketing practices and the industry in general.

Far from treating the Internet as an isolated factor in our industry, this edition deftly weaves new technology throughout the discussion of every direct marketing method, leaving no new or traditional method overlooked or underappreciated.

However, this thorough and "holistic" approach comes as no surprise for those of us who have known—and relied on—Bob Stone and his work over the decades. Bob has always had an uncanny ability to take the pulse of the direct marketing industry and predict where it is headed. It is a talent that has made him one of the most trusted and respected veterans of our industry. It also explains why Bob was one of the first industry leaders to be inducted into the Direct Marketing Association's Hall of Fame back in 1979.

Furthermore, in this edition for the 21st century, Bob's knowledge and understanding of the industry is complemented by the expertise of Ron Jacobs, an industry practitioner and educator whose influence and expertise are deservedly well-respected and widely recognized.

It is an amazing time to be a marketer. I envy those of you who are embarking on a career in this field, because the future is definitely going to be an exciting place to be.

Certainly, Bob Stone and Ron Jacobs have written a book that is a veritable map for the marketer who wishes to survive—and prosper—in the increasingly borderless Digital Marketplace. Read . . . and learn from the masters!

H. Robert Wientzen
President & CEO
Direct Marketing Association
New York City
Washington, D.C.

PREFACE

Welcome to the seventh edition of *Successful Direct Marketing Methods*. This marks the 26th anniversary of the first edition, published in 1975.

In 1975, SDMM was the only book published on the totality of direct marketing. Not so today. I have two shelves of books on the subject. That's testimony to the acceptance and growth of the discipline.

Each of the previous editions—published three to four years apart—was really a historic way of capturing the maturation of direct marketing. This, the seventh edition, has been created to be in cadence with what a new century has to offer. It is a new book in almost every way.

A new vocabulary has emerged, with new words and terms. Internet, website, E-mail, On-line, E-commerce, opt-in and opt-out, predictive modeling, regression analysis, data mining, data warehouses, data marts. Acronyms like CRM, LTV, RFM, ROI, CPO, CPI, and scores more.

As I contemplated a new millennium edition that would be state-of-the-art, it became obvious to me that the content of the edition could be maximized if I had an outstanding coauthor. As it turned out, I knew, without a doubt, who that person was.

My first and only choice was Ron Jacobs, President and CEO of Jacobs & Clevenger, Chicago. My experiences with Ron date back to 1990–91 when he rose from Account Executive to Account Manager at Stone & Adler. Among the accounts he served were Amoco Oil, AT&T, Meredith, and Old American Insurance Company.

In 1982, Ron Jacobs took the giant step: he started his own direct marketing advertising agency. The stature of clients Jacobs & Clevenger has served speaks for its success. They include the Americast division of Ameritech, American Dental Association, Baxter Healthcare, General Electric, Harris Bank, Hewlett-Packard, IBM, and Microsoft.

Not unlike many truly successful people, Ron gives freely of himself. He is a longtime member of the Direct Marketing Association. He is a past president of the Chicago Association of Direct Marketing, has been a trustee of the CADM Educational Foundation, and was selected as a Distinguished Direct Marketing Educator in 1994 by the Direct Marketing Educational Foundation. In 1998, Ron Jacobs received the Charles S. Downs Award as the Direct Marketer of the Year.

As impressed as I am with the business acumen of my coauthor, it was his ability to teach future direct marketing aspirants that made him my unquestioned choice. Ron has been Adjunct Professor at both DePaul University and Northwestern University.

Just how "new" is the seventh edition of *Successful Direct Marketing Methods*? New enough to encompass all of the topics whose vocabulary so impressed me. Every chapter takes into account, in some way, the astounding impact of the Internet on direct marketing.

Since there is emphatic treatment of new media in this edition, I feel it is important to point out that it is not our intent to favor "new" media over "old" media.

To put the value of new media in perspective with old media, consider these analogies: when TV came on the scene, it did not replace radio. When cable came on the scene, it did not replace standard TV. E-mail will not replace direct mail. Websites will not replace catalogs.

Newspapers and magazines, radio and television—all have made accommodations with the Internet, providing supplementary material on the Net to support lead stories and features. Bottom line, the integration of media has made communication more bountiful and more meaningful.

This preface prompts two questions: (1) How did direct marketing achieve the stature it enjoys today? And (2) where is direct marketing going from here? In my opinion, knowing how we got here is essential to determining where we are going.

The most precise way to measure growth, I have found, is to track it through the accomplishments of people who possess two vital traits—vision and passion. Direct marketing has been fueled by an abundance of visionaries whose passions have swept most obstacles aside.

The most active gestation period in my career has been from 1965 to the year 2000. All of the folks you are about to meet have been active within that time frame.

The year was 1965. Two visionairies were having lunch together. One was Ed Mayer, the guru of direct mail at the time. The other was Lew Kleid, a prominent list broker. They were bemoaning the paucity of direct mail education at the college level. No courses were being taught. Marketing textbooks gave little if any attention to direct mail.

Lew said to Ed, "If you will do a one-week seminar for college kids, I'll underwrite the cost." This led to the Collegiate Institute, which has introduced direct mail/direct marketing to thousands of college students.

In March 1967 the DMAA Educational Foundation was formed, and John Yeck of Yeck Brothers of Dayton, Ohio, became its first chairman. John's vision and passion—often at the expense of his direct marketing agency—kept him at the helm of the foundation's Board of Trustees until his death in 1999.

The most dramatic growth of the Educational Foundation took place in the 1980s. Two magnificent professionals came on board: Laurie Spar became a director and Dr. Richard Montesi became president.

Laurie Spar, always performing behind the scenes, has spent a major part of her career steering educators our way, all the while opening doors for college students. (See her dissertation on careers in direct marketing in the Appendix.)

The accomplishments of Dr. Montesi since his appointment as president are legend. From a handful of programs in 1980 (mostly for students), 15 years later DMEF would be holding more than 20 events each year.

And from 1980 to the year 2000, the number of students and educators on the alumni roster tripled. The number of direct marketing courses and degree, certificate, and diploma programs offered at colleges and universities expanded 1,000 percent.

The vision and passion that has taken the Direct Marketing Educational Foundation to where it is today could not have happened without the support of the Direct Marketing Association and Bob DeLay, who served as president of that association for 25 years.

When talking about Bob DeLay, in addition to his traits of vision and passion, you have to add guts. When he took over as president, he found the coffers depleted, the morale at low ebb, and the membership made up, for the most part, of firms of little distinction.

During his regime, the association became solvent, the number and quality of members improved substantially, government affairs committees were formed, seminars were put on in key cities, as well as public relations programs dealing with consumer issues and spring and fall conferences; all were professionally choreographed and staged. Education at all levels became a key goal.

Bob DeLay was the right person at the right time, as was his successor—Jonah Gitlitz. Jonah brought trade association experience to the job. Washington, D.C., was his home, and Jonah Gitlitz was at home in the area of government affairs.

Once more we seem to have the right person at the right time in Bob Wientzen, the current president of the DMA. Procter & Gamble bred, he espouses the one-page memo—Bob is high-tech personified. DMA is ready to take on the 21st century.

This preface would not be complete if I did not conclude it with another person driven by vision and passion—Martin Baier, a distinguished member of the Direct Marketing Hall of Fame. In 1969, Martin Baier was Vice President and Marketing Director of Old American Insurance Company of Kansas City, Missouri. Old American sold insurance by mail. An alumnus of the University of Missouri, Martin convinced the dean of the business school that the time had come to include a course on direct marketing. The course was called Elements of Direct Marketing and it rapidly became a popular elective.

Twenty years later Martin was teaching the same course, but as time went by, his vision had expanded to a degree program in direct marketing. In 1983 the Direct Marketing Educational Foundation became the catalyst for funding such a graduate program. The sum required was in the neighborhood of half a million dollars.

It was my privilege to write a fund-raising letter that fortunately brought an almost unbelievable response from members of the Direct Marketing Association. The mailing—a five-page letter—plus a number of personal solicitations, accomplished the financial goals. Thus did Martin Baier ignite the flame of many. It was the "impossible dream" come true.

I believe this answers the question: How did direct marketing reach the stature it enjoys today? The second question—Where is direct marketing going from here?—is in your capable hands.

My vision is one of decades and decades in which the bar will be raised higher and higher, peopled by successors in the images of Ron Jacobs, Ed Mayer, Lew Kleid, John Yeck, Laurie Spar, Dr. Richard Montesi, Martin Baier, Bob DeLay, Jonah Gitlitz, and Bob Wientzen.

May all your direct marketing methods be successful.

Bob Stone

ACKNOWLEDGMENTS

As with all editions of *Successful Direct Marketing Methods*, this seventh edition reflects the combined thinking of many outstanding authorities.

Particular thanks go to Laurie Spar, Vice President of the Direct Marketing Educational Foundation, for her contributions to the Appendix, as well as to the staff of the Direct Marketing Association, for their contributions to the text.

Academia in general has embraced direct marketing as an integral part of the total marketing curriculum, especially in the last decade. Hence this new edition benefits from cases not previously available. Special recognition goes to Steve Kelly, Director of the Institute for Interactive and Direct Marketing at DePaul University, as well as Assistant Director, Juliet Hart. And the following professors have been generous contributors as well: Professor Carla Johnson, St. Mary's College, Notre Dame, Indiana; Professor Donald W. Eckrich, Ph.D., Ithaca College, New York; Professor Eve Caudill, Mendoza School of Business, University of Notre Dame, Indiana; Professor Monle Lee, Indiana University—South Bend; Professor Scott Erickson, SUNY at Oneonta, New York; Sarah Wortman, formerly of DePaul University, Chicago; Professor Carol Ann Hackley, APR, University of the Pacific, Stockton, California; and Professor Mary Alice Shaver, Michigan State University, East Lansing.

However, lest anyone be concerned, we hasten to point out that this new edition, like all that preceded it, caters to the total needs of the practitioner. As a matter of fact, some of direct marketing's most respected practitioners have contributed to this book. Jack Schmid, for example, is known nationally and internationally as one of the foremost catalog authorities in the world. His agency, J. Schmid & Associates, Inc., of Shawnee Mission, Kansas, has clients such as Hershey Foods, Xerox Corporation, Fingerhut, Anheuser-Bush, New Pig Corporation, Sara Lee, Hallmark Cards, Marks & Spencer, Wolferman's Inc., Radio Shack (United Kingdom), and Sears (Canada). He is also the author of *Starting and Growing a Catalog Business*.

We can guarantee that his contribution to Chapter 15, "Creating and Managing Catalogs," is state-of-the-art.

Not to be overlooked in our acknowledgments is Rich Simms of Dial America, who helped bring new thinking to the teleservices chapter. We also appreciate contributions from Ron Bliwas, Ed Malthouse, Frank Mulhern, Bruce Wexler, and Bart Zeller in their respective fields of expertise.

John Miglautsch of Miglautsch Marketing, Waukesh, Wisconsin, has made major contributions to Chapter 3, "The Impact of Databases" and Chapter 19, "Modeling for Business Decision Support." John is a no-nonsense guy who takes the mystery out of theories.

Vic Hunter's contribution to Chapter Seventeen, "Business-to-Business Direct Marketing," is significant. Hunter, founder and president of Hunter Business Direct, Inc., clearly spells out the specific differences between consumer direct marketing and business-to-business direct marketing using an approach that has proved highly successful for many Fortune 500 companies. He is also the author of *Business-to-Business Marketing: Creating a Community of Customers* and a widely sought-after lecturer.

When it comes to lead-generation programs, on the other hand, there are specific techniques for both business-to-consumer and business-to-business. We are indebted to Bette Anne Duffy, senior partner and director of client services at OgilvyOne Worldwide, for major contributions to Chapter 18, "Managing a Lead-Generation Program." Her clients include IBM, AT&T, Sears, and Ameritrade.

For Chapter 20, "Mathematics of Direct Marketing," we are indebted to Bob Kestnbaum, founder of Kestnbaum & Company, and especially to Pamela Ames, vice president there for 22 years. The Kestnbaum organization has served all the major mail order houses and airlines, as well as telephone companies, banks, insurance companies, and automotive manufacturers.

Thanks also to our editors, Danielle Egan-Miller and Anne Basye, our draft editor, Nancy Snider, and typist, Shirley Bachrach.

Bob Stone
Ron Jacobs

DIRECT MARKETING
ESSENTIALS

THE SCOPE OF
DIRECT MARKETING

In little more than a century, direct marketing has grown beyond its roots in traditional mail order to embrace a host of new technologies, customer relationship-building techniques, and performance measures that set the bar for the future of marketing communications. It's become a powerful tool that every business should consider as part of an overall integrated marketing strategy.

Early Americans could order seeds and a host of products not available across the 13 colonies. By the end of the 19th century, many companies selling direct to consumers were serving the needs of a rapidly growing rural America. They brought convenience, breadth of style, and value to a rapidly expanding consumer population. Mail order companies offered ready-to-wear clothing, in the latest fashion, at a time when many Americans still wore clothing tailored from fabric purchased at a local dry goods store. They also sold a breadth of products for home or farm use—even prefabricated homes and barns.

A hundred years later, at the beginning of a new millennium, we see a resurgence of the traditional mail order business in the form of Internet E-commerce. Many of the marketing techniques, promotional tools, and analyses that these new electronic marketers are engaged in have been proven over many decades. These tools and techniques have been adapted and proven successful well beyond direct marketing's initial roots.

Much of direct marketing's recent growth has been in nontraditional business categories. Credit card companies, banks, investment companies, and insurance all are heavy users of direct marketing. Telecom, cable, and utility companies are users. Airlines, associations, and automobile manufacturers all use direct marketing. From computers to electronics, hardly a category is missed. Even retailers and shopping centers use direct marketing to drive traffic into stores.

Businesses selling to other businesses are also heavy users of direct marketing, and this is an area growing faster than business-to-consumer selling in both dollar volume and number of employees. It may surpass consumer direct marketing in total revenues in the near future.

Today it's hard to imagine an organization that doesn't use direct marketing in one form or another. Long trumpeted as a stand-alone discipline, direct marketing has matured and taken its place as a key driver in the total marketing mix.

Economic Impact of Direct Marketing

The size and economic impact of direct marketing in the United States has been debated for decades. The Direct Marketing Association (DMA) commissioned the first study in 1992 to analyze the extent of direct marketing in the United States and to develop an economic model for forecasting purposes. The WEFA Group—a collaboration of Chase Econometrics and Wharton Economic Forecasting—was selected to conduct the study, which continues to be updated regularly.

A breakout of the portion of U.S. sales revenue attributed to direct marketing is shown in Exhibit 1–1. Expectations put sales growth in direct marketing at 8.8 percent annually from 1999 through 2004, which is significantly greater than anticipated growth in total U.S. sales revenue for the same five-year period (5.3 percent). Total U.S. sales revenue in 1998 was more than $18 trillion; the projection for 2003 is $23.8 trillion.

According to the latest WEFA study, U.S. sales revenue attributed to direct marketing for 1999 was estimated to be $1.5 trillion, growing to $2.3 trillion by 2004. As companies adapt to even more direct-to-buyer channels (e.g., on the Internet), that number will continue to grow precipitously; it is estimated that the rate of growth will be 14.8 percent yearly between 1999 and 2004.

It is significant that growth in direct marketing sales, at an annual rate of 8.8 percent, is expected to outpace growth of 5.3 percent annually in total U.S. sales. In business-to-business direct marketing, sales are expected to total $1.1 trillion in 2004, an estimated 10.3 percent annual growth rate, which is almost double the projected rate of growth for total U.S. sales.

Direct Marketing Defined

Continuing growth and development in the field makes it more difficult to reach consensus on a standard definition of direct marketing. Such terms as *targeted marketing*, *relationship marketing*, *database marketing*, *one-to-one marketing*, or *integrated marketing* often are substituted. Indeed, these terms seem to share a number of common elements, such as the ability to reach a specific audience, create or enhance customer bonding, create dialogue, or combine various media and disciplines. While the definition of *direct marketing* has evolved over time, the authors believe that the term direct marketing is still the best description for the tools and techniques used in these various endeavors.

EXHIBIT 1-1

The Growth of Direct Marketing

DMA WEFA Studies tracking the growth of direct marketing show that overall direct marketing sales continue to grow at an enormous rate. The use of direct marketing in business-to-business, nonstore retail, and E-commerce all impact this growth.

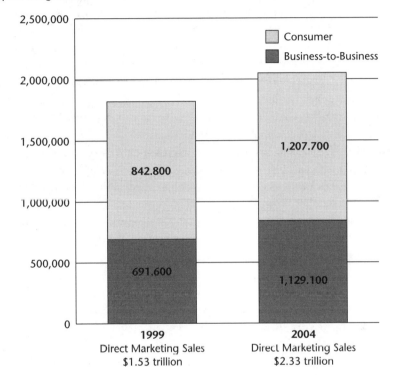

Source: DMA 1999 Economic Impact Study: US Direct Marketing & Interactive Today

The definition we have chosen is:

Direct Marketing is the interactive use of advertising media, to stimulate an (immediate) behavior modification in such a way that this behavior can be tracked, recorded, analyzed, and stored on a database for future retrieval and use.

While what direct marketing is called may be the source of some debate, the uniqueness of direct marketing is not. Let's elaborate on the chosen definition.

Interactive: One-on-one communications between marketer and prospect/customer is communication that initiates a dialogue. Two-way interaction is a fundamental building block of direct marketing.

Use of Advertising Media: Direct marketing is not restricted to any one medium. Indeed, direct marketers have discovered there is synergy among media. Using a combination of media is often more productive than using a single medium.

The variety of media available for direct marketing is ever expanding. Direct mail is just one medium. Magazines, newspapers, short form TV, infomercials, radio, transit advertising, and the telephone are all used. Much of the promotion on the Internet, from banner ads to E-mail, can be considered direct marketing.

Track, Record, and Analyze: Measurability is a hallmark of direct marketing. Every form of direct marketing activity, with rare exceptions, is measurable. Direct marketing programs become part of a history to learn from, with a variety of metrics that track spending, response, and return on investment. Internet marketing using E-mail or the World Wide Web is measurable, just like print advertising, telemarketing, direct mail, and broadcasting.

Stored in Database for Future Retrieval and Use: Databases are used to store compilations of known data about a prospect or customer, including their history of purchases, sources of response, credit rating, and so on. It's one thing to create history. A database stores this information in a way that it can be accessed—customer groups aggregated, segmented, identified—and used to make future programs more efficient. The use of a database is another fundamental building block of direct marketing.

Like most definitions of direct marketing, this one is media based. By using a media definition, it is easier to see how the objectives of direct marketing relate to other parts of the promotion mix (Advertising, Direct Marketing, Public Relations, Sales Promotion, Personal Selling).

However, direct marketing is more than just a media-based concept. Martin Baier, formerly vice president of marketing for Old American Insurance Company and now a consultant and educator, argues that this view sells direct marketing short. Baier argues for a more holistic view of direct marketing. In Volume 7, number 2 of the *Ruf Report*, Baier notes:

> *Direct marketing is a strategy . . . a discipline . . . a process . . . a philosophy of enterprise . . . an attitude . . . a collection of tools and techniques. Direct marketing is customer oriented, profit motivated, organizationally integrated, and strategy focused.*

> *Direct marketing is about creating new customers and cultivating current customers. Who are they? Where are they? How are they created? What is their lifetime value? These can be difficult questions to answer. Whether selling products or services electronically or by mail; generating leads for salespeople; creating retail traffic; fund-raising, or*

stimulating political action; direct marketing can be a powerful and highly effective tool.

Direct marketing is a philosophy and a process of marketing that has at its heart the needs, the desires, and the expectations of customers. It turns traditional views of business inside out by demonstrating that, instead of being in business to sell products or services, companies should be in business to establish and maintain relationships with customers. Customers are the lifeblood of any business. Without them, a business would languish and die.

Direct marketing can be traced back to mail order, a distribution system. Direct mail, an advertising medium, evolved from the mail order system. Today's direct marketing embraces both mail order and direct mail, along with all the other distribution channels and media.

The notion that direct marketing is "a collection of tools and techniques" resonates with longtime direct marketing practitioners. Seeing it as a purely media-based discipline limits the scope of direct marketing. What marketers have learned is that these various tools and techniques make up a kind of toolbox that can be translated across business categories, media, and marketing objectives.

As with any set of tools, you need to select the right ones for each program. Some will work; some won't. Some will work and others will work better. With the experience that comes from testing what works and what doesn't, direct marketing practitioners are able to select the most appropriate techniques for each objective, each campaign, each category, and each client. As new methods of marketing communications and selling evolve (e.g., banner ads, E-mail, E-commerce, etc.), many of the same tools and techniques are proving applicable.

The Basics of Direct Marketing

The basic purpose of any direct marketing program is to get a measurable response that will produce an immediate or ultimate profit. To create a measurable response, there must be an offer—a call to action. An offer to sell a product or service direct to a consumer or a business is but one way to create a measurable response. Offers that create leads for sales representatives, get people to inquire for information, build traffic in retail stores, and impel people to give to causes can also be measured.

Traditionally, direct marketers have identified lists/media, creative execution, and the offer as the key components to producing response. These decision variables can be divided into four parts, which we call the Elements of Promotion (see Exhibit 1–2), and ranked by importance: media/lists (40 percent), offer (30 percent), copy (15 percent), and layout (15 percent).

Elements of Promotion

This chart shows the weight given the elements of promotion in a direct marketing program. Creative (copy and layout) accounts for about 30 percent of the success of a program. The offer is equally important. However, unless you reach the right target group, even the best creative and offer will not work.

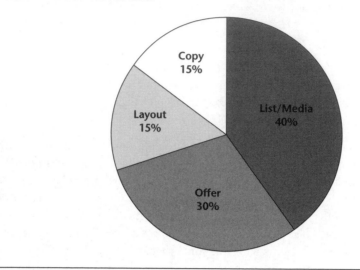

Choosing the best media/lists is the key to reaching the right target group. This is true whether you are mailing to prospects or trying to reach them with a television, radio, newspaper, or magazine campaign. Even on the Internet it's key to bringing together the right buyers and the right sellers.

The best creative or offer may not generate any response if the target group doesn't find the product or service relevant to its needs. Conversely, badly executed creative or a poorly formulated offer will depress response to the right target group, but not completely eliminate it.

Marketers continue to enhance their ability to reach the best target groups using direct mail. Lists that contain only names of individuals or business firms are being supplanted by enhanced databases that help profile prospects and customers and make it possible to target specific market segments. Profiling allows users to target prospects more effectively, identify and build relationships with their best customers, increase the relevancy of their offers, and improve their return on investment.

Many media forms can be selected geographically, demographically, or psychographically (by lifestyle). Newspapers can be selected by day of week or section to reach a target group (e.g., food day, business section, classifieds, Sunday magazine, etc.). Television can be selected by program type, day part, or network. Cable, local stations, and even major networks program against different demographics, targeting broad or narrow niches such as young adults, sports enthusiasts, women, families, and ethnic groups. The choices among consumer and business publications are incredibly broad and include thousands of titles.

The Internet has also grown into an advertising medium. Thousands of websites accept advertising, each serving different interests and niches. Much Web advertising is intended to generate a click to another website, an action that can be measured and tracked like other direct marketing media.

The offer, also known as the proposition, is another key to success. It is the terms under which a specific product, service, or brand is promoted, i.e., the promise of the transaction. It includes a mix of factors that motivate individuals within the target group to respond—the product or service, price, payment terms, guarantee, and incentives. Creative execution is used to package the offer in the most flattering way. If the offer doesn't convey perceived value, response suffers.

Creative execution, or the two elements of copy and layout or design, is not ranked as high as media or the offer. However, it is a mistake to assume that different degrees of creative make little or no difference. To the contrary, given the right lists and the right offers, superlative creative often increases response by 50 percent or more. Results like this are no accident. They start with customer insights that help the creative team get into the head of the reader. Creative must always be about how the customers' lives will be better, how the product or service solves their problems or will make them more successful at some endeavor. And it should involve the reader, stimulating emotions that can evoke response.

Brilliant direct marketing creative often starts with copy. To compel readers to respond, copy needs to give them rationales on why they should believe the offer, convince them they can trust the organization making the offer, and assure them that they won't make a mistake by responding.

Most direct response copy falls into four categories: benefits, description , support copy, and sweeteners and facilitators.

Benefits are the most important kind of copy, showing how the product or service will improve the potential responder's life. Descriptive copy replaces personal examination (i.e., the ability to touch, feel, or try out a product or service) before purchase. Support copy validates the claimed benefits (e.g., data, statistics, research, case studies, testimonials, etc.). Sweeteners and facilitators "sweeten" the offer. Sandra J. Blum, in *Designing Direct Mail That Sells*, declares that sweeteners give the reader more reasons to take the offer by using incentives, offering choices, reducing anxiety, and making it easier to respond or pay.

Direct marketing design builds on the copy. It should enhance the copy and graphics by making the most of the natural eye flow and eye path of the reader. Design should make it easier for the reader to continue reading, rather than putting the copy down and not continuing. Speaking of the elements within a direct mail package or in a complete campaign, Heiki Ratalahti, one of the foremost direct marketing designers, said, " . . . they should bear a family resemblance, or at least an interconnectedness." He continued, "To be successful, they should more or less tell the same story in more or less the same way. They should also more or less look like they've met before."

Measuring Customer Value

The ultimate objective of a successful direct marketing program is to build the long-term or lifetime value of a customer. This objective applies whether direct marketing methods are applied solely to a mail order business or to other channels of distribution. Either way, the customer database is available to cultivate customers.

As later chapters will reveal, direct marketers often avail themselves of rather sophisticated calculations. However, four terms—long-term or lifetime value (LTV), recency, frequency, monetary (RFM)—summarize the financial dimensions of direct marketing. Brief definitions will be sufficient at this point.

> *Lifetime value* (LTV) (also called long-term value): The total of financial transactions with a customer over the life of a relationship
> *Recency*: The amount of time since a person or firm last purchased
> *Frequency*: The number of times a customer buys within a season or a year
> *Monetary*: The amount of money a customer spends within a season or a year

Knowing the lifetime value of a customer reveals how much time and resources a marketer can afford to invest in a customer and still realize a satisfactory profit. A typical customer database includes information on recency (date of last purchase), frequency (number of purchases within a given period), and monetary (amount spent). Applying these criteria and looking at the results in different ways enables the marketer to identify segments of the customer base that offer the greatest profit potential. Practitioners of direct marketing have always pointed to measurability as a key reason for direct marketing's continued growth. As marketers have demanded more accountability from their advertising expenditures, direct marketing has benefited.

Marketers began to seek greater efficiency in their communications programs as a consumer marketplace dominated by nuclear families who could be reached through national media advertising vanished, replaced by a highly segmented marketplace served by a variety of media. Instead of seeking to capture as large a share of market as possible, marketers now seek to capture the greatest share of a particular customer segment. In many companies, promoting to prospects and customers is seen as an investment. And, like other investments, advertising dollars are held accountable for creating specific results.

Marketers are asking tough questions about their promotional programs. How do they make them measurable? How do they reach markets splintered into hundreds or thousands of subsegments? How do they use media fragmented to reach fewer and fewer people? And, how do they reach segments of one? For a growing number, the answer is applying the tools and techniques of direct marketing.

Building Customer Loyalty

Another of direct marketing's uses is in growing and maintaining customer loyalty. In many markets, such as long distance and wireless telephones, Internet service providers, and credit cards, "churn" (the rate of customer defection) is very high. Customers are often attracted by the use of low, short-term, promotional rates. Once these rates expire, customers exposed to similar rates from competitors often move to a competitor to take advantage of savings. In these cases, customer loyalty spells the difference between keeping and losing a customer.

Maintaining customer loyalty is important for all companies. It can cost five to ten times more to create a customer than it does to keep one. Ongoing customers are an important source of referrals and continued sales; they will pay increased prices if they believe they are getting value for the goods or services. As a result, reducing customer defections as little as 5 percent may increase profits by 25 to 85 percent.

A focus on profits or return on investment is important. Bob Stone discovered many years ago that, on average, 80 percent of profit from a customer base is likely to come from 20 percent of the total list.

The challenge is to identify the non-profitable segments of the customer base and to build their loyalty. The tools and techniques of direct marketing made such goals possible.

One-to-One and Customer Relationship Marketing

The tools and techniques of direct marketing also facilitate personalized customer communications. Using information in customer databases about customer behavior or demographics, companies can target the wants and needs of individual customers, thus building stronger customer loyalty and individualizing the total customer experience. This kind of marketing has become known as one-to-one marketing.

Many people use the terms one-to-one marketing and direct marketing interchangeably because many of the same tools and techniques are used for both. The difference between them is mainly in how solutions are approached. One-to-one marketing often involves direct interaction with an individual customer and then some form of mass customized treatment of that customer.

Don Peppers, a chief proponent of one-to-one marketing, believes that a diligent application of one-to-one marketing principles will prompt a business to find products and services for the customers it knows rather than finding customers for the products it has on hand: "The one-to-one marketer looks at the entire marketing proposition from the other end of the binoculars . . . from the customer's perspective."

Pepper's point, that the one-to-one marketer finds or creates product(s) for the customer rather than finding customers for the product(s), is valid. This is how traditional direct marketers built their businesses. Gaining customer insight through research that identifies the wants and needs of customers is key to the success of direct marketing. Mining the data that organizations already have about their customers is another.

Much information about customers has been locked up in databases created for purposes other than marketing. In the past these large mainframe "legacy systems" remained difficult if not impossible for marketers to gain access to. Marketing, sales, and customer service staffs were also often separated by hierarchies and silos that kept them from sharing information and ideas. This changed as top management in corporations began to adapt a concept known as Customer Relationship Marketing.

CRM practitioners use many of the same data technologies used in direct and database marketing. But they use this technology to seamlessly integrate every area of a business that affects customers, including marketing, sales, and customer service. CRM strives to make information a driving force within the organization, not just within the marketing department. Recovering, managing, and using information from legacy or from new systems becomes a goal of CRM. This is a fundamental shift in control of the demand side of business.

The success of the CRM concept is echoed by many of the ideas explored in this book. CRM uses contact strategies based on defining customer needs—identifying the value of a relationship; investing in customers according to their worth; integrating all contact channels in the plan (advertising, direct mail, promotion, sales, call centers, E-mail, Internet, etc.)—supported by sophisticated information systems, capable staff, and quantifying and measuring results.

These systems allow organizations that might not consider using "direct marketing" to market directly to consumers with ease. Pharmaceutical makers, tobacco companies, and automobile manufacturers have adapted CRM, as well as firms marketing directly to businesses. CRM communications programs use the tools and techniques of direct marketing to efficiently use the information that they have mined from their vast databases.

These concepts have gained rapid acceptance on the Internet. Popular websites have millions of click-throughs (CTRs) a day. The ability to capture new pieces of data about each user creates an astounding opportunity for direct marketers.

Successful CRM programs are a convergence of traditional direct marketing techniques, database marketing decision support tools, and digital marketing capabilities (see Exhibit 1–3). This convergence is creating new genres of direct marketing that approach the individual communications promised by customer relationship marketing.

Customer Relationship Marketing

The convergence of direct, database, and digital marketing is resulting in new forms of mass customized, customer-centric promotions. It is a way of linking strategic, creative, and technical expertise to develop stronger and more profitable customer relationships by enabling the tools of Customer Relationship Marketing.

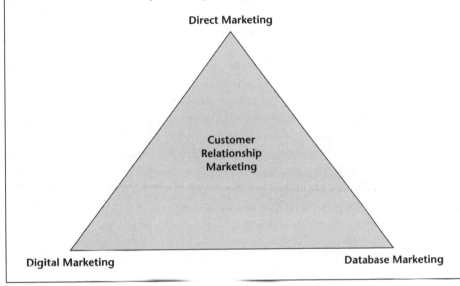

Mass Customization: Key to One-to-One Marketing

One-to-one marketers are increasingly using mass customization to provide customers with products and services that meet their needs.

In mass customization, mass market goods and services are individualized to satisfy a customer need at a reasonable price. Mass customization starts with a customer-company dialogue in which the company helps the customer articulate his or her needs and to identify the precise offering to fulfill those needs. The company then uses mass production techniques to create interchangeable parts, which keeps costs down while still giving the customer the choice that makes the product created for a market of one.

Motorola has used this collaborative built-to-order model to offer pagers in hundreds of combinations of cases, colors, and storage technologies. Dell has used this model for computers.

On the Internet, mass customization enables consumers to compile music CDs containing any combination of songs, obtain customized financial services (e.g., mortgages, investment services, credit cards, etc.), or design a one-of-a-kind Barbie.

Mass customized communications combine information technology and the creativity of advertising with the skill and focus of manufacturing and industrial engineering. Marrying these tools and techniques enables low-cost, totally customized messaging to deliver the "right message to the right person at the right time." This can be done with direct mail, E-mail, banner ads, and some forms of personalized print ads.

Integrated Communications

The tools and techniques of direct marketing work well alone for many kinds of offers. Mail order, financial services, insurance, lead generation, and traffic building are just some of the ways that direct marketing can be used successfully. Direct marketing is particularly powerful when used with customer segments where previous behavior can be used to predict future results.

The high cost-per-thousand of direct marketing media (e.g., direct mail, telemarketing, etc.) has made it more difficult for direct marketing to be used successfully to build awareness of brands. However, when direct marketing is combined as part of an overall campaign strategy with advertising, Internet marketing, sales promotion, public relations, and/or personal selling, it can be highly successful. The term most used to describe this is *integrated marketing communications*.

The American Association of Advertising Agencies (4As) defines integrated communications as:

> *A concept of marketing communications planning that recognizes the added value in a program that integrates a variety of strategic disciplines, e.g., general advertising, direct response, sales promotion, and public relations—and combines these disciplines to provide clarity, consistency, and maximum communications impact.*

Jerry Reitman, former executive vice president of Leo Burnett, paraphrases the definition by stating: "Campaigns should have the same tonality, the same creative direction . . . and, more importantly, the same strategic direction."

The integrated marketing communications process begins with a business problem, does not assume an advertising solution, takes the time necessary to research and develop an integrated strategy, puts all elements in place before pulling the trigger, measures everything, and accepts accountability. Exhibit 1–4 illustrates the ideal planning model for an integrated marketing communications program.

In this new environment, large global communications networks such as Interpublic, WPP, Young & Rubicam, Euro RSCG, and Publicis have acquired firms that specialize in many different marketing communications disciplines. This is understandable as more and more communication dollars move from traditional advertising to other disciplines. Many of the top direct marketing advertising agencies are part of these extended firms (see Exhibit 1–5).

EXHIBIT 1–4

Integrated Marketing Communications Planning

This chart, created by Don Schultz of Northwestern University, shows how Integrated Marketing Communications Planning for a brand can extend across customer segments, objectives, strategies, marketing tools, and disciplines. It starts with knowledge gained from a historical database, continues through program measurement, and ends by closing the loop and starting the process over for the next campaign.

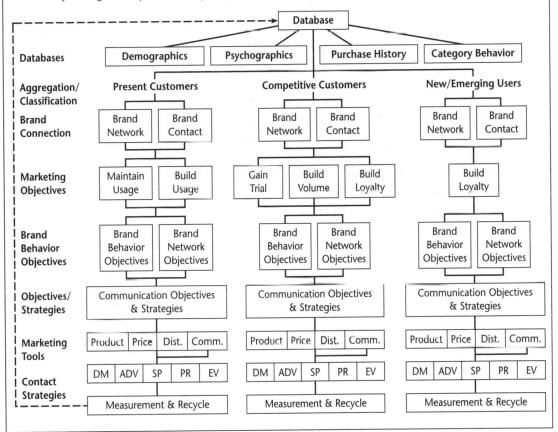

Affiliated agencies work together on clients, leveraging each of their own strengths to develop successful integrated marketing communications programs for their clients. Some clients choose to select their own agencies in each discipline, regardless of affiliations. These clients may choose agencies based on perceived strengths, category expertise, or past working experience. In this case, the clients take on the responsibility of ensuring that their programs are integrated.

Much progress has been made in the last decade in integrated marketing communications. Advertising firms such as Leo Burnett, Lintas, Ogilvy & Mather, Young & Rubicam, and others have been pioneers, helping their clients take

Top 10 Direct Marketing Agencies

Nearly all the top direct marketing agencies are affiliated with large global ad agency networks: Brann (Snyder Communications), Draft (Interpublic), Rapp Collins (Omnicom), Wunderman (Young & Rubicam), Grey (Grey), and Ogilvy One (Ogilvy & Mather).

Dollars are in thousands.

Rank '98	Rank '97	Agency	Direct Marketing Revenue '98	Percent Change	U.S. Agency Revenue '98	Percent Change
1	1	Brann Worldwide 1	$287,580	33.7	$287,580	33.7
2	4	Draft Worldwide 3	142,641	36.3	180,558	36.3
3	3	Rapp Collins Worldwide	126,148	18.1	167,148	18.1
4	5	Bronnercom 4	124,200	22.7	124,200	22.7
5	2	Wunderman Cato Johnson	120,495	11.9	140,110	12.3
6	6	Harte-Hanks/DiMark	90,538	19.8	90,538	19.8
7	7	Grey Direct Marketing	82,740	22.8	82,740	22.8
8	8	OgilvyOne Worldwide	77,200	25.3	77,200	25.3
9	9	Carlson Marketing Group	75,757	24.4	254,096	14.9
10	10	MRM/Gillespie 8	48,600	16.0	48,600	16.0

Notes: Specialty revenues are from an agency's U.S. operations only.
Source: Advertising Age, May 17, 1999.

advantage of media synergies and targeting efficiencies by integrating. However, integrated marketing is still hard to coordinate, whether there are many unaffiliated specialty firms or one large communications network involved. Issues of who takes the lead in planning, how budgets are divided, and how profits are distributed continues to be an internal problem for the success of integrated marketing.

Ogilvy & Mather Worldwide, New York, appointed a chief integration officer in March 1999 to coordinate the services of general agency Ogilvy & Mather, direct-shop OgilvyOne, Web-shop Ogilvy Interactive, corporate identity arm Brand Integration Group, and for collateral Design Direct. This formalized what was already being done for their major client, IBM Corp. This position reduced bottlenecks, improved communication, and decreased disagreements regarding direction among the groups.

For an understanding of how direct marketing integrates with other disciplines and new data technologies in integrated communications, let us look at the practices of E*TRADE, a stock brokerage that exists only on the Web.

CASE STUDY: E*TRADE Securities, Inc.

BACKGROUND

On-line stock brokerage is one of the most hotly contested categories on the Web. In 1999 there were more than six million wired investor households, more than 100 companies offered on-line brokerage services, and more than 30 percent of all retail stock trades were conducted on-line. An estimated additional seven million new customers will be in the market by 2002.

Price per trade is one of the driving forces in this market. The basic range of commissions for a basic trade goes from a low of $7.95 per trade to a high of $29.95. More than 20 companies offer trades in the $7.95 to $14.95 range. The number one on-line brokerage, Charles Schwab, charges $29.95.

Site access and reliability, important during normal times as well as during times of exceptionally high market activity, also influence the choice of E-brokers. Many brokerage sites have had problems with access to the site or slow speed. Other issues that affect the selection process include financial news, account minimums, hidden charges, reputation, variety of services, real-time stock quotes, and customer service.

E*TRADE was founded in 1982 as a brokerage service bureau. Its founder, Bill Porter, was a physicist and inventor with more than a dozen patents to his credit. The early E*TRADE provided on-line quote and trading services to brokerage companies such as Fidelity, Charles Schwab, and Quick & Reilly.

Bill Porter began to wonder why, as an individual investor, he had to pay a broker hundreds of dollars for stock transactions. He believed that someday most people would own computers, enabling them to invest with unprecedented efficiency and control.

In 1992, E*TRADE Securities, Inc., was launched as one of the first all-electronic brokerages offering on-line investing services through America Online and CompuServe. Four years later E*TRADE launched a Web version of its service at etrade.com.

In 1996 the top ten financial services companies on-line were all Internet-only companies targeting individual investors. By 1999 off-line financial service giants such as Merrill Lynch were moving on-line, recognizing that they could no longer ignore leaner, Net-based competitors such as E*TRADE, the number two on-line brokerage, behind Charles Schwab. Other on-line competitors include DLJ Direct, Discover Brokerage, Datek, and Waterhouse.

Charles Schwab, the on-line market leader, handled one-third of all on-line trades in 1999. E*TRADE per customer average assets were $30,000, versus Schwab at $200,000. While E*TRADE was gaining on Schwab, there was a cost. E*TRADE's average acquisition cost per customer in Q2 '99 was $250. During the same quarter, Schwab's cost to acquire a new customer was $130.

In 1999 the company became more diversified and made a number of strategic investments. These included on-line investment bank E-offering, transaction company ASB (formerly Archipelago Services), and financial advisory website ClearStation. E*TRADE also acquired Telebank, an on-line bank, thus enabling them to become a one-stop financial services brand providing mortgages, investment banking, retail brokerage services, commercial banking, and credit cards.

CHALLENGE

In September 1998, E*TRADE decided to increase its customer base by adding one million customers within eighteen months. E*TRADE's target demographic group was primarily males in their late 20s and 30s—high-income earners who were not experienced investors and were unlikely to be attracted to traditional stockbrokers. Research indicated that large numbers of this group had Internet access. While they might not be sophisticated investors, they were sophisticated Web users.

SOLUTION

To reach its goal, E*TRADE developed a comprehensive communication plan integrating television, print, Internet, sponsorships, and direct mail. The purpose of the ad program was to build E*TRADE's image. E*TRADE's market positioning was: "A service of the people for the people."

"[The Campaign was] meant to be unintimidating for people who aren't yet comfortable with transacting on the Net," according to Jerry Gramaglia, E*TRADE's senior VP of marketing, sales, and communications, as quoted in *The Industry Standard* magazine of September 27, 1999.

The company sought to find its audience beyond traditional financial-services ad outlets. "We want to be in places where Merrill Lynch or Charles Schwab would never be," noted Gramaglia. Direct mail included an offer of sign-up bonuses with United Airlines and Sprint.

An Integrated Campaign

The program included a number of components, each with a different objective:

- National advertising campaign: television, radio, print, Internet
- Direct mail to sign up new accounts
- Sales support material
- Internet sponsorship on the CNBC website
- Behind home plate at baseball parks, on billboards, in phone booths, and on buses in major metropolitan areas
- Sponsorship of the pregame show on Fox's broadcast of the World Series
- At the annual Comdex conference, sponsorship of the E*TRADE Oasis on the convention floor, where attendees could get foot massages, and complimentary limo rides between convention venues for attendees who signed up for an E*TRADE account

The campaign included a variety of media and techniques. Traditional TV and print were used to help build awareness of the E*TRADE brand and URL, while other media drove traffic to E*TRADE's website to sign up new accounts.

TV ads were the campaign's cornerstone. Seven spots, each with an antiestablishment feel, presented the common person cashing in on the on-line trading revolution. One spot, which integrated with E*TRADE's newspaper and radio campaign, hit on E*TRADE's fundamental sermon: boot your broker and do it yourself. "If your broker's so great, how come he still has to work?" it asked.

Another ad brought a cautionary message. It depicted a cubicle worker's stock going through the roof. Elated, he storms into the boss's office and quits. When he returns to his desk and sees that the stock has tanked, he panics and heads back to the boss to save his job. "Try not to get carried away," was the warning.

Print ads like the one shown in Exhibit 1–6 were image and message consistent with one of the television sports. Each repeated E*TRADE's fundamental sermon: boot your broker and do it yourself. Print ads were featured in financial, traditional business, and on-line business publications.

The direct mail program sought to entice prospects to sign up for E*TRADE accounts. The package consisted of a personalized letter, personalized application, and a brochure. The letter emphasized the ease of making stock trades and E*TRADE's low $4.95 (with rebate) offer for active investors.

The brochure showed the breadth of services E*TRADE offered, including security, research, etc. Positioning E*TRADE as more than just a stock brokerage site, it offered retirement planning, mutual funds, and a bond trading area.

The professionally written and designed mailing package, shown in Exhibit 1–7, spoke to key insights that E*TRADE has on its customers. It showed how easy it is to make trades from anywhere, at any time. A deadline was included to create a sense of urgency in responding.

List Selections. A mix of subscriber and compiled mailing lists targeted different market segments:

CASE STUDY: E*TRADE Securities, Inc. (continued)

- Small business owners
- High-income consumers
- Consumers who self-selected as active investors
- Financial publication subscribers
- Business publication subscribers
- Subscribers to on-line business publications
- Former customers and visitors to the website

Offer. The letter offered a bonus of as many as 50,000 United Airlines Mileage Plus miles for new accounts. A new individual account opened with a minimum of $1,000 earned 5,000 miles. Investors opening a joint account with a minimum of $50,000 earned an additional 25,000 miles. Investors who referred as many as four friends who opened individual accounts earned an additional 5,000 miles for referral.

Follow-up. Accounts that signed up received a fulfillment kit with complete instructions on how to use the features of their new account. It included

---

EXHIBIT 1–6

E*TRADE Print Ad

This print ad runs in traditional business publications like *Business Week* and nontraditional publications like *Business 2.0*. It continues E*TRADE's message that you need to plan your financial future, rather than rely on luck. This version has a bound-in reply card, which often improves response. Note the offer on the reply card.

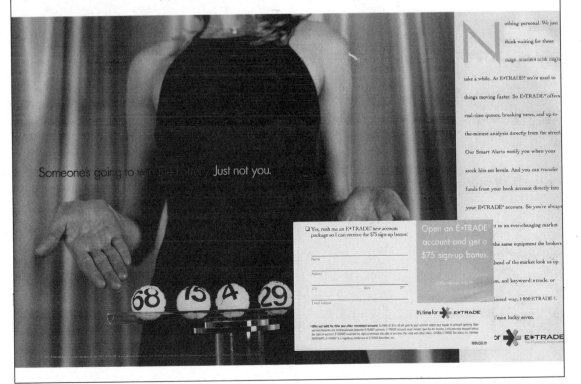

CASE STUDY: **E*TRADE Securities, Inc.** *(continued)*

cards with account number, user name, and personal pin number.

The E*TRADE campaign was a remarkable example of how contemporary organizations market direct to consumers. It featured an integrated marketing communications program that used a variety of media to build awareness of E*TRADE's URL (where it can be found on the Web) and key benefits. Direct mail and on-line programs provided the response mechanisms for account sign-up. Exhibit 1–8 shows the E*TRADE website.

RESULTS

There were 331,000 new accounts added in Q1 '99. E*TRADE was well on its way to pulling off its million-customer goal.

EXHIBIT 1–7

E*TRADE Direct Mail Package

This direct mail package prominently features the United Airlines mileage offer on the outer envelope, in the letter, and throughout the package.

CASE STUDY: **E*TRADE Securities, Inc.** *(continued)*

EXHIBIT 1–7   *(continued)*

E*TRADE Securities, Inc.
P.O. Box 3070
Menlo Park, CA 94026-3070
1 800 ETRADE

UNLTR/0899

Open an E*TRADE® account by October 15, 1999, and earn up to 50,000 Mileage Plus® miles.△△

••••••••5-DIGIT 60613
Ron S. Jacobs
Jacobs & Clevenger Inc.
3800 N Lake Shore Dr.
Chicago, IL 60613-3313

Dear Mr. Jacobs:

Why should you open an E*TRADE® account? For the same reason you fly United Airlines. You like to go with the best. And as the #1 – rated place to invest online,[†] no one makes it easier to take control of your financial future than **E*TRADE.**®

Open your account and start earning miles today. Thanks to E*TRADE's recent partnership with United Mileage Plus program, E*TRADE® account holders can earn up to 50,000 Mileage Plus miles per year—that's enough for two FREE round-trip tickets on United Airlines.

Already more than 1 million individual accounts have been opened online with E*TRADE.® And every hour of every day, they're taking advantage of the cutting-edge tools and technology that have helped level the playing field between full-service brokers and individual investors.

Active investors can buy and sell stocks from $ 1.95* a trade with rebate. We give you free unlimited real-time quotes to keep on top of your investments. Plus, you get Smart Alerts — our free e-mail or alphanumeric pager alerts that watch the markets and automatically notify you when stocks hit the price, volume, or P/E targets you set.

Plus, you can access more than 4,700 mutual funds through E*TRADE's Mutual Fund Center.[§] That includes 1,200 with no loads or transaction fees. And with our advanced screening tool, Power Search, you can evaluate in a matter of seconds which funds might be right for you.

There are many ways to earn 50,000 Mileage Plus miles in one year:	
Open an E*TRADE® Account	Mileage Plus Miles Earned
Individual account with a $1,000 minimum	5,000
Joint account with at least $50,000	25,000
Refer 4 friends who open accounts (5,000 miles each)	20,000
TOTAL ANNUAL MILES	50,000

Complete the enclosed Express Application and return it with your initial deposit of at least 1,000. Or you can complete the application online at *www.etrade.com/offer* — and be sure to enter the Special Offer Code printed above your name on the enclosed Express Application to get your Mileage Plus bonus miles. If you prefer, call 1-800-ETRADE-1, and we'll help you complete your application over the phone.

Sincerely,

Kathy Levinson

Kathy Levinson
President and Chief Operating Officer

P.S. Check out our newly designed Web site today, with faster research, easier navigation, and smarter services.

CASE STUDY: **E*TRADE Securities, Inc.** *(continued)*

EXHIBIT 1–7   *(continued)*

Express Application

1. Complete and sign.
2. Include a check to fund your account ($1,000 minimum), payable to E*TRADE Securities, Inc.
3. Mail your application and check to E*TRADE, P.O. Box 9206, Boston MA 02205-9891

Please review the E*TRADE Customer Agreement at www.etrade.com or contact us to receive by mail.

It's time for E*TRADE

1-800-ETRADE-1

Mileage Plus® Account Number: 00024 035 980
DWZ0899   **Special Offer Code: DWZ**

Ron S. Jacobs
Jacobs & Clevenger Inc.
3800 N Lake Shore Dr.
Chicago, IL 60613-3313

UNEXP/0899

Choose a Money Market Fund for Your Cash Balance

The cash balance in your account earns interest daily and is credited monthly. Tell us into which money market fund you would like us to deposit your cash. We will send you a prospectus for the fund you choose. Non-U.S. citizens are eligible only for the Credit Interest Program. Once your account is open, you can change your money market fund at any time. For current yield and fund descriptions, go to www.etrade.com/rates. Note: If you do not check a box, your uninvested cash will earn Credit Interest.

- [ ] Government Securities Portfolio
- [ ] Tax-Exempt Portfolio
- [ ] Money Market Portfolio
- [ ] Credit Interest *(not available in WI)*

E*TRADE® completes:

☐☐☐☐–☐☐☐☐   E*TRADE® account number

Account Type   For all other account types, please go to our Web site at www.etrade.com.

- [ ] Individual
- [ ] Joint (community property) — For AZ, CA, ID, LA, NM, NV, TX, and WA only.
- [ ] Joint (tenancy in common) — If one of the joint owners dies, his or her interest passes to his or her estate.
- [ ] Joint (rights of survivorship) — If one of the joint owners dies, his or her interest passes to the surviving owner(s).

Please Send Me Necessary Forms For:

- [ ] adding Margin or Options trading to this account
- [ ] an account transfer from another firm   [ ] an IRA

Or download forms from our Web site at www.etrade.com.

Free Checkwriting

We will mail your checks to you within three weeks of opening your account. Indicate the number of signatures required to process checks: [ ] One [ ] Two

Account Holder

Account Holder Name (if different from above)			
Address—cannot be P.O. box (if different from above)			Non-U.S. Citizens / Passport or ID #:
City	State	ZIP/Postal Code/Country	Country of Issuance:
Social Security Number	Date of Birth		Country of Legal Residence [ ] U.S. [ ] Other:
Phone Number	E-mail Address		Country of Citizenship [ ] U.S. [ ] Other:

Co-Account Holder

Co-Account Holder Name		Social Security Number
Non-U.S. Citizens / Passport or ID #: / Country of Issuance:		Date of Birth
Country of Legal Residence [ ] U.S. [ ] Other:	Country of Citizenship [ ] U.S. [ ] Other:	E-mail Address

Account Information Profile

	Account Holder	Co-Account Holder
Employer (If unemployed, self-employed, a student, or a homemaker, please specify.)		
Business Address (city, state, ZIP only)		
Occupation (If self-employed, please describe.)		
Is your employer a registered broker/dealer?	[ ] No [ ] Yes — If yes, include compliance letter.	[ ] No [ ] Yes — If yes, include compliance letter.
Are you a director, 10% shareholder, or policymaker of a publicly owned company? If yes, specify company.	[ ] No [ ] Yes	[ ] No [ ] Yes

Please Sign to Apply for Your E*TRADE® Account

I hereby request E*TRADE Securities, Inc., to open a Cash account in the name(s) set forth below. I am of legal age to contract. I acknowledge that I have received, read, and agree to be bound by the terms and conditions as currently set forth in the E*TRADE Customer Agreement [which is available online at www.etrade.com or contact us to receive by mail] and as amended from time to time. I ACKNOWLEDGE THAT E*TRADE DOES NOT PROVIDE INVESTMENT, TAX, OR LEGAL ADVICE OR RECOMMENDATIONS. Under penalty of perjury, I certify (1) that my Social Security (or taxpayer ID) number shown on this form is my correct number, and (2) that I am not subject to backup withholding because (a) I am exempt from backup withholding, or (b) I have not been notified by the Internal Revenue Service (IRS) that I am subject to backup withholding, or (c) I have been notified by the IRS that I am no longer subject to backup withholding [cross out item 2 if it does not apply to you]. [The Internal Revenue Service does not require your consent to any provision of this document other than the certifications required to avoid backup withholding.] I understand that you will supply my name to issuers of any securities held in my account so that I might receive any important information regarding them, unless I notify you in writing not to do so. I UNDERSTAND THAT THIS ACCOUNT IS GOVERNED BY A PREDISPUTE ARBITRATION CLAUSE, WHICH IS ON PAGE 7, PARAGRAPH 31b, OF THE E*TRADE CUSTOMER AGREEMENT, WHICH I WILL RECEIVE FROM E*TRADE UPON ACCOUNT ACTIVATION.

Account Holder Signature	Date
Co-Account Holder Signature	Date
E*TRADE® Completes: Principal Sign-off	Date

© 1999 E*TRADE Securities, Inc. Member NASD/SIPC. E*TRADE is a registered trademark of E*TRADE Securities, Inc.

But the marketing blitz came at a cost. E*TRADE was forgoing profits in order to invest in the brand. Roughly 40 percent of E*TRADE's $150 million budget went to TV, print, and outdoor buys. It's likely E*TRADE had to spend even more to hit the million mark, especially as competitors turned up the volume on advertising to build their own customer base.

EXHIBIT 1-8

E*TRADE Website

The E*TRADE website is the front door to its virtual store. With no bricks-and-mortar presence, the home page must be appealing and easy for customers to use. The Web is the ultimate customer-centric channel . . . competitors are just a click away!

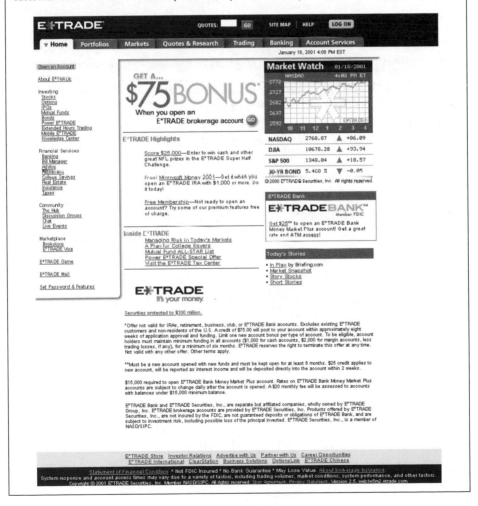

You are E*TRADE's marketing director. You've just learned that one of your competitors—a large, established bricks-and-mortar broker-age company that just opened an on-line brokerage—is offering free stock trades for a limited period of time. It wants to migrate its off-line customers on-line as well as take a bigger share of the on-line marketplace.

Your assignment is to maintain the loyalty of that important 10 percent of your customer base that provides 90 percent of your profits. Develop an outline of a program you would employ to retain the loyalty of your best customers. Hint: You'll want your customers to see the value of remaining an E*TRADE customer, while using some sort of incentives to encourage them to remain loyal.

Key Points

▶ The tools and techniques of direct marketing can be translated across business categories, media, and marketing objectives. Testing allows marketers to discover the most appropriate technique for each objective, campaign, category, or client.

▶ While tools and techniques change, the basic purpose of any direct market-ing program is still to get a measurable response that will produce an immediate or ultimate profit. The ultimate objective is to build the long-term or lifetime value of a customer. Both of these characteristics make direct marketing techniques attractive to traditional marketers whose advertising programs are held accountable for creating specific results.

▶ Direct marketing is an excellent tool for developing one-on-one customer relationships and for growing and maintaining customer loyalty—a critical factor in markets that experience high "churn," or customer turnover. In all industries, it costs five to ten times more to acquire a new customer than it does to retain an existing one.

▶ When combined as part of an overall campaign strategy with advertising, Internet marketing, sales promotion, public relations, and/or personal selling, direct marketing plays a key role in what is known as *integrated marketing communications*.

BUSINESS, STRATEGIC, AND DIRECT MARKETING PLANNING

Strategy and planning go hand in hand. Without a formal plan, even the best strategy may be doomed for failure. Plans are blueprints for taking an organization, business unit, or brand into the future. They plot a course to reach a set of stated objectives.

A plan will typically lay out a set of long-term objectives and provide guidelines for establishing short-term goals that need to be achieved along the way. Short-term goals act as benchmarks for measuring how far the plan has come toward achieving its overall objectives. Benchmarks help managers recognize when a plan needs adjustment or when a more complete change in direction may be necessary. Finally, plans provide a baseline managers can use to focus resources on the highest priority issues that they face to run a business effectively and achieve the best results.

The goal of planning is to make certain that an organization remains on track, stays up-to-date with emerging technologies, and optimizes its unique resources. Businesses once planned strategies three, five, or even ten years out based on assumptions about long-term growth prospects. Today, organizations review their plans annually, even quarterly, and make revisions based on a host of internal and external factors.

Businesses use many different types of planning tools. In a start-up organization, knowledge of business planning techniques is important. An established business will mobilize managers from different areas to develop a strategic plan to help shape the organization's long-term future. The marketing planning process is the mechanism by which many organizations analyze their markets, assess the impact of trends, and design a strategy to meet current and near-term needs of their customers.

All plans should use simple uncomplicated language. Major headings should be clear and followed by paragraphs that highlight the key points of the section. It should be easy for a reader to scan the document and decide which sections to devote more attention. The plan writer should give particular attention to grammar, spelling, structure, and punctuation—elements that have great impact on the overall impression of the document.

Plans need to be tested and proved on a continuous basis. They need to be reality-checked to gain support within an organization, and they need to be performance-tested in the marketplace. In evolving, emerging, or new marketplaces, several strategies or hypotheses are frequently tested at once. Through this process, organizations learn which strategies work and which don't. Successful organizations create an environment where experimentation and learning is approved of and rewarded.

There are many different schools of thought on business strategy. Some argue that businesses are too complex for deliberative and rational processes to have great impact. It's true that there is no simple prescription that works for every business. And, the best strategies sometimes wear out over time. In the real world, individuals within an organization make decisions about which corporate initiatives to emphasize, which customers to give the greatest attention to, and which companies to partner with. What's more, changes in the marketplace can render some strategies ineffective overnight.

This chapter looks at three kinds of plans: the business plan, the strategic plan, and the direct marketing plan. All three are critical to the organization using the tools and techniques of direct marketing.

Three Key Strategic Questions

Strategists often start a review by asking the three questions detailed in a white paper from the Harvard Business School, "Corporate Strategy: A Manager's Guide."

1. *Where should we focus the greatest effort and why?*
    This question goes to the root of how a company generates its revenue and profit. Often a company's profit center is not clear. Answering this question helps companies focus on strategies that garner the greatest reward. Today, theorists believe that companies must identify and make the most of their strengths while continuing to search for new profit opportunities from their existing value chain.

2. *What do we bring to the table?*
    This question puts the focus on the internal capabilities and strengths of an organization. The white paper points out that successful organizations like Federal Express have bundles of skills and technologies that affect and shape their strategies. In addition to core competencies, organizations have distinct capabilities that can't be easily duplicated by competitors—perhaps a recognized market position, strong brand, and a reputation over time.

3. *Do our core capabilities suit our position?*

Exploring this question helps organizations focus on capabilities that provide long-term opportunities. Companies shouldn't put effort into a marketing position that they can't sustain over time. Nor should they put resources into developing competencies from which they don't gain an advantage over their competitors.

Michael Porter, author of *Competitive Strategy*, believes that competitive advantage lies not in a single competency but in a whole system of activities. Amazon.com is a good example.

Amazon.com's strategy is to spread its resources over new business categories. Amazon is able to use the same systems to develop, promote, and fulfill products in these new categories while maximizing the customer base it has cultivated.

To outsiders it may appear that Amazon.com's chief competitive advantage is its large customer base. Not so. Amazon.com has developed a sophisticated business and technology infrastructure. Its merchandising skills and product offerings are important, as well as its customer base. But what sets it apart from competition is the combination of its efficient Web development process, ordering system, distribution capabilities, and customer service. Amazon.com maximizes the use of customer information, while building a business on systems that together give customers a real advantage in shopping with them.

It is hard for other companies to challenge Amazon's strategy. Few competitors have the resources to try to duplicate Amazon's mix of capabilities, which gives Amazon.com a unique advantage to capitalize on.

Can Amazon continue to expand globally using its competitive advantage? It has set up websites in Britain, France, and Germany, where the company believes that denser populations and shorter delivery distances create an ideal market for Internet sales. By contrast, the sprawling geography of the United States means that delivery times, using standard ground methods (e.g., UPS, USPS, etc.), can be several days, compared to overnight in much of Europe. Only time can tell how successful this strategy will be.

The Strategic Business Plan

A business plan is written to help attract outside investors and financing. It can help crystallize a fledgling organization's business model, market niche, organizational structure, and cash needs. It can also help reduce the risks associated with starting a business by including alternatives, a series of "what ifs" for the company's future.

A business plan answers questions an investor not familiar with the business might ask. Investors, who are the "customers" for the plan, want the plan to:

- Describe the key concepts of the business

- Establish that there is a market for the products and services the company sells

- Outline the organizational structure of the business

- Include financial projections that show the company's expected sales growth over a three-year period

The job of the business plan is to sell readers on the idea that the plan is worth investing in. One key to accomplishing this task is comprehensive research. Without it, a business plan will seem vague, shallow, or incomplete—causing the reader to doubt how much the writers know about their business, market, or customers. When doubts occur, the plan has not done its job.

The length of the finished business plan can vary. In some plans the marketing or product/service section may be detailed and complex, while in others it can be short and concise. The rule of thumb is that the plan must be long enough to communicate main ideas. It must contain enough information so that anyone who reads it will understand it, especially those unfamiliar with the concept.

There is no single "right" way to approach a business plan. Much depends on the kind of business or product/service that you plan to market. A plan for an Internet service business will surely be different from that of a manufacturing company selling mass customizing products created on an assembly line.

Elements of the Business Plan

The following elements, summarized in Exhibit 2–1, are included in most business plans:

Introduction. This short section describes in no more than a page why the plan is being written, its intended audience, and sets out the plan's business objectives and purpose as well as the business concept.

Executive Summary. To give the reader a clear picture of what the business is all about, this section includes the mission statement; the start date of the business; founders' names and functions; number of employees; location of headquarters and any branch offices; description/size of facilities; the products/services category; current investors; bank name(s); growth summary and plan; financial highlights; market potential; and a summary of management's plan.

Mission and Vision Statements. These statements set forth the central purpose of the business and its planned activities, as well as its major objectives, key strategies, and primary goals.

Market Analysis. The market analysis details the company's strengths, weakness, opportunities, and threats (SWOT); describes its competitive environment;

EXHIBIT 2-1

Elements of the Strategic Business Plan

Introduction
What is the purpose of the plan? Who is the audience?

Executive Summary
Summarizes the key elements of the plan (e.g., the mission statement; the products/services category; current investors; founder's names, financial and growth plans).

Mission and Vision Statements
What are the major objectives, key strategies, and primary goals of the business?

Market Analysis
Includes SWOT analysis, competitive analysis, likely target groups, research, and market share projections.

Customer Analysis
Who buys this product/service; are there multiple buyers, decision makers, or buying authorities; what is the size of the market, demographic or geographic dispersion, pricing analysis; what media or sales channels reach them?

Business Description
Describes the business, industry, developing trends, growth potential, emerging technologies, unique patents, trademarks, or names. What sets it apart from competitors?

Organization and Management
Outlines the organizational chart, staffing needs, job descriptions of top management, and biographies of founders and board of directors.

Integrated Marketing and Sales Plan
Includes detailed marketing plan, integrated marketing communications plans, methods of selling, distribution channels, pricing guidelines, expected competitive responses, budgets and timing, and rationales.

Funding Request
Details of the funding requirements, sources of funds, likely terms, and the projected return on investment (ROI).

Financial Projections
Three- to five-year forward-looking profit and loss statements, balance sheets, detailed cash-flow projections, and the path to profitability.

Appendix
Additional support materials, including research reports, specific product plans, samples of promotion materials, website, etc.

---

and defines the target group most likely to purchase the products/services offered and how the target group was determined. It also describes the share of the market the company hopes to gain and the share of market held by competitors.

Customer Analysis. Explains who buys this product/service, how many potential buyers there are, how much they typically spend for this product/service, and where buyers can be found. It also identifies whether multiple buyers, decision makers, and buying authorities are involved, and what brand contacts can be used to reach them.

Business Description. Describes what business the organization is in and includes information about trends in its industry. It also describes the products/services offered and explains what sets them apart from competitors, including any patents, trademarks, or names the organization holds.

Organization and Management. Details the anticipated organizational structure, staffing needs, and job descriptions of top management of the organization, as well as triggers for adding additional staff and management. It includes an organizational chart; details of compensation, incentive, and benefit plans; and biographies of top managers, as well as biographies and qualifications of the founders and board of directors.

Integrated Marketing and Sales Plan. This detailed summary of the marketing plan explains the methods of selling and channels of distribution, along with the rationale for the proposed mix of advertising, direct marketing, Internet, promotion, public relations, and events.

Its plans for selling and communications are compared with competitors. Other topics covered include credit and terms of receivables, credit approval procedures, pricing guidelines and markups, competitive response analysis, budgets and timing, and responsibilities and duties of involved staff. This section also explains what will be revised if anticipated growth is not met.

Funding Request. Details the funding requirements, potential sources of funds, likely terms, and the projected return on investment (ROI). This section needs to be realistic, as investors are unlikely to put money into something that doesn't make sense.

Financial Projections. A detailed accounting of how much money is needed, when it is needed, and when investors can expect a return on investment, usually in the form of a balance sheet and income statement (P&L) for the current period as well as for the future. Carefully developed financials show a firm grasp of the costs involved in operating the business. This section also includes a detailed cash-flow projection showing:

- Cash in (with all sources of cash identified)

- Cash out (with all uses of cash identified)

- Timing (when will each of the above occur?)

The financial projections should show the organization's path to profitability— an enduring key to success that is even more important in the post-Internet boom period.

Appendix. Appendices contain information referred to in the text of the business plan, such as research reports, tables, detailed market or sales projections, analyses, and exhibits.

What Investors Look for in a Business Plan

Investors want to know one thing: Will I recoup my investment?

To answer that question, they examine a number of areas closely. They want to know that the potential market for the product and services is sufficient. They look closely at the research and rationales for market size, expect to see growth options, and want to know what factors could impede success. And they look to see that the organization's value proposition is in alignment with the customers.

Investors want to see evidence that management is accomplished and dedicated. Besides business experience, they are looking for vision, diversity, competency, capabilities, and teamwork and networking skills. Networking ability is significant because business partnering is so important. Investors want to know if the company's partner set offers it a competitive advantage.

Investors also want to know the company's path to profitability. They peruse the financials to see if the revenue model is real. They test it to see if it makes sense, if growth projections are achievable, if profit projections can be reached, and if the overall financial plan is credible.

Lastly, investors look for plans that are truly unique. Recently, too many business plans have emphasized the uniqueness of the Internet rather than the uniqueness of the business proposition. In fact, it is more important to be different than to be digital.

Mohanbir Sawhney of the Kellogg Graduate School of Management has an interesting test for uniqueness. He asks entrepreneurs: "What would happen if your business plan were published in the Sunday paper?" If publication would be a disaster, Sawhney gives them only a slim chance for success. His rationale is that a business plan should be so unique that only the organization developing the plan should be able to execute it. This reinforces the importance to be in a business that is difficult, if not impossible, to replicate.

The Strategic Plan

A strategic plan is a blueprint of short- and long-term activities, strategies, and work plans, developed after considering external market forces and an organization's internal competencies and capabilities. One of the most useful tools for all organizations, strategic planning is an ongoing business process that enables an organization to make decisions about its vision and mission and develop the necessary procedures and operations to achieve that future, as well as determine how success is to be measured (see Exhibit 2–2).

EXHIBIT 2-2

Elements of the Strategic Plan

Introduction
- Describes the purpose of the plan and whether its scope is for the full organization, division, brand, or one product/service.
- Quantify how foward-looking it is (e.g., three years).

Executive Summary
- Summarizes the key elements of the plan (e.g., the scope, objectives, SWOT, mission, vision, the products/services category, current investors, founders names, financial and growth plans).

Goals and Objectives
- Highlights achievements to be realized over the next one to three years.
- Relates these to the business, customers, and other stakeholders.

Situation Analysis
- Competitive analysis—looks as far inside competitors as possible.
- Market analysis—includes market size and in-depth customer analysis.
- Environmental analysis—identifies key events and trends in the industry.

SWOT Analysis
- What are the key strengths and weaknesses of the organization?
- What are the key opportunities and threats in the marketplace?

Mission Statement
- What does this business really do and what does it hope to do?
- What makes this business, organization, or brand unique?

Vision Statement
- What will the business look like in one to three years? (This section can be aspirational.)
- This needs to be translatable into behavior within the organization.

Business Values
- What are the principles governing the business and its relationship with customers, partners, the community, and other stakeholders?
- This section is often included with the mission or vision statement.

Key Strategies
- Identifies what success looks like.
  Will the company build on strengths, resolve weaknesses, capitalize on opportunities, or avoid threats?
- Strategies can be organizational (e.g., diversification, organic growth, or acquisition) or functional (e.g., management, marketing, sales, operations, R&D, etc.).

Action Plans
- Outlines the major action programs in order of importance. Specifies what, who, where, how, and when for each.
- Prioritizes plans.

Financial Plans
- Identifies financial goals and creates P&Ls.
- Matches revenue and spending to period of the strategic plans.

Performance Measures
- Establishes measures to meet goals, complete strategies, improve or change direction.
- Identifies benchmarks, dates to know that plans are on track.

A strategic plan can bring together an organization's management, employees, stakeholders, and customers by communicating a common understanding of where the organization is going, how everyone involved can work to that common purpose, and how to identify the benchmarks for progress and success. Once written, it must be shared and reviewed with everyone constantly if it is to be a truly integrated, strategic plan. A plan that molders neglected in a drawer is no plan at all.

Increasingly, the voice of the customer drives the operations and charts the course for the future. Customer-driven organizations create plans while actively examining their products, services, and processes through the eyes of the customer. As part of the planning process, customer-driven organizations learn their customers' preferences and requirements, as well as their standards for performance, timeliness, and cost. And they not only listen to the expressed needs and expectations of the customers, but also gather independent information about the preferences of customers and categories they hope to serve in the future.

"Customer-driven" does not mean blindly taking action based upon the results of customer input. It means looking at what customers do—not just what they say—in determining their needs. For example, in new and emerging markets where customers are not familiar with a product or service, customers may not know what their needs really are. With new product introductions, customers may not know what kind of improvement to expect. It's important to match customer behavior to customer expectations when looking at results.

Two important elements of the strategic plan are the mission statement and the vision statement. The terms are often used interchangeably. However, there are differences in each type of statement worth noting.

Mission Statement

A mission statement should describe why an organization exists and what it hopes to achieve going forward. It should articulate the essence of an organization's nature, its values, and its business. To be effective, it must resonate with an organization's staff, as well as with prospects, clients, business partners, and others the organization hopes to affect. It must express the organization's purpose in a way that inspires commitment, innovation, and teamwork, and gains the broadest consensus.

An organization's mission statement should answer three key questions:

1. What is the purpose of the organization and what are the opportunities or needs that we exist to address?

2. What business are we in and what are we doing to address these needs?

3. What are the values, principles, and beliefs that guide the organization's work?

These questions should be answered in one or two brief paragraphs that are free of jargon and misleading business terms. A reader unfamiliar with a business should be able to decipher its mission statement without the need for additional learning. Without knowing that the following mission statement is for a company that provides E-commerce infrastructure support services, would you be able to identify its business?

We leverage eBusiness technology, innovative business processes, and new economy channel partners, to create the next generation Value Chain for the IT industry. As a result, everyone in the IT channel ecosystem wins.

Compare this to the mission statement for Hanna Andersson, a catalog and E-tail marketer of European clothes for children and their families:

We market clothes to enhance the lives of our customers through quality, functionality, durability, and design. We celebrate our beliefs with integrity. Our culture bears witness to our values. Our participation confirms our responsibility to the larger community.

Vision Statement

A vision statement is a fundamental tool for helping a company see into its future.

Visions are big pictures. They paint a picture of an organization's future through the eyes of that organization's leader or senior management team. They are often written by the CEO. At the very least, the effective leader will contribute ideas, concepts, and ways of thinking, staying at the center of development until the vision statement crystallizes. It's up to the CEO to translate the vision for employees and motivate them to embrace the vision.

A vision statement must be consistent with an organization's mission, goals, strategy, and philosophy. Its key objective is to guide an organization's behavior. A good vision statement is clear, concise, easily understandable, and memorable. It excites, inspires, and challenges an organization.

For a vision statement to be effective, it must be perceived as strategically sound. It must gain widespread support within an organization to become real and translate into behavior. Individuals within an organization must embody the vision by their actions, words, and deeds. In this way the vision is reinforced and becomes part of an organization's culture.

The importance of a powerful vision statement can't always be measured. However, consumer goods company Johnson & Johnson can attest to its value. It spent time and money building credibility with constituencies through its "Credo," a one-page vision statement outlining the company's value system. The credo reads in part:

We believe our first responsibility is to the doctors, nurses and patients, to mothers and fathers and all others who use our products and services. In meeting their needs everything we do must be of the highest quality . . . We are responsible to the communities in which we live and work and to the world community as well. We must be good citizens—support good works and charities and bear our fair share of taxes.

In 1982 and again in 1986, packages of the company's Tylenol® brand were adulterated with cyanide, causing the deaths of some customers. With Johnson & Johnson's name and reputation at stake, company managers and employees made countless decisions inspired by the philosophy in the Credo. As a result, customers were willing to give the company the benefit of the doubt in the Tylenol-tampering crisis and the brand was able to survive and even thrive.

SWOT Analysis

A strategic plan includes an analysis of an organization's internal strengths and weaknesses and external threats and opportunities. An effective process for identifying these elements is SWOT Analysis—Strengths, Weaknesses, Opportunities, and Threats. Research and analysis of the situation is often completed first. SWOT puts the information into a framework that reveals changes that can often be implemented without further analysis.

SWOT doesn't create answers; it allows the key issues to be identified, classified, and prioritized, which helps shed light on alternative solutions. When all elements have been identified, it is easy to establish points that balance strengths and weaknesses and opportunities and threats. These can then be plotted together, so decision makers can see how best to build on strengths and take opportunities while eliminating weaknesses and threats (see Exhibit 2–3).

A SWOT Analysis is usually completed in groups of no more than 10 people, to keep the discussion moving. Each of the four elements of the analysis is given its own section. Questions related to each section are written within the framework of that section. Questions should be considered from the organization's point of view as well as that of customers. Answers should be honest and realistic. Questions to address include:

Strengths:
What are the organization's real advantages?
What are the organization's core competencies? What does it
    do well?
Are we better financed than competitors, better able to retain
    key staff? Do we have a better reputation?

EXHIBIT 2–3

SWOT Analysis Template

This template allows for up to six items under each heading, but a business or brand can have many more. Limit the items to focus on the biggest issues, not smaller ones.

Instructions: Briefly list major *existing* Strengths, Weaknesses, Opportunities, and Threats. Strengths and Weaknesses are **internal** to the business. Opportunities and Threats are **external**.

Strengths	Weaknesses

Opportunities	Threats

Weaknesses:

What needs to be improved in products, services, processes, etc.?

What is it that we don't do very well?

Are there areas that should be avoided?

Do competitors have better market share and deeper market penetration, and is there one competitor that can't be unseated?

Opportunities:

Where are the bright spots in the organization's market?

Are there technologies or trends that favor the organization?

Do changes in population profiles, lifestyles, etc., offer an advantage?

Do changes in government policy, taxation, etc., benefit the organization?

Threats:
What obstacles does the organization face?
What is the competition doing to offset our gains?
What impact is the Internet, E-commerce, or other technology having
    on our industry?
Are changing marketing practices (e.g., the use of CRM, Sales Force
    Automation, etc.) threatening our position?
Do we have high bad debt, cash-flow problems, or an uncontrolled
    burn rate?

Completing a SWOT Analysis can be illuminating. It can point out what needs
to be done to improve an organization's performance. It is a way to take complex
business issues, sort them out in an orderly manner, and keep problems in perspective. It is a tool that can be used in developing situation analyses for strategic planning, business planning, even marketing plans.

The Direct Marketing Plan

Although the growth of the Internet as a marketing, distribution, and media channel has added many new twists to the traditional marketing planning process, this
chapter presents the elements of the direct marketing plan in a familiar way. The
direct marketing plan remains part of a common language that traditional marketers,
direct marketers, and Internet marketers can identify.

Like other kinds of plans, the direct marketing plan is a road map to be followed. Its content requires research, organization, and patience in its development
and execution. However, it is not a static document. It needs to be constantly
reviewed, updated, and revised as an organization's goals evolve with its marketplaces.

The direct marketing plan by its nature includes a strategic as well as tactical
side. The strategic side must be developed before an organization commits resources
to its exceptional elements. Inadequate or poorly thought-out strategic market planning means a company may invest in areas that are unlikely to ensure financial success. This is as true for Internet companies as it is for catalog businesses.

Developing the Direct Marketing Plan

When you take planning in context, it's easy to see the relationship among different
kinds of plans. For example, the financial projections contained in a business plan
are based on the assumptions contained in the marketing plan. The marketing plan
sets out where, how, and when promotional expenditures will be made, based on the
expected level of sales. Together, these are key elements of the financial projections.

Some elements in the direct marketing plan are simply reframed from the strategic or business plan. There is a synergy among plans that increases when members of an organization ask the same questions over and over again, and arrive at the same answers.

The direct marketing plan begins with a customer-centric approach to planning. The goal is to invest in the prospects, customers, and customer segments that the organization believes will help it reach the projected income-flow goals. To accomplish this, the organization begins by calculating or estimating the value of the prospects, customers, and segments to determine the right investment strategies for each group.

Elements of the Direct Marketing Plan

The elements of a typical direct marketing plan include:

Introduction. A short section describing the plan's purpose and its intended audience. It also sets out the business objectives and purpose of the plan, and often of the business concept.

Executive Summary. A short summary that gives the reader a clear idea of the plan's contents. It includes the objectives of the plan, the marketing strategies, key target groups and market segments, elements of the tactical plan, a budget summary, and rationales.

Situation Analysis. This section describes the marketing environment in which the organization operates and competes, as well as the results of any customer or market research. Its subsections include:

The macroenvironment of the marketplace, which describes demographic trends, economic indicators, relevant technologies; political, social, and cultural events; supply; and other forces that can impact the company.

The competitive situation, which includes information on major competitors with size, sales, goals, market share, product quality comparisons, marketing strategies, marketing spending, etc. Mapping out key competitors' marketing and business strengths as illustrated in Exhibit 2–4 will help illustrate where the best marketing positioning opportunity lies.

Target group analysis, which identifies demographic, psychographic, and behaviors of target buyers, decision makers, and end-users. It identifies the needs and wants of these groups and categorizes the most lucrative segments for marketing efforts.

Distribution channels, which provides information on size, trends, and importance of on-line, off-line, retail, or direct distribution channels for the company's products/services. It can include product/service or category demand analysis.

EXHIBIT 2–4

Competitive Analysis

To visualize the relative strengths of competitors, map key consumer decision variables into quadrants. This example plots competitors for high net worth financial planning services. Note the proposed positioning in a quadrant where there is little competition.

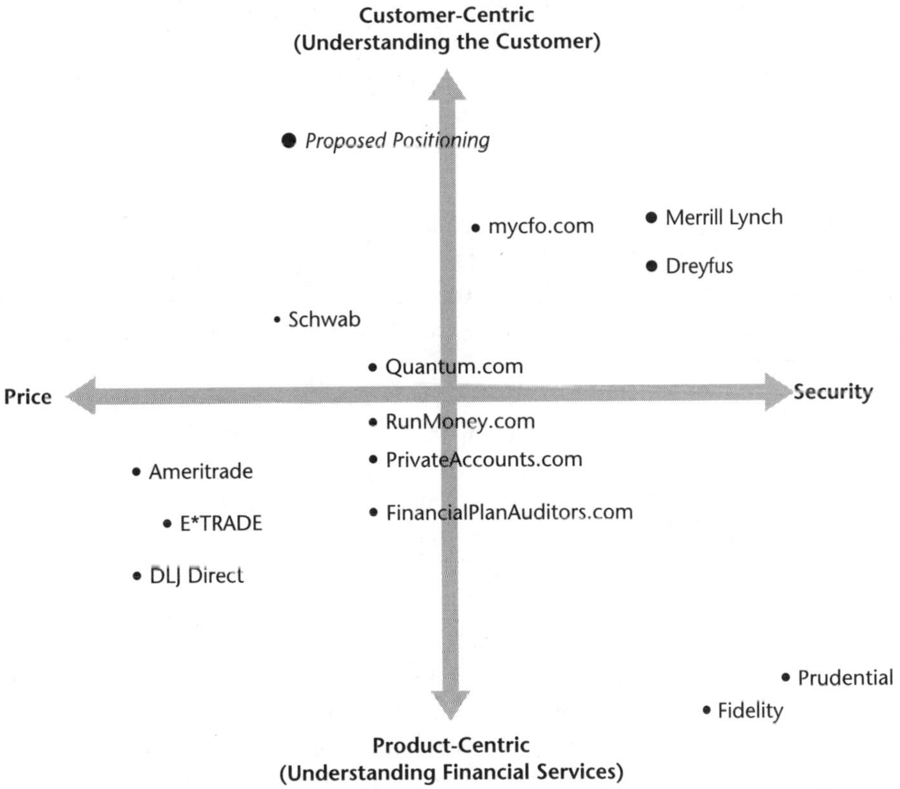

Customer-Centric
(Understanding the Customer)

● *Proposed Positioning*

● mycfo.com   ● Merrill Lynch

● Dreyfus

● Schwab

● Quantum.com

Price ←————————————————————→ Security

● RunMoney.com

● PrivateAccounts.com

● Ameritrade

● E*TRADE   ● FinancialPlanAuditors.com

● DLJ Direct

● Prudential

● Fidelity

Product-Centric
(Understanding Financial Services)

Product situation, which includes key aspects of the product, including sales, prices, and contribution margins as well as the net profits of each product line addressed in the marketing plan.

Research, which includes results of any primary or secondary research, prospect or customer surveys, or information gleaned from previous market tests conducted.

Opportunity and Issue Analysis.

This section includes the elements of the SWOT analysis germane to the marketing plan, using techniques similar to those discussed in the strategic planning section. Analyzing the internal strengths and weakness and external opportunities and threats to the organization in a competitive context is the first step. Once the key issues are described, the organization needs to address decisions to be made based on the SWOT analysis. This helps to determine objectives, strategies, and tactics for the direct marketing plan.

Goals and Objectives. This section outlines major company goals as well as marketing and financial objectives. A marketing objective must be quantified in terms of results and an achievable time or date. Results can be expressed in terms of results, sales, retention, etc. A quantified objective gives a benchmark on which to measure the success of the marketing plan. Examples of quantified objectives are "To get 30,000 click-throughs during the first month of operation," "To create 5,000 new customers during the second quarter," or "To generate 2,000 leads per week for next eight weeks."

The Marketing Strategy. This section orchestrates the elements of the marketing program. It includes a marketing strategy statement that summarizes the key target buyer description, explains how the organization plans to sell and market to those customers, and describes how the company wants prospects and customers to perceive it.

This can include the competitive market segments the company will compete in, the unique positioning of the company, brand or product/service, targeting strategies, benefit strategies, competitive price strategy, marketing and promotional spending strategy, and any possible R&D and market research expenditure.

Rationales for the marketing strategy may include an analysis and appraisal of the brand, category, multiline, product, price, and promotion strategies, and the rationale for why it is unique or compelling to buyers. This may include an analysis of competitive strategies as well.

A marketing strategy is successful when it is in alignment with the needs and wants of customers. This means the organization must have a clear understanding of its prospects', customers', and end-users' behavior. When possible, this should be gleaned from information on the database, past results, or current performance.

Tactics. This section details each specific marketing event and action planned, including media and mailing list plans, communications plans for direct mail, DRTV, response advertising, E-mail, and banner ad programs. It may include a summary of quarterly promotion and marketing communication plans, with spending, timing, share, sales, or product shipment goals, for each program and medium. It may also detail sponsorship, affiliate, event, or other kinds of programs planned.

It will include a description of each vehicle to be used in each program, with detail across media, disciplines, prospects, customers, the trade, etc. It will include separate tactics for acquisition, retention, activation, up-sell, cross-sell, or other kinds of programs planned.

Tactical marketing communications plans are the most detailed elements of the direct marketing plan. However, the whole of the plan should build into the communication plans. The communication tactics should simply flow from all that was written in support of them in the plan. This makes it a real working document, with a great chance of it translating into program success.

Budgets. There is no magic bullet for developing budgets. Budgeting usually starts with identifying the current or potential value of prospects, customers, and segments in order to estimate how much can be invested to achieve each goal. Competitive spending, changes in the market, and other uncontrollable forces impact budgets.

Budgets generally cover a calendar year, broken down by month or by quarter. They should contain a financial summary of quarterly promotion and marketing communication plans, broken down by program. They include spending, timing, sales, and share/shipment goals for each program.

Budgets are not static. They need to be updated quarterly and managed constantly against results. Budgets are often adjusted down or up as is necessary during the course of business. The impact of budget changes must be included in forecasts.

The Creative Strategy Plan

Not all plans are book-length manifestos rivaling the works of the greatest authors. Marketers often use a shorter type of plan, termed a marketing brief. A form of marketing brief used as an input document for creatives at agency Jacobs & Clevenger is called the Creative Strategy Plan.

This form, shown in Exhibit 2–5, fits on one side of an 8½ × 14 inch sheet of paper. It is meant to communicate in just a few lines the key elements that an individual needs to know to develop direct response creatives. No section of the plan has room for more than two or three lines of explanation.

There are two sections to the form. The marketing strategy section asks three questions that pinpoint the objectives of the creative assignment. The creative strategy section includes information on the target market as well as on what is to be communicated to prospects.

Elements of the Creative Strategy Plan

Key Fact. This is the single most important fact related to preparing this communication. In other words: Why are you doing a promotion? The answer to this could be to increase sales by x percent, to support other efforts, or to introduce a new product, service, brand, or line extension.

Consumer Problem This Creative Must Solve. The second question is related to the key fact. Its answer must be stated in consumer terms. It's not what the brand/product/service needs . . . it's what the customer needs! The answer might be, "High net worth consumers now have a website where they can access sophisticated financial tools previously only available through specialized financial

EXHIBIT 2–5

Creative Strategy Plan

JACOBS & CLEVENGER

Key Fact: (The single most important fact related to preparing this advertising)

Consumer Problem This Creative Must Solve: (Related to the key fact. State in consumer terms. Not what the brand/product/service needs . . . What the customer needs!)

Advertising Objective: (How this advertising/ direct marketing creative proposes to solve the problem stated above.)

Creative Strategy

• Prospect profile

• Competition

• Promise

• Reason why

• What is current perception of the brand?

• What perception of the brand do we want after this creative?

Legal & policy considerations/mandatory factors:

planners," or, "Now you can refinance your mortgage at 1 percent over prime rate with no points nor closing costs."

Advertising Objective. This explains how this creative proposes to solve the problem stated above. An example might be, "Develop a banner ad and E-mail campaign to drive on-line savvy, high net-worth prospects to the Envestnet.com website," or "Create a personalized direct mail with telephone follow-up campaign targeted at prospective home buyers."

Creative Strategy. This section asks for information on seven points that help to focus the creative strategy.

The prospect profile requires a few words about the demographics, psychographics, and/or behavior of prospects for the campaign. They may be customers or prospects. The more you know about them, the more targeted the promotion.

To pinpoint competition, consider what you have to replace to get people to purchase your product or service. Don't think of the competition too narrowly. Think of substitutes for your own product/service.

What promise are you making? What will prospects get if they purchase from you? What is the real benefit? Will their teeth be whiter? Will they be able to buy a car without the traditional middleman?

In the "Reason why" section, detail why prospects should believe the claims in the promise, and explain whether this rationale resonates with the prospect group.

Many questions make up the overriding question, "What is the current perception of the brand?" What do consumers think of your brand? Will what we propose be credible? Can we move the needle a little? It's easy for Amazon.com to make a customer service claim. It's much harder for a start-up to be credible with such a claim. A delivery guarantee might help overcome this.

Finally, consider how you want the brand to be perceived after the campaign ends. Do you have the credibility to get people to think differently about you? It's unlikely that you will convince foreign luxury car owners that an American luxury car is the equal of what they drive. It's clear that without credibility, you won't generate the results you hope for.

Legal & Policy Considerations / Mandatory Factors. In many categories there are legal and policy issues to be considered. Some companies prefer not to do sweepstakes for fear of blemishing their image. Insurance companies must create different forms for residents of different states. Interest rate ceilings vary from state to state. These are the kinds of issues dealt with here.

The creative strategy plan is an easy-to-use creative brief. It is a tool used by most agencies in the development of creative execution. It's one that you should try if you are responsible for giving input to creatives.

CASE STUDY: **Wells Fargo**

Written by Professor Mary Alice Shaver, Ph.D., Michigan State University, and Professor Carol Ann Hackley, Ph.D., APR, University of the Pacific, for the DePaul University Institute of Interactive and Direct Marketing's Case Writer's Workshop.

BACKGROUND

Home equity loans have become an important part of the bank consumer credit business, reaching new popularity with both customers and bankers at the end of the 20th century. But in Texas, laws dating from 1837 had prevented any borrowing against homestead property value, except for actual home improvement loans. After debating the issue for 25 years, the Texas legislature passed a Home Equity Law in May 1997 that left the issue up to the vote of the electorate. The law was accompanied by red tape that lenders viewed as "draconian." Still, if the law passed in the general election, the potential Home Equity Loan market in Texas could be as large as $10 billion in the first 24 months of the program.

CASE STUDY: **Wells Fargo** *(continued)*

Wells Fargo Bank, N.A. decided to move into the lucrative market in the summer of 1997. With just five months until the election, the company had to quickly learn as much about the market and the consumers as possible. Through the acquisition of First Interstate Bank, Wells Fargo had increased its branches in Texas, especially in Dallas–Fort Worth, Houston, and Austin. To move forward it needed to build an infrastructure for the home equity loan business that would allow it to compete and be a market leader if the law passed.

CHALLENGE

Wells Fargo needed to move quickly. In a matter of months decisions had to be made in the areas of consumer research, assessing the place of Wells Fargo in the consumer mind a year after the merger, budgeting for the campaign, deciding the appropriate level of spending necessary to gain a top market share, designing advertising, working against the competition, lobbying public officials, and positioning Wells Fargo as a leader in the home equity business.

Consumer research focused on brand name recognition and awareness of home equity loans. Research revealed low awareness, uncertainty, and fear of losing homes due to borrowing against them. Wells Fargo was seen as the bank that merged with First Interstate, but it had a favorable image associated with the values of the Old West. One strategic advantage for Wells Fargo was that consumers were neutral toward First Interstate, so there was no usurper image to overcome.

From its consumer research, Wells Fargo profiled the target customer as "a Texas homeowner who is looking to a trusted financial services provider for information about home equity loans, and who values excellent service and has demonstrated creditworthiness." It set out to create a direct marketing strategy to persuade the customer to seek a home equity loan from Wells Fargo.

SOLUTION

Wells Fargo decided to implement two direct mail home equity loan components. The first, labeled "Stampede," was sent on October 22, directly before the general election. On November 20, if the law had passed, a second mail initiative, termed "Dust," was to be sent to noncustomer homeowners in the Houston MSA. The goal was to profitably originate business through education on the new law, maintenance of strong customer focus, and low cost/expeditious production. Because Wells Fargo only had a 6 percent share of deposits, it had to go outside the customer base with direct mail.

"Stampede" was a combination Wells Fargo Bank customer cross-sell and prospect extract mailing. The plan was to target approximately 142,000 homeowners for the new Texas Home Equity Loan. The "Stampede" mailing base included 39,000 customers and 103,000 prospects. Because of the pending election, the mailing was a two-step prequalified mailing. To build the brand name and educate customers before the election, the customer first received an offer for a "Consumer Guide to Home Equity Loans." If the law passed, the fulfillment stage would be enacted. In this second step, the customer received a prequalified offer. Because the names had been prescreened, all respondents to stage one received the prequalified offer. No additional screening was done between the two stages.

The November mailing, "Dust," was a traditional prequalified mailing to noncustomer prospects in the Houston area. Several different letters were sent. The first solicited responses requesting the guide; the second accompanied the guide and invited recipients to call for additional information. Another mailing targeted prequalified homeowners and stressed both the low 7.99 APR rate and the after-tax translation of that rate to as low as 5.75 percent.

A telemarketing campaign was initiated once the law had passed on November 4. Of the approximately 192,000 direct mail pieces mailed, Wells Fargo

CASE STUDY: **Wells Fargo** *(continued)*

had telephone numbers for 150,000 for outbound follow-up telemarketing purposes.

Other advertising was also implemented. Teaser 60-second TV spots stated: "If you have questions about home equity in Texas, Wells Fargo has the answers. Kids, college, car, vacations." A tag line was: "For all your reasons why." The preelection teaser ads also offered a free guide to home equity loans.

The marketing strategy for the home equity loan mailings was:

- Develop an understanding of mailing home equity loan offers to Texas.
- Gain early market share.
- Test telemarketing for servicing noncustomer prospects. Explore early closing strategy through outbound telemarketing follow-up to customer applications.
- Build an understanding of response behavior.

RESULTS

By October 20 the phones were ringing. Although home equity loans could not be finalized until mid-January, approximately 4,000 applications had been submitted by January 1, 1998. In 10 weeks, Wells Fargo had 20,000 calls concerning home equity loans. The first people were hungry for credit.

Unfortunately, the quality of the applications was not as high as anticipated. Once approval could be given, the rate of completion was only 35 percent. Many of the applications below the Wells Fargo cut-off were referred to the Associates Home Equity Loan Service, which accepted these applications on a referral commission basis.

For the Texas campaign, the goals were twofold: volume of loans granted and market share. Although the market share goals were met initially—Wells Fargo attained an initial number one or two market share—only 50 to 60 percent of the target dollar/volume goal was met. Further, the market was softer than anticipated; market accep-

tance of the home equity packages was lower than projected. The direct mail campaign was not as successful as it had been in driving the customers into the branch banks to finalize the loans. Just when Wells Fargo adjusted its ad campaign expenditures and exposures downward, other banks in the market became more competitive in the home equity business and began advertising rates of .25 to .50 lower. The public perception was that Wells Fargo charged too much. Eventually, Wells Fargo dropped to number three or four in market share. However, although the volume of loans dropped off, the approval rate for loans rose as the market matured.

This was a situation in which decisions about start-up plans and costs, advertising spending levels, and the anticipated demand curve needed to be made before Wells Fargo even knew whether the product was going to be marketable. To be competitive in this lucrative market, Wells Fargo needed to move immediately after the May legislative decisions and to invest heavily, well in advance of the November referendum election. Although projections as to total market viability could be made using experience from other states—from population/home ownership figures and bank deposit levels—no firm data on demand existed for Texas. Other factors contributed to the failure to meet volume goals:

- Start-up costs to establish the working infrastructure were high. In June, Wells Fargo had one person on the Texas home equity account. In the next four months, over $1 million had been spent on research, advertising, call center development, and hiring and training 700 people.
- With the necessary heavy expenditures for the aggressive campaign, the cost for each loan application was approximately $200.
- Research showed Wells Fargo had little brand awareness, which had to be overcome with

advertising through both broadcast and direct mail.

- Many initial applications did not meet the minimum income or equity standards set by the bank.
- Competing banks entered the market aggressively, once the referendum had passed, with loan rates fractionally lower than Wells Fargo. This led to a public perception that Wells Fargo was expensive.

Valuable lessons were learned in the Texas campaign, however. The aggressive advertising did work to preempt the competition in the beginning. More important, the components that worked were introduced into other Wells Fargo market states. The marketing group was successful in using the strategy in Seattle, Phoenix, Denver, and in all nine states in the Wells Fargo region outside California. Profits missed in Texas were made up in the more mature markets.

PILOT PROJECT   In planning it's important to balance the desire for consensus with the need to explore diverse options. The problem is rarely a lack of strategies, but a lack of agreement around which one or ones to pursue and which to abandon. Your planning process needs to be capable of identifying the best strategy.

A. Using information provided in the Wells Fargo case as well as information gleaned from research on the Internet, develop a SWOT Analysis to explore the organization's strengths, weaknesses, opportunities, and threats related to marketing home equity loans.

B. Using the SWOT Analysis, develop a list of at least three possible marketing strategies for Wells Fargo to use in pursuing the market for consumer home equity loans. Write two or three paragraphs describing each strategy and explaining why it is worth testing.

C. Develop a compelling case for one of the three strategies. Compare the recommended strategy to the other two. Include rationales as to why this strategy is the one that should be adopted.

Key Points

▶ Planning helps an organization remain on track, stay up-to-date with emerging technologies, and optimize its unique resources. All plans need to be reviewed annually, even quarterly, and revisions should be made as external and internal factors change.

▶ To attract outside investors or financing, the business plan describes the key concepts of the business, establishes that there is a market for its products and services, outlines the organizational structure, and includes financial projections for three years. Its job is to persuade investors that they will recoup their investment.

▶ The strategic plan provides a blueprint of short- and long-term activities, strategies and work plans developed after considering external threats and opportunities and internal strengths and weaknesses.

▶ The direct marketing plan is strategic and tactical. It estimates the value of prospects, customers, and segments to determine the right investment strategies for each group; outlines measurable goals and objectives; and tells how the organization will compete.

▶ The elements of all three types of plans are linked. The financial projections contained in a business plan are based on the assumptions made in the marketing plan. The marketing plan sets out where, how, and when promotional expenditures will be made, based on the expected level of sales. Some elements in the direct marketing plan are simply reframed from the strategic or business plan. The synergy between the plans increases when members of an organization ask the same questions over and over again, and arrive at the same answers.

THE IMPACT OF
DATABASES

In the 19th century, shopkeepers pursued a highly personal "customer-centric" approach. Stores were small enough for shopkeepers to keep track of the preferences and proclivities of each individual they served.

Today's successful companies still apply a customer-centric approach, but it is driven by technology that allows organizations to identify, differentiate, and interact with millions of customers, and create customized communications for them.

Skillfully used, technology creates the impression that goods or services are offered for a specific customer's consideration. The truth is, *individual* customers are rarely *individually* identified. They are aggregated, then broken down into increasingly smaller groups that share similar behaviors, attitudes, demographics, or lifestyles. These elements are analyzed individually or combined to identify propensities for product demand, purchase, or defection. Once analyzed or combined, these elements can help organizations identify customer segments that can have remarkably different characteristics. Customers that have the greatest value to an organization can be differentiated from those with a lesser value or potential. Customers with different needs can be identified so that promotions, offers, and even products can be tailored to their specific needs. And customers who make major purchases can be acknowledged with thank-you letters, warranty cards, special offers for maintenance, and other communications designed to increase customer loyalty.

The knowledge that enables an organization to accomplish these goals is contained in a database—the heart of customer-centric strategies. While organizations use databases for a variety of business purposes, including order entry, billing, inventory management, and customer service, this chapter will focus on marketing databases—databases created to support marketing business processes.

Marketing databases are essential to the marketing process. The terms *direct marketing* and *database marketing* have often been used synonymously. Many companies have marketing databases but don't consider themselves users of direct marketing. Consumer goods companies use their databases for promotion programs.

Stockbrokers use marketing databases for prospecting, cross-selling, and up-selling. Semantics aren't important. Marketing databases enable the use of the tools and techniques of direct marketing. So long as these tools are carefully and profitably applied, companies can be successful.

Marketing databases are important to organizations that can no longer personally know their customers. The databases provide these organizations with the customer information necessary to support decisions that can help reduce the inherent risk in marketing programs. Marketing databases allow organizations to serve customers as individuals, creating ongoing dialogues to customize the relationships between marketer and customer.

There is no standard or "right" procedure for developing a marketing database. It is a customized application whose development must take many variables into consideration. A marketing database requires a complex group of inputs from promotions, external data, and internal systems (see Exhibit 3–1).

These databases can be created using off-the-shelf solutions, but they must be configured and integrated into the systems of users. Many vendors offer marketing database systems that run on mainframe computers, client server networks, or on PCs. Some are meant to stand alone, some to extract data from legacy systems (large computer systems that remain from a previous generation and time) or run with Internet applications.

Which system to select depends on a business's organizational structure, culture, and way of doing business. The number of records to be stored will impact the choice of a database. The kinds of marketing programs (e.g., brand building, promotion, direct mail, Internet) will impact database needs. The size, capabilities, and empowerment of the marketing staff is a driver for the choice of a marketing database. Most important, the sources of data will shape an organization's database needs.

The Internet is another factor to consider in creating a database. Both a boon and a complication, the Internet has created a virtual ocean of data for marketers to collect and try to make sense of. Marketers often have trouble synchronizing the information on databases within their firms. The deluge of information added from activity on the Internet has left many marketers unprepared and unable to take advantage of this rich new data source.

These are just a few of the factors that help make an organization a "market-intelligent enterprise." Every organization has its own needs that shape its unique marketing database. We'll look at some of those factors in this chapter. Most important, we will look at how to *use* the information stored in a database, especially in the era of the Internet.

What Is a Database?

In its simplest form, a database is a list. A card catalog could be considered a simple database sorted in alphabetical order, indexed by last name, and randomly accessed.

EXHIBIT 3–1

A Marketing Database System

A marketing database helps build customer relationships by capturing historical and behavioral data from an organization's marketing activities. Increasingly, information is a strategic resource, and databases are used to integrate the breadth of an organization's activities. Information can be used to drive product, channel, and marketing communications programs.

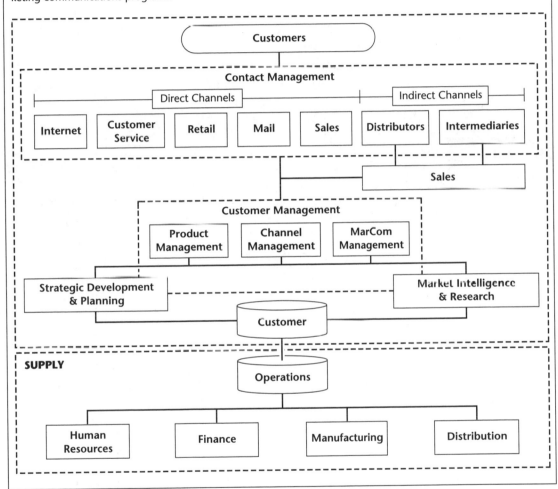

At the other end of the spectrum, a database is an engine that can link a virtually unlimited assortment of characteristics or variables together in a dynamic array.

There are two kinds of databases: *flat file* and *relational*.

A flat file database is a simple list that is sorted in one sequential order, most likely in customer number sequence. Each customer record must be kept in the same format. It would probably include a customer number, last name, zip code, and phone number indexes.

Because information is retrieved sequentially, as a flat file database grows it takes longer to run through the entire sequence in order to retrieve information. Thus, it is not useful for storing information that needs to be accessed quickly—in order for customers to place an order by phone or to check an order's status on the Internet. A flat file database is useful for storing information on promotional events for later analysis, for example, for modeling or future promotions.

The flat file approach becomes cumbersome when customer characteristics in addition to name, address, city, state, zip code, etc., are added. Marketers can add dozens—even hundreds—of customer variables related to behavior, demographics, and lifestyles. These variables, used mainly for marketing or financial analysis, are often maintained in secondary files called "tables." The order processing system doesn't have to wade through this data as a customer attempts to place an order.

EXHIBIT 3–2

Relational Database

A relational database structure reduces processing time by having a single element in a table relate to a single element in another table. While information in the tables can be extensive, only the information that "relates" is used in processing. This example shows a business-to-business database.

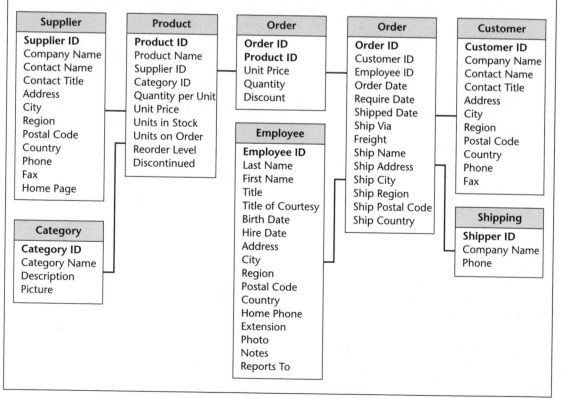

Supplier	Product	Order	Order	Customer
Supplier ID	**Product ID**	**Order ID**	**Order ID**	**Customer ID**
Company Name	Product Name	**Product ID**	Customer ID	Company Name
Contact Name	Supplier ID	Unit Price	Employee ID	Contact Name
Contact Title	Category ID	Quantity	Order Date	Contact Title
Address	Quantity per Unit	Discount	Require Date	Address
City	Unit Price		Shipped Date	City
Region	Units in Stock		Ship Via	Region
Postal Code	Units on Order	**Employee**	Freight	Postal Code
Country	Reorder Level		Ship Name	Country
Phone	Discontinued	**Employee ID**	Ship Address	Phone
Fax		Last Name	Ship City	Fax
Home Page		First Name	Ship Region	
		Title	Ship Postal Code	**Shipping**
Category		Title of Courtesy	Ship Country	
		Birth Date		**Shipper ID**
Category ID		Hire Date		Company Name
Category Name		Address		Phone
Description		City		
Picture		Region		
		Postal Code		
		Country		
		Home Phone		
		Extension		
		Photo		
		Notes		
		Reports To		

Secondary files are linked by a duplicate variable in each table (e.g., a customer ID number). Each table can have its own format. When these files are put into linked tables (a table is data put into rows and columns, like a spreadsheet) and placed within a larger database structure, it is called a "relational" database (see Exhibit 3–2).

The practice of Customer Relationship Management (CRM) requires sophisticated database systems that help marketers gain insight into customer behaviors, drive multichannel campaigns based on customer preferences, and track customer interactions across traditional and E-business initiatives. A system designed to support quarterly mailings for a small business won't need the same level of sophistication, but may result in a significant return on investment for the organization. A rudimentary knowledge of computers and information processing is helpful in assessing an organization's needs.

Sources of Information

Most of the information needed to begin a customer database is readily available within an organization. Accounting records, shipping and fulfillment records, service reports, inquiries, warranty cards, and survey research results can all yield valuable marketing information (see Exhibit 3–3).

But just because the information is there does not automatically qualify it for entry into a marketing database. Some information is unnecessary; other information is too expensive to acquire. A guideline to follow is this: collect the relevant data you think you'll need to know . . . and no more. Usually this will be information

---

EXHIBIT 3–3

Types of Data
Both consumer and business databases usually combine internal and external data, but the sources and types of data vary.

Internal Data (Customer)	External Data
• Purchases	• Address (street, telephone, E-mail)
• Customer transactions	• Household
• Amount spent	• Demographics
• Transaction dates	• Socioeconomic data
• Promotion history	• Lifestyle psychographics
• Customer services	• Firmographics technographics (Business data)
• Profitability	• Geo-demographics
• Lifetime value	

necessary to better understand individual prospect or customer needs, better assess their possible value, or identify their propensity for future response.

Many kinds of data are stored on a marketing database. For companies selling direct, the most useful information is historical purchase data: the first date and the subsequent date(s) of activity, the dollar amounts of each purchase, and products purchased (recency, frequency, monetary, and type).

Promotion history adds information on customer behavior that can also be used to improve future programs. Maintaining a record of the campaigns, offers, or types of promotions that a customer has responded to adds information that can be used to segment customer groups.

Customer data are often limited to name, address, city, state, and zip code. To give a clearer picture of customers, demographic and lifestyle data can be appended to a database: age, income, gender, marital status, home value, presence of children, education, hobbies, interests, etc. Demographic and lifestyle data often close the loop on customer knowledge.

A large credit card company was designing a marketing database. Its records contained only the merchant number, date, and amount of a purchase, not what was purchased with their card. The records indicated if the customer bought from a major vendor like an airline or from a chain store like K mart or Pizza Hut. Instead of trying to discover more about customer buying behavior, the company appended data to each record, adding more than 250 individual-level variables like type of car, age, income, etc. While appending data was an important element for identifying the heaviest users and for developing programs for the future, it would have been far better for the company to take what it did know about customer behavior (even if it took some creativity to decipher).

Attitudinal data—data on brands, category usage, purchase motivators, purchases barriers, customer satisfaction, etc.—can help an organization leverage the equity it has built with customers and determine new segmentation strategies. When gleaned from surveys or other research and added to demographic data, attitudinal data can be a powerful tool for identifying loyal customers, swing users, or potential changers.

Business and industrial databases require unique data. Customers are often not the end-user, but rather, a buying authority. It is important to capture multiple names within a company so that decision makers, decision influencers, and buying authorities can be tracked. In addition, relevant data for industrial databases include standard industrial classification (SIC), headquarters or branch office, revenues, number of employees, length of time in business, socioeconomic information about the organization's location, and even data about the personality of individual buyers.

Today's technology encourages the collection of vast quantities of data—but what data a database should include depends entirely on its future value in use. "Nice to know" or "We may need that somewhere down the line" are not valid reasons for accumulating data. Information costs money, and that cost must return a value.

Information is also a perishable commodity. Not only does the degree of customer activity (or inactivity) fluctuate, but the people and organizations comprising a database are far from static. Customers' demographics change as they go through various life stages or raise families. Business buyers change jobs, within as well as between organizations. Customers' attitudes and preferences change. They die. They move. In 12 months, 20 percent of an average customer list could change addresses.

Such volatility demonstrates the importance of adequate mailing list maintenance. It demonstrates, too, that customer lists that are mailed and maintained religiously have greater deliverability value to the direct marketer than lists compiled without data qualification, from directories or rosters.

Data about customers and their transactions must be kept up-to-date. No advertiser wants to distribute communications indiscriminately. It is important to make sure that the message is not only deliverable, but also properly targeted. Cost without benefit is to be avoided. To achieve this end, you need to be concerned with maintenance as well as with ongoing updating of transactions and other data contained within each customer record.

Marketers must often choose between a simple database and simple analysis. Experience shows that the greatest success comes from continuously expanding the variables in a database. Adding appended and census variables does not mean that recency won't be the most powerful and predictive variable. But if the variables are not added in, a marketer may never know.

Database Marketing and Customer Relationships

The first sale to a newly acquired customer is but a forerunner of additional sales to that customer in the future. Additional sales are key to the customer relationship marketing process. Because it costs far less to keep a customer than to acquire a new one, increasing numbers of companies are focusing extensive resources on customer loyalty, seeking to retain customers through programs and incentives driven by their marketing database.

From the outset, customers are not homogeneous. Their one common characteristic is the relationship or affinity they form with companies they favor with their business—and often their continued loyalty. When customers perpetuate such relationships, they expect in return to receive quality, value, and service. Organizations, in turn, seek customer loyalty in the hope of cementing the relationship, so that customers keep coming back.

Relationships or affinities with customers can be developed to such a degree that loyal customers trust and buy the company's brands above all competitive offerings. Affinity and good customer relationships extend their value, too, well beyond the first sale . . . to cross-selling of unrelated products/services, even from unrelated organizations. The power of the marketing database makes all of this, and more, possible.

EXHIBIT 3–4

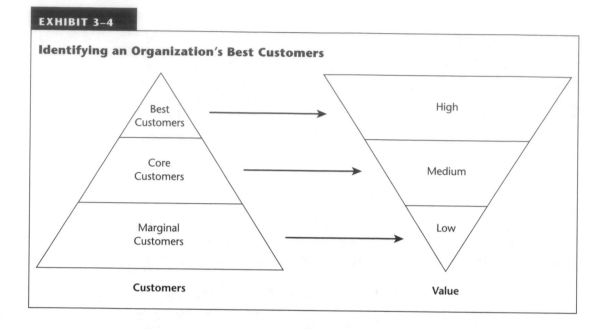

Identifying an Organization's Best Customers

Defining an organization's best customers is often not easy. Most organizations identify their most profitable customers as their best customers. There is a good reason for this. As noted by David Ogilvy, as few as 10 percent of an organization's customers contribute 90 percent of its profits. A second group of core customers, with average profitability, make up the largest group of customers. A final group of marginal buyers, often infrequent or high maintenance customers, usually provide little or no profit (see Exhibit 3–4).

Yet many organizations strive to retain money-losing clients. These "marquee clients" may give the organization credibility even as they drain profitability. Some large advertising agencies, for example, keep their largest and least profitable clients because they are household names or longtime clients who provide high visibility in local markets, assignments in a prestigious category, or unique opportunities for creativity.

Such behavior may seem illogical, but it isn't uncommon. In fact, every organization actually has a small core group of highly loyal customers that provides the majority of its profit. What often seems illogical is that few organizations develop retention programs that distinguish their most profitable customers from their least profitable.

The first step in leveraging an organization's core group of loyal and profitable customers is to understand their motivations. Some customers are easily predictable, preferring long-term, stable relationships. Other customers may spend more, pay their bills more promptly, or require less maintenance. Others may value the organization's products or services over all others. These different groups make up an organization's best customers, and the more of them an organization can acquire and keep, the more profitable the organization will be.

Customer Relationships and Lifetime Value (LTV)

In the past, it was difficult to evaluate how well a company nurtured its customer relationships. Though businesses knew that the number of customers increased or decreased, that advertising attracted some new customers, or that competitors took away others, there were few ways of knowing which customers came or went, or why.

But database technology has changed that. An organization can at last identify its loyal customers, its repeat purchasers, and its one-time-only "triers," especially within well-defined market segments. Moreover, marketers can now trace each customer's actions and transactions. This ability makes customers a significant—and measurable—asset like buildings, equipment, inventory, and accounts receivable.

Customers are a source of future revenues and future profits that can go well beyond recovering the initial costs of acquiring these customers through selling, advertising, and other sales promotions. However, generally accepted accounting principles actually hide the value of customers on a line on balance sheets called "goodwill." The investments in programs to reduce customer defections and improve customer loyalty are written off as an expense rather than an investment that can have a long-term impact on profits. When the high costs of creating a marketing database are simply seen as an expense, they easily fall victim to marketing budget cuts. When seen as part of a customer loyalty effort, the impact of marketing databases is no longer hidden.

The concept of lifetime value of a customer (LTV), adopted long ago by mail order firms to guide marketing decision-making, also applies to the value of the database. More companies began adopting the LTV concept after the Supreme Court ruled in favor of a New Jersey newspaper that claimed depreciation deduction for its acquisition of a paid-subscriber customer list as part of a sale transaction. In reaching its decision, the court rejected the IRS argument that customer lists are a form of goodwill and therefore never depreciable.

Direct marketers truly appreciate LTV when they engage in both continuity selling and cross-selling, and when they develop a database of customers. The LTV approach, too, is ideally suited to determining the market value of an enterprise in cases where an acquisition or a sale is contemplated. Since such an asset valuation of a database reflects anticipated future performance, it can be a better gauge of value than the commonly used multiples of sales or profits. The arithmetic involved in determining LTV is calculated in Chapter 20, "Mathematics of Direct Marketing."

Accessing Data Through Data Warehouses and Data Marts

All database systems have trade-offs. One of these involves ease of access to data. Marketers ask for such access to get closer to answers about customers, segments, and program results. This usually requires significant time and expense, including vendor evaluation, hardware, and software implementation. Often, marketers are able to get slick point-and-click query tools that require days or weeks of staff training, only to discover that this is not what they were looking for.

Most databases maintain data as rows and columns of numbers and words. Queries to the database return data in the same way. In addition, queries must be constructed carefully to return the information that marketers are really looking for. What marketers would prefer is to ask questions and get answers in the form of charts, graphs, and maps.

Decision Support Systems and Executive Information Systems (EIS) provide access that is quick and easy use, but the trade-off here is that charts and graphs must often be preprogrammed to some degree. Quick count engines are another technology for doing data analysis and extraction. These tools often feed into an EIS system but reduce the limits on ad-hoc queries and reports or questions of the database that allow for unlimited exploration.

Many large organizations have data helpful to marketing locked up in systems designed for such operational purposes as order entry, purchasing, logistics, or transaction processing. These so-called *legacy systems* are often added at different times, created on different hardware platforms, and run software optimized for the purpose of that system.

Legacy systems offer a challenge to marketers. While they contain information that may be important for marketing, this information is not easily accessible. Information from multiple systems simply multiplies the problem.

One solution to this problem is the *data warehouse*—a storage facility that takes data from a number of transaction systems and brings it together into a central repository. The job of the data warehouse is to create a set of standardized fields for all of the different data elements in the various legacy systems.

A data warehouse is often designed for a whole host of corporate needs and departments. A separate system can house all the customer and transaction data along with accounting, manufacturing, and any number of other data. Data warehouses can make it easier to query and report data from multiple transaction processing systems and external data sources.

The data warehouse is a good data storage and reporting system, but it is not easy or flexible to use for heavy data processing or modeling. A better solution is to extract information from the data warehouse and put it into a *data mart*: a database system designed for a smaller number of users with more specialized data uses.

The warehouse feeds relatively raw data into the mart—leaving out accounting data, perhaps, but including those data fields that marketing is genuinely interested in. Inside a data mart, marketing can use the analysis tools best suited to specialized tasks. Data can be summarized to suit need, and new variables can be created or appended (bought from outside data providers and added to the customer records).

Although marketing databases have come a long way, there is no simple way to gain access to all the data necessary to make decisions. There is a great demand for specialists who are trained in database design, execution, and analysis, and who can work hand in glove with marketing departments. The explosion of data created by the growth of the Internet has added even more demand for such individuals. Marketers embarking on a database project would be wise to work with specialists either inside or outside of their firms.

Using Data Mining to Make Decisions

Many marketers busy themselves looking at their data in an almost endless process of discovery. Data is infinite; that is, there are an infinite number of variables that can be gathered about any particular item or event. Data is also historical. It is a collection of facts about events that have already transpired. At the same time, decisions are finite and must be made in time.

When tracking history, there is always a gap between yesterday and tomorrow. There is always something else that can be taken into consideration. This means that no matter how much data you have, there is never enough data to make a decision.

The growth of the Internet has exacerbated this quandary. Organizations with busy websites can capture millions of pieces of data about users each day. So can retail marketers, consumer goods companies, and many other users. Kraft Foods, for example, has captured information on more than 30 million respondents to promotional offers. Large data sets such as these are difficult to maintain but even more difficult to gain knowledge from. That's why marketers who are swimming in data need tools that let them use the right data to make decisions that impact the bottom line.

Data mining is a process for discovering patterns and trends in large database sets to find useful decision-making information. There are a number of data mining tools and techniques. Some are used to identify significant relationships that exist among variables. Such tools are useful when there are many possible relationships. For instance, a packaged goods company may track up to 200 variables about each customer on its file. There are many possible ways of combining 200 variables. A data mining application can quickly help recognize which patterns of relationships among the variables are significant. Once these relationships are identified, other types of tools are then used to understand the nature of the relationships.

There is no one best data mining technique; different techniques work better with different types of data. Four of the most common are Cluster Analysis, Daisy (Data Analysis Interactively) graphical analysis, Market Basket Analysis, and neural networks.

Cluster Analysis

Cluster Analysis is a data reduction technique that groups variables based on similar data characteristics. It is useful for segmenting customer groups based on demographic, financial, or purchase behavior characteristics. A bank used Cluster Analysis to identify three groups of customers based on the types of accounts they had opened. The first group, labeled "General Customers," opened equal percentages of accounts of all types. The second group, "Long-term Customers," opened more mortgages, investment accounts, home improvement loans, and CDs, and had a higher lifetime value and a longer customer life cycle. The third group, "Short-term Customers," opened more checking and savings accounts and personal loans. They had a lower lifetime value and were more likely to switch accounts or institutions. Once data from the Cluster Analysis helped the bank identify differences in behavior (especially attrition) between the groups, it was able to treat each segment differently, creating specific offers and promotions for each group and adjusting the promotional budget for each.

Daisy Charts

Data visualization tools let users easily and quickly view graphical displays of information from different perspectives using graphs and summaries of different subsets of data. Exhibit 3–5 shows a Daisy (Data Analysis Interactively) graphical analysis. Daisy Charts help marketers discover underlying patterns in data that are not necessarily statistically significant but can dramatically affect business, research, and strategies. These hidden links are shown in colored Daisy Charts.

The Daisy Chart shows an analysis of Sales and Inventory by Shop, Product Type, and Supplier. Sales and Inventory are shown as histograms that enable a visual assessment of performance. The links among variables show which are the strongest patterns. This analysis can even show which are the least profitable.

The real benefit from this kind of analysis comes from looking at Daisy Charts over successive days. Subtle changes become obvious. Problems, strengths, and possible weaknesses can be identified before they become substantial. For example, to reduce customer churn, a wireless phone company identified variables related to attrition and plotted total minutes used in each customer's first six months of business. Daisy Charts plotted the changes in customers' regular usage, roaming charges, and long distance during each of these six months and tracked changes from month to month. The company also plotted positive or negative responses to bonding mailings and phone or mail retention efforts, and compared tests against con-

EXHIBIT 3–5

Daisy Chart

A Daisy Chart is a visualization tool that shows the relationship among variables. Related variables are linked, and the strength of the variables shown with histograms (bar charts that show frequency data). This example analyzes traffic to a website.

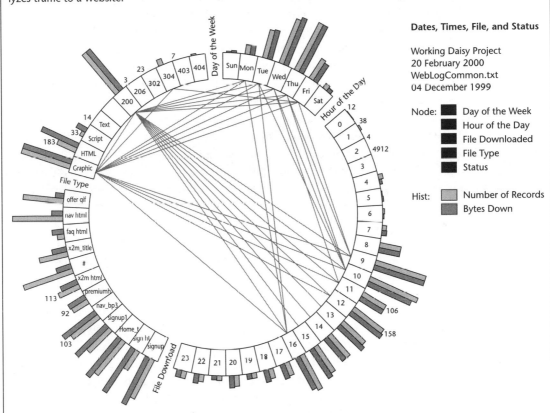

trols. Daisy Charts revealed correlations among variables that could improve the timing and efficiency of promotions. They also identified customer segments whose lifetime value was less than the cost of retention—substantially changing the company's approach to customer churn.

Market Basket Analysis

Market Basket Analysis is one of the most common data mining techniques. Named for the cart that customers use while shopping, its purpose is to determine what products or services customers purchase together.

Instead of making marketers guess what customers should logically buy together, Market Basket Analysis lets customer sales data provide the information. Developed as a means for retail marketers to interpret checkout scanner data, Market Basket Analysis can be used to help stores place products that are frequently purchased together in the same area. A mail order company, cataloger, or E-commerce company can use Market Basket Analysis to determine the layout of a catalog, website, or order form. Direct marketers can use the results to determine what new products to offer their prior customers or which products to offer as an add-on when customers call or complete an on-line transaction.

Some related products are obvious. It's hard to imagine a fast-food restaurant failing to ask, "Would you like fries with your order?" Other associations are not so obvious. For example, a company that sells wine direct learned that buyers of champagne were likely to add glassware, chocolates, or gift items to their order. Buyers of California wines would often add other California wines to their orders. Red wine buyers were more likely to take advantage of full case discounts. By matching offers to various behaviors, the company was able to substantially increase overall sales.

Neural Networks

Neural networks are used to discover and predict relationships in the data. Unlike traditional statistical modeling, neural networks can be "trained" to discover relationships that cannot be described with linear algebra and can often compensate for low quality data. Neural networks are the ultimate black box. They build complex formulas that are nearly impossible to decipher but seem to work in many cases. They are certainly worth testing where large amounts of data exist.

Neural networks can effectively reveal what elements of a company's total offering affect customer satisfaction. One midwestern utility company used neural networks to analyze customer satisfaction surveys in order to identify the specific service elements that had the greatest impact on overall customer satisfaction and to measure how those elements changed over a period of time. This information was then used to target areas of improvement that could lead to increased customer satisfaction ratings.

Because the utility was going through deregulation, it would face real competition for the first time. Hot summers and an aging power grid had given the utility a dubious reputation with customers. In order to remain competitive, the utility conducted a series of surveys the year before restructuring was to take place.

Neural networks were chosen to analyze the answers because of their ability to measure multiple and complex interactions between variables. A model was created that compared answers about various facets of customer service, perceptions of the company and its concern for the community, and customer demographics over time. Many questions had multiple levels of response. The neural network was able to discern between different overall ratings of satisfaction by customers, and key predictors of satisfaction were extracted from the models.

This analysis revealed key elements of service that customers found most important. It identified demographic segments that were most and least likely to be satisfied by company efforts. And it helped determine the most effective message delivery channels for reaching customers. This important information was used by marketing communication decision makers to develop direct marketing strategies for improving customer satisfaction and retention.

Taking Your Database Global

Creating a database for global use, particularly on the Internet, adds many complications.

A look at websites from companies like Cisco Systems, Microsoft, National Semiconductor, and Outpost.com shows the flags of many countries. Often, these large companies accept and ship orders to customers around the globe. Information on these customers is collected and stored in a marketing database.

To accommodate this information, a number of changes must be made. Name fields must be enlarged, as it is common in some countries to use a maternal family name as well as a paternal family name. One or more middle names are quite common in some countries, as are longer names than those used in the United States. Character sets must be added to accommodate language differences. Languages that share Roman characters with English often use different accent marks and punctuation. Spelling the name of customers properly is a worldwide courtesy.

Postal and address coding is another issue. According to the Universal Postal Union—a specialized institution of the United Nations that regulates postal conventions in its 189 member countries—only 69 countries, including the United States, have sophisticated postal delivery systems. Of those, only 30 use street names for identifying addresses.

International mail codes (e.g., in the United States, the five- or nine-digit zip code) come in various lengths, can have different placement within an address, and can be numeric, alpha, or alphanumeric. Databases that capture international data must be flexible and designed with the needs of different countries in mind.

Databases Raise Privacy Concerns

While marketing databases create benefits for both consumers and organizations by reducing wasted promotion, increasing targeted products/services, and personalizing customer service, their use also raises privacy concerns. These concerns collide when consumers' expectations of privacy conflict with what organizations believe are fair commercial uses of personal information.

Marketers in the United States prefer to apply self-regulation to balance the scales. But the global reach of the Internet means that companies may be subject to privacy legislation in jurisdictions where they market outside of the United States. European Union (EU) data rules, for example, are very stringent. The EU Data Protection Directive calls upon member states to protect the "right to privacy with respect to the processing of personal data." It requires EU member countries enact legislation requiring that on-line and off-line data is:

- Processed fairly and lawfully

- Collected and possessed for specified, explicit, legitimate purposes

- Accurate and kept current

- Kept no longer than deemed necessary to fulfill the stated purpose

Users are given the explicit right to access information, correct or block inaccuracies, and object to the information's use. An individual's consent is required to collect sensitive information (e.g., race, religion, etc.), and these rules forbid the transfer of personal data to any country outside the EU that does not guarantee similar safeguards are in place. This view of privacy is different than in the United States.

U.S. companies that do business within the European Union are subject to these rules for data collected within the EU, according to Peter Swire, a law professor at Ohio State University. Swire notes that an airline reservations system was prohibited in one European country from transferring personal data to the United States, such as a passenger's preference for a kosher meal because that might imply that he or she is Jewish.

CASE STUDY: 3Com: Building a Global Database

BACKGROUND
Global corporations face unique challenges in developing marketing databases. The development of 3Com's database reveals critical issues managers and executives must deal with.

The 3Com company is a worldwide supplier of data, voice, and video communication technology, with more than 200,000 million customers. Through a number of sales channels, including on-line selling, phone orders, and retailers, 3Com sells to consumer and business-to-business customers. It sells direct to business customers, including large enterprises, carriers, OEMs (original equipment manufacturers), and small to medium businesses.

CASE STUDY: **3Com: Building a Global Database** *(continued)*

CHALLENGE

The 3Com marketing database needed to accommodate its growing business and be able to manage information from many different sources—customers and prospects, consumer users, business users, international addresses, on-line users—in real time.

SOLUTION

The company defined corporate, organizational, and departmental goals that were critical to the success of the project. The database would have to meet three key criteria:

1. Accommodate global responses
2. Link with all off-line and E-commerce initiatives
3. Have short refresh cycles

This database should have integrating systems that provide different views of marketing information; for example, demand generation (that is, pulling prospect information out of the database in order to create new business opportunities), lead cultivation, and Sales Force Automation (SFA). Each of these views contained different information and required a different type of processing. Hence, 3Com decided to build its marketing database to support more targeted and measurable demand generation, and to integrate with other functions.

The output of the database was critical in the implementation process, and 3Com made sure that the output data matched its business needs (ability for users to extract their own data 24/7, Web-based access, and flexibility). Moreover, regular and accurate data input was the key to useful output. Decisions made by 3Com on data input included the daily update cycle, company standard format, and the use of key codes to ensure accurate data entry.

To achieve an operational global database, 3Com created systems to ensure that data sources were reliable and in a country-compliant format. That database was designed to store international data and to maintain and clean the data without losing unnecessary data or losing the identification of countries of origin.

To support Web access, 3Com designed a simple interface and a set of reporting rules that allowed it to support multiple campaign results.

While most databases are updated quarterly, 3Com knew its database would capture so much information that new "data builds" would be needed almost continually in order to add new fields and refine old ones. Cycle times and audits were accelerated with continuous updates and frequent data builds. Also, 3Com continuously audited its processes to make sure they were working properly and to ensure consistency, accuracy, and clarity of data.

RESULTS

The strategy that 3Com followed to develop its new marketing database produced many successful results.

The company was successful in solving the issues (language, address format, etc.) that a centralized global database faces. The 3Com website, one of the key inputs into the database, allows unique access for visitors from 25 countries, including the United States. Each Welcome Page is written in that country's language, if different from English (see Exhibits 3–6 and 3–7).

The 3Com database was customized for its employees, corporate customers, and partners. Business customers are able to connect through a customized extranet connection by logging on to its website using a personal password. They can check on product availability, contract status, order status, etc., in real time (see Exhibit 3–8).

The 3Com E-commerce infrastructure and its database were fully integrated in order to manage customer relationships. Through the connectivity and integration of its systems, 3Com is able to identify repeat purchase customers, onetime customers, how many times a customer orders, and other data that help manage its marketing campaigns.

CASE STUDY: 3Com: Building a Global Database *(continued)*

EXHIBIT 3-6

3Com Home Page

The 3Com home page (also the Welcome Page for English-language users) is easy to navigate and use. Light graphics and generous white space make it load quickly no matter what kind of connection the user has—important when a site is accessed from countries with slower connections.

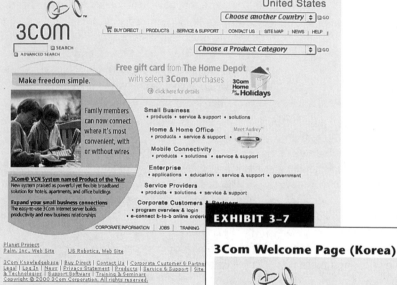

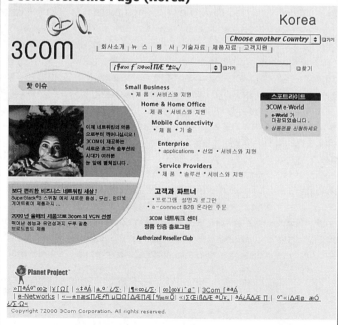

CASE STUDY: **3Com: Building a Global Database** *(continued)*

EXHIBIT 3-8

3Com Customer Page

The 3Com case focuses on some of the issues facing companies that market globally as well on the Internet. But there is one additional complicating factor.

Most businesses market only to other businesses or only to consumers. But 3Com, as well as companies such as Dell, Microsoft, and OfficeMax, markets to both consumers and businesses. This adds a significant level of complexity to the database's storage and access capabilities.

Define the main differences in building a marketing database for consumers versus businesses. Think in terms of the sources of this data, the differences in data fields, and the kinds of information that are specific to maintaining information about consumers versus businesses. Are the marketing programs done for consumers different from those for businesses? If so, what are the implications of that for a marketing database?

Key Points

▶ Databases aggregate customers and break them down into increasingly smaller groups that share similar behaviors, attitudes, demographics, or lifestyles. Analyzing or combining these elements helps identify customer segments with similar needs so promotions, offers, and products and services can be tailored to their needs.

▶ Look for customer database information in your organization's accounting records, shipping and fulfillment records, service reports, inquiries, warranty cards, and survey research results. Add historical purchase and promotion history, attitudinal data, and demographic information to segment customer groups. Steer away from data that is merely "nice to know" and seek information that returns a value.

▶ By combining data from a number of transaction systems, a data warehouse can make it easier to query and report data from multiple transaction processing systems and external data sources. For heavy data processing or modeling, extract information from the data warehouse and put it into a data mart that can summarize and analyze data and create or append new variables.

▶ Four data mining techniques—Cluster Analysis, Daisy (Data Analysis Interactively) graphical analysis, Market Basket Analysis, and neural networks—can help marketers discover patterns and trends in large database sets to find useful decision-making information.

▶ Building a global database involves a host of considerations: larger name fields, additional character sets, address coding variations, international mail codes, and privacy laws that vary from country to country.

CONSUMER
AND BUSINESS
MAILING LISTS

Should we invest more in creating new customers or in building better relationships with our existing customers?

This question is nearly impossible to answer.

If the program is mature, if there are a large number of customers, and if profit is the key focus, the common wisdom would argue for building better customer relationships. The tools and techniques of direct marketing are well used when targeting consumers or businesses where there is an established relationship. Results will be significantly greater and profits higher when customers are targeted. Even former buyers will respond better than individuals who have no previous experience with an organization.

But creating new customers is also essential.

To promote a new product or service or a new venture, or to thrive in the growth stage of a business, an organization needs to prospect for new customers. Even established organizations need new prospects to replenish their customer base. Successful customer retention programs don't keep 100 percent of customers. Maintaining a balance between customer and prospect marketing efforts is one of the keys to business success.

Many organizations rely upon direct mail for their main medium or as a support medium for their prospecting efforts. Mailing lists can help them target businesses or consumers, sell a product or service direct, generate a lead, drive traffic into an on-line or off-line store, sell subscriptions, or persuade contributors. They may also use television, radio, print advertising, co-ops, the Internet, or other media to create new customers. They may even supplement with trade shows or events. However, if organizations use direct mail, they will likely need to use mailing lists. A thorough understanding of traditional list practices is a building block of direct marketing, and the goal of this chapter. (E-mail lists are discussed in Chapter 12.)

Mailing List Basics

Mailing lists are not sold but rented, typically for a onetime use. If after testing a portion of a list, the renting organization wants to remail or roll out the list (e.g., in continuation), it must pay an additional rental fee.

The list provider *seeds* the list with names that come back to it in order to monitor list usage. Companies that repeatedly violate the rental agreement soon find they are unable to rent lists from any organization. Seeding is a significant deterrent to abuse.

Many organizations rent their lists. According to the Direct Marketing Association (DMA), the practice of making lists available for rental or exchange has remained consistent over the past few years. The number of names rented by companies has increased (see Exhibit 4–1). Companies find it a significant additional revenue source. The average lists rent for $70 per thousand but may cost $100 or more per thousand depending upon the number of names rented and the selection criteria. The more responsive the names on the list, the more it costs and the more likely that the list will be rented frequently.

EXHIBIT 4–1

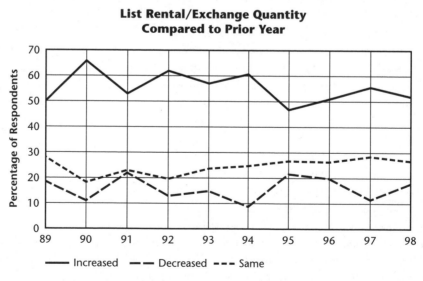

List Rental Growth

According to the DMA, list rental usage continues to grow, especially in the business-to-business segment.

List & Database Council. Annual List Usage Study.

Specialty lists of hard-to-get names—such as buyers of airplanes, sailboats, and exotic cars; small and large cap investors; and foreign lists—may rent for three to four times premium! The quality of the names and difficulty in acquiring them is always a major factor in list rental costs.

Hot-line names also are rented at premium price. These are names with the most recent activity on file, typically defined as added within the last 90 days. It can be up to six months or a year, depending upon how the list owner defines it. Hot-line names remain a very popular category of names to rent.

An organization with a list of one million names may be able to rent every name on the list seven or more times a year. At an average cost of $70 per thousand, turning the list seven times annually would generate gross revenue of $490,000. While the list owner might have to pay fees, commissions, and some processing costs, this list becomes incremental income to the business. It's easy to understand why organizations are involved in the practice of renting their list of customers or members.

Some organizations choose not to rent their lists. But even they will often exchange lists with other companies that have noncompetitive offers. Organizations usually exchange an even number of names. Some organizations won't exchange their hot-line names or will only exchange names of former buyers. This dilutes the value of the exchange, but it still may be worth testing in categories where new names are difficult to acquire.

Types of Mailing Lists

There are three kinds of mailing lists: house lists, response lists, and compiled lists. Each type offers advantages but may have drawbacks. However, all lists must be maintained, kept up-to-date, to provide value or offer competitive advantage.

House Lists

House lists are simply the databases of an organization. Considered the key asset of any organization, they include current customers, former customers, and inquiries (i.e., prospects). Because the house list is so important, it must be maintained and updated constantly.

Each organization builds its house list to fit its unique needs. Records may be gleaned from a variety of internal sources, such as direct mail, phone, retail, or Internet transactions. A company may have more than one business unit and maintain purchase records separately or aggregate them. Even the definition of a customer varies from company to company.

The word "customer" usually refers to an "active" buyer. In mail order companies this usually means someone who has purchased within the last 12 months.

It is the same for contributors to causes. Subscribers to publications have finite expiration dates. They may be considered "active" and sent copies of the publication for as long as three months after the expiration date. Purchasers of long-life high-ticket items, such as computers or automobiles, may be considered active for the years that they own the product.

Although it also varies, former customers fall outside of an organization's definition of active. Former customers are valuable because they are more likely to purchase, subscribe, or contribute than prospects. The longer it has been since a transaction, the less likely it is that a former customer will purchase again. This is true in both the consumer and business markets. Recency of purchase, frequency of purchase, type of product purchased, and monetary value of transactions are clues to a customer's propensity to purchase again.

In our mobile society where up to 20 percent of the population moves annually and frequent job changes are commonplace, house lists can age quickly. Publications will remail lapsed subscribers within six months of expiration. Most organizations continue to mail former customers for up to three years. It is different for every organization.

Not all organizations maintain lists of inquiries or prospects. The benefit of prospect files is that the prospects have indicated some interest in the products or services offered by the organization. It is more common to maintain prospect files in the business marketplace, where qualified leads are often promoted for up to a year after first being identified.

Response Lists

Response lists are the house lists of other organizations. They are made up of individuals with an identifiable product interest and a proven willingness to buy, subscribe, join, contribute, inquire, or otherwise respond to specific offers. Response lists are most often used in the consumer marketplace, where customer files are larger than in the business market.

Response lists are made up of individuals who have exhibited a particular kind of behavior. They may have responded to a direct mail offer, a print ad, a broadcast commercial, via telephone, or on the Internet. Marketers have learned that previous behavior is the greatest predictor of future behavior. Someone who has responded by mail once is likely to do it again. Someone who has responded to an outbound telephone call is more likely to duplicate this action. And someone who has purchased a product from a certain category is more likely to purchase that category again.

Because marketers can select lists where specific behaviors have been exhibited, response lists are popular. While this is not a perfect science, it is clear that someone who has responded to a certain medium, a certain kind of offer (e.g., a sweepstakes), or a particular product category, is more likely to respond to similar future promotions than when knowledge of such behavior is absent.

Marketers try to match up previous behaviors with the kinds of behaviors they are trying to duplicate. Broad categories reflect this behavior. Response lists can be broken into a number of further categories.

Buyer Lists. These are lists of individuals who have purchased something direct, through a solo direct mail offer, a catalog, a print ad, a website, a short-form television commercial (30, 60, or 120 seconds in length) or an infomercial (10, 15, or 30 minutes in length).

Attendee/Membership/Seminar Lists. These are lists of individuals who have attended a conference, trade show, or industry event. Such individuals are extremely valuable, since they often spend hundreds, even thousands, of dollars to increase their knowledge about specific subjects. Individuals on these lists are likely to respond to offers that closely match their identified fields of interest.

Subscription Lists. These consist of individuals who have subscribed to business or consumer publications or newsletters. There are two kinds of subscription lists: *controlled circulation* and *paid circulation*.

Controlled circulation publications, common in business, are free to qualified readers. To qualify, subscribers must fall into a certain professional or managerial category and certify that they are decision makers or influencers for products offered by advertisers in the publications. Proof is accomplished by completing and signing a subscription request form, or "qualification card." Subscribers are asked to give their name, address, phone number, job title, job function, size of company, and the type of products they purchase. Typically, controlled circulation lists are selectable by all of these characteristics.

With paid circulation publications, subscribers pay a fee and are not required to provide information in addition to their name and address. Both business and consumer publications use this model. Paid publication titles often reach individuals with very specific interests. These lists can be highly responsive if the interests of subscribers are a good match for a product or service offered.

Donor Lists. Fund-raisers use donor lists because they contain the names of people who have contributed money to charities and nonprofit organizations. Political parties, special interest groups, religious assemblies, and cause-related organizations all use these lists. Knowing the source of names (direct mail, television, telephone, etc.) is important. When sending a request for contributions by mail, use names solicited by direct mail.

Credit Card Holder Lists. These names are useful because most credit card solicitations are sent and responded to by mail, and most direct offers require a credit card. Although credit cards seem ubiquitous, they are not. Active credit card users often fit a profile similar to direct mail buyers.

Merged Database Lists. This type of list includes the merged lists of companies that often won't rent their lists individually. Using the merged list simplifies the selection process because duplicate names are eliminated; therefore, the list owner can offer the remaining names as a single, unduplicated list at a higher rental fee. Abacus is one such list, aggregating consumer catalog lists. Cahners, a publisher of qualified trade publications, aggregates its various lists. These databases allow users to reach a large portion of a specific market segment without having to track down many hard-to-find lists.

Compiled Lists

Compiled lists are made up of individuals or companies without any previous indication of willingness to respond, but with some defined and identifiable characteristic(s) such as demographics, psychographics, zip code, etc. Compiled lists offer broad national coverage. Some pieces of demographic information are available on nearly every consumer, household, and business in the United States.

Compiled lists are useful for retail, consumer goods, and business offers where reaching the right target group is more critical than knowing that they have previously responded to a direct-response offer. They can also be used to enhance or profile house files, or are combined with response lists to add missing consumer demographic or business firmagraphic (e.g., business demographic) data.

There are three kinds of compiled lists: consumer compiled lists, consumer lifestyle enhanced lists, and business compiled lists.

Consumer Compiled Lists. Many consumer product marketers have developed clear pictures of their best customers. This picture may include demographics and psychographics, and may be limited to specific geographic areas. For example, an automobile manufacturer may have a clear demographic picture of the buyers of its brand. There may be differences among purchasers of different models of the brand (e.g., convertibles, family sedans, and sport utility vehicles). There might be differences in the popularity of each model in different geographical regions of the country. It is imperative for this marketer to reach the right target groups. Compiled lists are the only rented lists that would yield broad national or geographic penetration and pinpoint targeting (see Exhibit 4–2).

Consumer compiled lists are created from a number of different public and private sources. Name, address, and phone numbers are gleaned from telephone directories and credit bureau records. (Note: Credit bureau data may be used for name and address, but the Federal Trade Commission forbids the use of private financial data on these files for marketing purposes.)

Additional information comes from other sources. Home owner data (e.g., home value) is compiled from county property records. Driver's license and auto registration data is available from many states and added to the mix. Income and demographic information is derived from U.S. Bureau of the Census data. Com-

EXHIBIT 4–2

Consumer Compiled List Segments

Demographic data is compiled from public sources, while lifestyle information is usually compiled from surveys and other self-reported sources. Not all segments are available for every prospect. Choosing more segments gets you closer to your primary target market, but it also reduces the available universe.

Demographic
- Age
- Household Income
- Gender
- Marital Status
- Family Composition (e.g., presence of children, 0–1 people HH, etc.)
- Dwelling Unit Type
  - Single Family Dwelling Unit (SFDU)
  - Multiple Unit Dwelling (MUD)
- Home Value
- Credit & Savings
- Occupation
- Education
- Mail/Phone Responsive
- Telephone Number
- Auto Registration
  - Not available in all states
  - No lease car data

Lifestyle Interests
- Brand/Category Usage
- Ailments
- Financial/Stocks
- Household Income/Home Ownership
- Presence of Children
- Pet Ownership
- Mail Order Shopping (i.e., has responded to direct mail in the past)
- Travel (domestic, international, ecotourism)
- Sports (e.g., golf, skiing, cycling)
- Books
- Wine
- Gourmet Food/Cooking
- Fine Dining

pilers create elaborate algorithms to combine census data, property owner records, and automobile registrations to create even more accurate household profiles. Children's age data is collected from different sources and included on some list databases.

Consumer Lifestyle Enhanced Lists. Sometimes knowing customer demographics isn't enough. Many of the large compilers use syndicated surveys or warranty cards to capture a broad range of consumer information, including hobbies, personal interests, pet ownership, category and brand usage, and additional demographic information. This information is usually rented at the household level.

Often, this compiled list is a terrific way to identify households that have specific sports interests such as golf, fishing, or biking, or are pet owners (e.g., dogs, birds), or are mail order buyers. Consumers will identify themselves as health conscious, having a diet interest, or as users of a particular product category.

Self-reported data may not be totally accurate. They reflect an individual's perception of self. Individuals who say they are avid readers may not be, but they may be heavy buyers of books. Income may be overstated, but individuals may live a lifestyle that meets this exaggeration. While such lists may cover only 18 to 20 million U.S. households (less than 20 percent), these households tend to be some of the most promotionally responsive names available.

Business Compiled Lists. Business lists, compiled from a number of sources, contain addresses and phone numbers and key firmagraphics that describe the size of a company and its type of business. Typical firmagraphics include:

- Standard Industrial Classification (SIC)

- Annual Sales

- Number of Employees

- Headquarters or Branch Office

- Geography

- Business Structure (e.g., corporation, subsidiary)

- Recent Relocation

Where business compiled lists often fall short is in reaching an individual decision maker. Typically, the names of only a few top officers of a company appear, forcing users to mail to "premium buyer," "office manager," or "President"—which greatly reduces response. Combining compiled lists with lists that provide specific executive names (e.g., house files, trade publications, other response lists) may help to better target promotions. This is often done through profiling.

Profiling

Profiling is a first step in understanding an organization's customers by identifying demographics, firmagraphics, or lifestyle attributes of each customer. Appending this information to the customer file adds valuable information for targeting future promotions, understanding customer defections, and identifying cross-selling and other new business opportunities.

Business-to-business house files can be matched against a national database of businesses such as Dun & Bradstreet or InfoUSA. This profiling process will result in a more thorough knowledge of the current client base—a well-defined target market for future prospecting. With this knowledge comes a better understanding of the marketing and communications programs necessary to more effectively penetrate the desired segments (see Exhibit 4–3).

The information and insights obtained through profiling can help the business-to-business marketer accomplish a number of objectives and is usually developed in three phases:

Phase I: Account identification and matching. Consists of linking the national database operations files to the business-to-business house file.

Phase II: Appending data from the national database to the business-to-business house file. Utilizes the existing compiled business establishment data (e.g., geographic, type of business, size of business, and type of location) from the national database.

Phase III: Development of market segmentation profiles. Consists of analyzing the business-to-business customer file on the basis of the distribution and concentration of customers within specific market segments (e.g., the extent to which the current best customers are concentrated within certain areas, such as SIC codes, geographic areas, company size, and revenue contribution groups).

Another way of analyzing the activities of current customers and assessing their potential value is by drawing maps or creating matrices of current purchasing activities, as shown in Exhibit 4–4. Based on the purchase activity quadrant in which the customer falls, customer files can be segmented and specific messages and offers can be targeted to best leverage the different opportunities.

Quadrant 1 represents the best customers, those who spend the most dollars and purchase the most frequently. Clearly, the emphasis in this segment is on maintaining loyalty and providing rewards for continuity.

Quadrant 2 represents customers who spend a lot of dollars but spend infrequently. Large average-order sizes combined with low levels of purchase frequency indicate that the customer might be using this vendor for a few specialized purchases. Supplementary research, such as in-depth personal interviews among a sample of customers in this quadrant, can help uncover the reasons they buy on an infrequent, specialized basis. These issues can then be addressed in both the creative and the offer to move customers into Quadrant 1.

Quadrant 3 represents customers who spend just a few dollars but make purchases relatively frequently. Small average-order sizes combined with high levels of purchase frequency indicate that these customers are "cherry picking," concentrating on the lowest-cost sales items. Again, supplementary research, such as in-depth personal interviews among a sample of customers in this quadrant, can help

EXHIBIT 4–3

Customer Profiling

Customer profiling is completed by overlaying additional data to a customer or prospect database. The "best" customer segments can be identified and segmented with the appended data added to the known customer information.

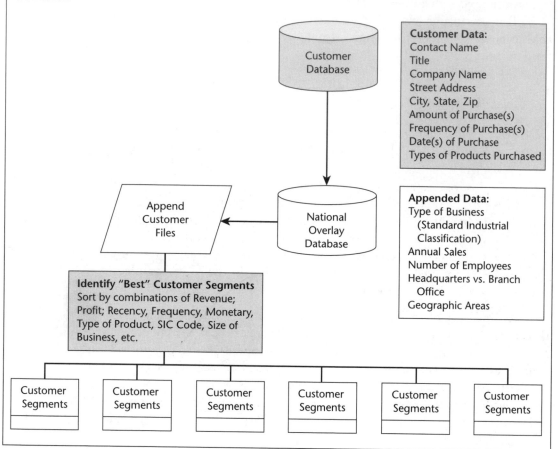

uncover problems to be addressed with both creative and offers to stimulate purchases of a wider range of merchandise, particularly higher-ticket items.

Quadrant 4 represents the worst of all worlds, the customer who doesn't spend very much or very often. The potential payoff in identifying these customers is in saving money by targeting a higher proportion of spending toward customers in the first three quadrants.

The potential of these customers can be further assessed by observing the degree to which companies with certain characteristics, such as SIC code, size, and geographic location, tend to be concentrated in certain quadrants. For example, if customers from four SIC codes are predominant within Quadrant 1 (highest sales volume, greatest purchase frequency), then the share of market or degree of penetration in each of the four SIC codes can be analyzed. By comparing the customers in the house file against the total number of businesses within each SIC code on the national database, a profile of market penetration can be drawn, as shown in Exhibit 4–5.

List Selection Guidelines

Evaluating list selections is not easy. There are many categories and types of lists, and ways of creating them. There is no perfect way to select information from lists, but some guidelines based on experience are helpful.

Description. Who is on the list? There may be mail order buyers, former buyers, subscribers, expires, donors, former donors, inquiries, coupon redeemers, etc. It's important to match the offer and target group as closely as possible to the description of those on lists that are mailed.

Affinity. A close relationship with the target group that the marketer is trying to reach. It's not possible to rent competitive response lists. It's not likely that a perfect match exists. Marketers try to rent relevant list choices that approximate their target group as closely as possible. A marketer of holiday fruit baskets might test lists of other food products sold at holiday time. Opera season ticket holders might be targeted for a subscription to the symphony. A marketer of waterproof

---

EXHIBIT 4-4

Purchase Activity Matrix

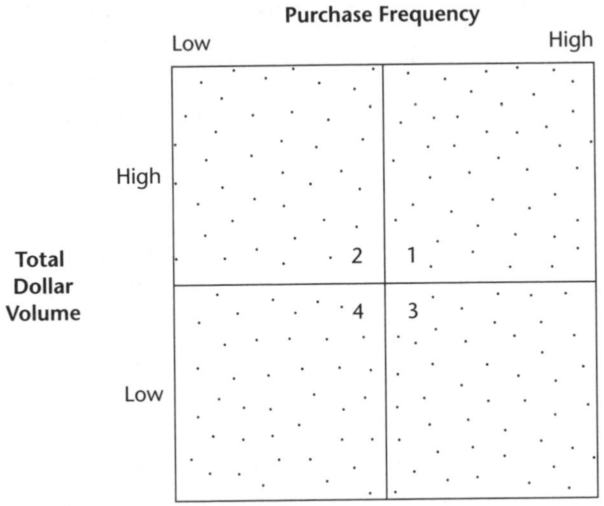

Purchase Frequency

Low — High

Total Dollar Volume: High, Low

2 | 1
4 | 3

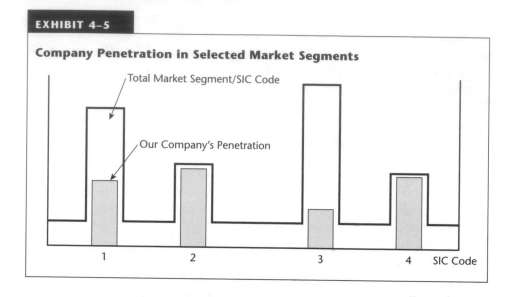

EXHIBIT 4–5

Company Penetration in Selected Market Segments

Total Market Segment/SIC Code

Our Company's Penetration

1   2   3   4   SIC Code

sport boots might mail to readers of outdoor and sporting magazines, buyers of outdoor clothing, or those who have purchased shoes direct.

List Source. The origin of the names on the list. Knowing the source of a list is important. Individuals who purchased via direct mail or a catalog are more likely to respond to direct mail than a buyer who responded to a print ad, television, etc. It's also a clue to the accuracy of the information.

Renting Mailing Lists

Mailing lists may be rented from list owners, list managers, and list brokers. Each source has its strengths and weaknesses.

List owners make the final decisions on any list rental, and determine the appropriateness or competitiveness of a prospective renter's request. They generally ask for, or require, a sample mail piece before agreeing to rent their lists. If there is any concern that an offer might offend the list owner's customers, they will reject the request.

Some response list owners rent their own lists, but most use intermediaries and will only negotiate large, multiuse deals. Compiled list owners are the exception. Organizations such as Donnelly Marketing, Experian, RL Polk, InfoUSA, and Dun & Bradstreet rent their own lists. Their sales forces tend to focus on large customers. Compiled lists are available from other sources as well.

List managers administer the lists for list owners. They generally manage a number of lists and handle fulfillment, billing, and list hygiene. Typically, list managers get monthly updates from the list owner. Because they maintain the list outside of the list owner's system, they benefit both the list owner and renter by speeding up the processing of list orders. Many list managers rent lists other than their own as well. However, they have a vested interest in renting the lists that they manage, and thus should not be considered impartial list sources.

List brokers are the key link in the list rental process. They provide timely and informed recommendations about which lists should be tested and why, and will provide a detailed report on each list recommended. Brokers also handle the administrative aspects of list rental and fulfillment. Most brokers are paid a commission by the list owner or manager and do not charge list renters. Brokers may require a minimum order of 5,000 names per list (not per order). For large orders, volume discounts ranging from 10 to 60 percent are available.

Some brokers ask to be compensated for the consulting service they provide, not just for net names rented. This fee is usually credited toward list rental as an incentive to rent from the broker. This method ensures that the broker's consulting time is compensated whether a list order is placed or not.

The best way to find a good list broker is through referral. Ask colleagues or associates for their recommendations. Many brokers specialize. Finding one with experience in a particular category is important.

Evaluating Mailing Lists

A good starting point for list evaluation is the Standard Rate and Data (SRDS) Direct Marketing List Source. Subscribers receive a printed volume, and have access to the same information on-line. Although it is comprehensive, SRDS information is timely only immediately after publication. Rates and other information still need to be confirmed through a list professional. Because SRDS organizes all the information for every list in exactly the same way, it is very easy to compare lists. Exhibit 4–6 is a sample page from SRDS.

List information can also be found on "data cards" provided by list owners and brokers. (A sample is shown in Exhibit 4–7.) Because information is not presented in a standard format, comparisons can be difficult. Stevan Roberts, president of list brokerage Edith Roman Associates, Inc., notes that the following information, included in most data cards, should be evaluated when deciding upon a list rental.

- List size. Lists range in size from less than 2,000 names to 1 million names or more. The traditional approach to direct mail is to test a small portion of the list, then mail to a larger portion if the test is successful. For this reason, some mailers avoid small lists—because the opportunity to expand after a successful test is limited by the total number of names available. On the other hand, to the mailer seeking unusual or hard-to-find prospects, such small specialized lists may be the only means of reaching certain markets.
- Cost per thousand. Prices typically range from $50 to $85 per thousand names, with specialized lists going for $100 to $150 per thousand and more. Be wary

EXHIBIT 4–6

Sample Entry from Standard Rate and Data Services (SRDS)

While its information is not always up-to-date, SRDS is a useful compendium that allows multiple lists to be quickly compared.

6. METHOD OF ADDRESSING
Cheshire labels, 4-up; pressure sensitive labels, 7.50/M extra; mag tape, (9TR/1600 BPI), 25.00 fee.
7. DELIVERY SCHEDULE
10 working days.
8. RESTRICTIONS
Two sample mailing pieces required.

EARTH CARE CATALOG

Data Verified: Jan 19, 2000.
Location ID: 10 DCLS 553 **Mid 065777-000**
1. PERSONNEL
List Manager
D-J Associates
75 Danbury Rd., P. O. Box 2048, Ridgefield, CT 06877. Phone 203-431-8777. Fax 203-431-3302.
E-mail: info@djassoc.com
2. SUMMARY DESCRIPTION
Catalog buyers of and inquirers about recycled paper gifts, practical household and personal products, paper notecards and gift wraps.
70% female.
Average unit of sale 58.00.
3. LIST SOURCE
Direct mail.
4. SELECTIONS WITH COUNTS
Updated: Feb 8, 1999.
Counts Thru: Oct 1998.

	Total Number	Price per/M
Buyers (24 month)	53,364	*85.00
12 month	28,177	*90.00
6 month	24,625	*95.00
3 month	10,216	*100.00
Inquiries (6 month)	9,892	70.00

(*) Fundraisers/publishers, 70.00/M.
Minimum order 7,500.
4A. OTHER SELECTIONS
Key coding, , 2.00/M extra; state, SCF, Zip, 6.00/M extra; 25+, 16.00/M extra; 50.00+, 21.00/M extra; 75.00+, 26.00/M extra.
6. METHOD OF ADDRESSING
Cheshire labels, 4-up; pressure sensitive labels, 7.00/M extra; mag tape, nonrefundable, 25.00 fee.
8. RESTRICTIONS
Sample mailing piece required.
11. MAINTENANCE
Updated quarterly.

EDDIE BAUER CATALOG BUYERS

Data Verified: Jan 19, 2000.
Location ID: 10 DCLS 553 **Mid 020973-000**
1. PERSONNEL
List Manager
Direct Media Consumer List Management
P.O. Box 4565, 200 Pemberwick Rd., Greenwich, CT 06830. Fax 203-531-1452. Phone 203-532-1000.
URL: http://www.directmedia.com
E-mail: rmontr@ix.directmedia.com
2. SUMMARY DESCRIPTION
Buyers of men's and women's apparel as well as home furnishings, gifts, domestics, etc.
24% male, 73% female; average age 47.
Average unit of sale 95.00.
3. LIST SOURCE
100% direct mail buyers, direct mail requests, space ads pip's.
4. SELECTIONS WITH COUNTS
Updated: Jan 3, 2000.
Counts Thru: Nov 1999.

	Total Number	Price per/M
Buyers (12 month)	2,509,639	*105.00
6 months	1,504,986	+10.00
3 months	909,336	+15.00
Hotline (monthly)	319,727	+20.00
3 month catalog requestors	135,000	*65.00

(*) Publishers/fundraisers/insurance/video/tape club, 65.00/M.
Minimum order 5,000.
4A. OTHER SELECTIONS
Credit card, multi's, sale/clearance, 10.00/M extra; key coding, 1.00/M extra; state, SCF, Zip, gender, 5.00/M extra; monthly change of address, merchandise, 20.00/M extra; dollar amount : 25.00+, 10.00/M extra; dollar amount : 50.00+, 20.00/M extra; dollar amount : 75.00+, 25.00/M extra; dollar amount : 100.00+, 40.00/M extra.
5. COMMISSION, CREDIT POLICY
20% commission to brokers. Cancel charges: A 50.00 flat fee plus all other appropriate charges will apply on all cancelled orders.
6. METHOD OF ADDRESSING
Cheshire labels, 4-up, 2.00/M extra; pressure sensitive labels, 7.00/M extra; mag tape, 25.00 fee.
8. RESTRICTIONS
Two sample mailing pieces required.

EDDIE BAUER CATALOG BUYERS W/Z - 24 DATABASE ENHANCEMENTS

Data Verified: Jan 19, 2000.
Location ID: 10 DCLS 553 **Mid 219419-000**
1. PERSONNEL
List Manager
Direct Media Consumer List Management
P.O. Box 4565, 200 Pemberwick Rd., Greenwich, CT 06830. Fax 203-531-1452. Phone 203-532-1000.
URL: http://www.directmedia.com
E-mail: rmontr@ix.directmedia.com
2. SUMMARY DESCRIPTION
Eddie Bauer is one of many participants in the Direct Tech Z-24 database who have their names available for outside list rental; 65% women.
65% female.
3. LIST SOURCE
Direct mail.
4. SELECTIONS WITH COUNTS
Updated: Jun 10, 1999.
Counts Thru: Mar 1999.

	Total Number	Price per/M
Buyers (3 month)	738,720	*105.00
6 months	1,596,620	"
12 months	2,338,160	"

(*) Z-24 enhancement fee, 35.00/M extra; fundraisers, publishers, memberships, 65.00.
Minimum order 5,000.
4A. OTHER SELECTIONS
Recency, dollar select (cum)- n/c, age, child's age, 6.00/M extra; Zip, (50.00 minimum), 5.00/M extra.
5. COMMISSION, CREDIT POLICY
Cancel charges: All cancelled orders charged a 50.00 flat cancellation fee, plus appropriate running and shipping charges.
6. METHOD OF ADDRESSING
Cheshire labels, 4-up; pressure sensitive labels, 6.00/M extra; mag tape, non refundable charge(9T 1600 BPI), 25.00 fee.
8. RESTRICTIONS
Sample mailing piece required.
11. MAINTENANCE
Updated bimonthly.

EDDIE BAUER-CHANGE OF ADDRESS

Data Verified: Jan 17, 2000.
Location ID: 10 DCLS 553 **Mid 219519-000**
1. PERSONNEL
List Manager
Direct Media Consumer List Management
P.O. Box 4565, 200 Pemberwick Rd., Greenwich, CT 06830. Fax 203-531-1452. Phone 203-532-1000.
URL: http://www.directmedia.com
E-mail: rmontr@ix.directmedia.com
2. SUMMARY DESCRIPTION
Eddie Bauer customers who have submitted their address changes.
22% male, 72% female; average age 47.
Average unit of sale 95.00.
4. SELECTIONS WITH COUNTS
Updated: Jan 3, 2000.
Counts Thru: Nov 1999.

	Total Number	Price per/M
Change of address (12 month)	1,046,082	*105.00
6 month	481,887	+10.00
3 month	243,645	+15.00
1 month	45,644	+20.00

(*) Publishers/fundraisers/insurance/video/tape club $65/M (available upon request).
Minimum order 5,000.
4A. OTHER SELECTIONS
State, SCF, Zip, 50.00 minimum, gender, 5.00/M extra; multi's, credit card, 10.00/M extra; merchandise selects, 20.00/M extra; key coding, 1.00/M extra; dollar amount:; 25.00+, 10.00/M extra; 50.00+, 20.00/M extra; 75.00+, 25.00/M extra; 100.00+, 40.00/M extra.
5. COMMISSION, CREDIT POLICY
Cancel charges: All cancelled orders are subject to a $50 charge plus applicable running and shipping charges.
6. METHOD OF ADDRESSING
Cheshire labels, 4-up, 2.00/M extra; pressure sensitive labels, 7.00/M extra; mag tape, non refundable charge(9T 1600/800BPI), 25.00 fee.
8. RESTRICTIONS
Two sample mailing pieces required.

EDDIE BAUER CLEARANCE AND SALE CATALOG BUYERS

Data Verified: Jan 19, 2000.
Location ID: 10 DCLS 553 **Mid 070662-000**
1. PERSONNEL
List Manager
Direct Media Consumer List Management
P.O. Box 4565, 200 Pemberwick Rd., Greenwich, CT 06830. Fax 203-531-1452. Phone 203-532-1000.
URL: http://www.directmedia.com
E-mail: rmontr@ix.directmedia.com
2. SUMMARY DESCRIPTION
Buyers of clearance merchandise reduced 15% to 45%.
19% male, 78% female.
Average unit of sale 70.00.
3. LIST SOURCE
Direct mail.
4. SELECTIONS WITH COUNTS
Updated: Jan 3, 2000.
Counts Thru: Nov 1999.

	Total Number	Price per/M
Total list (12 months)	975,282	*105.00
6 months	704,757	+10.00
3 months	425,643	+15.00

(*) Publishers/fundraisers/insurance/video/tape club, 65.00/M.
Minimum order 5,000.
4A. OTHER SELECTIONS
State, SCF, Zip, 50.00 minimum, gender, 5.00/M extra; special clearance / sale select, multi's, method of payment, 10.00/M extra; key coding, 1.00/M extra; 25.00+, 10.00/M extra; 50.00+, 20.00/M extra; 75.00+, 25.00/M extra; 100.00+, 40.00/M extra.
5. COMMISSION, CREDIT POLICY
Cancel charges: All cancelled orders are subject to a 50.00 charge plus applicable running and shipping charges.
6. METHOD OF ADDRESSING
Cheshire labels, 4-up, 2.00/M extra; pressure sensitive labels, 7.00/M extra; mag tape, non refundable harge (9T 1600/800bpi), 25.00 fee.
8. RESTRICTIONS
Two sample mailing pieces required.
11. MAINTENANCE
Updated monthly.

EDDIE BAUER - LIFEPHASES

Data Verified: Jan 19, 2000.
Location ID: 10 DCLS 553 **Mid 219569-000**
1. PERSONNEL
List Manager
Direct Media Consumer List Management
P.O. Box 4565, 200 Pemberwick Rd., Greenwich, CT 06830. Fax 203-531-1452. Phone 203-532-1000.
URL: http://www.directmedia.com
E-mail: rmontr@ix.directmedia.com
2. SUMMARY DESCRIPTION
Enhanced file of Eddie Bauer buyers.
23% male, 72% female.
Average unit of sale 95.00.
4. SELECTIONS WITH COUNTS
Updated: Jan 3, 2000.
Counts Thru: Nov 1999.

	Total Number	Price per/M
Total list (12 month)	2,509,639	*105.00
6 month	1,504,986	+10.00
3 month	909,336	+15.00
Exact age (12 month buyers):		
25-34	353,224	+15.00
35-44	564,829	"
45-54	526,173	"
55-64	224,739	"
65+	153,052	"
Parent of children (12 month buyers):		
0-3	139,060	+15.00
4-6	173,545	"
7-9	160,275	"
10-12	136,893	"
13-18	224,225	"
Income (12 month buyers):		
0-15,000	53,057	+10.00
15,000-34,999	495,652	"
35,000-74,999	1,448,905	"
75,000+	529,032	"

(*) Publishers, fundraisers, insurance, video, tape club, 65.00/M.(Available upon request).
Minimum order 5,000.
4A. OTHER SELECTIONS
State, SCF, Zip, or 50.00 minimum, 5.00/M extra; credit card, 10.00/M extra; gender, dwelling type, length of residence, 6.00/M extra; household size, 5.00/M extra; merchandise, 20.00/M extra; exact age, parents, 15.00/M extra; dollar amount; 25.00+, 10.00/M extra; 50.00+, 20.00/M extra; 75.00+, 25.00/M extra; 100.00+, 40.00/M extra; key coding, 1.00/M extra.
5. COMMISSION, CREDIT POLICY
Cancel charges: All cancelled orders are subject to a 50.00 charge plus applicable running and shipping charges.
6. METHOD OF ADDRESSING
Cheshire labels, 4-up, 2.00/M extra; pressure sensitive labels, 7.00/M extra; mag tape, non returnable (9T 1600/800 BPI), 25.00 fee.
8. RESTRICTIONS
Sample mailing piece required.

EDDIE BAUER-IB LIFETRENDS

Data Verified: Jan 19, 2000.
Location ID: 10 DCLS 553 **Mid 253272-000**
1. PERSONNEL
List Manager
Direct Media Consumer List Management
P.O. Box 4565, 200 Pemberwick Rd., Greenwich, CT 06830. Fax 203-531-1452. Phone 203-532-1000.
URL: http://www.directmedia.com
E-mail: rmontr@ix.directmedia.com
2. SUMMARY DESCRIPTION
Masterfile of the interests and lifestyles of Eddie Bauer's mail order buyers.
21% male, 64% female.
Average unit of sale 95.00.
3. LIST SOURCE
Direct mail, pip's, space ads.
4. SELECTIONS WITH COUNTS
Updated: Dec 29, 1999.
Counts Thru: Nov 1999.

	Total Number	Price per/M
Buyers (12 month)	3,443,365	*105.00
6 month	1,935,878	+15.00
3 month	1,169,662	"
Hotline (1 month)	493,350	"

(*) Publishers, fundraisers, insurance, video, tape club, 65.00/M.
Minimum order 5,000.
4A. OTHER SELECTIONS
State, SCF, Zip, multi- buyers, 5.00/M extra; dollar, method of payment (select or omit), 10.00/M extra; running charges, 7.00/M extra; key coding, 1.00/M extra; zip 50.00 minimum, maximum selection cap of 35.00/m, maximum two interest selects per order; interest selections:, 20.00/M extra; crafts & hobbies, donors, financial, fitness, good life, home & garden, home entertainment, home office, outdoor recreation, pet people , readers.
5. COMMISSION, CREDIT POLICY
Cancel charges: Cancelled orders will be charged a 50.00 flat cancellation fee, plus appropriate running and shipping charges.
6. METHOD OF ADDRESSING
Cheshire labels, 4-up, 2.00/M extra; pressure sensitive labels, 7.00/M extra; mag tape, nonreturnable fee(9T 1600/800 BPI), 25.00 fee.
8. RESTRICTIONS
Two sample mailing pieces required.
11. MAINTENANCE
Updated quarterly.

E4L INC.'S QUANTUM MARKETING MASTERFILE

Data Verified: Aug 16, 1999.
Location ID: 10 DCLS 553 **Mid 650910-000**
1. PERSONNEL
List Manager
List Services Corporation
6 Trowbridge Dr., P.O. Box 516, Bethel, CT 06801-0516. Phone 203-743-2600. Fax 203-743-0589. Fax 203-778-4299.
URL: http://www.listservices.com
E-mail: lscmgmt@listserv.com
Key Contact: Brian DiMarino, Phone 203-791-4454.
E-mail: dimarino@listserv.com
2. SUMMARY DESCRIPTION
Infomercial buyers of innovative products.

Access the SRDS Direct Marketing List Source® Online at www.srds.com

continued
2153

of firms offering so-called "bargain lists" selling for $5, $10, or even $25 per thousand; often, these are absolutely worthless.

- List description. Each data card contains a paragraph or two about the background of the list: its source, history, a profile of the type of buyers it represents, and a description of the product they bought, the publication they subscribe to, or the seminar they attended. Read the description to get a "feel" for the market represented by the list.

- Average order size. Given as a dollar amount, this represents the average size of the mail order purchase made by the buyers on the list. Average order size is a good indication of how much individuals on a list might be willing to spend via direct mail. It's unlikely that individuals who have spent $25 will respond to offers for $100.

- Percentage of the list that is direct mail–generated. Data cards often contain the phrase "95 percent direct mail–generated" or "100 percent direct mail–generated." This indicates the percentage of the names on the list obtained through response to direct mail. Higher percentages are better because direct mail–generated prospects and customers are more likely to respond to direct mail than people who became prospects or customers through other avenues. (Surveys indicate that as many as one-third of Americans do not respond to direct mail solicitations.)

- Hot line. The segment of the list containing customers who made a mail order purchase within the last 30 to 90 days (the more recent, the better). Hot lines typically rent for $5 to $10 more per thousand than the rest of the list.

- Active versus inactive, buyer versus prospect. Customer lists almost always pull better than prospect lists. When testing a list of newsletter subscribers, first select the current (active) subscribers rather than the former (inactive) subscribers. When renting a list from a mail order catalog company, obtain the names of people who actually bought from the catalog, not those who merely requested a free catalog but did not buy. The rule of thumb is to test the most likely group first and then test the others after the best names have been exhausted.

- List usage report. Try to get the list supplier to tell you how well the list pulled for others who rented it—especially those with similar offers. This information probably won't appear on the data card but it may be contained in a separate List Usage Report available from the broker. These reports usually show rental activity by tests (initial mailings) and continuations (rental of additional names following a successful test). If a high percentage of the mailers who tested are also listed under continuations, they are getting test results profitable enough to warrant continued use of the list—a good sign.

- Selections available. The data card indicates the selection criteria by which the list can be segmented. In general, the more selections, the better, because selectability allows you to mail only to those names closest to a marketer's target profile.

- Frequency of updating. Are the names current and is the list frequently updated? Some list suppliers may guarantee their lists to be clean and will refund postage costs on pieces returned as "undeliverable" (called nixies) in excess of some certain small percentage. The fewer nixies per list, the cleaner the list. The U.S. Postal Service considers returns of 2 percent or less of the mailing as very good; in other words, a clean list.

EXHIBIT 4–7

Sample Data Card

This data card for Eddie Bauer Catalog Buyers includes a description of the list, average order size, the source of names on the list, available list quantities, selections available, and other information.

EDDIE BAUER CATALOG BUYERS

DM06890   MN05063

```
EDDIE BAUER CATALOG BUYERS

2,586,544  12 MONTH BUYERS (THROUGH 1/00)    $105.00/M
1,864,738   6 MONTH BUYERS             ADD     $10.00/M
1,278,180   3 MONTH BUYERS             ADD     $15.00/M
  357,064   MONTHLY HOTLINE BUYERS     ADD     $20.00/M
            MONTHLY CHANGE OF ADDRESS  ADD     $20.00/M
  135,000   3 MONTH CATALOG REQUESTORS         $65.00/M
```

THE EDDIE BAUER CATALOG FEATURES HIGH QUALITY MEN'S AND WOMEN'S APPAREL AND HAS EARNED A REPUTATION AS AMERICA'S PREMIER OUTFITTER. THEY ALSO CARRY A VARIETY OF FOOD/GIFT ITEMS, HOME FURNISHINGS, CAMPING ACCESSORIES, SPORTS EQUIPMENT, DOMESTICS, ETC. THE MEDIAN AGE OF THE EDDIE BAUER CUSTOMER IS 47; MEDIAN HOUSEHOLD INCOME IS $50,000; 74% ARE HIGHLY EDUCATED.
.
PACKAGE INSERT PROGRAM ALSO AVAILABLE.

```
SELECTIONS:  STATE, SCF $5.00M; ZIP $5.00M OR $50.00
             MINIMUM; SEX $5.00M; MULTI'S, CREDIT
             CARD $10.00M; DOLLAR AMOUNT (LAST
             PURCHASE): $25+ $10.00M, $50+ $20.00M,
             $75+ $25.00M, 100+ $40.00M; SALE/
             CLEARANCE $10.00M

SOURCE:      BUYERS - 100% DIRECT MAIL
             REQUESTS - DIRECT MAIL; PIP'S; SPACE ADS
```

MERCHANDISE SELECTS $20.00M:
FOOD/GIFT, FIELD HARDWARE, HOME FURNISHINGS, LUGGAGE, MEN'S ACCESSORIES, WOMEN'S ACCESSORIES, SPORTS EQUIPMENT, WOMEN'S FOOTWEAR, MEN'S FOOTWEAR, WOMEN'S FASHIONS, MEN'S FASHIONS, DOMESTICS, AND MUCH MORE.
.
*******INQUIRE FOR ADDITIONAL APPAREL SELECTS*****
*******INQUIRE FOR ENHANCEMENTS******************
.
PUBLISHERS/FUNDRAISERS/INSURANCE/VIDEO/TAPE CLUB
$65.00/M - (AVAILABLE UPON REQUEST).
.
ALL CANCELLED ORDERS ARE SUBJECT TO A $50 CHARGE PLUS APPLICABLE RUNNING AND SHIPPING CHARGES.

```
002, BCLR

***UNIT-OF-SALE***
$95.00 AVERAGE

*******SEX********
72% WOMEN, 23% MEN

****ADDRESSING****
4-UP CHESH. $2.00M
MAGNETIC TAPE**
9-TRACK 800 BPI
9-TRACK 1600 BPI
PRES. SENS. $7.00M

*****KEY-CODING***
$1.00M

***MINIMUM-ORDER**
5,000

2 SAMPLE MAILING
PIECES REQUIRED

**MAG-TAPE-INSTR**
**$25.00 NON-
REFUNDABLE CHARGE
```

Direct Media - A Division of Acxiom/Direct Media
200 Pemberwick Rd, Greenwich, CT 06830 Tel: (203)532-1000 Fax:(203)531-1452

Because approximately one-fifth of the population moves every year, compiled and prospect lists get outdated quickly. As a rule, a list should be updated (meaning that names no longer current are removed) at least twice a year, if not quarterly. The National Change of Address file (NCOA), for example, is updated every two weeks. Updating frequently lowers the cost for address corrections.

Mailing Formats

In the past, the most common format for receiving rented lists was pressure sensitive or paper Cheshire mailing labels, the format preferred by letter shops that used automated equipment to cut the paper into single labels and affix these labels to envelopes.

Today, lists are more likely to be delivered on magnetic tape, cartridge, CD, regular or zipped diskette. In addition to the names ordered, each mailing record may include a key code to identify the list source (essential for determining response when testing several mailing pieces or lists).

For most mailing programs, a number of lists may be ordered. If the lists are similar, names may be duplicated from one list to another. This is to be expected when trying to reach a specific target group. Sometimes unexpected duplication occurs. Several brokers may release data cards for the same list under different titles with varying descriptions. Or, a list owner will market different parts of a single file as separate lists. Mailers protect themselves in two ways.

Net name arrangements can be negotiated with brokers so that only unduplicated names are paid for. These agreements may be negotiated at a flat rate (e.g., a marketer may only pay for 80 percent of names ordered) or at a discount based on all of the duplicate names where the list owner controls the deduping of the lists. Whether a net name arrangement is negotiated or not, some duplication is likely to exist. To reduce duplication, multiple lists go through a process known as merge/purge. Merge/purge is part of a broader area known as list hygiene

List Hygiene

According to the Direct Marketing Association, "The most important step every mailer can and should take is to improve list hygiene." Standardizing formats, merging multiple files, eliminating duplicates, and updating and verifying address elements are all critical steps essential to maximizing deliverability.

The USPS also offers discounts to mailers for helping to automate mail distribution by presorting and bundling mail. There are discounts for presorting by three-digit zip code (SCF), five-digit zip, zip+4 (nine-digit zip), and carrier route. Carrier route and zip+4 coding offer the lowest postal rates in all classes. Mail rates are based on service labeled First Class, Periodicals (the former Second Class), or Standard Class, which includes Nonprofit (formerly Third and Fourth Classes), as shown in Exhibit 4–8.

EXHIBIT 4–8

Postal Regulations

Postal regulations are very stringent. Check with a letter shop or the USPS website (usps.com) to determine which discounts a mail piece qualifies for.

Postal Rates

First Class Rates

Weight (oz.)	Non-Automation		Automation						
			Letter-Size				Flat-Size		
	Single-Piece	Presorted	Basic	3-Digit	5-Digit	Carrier Route	Basic	3/5	
1	$0.330	$0.305	$0.270	$0.261	$0.243	$0.238	$0.300	$0.270	
2	$0.550	$0.525	$0.490	$0.481	$0.463	$0.458	$0.520	$0.490	
3	$0.770	$0.699	$0.664	$0.655	$0.637	$0.632	$0.694	$0.664	
4	$0.990	$0.919	$0.884	$0.875	$0.857	$0.852	$0.914	$0.884	

Standard Mail (formerly Third Class Mail) Letter Size Rates
(pieces 3.3087 oz. or less)

Presorted		Automation		
Basic	3/5	Basic	3-Digit	5-Digit
$0.235	$0.207	$0.183	$0.176	$0.160

Non-Profit Standard Mail, Letter Size Rates
(pieces 3.2873 oz. or less)

Presorted		Automation		
Basic	3/5	Basic	3-Digit	5-Digit
$0.169	$0.142	$0.119	$0.114	$0.093

Non-Letter Size Rates
(pieces 3.3087 oz. or less)

Presorted		Automation	
Basic	3/5	Basic	3/5
$0.304	$0.240	$0.245	$0.203

Letter-Size, Enhanced Carrier Route Rates
(pieces 3.3062 oz. or less)

Non-Automation			Automation
Basic	High Density	Saturation	Basic
$0.162	$0.139	$0.130	$0.156

Non-Profit Enhanced Carrier Route Letter Size Rates
(pieces 3.3103 oz. or less)

Non-Automation			Automation
Basic	High Density	Saturation	Basic
$0.099	$0.078	$0.072	$0.092

EXHIBIT 4–9

The Economics of Merge/Purge

Removing duplicate names can greatly improve marketing efficiency. In this example, the savings from running the merge/purge are far greater than the cost of analysis.

	With Merge/Purge	Without Merge/Purge
Quantity to mail	128,426.00	180,269.00
Cost to Print & Mail at 65¢ each	$83,476.90	$117,174.85
Cost to run Merge/Purge	$350.00	Not Applicable
Total Costs	$83,826.90	$117,174.85
Cost Savings	**$33,347.95**	

Please note that prior to Merge/Purge all lists have been run through National Change of Address Postal Software and standardized for addressing. It is important to start with the cleanest names and addresses to ensure the best deliverability.

Proper care in the creation and maintenance of prospect and customer files has become more important than ever. Taking steps to ensure the maximum USPS discount rates can result in savings of thousands of dollars, not to mention a better return on investment.

A typical list cleaning exercise, for example, is shown in Exhibit 4–9, "Economic Impact of List Hygiene." On a 1 million piece mailing with a $1 per-piece cost, a 2 percent response rate, and a $55 average-order value, the combination of cost avoidance and additional revenue generated through proper list hygiene provides a return on investment of $64,250 on the first mailing. Subsequent mailings increase these returns.

Applying List Hygiene

There are a number of steps that can be taken to clean lists before mailing. Planning these steps carefully can help a marketer derive more marketing information from the hygiene process. For example, if a marketer is doing site planning, media selections, or risk assessment, longitude and latitude data can be appended onto each household record to allow for geographic analysis. Finding ways to combine steps can save considerable time and money.

List Standardization. Standardization is the process of normalizing data records from multiple sources to ensure completeness and standard formatting for each data element. The outcome of this process should be to flag affected records to be fixed or eliminated.

Editing and Reformatting. This process involves editing and reformatting records so every field is handled uniformly. To do that, the standardization routine must first parse out every element in the name and address. Additional fields can be appended to the records during the editing and formatting procedure.

Merge/Purge. Duplicate identification is particularly important for Periodicals and Standard Class mailers. Good merge/purge systems eliminate duplicates, improve targeting, and increase response rates. The system must be flexible and customizable to accommodate unique situations based on marketing objectives. Multifamily dwellings, rural addresses, prestige addresses, cohabitants, married versus maiden names, misspellings, previous versus current occupants, and other common address problems must be considered. Merge/purge flags dupes and permits intelligent marketing decisions (see Exhibit 4–10).

Verification and Correction. To identify and correct bad addresses, use USPS-certified address-matching services offered by commercial vendors or service bureaus.

EXHIBIT 4–10

Merge/Purge Report

There is always duplication among lists targeting individuals with similiar demographics, psychographics, or affinities. In this example, there is duplication within and among the lists in a 150,000-piece mailing.

List Name	List Quantity	Interdupes*	Intradupes**	Total Dupes (Inter and Intra)	Total Unique Records
House File	61,782	0	0	0	61,782
List 1	12,685	125	5,640	5,765	6,920
List 2	13,076	336	7,533	7,869	5,207
List 3	12,989	414	2,027	2,441	10,548
List 4	12,954	223	5,672	5,895	7,059
List 5	13,305	19	3,405	3,424	9,881
List 6	12,955	26	5,671	5,697	7,258
List 7	14,723	17	4,299	4,316	10,407
Lisy 8	13,798	235	7,988	8,223	5,575
List 9	12,002	2	8,211	8,213	3,789
Totals	**180,269**	**1,397**	**50,446**	**51,843**	**128,426**

* Interdupes are duplicates found within a single file.
** Intradupes are duplicates found from multiple files during Merge/Purge.

Merge/Purge Criteria: One mailing piece should deliver to a single household.
Address, city, state, and zip code will determine each household location.

List Criteria: House File has the highest priority. All additional lists should be purged against the House File.

Coding Accuracy Support System (CASS) software identifies and corrects bad addresses to the carrier route and zip+4 level. It is used for all classes of mail and is updated every three months. Mailers use CASS zip-code corrections in updating lists to receive an automatic discount or lower rate. However, the updates must have been made less than 90 days prior to mailing for the discount or lower rate to apply. For mailings with "old" CASS updating (more than six months), there is no discount or lower rate.

Delivery Sequence File (DSF) contains every deliverable address in the country (at the mailbox level). It has more than 125 million addresses on file, offering nearly 100 percent of all city-style, rural route, highway contract, P.O. box, and standardized business addresses. It is the most complete address database available, and will fix between 1 and 3 percent of the bad records in a file.

Locatable Address Conversion System (LACS) converts rural routes with box numbers and other addresses the USPS considers "nonstandard" into city-style or standard address delivery points. This USPS database currently includes more than 2.3 million records, covering mostly southern and midwestern regions.

The National Change of Address (NCOA) file contains more than 120 million address changes (all of the address changes occurring in the past three years) and is updated weekly. Matching files against NCOA improves address hygiene by reducing undeliverables (nixies). Many mailers routinely find about 7 to 10 percent of their file comprised of nixies each year if they do not update. Typically 1 to 3 percent of addresses in a list will change every six months. NCOA is required for First Class mailing discounts.

Privacy

Questions of data compilation and usage are sensitive. Many consumers and businesses alike view them as privacy issues. When carelessly asked questions about age, marital status, or children are included as part of a general direct marketing program, they seem out of context and may reduce response. A consumer may ask, "Why do they need to know the value of my home to complete an order for a pair of jeans?"

Such questions can't be taken lightly. Information privacy is a significant issue for marketers. Most consumers want some control of the terms under which their personal information is acquired by others and used. At the very least, research shows that most individuals want marketers to disclose how their information will be used.

Mary J. Culnan, a professor at Georgetown University, has done extensive research into consumer privacy. Culnan points out that information privacy concerns can arise in different contexts.

Consumers understand that there are times when they need to disclose personal information. Financial information may be necessary to qualify for automobile insurance, a mortgage, a credit card, or to open a bank or a brokerage account. Medical information may be necessary when applying for health or life insurance, a new job, or before being exposed to physically stressful situations (e.g., a ride in a fighter plane). Surveys show that people do not object to this. It is secondary use of the information provided that raises privacy concerns.

Secondary use refers to collecting information for one purpose and subsequently using the information for other purposes. It also includes unrelated use by the organization that collected the information, e.g., for the creation of rented mailing lists, as well as sharing the information with third parties—especially personal information contained in public records, credit reports, and other databases used for credit or hiring decisions. Privacy concerns arise when this reuse is unrelated to or incompatible with the purpose for which the information was originally collected, and the mailer or list renter does not offer consumers the opportunity to object to this reuse.

Culnan notes that public opinion surveys and her own research have shown that firms can balance these privacy concerns with their legitimate business need for the information by observing fair information practices. When consumers are offered notice and choice (e.g., to opt out), privacy concerns are no longer significant and a majority of consumers do not object to secondary use of personal information.

Another concern for consumers is the unauthorized access to their personal information. This can come through a security breach or because the custodian of the information has not implemented appropriate internal controls (e.g., pretext calling, identity theft, or having one's credit card number stolen on-line by hackers).

Unauthorized access is focused in three areas:

1. *Fraud.* Consumers are greatly concerned with the misuse and abuse of data and information. Health-care, personal, and financial information must be carefully protected. New media and the proliferation of data sources keep this a top-of-mind concern among everyone.

2. *Identity theft.* The incidence of outright theft of an individual's name, credit history, etc., has been growing. Credit card theft has become a major concern of consumers and law enforcement agencies. New ways of protecting against identity theft seem to be met with new ways of capturing this information. This could be a barrier to increased on-line commerce.

3. *Anonymity.* Phone calls, unsolicited mail, and spam have all contributed to the increasing desire of a growing number of consumers to remain unidentified. For evidence, consider the increased number of unlisted phone numbers. In California as many as 60 percent of phone numbers are unlisted. It may be as high as 30 percent across the country. This is a clear message that marketers must begin to heed.

Observing information practices that consumers view as fair is a win-win solution for consumers and businesses. Disclosure and options such as opt-out reduce the perceived risk to consumers, while allowing an individual to control the use of his or her personal information.

Most marketers allow consumers and businesses to opt out of promotions. To do so, an individual must ask to be excluded from future promotions from the organization, cross-sell opportunities from the organization, and/or the renting of his or her name to other organizations. This is good for the marketers, since they don't spend money to send promotions to individuals who would prefer not to receive them.

The DMA's "Consumer Marketer's Promise" requires all of its members that market to consumers to give notice and choice if personal information is shared with third parties and to respect consumer requests not to receive solicitations from the company or its affiliates. (This promise is reproduced in Chapter 12.)

Opt-out is not without controversy. In the on-line realm, opt-in is the standard, and individuals must give their permission in order to receive promotional offers of any kind. This proactive approach reduces the number of people on such lists. Informed consent (i.e., opt-in) is required in certain regulated markets. Considering list rental revenue, the number of lists available, and the history of opt-out in traditional direct marketing, it is unlikely opt-in will ever be adopted.

Reducing Mail Volume

For those who prefer to substantially reduce the amount of national advertising mail and telephone offers they receive, the Direct Marketing Association has two services available free of charge for consumers:

1. Mail Preference Service (MPS) enables individuals to receive less national advertising mail by having their names removed from many national mailing lists. Established in 1971, this consumer program is used by about 2 percent of the American adult population. Not all organizations participate in MPS, although DMA members do. Consumers can write directly to marketers that don't participate and ask to be removed from their lists.

2. Telephone Preference Service (TPS) enables people to receive fewer telephone sales calls in their homes by removing their names from many national telephone sales lists. Local telephone marketers, as a rule, do not participate in national name removal programs. Consumers can contact them directly, or when they call ask that their name be deleted from their list.

When consumers register with MPS and/or TPS, their names are placed on a name removal file that is made available to participating marketers on a monthly or quarterly basis. It may take a few months before consumers notice a decrease in the advertising mail and telemarketing calls received.

Although the efficacy of such self-regulation can be questioned, these programs do address consumer concerns. It is one reason that the use of mailing lists has not been severely regulated. There is regulation on some kinds of data (e.g., credit bureau, driver's license, etc.), and in the future there may be additional regulations. In the meantime, marketers will continue practices that are virtually unchanged over the last hundred years.

Case Study: Staples Direct

Adapted from Acxiom Case-in-Point, Volume 4, Issue 5: Sept/Oct 1998

BACKGROUND

Direct marketers rely on lists to tease the best prospects out of every mail or telemarketing campaign. The growing availability of mailing lists in the United States in some ways only makes that job harder, as it increases the total universe of potential names that marketers must comb through to find responsive prospects that can be converted into profitable customers.

This challenge is compounded by U.S. direct marketing economics: a dramatic increase in direct-response marketing over the past 10 years has contributed to oversaturation in both the consumer's and the business executive's mailbox, making both markets less responsive overall. At the same time, steadily increasing postage and paper costs have pinched the profitability of customer acquisition efforts.

CHALLENGE

Direct-sales operations like Staples Direct, the $500 million division of $5 billion office supply retail leader Staples, Inc., have developed sophisticated marketing techniques to reduce waste and maximize profit. This sophistication extended to mailing lists. The challenge was to build a predictive model to extract the names of individuals most likely to respond to a Staples Direct catalog.

Thanks to a customer loyalty program introduced early in its history, the company has reams of data about its customers' buying habits and preferences, and has used that information to position itself for dominance against aggressive discount competitors and catalogers targeting its markets.

Inaugurated in 1992, Staples Direct's multiproduct catalog, mailed to existing customers and targeted prospects, now generates 10 percent of Staples' total revenues. It is growing faster than either the 5.1 percent industry average for U.S. consumer catalog retailers or the 6.1 percent business catalog retailers.

SOLUTION

Staples Direct started with two million prospect names that were matched against Acxiom's multisourced business-to-business compiled lists, the Database Prospecting Alliance (DPA). This match yielded a 500,000-name prospect file enhanced with DPA variables such as the SIC, employee size, title, gender, and credit code. Additional variables from Staples Direct's file were also retained in the output file.

A separate file of responders to a recent Staples Direct mailing was then matched to the DPA and to the half-million prospect names produced by the first DPA match. This produced a multivariable master file of Staples Direct responders and nonresponders.

To identify the predictive variables, a multivariate regression model was applied to half of the names in this master file and tested on the other half. All of the names in the master file were scored into one of ten deciles, based upon their predicted level of purchases in response to a catalog mailing. The resulting gains were presented as a table that indicated minimal variance and good predictability.

The model was tested on a live mailing, scoring the entire circulation file for one Staples Direct catalog mailing. The result of this test was that the top decile outperformed the lowest by four times and outperformed the average by double.

The model was also used on test lists, including both continuation lists (lists tested previously) and new lists never tried before. Encouraged by the results of the first test, the model was deployed as a name selection tool with the next mailing.

The model was applied to the DPA and other test lists. The bottom-performing decile from the prospect file was eliminated and Staples mailed proportionately more to the top-performing deciles. Increasing the prospect file, deciles were selected according to historical responsiveness of each test list. The model was also tested on compiled names, which generally don't work as well as response lists.

Case Study: **Staples Direct** *(continued)*

RESULTS

The model has proven its worth. It has been used to mail different decile ranges within different geographic markets, and to successfully test additional multisourced business files. It has proven effective in scoring inactive customers to select those most likely to respond to a reactivation campaign. And it has helped the firm refine its mailing strategy to hone in on prospects within driving distance of Staples retail stores.

In its first year, the model improved performance by 15 percent while increasing circulation signifi-cantly. By transferring those costs into mailing prospects who are more receptive to their offer, Staples increased sales response and sales per book.

Over the course of only the first two mailings constructed with the model in place, Staples saw a significant reduction in waste and a significant lift in response from this acquisition effort. Subsequent efforts continued that trend, even as the firm increased its overall mailing volume. The model has enabled Staples to reduce the quantity of names selected from rollout and test lists.

You are a regional marketing director of a firm that specializes in installing central air-conditioning in homes. The market you are targeting is Milwaukee, Wisconsin. Based on research of your customer base, the profile of your customers is as follows:

- Lives in a house ten years old, or more

- Has a household income of $35,000 a year, or more

- Has lived in the same house for five years, or more

Identify the sources you might use to build a list meeting these criteria.

Key Points

▶ There are three kinds of lists: house lists, which are the customer databases of organizations; response lists, or house lists of other organizations; and compiled lists of individuals or companies without any previous indication of willingness to respond, but with some defined and identifiable characteristic(s), such as demographics, psychographics, or zip code.

▶ Profiling is the process of understanding customers by identifying their demographics, firmagraphics, or lifestyle attributes. Appending this information to the customer file adds valuable information for targeting future promotions, understanding customer defections, and identifying cross-selling and other new business opportunities.

▶ Mailing lists are rented, typically for a onetime use, and supplied on magnetic tape, cartridge, CD, or regular or zipped diskette. If after testing a portion of a list, the renting organization wants to remail or rollout the list (e.g., in continuation), it must pay an additional rental fee. List owners make the final decisions on any list rental and may reject rental requests that are inappropriate or competitive.

▶ Data cards provide details on the list size, cost per thousand, its source and history, the average size of the mail order purchase made by the buyers, and the percentage of the list that is direct mail–generated. Data cards also indicate the presence of hot-line names—customers who made a mail order purchase within the last 30 to 90 days—and the selection by which the list can be segmented.

▶ Lists age quickly and should be updated (meaning that names no longer current are removed) at least twice a year, if not quarterly. Updating frequently lowers the cost for address corrections. Service bureaus can also prevent address corrections by standardizing names, editing and reformatting records, purging lists of duplications, and verifying and correcting addresses.

▶ Privacy concerns often arise when information collected for one purpose is subsequently used for other purposes. Concerns abate when mailers and list renters offer consumers the opportunity to object to this reuse. The DMA's Mail Preference Service and Telephone Preference Service enables consumers to remove their names from many national mailing lists.

THE OFFER

It has often been said that a dynamic offer can succeed even if selling copy is fair to poor. But the most dynamic of copy cannot be powerful enough to make a poor offer succeed. The ultimate, of course, is a dynamic offer supported by dynamic copy.

Factors to Consider

When a direct sale is the objective, there are ten factors to consider when creating an offer.

1. *Price.* Nothing is more crucial than setting an appropriate price. Does the price allow for a sufficient markup? Is the price competitive? Is the price perceived by the consumer to be the right price for the value received? If you want to sell your item for $7.95 each, how about two for $15.90 (same price, but you get twice the average sale)? How about selling the first for $11.95 and the second for $3.95 (same total dollars if you sell two units—and if you don't sell two units, you get a higher price for a single unit)? Testing to determine the best price is vital to maximizing long-term payoff.

2. *Shipping and Handling.* Where applicable (usually not for a publication or service), shipping and handling charges can be an important factor in pricing. It's important to know how much you can add to a base without adversely affecting sales. Many merchandisers follow a rule of thumb that shipping and handling charges should not exceed 10 percent of the basic selling price. But again, testing is advisable.

3. *Unit of Sale.* Will your product or service be offered "each"? "Two for"? "Set of X"? Obviously, the more units you can move per sale, the better off you are likely to be. But if your prime objective is to build a large customer list fast, would you be better off to offer single units if you got twice the response over a "two for" offer?

4. *Optional Features* include such things as special colors, odd sizes, special binding for books, personalization, and the like. Optional features often increase the dollar amount of the average order. For example, when the publisher of a dictionary offered thumb indexing at $2 extra, 25 percent of total purchasers opted for this added feature.

5. *Future Obligation.* Common are book and tape offers that commit the purchaser to future obligation. ("Take ten tapes for $1 and agree to buy six more in the coming 12 months.") A continuity program offer might state: "Get Volume one free—others will be sent at regular intervals." Future obligation offers, when successful, enable the marketer to "pay" a substantial price for the first order, knowing there will be a long-term payout.

6. *Credit Options.* It's rare today to receive a catalog that does not contain one or more of these options: "Charge to American Express, Diners Club, Visa, Master Card, Discover." It pays. The average charged order is usually at least 15 percent larger than a cash order. Some major direct marketers offer credit for 30 days, others offer installment credit with interest added (oil companies are a good example). Whether it's commercial credit cards or house credit, history says credit options increase revenue.

7. *Incentives* include free gifts, discounts, and sweepstakes. Toll-free or on-line ordering privilege is likewise an incentive—ease of ordering. Not unlike credit options, toll-free ordering privileges tend to increase the average order 15 percent and more. But incentives must be tested front-end and back-end. Are people "buying" the free gift or sweeps? Will they be as good repeat customers as those who bought in the first instance without incentive?

8. *Time Limits* add urgency to an offer. One word of caution: If you establish a time limit, stick to it.

9. *Quantity Limits.* One of the major proponents of quantity limits is the collectibles field. ("Only 5,000 will be minted. Then the molds will be destroyed.") There is something in the human psyche that says, "If it's in short supply, I want it." Even "Limit—two to a customer" often outperforms no limit. But if you set a limit, stick to it.

10. *Guarantees.* Of the 10 factors to be considered in structuring an offer with the objective of making a sale, there is one that should never be passed up—the guarantee. Hundreds of millions of people have ordered by phone or mail over the decades with the assurance their satisfaction is guaranteed. Don't make an offer without a guarantee. Nothing should happen in the creative process until you have structured an offer, or offers, that will make the creative process work. But remember this—what you offer is what you live with.

Selecting Response Channels

Today, marketers may give prospects and customers a wide variety of media to respond to an offer. The four primary channels are mail, phone, fax, and Internet.

By mail, the marketer can provide a postage-free card or envelope, or can specify that the responder provide the postage. We're talking about pennies here, but surprisingly, the postage-free card or envelope usually pulls better.

Order forms are another mail response vehicle. The number one rule in creating an order form is that it must look too important to throw away. Close to that rule is: you should make it easy for the prospect to respond. Challenging the second rule are order forms that seem quite complicated. Publishers Clearing House comes to mind. Their order forms certainly look too important to throw away, plus they are loaded with *involvement devices*—various stamps that must be affixed to the order form prior to returning it.

As one would expect, offers that provide a toll-free number appeal particularly to prospects who have an urgent need for a particular product or service. On the other hand, those who have more curiosity than an urgent need would prefer to respond by mail. This group might be of a mind-set that says, "Why should I voluntarily submit myself to a phone sales pitch?"

Happily, there's no reason to test one against the other. Offer both postage-free and toll-free. Let the market make its own choices.

The medium of the fax still carries with it a special feeling of importance and urgency. Therefore, it behooves the marketer to respond quickly to inquiries or orders initiated by fax.

Finally, any marketer who ignores the power of the Internet does so at his or her own peril. Here again it is imperative for marketers to respond quickly. Companies that conduct business on-line should confirm orders by E-mail just a few minutes after they have been placed. Companies that still batch Internet orders and enter them off-line—and there are a few—should confirm as soon as possible via E-mail.

An In-Depth Look at Unique Offers

Before going over the following offers, review each with the basic question: How can I adapt this offer to my line of business?

Exhibit 5–1 is a newspaper insert from a suburban edition of the *Chicago Tribune* newspaper. This is a targeted insert in that a list of 25 dealers within the segmented area appears on the back of the insert. The offer includes a $50 rebate as an incentive. The expiration date is designed to overcome human inertia.

EXHIBIT 5–1

Rebate Offer

Sprint PCS

Get a
$50 Mail-In Rebate
on any Sprint PCS Phone™

- Buy any **Sprint PCS Free & Clear Plan**™ starting at $29.99 and get a $50 mail-in rebate on any Sprint PCS Phone.

- The Sprint PCS Free & Clear Plan includes **free long distance**. Use all of your minutes for local or long-distance calls from anywhere on the all-digital Sprint PCS Nationwide Network, serving over 280 major metropolitan areas.

- Plus, pay as little as **A Dime Anytime** on plans starting at **$50 a month/500 minutes** for a limited time.

- With Sprint PCS, there are no annual contracts required and no hidden charges. Plus, features like Voicemail, Caller ID and Call Waiting are included.

$99⁹⁹ Everyday low price
−$50⁰⁰ mail-in rebate
$49⁹⁹ Final Price
Sprint PCS Phone by Samsung™

Sprint PCS Phone™ By Samsung® (model # SCH-2000)
- Voice-Activated Dialing
- Up to 4 hours of continuous talk time
- Only 5.4 oz.

Phone purchase and activation required. Restrictions apply. See printed materials in store for details.

◆ **Sprint**   The clear alternative to cellular.™   **Sprint PCS**

Hurry Rebate Offer ends August 19th

For the Sprint PCS Select Retailer nearest you , see Retailer list on reverse side

EXHIBIT 5-1 *(continued)*

Sprint PCS Select Retailers near you.

Krystel Wireless	5501 N.W. HWY	Crystal Lake	60014	(815) 459-9755
Alpine Camera/Northshore Camera of Des Plaines	686 Lee St.	Des Plaines	60016	(847) 229-6181
K&H Electronics dba Cellupager	2606A Dempster St.	Des Plaines	60016	(847) 299-5701
PC Comm	Gurnee Mills Mall	Gurnee	60031	(847) 856-1720
Audiosmith	755 N. Miluakee Ave.	Libertyville	60048	(847) 816-1900
Extreme Mobile Sound	5838 Dempster	Morton Grove	60053	(847) 966-3800
Spoke & Ski	701 N. Milwaukee Ave.	Vernon Hills	60061	(847) 816-0084
CSSINET	3073 Dundee Rd.	Northbrook	60062	(847) 498-0061
Wireless Cellutions	1137 Northbrook Court	Northbrook	60062	(847) 498-1188
The Page Center	1713 N. Rand Rd.	Palatine	60074	(847) 358-2666
MiCom	8404 Gross Point Rd.	Skokie	60077	(847) 663-1194
Best Com	2011 Belvidere Rd.	Waukegan	60085	(847) 336-0119
Communication Concepts Inc.,	102 Washington St.	Waukegan	60085	(847) 360-8600
AB Distributing	300 Lexington Drive	Buffalo Grove	60089	(847) 215-9009
Planet Wireless	1503 W. Dundee Rd.	Buffalo Grove	60089	(847) 368-1400
Extreme Mobile Sound	89 East Dundee Rd.	Wheeling	60090	(847) 520-9500
SBBS	444 Skokie Blvd.	Wilmette	60091	(847) 256-4600
DC Cellular	140-8 Barrington Rd.	Streamwood	60107	(630) 213-6120
Mason's Car Wash,	14 e. Irving Rd.	Streamwood	60107	(630) 289-7522
Cellular.com	547 South Eighth St.	West Dundee	60118	(847) 836-6666
Communication Concepts Inc.,	33 Clocktower Plaza	Elgin	60120	(847) 931-7000
Absolute Wireless	145 S. Randell Rd.	Elgin	60123	(847) 742-7900
Communication Next	845 E. Schaumburg Rd.	Schaumburg	60194	(847) 895-1860
Int Communication Corp.	2305 Ridgeway	Evanston	60201	(847) 328-6882
Adcom PCS, Inc.	8512 Golf	Niles	60714	(847) 583-1577

Exhibit 5–2 is a USPS offer of a free kit to general advertising agencies and direct marketing agencies. Answering research questions becomes a condition of receiving the free kit.

Exhibit 5–3 is taken from Steve Forbes's political fund-raising effort. Note that there are suggested amounts ($25 and $30), but the opportunity to give a different amount, either more or less, is also given. Experienced fund-raisers know the average donation is larger if one or more amounts are suggested.

Exhibit 5–4, the Multi-Book Offer, reflects the common knowledge among book clubs that the number of new members acquired from a given ad is positively or negatively affected by the number of books offered. Fifty-three books are offered in this full-page, four-color ad by the Mystery Guild. The choice of titles is enhanced even more by encouraging the prospect to consider additional titles on the website.

The basic offer is loaded with incentives: (1) A $25.95 book FREE just for subscribing. (2) Five more books for 99 cents, (3) plus a FREE umbrella and tote set or an extra book. (4) Satisfaction guaranteed (return books within 10 days at club's expense, but keep free gifts). (5) Save up to 60 percent off of publishers' hardcover edition prices. (6) Extra bonus: take an additional book now for $3.99 plus shipping and handling; reduce membership book purchase requirement to only three books. (7) A FREE club magazine up to 17 times a year. (8) On-line convenience: join at website, get an even larger selection of books.

Exhibit 5–5, a survey/contribution offer for the National Parks and Conservation Association, contains no separate response form; instead, a response form asking for a contribution follows the last survey question quite logically.

EXHIBIT 5–2

Free Kit Offer

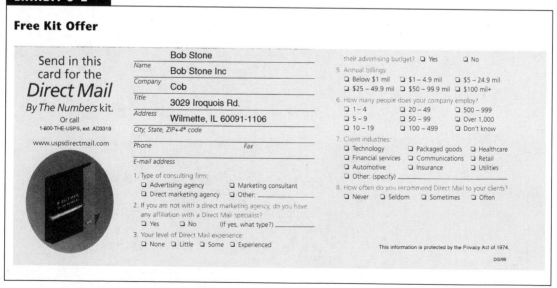

EXHIBIT 5-3

Fund-Raising Response Card

URGENT NOTICE

Forbes 2000
HE WANTS YOU TO WIN
Charter Member
MEMBER NAME
MEMBER NUMBER

Your official 1999 Forbes 2000℠ Charter Membership Card was mailed to you on July 26, 1999. If you received your Card, but have not yet mailed your special support contribution, please use the bottom portion of this form to respond by September 30, 1999. It is essential to the success of Steve Forbes's presidential campaign to have the largest possible base of grassroots contributors by the September 30 federal election commission quarterly reporting deadline. 100% of your contribution will be put directly to use co-sponsoring radio and television advertising and building the campaign grassroots organization nationwide.

Detach and keep this portion with your records.   CARD RECEIVED __/__/__ CONTRIBUTION SENT __/__/__ AMOUNT SENT $_____
                                      MO DY YR   MO DY YR

```
Mr. Robert Stone                              102004652
3029 Iroquois Rd                              HAM45
Wilmette, IL  60091-1106
```

SUPPORT REPLY FORM

☐ I understand how important it is to help show the public that support for Steve Forbes's agenda is wide and deep, and to co-sponsor TV and radio advertising and grassroots organizing activities, I have enclosed a special contribution of:

        ☐ $25   ☐ $35   ☐ Other $_____

☐ I did not receive my Charter Membership Card. Please send a replacement card to me at the above address.

Please make checks payable to: **Forbes 2000, Inc.**

To make a credit card contribution, please complete the information on the reverse of this form.

Paid for by Forbes 2000, Inc. Contributions are not tax deductible as charitable contributions for federal tax purposes. Corporate contributions and contributions from foreign nationals are prohibited by law.

WE ARE MAKING STRONG GAINS IN THE POLLS IN EARLY PRIMARY AND CAUCUS STATES, BUT WE NEED TO KEEP ADVERTISING AND ORGANIZING. IF YOU CAN MAKE ANOTHER CONTRIBUTION, I HOPE YOU WILL DO SO TODAY. MANY THANKS! —Steve

Please enclose your check and this portion of the Support Reply Form in the orange envelope for immediate processing. If you wish to make your contribution by credit card, complete the information on the reverse of this form. Thank you!

The response form itself follows the basics of a good fund-raising effort. It gives five different amounts of contributions to consider and circles an amount that suggests this should be the minimum amount to consider. A fanny pack is offered for giving a contribution of $15 or more. And, to make it easy to respond, the opportunity is given to contribute through one of three credit cards. (A contribution through a credit card is likely to increase the gift by 15 percent or more over a cash contribution.)

Bingo cards constitute an offer. The card is a service provided by many publications with numbers for specific advertisers' literature, which makes it more convenient for readers to get further information. All the reader has to do is circle the numbers assigned to ads that interest him/her and the publisher sends the inquiries to the advertisers to fulfill.

Exhibit 5–6 illustrates a bingo card bound into *Selling Power*, a trade publication for sales and marketing people. A word of explanation—there is a sound

EXHIBIT 5-4

Multi-Book Offer

EXHIBIT 5-5

Survey/Contribution Offer

7. The National Park Service says that pollution from power plants and industries significantly worsens the visibility at Grand Canyon, Great Smoky Mountains, and other national parks. Should companies be required to clean up their pollution, even if it meant that you might pay more for utilities and consumer products?

☐ Yes   ☐ No

8. Would you be willing to use a shuttle bus in popular parks during peak season to reduce traffic congestion and help protect park resources?

☐ Yes   ☐ No

9. At national parks like Grand Canyon and Great Smoky Mountains, companies offer low-flying airplane or helicopter sightseeing trips. Some people believe these trips should be allowed because they offer access to the parks to those who might not otherwise be able to see them. Others believe that flights should be limited or banned because the sight and sound of low-flying aircraft keep other visitors from enjoying the peace and natural sounds of the park. What do you believe?

☐ Sightseeing flights should be banned

☐ Sightseeing flights should be limited

☐ Sightseeing flights should not be banned or limited

10. The National Park Service says it will take more than 5 billion dollars to meet its backlog of needs. People differ on whether they believe that the U.S. Congress should allocate more money to national parks, given other national priorities. What do you believe?

☐ Yes, Congress should allocate more money to national parks

☐ No, Congress should not allocate more money to national parks

☐ **Yes,** I'll gladly do my share to help protect America's national parks. Please enroll me as a conservator as well as a user of America's most beautiful wild lands and most meaningful historic heritage. I have enclosed my membership contribution of:

☐ $100   ☐ $50   (☐ $25)   ☐ $20   ☐ $15   ☐ Other $_____

YOUR GIFT AT THIS LEVEL WILL REALLY HELP!

In thanks for your gift of $15 or more, you'll receive a NPCA's FANNY PACK, our bimonthly four-color magazine *National Parks,* information on PARK-PAK, and many other member benefits.

☐ I prefer to charge my dues to: ☐ VISA   ☐ MasterCard   ☐ American Express

Account No._____ Exp. Date _____

Signature _____

We have made our best effort to avoid duplication of mailings to members. If you have received a duplicate mailing, please pass this package to a friend. All but $3, which covers a subscription to *National Parks,* and the $5.95 retail value of the free fanny pack are tax-deductible to the extent allowed by law.

On a selective basis, NPCA makes its membership list available to organizations whose mailings we think you will find of interest. If you prefer that your name be omitted from this list, please check the box on your address label.

Yours Free...
as a new member of NPCA

reason for limiting the reader to ten or fewer choices: for some reason, a surprising number of people just "love to collect literature." They will circle practically every number on a bingo card. Needless to say, they are poor prospects.

Finally, with few exceptions, you will get more responses on bingo cards than you will directly from your ads. The quality of leads, on the other hand, tends to be better from those who respond directly from the ads.

Exhibit 5–7 is an example of an incentive for providing an E-mail address. Sharper Image, recognizing the value of E-mail contact with its catalog customers, forthrightly gives customers an opportunity to win a $3,195 sweepstakes prize if they will voluntarily provide their E-mail address.

Exhibit 5–8 shows how free services are offered in exchange for providing an E-mail address. DMA and its subsidiary association offer free services for an undisclosed period of time.

There are some subtleties involved in this combination offer:

1. The request for the E-mail address appears "matter of fact" in that E-mail address is required in the normal sequence of name, company, and phone number.

EXHIBIT 5–6

Bingo Card

FREE INFORMATION FROM OUR ADVERTISERS

It's easy to get information on products, services and companies advertised in this issue. Simply circle the number on this postage-paid card that corresponds to the number printed below the advertisement. Then detach your completed card and drop it in the mail today. Please limit your selection to no more than 10 choices. Only cards with 10 or fewer choices will be processed. Please print legibly to aid processing.

NAME
TITLE
COMPANY
ADDRESS
CITY/STATE/ZIP
PHONE # (   )
E-MAIL ADDRESS:
WEB ADDRESS:

PLEASE INDICATE YOUR INDUSTRY:
☐ Manufacturing   ☐ Financial or insurance
☐ Service organization   ☐ Wholesale or distribution
☐ Retail trade   ☐ Transportation/communication
☐ Education, library, or government   ☐ Other

You may also fax this coupon to 203/743-0042
For subscriptions call 1-800-752-7355
Visit our Web site: www.sellingpower.com

Send more information about the products or services circled below
ONLY CARDS WITH 10 OR FEWER CHOICES WILL BE PROCESSED.

1	2	3	4	5	6	7	8	9	10
11	12	13	14	15	16	17	18	19	20
21	22	23	24	25	26	27	28	29	30
31	32	33	34	35	36	37	38	39	40
41	42	43	44	45	46	47	48	49	50
51	52	53	54	55	56	57	58	59	60
61	62	63	64	65	66	67	68	69	70
71	72	73	74	75	76	77	78	79	80
81	82	83	84	85	86	87	88	89	90
91	92	93	94	95	96	97	98	99	100
101	102	103	104	105	106	107	108	109	110
111	112	113	114	115	116	117	118	119	120
121	122	123	124	125	126	127	128	129	130
131	132	133	134	135	136	137	138	139	140
141	142	143	144	145	146	147	148	149	150

Save time!
Check below to get information about all advertisers from the following product categories:

801 ☐ Sales automation   804 ☐ Incentive travel   806 ☐ Group meetings
802 ☐ Sales incentives/gifts   805 ☐ Individual business   807 ☐ Fleet
803 ☐ Sales training   travel

EXHIBIT 5–7

E-Mail Address Solicitation

THE SHARPER IMAGE®
650 Davis Street
San Francisco, CA 94111
(415) 445-6000

Richard Thalheimer
Chairman and Founder

Win-The-Chair!
SWEEPSTAKES

Dear Sharper Image Customer,

We're giving away a luxurious new "Ultimate" Get-A-Way® Chair — worth $3,195 — every month for the next six months with our Win-The-Chair e-mail sweepstakes!

To enter, give us your e-mail address by going to our Website at www.sharperimage.com and clicking on the sweepstakes button. Or fill out the reverse side of this letter and bring it to one of our stores.

Best of luck!

Richard

Richard Thalheimer

No purchase necessary. Void where prohibited. Sweepstakes ends January 31, 2000. Open to legal residents of the United States and Canada, eighteen years of age and older as of August 1, 1999, excluding residents of Quebec.

sharperimage.com

See the flap end of this letter for official rules or visit http://www.webstakes.com/sharperimage2/rules.html

2. The free services checklist follows. In reality the AIM services are being introduced to DMA members, and the E-mail address of the member is being picked up in the process.

3. All concern about the DMA or AIM renting out E-mail addresses is covered in advance with this declaration: "AIM respects your privacy. We will never release your E-mail address to anyone."

Exhibit 5–9 is a credit card/catalog offer with involvement device. Involvement devices have long been used to move the prospect one step further toward accepting an offer.

EXHIBIT 5–8

Free Services Offered in Exchange for E-Mail Address

Internet & Direct Marketing

ASSOCIATION
for **AIM**
INTERACTIVE
MEDIA
www.interactivehq.org

AND

DMA
Direct Marketing Association

Dear Bob:

Every day your competitors are getting important inside information about the Internet business from the Association for Interactive Media (AIM). More than 28,000 senior new media executives read these publications — you can get your free subscriptions today!

Now that AIM is an independent subsidiary of the Direct Marketing Association, you are able to receive your own copies of this valuable market research about the Internet.

Fax this form to us today so we can add you to the distribution lists. This free offer is for a limited time only.

AIM publishes these email newsletters as a service exclusively for senior executives in the new media business. There are no hidden costs, no obligation to join AIM, and no strings attached. You can unsubscribe to these publications at any time.

Thank you and enjoy!

**AIM respects your privacy. We will never release your email address to anyone.

**FREE NEWSLETTERS
STAY INFORMED**
Quick Response Form — Fax to 202-408-0111

Name: _____

Company: _____

Email: _____

Phone: _____

Please sign me up for:

☐ **RESEARCH UPDATE SERVICE:** Summaries of the newest, most important research about the Internet market.

☐ **WHO'S NEWS:** The Internet's best tip sheet — your weekly guide to deals, dealmakers, movers & shakers.

☐ **POLITICS INSIDER:** Weekly guide to the wheeling & dealing in the smoky back room.

☐ **AIM/DMA SCHEDULER:** AIM and DMA's emailed event calendar.

☐ **Save $500 on AIM membership:** Receive information on how your company can be more profitable online through a half-price AIM membership — for DMA members only.

1301 Connecticut Avenue, NW • 5th Floor • Washington, DC 20036 • 202-408-0006 • fax: 202-408-0111
www.interactivehq.org

In this case, Spiegel features an "Approved" sticker that, when removed and transferred to the acceptance form, brings the prospect a charge card and the 572-page fall catalog free. Note the alternative way to receive the charge card and catalog—"Call toll free 1-800-541-4445." Finally, note the simple statement designed to overcome human inertia: "All we ask is that you return the form below or call before September 25, 1999."

Exhibit 5–10 shows a "name your price offer," one of the most exciting new offers to make the scene in the past decade. This name your price offer is for domestic and international airline flights. Noting that the same bidding concept will soon be applied to hotels causes one to ask, "Will the same type of offer be applied

EXHIBIT 5–9

Credit Card/Catalog Offer with Involvement Device

Ms. Barbara Stone
3029 Iroquois Rd
Wilmette, IL   60091-1106

l.lll.ll..ll..l.l..l...ll..ll...llll...ll...ll..ll.l..l.l.l

Approved

Place this sticker on the form below
to accept your charge card and
FREE 572-page Fall Catalog.

Dear Ms. Barbara Stone,

   You have been pre-approved to receive a new Spiegel® FCNB Preferred® Charge Card. It will arrive
with a credit line up to **$825**, which is immediately available. You'll also receive a *free* copy of the
Spiegel 572-page Fall Catalog (a $10 value).

No Annual Fee

   Just complete and return the Pre-approved Acceptance Certificate below. Or, to receive your new charge
card and catalog even faster, call toll free **1-800-541-4445**. Tell your Sales Associate:

- your **Application Code** is **22603232**
- you want **Offer Number F1473**

   Once your card and catalog arrive, you can use them to shop for women's and men's fashions ... home
furnishings ... electronics ... and more.

   Your charge card and your free catalog are ready now. All we ask is that you return the form below or
call before September 25, 1999. Thank you for your time.

Sincerely,

Christian Feuer
Vice President, Marketing

P.S. You can call now to accept your card and catalog: **1-800-541-4445**.

992-MOD

Place sticker below, complete and return form
in enclosed postage-paid envelope.

0106193

Yes, I accept the Spiegel® FCNB Preferred® Charge Card and
FREE 572-page Fall Catalog.
Please make any necessary address corrections below. (Courtesy titles are optional.)

Ms. Barbara Stone
3029 Iroquois Rd
Wilmette, IL   60091-1106

Pre-Approved Credit Line Up To: $825
Appl. Code: 22603232   Offer #: F1473

Approved

Day Phone		Home	Evening Phone		Home
Area Code ( )		Work	Area Code ( )		Work
		Social Security Number (Required)			
Date of Birth					

Employer   How Long?

Employer's City   State

Total Annual Household Income All Sources

- $0-15,000 $15,001-25,000 $25,001-35,000
- $35,001-45,000 $45,001-55,000 $55,001+

You need not supply any alimony, child support or separate maintenance income if you do not want
us to consider it in evaluating your application.

Name of other
authorized buyer

Social Security Number

FCNB PREFERRED Charge is available to Spiegel customers through
First Consumers National Bank® of Portland, Oregon.

X _____ Date _____
SIGNATURE — SEE OPPOSITE SIDE FOR IMPORTANT NOTICES AND CREDIT INFORMATION   06/99-UCA

6014739

EXHIBIT 5–10

Name Your Price Offer

Albuquerque	Name your price!
Anchorage	Name the price you want!
Aspen	Name your own price!
Atlantic City	Name your price!
Baltimore	Name your own price!
Baton Rouge	You name the price!
Billings	Name your own price.
Birmingham	You name the price!
Boise	Name the price you want!
Boston	You name it!
Buffalo	Name the price you want!
Cedar Rapids	It's your price!
Charleston	Name the price!
Charlotte	Why not name your price!
Chattanooga	Name the price you want to pay!
Chicago	Name your own price!
Cleveland	Just name your price!
Colorado Springs	Name the price!
Columbus	Name your price!
Dallas	You name it!
Daytona Beach	Name your own price!
Denver	Just name the price!
Des Moines	Name your own price!
Detroit	Have you named your price?
El Paso	Name your own price!
Erie	You name the price!
Fairbanks	You name the price you want!
Fargo	Name it.
Fayetteville	Name the price you want!
Fort Lauderdale	You name the price!
Fort Myers	You name it!
Fresno	Name your price!
Grand Rapids	Why not name your price?
Green Bay	Name your own price!
Hartford	Just name the price!
Honolulu	Name your own price!
Houston	You name the price!
Idaho	Name the price!
Indianapolis	You name it!
Jacksonville	Just name your own price!
Key West	Name your price!
Knoxville	Name the price!
Lafayette	Why not name the price?
Lake Tahoe	Name your best price!
Las Vegas	Have you named your price today?
Lincoln	Name the price you want to pay!
Long Beach	It's your price!
Los Angeles	Name your own price!
Louisville	Name your own price!
Memphis	Name the price you want!
Miami	You decide!
Milwaukee	Name your price!
Minneapolis/St. Paul	Name your own price!
Mobile	Pick the price!

Incredible prices on airline tickets to over 346 cities!

How much do you want to pay for airline tickets? With priceline.com, it's up to you!

If you haven't used priceline.com to name your own price for airline tickets, you're missing out on a great way to save money. And there's no better time than now to book tickets for your next trip. Name your own price to virtually anywhere in the U.S. or worldwide—free of charge—and get an answer in just *one hour* for domestic travel, 24 hours for international travel.

So what are you waiting for? Join over 60,000 satisfied priceline.com customers. Just give us a call toll-free at 1-800-PRICELINE (774-2354), or visit us on the Web at www.priceline.com. It's fast, easy and the service is free. So, if you're ready to buy airline tickets to any of over 346 cities, come to priceline.com. After all, there's no better price than *your* price.

Nashville	You name the price!	San Francisco	It's your price!
New Orleans	Just name your own price!	Santa Barbara	Name your own price!
Newark	Name your own price!	Savannah	Name your best price!
New York	You name the price!	Seattle	Name your price!
Norfolk	Name your price!	Sioux City	Name the price!
Oklahoma City	Name your own price!	South Bend	Name your own price!
Omaha	You name the price!	Syracuse	Name your own price!
Orlando	You name the price!	Tampa	Name your price!
Palm Springs	You name it!	Toledo	Have you named your price?
Philadelphia	Name your price!	Tulsa	You name the price!
Pittsburgh	You decide!	Tucson	Name your price!
Portland	Name the price you want!	Washington	Name your own price.
Raleigh/Durham	Name your own price.	West Palm Beach	Name it.
Sacramento	Name your price!	Yuma	You name the price!
San Antonio	Name the price you want!		
San Diego	Have you named your price?		

. . . And hundreds of other U. S. cities!

Name Your Price to These International Cities:

Amsterdam	You name the price!
Athens	Name the price!
Auckland	Why not name your price!
Bangkok	Name your own price!
Barcelona	Name the price you want to pay!
Berlin	Name your best price!
Bombay	Name the price!
Brussels	Just name your price!
Budapest	Name the price!
Buenos Aires	Name your own price!
Cancun	Name your price!
Caracas	Name your price!
Copenhagen	You name the price!
Dublin	You name it!
Frankfurt	Name your own price!
Geneva	Just name the price!
Glasgow	Name your price!
Helsinki	How you named your price?
Hong Kong	Name your own price!
Istanbul	You name the price!
Ixtapa	Why not name your price!
Johannesburg	Name your price!
Kuala Lumpur	Name you own price!
Lisbon	Name it.
London	Name the price you want!
Madrid	You name the price!
Mexico City	Name your price!
Paris	Name the price you want!
Milan	Name your price!
Nice	Name the price!
Paris	Name your price!
Prague	Why not name your price!
Puerto Plata	It's your price!
Rio de Janeiro	Name your own price!
Rome	You name it!
Santo Domingo	Name your own price!
Santiago	Name the price!
Sao Paulo	Just name the price!
Shannon	Name your price!
St. Maarten	Name your own price!
Stockholm	You name the price!
Sydney	Name your price!
Tokyo	You name the price!
Tel Aviv	You name it!
Warsaw	You name it!
Zurich	Name your own price!

. . . And hundreds of other destinations worldwide!

1.800.priceline | priceline.com™
Name Your Own Price™

Coming Soon...priceline Hotels Save by naming your own price for quality hotel accommodations in 26 U.S. cities! Visit us at priceline.com for all the details.

to ocean cruises?" This is where we should apply the magic question: How can I adapt that idea to my line of business?

Merchandising the Offer

Each of the offers just reviewed has wide application. As a matter of fact, many of the offers can be used successfully in combination. However, as powerful as many of these offers are, one must keep in mind that to maximize success, the offers must be merchandised properly to target markets.

Free-Gift Offers

Giving free gifts for inquiring, for trying, and for buying is as old an incentive as trading stamps. It is not at all unusual for the right gift to increase response by 25 percent and more. On the other hand, a free-gift offer can actually reduce response or have no favorable effect on the basic offer. This is particularly true where the unit of sale or amount of sale consideration overshadows the appeal of the free gift.

What's more, there is a tremendous variance in the appeal of free gifts. For example, the Airline Passenger Association tested two free gifts along with a membership offer: an airline guide and a carry-on suit bag. The suit bag did 50 percent better than the guide. A fund-raising organization selling to schools tested three different gifts: a set of children's books, a camera, and a 30-cup coffeemaker. The coffeemaker won by a wide margin; the children's books came in a poor third.

Testing for the most appealing gifts is essential because of the great differences in pull. In selecting gifts for testing purposes, follow this rule of thumb: gifts that are suited to personal use tend to have considerably more appeal than those that aren't.

There is yet another consideration about free gifts: Is it more effective to offer a selection of free gifts of comparable value than to offer only one gift? The answer is that offering a selection of gifts of comparable value usually reduces response. This is perhaps explained by the inability of many people to make a choice.

Adopting the one-gift method (after testing for the one with the most appeal) should not be confused with offering gifts of varying value for orders of varying amounts. This is quite a different situation. A multiple gift proposition might be a free travel clock for orders up to $40, a free miniature sports radio for orders from $40 to $75, and a free camera for orders over $75. Offering gifts of varying value for orders of varying amounts is logical to the consumer. The advertiser can afford a more expensive gift in conjunction with a larger order. The prime objective is accomplished by increasing the average order above what it would be if there were no extra incentive.

The multiple gift plan works for many, but it can also boomerang. This usually happens when the top gift calls for a purchase above what most people can use or afford. The effect can also be negative if the gift offered for the price most people can afford is of little value or consequence. The multiple gift plan tied to order value has good potential advantages, but careful tests must be conducted. An adaptation of the multiple gift plan is a gift—often called a "keeper"—for trying (free trial), plus a gift for keeping (paying for the purchase). Under this plan the prospect is told he or she can keep the gift offered for trying, even if the product being offered for sale is returned. However, if the product being offered is retained, the prospect also keeps a second gift of greater value than the first.

Still another possibility with gift offers is giving more than one gift for either trying or buying. If the budget for the incentive is one dollar, for example, the advertiser can offer one gift costing a dollar; two gifts combined, costing a dollar; or even three gifts totaling a dollar. From a sales strategy standpoint, some advertisers spell out what one or two of the gifts are and offer an additional "mystery gift" for prompt response. Fingerhut Corporation of Minneapolis is a strong proponent of multiple gifts and "mystery gifts."

Free gifts are a tricky business, to be sure. Gift selection and gift tie-ins to offers require careful testing for best results. The $64,000 question is always: "How much can I afford to spend for a gift?" Aaron Adler, cofounder of Stone & Adler, maintains that most marketers make an erroneous arbitrary decision in advance, such as, "I can afford to spend 5 percent of selling price." He maintains that a far more logical approach is to select the most appealing gift possible, without being restricted by an arbitrary cost figure, rather than being guided by the net profit figures resulting from tests. For example, Exhibit 5–11 shows a comparison of net profits for two promotions on a $29.95 offer; one with a gift costing one dollar and the other with a gift costing two dollars, given a 50 percent better pull with the two-dollar premium.

In this example, it is interesting to note that when the one dollar gift was offered, the mailing just about broke even. But when the cost of the gift was doubled, the profit jumped from $4.52 to $52.16 per thousand mailed. Another advantage of offering more attractive gifts (which naturally cost more) is to offer gifts of substantial value tied to cumulative purchases. This plan can prove particularly effective when the products or services being offered produce consistent repeat orders. A typical offer under a cumulative purchase plan might be: "When your total purchases of our custom-made cigars reach $150, you receive a crystal decanter absolutely free."

EXHIBIT 5–11

Comparison of Profits from Promotions with Free Gifts of Different Costs

Item	$1 Gift	$2 Gift
Net pull of promotion	1%	1.5%
Sales per thousand pieces	$299.50	$449.25
Less		
Mailing cost	120.00	120.00
Merchandise cost (45%)	134.98	202.16
Administrative cost (10%)	30.00	44.93
Premium cost	10.00	30.00
Total costs	$294.98	$397.09
Profit per thousand pieces	$4.52	$52.16

Get-a-Friend Offers

One overlooked and profitable offer is the get-a-friend offer. If you have a list of satisfied customers, it is quite natural for them to want to let their friends in on a good thing. The basic technique for get-a-friend offers is to offer an incentive in appreciation for a favor. Nominal gifts are often given to a customer for the simple act of providing friends' names, with more substantial gifts awarded to the customer for friends who become customers.

Based on experience, here is what you can expect in using the get-a-friend approach: you will get a larger number of friends' names if the customers are guaranteed that their names will not be used in soliciting their friends. Response from friends, however, will be consistently better if you are allowed to refer to the party who supplied their names. To get the best of two worlds, therefore, you should allow customers to indicate whether their names may be used in soliciting their friends. For example: "You may use my name when writing my friends" or "Do not use my name when writing my friends."

Response from friends decreases in proportion to the number of names provided by a customer. One can expect the response from three names provided by one person to be greater than the total response from six names provided by another person. The reason is that it is natural to list the names in order of likelihood of interest.

Two safeguards should be applied to get the maximum response from friends' names: (1) limit the number of names to be provided, for example, to three or four, and (2) promote names provided in order of listing, such as all names provided first as one group, all names provided second as another group, and so forth. Those who have mastered the technique of getting friends' names from satisfied customers have found that, with very few exceptions, such lists are more responsive than most lists they can rent or buy.

Short- and Long-Term Effects of Offers

A major consideration in structuring offers is the effect a given offer will have on your objective.

1. To get a maximum number of new customers for a given product or service as quickly as possible

2. To determine the repeat business factor as quickly as possible

3. To break even or make a profit in the shortest time

So, the key question to ask when designing an offer is: How will this offer help to accomplish my objective? Say you are introducing a new hobby magazine. You have the choice of making a short-term offer (three months) or a long-term offer

(12 months). Because your objective is to determine acceptance as quickly as possible, you would decide on a short-term offer. Under the short-term offer, after three months you will be getting a picture of renewal percentages. If you have made an initial offer of 12-month subscriptions, you would have to wait a year to determine the publication renewal rate. In the interim you would be missing vital information important to your magazine's success.

If the three-month trial subscriptions are renewed at a satisfactory rate, you can then safely proceed to develop offers designed to get initial long-term subscriptions. It is axiomatic in the publishing field that the longer the initial term of subscription, the higher the renewal rate is likely to be. Circulation professionals know from experience that if they are getting, say, a 35 percent conversion on a three-month trial, they can expect a conversion of 50 percent or more on 12-month initial subscriptions. This knowledge, therefore, can be extrapolated from the short-term objective to the long-term objective.

Sol Blumenfeld, a prominent direct marketing consultant, when addressing a Direct Mail/Marketing Association convention, made some pertinent remarks about the dangers of looking only at front-end response. Blumenfeld stated: "Many people still cling to the CPA (cost per application) or CPI (cost per inquiry) response syndromes. In their eagerness to sell now, they frequently foul up their chances to sell later."

He then asks: "Can the practice of those who concern themselves only with front-end response at least partially explain book club conversions of only 50 to 60 percent? Magazine renewal rates of only 30 percent? Correspondence school attrition factors of as much as 40 percent?"

Blumenfeld gives us a case in point. A control for the Britannica Home Study Library Service (a division of Encyclopedia Britannica) was run against several test ads developed by the agency. Control ads offered the first volume of Compton's Encyclopedia free. Major emphasis was placed on sending for the free volume; small emphasis was placed on the idea of ultimately purchasing the rest of the 24-volume set. Front-end response was excellent; the rate of conversion to full 24-volume sets was poor. Profitability was unacceptable. Against the control ad, the agency tested several new ads that offered the first volume free but also revealed the cost of the complete set in the headline. The cost per coupon for the new ads was 20 percent higher than for the control ad, but conversions to full sets improved a full 350 percent.

Ways to Hype Response

Once you have decided on your most appealing offer, either arbitrarily or by testing, you should ask a very specific question: How can I hype my offer to make it even more appealing? There are several ways: terms of payment, sweepstakes, umbrella sweepstakes, toll-free response, publisher's letters, and the guarantee.

Terms of Payment

Where a direct sale is involved, the terms of payment you require can hype or depress response. A given product or service can have tremendous appeal, but if payment terms are too stringent—beyond the means of a potential buyer—the offer will surely be a failure. Five general categories of payment terms may be offered: (1) cash with order, (2) cash on delivery (COD), (3) open account, (4) installment terms, and (5) revolving credit.

If a five-way split test were made among these categories, it is almost certain that response would be in inverse ratio to the listing of the five categories. Revolving credit would be the most attractive and cash with order the least attractive. With each loosening of terms, the appeal of the offer is hyped.

In a four-way split test on a merchandise offer, here's how four terms actually ranked (the least appealing terms have a 100 percent ranking): cash with order, 100 percent; cash with order—free gift for trying, 144 percent; bill-me offer (open account), 177 percent; and bill-me offer (open account) and free gift, 233 percent. As the figures disclose, the most attractive terms (bill-me offer and free gift) were almost two and a half times more appealing than the least attractive terms (cash with order).

Although COD terms are generally more attractive than cash-with-order requirements, such terms are rarely offered these days, for two reasons. First, non-deliveries are high because most households have two working adults, negating the opportunity to collect upon delivery. Second, even when at least one adult is home, a high percentage of those who ordered with enthusiasm lose the desire to accept and pay for the merchandise.

When merchandise or services are offered on open account, payment is customarily requested in 15 or 30 days. Such terms are naturally more appealing than cash with order or COD. Open-account terms are customary when selling to business firms. When used in selling to the consumer, however, such terms, while appealing, can result in a high percentage of bad debts, unless carefully selected credit-checked lists are used.

The best appeals lie in installment terms and revolving credit terms. Both mechanisms require substantial financing facilities and a sophisticated credit collection system. Installment selling in the consumer field is virtually essential for the successful sale of "big ticket" merchandise—items selling for $69.95 and up.

One can have the best of two worlds—most appealing terms and no credit risk—by allowing customers to charge purchases to a credit card such as American Express and Discover, or one of the bank cards: Visa or MasterCard. It is not unusual to hype the average order from a catalog by 15 percent when bank card privileges or travel-and-entertainment card privileges are offered. Not only do these privileges tend to increase the amount of the average order, but they also tend to increase the total response.

Sweepstakes

Since the 1970s, sweepstakes offers have been almost standard for mass mailers like *Reader's Digest* and Publishers Clearing House. The prize structures for those firms and their ilk have promised and delivered grand prizes that fulfill the giddy dream of becoming an instant multimillionaire.

The hype of the basic offers is the sweepstakes. It is generally known by the general public that "you need not purchase to win." However, consumer behavior being what it is, there is an uncalculated percentage of the general public that does buy because they think that will increase their opportunity to win.

Hundreds, perhaps thousands, of tests have been made to compare order percentage with and without a sweepstakes overlay. Speaking in generalities, order percentage usually increases 30 percent or more.

Sweepstakes are not likely to go away, but Congress is watching. So it behooves the marketer to play by the rules.

Toll-Free Response

Toll-free telephone response (800 numbers) offers the opportunity to hype the response from just about any offer. (See Chapter 10, "Telemarketing/Teleservices.")

Publisher's Letter

Another innovative device for hyping responses is an extra mailing enclosure known as the "publisher's letter." It gets its name from its first usage—a short letter from a magazine publisher enclosed in the basic mailing package.

The publisher's letter usually carries a headline: "If you have decided not to respond, read this letter." The letter copy typically reinforces the offer made in the basic mailing packages, assures the reader it is valid, and guarantees the terms. This extra enclosure often increases response by 10 percent and more. While the publisher's letter was originated for subscription offers, this device was soon adopted by other direct marketers selling goods and services. Results have been equally productive.

The Guarantee

As mentioned at the outset, no matter what the terms or basic offer may be, a strong guarantee is essential when selling products or services direct. For more than 100 years Sears, Roebuck and Company has guaranteed satisfaction for every article offered (see Exhibit 5–12). Over the years, no one else has ever succeeded in mail order operations without duplicating the Sears guarantee or offering a similar assurance.

The importance of the guarantee is perhaps best understood by recognizing a fact of life: people are hesitant to send for merchandise unless they know that the

---

EXHIBIT 5–12

Sears Guarantee

SEARS GUARANTEE

Your satisfaction is guaranteed or your money back.

We guarantee that every article in this catalog is accurately described and illustrated.

   If, for any reason whatever, you are not satisfied with any article purchased from us, we want you to return it to us at our expense.

   We will exchange it for exactly what you want, or return your money, including any transportation charges you have paid.

SEARS, ROEBUCK AND CO.

---

product may be returned for full credit if it does not meet their expectations. Guaranteed satisfaction should be a part of any offer soliciting a direct sale.

Danger of Overkill

The power of an offer cannot be overestimated. But there's such a thing as too much of a good thing—offers that sound too good to be true, or that produce a great front-end response but make for poor pay-ups or few repeat customers. Here are two thought-provoking examples.

    1. A comprehensive test was structured for a fund-raising organization to determine whether response would best be maximized by (a) offering a free gift as an incentive for an order, (b) offering a combination of free gift plus a cash bonus for completing a sale, or (c) offering a cash bonus only. The combination of free gift plus cash bonus pulled the lowest response by far; the free-gift proposition far outpulled the cash-bonus proposition.

    2. A $200-piece of electronic equipment was offered for a 15-day free trial. This was the basic proposition. But half the people on the list also were invited to enter a sweepstakes contest. Those on the portion of the list not invited to enter a sweepstakes responded 25 percent better than those on the portion invited to enter.

    In both these examples the more generous offer proved to be "too much." One must be most careful not to make the incentive so overwhelming that it overshadows the product or service being offered. Another important consideration in structuring offers is the axiom, "As you make your bed, so shall you lie in it." Here's what we mean: if you obtain thousands of new customers by offering free gifts as incentives, don't expect a maximum degree of repeat business unless you continue to offer free gifts. Similarly, if you build a big list of installment credit buyers, don't expect these buyers to respond well to cash-basis offers, and vice versa.

The offer—it is the carburetor with just the right mix that powers the driving machine.

CASE STUDY: Simple Pleasures Light

BACKGROUND

The line between sales promotion and direct marketing is often thin, especially when both are included in an integrated marketing communication campaign.

There are many similarities between the two disciplines. Both are measurable and accountable, and can provide large amounts of results to be analyzed. Both promote value-added approaches, especially incentives targeted at targeted prospect groups, and both have tools and techniques that are applied in specific ways.

There are differences as well. The objectives of sales promotion are often short term—for example, to increase sales during a specific sales cycle. Sales promotion has many tactics, some of which are not applicable to direct marketing. On-pack promotions, point of purchase, end caps (displays at the end of an aisle in a retail store), events, etc., have no corollaries in direct marketing.

Direct marketing focuses on long-term gains, creating sales where the expenditures are based on the potential "lifetime value" of the customer. It works backward, first learning about customers, deciding how to use that information in the future, and then capturing the raw data for future campaigns.

This case shows how the targeted use of coupons was included among the tools and techniques of direct marketing in order to reach specific target groups, capture information for a database, and test various promotional offers for a consumer goods product.

CHALLENGE

Simple Pleasures Light is a fat-free, sugar-free, frozen dessert product. It competes in the crowded frozen desserts and novelties segment with light (e.g., low-fat) ice creams, sugar-free ice creams, frozen yogurt, sorbets, and a host of other products designed to satisfy Americans' sweet tooth.

Simple Pleasures cannot be called ice cream because it does not contain at least 10 percent butterfat as required by the FDA's standard of identity for ice cream. It is made with Simplesse, a fat substitute made from egg white and milk protein blended and heated in a process called microparticulation, in which the protein is shaped into microscopic round particles that roll easily over one another. The aim of the process is to create the feel of a creamy liquid with the texture of fat. Simple Pleasures is also sweetened with Nutrasweet (aspartame), allowing it to make its sugar-free claim.

First introduced as a line extension, Simple Pleasures is targeted at diet- and weight-conscious consumers, who are highly concerned with the sugar and fat content of products that they consume. Regular ice cream has approximately 10 percent fat and contains about 7 grams of fat, 30 milligrams of cholesterol, and 135 calories per 4-ounce serving. A super-premium ice cream may contain 16 percent butterfat, with a 4-ounce serving providing 19 grams of fat, 97 milligrams of cholesterol, and 274 calories. A 4-ounce size of Simple Pleasures Light contains less than 1 gram of fat, 14 milligrams of cholesterol, and 80–90 calories (depending on the flavor).

CASE STUDY: **Simple Pleasures Light** *(continued)*

The diet-and-weight-conscious segment should not be confused with the health-conscious segment. While many health-conscious consumers are concerned with their intake of sugars and fats, they are also concerned about product ingredients and favor organic or natural ingredients. It is unlikely that a product with both a fat substitute and sugar substitute would appeal to this segment.

Through research, it was determined that the primary target group for this product would be single women ages 25–35 who are diet and weight conscious. It was agreed that testing needed to be done to learn more about the demographics of the target group as well as to determine what value coupon would produce the optimal results. The offer tested a 50-cent coupon versus a 35-cent coupon.

SOLUTION

The agency chose a highly targeted, solo direct mail campaign to introduce Simple Pleasures Light. Direct mail could target the specific demographics better than freestanding inserts or coop direct mail coupon programs. It could also accomplish another key strategy of the launch: to build a database of customers whose behavior could be tracked over time.

The direct mail program's main objective was to educate target consumers as to the product's benefits, and "incent" them—jargon for "provide an incentive that persuades"—to gain trial of the product. The incentive was a cents-off coupon. Additional awareness was created by a self-liquidating premium offer (paid for by the consumer, with the sales transaction covering the product cost and handling fees).

The program was targeted at consumers in key geographic markets based on product distribution, potential market share, and a high concentration of prospects who fit the demographics.

The program sought to:
- Gain trial of simple Pleasures Light among 150,000 new users
- Build awareness of product benefits: low

calorie, all natural, great taste, and fat free
- Reach the target market
- Achieve high response rate measured by coupon redemption and premium response
- Build a database of customers who had bought the product

In order to achieve these objectives, the agency selected image and positioning consistent with the integrated marketing campaign. To establish a fun, humorous tone and educate the consumer on the product, the agency chose the comic strip character "Cathy" as the spokesperson for Simple Pleasures Light. "Cathy," created by former advertising copywriter Cathy Guisewite, chronicles the trials, tribulations, and inherent humor in the life of a single career woman, a key demographic among diet and weight conscious consumers.

The "Get Your Spoon Ready" creative features a self-mailer designed to break through consumer clutter by featuring personalized copy on the front and back. "Cathy" is featured prominently, with a personal call to action on the front directing consumers to "get their spoons ready," and on the back promoting that inside is a coupon, a Cathy premium offer, and a FREE personalized *Cathy* cartoon. Personalization was used to spark the target consumer's curiosity and involvement with the piece, with the hope that she would tear off the comic and adhere it to her refrigerator as a continual reminder of product (see Exhibit 5–13).

In addition, each coupon had a "match code" imaged onto its back. The "match code" is a unique number that *matches* a prospect record (name, address, list source, etc.) of those mailed the direct mail piece. A "match code" file of those sent the mailing is kept, and the "match code" number from redeemed coupons is used to create a database of respondents to the promotion (see Exhibit 5–14).

The strength of this strategy is that the consumer has nothing to fill out when redeeming the coupon, which typically improves redemption. The weakness

CASE STUDY: Simple Pleasures Light *(continued)*

of this strategy is that you don't know who actually redeemed the coupon at retail. The "match code" contains the name of only those who were sent the mailing. Nonetheless, this is a good strategy for build-ing a database of promotionally responsive buyers with interest in a product or service.

A key element of the launch was a test that pit-ted two coupon values against each other: 35 cents

EXHIBIT 5–13

Direct Mail Package for Simple Pleasures Light

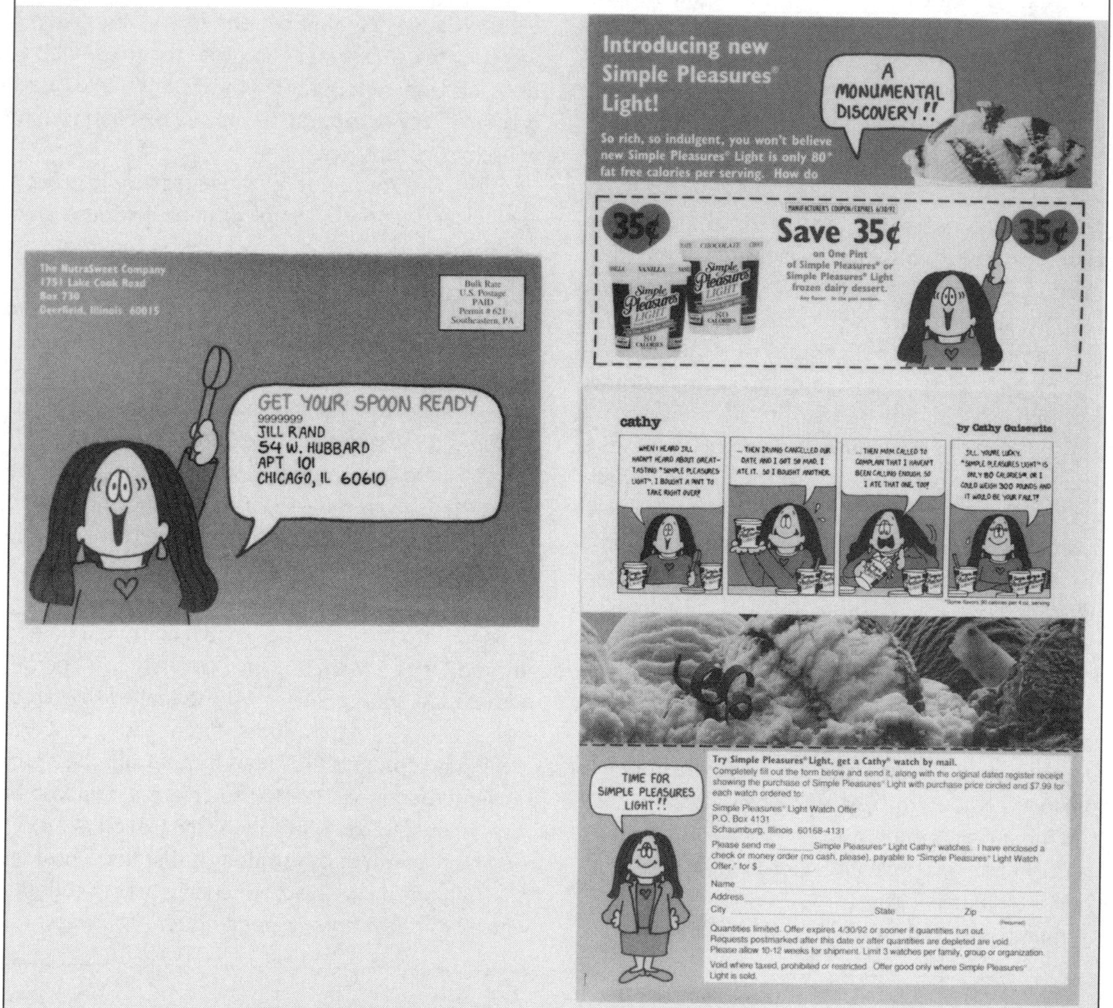

CASE STUDY: **Simple Pleasures Light** *(continued)*

EXHIBIT 5-14

List Test Matrix

List Name & Description*	Coupon Amount	Metro Area Universe	Boston	Chicago	Los Angeles	Miami	New York	San Diego	San Francisco	Washington, D.C.	Total Test City
DM	50¢	1,024,166	45,000	70,000	70,000	41,000	120,000	29,000	42,000	16,000	433,000
DM	35¢	1,024,167	45,000	70,000	70,000	41,000	120,000	29,000	42,000	16,000	433,000
MM	50¢	282,530	13,000	22,000	9,000	4,000	5,000	3,000	3,000	16,000	75,000
MM	35¢	282,000	13,000	22,000	9,000	4,000	5,000	3,000	3,000	16,000	75,000
ND	50¢	388,900	19,000	24,000	34,000	5,500	62,700	5,000	9,800	17,000	177,000
ND	35¢	305,690	4,500	7,900	7,800	1,500	7,500	2,500	2,000	3,000	36,700
BB	35¢	305,690	4,500	8,000	7,800	1,500	7,500	2,500	2,000	3,000	36,800
SE	35¢	388,900	19,000	24,000	30,000	5,200	6,000	5,000	9,000	15,000	113,200
SH	35¢	584,000	3,500	6,000	13,000	22,000	9,000	4,000	9,000	6,000	72,500
NY	35¢	255,000	4,000	10,000	11,000	3,000	10,000	3,000	6,000	800	47,800
Total	$.50	1,695,596	77,000	116,000	113,000	50,500	187,700	37,000	54,800	49,000	685,000
Total	$.35	3,145,447	93,500	147,900	148,600	78,200	165,000	49,000	73,000	59,800	815,000
TOTAL		4,841,043	170,500	263,900	261,600	128,700	352,700	86,000	127,800	108,800	1,500,000

*Key

BB - Behavior Bank psychographic survey respondents, Females Age 25–46, 1–2-person households, $30M+ income.
DM - Donnelly Marketing compiled demographic list; Females, Age 26–45, 1–2-person households, $25M+ income, mail order buyers.
MM - Metromail compiled demographic list; Females, Age 26–45, 1–2-person households, $30M+ income, mail order buyers.
ND - National Demographics and Lifestyles; Females, Age 26–45, 1–2-person households, $30M+ income, artificial sweetener look-alikes.
NY - New York Magazine; Female subscribers.
SE - SELF; Female subscribers.
SH - SHAPE; Female subscribers.

CASE STUDY: **Simple Pleasures Light** (continued)

and 50 cents. The objective was to learn which amount achieved the lowest cost per unit of product sold when including the promotion, incentive, and redemption costs. The agency and company also wanted to learn which offer would provide both the greatest short-term trial and long-term customer value.

Because the program was a trial builder among new target users, a segment not as coupon responsive as other age and income segments, it was imperative that the offer have a desirable perceived value. Grocery stores in some of the most promising markets double the value of coupons. That is, when a consumer redeems a coupon worth 25 cents, the grocery store adds another 25 cents. The consumer saves 50 cents. Policy varies widely, from stores that double every day, to stores that limit how many coupons can be doubled, to stores that only double coupons once each month.

Most stores won't double coupons worth more than 50 cents. In cities where grocery chains double coupons, there are few coupons worth 50 cents or more. From the view of many promotionally responsive consumers, a 55-cent coupon has a lower value than a 50-, 40-, or 35-cent coupon. Marketers have to be aware of this when testing coupon offers. The tested offers of 35 cents vs. 50 cents were created with this in mind.

List recommendations included a mix of compiled, lifestyle, and response lists. The List Test Matrix shown in Exhibit 5–14 summarizes the lists and counts.

RESULTS

In this test, the 50-cent coupon offer pulled a 7 percent redemption rate, while the 35-cent coupon offer pulled a 5.4 percent redemption rate. This 30 percent increase for the 50-cent offer helped offset the higher face value. The total cost per coupon redeemed was $4.81 for the 50-cent offer versus $6.05 per coupon redeemed for the 35-cent offer.

TOTAL CIRCULATION	1,500,000	
50-CENT FACE VALUE		
Circulation 50-Cent		
Face Value	685,000	
Redemptions	7.00%	47,950.00
Handling Fee	$ 0.12	$ 5,754.00
Redemption Cost	$ 0.50	$ 23,975.00
Production/Media Cost		
(CPM)	$ 293.03	$ 200,725.55
Total Costs		$ 230,454.55
Cost/Unit Redeemed		$ 4.81
35-CENT FACE VALUE		
Circulation 35-Cent		
Face Value	815,000	
Redemptions	5.40%	44,010.00
Handling Fee	$ 0.12	$ 5,281.20
Redemption Cost	$ 0.50	$ 22,005.00
Production/Media Cost		
(CPM)	$ 293.03	$ 238,819.45
Total Costs		$ 266,105.65
Cost/Unit Redeemed		$ 6.05

PILOT PROJECT You have been given an important assignment: to launch a new publication called *Prime Time* for the over-50 market. This is to be a monthly publication, carrying a cover price of $2.50, with a mail subscription rate of $24 a year. The publisher is anxious to (1) reach a subscription base of 100,000 subscribers before the first issue appears and (2) determine the renewal rate as quickly as possible. There will be no newsstand distribution.

Keeping the publisher's objectives in mind, develop three different offers that might be tested.

Key Points

▶ A dynamic offer can succeed even if selling copy is fair to poor—but dynamic copy cannot make a poor offer succeed. The ultimate, of course, is a dynamic offer supported by dynamic copy.

▶ Use testing to find the offer that best matches your target audience and accomplishes your objective: getting a maximum number of new customers for a given product or service as quickly as possible, determining the repeat business factor as quickly as possible, or breaking even or making a profit in the shortest time.

▶ Consider using terms of payment, sweepstakes, umbrella sweepstakes, toll-free response, publisher's letters, and guarantees to "hype" your offer and make it even more appealing. But don't make the incentive so overwhelming that it overshadows the product or service being offered.

▶ Consider the long-term effects of your offer. If you obtain thousands of new customers by offering free gifts as incentives, you will need to continue to offer free gifts to get repeat business. Similarly, installment credit buyers will continue to respond to installment terms, not cash-basis offers.

MEDIA OF DIRECT MARKETING

MAGAZINES

In days gone by a major mission of general advertising was to establish and reinforce brands. Mail order ads, on the other hand, had a different mission: to sell goods and services. Period.

After decades of hard sell, direct marketers are beginning to realize you can practice branding and sell, too. Let us scrutinize two magazine ads, Exhibits 6–1 and 6–2.

Exhibit 6–1 is a direct response ad for Harley-Davidson, one of the most recognized brand names in the world. It plays off its recognition by promoting a safety program and dealer traffic at the same time.

Exhibit 6–2, Discover Brokerage, was created by Black Rocket of San Francisco. Discover Brokerage's challenge was to overcome the fact that it was not a well-established brand. It did not enjoy the recognition of a Merrill Lynch or an A.G. Edwards.

This relatively unknown firm had to build awareness and gain consideration in a category of well-established players that had larger budgets and built-in customer basics from their off-line businesses.

After two months, brand awareness tripled and average daily account acquisitions grew fivefold, overall accounts increased by 23 percent, and assets managed grew by 14 percent. Discover Brokerage was a finalist in the prestigious Magazine Publishers of America Kelly Awards.

These two direct response ads are a far cry from the copy-jammed ad with the famous headline, "They Laughed When I Sat Down At the Piano But When I Started to Play!—" written by the great John Caples (see Exhibit 6–3) in the 1920s.

Magazines are a study unto themselves. How you test and use the medium depends upon your objectives and how successful you are in matching product profiles with customer profiles.

Harley-Davidson Ad

Consumer publications tend toward larger circulation; business-to-business publications tend toward smaller circulation. Mail order ads are more likely to appear in consumer publications; lead generation ads are more likely to appear in business-to-business publications.

The Internet has had a definite effect upon editorial content of magazines, in that it is commonplace for magazines to have one or more websites through which they offer more information about given articles, additional news and features, and links to past articles on a subject. Many of these sites generate additional income through advertising, which is often offered in combination with print advertising.

Testing Regional Editions

For the buyer of space in magazines today, most publications with circulations of more than 1.5 million offer the opportunity to buy a regional portion of the national circulation.

EXHIBIT 6–2

Discover Brokerage Ad

Regional editions offer important opportunities to the mail order advertiser. Here are a few of the advantages of regional buys:

1. It is not necessary to invest in the full national cost of a publication to get some indication of its effectiveness for your proposition. In magazines such as *Time* or *TV Guide*, running in a single edition allows determination of relative response with an investment at least 20 percent less than what it costs to make a national buy.

2. Some regions traditionally pull better than others for the mail order advertiser. For many mail order products or services, nothing does better than the West Coast or worse than the New England region. Select the best response area for a particular proposition.

Most publications charge a premium for the privilege of buying partial circulation. When testing a publication, put the advertising message in the better-pulling region to offset much of this premium charge.

3. Availability of regional editions makes possible multiple copy testing in a single issue of a publication. Some magazines offer A/B split-run copy testing in each

EXHIBIT 6-3

Classic Direct Response Ad

"Can he really play?" a girl whispered. "Heavens no!" Arthur exclaimed. "He never played a note in his life."

They Laughed When I Sat Down At the Piano But When I Started to Play!—

ARTHUR had just played "The Rosary." The room rang with applause. I decided that this would be a dramatic moment for me to make my debut. To the amazement of all my friends, I strode confidently over to the piano and sat down.

"Jack is up to his old tricks," somebody chuckled. The crowd laughed. They were all certain that I couldn't play a single note.

"Can he really play?" I heard a girl whisper to Arthur.

"Heavens, no!" Arthur exclaimed. "He never played a note in all his life... But just you watch him. This is going to be good."

I decided to make the most of the situation. With mock dignity I drew out a silk handkerchief and lightly dusted off the piano keys. Then I rose and gave the revolving piano stool a quarter of a turn, just as I had seen an imitator of Paderewski do in a vaudeville sketch.

"What do you think of his execution?" called a voice from the rear.

"We're in favor of it!" came back the answer, and the crowd rocked with laughter.

Then I Started to Play

Instantly a tense silence fell on the guests. The laughter died on their lips as if by magic. I played through the first few bars of Beethoven's immortal Moonlight Sonata. I heard gasps of amazement. My friends sat breathless—spellbound!

I played on and as I played I forgot the people around me. I forgot the hour, the place, the breathless listeners. The little world I lived in seemed to fade—seemed to grow dim—unreal. Only the music was real. Only the music and visions it brought me. Visions as beautiful and as changing as the wind blown clouds and drifting moonlight that long ago inspired the master composer. It seemed as if the master

musician himself were speaking to me—speaking through the medium of music—not in words but in chords. Not in sentences but in exquisite melodies!

A Complete Triumph!

As the last notes of the Moonlight Sonata died away, the room resounded with a sudden roar of applause. I found myself surrounded by excited faces. How my friends carried on! Men shook my hand—wildly congratulated me—pounded me on the back in their enthusiasm! Everybody was exclaiming with delight—plying me with rapid questions... "Jack! Why didn't you tell us you could play like that?"... "Where did you learn?"—"How long have you studied?"—"Who was your teacher?"

"I have never even seen my teacher," I replied. "And just a short while ago I couldn't play a note.'.

"Quit your kidding," laughed Arthur, himself an accomplished pianist. "You've been studying for years. I can tell."

"I have been studying only a short while," I insisted. "I decided to keep it a secret so that I could surprise all you folks."

Then I told them the whole story.

"Have you ever heard of the U. S. School of Music?" I asked.

A few of my friends nodded. "That's a correspondence school, isn't it?" they exclaimed.

"Exactly," I replied. "They have a new simplified method that can teach you to play any instrument by mail in just a few months."

How I Learned to Play Without a Teacher

And then I explained how for years I had longed to play the piano.

"A few months ago," I continued, "I saw an interesting ad for the U. S. School of Music—a new method of learning to play which only cost a few cents a day. The ad told how a woman had mastered the piano in her spare time at home—and without a teacher! Best of all, the wonderful new method she used, required no laborious scales—no heartless exercises — no tiresome practising. It sounded so convincing that I filled out the coupon requesting the Free Demonstration Lesson.

"The free book arrived promptly and I started in that very night to study the Demonstration Lesson. I was amazed to see how easy it was to play this new way. Then I sent for the course.

"When the course arrived I found it was just as the ad said — as easy as A.B.C! And, as

the lessons continued they got easier and easier. Before I knew it I was playing all the pieces I liked best. Nothing stopped me. I could play ballads or classical numbers or jazz, all with equal ease! And I never did have any special talent for music!"

* * * * *

Play Any Instrument

You too, can now teach yourself to be an accomplished musician—right at home—in half the usual time. You can't go wrong with this simple new method which has already shown 350,000 people how to play their favorite instruments. Forget that old-fashioned idea that you need special "talent." Just read the list of instruments in the panel, decide which one you want to play and the U. S. School will do the rest. And bear in mind no matter which instrument you choose, the cost in each case will be the same—just a few cents a day. No matter whether you are a mere beginner or already a good performer, you will be interested in learning about this new and wonderful method.

Send for Our Free Booklet and Demonstration Lesson

Thousands of successful students never dreamed they possessed musical ability until it was revealed to them by a remarkable "Musical Ability Test" which we send entirely without cost with our interesting free booklet.

If you are in earnest about wanting to play your favorite instrument—if you really want to gain happiness and increase your popularity—send at once for the free booklet and Demonstration Lesson. No cost — no obligation. Right now we are making a Special offer for a limited number of new students. Sign and read the convenient coupon now — before it's too late to gain the benefits of this offer. Instruments supplied when needed, cash or credit. U. S. School of Music, 1831 Brunswick Bldg., New York City.

Pick Your Instrument

Piano	'Cello
Organ	Harmony and
Violin	Composition
Drums and	Sight Singing
Traps	Ukulele
Banjo	Guitar
Tenor	Hawaiian
Banjo	Steel Guitar
Mandolin	Harp
Clarinet	Cornet
Flute	Piccolo
Saxophone	Trombone
Voice and Speech Culture	
Automatic Finger Control	
Piano Accordion	

U. S. School of Music,
1831 Brunswick Bldg., New York City.

Please send me your free book, "Music Lessons in Your Own Home", with introduction by Dr. Frank Crane, Demonstration Lesson and particulars of your Special Offer. I am interested in the following course:

....

....

Have you above instrument? ....

Name ....
(Please write plainly)

Address ....

City.......................... State..............

of the regional editions published. For example, in *TV Guide* you can test one piece of copy against the control in one edition, another against the control in a second edition, another against the control in a third, and so on. As a result, you can learn as much about different pieces of copy in a single issue of one publication as you could discover in several national A/B copy splits in the same publication over a span of two years or more.

4. Don't make the mistake of testing too small a circulation quantity. It is essential to test a large enough circulation segment to provide readable results that can be projected accurately for still larger circulations.

Warning: buying regional space is not all fun and games. You will have to pay for the privilege in a number of ways. As mentioned, regional space costs more.

Another factor to keep in mind is the relatively poor position regional ads receive. The regional sections usually appear far back in the magazine or in a "well" or signature of several consecutive pages of advertising with no editorial matter to catch the reader. Poor location can depress results as much as 50 percent below what the same advertisement would pull if it were in the first few pages of the same publication. When using regional space for testing, be certain to factor this into the evaluation.

Exhibit 6–4 shows how various factors must be weighed in utilizing regional circulation for test purposes. Because full-page, four-color inserts have been

---

EXHIBIT 6–4

Regional Test Schedule for XYZ Yarn & Craft Company

Redbook

Space:	Full-page, four-color insert
Position:	Back of main editorial (regional forms)
Issue:	June
Space cost:	$14,235 (printing cost not included)
Editions used:	New England, Mid-Atlantic, South Atlantic
Total test circulation:	1,121,000 (35 percent of total circulation)
Regional premium:	None

Family Circle

Space:	Full-page, four-color insert
Position:	Back of main editorial (regional forms)
Issue:	June
Space cost:	$3,800 (printing cost not included)
Editions used:	Los Angeles (383,000), San Francisco (209,000)
Total test circulation:	592,000 (15.3 percent of total circulation)
Regional premium:	None

extremely profitable for some of the large mail order advertisers, this size unit was tested for the XYZ Yarn & Craft Company to see whether such inserts could bring in a lower lead cost than could be obtained from a black-and-white page and card.

Because women's publications are the most successful media for this advertiser, the company went to two such publications that offered the mechanical capabilities for regional testing of an insert. Although May and June are not prime mail order months, it was necessary to test then in order to allow turnaround time for the next season's scheduling. Therefore, the following factors were taken into consideration in projecting test results to learn whether this unit would be successful in prime mail order months with full circulation: (1) regional premium, (2) month of insertion, (3) position in book, and (4) relative value of specific media.

Pilot Publications

When planning your direct marketing media schedule, think about the media universe the way you think about the view of the sky in the evening. If you have no familiarity with the stars, the sky appears to be a jumble of blinking lights with no apparent relationship. But as you begin to study the heavens, you are soon able to pick out clusters of stars that have a relationship to one another in constellations.

The magazine universe is no different. There are nearly 400 consumer magazines with a circulation of 100,000 or more. The first step in approaching this vast list is to sort out the universe of magazines into categories. Although this process is somewhat arbitrary, it is useful to have a mental map of major magazine groupings.

Once you begin to think of magazines as forming logical groupings within the total magazine universe, you can begin to determine the groupings offering the most likely marketplace for your product or proposition. Exhibit 6–5 is a basic magazine category chart and lists of some of the publications currently available for the direct response advertiser.

Within each category there are usually one or more publications that perform particularly well for the direct response advertiser at a lower cost than other publications in the group. We call those magazines the *pilot publications* for the group. If you use the pilot publications and they produce an acceptable cost per response, you can then proceed to explore the possibility of adding other magazines in the category to the media schedule.

In selecting the pilot publications in a category, keep in mind that you are not dealing with a static situation. A publication's mail order advertising viability changes from year to year, and what is a bellwether publication this season may not be the one to use next year. It is important to check your own experience and the experience of others in determining the best places to advertise first in each category, and the next best, and the next best, and so on.

EXHIBIT 6–5

Basic Consumer Magazine Categories

Demographic	Category	Sample Publications
Dual audience	General editorial/ entertainment	Grit, National Enquirer, National Geographic, New York Times Magazine, Parade, People, Reader's Digest, TV Guide
	News	Time, Newsweek, Sports Illustrated, U.S. News & World Report
	Special interest	Architectural Digest, Business Week, Elks, Foreign Affairs, High Fidelity, Modern Photography, Natural History, Ski, Travel & Leisure, Wall Street Journal, Yankee
Women	General/service/ shelter (home service)	Better Homes & Gardens, Cosmopolitian, Ebony, Family Circle, Good Housekeeping, House Beautiful, House & Garden, Ladies' Home Journal, McCall's, Redbook, Sunset, Woman's Day
	Fashion	Glamour, Harper's Bazaar, Mademoiselle, Vogue
	Special interest	Brides, MacFadden Woman's Group, McCalls Needlework & Crafts, Parents, Working Woman
Men	General/entertainment/ fashion	Esquire, Gentlemen's Quarterly, Penthouse, Playboy
	Special interest	Field & Stream, Home Mechanics, Outdoor Life, Popular Mechanics, Popular Science, Road & Track, Sports Afield
Youth	Male Female Dual audience	Boy's Life Teen, YM Scholastic Magazines

Think of the media-buying program as an ever-widening circle, as illustrated in Exhibit 6–6. At the center is a nucleus of pilot publications. Each successively larger ring includes reruns in all profitable pilot publications plus new test books. In the same way, you can expand from campaign to campaign to cover wider levels of the various media categories until you have reached the widest possible universe.

EXHIBIT 6–6

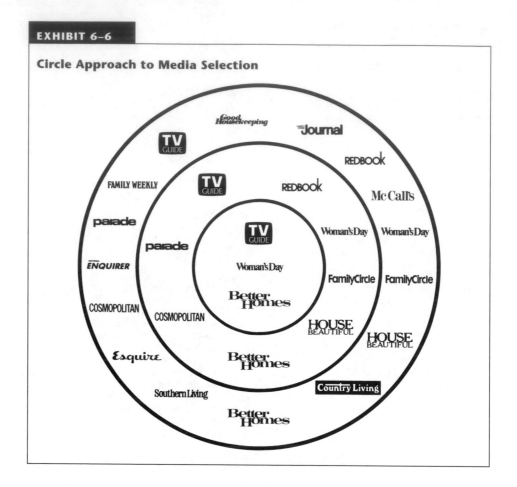

Circle Approach to Media Selection

Bind-In Insert Cards

The reason for the success of the insert card is self-evident. Pick up a magazine, thumb through its pages, and see for yourself how effectively the bound-in cards flag down the reader. Each time someone picks up the publication, there is the insert card pointing to your message. Another reason is the ease with which the reader can respond. The business reply card eliminates the trouble of addressing an envelope, providing a stamp, and so on.

Before the advent of the insert card, the third and fourth covers of a magazine were the prime mail order positions and were sold at a premium. The bind-in insert card has created a world in which three, four, five, or more direct response advertisers can all have the position impact once reserved for the cover advertisers alone.

When you go to purchase space for a page and an accompanying insert card, you must face the fact that the best things in life are not free. Insert card advertising costs more. You must pay a space charge for the page and the card and sometimes a separate binding charge, and you must then add in the cost of printing the cards. How much you pay, of course, depends on the individual publication, the size of the card, and a number of other factors. There is no rule of thumb to follow in estimating the additional cost for an insert card. Space charges alone for a standard business reply card can be as much as 40 percent of the black-and-white page plus additional binding charges.

When the cost of the insert unit adds up to as much as four times the cost of a black-and-white page, you will have to receive four times the response to justify the added expense.

For most direct response advertisers, the response is likely to be six to eight times as great when pulling for an order and as much as six to eight times as great in pulling for inquiries. As a result, you can expect to cut your cost per response by 50 percent or more with an insert card as opposed to an ordinary on-page coupon ad.

Bingo Cards

Insert cards have a dramatic effect on response, and so do bingo cards. Bingo cards, often referred to as *information cards*, were developed by magazine publishers, both consumer and business, to make it easy for the reader to request more information. *Bingo card* is really a generic term for any form of reply card, or printed form on a magazine page, on which the publisher prints designated numbers for specified advertisers' literature. The reader simply circles the number designated for the literature desired.

Typically, an advertiser placing a specified unit of space in a magazine is entitled to a bingo card in the back of the publication. Ads reference these bingo cards with statements such as, "For further information, circle Item No. 146." The cards are sent directly to the publisher, which sends compiled lists of inquiries to participating advertisers. The respective advertisers then send fulfillment literature to all who requested it.

Magazine Advertising Response Pattern

There is a remarkable similarity from one insertion to another in the rate of response over time for most magazines. Monthly publications generally have a similar pattern for the rate of response from week to week. However, the pattern of response for publications in different categories can vary. For example, a mass circulation weekly magazine (such as *TV Guide* or *Parade*) will pull a higher percentage of the total response in the first few weeks than a shelter book (such as *House & Garden* or *Better Homes & Gardens*). A shelter book has a slower response curve but keeps pulling for a long time because it is kept much longer than a mass circulation magazine.

Also, subscription circulation will pull faster than newsstand circulation. All subscribers usually receive their copies within a few days, whereas newsstand sales are spread out over an entire month. Consequently, the response pattern is spread out as well.

For an ad calling for direct response from a monthly magazine, here is a general guide to the likely response flow:

After the first week	3 to 7%
After the second week	20 to 25%
After the third week	40 to 45%
After one month	50 to 55%
After two months	75 to 85%
After three months	85 to 92%
After four months	92 to 95%

From a weekly publication such as *Time* or *TV Guide*, the curve is entirely different; 50 percent of the response usually comes in the first two weeks.

These expectations, of course, represent the average of many hundreds of response curves for different propositions. You will see variations up or down from the classic curve for any single insertion.

As a general rule for monthlies, you can expect to project the final results within 10 percent accuracy after the third week of counting responses. If you are new to the business, give yourself the experience of entering daily result counts by hand for dozens of ads. Before long you will develop an instinct for projecting how an ad for your particular proposition is doing within the first 10 days of measured response.

Timing and Frequency

Once you determine where you want the ad to run, timing and frequency are the two crucial factors in putting together an effective print schedule. Some propositions will do best at one specific time of the year. For example, novelty items are likely to be purchased in October and November, or even as early as late September, for Christmas gifts. But for nonseasonal items there are two major print advertising seasons for direct response.

The first and by far the most productive time for most propositions is the winter season, which begins with the January issue and runs through the February and March issues. The second season begins with the August issue and runs through the November issue. The best winter months for most people are January and February. The best fall months are October and November. For schools and book continuity propositions, September frequently does as well or better.

If you have a nonseasonal item and you want to do your initial test at the best possible time, use a February issue with a January sale date or a January issue with a late December or early January sale date of whatever publication makes the most sense for your proposition.

How much of a factor is the particular month in which an ad appears? It could make a difference of 40 percent or even more. Exhibit 6–7 shows what the direct response advertiser can expect to experience during the year based on the costs per response (CPR).

These hypothetical relative costs are based on the assumption that the insertion is run one time in any one of the 12 issues of a monthly publication. But of course, if you are successful, you will want to run your copy more than once. So now you are faced with the other crucial question: What will various rates of frequency do to your response? Should you run once a year? Twice? Three times? Or every other month?

The frequency factor is more difficult to formulate than the timing factor. Optimum frequency cannot be generalized for print media advertising. Some propositions can be run month after month in a publication and show very little difference in cost per response. At one time, Doubleday & Company had worked out optimum frequency curves for some of its book club ads that required a 24-month hiatus between insertions.

How, then, do you go about determining ideal frequency of insertions? Try this procedure: the first time your copy appears in a publication, run it at the most

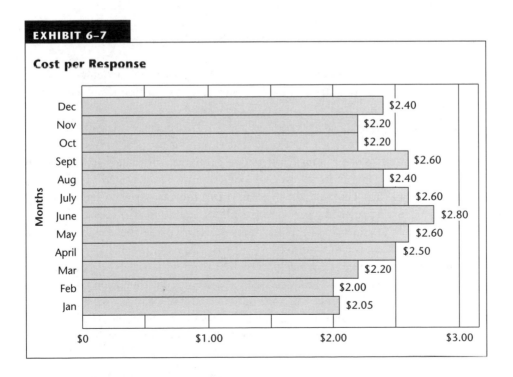

EXHIBIT 6–7

Cost per Response

Months	Cost per Response
Dec	$2.40
Nov	$2.20
Oct	$2.20
Sept	$2.60
Aug	$2.40
July	$2.60
June	$2.80
May	$2.60
April	$2.50
Mar	$2.20
Feb	$2.00
Jan	$2.05

favorable time of the year for your special appeal. If you have a nonseasonal proposition, use January or February issues.

If the cost per response is in an acceptable range, or up to 20 percent better than expected, wait six months and follow with a second insertion. If that insertion produces results within an acceptable range, you probably are a twice-a-year advertiser. If the first insertion pulls well over 20 percent better than the planned order margin, turn around and repeat within a three- or four-month period. If the response to the test insertion in January or February was marginal, it usually makes sense to wait a full year before returning for another try in that publication.

The best gauge of how quickly you can run the next insertion aimed at the same magazine audience is the strength of the response from the last insertion. What you are reading in the results is a measurement of the saturation factor as it relates to that portion of the circulation interested in your selling message.

Of course, like all the other factors that affect response, frequency does not operate in a vacuum. The offer of a particularly advantageous position in a particular month, or a breakthrough to better results with improved copy, can lead you to set aside whatever carefully worked-out frequency you had adopted earlier.

Determining Proper Ad Size

A crucial factor in obtaining an acceptable cost per response is the size of the advertising unit you select. Ordinarily, the bigger the ad, the better the job the creative people can do in presenting the selling message. But there is one catch: advertising space costs money. And the more you spend, the greater the response you need to get your money back.

What you want to find is the most efficient size for your particular proposition and for the copy approach you have chosen. Just as with frequency, there is no simple rule of thumb here.

Generally speaking, advertising for leads, or prospects, or to gain inquiries, requires less advertising space than copy that is pulling for orders. Many companies seeking inquiries or running a lead item to get names for catalog follow-up will make use of advertising units of less than one column. Only a handful of companies looking for prospects can make effective use of full-page space. Going one step further and using a page and insert card to pull for leads runs the risk of being too effective. This unit can bring in inquiries at very low cost at the possible expense of good quality. Find out at your peril.

For example, if you use a black-and-white page with a tear-off coupon that generates leads at $5 each and that converts at a 10 percent rate, then your advertising cost per sale is $50. Take the same insertion and place it as a page and insert card, and the cost per response could be as low as $3. If the conversion rate held up at 10 percent, the advertising cost per sale would be only $30. But it is more likely that the advertiser would experience a sharp conversion rate drop, to perhaps 5 percent, with a resultant $60 cost per sale plus the cost of processing the additional leads.

When a direct sale or a **future** commitment to buy is sought, the dynamics usually are different than when inquiries are sought. As a general rule, the higher the unit of sale or dollar volume commitment, the larger the unit of space that can be afforded, right up to the double-page spread with insert card. However, there are a number of additional factors to be considered:

1. The nature of the product presentation might require a particular space unit. For example, in tape club and book club advertising, experience has shown that a maximum number of books and tapes should be displayed for best results. As a consequence, many of these clubs run a two-page spread as their standard advertising unit. And in a small-size publication such as *TV Guide*, they might take six or even eight pages to display the proper number of books and tapes.

2. Some propositions, such as Time-Life Books in the continuity book-selling field, require four-color advertising in order to present the beautiful color illustrations that are an important feature of the product.

3. Usually, full-page ads appear at the front of a publication and small-space ads at the back. So going to a full-page unit is often related to the benefits you can expect from a premium, front-of-publication position.

4. If you are successful with a single-page ad with coupon, test using an insert card before you try to add a second page. If the page and insert card work for you, give the spread and card a try.

5. Most mail order advertising falls into one of three size categories: (a) the spectacular unit—anything from the page and standard card insert to the four-page preprinted insert, (b) the single full-page unit, or (c) the small-space unit, less than one column in size.

The awkward sizes in pulling for an order appear to be the one-column and two-column units. These inserts seldom work better than their big-brother pages or little sister 56-line, 42-line, and 21-line units, although a "square third" (two columns by 70 lines) can be a very efficient space unit.

Always remember that space costs money. The objective is to take the minimum amount of space needed to express the proposition effectively and to return a profit. Start by having the creative director at your advertising agency express the proposition in the amount of space needed to convey a powerful selling message. Once you have established the cost per response for this basic unit, you can experiment with other size units.

If you have two publications on your schedule that perform about equally well for the basic unit, try testing the same ad approach expressed in a smaller or larger space size in one of those two publications. At the same time, run the basic control unit in the same month in the other publication.

Four-Color, Two-Color, Black-and-White

All magazines charge extra for adding color to your advertising. And there will be additional production expense if you go this route. Usually the cost of adding a second color to a black-and-white page does not return the added costs charged by the publication for the space and the expense of producing the ad. If the copy is right, the words will do their job without getting an appreciable lift from having headlines set in red or blue or green. An exception might be the use of a second-color tint as background to provide special impact to the page.

It is with the use of four-color advertising that the direct response advertiser has an opportunity to profit on an investment in color. A number of publications (*Woman's Day*, *Ladies' Home Journal*) allow you to run a split of four-color versus black-and-white, in an alternating copy A/B perfect split-run. Test results indicate an increase of anywhere from 30 percent to almost 60 percent where there is appropriate and dramatic utilization of the four-color process.

Given a striking piece of artwork related to the proposition or an inherently colorful product feature to present, you can expect an increase in response when you use four-color advertising. You will need more than a 20 percent increase in most publications to make the use of color profitable, so it is wise to pretest the value of this factor before scheduling it across the board. Some products, such as insurance, simply do not benefit from color.

The Position Factor

Position in life might not be everything, but in direct response it often means the difference between paying out or sudden death. By *position* we mean where an advertisement appears in the publication. There are two rules governing position.

First, the closer to the front of the publication an ad is placed, the better the response will be. Second, the more visible the position, the better the response.

The first rule defies rational analysis. Yet it is as certain as the sun rising in the morning. Many magazine publishers have offered elaborate research studies demonstrating to the general advertiser that an ad in the editorial matter far back in a publication gets better readership than an ad placed within the first few pages of the publication. This could well be true for the general or institutional advertiser, but it is not true for the direct response advertiser.

Whatever the explanation is, the fact remains that decades of measured direct response advertising tell the same story over and over again. A position in the first seven pages of the magazine produces a dramatically better response (all other factors being the same) than if the same insert appears farther back in the same issue.

How much better? There are as many answers to this question as there are old pros in the business. However, here is about what you might expect the relative response to be from various page positions as measured against the first right-hand page, arbitrarily rated at a pull of 100:

First right-hand page	100
Second right-hand page	95
Third right-hand page	90
Fourth right-hand page	85
Back of front of the publication (preceding editorial matter)	70
Back of the publication (following main body of editorial matter)	50
Back cover	100
Inside third cover	90
Page facing third cover	85

The second rule, concerning visibility, is more easily explained. An ad must be seen before it can be read or acted on. Right-hand pages pull better than left-hand pages, frequently by as much as 15 percent. Insert cards open the magazine to the advertiser's message and thereby create their own "cover" position. Of course, the insert card introduces the additional factor of providing a postage-free response vehicle as well. But the response from insert cards is also subject to the influence of how far back in the magazine the insert appears. Here is what you can expect in most publications (assigning a 100 rating to the first card):

First insert card position	100
Second insert card position	95
Third insert card position	85
Fourth insert card position	75*
Fifth insert card position	70*
* If position follows main editorial matter	

How to Buy Direct Response Space

Because mail order advertising is always subject to bottom-line analysis, the price you pay for space can mean the difference between profit and loss. Before you place space, ask the publisher or the publisher's agency these basic questions:

1. Is there a special mail order rate? Mail order rates are usually 10 to 30 percent lower than general rates.

2. Is there a special mail order section, a shopping section where special mail order ads are grouped? This section is usually found in the back of the magazine.

3. Does the magazine have remnant space available at substantial discounts? Many publishers offer discounts of up to 50 percent off the regular rate.

4. Is there an insertion frequency discount or a dollar volume discount? Is frequency construed as the number of insertions in a time period or consecutive issues? Many publishers credit more than one insertion in an issue toward frequency.

5. Do corporate discounts apply to mail order? Sometimes the corporate discount is better than the mail order discount.

6. Are there seasonal discounts? Some publishers have low volume advertising months during which they offer substantial discounts.

7. Are there spread discounts when running two pages or more in one issue? The discount can run up to 60 percent on the second page.

8. Is there a publisher's rate? Is this in addition to, or in lieu of, the mail order rate? It can be additive.

9. Are per inquiry (PI) deals accepted? In PI deals the advertiser pays the publisher an amount for each inquiry or order, or a minimum flat amount for the space, plus so much per inquiry or order.

10. Are "umbrella contracts" accepted? Some media-buying services and agencies own banks or reserves of space with given publications and can offer discounts even for onetime ads.

11. Is bartering for space allowed? Barter usually involves a combination of cash and merchandise.

CASE STUDY: State Farm

Written by Carla Johnson, St. Mary's College, Notre Dame; Don Eckrich, Ithaca College; and Monle Lee, Indiana University, South Bend, for the DePaul University Institute of Interactive and Direct Marketing Case Writer's Workshop.

BACKGROUND

The State Farm Group of companies is very midwestern, conservative, and family-, community-, and agent-focused. It seeks to live by its tag line, "Like a good neighbor, State Farm is there." One of State Farm's greatest strengths is in its selection, training,

and overall maintenance of an exclusive system of almost 17,000 multiline agents across the country.

While life insurance is a major component of the State Farm Group of companies, State Farm's reputation and heritage is directly linked with auto and homeowners insurance. The company ranks number one in market share for both categories, and State Farm agents have long focused on selling these two lines of insurance. The company's auto and homeowners policyholders generally go somewhere else for life, even though State Farm has offered agents life insurance promotions to help sell life insurance.

The insurance industry is cyclical, especially for home and auto insurance. As part of this cycle, the industry may experience a bad accident or disaster year. For instance, El Niño created a bad year for home insurance because of weather-related disasters. Since State Farm was in a bad cycle for home and auto, the company realized that 1997 would have to be a good year for life insurance. The objective was straightforward: increase State Farm's life insurance sales. The problem was that State Farm agents found it difficult to bring up the subject of life insurance with their clients because life insurance actually deals with death.

Also, in recent years the trend has been away from life insurance to annuities and tax-advantaged retirement vehicles. Sales of these "accumulation products" for retirement have grown, while life insurance sales have declined.

State Farm's vast network of multiline agents has been able to establish a leadership position in the life insurance industry in the United States, with a customer base of almost 28 million households. Nevertheless, by State Farm's own standards (the percentage of customers who own at least one State Farm life insurance product), its penetration of the life insurance market is well below management's aspirations.

Industry analysts confirm that a "vast, relatively untapped market" exists in the sales of life insurance products well into the foreseeable future. In a 1997 LIMRA study, 35 percent of respondents said they needed more life insurance, yet only 24 percent said they had been approached to buy life insurance. Demographic changes also favor more life insurance sales. Buyers today have more disposable income; the traditional family model still exists, although it starts later; and extended life spans do not diminish the need for life insurance.

CHALLENGE

In early 1997, State Farm challenged advertising agency DDB Needham, and Needham's integrated communications division, to create an innovative and multifaceted campaign to excite and inspire State Farm's generally underperforming multiline agencies. Specifically, DDB Needham was asked to catalyze increased discussions between agents and existing auto and homeowner policyholders on the topic of purchasing life insurance. But the agency needed to find a way to both motivate agents and provide them with a means to "break the ice" about life insurance products with their clients.

SOLUTION AND RESULTS

Part of the solution occurred almost by accident. At about the same time State Farm was pondering its problem, *LIFE* magazine approached the insurance company with an invitation to be sole sponsor of a special issue of the magazine honoring American heroes as well as a television special called "*LIFE's* Greatest Holiday Stories." Special-issue sponsorships are not uncommon in the magazine business, and provide an important means of rewarding loyal advertisers. In this case, the sole sponsorship offer meant that State Farm would partner with *LIFE* magazine and be identified as the exclusive sponsor of the two prominent and highly visible specials—one on television and the other in print.

State Farm recognized the opportunity as a high potential platform for promoting life insurance and agent involvement. Any association with *LIFE* magazine would offer several obvious benefits. First, State Farm would receive the equity of a well-known and highly respected media partner. Whatever the State Farm message, it would be amplified by the credibility and respect generally associated with *LIFE* magazine. Second, the personalities and values of the two companies were very similar and complementary. The concept of honoring and saluting American heroes (people having had a positive impact on our lives and society) would resonate well with State Farm's "Like a Good Neighbor" motto. In particular, it was felt that the "historical nature" and "talk value" of such a prestigious campaign would provide a natural and comfortable means for agents to broach the issues of life insurance. Third, it would bring the additional clout and credibility of *LIFE*'s owner, Time Inc./Time Warner, as well as potential access to its vast resources.

State Farm promptly accepted the offer. The theme selected for the promotion was "State Farm Salutes *LIFE*'s Heroes," and it included a variety of elements built into and around the special *LIFE* magazine issue and the one-hour, prime-time network TV special. For instance, print-spread "advertorials" were created to promote awareness of the two events. Suitable heroes were selected by *LIFE*, and their respective profiles were created and prepared for

magazine and television delivery. A website dedicated to *LIFE* heroes was developed, and several Internet advertisements were also created and placed. DDB Needham used the *LIFE* campaign to convey the positive message that by buying life insurance, life's heroes protect their families' futures.

The target publication date for the special issue of *LIFE* magazine was May 1997, while the television special, "*LIFE*'s Greatest Holiday Stories," was to air on CBS, December 22, 1997. *LIFE* magazine and State Farm were the only sponsors.

Various disciplines/departments at DDB Needham became involved in the launch of these two media events. Account Management and Media worked hand in hand to develop the concept with

EXHIBIT 6–8

State Farm Promotional *LIFE* Magazine Cover Wrap

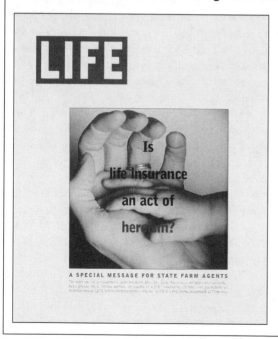

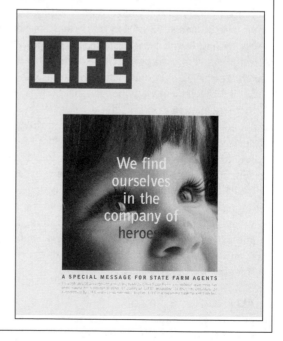

CASE STUDY: State Farm *(continued)*

LIFE. Account Management and Strategic Planning worked together to develop the overall campaign and test consumer reactions to the creative. The creative group developed all consumer creative materials (TV, radio, and print). DDB Interactive created and developed the Internet banners and buttons that were placed by Media in a Pathfinder Internet buy.

Beyond DDB, the integrated communications group was charged with creating and producing a variety of unique "ice breakers" and other promotional tie-ins, including all ancillary support materials for both agents and clients. The goal was to catalyze dialogue between historically reluctant agents and clients more likely interested in auto and homeowners insurance than life insurance. Promotional and educational materials were made available to complement the special Heroes issue of *LIFE* magazine coming out in May 1997 and the TV special in December 1997.

The magazine itself proved a popular ice breaker. *LIFE* provided each agent with a six-month complimentary subscription to the magazine beginning with the May 1997 special issue. The regular issues for May, July, and September featured special cover wraps that carried messages to create agent enthusiasm for the campaign (see Exhibit 6–8). A response vehicle enabled DDB Needham to track which agents participated in the Heroes campaign.

PILOT PROJECT

You are the advertising manager for a publisher of children's books. It is your assignment to test market for a new continuity series of 10 books written for age levels 6 to 10. Each book in the series will sell for $4.95. Outline a plan for test marketing in magazines.

1. What pilot publications would you schedule for testing?

2. Will you use any regional editions? Why or why not?

3. Do a circle approach to media selection indicating what additional publications you will expand to if the pilot publications prove successful.

4. Prepare a timing schedule, indicating when your pilot ads will break and when your expanded media-buying program will take place.

5. What ad size will you use? Will the ad be black-and-white, two colors, or four colors?

Key Points

▶ Test the "pilot publications" in magazine categories—publications that perform particularly well for the direct response advertiser at a lower cost than others in the group. If they produce an acceptable cost per response, consider adding other magazines in the category to the media schedule.

▶ Insert cards can increase response six to eight times and cut cost per response by 50 percent as opposed to an ordinary on-page coupon ad. Bingo or information cards can also greatly increase requests for information.

▶ For monthly magazines, 50 percent of the total response comes in the first month after publication; for weekly publications, 50 percent comes in the first two weeks. For monthlies, final results may be projected within 10 percent accuracy after the third week of counting responses.

▶ Advertising for leads, prospects, or inquiries requires less space than advertising for orders. The higher the unit of sale or dollar volume commitment, the larger the unit of space that can be afforded. Take the minimum amount of space needed to express the proposition effectively and to return a profit.

▶ A four-color ad can increase response but requires more than a 20 percent increase in most publications to make color profitable.

▶ The closer to the front of the publication an ad is placed, or the more visible its position, the better the response will be. Right-hand pages pull better than left-hand pages, frequently by as much as 15 percent. Insert cards also pull better because they open the magazine to the advertiser's message, thereby creating their own "cover" position.

▶ When purchasing space, inquire about special mail order rates and insertion frequency discount or a dollar volume discount. Corporate and seasonal discounts, publisher's rate, per inquiry deals, and barter are also worth investigating.

NEWSPAPERS

Despite the influx of cell phones, pagers, and palm computers that can send and receive messages and download information—even in spite of ambitious on-line news organizations like MSNBC.com—the local newspaper remains an integral part of practically everyone's daily life.

Couple its familiarity with its enormous circulation—together, the 1,600-plus daily newspapers in the United States reach approximately 63 million—and it's clear why newspapers remain one of the best direct marketing media.

Direct marketers have lots of options when considering newspapers. Newspapers can be thought of as a separate advertising medium, running ads within categories such as the Women's Section, Business, Sports, etc. Or newspapers can be thought of as distribution channels carrying their preprints, or ads in syndicated newspaper supplements, Sunday comics sections, local TV books, or local magazines.

ROP (run of paper) ads are usually restricted to ads that can be effective without a need for quality four-color printing. A good example of a direct response advertiser who has been very successful with black-and-white newspaper ads is Oreck Vacuum (see Exhibit 7–1).

On-line newspaper editions offer special content on restaurants and entertainment that is highly targeted to local readers. Newspapers generally offer classified ads, their number one revenue and profit center, on-line as well as off-line, as they try to stave off competition from job, real estate, auto, and auction sites. Some newspapers are even helping loyal advertisers—especially small retailers—develop their own websites by providing Web design templates, computer space, and a URL.

EXHIBIT 7–1

Oreck Full-Page Ad in *Chicago Tribune*

Newspaper Preprints

Newspaper preprints are at the top of the printing quality scale. Preprints offer few format restrictions and several advantages:

1. Quality of paper and printing is controlled by the marketer.

2. While the "life" of a newspaper is rarely more than a day, preprints take on a lifetime of their own, depending upon the interest of the reader.

3. Involvement devices, which have proved so successful in direct mail packages, can be used effectively with newspaper preprints as well.

4. Testing of preprints—testing one version against one or more different versions—is within the control of the marketer since splits can be prearranged at the printing plant.

The cost of printing preprints is borne by the marketer; the newspaper charges for circulation of the preprint based upon the size and number of pages. The preprint can be as simple as one sheet of board stock or a multipage brochure (see Exhibits 7–2, and 7–3).

Syndicated Newspaper Supplements

Imagine, if you will, placing two space-insertion orders, and buying newspaper circulation of 58 million plus! It is possible by buying space in *Parade* and *USA Weekend*. Both publications enjoy a good track record for direct response advertisers. To compare the two publications, here are some figures, assuming a four-color, full-page ad has been placed.

TABLE 7–1

Comparison of Circulation and Rates for Full-Page Four-Color Ads

PUBLICATION	CIRCULATION	FOUR COLOR	
		Page	*CPM*
Parade	37,000,000	$694,900	$18.79
USA Weekend	21,918,303	$436,170	$19.91

Source: SRDS (Standard Rate & Data Service), September 1999

Parade is generally distributed among the top 100 metro areas. *USA Weekend* is generally carried by newspapers with smaller locations, basically "C" and "D" counties. The majority of newspapers distributing *USA Weekend* are outside the top

EXHIBIT 7–2

An 8½ × 11 Insert in the *Chicago Tribune*

150 metro areas. However, in two-newspaper markets, one newspaper will carry *Parade* and the other *USA Weekend*. Both syndicated supplements provide an excellent mail order atmosphere.

While Table 7–1 shows the cost of a four-color page ad going to total circulation of both publications, there is no way this would take place in the real world unless prior testing of the ad and the publications warranted the full runs.

Front Cover of 12-Page Insert Promoting Three-Day Sale

THE GOOD LIFE AT A GREAT PRICE. GUARANTEED.

SEARS

Thursday, Friday and Saturday
use your Sears card and take

10% off

everything...even sale prices

3 Days Only

Apply for the Sears Card and you also get 10% off.
See page 10 for offer details.

IYX025A Z123-Z123

Assuming that both the ad and the publications are unproved, here are some first steps the marketer might take:

1. Negotiate a "mail order rate," usually less costly than general advertising rates.

2. Run the ad as a test in three regions: West, Central, Eastern.

3. Limit the three-region test to either *Parade* or *USA Weekend*, depending upon small market/large market experience.

4. Bargain for remnant space. (Remnant space is usually created when package goods advertisers, who do not have total national distribution for a given brand, eliminate certain cities or regions from the schedule. Thus the publishers sell the remnants at bargain rates.)

Local Newspaper Magazines

Several steps closer to local markets are newspaper-inserted magazines published by leading newspapers in major markets (see Exhibit 7–4). A case can be made for readership of magazines that cater to local markets from an editorial standpoint.

A "cousin" to local newspaper magazines are the weekly TV books produced by local newspapers containing the local TV and radio schedules. While most of the advertising in these books promote local TV and radio programming, back cover space for direct response ads is usually available.

Comics as a Direct Marketing Medium

Perhaps the biggest sleeper as a medium for direct marketers is the comic section of weekend newspapers. Comics are not glamorous, nor are they prestigious. But their total circulation, readership, and demographics constitute an exciting universe for the direct response advertiser.

The Metro-Puck Comics Network, being the largest, distributes through 150-plus Sunday newspapers. Their circulation as of September 1999 was 41,310,961. A one-page, four-color ad sold for $831,546.

The demographic characteristics of comics readers are quite a surprise to most advertisers, who seem to have ill-conceived ideas about this type of reader. The median age of the adult comics reader is 39 years, just slightly younger than the U.S. median age.

One of the major misconceptions about comics readership is that the higher one's education, the less likely one is to read the comic pages. Statistics from *Simmons Total Audience Study*, as illustrated in Table 7-2, dispute this.

Finally, there is the misconception that the higher one's income, the less likely one is to read comics. Again, the figures refute this.

EXHIBIT 7–4

Direct Response Ad from *Chicago Tribune* Magazine

Critics Agree:

MailStation

is the *perfect gift*:
E-mail
without the PC!

"This wonderfully uncomplicated device is aimed at those who don't need or want to buy a computer but who nevertheless want to **get in on the fun and power of e-mail.**" *The Seattle Times*

"**It's a terrific gift** or productivity purchase for anyone who wants to communicate in cyberspace with a single-purpose device." *PC Magazine*

"**I am impressed.** The **MailStation** does what it promises to do, and **my mother is delighted with it.**" *Wall Street Journal*

"I'm delighted with **MailStation.**" *Mom*

Give family and friends the gift of E-mail with the revolutionary new MailStation™ – E-mail without the PC!

It seems that everyone you know - family, friends, even your Mom and Dad - are all on a busy schedule. Well, here's a way that they can stay in touch with you using e-mail, without the complications of a PC. What's more, it's fun! And the gift of e-mail is as easy as calling our toll-free number, 1.800.718.1293.

E-Mail is now simple for everyone!

MailStation is the friendly, easy-to-use, inexpensive device that lets anyone with a phone line have e-mail. MailStation has a comfortable keyboard with a picture driven menu and simple to understand buttons that make sending and receiving e-mail a breeze. The device takes up about the same space as a regular sheet of paper and has a clear, easy-to-read screen. Text size on the screen can be increased for even easier reading.

The perfect gift for everyone in your life.

Even if your family and friends don't have a PC, they can have e-mail. There's no software to figure out. No setup. No high costs. No hassles. MailStation gets everyone in on the e-mail revolution, inexpensively and simply. It lets your family and friends save on long distance phone calls. Best of all, it's convenient because they can send and receive e-mail any time of the day or night. MailStation is the perfect gift.

The affordable way to e-mail.

As a special introductory offer, the MailStation itself is now just '99', *a savings of $50 off the regular price.* The only other cost is the monthly e-mail service. And the monthly charge is always the same, no matter how many e-mail messages they send or receive, whether they e-mail down the block or around the world. Remember, with MailStation they can communicate to anyone with e-mail.

Call 1.800.718.1293 to get e-mail NOW!

Giving MailStation is easy. Have your credit card handy, then simply call toll-free 1.800.718.1293 and an associate will help you create an e-mail address for your family or friend on the spot. MailStation will then be sent out all ready to go. They will be able to plug it in to the phone jack, power it up, and then e-mail instantly! If they have questions or need help, they can call us toll free. And there is no charge for technical help.

CALL NOW! 1.800.718.1293. Or visit us on the web at www.mymailstation.com/293. Give the perfect gift today!

MailStation™
E-mail Made Easy
1.800.718.1293

SPECIAL INTRODUCTORY OFFER

$99*

Save '50 now.

Device only. Please call for a service plan that works for you!

*Plus shipping and applicable sales tax.

NOT SOLD IN STORES
Only available by mail order.

TABLE 7–2

Demographic Characteristics, Readers of Comics Compared with U.S. Population

CHARACTERISTICS	COMICS READERS	U.S. POPULATION
Age		
18–24	20.5%	18.4%
25–34	21.7	22.1
35–49	23.9	23.3
50–64	20.9	21.5
65, and above	13.0	14.7
	100.0%	100.0%
Education		
Graduated from college/attended college	39.1%	33.3%
Graduated from high school	40.3	39.5
Did not graduate from high school	20.6	27.2
	100.0%	100.0%
Income		
$50,000 and above	22.6%	18.5%
$40,000–49,999	15.3	13.6
$35,000–39,999	9.3	8.4
$30,000–34,999	10.1	9.6
$25,000–29,999	9.2	9.7
$20,000–24,999	9.3	9.9
$10,000–19,999	16.3	18.7
$9,999 and under	7.9	11.6
	100.0%	100.0%
Median Income	$31,837	$22,415

Developing a Newspaper Test Program

When direct response advertisers first consider testing newspapers as a medium, they have myriad decisions to make. Should they go ROP, the newspaper preprint route, local Sunday supplements, syndicated supplements, TV program supplements, comics? What papers should they test? Putting ad size and position aside for the moment, there are two initial considerations: the importance of advertising in a mail order climate, and the demographics of markets selected as they relate to the product or service being offered.

If you had one simple product—a stamp dispenser, for instance—and a tiny budget, you might place one small ad in one publication. You could run the ad in the mail order section of the *New York Times Sunday Magazine*. Generally, if you don't make it there, you won't make it anywhere. Running such an ad would give a "feel." If it worked, it would be logical to test similar mail order sections in major cities such as Chicago, Detroit, and Los Angeles.

Simple items, which are suited to small-space advertising in mail order sections, greatly simplify the testing procedure. But more often than not, multicity testing in larger space is required. Prime direct response test markets in the United States include Atlanta, Buffalo, Cleveland, Dallas–Fort Worth, Denver, Des Moines, Indianapolis, Omaha, and Peoria. In the selection of test markets, you should analyze the newspaper to make certain it has advertising reach and coverage and offers demographics that are suitable to your product. If there are two newspapers in a market, it is worthwhile to evaluate both of them. Let us say that because of budget limitations advertising can be placed in only a limited number of markets. Such criteria as circulation, household penetration, male or female readers, and advertising linage relating to the product to be advertised should be measured.

A number of sources will provide the data necessary for evaluation. You would begin with the SRDS *Newspaper Rates and Data* for general cost and circulation information. *SRDS Circulation Analysis* would provide information about metro household penetration. *Simmons Total Audience Study* could then be used to isolate male or female readers of a particular age group. Other criteria to be measured are retail linage in various classifications, and spendable income by metro area.

Demographics are a major consideration whether you are using ROP, preprints, local supplements, syndicated supplements, or TV program supplements. Once an advertiser develops a test program that closely reflects the demographics for the product or service, expansion to similiar markets makes possible the rapid acceleration of a full-blown program. But selecting newspapers is tedious, because there are hundreds from which to choose, as compared to a relative handful of magazines whose demographics can be more closely related to the proposition. As an example, a test newspaper schedule could be placed in the following markets: Atlanta, preprint; Cleveland, Metro comics; Dallas–Fort Worth, ROP; Denver, preprint; Des Moines, ROP; Indianapolis, preprint; Omaha, Metro comics; and Peoria, *Parade* remnant. If there is more than one newspaper in a test market, the paper with the most promising demographics should be selected.

A test schedule like this would be ambitious in terms of total dollars, but it would have the advantage of simultaneously testing markets and formats. Once a reading has been obtained from the markets and formats, the advertiser can rapidly expand to other markets, and will have the advantage of using the most productive formats.

Advertising Seasons

As in direct mail and magazine direct response advertising, there are two major newspaper direct response advertising seasons. The fall mail order season begins roughly with August and runs through November. (A notable exception is a July insertion, which is often useful, especially when using a pretested piece.) The winter season begins with January and runs through March.

Exceptions to the two major direct response seasons occur in the sale of seasonal merchandise. Christmas items are usually promoted from September through the first week of December. A nursery, on the other hand, will start promoting in late December and early January, then again in the early fall. Many nurseries follow the practice of promoting by geographic regions, starting earlier in the South and working up to later promotion in the North.

Timing of Newspaper Insertions

Besides the seasonal factor, timing as it relates to days of the week is important. According to the *E&P Yearbook*, *Bureau of Advertising Circulation Analysis*, the number of copies of a newspaper sold per day is remarkably constant month after month, despite such events as summer vacation and Christmas holidays. People buy the newspaper to read not only the editorial matter but also the ads. While magazines are often set aside for reading at a convenient time, newspapers are read the day they are delivered or purchased or are not read at all.

According to an *Audits & Surveys Study*, the percentage of people opening an average ad page any weekday, Monday through Friday, varies less than 3 percent, with Tuesday ranking the highest at 88 percent.

Monday through Thursday are favorite choices of many direct response advertisers for their ROP advertising. Many direct response advertisers judiciously avoid the weekday issue containing grocery advertising.

More and more newspapers are accepting preprints for weekday insertions. This can be a major advantage, considering the larger number of preprints appearing in most metro Sunday newspapers.

The Position Factor

Newspapers and magazines have many similarities in respect to the importance of position in direct response advertising. Research has demonstrated high readership of newspaper ads, whatever the position. However, direct response advertisers still prefer right-hand pages. Generally, such advertisers find that ads are more effective if they appear in the front of the newspaper rather than in the back. Placement of coupon ads in the gutter of any newspaper page is almost always avoided.

All newspapers are printed in sections. Special consideration should be given to the reading habits of men and women as they relate to specific sections of a newspaper. Readership habits of men and women are similar, with the exception of four sections: food and cooking, home furnishings, gardening, and sports.

Color versus Black-and-White

The possibilities of using color in newspaper advertising may be regarded as similar to those for magazine advertising, with one major exception. If you plan to use one or more colors other than black in an ROP ad, you simply can't get the quality that you can in a color magazine ad. This does not mean that ROP color shouldn't be tested. A majority of newspapers that offer color will allow A/B splits of color versus black-and-white.

Studies have used split runs and the recognition method to test the attention-getting power of both two-color and full-color ROP ads. These studies show increases of 58 percent for two-color ads and 78 percent for full-color ads above the level of results for black-and-white versions of the same ads. Comparable cost differences are 21 percent and 25 percent, respectively.

When Starch "noting score" norms are used to estimate the same attention-getting differential, a different conclusion is reached. The differences are about 10 percent and 30 percent, respectively (when size and product category are held constant). Using norms means comparing a black-and-white ad for one product in another city at another time. These variables inevitably blur the significance of comparisons.

For the direct response advertiser, these studies are interesting. However, you should remember that genuine controlled testing is the only way to get true figures.

CASE STUDY: **Outsourcing a Newspaper Campaign**

Considering the complexities of putting a newspaper campaign together, there is much to be said about the wisdom of outsourcing. The Newspaper Network (TNN) of Sacramento, California, offers direct marketers and their agencies a planning and order placement process that greatly simplifies scheduling. New Media Director Kimberly Zercie developed several scenarios indicating how the process, called Merlin, would function in several marketing situations. This scenario involves the auto aftermarket.

BACKGROUND

You are the media planner/buyer for an auto parts store. Your chain has stores in three southeastern states (Alabama, Georgia, North Carolina), mostly around major cities. A large category killer, Auto Parts

Warehouse, has opened three locations in your three largest markets.

CHALLENGE

As a defensive measure, your advertising director has planned a major advertising/marketing effort to raise awareness of your chain and emphasize your reputation for quality and service (characteristics that will differentiate you from the price-driven competition). Because this is an eleventh-hour solution, it is not in the budget. The ad director has requested an analysis and costs for this plan by the end of the day.

SOLUTION

- Log onto *tnninc.com*, click on "tools," and click again on "Merlin."

CASE STUDY: Outsourcing a Newspaper Campaign *(continued)*

- Enter your user ID and password, and click "login."
- Because your plan is clearly tied to geography and a specific industry category, Quick Quote isn't the best tool . . . you choose "select by geography, and demographics."
- Click "next."
- Again, your campaign will be tightly tied to your store locations, even though you're in three states. To minimize waste, choose MSAs.
- While you can easily identify the MSAs where you have stores, you choose all of the MSAs in your three states. This way you can include other, contiguous MSAs with high propensities to be your customer.
- Click "next."
- You'll be sorting your selection on the next screen, so click next again to ignore the demographics option.
- Because you're promoting quality and service, you'll be looking for a combination of markets with high automotive aftermarket spending and higher median household incomes (not lower, price-driven incomes). Click twice at the top of the "Media HHI" column to sort the markets in descending order.
- Select all of the MSAs in which you have stores, and the top five MSAs that have high auto aftermarket spending and high median household incomes (to show your director that you've done your homework, and are looking for ways to increase your awareness). You can do this by clicking the check boxes next to your choices.
- Scroll to the bottom of the screen and click "next."
- Now, you have a list of all the daily newspapers that have circulation in these markets. But since efficiency and economy are critical (as usual), you want to choose only the best penetrating

papers. Since Sundays generally have the highest circulation, double-click on the "Sunday Penetration" column to sort in descending order.
- Select the single, best-penetrating newspaper in each MSA, scroll to the bottom of the screen, and press "next."
- A list box displaying your selections follows. Here you highlight the ones you want, and click "Submit Publications."
- Now, build your schedule for these papers. Enter the insert date, insert size, whether you want to repeat the insertion, and whether or not you want color. Each paper must be updated one at a time by editing the appropriate fields, and pressing "UPD" (the update button) next to each selection.
- Choose "Summary" from the menu on the left.
- Now you're looking at your total schedule. What's the cost? Look at the budget calculator in the upper right-hand corner of the screen (since this is an unbudgeted item, the cost is represented as a negative number).
- Are there some papers/markets that are clearly bad buys? Look at your CPMs. If there are, delete them by clicking the check box next to the unwanted newspapers, and then clicking the "delete" button.
- Now that you've outlined the buy, click on the "detail" button at the left.
- At the top of this page, click on "CSV." This will launch an Excel file *or* a comma-delimited text file. Save as "Operation Category-Killer."
- Format this file, and submit it to your director. Tell her that these are national open rates—the worst case scenario budgetwise.
- When she says it's a go, attach it to an E-mail and send it to your account coordinator at TNN. TNN will negotiate the campaign based on your contract levels *or* a potential test.

PILOT PROJECT You are the advertising manager of a mail order operation selling collectibles. You have been successful in magazines offering a series of historic plates. You have never used newspapers, but now you have a $75,000 budget to test the medium.

Outline a newspaper test plan. (Note: If you use preprints, your total space budget should cover printing costs.)

1. Select your test cities.

2. Will your test run in the Sunday edition or the weekday edition, or both?

3. What formats will you test: preprints, supplements, comics, local TV guides, ROP?

4. What size preprints or ads will you test?

5. At what time of the year will you run your tests?

Key Points

▶ Newspapers remain one of the best direct marketing media. Preprints, syndicated supplements, local newspaper magazines, even the comics, offer opportunities for direct marketers.

▶ To select test markets, analyze the newspaper to make certain it has advertising reach and coverage and offers demographics that are suitable to your product. Measure such criteria as circulation, household penetration, male or female readers, and advertising linage relating to the product to be advertised.

▶ As in direct mail and magazine direct response advertising, there are two major newspaper direct response advertising seasons. The fall mail order season begins roughly with August and runs through November. (A notable exception is a July insertion, especially useful when using a pretested piece.) The winter season begins with January and runs through March.

▶ While color ads do draw more attention, it is difficult to get the same quality that you can in a color magazine ad. Two-color ads can cost 21 percent, and four-color ads 26 percent, more than black-and-white advertising.

TV/RADIO

Broadcast Applications

Broadcast TV, both local and network, has long been a major medium for consumer direct response advertisers, producing inquiries, supporting other media, and selling goods and services to the consumer. More recently, cable has come on strong.

The range of TV direct response offers has greatly expanded in recent years. Although magazines, tapes, CDs, and innovative products certainly continue to be sold direct, many different types of direct response offers have surfaced.

Lead-generation commercials for high-ticket products and services such as home mortgages, insurance, and exercise equipment are now common. In addition, many Fortune 500 companies have started incorporating TV direct response into the marketing mix.

A truly unique application of broadcast TV involves White Castle. Hundreds of thousands of midwesterners were practically raised on White Castle hamburgers. Each year many of those same midwesterners moved to other regions of the country. Even without a White Castle nearby, the taste lingered on.

White Castle solved the availability problem by initiating a unique TV campaign with the theme, "White Castle has the taste some people won't live without" (see Exhibit 7–1). Outside of the White Castle trading area, commercials ended with this tag line: "Hamburgers to Fly. Call 1–800–W CASTLE." More than 10,000 hamburgers were sold weekly, with a minimum order of 50 hamburgers for $57!

Cable TV looks like broadcast TV, but it is different in many ways. First, the cable TV audience is highly defined. Cable operators know who is tied into the system. They send them a bill every month. This demographic information and some psychographic information is available to the advertiser. With many more channels available, cable, not unlike the audience selectivity traits of radio and niche

EXHIBIT 8-1

White Castle Campaign

DAUGHTER: I miss you, momma. I miss the city, too.

MOMMA: What if we sent you a little bit of your home town.

DAUGHTER: Now, how are you gonna do that?

White Castle hamburgers from back home! You can't get them out here.

My folks sent them!

ROOMMATE: Hey! Johnson's got White Castles!

GANG: White Castles!

DAUGHTER: You know, on my first date we stopped at a White Castle.

SINGERS: WHITE CASTLE HAS THE TASTE SOME PEOPLE WON'T LIVE WITHOUT.

magazines, provides more special interest programming. Thus, the direct response advertiser can tie offers to predefined audiences with a proclivity toward special interests such as sports, news, or entertainment.

One of the most firmly established special interest channels is Home Box Office (HBO). Its appeal is to those who have a particular interest in movies, sports, and special events. To be successful, not only must HBO offer superior programming, but it must also sell subscriptions for the programs.

A phenomenon of our times is the home shopping TV show. The telephone is integral to its explosive growth. The pioneer was HSN (Home Shopping Network). A later entrant, QVC Network, broadcasts its shopping channel live 24 hours a day, seven days a week. QVC built its huge volume by featuring presched-

Cover Panel of Folder Announcing Free Prizes to Cable Viewers

uled programs, offering products from specific product categories such as jewelry, electronics, and apparel.

Customers may order any item presented on QVC at any time that's convenient to them, providing the item is still in stock. Throughout all TV broadcasts, the QVC toll-free number is flashed constantly. Phone response is almost instantaneous. To promote viewership, QVC mails extensively to cable subscribers, providing them with free memberships in the QVC Shoppers Club and notifying them about free prizes awarded each day (see Exhibits 8–2 and 8–3).

Infomercials

The infomercial is no longer "the new kid on the block." The kid, so to speak, is now a grown-up with impressive credentials. It is estimated that infomercials collectively generate more than $1 billion in sales and at least $500 million in media time expenditures on cable and broadcast television. The number of Fortune 500

EXHIBIT 8–3

First Page of Two-Page Letter to Cable Subscribers with Free Membership Card for QVC Shoppers Club

```
MultiVision
QVC Network
Channel 23


1-800-345-1515      1-800-345-1515
QVC MEMBERSHIP NO.       QVC MEMBERSHIP NO.

1449-3828           1449-3828


1-800-345-1515      1-800-345-1515
QVC MEMBERSHIP NO.       QVC MEMBERSHIP NO.

1449-3828           1449-3828
```

QVC SHOPPERS CLUB

★ MEMBERSHIP CARD ★

MEMBERSHIP NUMBER   1449-3828

Mr. Don Corley
P.O. Box 641
Cambria, IL 62915

QVC - Cable Channel 23

```
        CAR-RT SORT  **B009
                                  ~ Place these stickers on your phones so you'll
Mr. Don Corley                      always have your membership number and
P.O. Box 641                        QVC phone number handy!
Cambria, IL 62915

Dear Cable Subscriber:

    Because you're a MultiVision cable subscriber,
we're pleased to award you a FREE membership in
the QVC Shoppers Club!

    Your exclusive membership number is valuable.
It's your key to winning great prizes on QVC.  And
you'll have lots of opportunities to win, because
QVC GIVES AWAY HUNDREDS OF PRIZES EVERY DAY!

    Hourly $25 prizes.  Daily $1000 shopping sprees.
And weekly grand prizes such as new cars and dream
vacations -- all to help introduce cable viewers to
QVC, the new way of shopping, on Cable Channel 23.

    QVC stands for Quality, Value and Convenience.
Tune in to channel 23 anytime, day or night,
for a wide variety of high-quality products to
help you look your best, beautify your home and
make your life easier.  You can order any item
by phone, with a 30-day money-back guarantee.

    However, you don't have to buy anything to win
prizes on QVC.  Here's just one way you could win:

    Tune in for QVC's hourly Lucky Number drawings.
Every time the number drawn matches either the
first 4 digits or the last 4 digits of your QVC
membership number, YOU'RE A WINNER!  Just phone
QVC before the next Lucky Number is drawn and
you'll instantly win $25 credited to your QVC
account.  Plus, you'll automatically be entered
in QVC's DAILY $1000 GRAND PRIZE DRAWING!

    Your membership number is 1449-3828, which gives
you two opportunities to win during each drawing!
Every time 1449 or 3828 is drawn, YOU'RE A WINNER!

                            Over, please...
```

firms using infomercials as a direct marketing tool has doubled in recent years. There are infomercials running somewhere on broadcast television or on cable every hour of the day, 24 hours a day, seven days a week, nationally and internationally—between 150 and 300 actively on the air at any one time.

But selling or traffic building with infomercials is no sure thing: a gambling spirit with fairly deep pockets to match is required. Infomercials can cost up to $500,000 to produce, and testing to determine performance will run $30,000 to $40,000.

To test retail sales impact, an infomercial should run ten times per market per week for a minimum of four weeks, so the before and after impact can be measured. Depending on the size of the market, the media cost can range from $5,000 to $50,000 per market per week. A typical retail sales test runs in two to four markets.

Radio

Radio has two things going for it over broadcast TV: (1) program formats to which advertisers can better target, and (2) much lower costs for similar time periods. Targeting to the right program formats is the key.

For example, if an advertiser is soliciting phone-in orders for a rock album, there's no problem running a radio commercial on scores of stations that feature rock music; these listeners are the very audience the advertiser is seeking. Or if a financial advertiser is soliciting inquiries from potential investors, there are program formats that help the advertiser reach a target audience: "Wall Street Report" for example, or FM stations with a high percentage of upper-income listeners.

This 60-second radio commercial by Merrill Lynch ran in conjunction with program formats with a high percentage of listeners who matched its customer profile:

(Music up and under)

ANNOUNCER: A word on money management from Merrill Lynch. Today, many banks are trying to copy our revolutionary Cash Management Account financial service. Here's why they can't. Bank money market accounts are simply that: bank accounts. A Merrill Lynch CMA gives you access to the entire range of our investment opportunities. Instead of just an account, you get an Account Executive, backed by the top-ranked research team on Wall Street. Idle cash is automatically invested in your choice of three CMA money market funds. You enjoy check writing, a special Visa card, automatic variable-rate loans up to the full margin loan value of your securities—at rates banks aren't likely to match. So give your money sound management and more to grow on. The all-in-one CMA financial service.

(Music) From Merrill Lynch. A breed apart.

LOCAL ANNOUNCER: For more complete information and a free prospectus, including sales charges and expenses, call 000–0000. Read it carefully before you invest or send money. That's 000–0000.

Videocassettes

The proliferation of VCRs may be bad news for movie theaters and television networks, but for the direct marketer, VCRs are an opportunity rather than a threat: Direct marketers have the opportunity to become sponsors of videocassette programming.

By incorporating commercial messages in the program, producers can defray the high cost of production and sell their tapes at a lower price. In addition, they might be able to open new distribution outlets. As an example, the hour-long "Mr. Boston Official Video Bartender's Guide," sponsored by Glenmore Distilleries, is available through liquor stores as well as the more usual outlets. Along with the cassette goes an eight-page catalog featuring each Glenmore product.

With such a catalog, or with specific sales and response information incorporated into a taped presentation, a sponsored videocassette might prove so productive for an advertiser that it could afford to sell the tape cheaply, use it as a self-liquidating premium, or even give the tape to videocassette outlets for low-rate rental. Videocassette catalogs also show potential for high-ticket items that benefit from demonstration.

Basic Broadcast Concepts

Buying and scheduling TV and radio time is best left to the experts—direct marketing agencies and some select buying services. But for a direct marketer to recognize the opportunities and pitfalls of advertising in these media, it is imperative that the basics be understood. The following comments about buying and scheduling TV apply equally to radio.

Ratings

It is important to keep in mind that the cost of a commercial time period is based on its rating. This is a measure of its share of the total TV households viewing the show. The more highly rated the show, the higher the cost. One rating point equals 1 percent of the total households in the market. A show with a 20 rating is being watched by 20 percent of TV households.

When the total ratings of all the time periods in a schedule are combined, the result is called gross rating points. Simply stated, if a television schedule has 100

GRPs per week, it is reaching the equivalent of 100 percent of TV households in the market in that week. Obviously, this is a statistical reach with varying degrees of duplication. It does not guarantee that 100 percent of the individual homes will be reached.

Commercial Lengths

Although 15 or 30 seconds is the most common length for general or image advertising, direct marketers seldom find it adequate to tell their selling story in a persuasive way. Ninety to 120 seconds is usually required for a direct sale commercial, and 60 to 90 seconds is usually required for lead-generation commercials. On the other hand, support commercials with sufficient GRPs prove effective with a combination of 10-second and 30-second commercials. But key outlet marketing usually requires longer lengths.

Of course, with the popularity of 30-second announcements, and the premium broadcasters can get for them, it is not always possible to clear longer-length commercials, particularly during periods of high demand.

Reach and Frequency

TV advertisers use two terms in measuring the effectiveness of their television schedules:

Reach refers to the number of different homes exposed to the message within a given time segment.

Frequency is a measure of how many times the average viewer will see the message over a given number of weeks. Frequency also can be measured against viewer quintiles (e.g., heaviest viewers, lightest viewers).

The combination of reach and frequency will tell you what percentage of the audience you are reaching and how often on average they will see your message. Television schedules often are purchased against reach and frequency goals; actual performance is measured in postanalysis.

For most direct marketers, reach and frequency are not as important as actual response rates, which represent a true return on the media dollar. But knowledge of reach and frequency is critical when television is used in a supporting role.

Buying Time

Buying specific time periods is the most expensive way to purchase television time. You pay a higher price to guarantee your message will run at a precise time within a predetermined program environment.

Television time also can be bought less expensively. Stations will sell run-of-station (ROS) time—time available during periods the station has been unable to sell at regular rates. This is particularly true with independent (non-network) stations, which often have sizable inventories of unsold time. If the station, however, subsequently sells the time to a specific buyer, your commercial will be preempted.

Preemptible time can be an excellent buy for direct response advertisers because of the combination of lower cost and quite respectable response rates. When buying preemptible time, it also is possible to specify the day parts (daytime, early fringe, late fringe, and so on) for slightly more than straight ROS rates. This can be important for direct marketers with a specific target audience for their product. Such spots still may be preempted at any time, however.

Television time also can be purchased on the basis of payment per inquiry (PI) and bonus-to-payout. PI allows the station to run as many commercials as it wishes, whenever it wishes. There is no charge for the time, but the station receives a predetermined sum for every inquiry or sale the advertisement generates for the advertiser. The advertiser is not committed to pay for a spot until it delivers an inquiry or sale, and then only in relation to responses.

But there are disadvantages. It is almost impossible to plan methodically for fulfillment. Such programs cannot be coordinated reliably with other efforts or promotion timetables. And because the station will run the commercials that it thinks will perform best for it, your spot might never run and you will not know it until your entire selling program has been jeopardized.

Bonus-to-payout involves a special arrangement with the station to deliver a certain number of responses. A schedule is negotiated with the station to guarantee a certain minimum schedule. If at the end of the schedule the response goal has not been reached, the station must continue to run the commercial until it is reached. This method provides a better planning base for the direct marketer.

With television time in high demand, such opportunities are not as available as they once were. But if they can be located, they can be a superb vehicle for direct marketers.

TV Schedules

What kind of broadcast TV schedule is most productive and/or efficient for the direct marketer? It depends on the objective. For direct sale or lead-generation commercials, which require the viewer to get up and take some action within minutes, certain criteria apply. For example, the TV viewing day is divided into various day parts: weekday daytime, early evening or fringe, prime time, late night or fringe, and weekend. Each day part tends to reach one group or combination of viewers better than the others.

It is important to know your primary target group so you can select the most appropriate day part. Prime time is so called because it reaches the largest audience with the most exciting shows. It is also the most expensive. The more attentive viewers are to the show, the less likely they are to respond immediately. Therefore, times of lower viewer involvement and attentiveness are better and less expensive for the advertiser who expects a direct response. Reruns, talk shows, old movies, and the like often are the best vehicles for direct response advertising. These tend to run predominantly in daytime, fringe, and late-night time slots.

Similarly, because independent stations tend to run a higher percentage of syndicated reruns and movies, their viewers tend to have a lower level of attentiveness to the programming. But even on independent stations, avoid news shows and other high-interest programming. Check the ratings. They are a good guide.

Seasonality is another factor in direct response TV. The first and third quarters are the best seasons for television response, just as they are for print and mail. Moreover, television time pricing is related to viewing levels, which are seasonal and vary month to month as well as by day part.

Market Performance

Some geographic locations are good for certain products or offers. Others are simply not receptive. It pays to know ahead of time what a market's propensity is. Previous experience with mail or print can be a reasonably reliable guide.

In any event, it is not necessary to jump in up to your neck. Start with a handful of markets—say, two to five—and test the waters. Try a one- or two-week schedule. As few as ten commercials per week can give you a reading. Monitor your telephone response daily. You'll know within two or three days if it's bust or boom. After a week or so you'll have an even more precise fix on how well your commercial is doing. If it holds up, stay with it until it starts to taper off. Then stop. Don't try to milk a stone.

Meanwhile, move on to other markets in the same methodical and measured way. You always can return to your most successful markets later in the marketing year, after your commercial has had a rest. Or you can come back with a new offer.

Advantages and Disadvantages of Different Types of Stations

Media-buying decisions have become more complex because of the expansion and success of various cable and broadcast stations and programming packages. Let's examine the advantages and disadvantages of the five major options for most TV direct response offers.

Network. The four major networks are ABC (195 affiliated stations), CBS (189 affiliated stations), NBC (186 affiliated stations), and Fox (134 affiliated stations). The advantage of the network option is that network reaches 95 percent of the potential U.S. TV households with each spot. The disadvantages are:

1. There are few, if any, 120-second spots available.

2. It is generally cost prohibitive.

3. Telemarketing blockage problems would occur in most day parts.

4. Talent payments could present a problem.

Though once considered prohibitively expensive, with astute planning the network option can be a viable direct response vehicle.

Spot TV. The use of spot TV is a localized way of making a buy that can be done through independent stations and/or affiliates. Whether you buy one or five stations in a spot market, you are reaching only one TV market. Rates vary greatly, depending on the station's ranking in and the size of the market.

One advantage of spot TV is that it is cost efficient. Because of competition within a market, reasonable buys generally can be made. Also, you can maximize efficiencies in the better-performing markets and on the better-performing stations. The disadvantage is that for a national campaign, it's more labor intensive to buy each market individually. Spot TV is the common approach for most direct response television campaigns.

Network Cable. The total cable penetration in the United States is 61 percent. There are 32 advertiser-supported cable networks and 16 regional cable networks. The advantages of network cable are:

1. It is cost efficient.

2. It enables targeting an offer to a cable network's audience.

3. Back-end tends to be better on cable than on broadcast TV because cable has a more upscale audience.

The disadvantage is that there are limited availabilities, especially if you have a two-minute spot. Network cable is especially appropriate if you have a one-minute spot and an offer perfectly matched to a cable network's audience.

Local Cable. Unlike cable network, local cable enables you to buy on a market basis or, in some instances, on a neighborhood basis. One advantage of local cable is that it allows a very targeted approach that works for products with narrow market segments. Also, it allows securing of additional cable time when networks are tight. The disadvantages include:

1. There are no two-minute breaks.

2. Rates aren't particularly cost efficient.

3. You have to work with five or more cable operators to cover one market.

4. It offers a very fragmented audience.

Local cable is best used for offers that target a narrowly segmented market.

Syndication. Syndication is the sale of a TV program for airing on a market-by-market, station-by-station basis. Though generally associated with reruns and game shows, syndication can include first-run movies and original, first-run TV shows. Some direct marketing agencies have also been able to buy time within a syndicated program, ensuring that the spot will air every time the show runs.

The advantages of syndication are:

1. It is difficult to preempt a syndicated program.

2. It reaches 80 to 90 percent of the country (similar to network).

3. There are no telemarketing headaches, because each station airs a particular show at a different time of day or on a different day of the week.

4. It allows product-to-program matching—a useful targeting tool.

The disadvantages are that it usually accepts only 60-second spots; therefore, for cost efficiency, buyers often have to wait for "distressed" or unsold time within a syndicated program. Syndication is well-suited to one-minute offers that are matched to a specific program and is a good choice for direct marketers having problems with preemptions.

Creating for Direct Response TV

Television is a visual medium and an action medium. And you are using it in a time of great video literacy. Your concept must be sharp and crisp. It must be designed to jar a lethargic and jaded audience to rapt attention. Your concepts, therefore, require the best and most knowledgeable of talent.

When you have arrived at your concept, it's time to write a script and do a storyboard. The script format is two adjacent columns, one for video descriptions and one for copy and audio directions. The two columns track together, so the appropriate words and sounds are shown opposite the pictures they will accompany. Video descriptions should make it possible to understand the general action in any given scene. It is not necessary at this point to spell out every detail.

Some people prefer to work only with storyboards, while others combine scripts and storyboards. The storyboard is a series of artist's drawings of the action and location of each scene. There should be enough individual pictures (called frames) to show the flow of the action and provide important visual information. Most concept storyboards run 8 to 16 frames, depending on the length of the commercial, the complexity of the action, and the need to show specific detail.

Novices make two important errors when preparing TV storyboards. One is failure to synchronize the words and the pictures. At no point should the copy be talking about something different from what the picture is showing, nor should the picture be something unrelated to the words.

The second mistake is failure to realize that most people who evaluate a storyboard equate frames with the passage of time. Each frame in an eight-frame storyboard will often be interpreted as one-eighth of commercial time. If some intricate action takes place over five seconds, it could take four or five frames to illustrate. Meanwhile, a simple scene that may run ten seconds can often be illustrated with one or two frames. Imagine the confusion the reviewer of the storyboard faces. Make sure your storyboards show elapsed time. Often an elapsed time indicator next to the picture will do the trick.

Of course, these criteria are guidelines, not rules. Even if they were, the essence of all great advertising, including direct response, is to break the rules to reach people in a way they haven't been reached before. But it is something quite different to violate principles that have been developed over years of observation. Do so only at your own peril.

There is a set of rules that relates to laws. Various industry self-regulatory bodies and instruments of the government watch over the airwaves. They require that advertising be truthful and not misleading. Don't say (or picture) anything in your commercial that you can't substantiate or replicate in person. And don't make promises your product or service can't deliver.

As you design your direct response commercial, there are some important techniques to keep in mind. If at all possible, integrate your offer with the rest of your commercial. It will make it easier for the viewer to comprehend and respond. And it will give your offer and your product or service the opportunity to reinforce each other in value and impression.

Also, if possible, integrate the 800 toll-free number into the commercial. You should plan to have the telephone number on the screen for at least 25 seconds or more, depending on the length of the commercial. Try to find ways to make it "dance" on the screen. Bring it on visually as it is announced on the sound track. Apply similar connection to visual and voice for announcing your website.

Once you have developed a television storyboard that you believe is a good representation of what you want to accomplish, it is possible to evaluate it using the following criteria:

1. *Immediacy.* Is there a sense of urgency to "Call this number now"? Does it make viewers feel that an opportunity will be lost if they don't run to the phone?

2. *Clarity.* Is the offer clear? Do people understand exactly what they will receive, or is there room for doubt and ambiguity?

3. *Lack of retail availability.* If the advertised product is not available in any store, make sure that point is communicated to the viewer.

4. *Increased value.* Many tactics can heighten the offer's value; for example, making a "special television offer" and stating "for a limited time only."

5. *Limited options.* If the spot provides viewers with too many choices, they will be confused. Yes-or-no offers usually do better than multiple-choice ones.

6. *Early close.* Ask for the order early and often. If the commercial waits until the final seconds or makes only one request for the viewer to call, it is usually too late.

7. *Less is more.* If you're asking for installment payments, focus the viewer's attention on the installment amount. Do not emphasize the sum total of all the installments.

8. *Show and tell.* If the product does more than one thing, show it. This is the only way viewers will become familiar with the product. Demonstrations work. Make sure the commercial conveys exactly what viewers are getting when they buy the product.

A support television commercial differs from a straight response commercial in ways worthy of note. Because it seeks to reach the largest number of people, it usually runs in time periods when 30 seconds is the prevalent availability. It must have a greatly condensed message, placing a premium on simplicity. As it seeks no immediate response, but directs the viewer elsewhere, such as to a newspaper insert, memorability and a positive attitude about the advertiser become extremely important.

Creating for Radio

In its early days television was perceived by many copywriters as nothing more than illustrated radio. With the evolution of the medium, we learned how limited that vision was. Now, in this age of video, there is a tendency to think of radio as television without the pictures. That perception is equally wrong.

Radio is the "writer's medium" in its purest sense. Words, sounds, music, and even silence are woven together by the writer to produce a moving tapestry of thought, image, and persuasion. Connection with the listener is direct, personal, emotional, primal.

In writing for radio it is important to consider a station's format. The country-and-western station has a different listening audience from the all-news station. Different people listen to classical music than talk-back or rock programming. Tailor your message and its style to the format of the station it is running on. That doesn't necessarily mean make it sound exactly like the station's programming. Sometimes it makes sense to break the flow of programming to stand out as a special message, but only within the framework of the format that has attracted the station's listeners.

Remember also that radio is more personal than TV. Radios are carried with the listener—in a car, at the beach, at the office, in the bathroom—and even joggers with their earphones are tuned into the radio cosmos. Moreover, because the radio listener can supply important elements in the message mosaic, the conclusion drawn from it is likely to be more firmly held than that which the individual has not participated in. Do not fill in all the blanks for your listeners. Let them provide some of the pieces. At the same time be sure the words you use are clear in their meaning and emotional content. Be sure the sounds are clearly understandable and recognizable. If not, find some way to augment them with narrative or conversation that establishes a setting that is easy to visualize.

Use music whenever you can justify its cost and consumption of commercial time. Music is the emotional common denominator. Its expression of joy, sorrow, excitement, romance, or action is as universally understood as any device available to you. When it comes time to consider music, contact a music production house. There usually are several in every major city. Los Angeles, New York, and Chicago have scores of them. Or consider library music that can be purchased outright at low cost.

Another aspect of radio is its casualness. Whereas television tends to command all of our attention and concentration, radio usually gets only a portion of it. It is important to keep radio commercials simple and intrusive. Devices such as special sounds (or silence) can arrest your listener's attention. To hold it, the idea content must be cohesive and uncomplicated. Better to drive one point home than to flail away at many. If many points must be covered, they all should feed to a strong central premise. This advice is appropriate for all advertising, but for radio it is critical.

The length a radio commercial runs is usually 60 seconds. This not only should be adequate for most commercial messages, but it also is the time length listeners have become accustomed to. Thirty-second commercials are available but are not a good buy for direct response purposes.

One other thing that everyone who listens to radio will appreciate is that the medium lends itself to humor. For some reason we have become used to hearing humor on radio and we respond positively to it. The following radio commercial employs humor effectively to address small business owners while talking to the public at large.

> Husband: How did we get into this anyway?
> Wife: Who knows, we tried to make it work.
> Husband: Well, I guess it's over.
> Wife: We better get on with it.

Husband: Okay, you get the car.

Wife: Right.

Husband: I get the sofa bed. You get the fridge.

Wife: Right.

Husband: I get the Bell System yellow pages directory. You get the—

Wife: Hold on—that doesn't mean the Gold Pages Coupon section, does it?

Husband: Why, sure it does.

Wife: I get the Gold Pages Coupons.

Husband: Well, come on—you're getting the bedroom set, too.

Wife: You can have the bedroom set. I want the Gold Pages Coupons good for discounts at local merchants.

Husband: I'll tell you what . . .

Wife: What?

Husband: I'll throw in the oil painting and the end tables.

Wife: I want the Gold Pages.

Husband: Look, you can have everything else. Just let me keep the Gold Pages Coupons.

Wife: Get off your knees. You really want them that bad?

Husband: I do absolutely.

Wife: We could split them.

Husband: You mean . . . tear them apart?

Wife: You're right . . . it won't work.

Husband: No. Neither will this.

Wife: It won't work.

Husband: You mean ...

Wife: We'll just have to stay together.

Husband: Dolores—what a mistake we almost made.

Wife: Lorraine.

Husband: Lorraine—what a mistake we almost made.

Wife: Who's Dolores?

TV in the Multimedia Mix

For decades marketers have regarded electronic media as stand-alone media. But astute marketers have joined the trend toward integrated communications. A classic example of this trend was the multimedia campaign for Ryder used trucks, created by Ogilvy & Mather Direct.

Exhibit 8–4 gives a precise description of the campaign, which included direct mail, direct response, TV, print, and radio.

Exhibit 8–5 shows a print ad that appeared in ensuing vertical publications. A vertical publication is one that caters to a specific category of business, such as

EXHIBIT 8–4

Description of Ryder Campaign

Product or Service

Used vehicle sales, including vans, gas and diesel straight trucks, refrigerated trucks, tractors, and trailers. Range in price from $7,000 to $35,000.

Target Audience

- Owners/presidents of small service businesses, small wholesalers/retailers, small trucking companies and light manufacturing companies (cabinetry, auto parts, electronic parts, clothing/candy)
- Owner/operators
- Used truck purchasers in large companies with 10+ vehicle fleet size

Medium/Media Used

Direct mail: 300,000 pieces. Lists included previous customers, Dun & Bradstreet selects (targeted industries; less than 100 employees; transportation titles), *Fleet Equipment* subscribers, *Fleet Owner* subscribers, *Allied Truck Publication* subscribers.

DRTV: :60 and :120 local television in spot markets, 3–5 stations/market, 10–15 spots/week/station, for 2–4 week flights

Print: local trade publications (*Truck Trader*)

Radio: local; spot stations

Marketing Strategy

To remain competitive in its primary business—truck rental and leasing, Ryder needs to keep its truck fleet current. Selling its used vehicles helps Ryder fund the purchase of new vehicles while providing an additional source of revenue.

Problem:
- Increasingly depressed market for used vehicle sales
- Aggressive sales objectives within a more competitive category environment
- Inconsistent awareness that Ryder also sells trucks

Solution:
- Leverage Ryders' reputation for quality in truck rental and leasing to sell its vehicles at a premium price.
- Establish "Road Ready" as a symbol of reliability, safety, and value through a lifetime of maintenance.
- Provide a continuous presence in the marketplace to generate awareness that Ryder sells trucks.
- Generate immediate, qualified leads through an offer of a free "How to Buy a Used Truck" booklet.

banking or a specific interest like jogging, boating, etc. The headline "Buy a Ryder Road Ready Used Truck and you'll find one problem. The mechanics hate to see them go" carries the campaign theme.

Exhibit 8–6 reveals the 120-second TV commercial. It was tagged "The Crying Commercial" because it paid off on the theme "The mechanics hate to see them go."

How successful was this multimedia campaign? The combination of direct mail, print, TV, and radio produced a total of 46,046 responses, beating the previous controls by 245 percent.

EXHIBIT 8–5

Print Ad for Ryder Campaign

EXHIBIT 8–6

The Crying Commercial

Ogilvy & Mather Direct

CLIENT: RYDER
PRODUCT: USED TRUCK SALE
TITLE: "CRYING"
COMML No.: RTLR 0111 :120

(SFX-TRUCK HORN) (MUSIC UP-SENTIMENTAL THEME)
MECHANIC #1: There goes my baby.

STEVE: Here we go again. I knew it, every time Ryder sells a used truck this happens.
(SFX-SOBBING, BLOWING NOSE)

STEVE: Alright, there, there.

You didn't know Ryder sells trucks? They do, they sell them. Excuse me.
(SFX-SOBBING)

The same quality trucks they rent and lease to businesses, they also sell to businesses.

Makes these guys fall apart.

MECHANIC #2: We've been caring for them since they were new.

STEVE: See what I mean? They look after these trucks like they were their own.

MECHANIC #3: They've got their whole lives ahead of them.

STEVE: You're going to be okay, don't worry about it. Do you believe these guys?

Ryder sells more kinds of used trucks than anyone. Trucks, vans, tractors, trailers.

Even specialized equipment.

Just call and they'll tell you where to get 'em. They'll even--

MECHANIC #1. (VO) Steve, not the book!
STEVE: Eh, I have to do this.

They'll even give you free advice before you look. It's in here: "How to Buy a Used Truck."

You gotta get this. It's the inside story. What to look for, and avoid. Whether you're buying now or just kicking some tires.

Course, with a Ryder used truck you know what you're getting into.

See this tag. "Road Ready." It means this truck has been maintained at the highest standards since it was new.

Ryder has the records to prove it. And a limited warranty to back it. Impressive stuff.

How ya doin'? (MUSIC UP-SENTIMENTAL THEME)
MECHANIC #4: Great.

EXHIBIT 8–6 *(continued)*

RYDER–"CRYING"

STEVE: These guys put their hearts into these trucks. They even fix things before they go wrong.

MECHANIC #4: Brakes. Steering. Engine.

STEVE: You'll love your Road Ready truck as much as they do.

MECHANIC #2: Oh please, I don't want to see you go.

STEVE: Only you'll get to keep yours. So call for the Ryder Road Ready Center near you. Ask about financing.

MECHANIC #1: (VO) Steve! STEVE: It's okay, relax.

MECHANIC #1: Don't give him the number, please.

Just call for the free book: "How to Buy a Used Truck."

Even if you're not buying now, you'll be an expert.

But you gotta call.

MECHANIC #4: Please take good care of them.

STEVE: Don't worry. They'll get more trucks. Sorry, I'm out of tissues.

It's a new jacket, get off me. I'm not kidding!

(SENTIMENTAL MUSIC UP AND OUT)

CASE STUDY: Surety, Inc.

Written by Donald W. Eckrich, Ithaca College; Scott Erickson, SUNY College at Oneonta, New York; and Sarah Wortman, DePaul University, for the DePaul University Institute for Interactive and Direct Marketing Case Writer's Workshop

BACKGROUND

Surety, Inc., a $500 million wholly owned subsidiary of The Randall Walker Company, a 90-year-old Chicago-based retail department chain, is one of the premier direct marketing companies in the world. The nation's second largest telemarketer, it makes well over 60 million scripted telephone presentations a year, and also delivers more than 400 million mail solicitations annually.

Surety's products include continuity clubs, credit card insurance, and health and life insurance. Now the company would like to introduce a new product, a life insurance plan specifically designed to cover funeral and/or burial expenses. While this product had been around for many years and was offered by some prominent competitors, the presumed competitive advantage for Surety would be the brand equity available through the Randall Walker name.

Randall Walker Life Insurance Company's Mature Life Plan, as it would be called, would appeal to older adults concerned with both the increasing costliness of funeral and burial services and the financial consequences of being underinsured. Impulse purchase behavior would likely play an important role. Potential enrollees would hopefully be impressed, if not excited, by the connection of this product to the Randall Walker name, and they further would be able to respond spontaneously, anonymously, and without risk, using an 800 number.

CHALLENGE

Randall Walker challenged its subsidiary to develop a direct response TV campaign, the first of its kind for Randall Walker.

Generating a large lead pool would not be enough. The key to a successful product launch would be in the number of conversions from leads to paid applications. Achieving close to a 7 percent conversion rate of leads to paid applications would be necessary to succeed.

Randall Walker was excited about the project because it offered a way to develop markets away from the existing customer file. All respondents to the direct response TV campaign, whether qualified for the insurance or not, could be captured and placed in a new data file. As this database grew, the company could develop even more new products and promote them through direct response TV.

SOLUTION

The company and its agency decided to test market a direct response TV campaign in Chicago, where it rated extremely high in store presence. The rationale was simply that if the campaign showed signs of weakness or failed outright, there would be no reason to expand it elsewhere. QST Inc., a major player in the development of direct response TV programming and well known throughout the industry, was retained to help develop and implement the Chicago test. Randall Walker agreed to pay for the production of three spots—one 2 minutes, one 90 seconds, and one 1 minute—to be broadcast on Chicago TV at those off-peak times determined most appropriate by QST. The out of pocket costs for producing the spots ranged between $9,500 and $15,000, well below industry averages for such productions. Ownership rights to the spots remained with QST, and Surety further agreed to pay a fixed fee of $20 per lead generated by the spots.

The Chicago test resulted in a three-pronged, direct mail-based strategy. Despite having one of the world's foremost outbound telemarketing capabilities, Surety outsourced the handling of all inbound telemarketing communications to inbound telemarketing communication specialists DATA-MARK. QST bought the media time and placed the test spots; DATAMARK received, processed, and tabulated all inbound telecommunications and modemed the data to Surety, which entered it into the new database.

The first TV test spots were aired in October of a nonelection year—not ideal, for the fourth quarter is generally considered the worst quarter for generating insurance leads. The first batch of outbound correspondence was mailed shortly thereafter. The packets included a personalized letter and a "Benefits Kit" that included a 50-page *Guide to Social Security and Medicare*, a three-page foldout titled "The Benefits of Mature Life," an enrollment form, a separate insert describing an offer to receive a free issue of the *Consumer's Guide Prescription Drug Book*, another insert describing an offer of a free Diamond Dial Watch for including the first premium's payment (using any payment method), and a self-addressed stamped envelope. Subsequent mailings were not as elaborate but helped reinforce the primary benefit of the Mature Life Plan—responding to the shortfall in Social Security's lump-sum death benefit.

RESULTS

Results were good, and it was determined that had this been an actual rollout, it would have been a complete success. But second-phase tests performed in the first quarter of the year in other geographic areas consistently fell short of baselines and offered a sharp contrast to the first test. Adding a follow-up telemarketing call did not help.

A Second Attempt

A second firm was hired to produce and air its own spots, hire an independent media buyer to negotiate rates and buy time, and handle fulfillment. The new agency planned to bill Surety for the actual amortized cost per lead.

The new test aired in the fourth quarter of an election year. Spots aired on stations in or near cities with a Randall Walker location. Surety took advantage of the situation to test both approaches. QST had an opportunity to air its spots in some markets, while the new agency's spots aired in others. The new agency,

MARFAX, took over fulfillment and data collection activity.

Better Results

Within a month of test start-up, QST had exceeded its quota of leads while maintaining the $20 per lead charge. The test plan had projected QST to generate 2,150 leads over the fourth quarter, and it generated 2,451 leads in less than a month. Meanwhile, MARFAX had generated 1,712 of its expected 2,850—over 60 percent of its quota in roughly one-third of the plan's time frame. Based on the preliminary data, it was concluded that both approaches could generate large numbers of leads in a national, cross-sectional test. In its final form, leads were generated from TV spots in over 23 cities with Randall Walker locations, utilizing 32 TV stations. QST was instructed to put an immediate hold on any further broadcast, while MARFAX was given three additional weeks to bolster its lead-generation performance. Both organizations were out of the field by the end of November.

The results looked good, but there were some concerns. For one, not only had both tests been conducted during the fourth quarter, but also during an election year—raising concerns of diminished market performance for direct-marketed insurance products in general, and the problems associated with placing TV spots in direct competition with heavy-spending candidates for political office.

However, one of the most important reasons for the product launch was its capacity to initiate a new database. Even a marginally performing product could be accepted, provided it contributed to the outstanding success of another. On the positive side, during the tests, over 15 percent of conversions paid their policy premiums immediately using the Randall Walker Credit Card—proof that the Randall Walker name provided significant brand equity for this insurance product. Surety and Randall Walker planned to stick with their direct response TV strategy.

PILOT PROJECT Your assignment is to create a 60-second radio spot for a long-awaited CD DanceFest 2001 from legendary Chicago DJ, IM2 Cool. Filled from start to finish with hefty beats and solid, move-busting tunes, this two-CD compilation shows off the turntable skills that brought DJ IM2 Cool from obscurity to dance floors everywhere.

DanceFest 2001 includes 24 tracks that starts out big, gets bigger, then changes gears to keep things interesting. It includes cuts such as Plump DJs' "The Push," Orbital's "Nothing Left," Aziddo Da Bass's "Dooms Night," DJ Icey's "Low Tide," and 20 additional tracks that will leave the listener begging for more.

The regular price for this two-CD set is $29.95, but it will be offered for $19.95 plus $3.95 shipping and handling. Only credit cards Visa, MasterCard, and Discover card will be accepted for payment. The toll-free phone number for ordering is 1-800-IM2-Cool (1-800-462-2665). Or it can be ordered from IM2 Cool's website www.IM2Cool.com. A free MP3 download of Cool's favorite mix from the CD is available at the site. The CD is not available in stores.

Key Points

▶ The cost of a commercial time period is based on its rating, the measure of its share of the total TV households viewing the show. The more highly rated the show, the higher the cost. More important than reach and frequency are actual response rates, which represent a true return on the media dollar.

▶ To buy time economically, ask about preemptible time and payment per inquiry (PI) and bonus-to-payout arrangements. For best response, schedule commercials during fringe day parts and programs with lower viewer involvement, like reruns, talk shows, and old movies.

▶ The first and third quarters are the best seasons for television response.

▶ Test TV commercials in two to five markets for one or two weeks. As few as 10 commercials per week can give you a precise fix on how well the commercial is doing. If it holds up, stay with it until it starts to taper off, and move on to other markets in the same methodical and measured way.

▶ Integrate the offer with the product or service so they reinforce each other in value and impression. Show the 800 toll-free number or the Web address on the screen for at least 25 seconds, depending on the length of the commercial.

▶ Radio costs less than television and offers more targeted program formats. The message and style of a 60-second radio commercial should be tailored to the format of the station it is running on. Keep radio commercials simple and intrusive. Use special sounds to arrest your listeners' attention, but keep the main idea uncomplicated. Better to drive one point home than to flail away at many.

CO-OPS

Co-op mailings include two or more offers in the same envelope or other carrier, with each participating mailer sharing the mailing cost based on a predetermined formula.

Co-ops, in various formats, have been available to marketers for decades. Among the most popular are postcards—3½ × 5½ inch—assembled three to the sheet or loosely. In an effort to make more selling space available, many co-ops accept printed lithographed sheets that measure 8½ × 11 inches, folding down to 5½ × 8½ inches. But the ultimate in size is the 24-page minicatalog with a page size of 5½ × 7½ inches.

It is estimated that more than 1,000 co-ops are available at any one time. Their basic appeal is that you share the cost with other marketers, thus attaining a much lower cost per thousand circulation. Rule of thumb is that participation in a co-op costs about one-fourth as much as a solo mailing. That's the good news.

The bad news is that on average, response rate from a co-op is about one-fourth as much as you would get with a solo mailing. But that's the average. The purpose of this chapter is to discuss how to beat the averages.

Getting Co-ops Read

Participants in co-ops face fierce readership competition. You can greatly improve your chances for getting your piece read and acted on by knowing the behavior patterns of people who receive co-ops.

In focus group research interview sessions in which groups of housewives were brought in and handed co-op envelopes filled with discount coupons and other offers, there was an amazingly consistent behavior pattern. The participants, without exception, sorted each envelope's contents into two piles. Later, when they were asked the basis for the two piles, they answered: "Interesting—not interesting; like—dislike; value—no value." Your offer must find its way to the right pile during that initial sorting.

The way to get into the first pile is to have a simple message clearly stated with effective graphics. The more alternatives you offer, the less your response might be. In a phrase, don't get sorted out; keep it simple. You only have a few seconds to make an impact. Inserts in direct mail co-ops are more like ads in a magazine than like regular direct mail. If the offer appears to be too much trouble, if it appears that the message is going to take some time and effort to get at, the home shopper goes to the next offer.

Generally, in co-op direct response advertising the recipient sees little and remembers less. Any purchase is basically made on impulse, and response levels can be seriously impacted if the potential respondent does not act within a short time span. The products and services should fall into the pattern of something wanted or needed now. This is true whether the marketer is seeking an inquiry or a direct sale.

Consumer Co-ops

When consumer co-ops first came on the scene, the mailing lists they used were for the most part compiled lists. Driver's license names constituted a major portion of the compilation.

These were good, clean lists, current for the most part, but little was known about the demographics. If you wanted the names of people who owned a Model A Ford, by gosh—they were available. But if you wanted to know the names of Model A Ford owners who were mail order responders—forget it!

Well, times do change. The large consumer co-ops like ValPack and Carol Wright offer a number of selects within their massive consumer list. Using Carol Wright as an example, here are some of the selects available in its 25-million-name list.

- Heads of Household, ages 18 to 60

- PC Owners

- Females, ages 18 to 44; Females, ages 25 to 54

- Mail Order Responders

- Seniors, ages 50 to 64

- Pet Owners

The Tropicana insert, Exhibit 9–1, is one of 30-plus offers in one mailing. Note the cents-off coupon plus the free movie tickets.

EXHIBIT 9–1

Tropicana Insert in 30-Piece Co-op Mailing

Business-to-Business/Professional Co-ops

There are hundreds of co-ops catering to professionals and manufacturing management. The circulation isn't even close to consumer co-ops, but in business-to-business the units of sale can be many, many times a consumer sale. So smaller numbers can be very much worthwhile.

Many of the card decks on the market have emanated from publishing firms. One of the most remarkable phases of Prentice Hall's card deck program is that it delivers 100 percent direct response buyers for every card deck offered. Exhibit 9–2 shows the variety of card decks offered, the circulation, and when they are mailed.

Exhibit 9–3 gives full particulars about the *Business Management* card deck. (The same format is used in giving particulars about all card decks.) Exhibit 9–4 shows the postcard of a co-op advertiser seeking catalog requests.

EXHIBIT 9–2

Sample Card Decks and Their Circulation

Prentice Hall 1999
Card Deck Schedule

#	Deck Title/Name	Published Tag Line	Deck Circulation	Deck Orders Due	Material and Inserts Due	MAIL DATE
1	AICPA & PH Accounting	PH/AICPA	100,000	11/24/98	12/01/98	Early Jan
2	Elementary Educators	PHED	200,000	12/01/98	12/05/98	Early Jan
3	Sports & Coaching	PHSC	75,000	12/08/98	12/12/98	Mid Jan
4	Business Management	PHBM	175,000	12/15/98	12/22/98	Late Jan
5	Health & Natural Healing	PHHN	100,000	12/29/98	01/05/99	Early Feb
6	School Librarians	PHSL	50,000	01/06/99	01/13/99	Mid Feb
7	Plant & Manufacturing	PHPM	105,000	01/14/99	01/21/99	Mid Feb
8	Science Teachers	PHST	100,000	01/26/99	02/02/99	Early Mar
9	Music Educators	PHME	50,000	02/02/99	02/09/99	Early Mar
10	English Teachers	PHET	100,000	02/09/99	02/17/99	Mid Mar
11	Early Childhood	PHEC	100,000	02/15/99	02/22/99	Mid Mar
12	Human Resources	PHHR	50,000	02/23/99	03/02/99	Late Mar
13	Social Studies Teachers	PHSS	75,000	03/02/99	03/09/99	Early Apr
14	Women-At-Work	PHWW	100,000	03/15/99	03/22/99	Mid Apr
15	Finance & Accounting	PHFA	80,000	03/24/99	03/31/99	Late Apr
16	Health & Natural Healing	PHHN	100,000	04/12/99	04/19/99	Mid May
17	Business Management	PHBM	175,000	04/23/99	04/30/99	Late May
18	School Administrators	PHSA	100,000	05/03/99	05/10/99	Early Jun
19	Plant & Manufacturing	PHPM	105,000	05/11/99	05/18/99	Mid Jun
20	Career & Personal Adv	PHCP	75,000	05/26/99	06/02/99	Late Jun
21	Ed-At-Home/Back to Sch	PHAH	100,000	06/07/99	06/14/99	Mid Jul
22	Sports & Coaching	PHSC	75,000	06/29/99	07/06/99	Early Aug
23	Elementary Educators	PHED	200,000	07/08/99	07/15/99	Mid Aug
24	Art Educators	PHAE	75,000	07/16/99	07/23/99	Mid Aug
25	Early Childhood	PHEC	100,000	07/23/99	07/30/99	Late Aug
26	AICPA & PH Accounting	PH/AICPA	100,000	08/02/99	08/06/99	Early Sep
27	Secondary Educators	PHSE	150,000	08/06/99	08/13/99	Early Sep
28	Canadian Educators	PHCE	20,000	08/11/99	08/18/99	Mid Sep
29	Women-At-Work	PHWW	100,000	08/11/99	08/18/99	Mid Sep
30	Plant & Manufacturing	PHPM	105,000	08/16/99	08/23/99	Mid Sep
31	Health & Natural Healing	PHHN	100,000	08/30/99	09/06/99	Early Oct
32	Guidance & Counseling	PHGC	100,000	09/01/99	09/04/99	Early Oct
33	School Librarians	PHSL	50,000	09/04/99	09/11/99	Mid Oct
34	Business Management	PHBM	175,000	09/16/98	09/23/98	Late Oct
35	Special Educators	PHSP	150,000	09/27/99	10/04/99	Early Nov
36	Music Educators	PHME	50,000	10/04/99	10/11/99	Mid Nov
37	Ed Hotline	PHEH	125,000	10/11/99	10/18/99	Mid Nov
38	Human Resources	PHHR	50,000	10/15/99	10/22/99	Mid Nov
39	Career & Personal Adv	PHCP	75,000	10/25/99	11/01/99	Late Nov
40	School Administrators	PHSA	100,000	11/02/99	11/09/99	Early Dec

NOTE: All side-by-side (6" x 7") formats anticipated except for non-domestic mailings

PRENTICE HALL DIRECT • 1-800-937-9970
240 Frisch Court, Paramus, NJ 07652-5240 • Fax: 201-909-6378 • e-mail: catherine_rogers@prenhall.com

EXHIBIT 9-3

Rate Card, *Business Management* Card Deck

BUSINESS SELF IMPROVEMENT

Business Management

GUARANTEED CIRCULATION RATE BASE OF 175,000

1999 Rates & Data

Card #7

Issue and Closing Dates

Issue	Orders	Material/Inserts	1999 Mail Date
Winter	12/15/98	12/22/98	late January
Spring	4/23	4/30	late May
Fall	9/16	9/23	late October

Market Profile

Reach a proven, direct mail responsive list of 175,000 executives, managers, consultants, and entrepreneurs at business addresses. These ambitious professionals are employed in the service, manufacturing, and wholesale industries.* They have spent from $29.95 to $125.00 for Prentice Hall business references and manuals including Manager's Troubleshooter, Advertising Manager's Handbook, Labor & Employment Law Deskbook and many others. These loyal mail order buyers are ideal prospects for products and services that can improve their job performance and their company's bottom line. This list is cleaned and updated monthly.

*With 65% in small to mid size companies and 35% large (over 100 employees)

Advertising Rate

Black & White base rate
(std. card) $5600

Black & White base rate
(jumbo card) $7875

Frequency Discounts (applied to base rate)

2-6 cards, per card 10%

7-15 cards, per card 15%

16-25 cards, per card 20%

26 or more cards .... Inquire

Note: Insertions in one or more Prentice Hall Target Market Card Decks can be combined to achieve a higher discount. Earned frequency discounts apply to base rate and remain applicable for 12 months. Discounts will be short-rated if not fulfilled within a 12-month term.

Premiums

Color: (commissionable)

	Std.	Jumbo
2/Color (black & 1 other color), publisher's standard of reflex blue, process blue, PMS 185 red, PMS 347 green or process yellow,
additional per side $250 $400

3/Color or 4/Color (separations & color key required),
additional per side $450 $600

Matched color,
additional per side $325 $500

Split Runs (50/50):
Net cost per B+W, 2/C card $250
Net cost per 4/C card $350

Inserts/Preprinted and Supplied

Preprinted Inserts weighing 1/4 ounce (.25 oz.) or less, the B&W base rate, less applicable discounts apply. Inserts weighing more than 1/4 ounce, inquire for rate. Sample to publisher required for approval and proper price quote. Production slowdowns may incur additional costs. Trimmed or folded size not to exceed 6" x 7". Call Prentice Hall for insert shipping address.

Note: Please supply a minimum of 3% over the guaranteed circulation for overage, spoilage and samples.

Commissions/Cash Discounts

15% to recognized agencies/brokers, if paid within 30 days of invoice date. No cash discount. For payment in full with order, $200 cash discount applied.

Mechanical Requirements

Jumbo cards:

Dimensions - Trim size: 5-3/8" x 7"

Copy area - 5-1/8" x 6-5/8"

Standard cards:

Dimensions - Trim size: 5-1/2" x 3-1/2"

Copy area - 5-1/8" x 3-1/8"

Production method - Offset

Binding method - Loose deck

Line Screen - 133

Max Ink Density - 240%

Paper stock - White, .007 hi-bulk, non-coated stock

Digitized material preferred (disk output form and laser separated proofs required). Negatives (right reading emulsion side down) or camera-ready art also acceptable. No bleeds.

Note: Material that needs to be reduced or enlarged, or requires any other preparation to "make ready" for production may incur additional charges.

(see page 29 for more information)

Policy

Publisher reserves the right to refuse any advertisement. Agency/client are jointly liable for payment on orders received and accepted. All orders are subject to terms of rate card. Cancellations after closing date are not acceptable. Prepayment required until credit is established. Publisher cannot guarantee results or outcome of this mailing.

PRENTICE HALL DIRECT • 1-800-937-9970

240 Frisch Court, Paramus, NJ 07652-5240 • Fax: 201-909-6378 • e-mail: catherine_rogers@prenhall.com

20

Other Channels of Distribution

Co-ops are in no way limited to circulation by mail. Let's take a look at some other channels of distribution.

Package Stuffers

There is a saying that the best time to sell someone is right after they have bought something. Based upon the theory, many direct marketers do well by providing package stuffers to mail order companies who will put them into their outgoing packages. (There is a charge for this, of course.)

When computing percent of response from package stuffers, it should be noted that stuffers are used up over time. Thus, a count of inventory at the present time must be subtracted from the last inventory of cards in order to produce a valid analysis.

Newspaper Inserts

A long-running newspaper co-op is Valassis. Running 16 pages plus, and inserted into Sunday newspapers, it is loaded with cents-off coupons. Typical among package goods advertisers are Welch's, Oreo cookies, Stouffer's, Wheaties, Cheerios, A&W Root Beer, Healthy Choice soups, Arm & Hammer, and scores more.

While Valassis is an old standby in newspaper co-ops, it is significant to note a newspaper insert named "The Net Best," where the only address given for most participants is its E-mail address. There's a sweepstakes to add interest to the insert, but it is called "Webstakes.com." (No purchase necessary.) The slogan for the co-op is: "Great Buys from the Internet's Top Retailers." Signs of the times?

E-Mail Co-ops

Only one step removed from a co-op that excludes households without computers is a co-op mailed solely to E-mail addresses. E-mail address lists of consumers who have opted in (given permission) to receive E-mail are becoming abundant.

On-line Coupon Distribution

Many on-line companies and consumer brands have tested on-line coupon distribution, including JCPenney, K mart, Kids 'R' Us, CDW, Disney, Kodak, and AT&T. The coupon site Coolsavings.com features offers from such prominent direct marketers as Geico Direct, the on-line insurance company InsWeb, and Andysgarage.com, where catalog giant Fingerhut liquidates its inventory (see Exhibit 9–5).

There are three major promotional models for on-line coupon activity:

1. *In-store redemption.* Users print coupons from a site and redeem the coupons at a retail location.

2. *On-line redemption.* When users click on E-commerce coupons placed on coupon sites, the coupons are applied to offers right there on the site.

3. *Continuity/Affinity programs.* These sites provide offers worth a predesignated amount with an off-line purchase. Site visitors print these coupons and give them to the off-line retailer at checkouts. Like affinity programs, these programs allow Web surfers to earn points toward future purchases of products and services while coincidentally building the lifetime value of customers overall.

Why Offer Coupons?

Whatever the channels of distribution, the bottom line is that hundreds of millions of coupons are offered and used each year. The question is, why?

Cox Direct, publishers of the Carol Wright co-op, gives these major reasons why package goods firms use couponing:

EXHIBIT 9–5

On-line Coupon Distribution

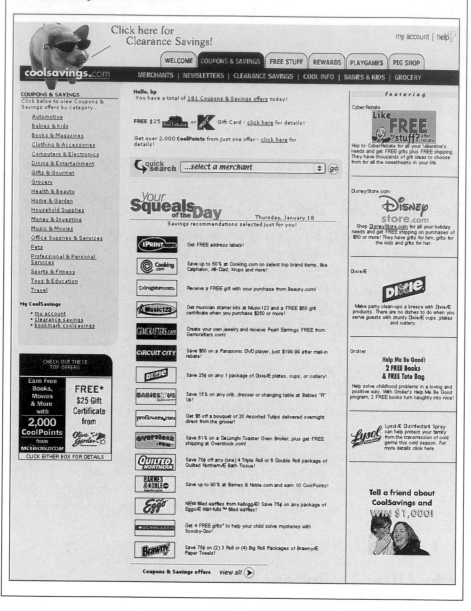

- To generate short-term incremental volume

- To reward loyal users

- To counteract competitive coupon pressure

- To support retail merchandising events (synergy)

- To build the brand franchise base, attracting new users through the communication of added value

- To generate trial and optimize repeat for a new brand

- To build brand/corporate equity with the retailer/consumer

- To preempt competitive promotional, introductory activity by "protecting" current users

Co-ops are a major tool for direct response advertisers when used correctly. They are not suitable for selling a $400 camera, but they are excellent for getting inquiries about a $400 camera or selling a lower-priced product or service. Co-ops are highly preferred for in-store coupon redemptions and for scores of direct response offers requiring a minimum of information for a target audience.

Co-op Testing Rules

Testing co-ops is a tricky business. When you test an insert in a co-op, you are doing so with one group of partners; when you "roll out," you are likely to be participating with a different group of partners. So you must live with this variable. Here are a few simple rules for testing co-ops:

- Because testing is a trial for a subsequent major promotion, it is important to ensure that conditions for the major promotion will be as close to those of the original as possible.
- Know what your break-even point is and test a sample large enough so your result can be acted on.
- Test the co-op first and leave the segments for later unless your product clearly suggests a particular segment. For example, if your product is aimed entirely at a female market, test only the female portion of a co-op mailing.
- Test a cross section of the complete co-op list. If no "*n*th" sample is available, request distribution in several different markets—all widely dispersed.
- Don't let too much time elapse between your test and your continuation, especially if the item you are testing is of a seasonal nature.

CASE STUDY: WEB Direct Marketing/Hanover House

BACKGROUND

About 20 years ago WEB Direct Marketing, Inc., of Wheeling, Illinois, started working with Hanover House of Hanover, Pennsylvania. Hanover had 21 catalogs at the time, each with a different name and each targeted to a different audience. Hanover needed an alternative to the expensive, time-consuming, two-step catalog process.

CHALLENGE

The challenge was to develop a low-cost, miniature, four-color catalog with a built-in envelope and coded order form that weighed less than one-third ounce. WEB met the challenge at the budgeted cost with a 3¼ × 7 inch catalog of 16 pages plus envelope and order form. The catalog was dubbed the "mini storybook."

Featuring Hanover's best values and hottest-selling items at a variety of price points, the mini storybook was tested in 100 different package insert programs for a total cost of less than 10 cents each to create, print, insert, and deliver to a targeted audience of proven mail order buyers.

RESULTS

The program was a big success. On average, across all programs, the profit from the sale of merchandise featured in all of the mini storybooks exceeded Hanover's total print and media costs. The company actually began to make a profit prospecting for new customers.

Hanover didn't stop with package inserts. Since it weighed so little, the mini storybook could ride along with an order acknowledgment, an invoice,

EXHIBIT 9–6

A 24-Page Mini Storybook Catalog for Reliable

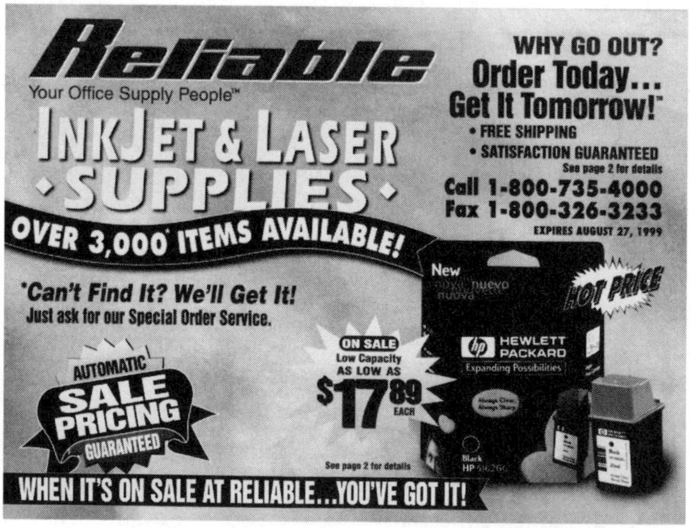

a statement, a dun notice, or other customer correspondence.

WEB Builds on Success

As for WEB Direct Marketing, with the success of Hanover House under its belt, the firm decided, as the saying goes, "We're in business." It went on to develop a business plan that married alternative media with the mini storybook to create a unique marketing approach. Multi-page mini storybooks have been used successfully by both consumer and business-to-business marketers. (See Exhibit 9-6.) Mini storybooks are distributed using alternative media, including:

- Card decks
- Co-op mailings
- Cable billing statements
- Magazine bind-ins
- Package inserts
- First-class billing statements
- Take-ones
  The heaviest users of alternative media are:
- Catalog firms
- Office suppliers
- Credit card companies
- Phone companies
- Mortgage bankers
- Hotels and travel packages
- Health care programs
- Book publishers
- Major service organizations
- Merchandise clubs
- Sales organizations seeking leads, both consumer and business-to-business

With its business plan in hand and a marketing plan to go with it, WEB's major target was card decks. As WEB partner Joe Kallick pointed out, circulation is huge: total circulation of 1,000 card decks is nearing 300 million.

The WEB strategy went beyond being included in a card deck. Instead, WEB told card deck publishers that it wanted to purchase the window position for its mini storybook clients in co-ops to ensure high visibility. WEB was willing to pay a premium for this position. Kallick's position with the card deck publishers was that WEB's attractive four-color mini storybooks induce the recipient to open the deck, and that other participants with one- and two-color cards benefit thereby. The publishers bought into that.

Kallick's enthusiasm for the use of card decks is based in large part on their lists. Deck publishers update with each mailing, ensuring freshness, and utilize mostly direct-response-generated names. Further, they employ four-line addresses, thereby mailing to an individual.

After the success of its standard 16-page, $3\frac{1}{2} \times 5\frac{1}{2}$ inch mini storybook, marketers urged WEB to provide more selling space. Despite weight and size restrictions in some media, WEB was able to develop a $5\frac{1}{4} \times 7$ inch digest-size format containing up to 24 pages that was accepted. This enhanced version has significantly improved response rates, yet can be produced for 15 to 17 cents, including the cost of media, tracking codes, and shipping charges.

Second Target Strategy: Cable Companies

In its Hanover House program, a second major target for WEB was cable companies. Cable companies combined mail 60 million statements a month.

After analyzing the cable market and negotiating with cable system operators, WEB developed more than 600 market selections from a 30 million universe that they could target on a national, regional, or local basis. To further enhance response, WEB overlaid the markets with 29 demographic selections that included age, income, education, housing, and even a special affluence index.

Cable bills are mailed first class to ensure rapid, timely delivery. Clients' offers enjoy quick recognition since only one outside advertiser is allowed in the monthly statement.

Testing Alternative Media

How does a direct marketer match its profile against the total alternative media available? WEB recognized this problem at the outset and included profiling against media as part of its total service operation.

To illustrate the testing procedure for the mini storybooks, WEB was asked to prepare a test budget for a hypothetical marketer of credit cards using four media alternatives: (1) cable billing statements, (2) card packs, (3) package inserts, and (4) first-class billing statements (to publication subscribers, or for utilities, cellular services, etc.). The test budget is shown in Exhibit 9–7.

The recommendations are "turnkey in the mail" costs. They include media research, media recommendations and placement, as well as complete print production, tracking codes, and shipping charges. There are no extras except for creative and film. A two-way perfect split for testing is available.

To zero in on a specific category of the hypothetical credit card company—small-business package insert programs—we asked for insert recommendations. Exhibit 9–8 lists the recommendations.

EXHIBIT 9–7

Test Recommendations for Using a Mini Storybook in Alternative Media

Medium	Circulation	Cost per Thousand	Budget
Cable Billing Statements	1,000,000	$100/M*	$100,000
Card Packs (10 decks)	1,000,000	$90/M	$90,000
Package Inserts (20 programs)	1,000,000	$110/M	$110,000
First Class Billing Statements	1,000,000	$100/M	$100,000

*The per-thousand prices are based on a combined test circulation of 4 million.

PILOT PROJECT   You have become promotion director of *Advertising Age* magazine. Management has decided to develop a co-op postcard program to be mailed four times a year to their 70,000-plus subscribers.

As a prelude to launching, you have been charged with developing a list of products and services that you believe will appeal to the *Ad Age* audience.

Break your product and service categories into two groups: primary and secondary. Expand the list for each to 10, using the first three as starting points.

Primary	Secondary
1. Advertising and marketing books	1. Investment opportunities
2. Premiums	2. Office forms
3. TV production	3. Office equipment
4. _____	4. _____
5. _____	5. _____

EXHIBIT 9-8

Overview for Package Insert Media Recommendations

Program Name	Annual Circulation(000)	Distributed
1. Viking Office Supplies	2,400	Daily
2. NEBS—Small Business Resource PIP	1,200	Daily
3. PaperDirect Catalog PIP	600	Daily
4. Delux Business Checks & Forms PIP	1,200	Daily
5. PC Mall/Mac Mall PIP	720	Daily
6. PC Zone PIP/Mac Zone PIP	600	Daily
7. PC Connection PIP	1,000	Daily
8. Fast Company Premium PIP	400	Daily
9. Safeguard Business Systems PIP	1,300	Daily
10. Reliable Office Supplies PIP	2,200	Daily
11. Newsweek Movers & Shakers PIP	600	Daily
12. Rapidforms PIP	600	Daily
13. Darby Medical & Dental supply PIP	900	Daily

Total Annual Circulation: 13,720,000

*PIP (Package Insert Program)

6. _____   6. _____
7. _____   7. _____
8. _____   8. _____
9. _____   9. _____
10. _____   10. _____

Key Points

▶ Co-op mailings allow marketers to share costs, thus attaining a much lower cost per thousand circulation. But while participation in a co-op costs about one-fourth as much as a solo mailing, response rate from a co-op is also only one-fourth as much.

▶ To ensure readership, use a simple message clearly stated with effective graphics. More alternatives means less response. If the offer appears to be too much trouble, the home shopper goes to the next offer.

▶ Coupons are an excellent way to generate inquiries for a high-priced item or to sell a lower-priced product or service. They work well for offers requiring a minimum of information for a target audience.

▶ To test co-ops, know what your break-even point is and test a sample large enough so your result can be acted on. Test a cross section of the complete co-op list. If no "*n*th" sample is available, request distribution in several different markets—all widely dispersed. Don't let too much time elapse between your test and your continuation.

TELEMARKETING/ TELESERVICES

Telemarketing is as much an advertising medium for direct response advertisers as print, broadcast, E-mail, or direct mail.

In a world that places a premium on anything "interactive," telemarketing has a distinct advantage over most of these media. Because both outbound and inbound telemarketing are live, interactive events, they are well-suited to promoting the interactive business models now emerging on the Internet.

Once thought to work only in conjunction with other media, telemarketing has proven itself a stand-alone method of marketing. The limitations were lifted during the early 1990s, when this medium experienced 20 percent annual growth, leveling off at 6 to 8 percent by the end of the decade. It has become the largest medium within the direct marketing industry (see Exhibit 10–1).

Telemarketing today includes everything from broadcasting an 800 number on an infomercial to placing outbound calls to determine the political preference of a household. As call centers transform themselves to meet the needs of consumers who can communicate through a number of media—even simultaneously—telemarketing is stretching to embrace E-mails and Web chats.

There is a growing movement to change the name *telemarketing* to *teleservices* or *customer relationship management*. The first identifier for the medium was telephone marketing, which pretty well described it. AT&T introduced a new name, telemarketing, which flourished as a sales medium, particularly in the sale of consumer goods. This chapter uses the expanded reference, teleservices.

In the year 2000 the focus of the industry changed to include service. In the past, most phone calls were made for the purpose of taking an order or at least attempting to get an order. Now, companies have realized that a call to develop a relationship with the customer is just as important as the actual sales call. More and more attention is given to customer relationship management. Thus the emergence of the term *teleservices*. As the Internet grows, we might anticipate still another name change: *electronic services*, perhaps.

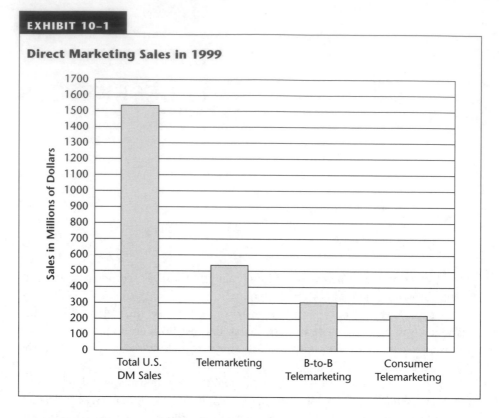

EXHIBIT 10–1

Direct Marketing Sales in 1999

Why do companies continue to telemarket their products or services? The answer is quite simple: because it works!

A Study of Human Perception

In late 1995, Reese Brothers, Inc., a Pittsburgh-based service agency, conducted a research project to determine the consumer's perception of phone calls received. Its survey focused on such questions as:

- What types of calls do consumers receive in their homes?

- Which of these calls do consumers find most satisfactory and least satisfactory?

- Do consumers distinguish between types of calls made, such as those to sell them goods or services or to raise funds?

- How do the behaviors and opinions of people with unlisted numbers compare to people with listed numbers?

This survey was not designed to determine whether consumers would buy over the phone. Rather, it examined attitudes and behavior with respect to different categories of telemarketing. Ultimately the survey responses provided a measure of the relative importance of these categories to one another in respect to satisfaction. The goal was not to develop a "model" that would predict human behavior, but simply to determine whether public attitudes were related to categories of telemarketing or to the industry itself.

Key Findings

A. Are public attitudes related to categories of telemarketing, rather than telemarketing in general?
Yes. The survey clearly indicated that the public does think of different calls in different ways, based upon the source and content of the call.

B. Who calls the most people?
More people (50 percent) have received calls offering long distance services than any other type of call. Calls from a local charity were a close second.

C. Who calls the same people most often?
It is most likely that a repeat call is made from a firm selling household repair items such as windows or siding. For those with unlisted numbers, the most frequent call was for long distance service.

D. What calls does the public like best?
Calls for charities and educational foundations were overwhelmingly preferred as the most satisfying call to receive. A composite of three independent measures of satisfaction showed a 350 percent greater likelihood of being satisfied with a call requesting a donation than with calls selling goods and services.

E. Is the public aware of, and do they use, a "do not call" list?
Of those with listed numbers, 24 percent have asked to be placed on a do not call list; 32 percent of those with unlisted numbers have made the same request at one time or another. Calls regarding investment opportunities and free vacations are most likely to receive a do not call request.

F. After saying no to an initial offer, do consumers welcome future calls from the same merchant or charity?

    1. People with listed numbers are equally likely to find it as acceptable to be called back within 30 days as they are to ask to be put on a do not call list. People with unlisted numbers are half as likely.

    2. People with listed numbers are twice as likely to find call-backs acceptable as to ask to be put on a do not call list.

G. There is little or no difference between people with listed versus unlisted numbers with respect to the following:

    1. Sixty-six percent have answering machines.

    2. Sixty-three percent have used a credit card to make a purchase over the phone at some time.

H. With regard to legislation and charitable telephone fund-raising:

    1. Thirty percent of the responders felt that charitable fund-raisers should be regulated in the same way as all businesses.

    2. Eight percent felt that charitable fund-raisers should be regulated because there is no difference.

I. What type of calls do consumers like to receive?
In order from like to least like:

    1. National and local charities

    2. Magazines

    3. Long distance

    4. Credit card offers

    5. Household items

    6. Household services

    7. Sweepstakes

    8. Free vacations

    9. Investments

There is a natural survey bias to rate calls as "unsatisfactory" because most people do not purchase when given the opportunity to buy over the phone. On any given calling program, about 80 to 95 percent of the people called do not purchase; therefore there is a high predisposition to be dissatisfied. Even if a call were conducted in a satisfactory manner, the outcome itself is not totally positive because the sale was not made.

Overall, very few people who refuse a telephone offer would prefer "never to be called again." They may be receptive to a different product or service in the future. It's worth placing a call to this group of customers again—unless they have asked to be placed on "do not call" lists.

This survey represents original research that supports the idea that the medium is noninvasive for the majority of consumers. It should be noted that this research concentrated on one small segment of the medium, that of outbound consumer calling.

Teleservice Applications

Although technology has caused a number of changes in the teleservices industry, the applications for the medium have remained quite constant. With the Internet come new opportunities, which are still being explored.

Basically there are two disciplines in teleservices: outbound and inbound calling. Outbound is very much proactive while inbound is reactive. Both have applications in the consumer as well as the business-to-business markets. Regardless of the discipline used, the objectives are very similar. The following list demonstrates the basic objectives for using teleservices:

- Sell a product
- Take an order
- Generate leads
- Qualify leads
- Market research
- Up-sell
- Cross-sell

- Political campaigns
- Fund raising
- Subscriptions and renewals
- Account management
- Customer retention
- Customer relationship marketing

This list is not meant to be all-inclusive for teleservices. New applications are being developed on a regular basis. Teleservices was introduced as a way to increase response rates for direct mail; today it survives and thrives on its own, as well as when used with other media. Teleservices continues to be a medium that produces measurable results in a very short period of time, which is what separates it from most other media.

Inbound Teleservices

Inbound teleservices may be the area most profoundly impacted by the Internet. Industry is now gearing up for a world in which customers and businesses communicate through a whole host of media, often simultaneously. In order to serve customers better, companies must seamlessly integrate these contact points. Call centers that once focused on receiving inbound telephone calls are positioning themselves to respond to E-mails, participate in Web chat requests, and respond to "call me" buttons now appearing on E-commerce websites. These "customer contact centers" are investing heavily in technology that facilitates contacts in many media.

Inbound telephone calls are still the medium of choice for many consumers. Calls are usually generated from a catalog, an infomercial, direct mail, or a print ad. Customers like this discipline because they have full control. They decide when to place the call, already have some idea of the product or service offered, and normally do not need to be sold on the product being featured. Ads often use terms such as: "Act now" . . . "Operators are standing by" . . . "You have ten minutes to call" . . . and, of course, "Hurry, before it's too late." All of these phrases convey a sense of urgency because chances are the prospect will not order if the call is not made shortly after reading or viewing the material.

While the customer is on the phone is an excellent time to offer other pieces of equipment. This "add-on" sale is a great way to increase the revenue of the basic sale using low-pressure selling tactics. Most inbound telemarketing centers have the technology to suggest additional products based upon the original order. If a customer is ordering golf clubs, the computer may trigger a question about also ordering golf balls. Another successful add-on technique is to offer a phone special after taking the phoned-in order. This technique, on average, will add one additional sale for every ten people who order by phone.

The consumer who enjoys shopping by catalog expects the convenience of ordering via a toll-free number. Catalogs will normally present their toll-free number on every page as well as on the cover.

Exhibit 10–2 is an example of how AT&T advertises its toll-free number for the purpose of enrolling individuals for long distance service. What better way for a company in telecommunications to advertise! The representatives for AT&T must be prepared to discuss the advantages of their program and attempt to close the sale on the phone.

A very widespread use of inbound teleservices can be found in Exhibit 10–3. Dealer locator programs are very beneficial to the consumer because most of these calls are handled with some type of automatic attendant type service. By entering a zip code on the touchpad of the phone, the computer identifies the pharmacy closest to the caller's location. For the company, this requires updated technology, but little if any personal interface.

Outbound Teleservices

Outbound business-to-business calling is the fastest growing segment of the teleservice industry. One reason for this is the continued increase in the cost of making face-to-face sales calls. Companies seek new methods of contacting prospects and existing customers in a more cost-effective manner. Outbound is completely controllable in that it usually has a set number of people to contact and a calling window that establishes a definite end date. It can be used alone or in combination with other direct marketing media.

Outbound teleservices is also preparing itself for new technological applications. Already, companies are trying to determine how to stay in touch with customers who forgo "land lines" altogether in favor of cellular telephones. Under what terms and conditions may a company contact cellular customers, who often pay for every incoming call and may answer the phone in places where it is simply not possible to conduct a conversation with a telephone sales representative? How will outbound telemarketers be affected by the emerging Voice Over Internet Protocol (VOIP) technology, or by communications appliances that transfer voice, data, and video? The answers will emerge as new technologies are adapted.

EXHIBIT 10–2

AT&T Long Distance Ad

When is

7¢

less than a

nickel?

When it's...

All day. Every day.

INTRODUCING
AT&T
One rate
7¢ plan

With the new AT&T One Rate® 7¢ plan, all your state-to-state calls from home all day, every day, are just 7¢ a minute.* Unlike those nickel rates that can sometimes cost you a quarter. AT&T has made real savings simple once again. To enroll, call 1 800 4 ONE RATE.

CALL NOW **1 800 4 ONE RATE** TO ENROLL

1 800 4 663-7283

www.att.com/7cents

 AT&T

95 monthly fee applies. Available in most areas. © 1999 AT&T

EXHIBIT 10–3

Kmart Dealer Locator Ad

The List Is the Most Important Element

A successful outbound program depends upon four basic elements, all of which must be analyzed prior to the implementation of the program:

- List or target audience

- Offer being communicated

- Telephone sales representative

- Script or message to be communicated

Of these four elements, the list is the most important. Says Rich Simms, Development Manager of DialAmerica: "If a list is well-targeted, a promotion can still be successful even if the product is less than terrific, the script is weak, the TSRs are not top-notch, and fulfillment is inefficient." The reverse is also true: a poorly targeted list can doom a great product, script, TSR force, and fulfillment.

A name is not just a name as it once was. Companies using teleservices want to know as much as possible about the names about to be called—both demographics and psychographics. The best list to call is existing customers, because they have already demonstrated that they will buy the product. Now the only question is whether they will buy over the phone.

Companies can no longer succeed with prospect lists that are not a close match to customer list profiles. Modeling programs have to be developed. The result of this sophisticated approach is less calling and better results. Research is now being implemented to determine if the characteristics of a phone buyer are the same as the direct mail customer. Sounds simple, but the industry is very concerned about calling individuals who have little if any likelihood of purchasing the product being marketed.

Most credit card issuers rely heavily on outbound teleservices for ongoing acquisition programs. The typical list is a preapproved audience. The screening process eliminates those individuals with poor credit ratings. Since "list" is one of the most important criteria in a successful program, it is easy to observe that preapproved prospects increase the chances for success.

The offer is usually a short-term, very low interest rate that includes balance transfers from other credit cards as well as current purchases. After the introductory interest rate expires, the interest rate increases to a competitive rate. The goal of the credit card companies is to get the new customer to transfer balances or even cancel other cards, leaving their card as the customer's card of choice. On this type of program, a teleservice representative is able to contact approximately 14 to 16 decision makers in an hour. In that hour of calling, a normal sales-per-hour rate of .75 to 1.0 would be expected. This response rate far exceeds a similar direct mail program with the same offer.

Using Outbound to Qualify Leads

Companies with a field sales force have discovered a unique application for outbound teleservices: generating sales leads. In any given mail response, some responses are very "hot" leads while others are just looking for information. There is a big difference between a generated and a qualified lead. One phone call by a screener gets rid of the "suspects" and identifies the real.

Most salespeople do not like to "prospect" or spend time on the phone because they feel they are more effective when they can see the body language of their prospects. A leading insurance company supplies its sales force with leads on a weekly basis. Over the past two years, each sales representative has received an average of seven to ten leads per week, which produce far more sales than "cold" calls.

The phone is quick, and a phone representative is able to make more contacts in a given morning than a sales representative can make face-to-face in a week.

But leads can cool quickly if the lead-generation program outpaces the ability of the sales force to turn leads into business. (See Chapter 18 for a discussion of managing lead flow to avoid this problem.) In a study of its inbound 800 customer contact centers, which generated leads for its value-added resellers, Xerox discovered that the life of its leads was a mere three hours! To avoid losing sales, Xerox required its VAR sales representatives to place follow-up calls within three hours and notify Xerox that the contact had occurred. If three hours passed without confirmation from the VAR, Xerox retrieved the lead and had an in-house sales rep place the follow-up call.

Using Outbound Teleservices for Market Research

Market research can be as simple as a follow-up to attending a seminar or as complex as a 20-minute telephone survey. Nissan and Subaru, which pride themselves in customer follow-up, send a survey to all new car buyers with a follow-up call if necessary. They are most interested in learning the customer's perceptions about their dealer, and the manner in which the selling process took place. Their data is collected, analyzed, and a Dealer of the Year is identified. Many automobile dealers will call their service customers one week after a car is serviced. These dealers are looking for information that will result in providing better service to the customer.

Outbound Business-to-Business

Outbound business-to-business teleservice opportunities far exceed those of the consumer market. In the business sector, the telephone is an acceptable way to do business. Very often companies decide to use manual dialing as opposed to predictive or power dialing because businesses will answer the phone, thus eliminating the need for costly equipment.

Some companies will use an existing customer list to call, while others may purchase a list of businesses that match their requirements. In either case, it may be more difficult to reach the decision maker.

Business calling tends to be more account management as opposed to direct sales. The typical outbound call to a consumer is a onetime call that results in a decision to buy or not. In business calling it is more important to develop a rapport with the decision maker and periodically make calls where no sale is attempted. An outbound representative should be able to manage approximately 400 accounts on a monthly basis. It is a more relaxed environment than the consumer-calling unit.

The key to successful customer relationship management is a commitment from the company to continue the program. It should not be done on a short-term test basis, because it will take some time for customers to appreciate regular contacts from the company. A minimum amount of time to test the concept would be one year. In that year, a teleservice representative should be able to contact each account a minimum of four to five times. This will provide the marketing department with ample statistics to make an intelligent business decision. One method of analyzing this activity is to survey your customer base and obtain feedback from them. Perception is reality, and if the customer feels the regular contact is beneficial then it must be considered a positive.

American Hotel Register markets to the hospitality market. Its primary marketing vehicle is a catalog with thousands of products. Initially AHR designed and implemented an inbound order-taking department, which was so successful it was expanded to more than 64 workstations. Although successful, AHR felt it was still missing business opportunities.

AHR acquired a consultant who designed an outbound customer contact program that centered around making "warm and fuzzy" phone calls. The program was designed to introduce the customer contact representative during the first calls and ultimately to feature items on sale. For specific products such as lightbulbs, ironing boards, and in-room safes, the department sold more of these products in a month than had been sold in the past year. Today, the department has expanded and the customer contact program is generating record sales.

Hiring: The Lifeblood of the Call Center

Many companies outsource their teleservices work to customer contact centers. While outsourcing is predicted to rise 20.4 percent by the year 2002, the overall call center growth rate will approximate 6.5 percent. "Outbound activities are particularly attractive to outsource as they tend to be more prone to volume fluctuations than their inbound counterparts," says *Datamonitor*. However, the industry is moving away from outsourcing cold calling on an outbound basis and gravitating to more customer relationship management.

The success of a call center, whether it is a vendor or an in-house operation, depends upon the individual on the phone. Companies are spending large amounts of money in developing "training" programs, but few are doing anything about the selection process. Some just accept the fact that there is high turnover, and plan for it. When selecting a location for a service station or restaurant, the secret is: "location, location, location." In teleservice the secret to longevity of representatives is: "selection, selection, selection."

A phone representative must have three attributes:

1. Verbal communication skills

2. Ability to read a script or call guide with enthusiasm

3. Willingness to overcome objections

While there are a number of other attributes the rep must possess, if these three are present, the training job becomes much easier. Instead of investing major amounts in training programs, the bulk of the human resources (HR) budget should be spent on the selection process. If a better method is found for hiring people who will stay longer, then the investment has been more than worth it.

One suggestion to improve the hiring process is to require two phone interviews prior to having a personal interview. During these two interviews, the HR specialist should be able to determine:

Communication skills of the individual. Can I understand her/him with little if any difficulty?

Ability to read a script. This is done by sending out a script that is to be read during the second interview.

Willingness to follow directions. The HR specialist should ask the candidate to call on a specific day and time.

Each of these steps will go a long way toward determining if a candidate is qualified or can do the job. This process also eliminates the initial "first impression" that a candidate normally makes at an in-person interview.

An additional method for improving selection is by administering a written test to candidates who are given a personal interview. Some companies have developed their own test, which parallels the skill sets they seek. The more objective steps . . . the better the rep. Companies should also take the time to check references in writing. Most will not respond to a telephone interview. However, a great deal of information can be gotten in a conversation.

Once the individual has been hired, the real screening process begins. The trainer is responsible for "washing out" inappropriate new hires who happened to get by the recruiter. The trainer may miss a few, because he or she has been told to fill the seats. So the ultimate responsibility falls on the supervisor. If a company pays attention to the selection process and uses the training and coaching periods to eliminate those who should not remain, then a significant improvement in retention should take place.

Research shows that the skill sets for an outbound caller are not the same as the inbound representative. However, with ever-changing technology, the skill sets necessary to do either job will become more advanced. Outbound calling requires individuals who have little if any concern about hearing people say "no" on the phone. The majority of outbound calls, sometimes as high as 95 percent, will result in a "not interested" response. Rather than take it personally, the representative must be ready to take the next call with as much personality and expression as the first call.

Other ways to combat representative turnover are:

1. Develop a career path that is attainable and one that others have followed.

2. Show the new representative that the company really cares whether he/she is successful through the use of coaching, monitoring, and critiquing.

3. Make the call center a fun place to work by implementing games, contests, and other motivational devices.

4. Move representatives from one program to another in order to eliminate staleness or boredom.

5. Develop competition between different call centers or within calling groups.

Call center representatives do want to succeed. They need constant reinforcement that their performance is vital to the success of the company. Implementation of the above ideas should go a long way to reducing turnover.

Training for New Hires

A job description for a new teleservice representative will be found in Exhibit 10–4, and Exhibit 10–5 contains a diagram of a typical outbound consumer call. The new hire is the most important position within a call center because it is the representative who makes things happen over the phone.

The depth of training programs varies widely. The AT&T program is said to cover a period of 18½ days. This is comprised of 4 days for orientation, 2½ days for network services, 3½ days devoted to selling skills, 2 days devoted to teleservice applications, 3 days for account management (basic), and 3½ days on advanced account management.

Most companies will spend a minimum of 10 days in the training process. Lesser training simply involves observing a veteran on the phone followed by explanation of technique applied. Many companies monitor phone calls routinely, then discuss flaws in approaches.

EXHIBIT 10–4

TSR Job Description

JOB DESCRIPTION: TSR

DATE

Telemarketing Service Representative   Unit Supervisor

JOB TITLE   **REPORTS TO**

BROAD FUNCTION: To make quality presentations and maintain an acceptable OPH/Conversion Rate

KEY DUTIES AND RESPONSIBILITIES:

- Arrive to work at least 15 minutes before calling shift starts
- Work the schedule shift as designated by the facility supervisor to whom you are assigned
- Follow script verbatim
- Maintain OPH/Conversion rate
- Maintain quality presentations
- Code calls properly
- Fill out tally sheet completely
- Fill out sales logs and tapes completely
- Follow tape recording procedures accurately if applicable
- Keep work stations clean at all times
- Be professional and courteous at all times
- Remain seated during calls
- Remain on premises during shift

TECHNICAL SKILLS: Computer Aptitude

SCOPE DATA: None

DIRECT REPORTS: None

JOB RELATED BEHAVIOR:

- Good communication skills
- Enthusiasm
- Above average reading ability
- Courteous

EXHIBIT 10–5

Flowchart of Telephone Sales Process

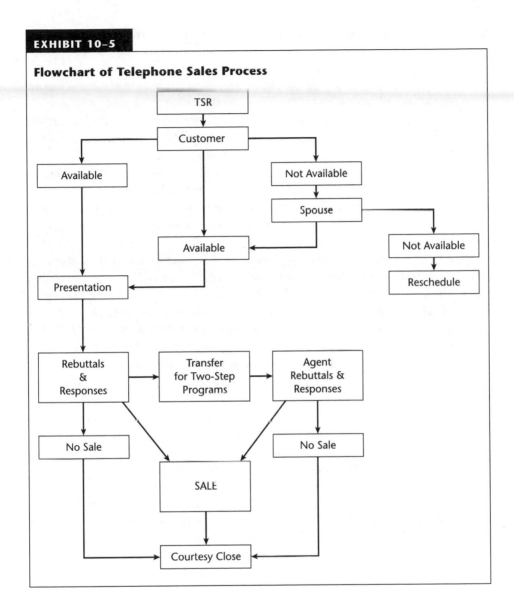

Scripting

Using a script does not suppress the personality of the representative or place the representative in a straitjacket. In the early '90s, verbatim scripting was the only type of script allowed in the call center. Today, unless the outbound calling is being conducted in a regulated industry, a call guide will generally produce results that exceed the verbatim.

Insurance and investment calling requires a verbatim approach because creative material has to be approved both by the client's legal staff as well as the

Commissioner of Insurance's office. In the case of a credit card solicitation, a portion of the verbal authorization must be read verbatim in order to meet the requirements set forth by Truth and Lending regulations.

Call guides are prevalent in the business segment because they are well-suited for consultative selling, which requires the representative to discuss various products as well as past purchases with the customer. A genuine rapport must be developed, and it can only be done through conversation. The goal is to make the call so pleasant that the customer does not look at it as a sales call.

A conversational, flexible approach works well when services such as a credit card are being promoted. When a prospect indicates that he or she has no interest in a credit card, it is important to identify the reason why there is no interest. This is done by asking basic questions such as: "Is that because you are already carrying other credit cards?"

Most of the time, the prospect doesn't want another credit card for that reason. At this time, the representative has to find one feature of the credit card that would change the prospect's mind. This has to be done at the option of the representative as opposed to verbatim scripting. Perhaps the question would be: "Are you currently using cards that have an annual interest higher than 10 percent?" Or: "Do you use your cards when you travel?" Each question is directed to create a conversation that will lead to some indication that the credit card may in fact be a good one for the prospect. If there is a second "not interested," then it is in good taste to terminate the conversation.

Most sales in outbound teleservices are made after the prospect has given an initial response of "not interested." Research indicates that it is the same reaction as when a salesperson in a retail store asks: "May I help you?" The knee-jerk response is: "No thank you, I am just looking." On the phone, most people are really not concentrating on what is being said. If they can get off by replying "I'm not interested," they can avoid getting involved in the conversation. After the first "not interested," the representative has approximately 20 seconds to create interest or the possibility of making a sale is very remote.

One final point: keep in mind that scripts can be modified in one day and the entire presentation can be quickly changed if results aren't successful.

The Mathematics of Telemarketing

The power of telemarketing is beyond question. Its place in the totality of direct marketing is firmly established. But the mathematics of telemarketing is not clearly understood by many. For starters, the telephone is the most expensive advertising medium on a per-thousand basis after face-to-face selling. So telemarketing has to be very cost effective to be successful, and for thousands of marketers it is.

Inbound/Outbound Costs

Two sets of numbers are key to estimating telemarketing costs:

- Cost per call for handling *inbound* calls from business firms and consumers

- Cost per decision-maker contact in making *outbound* calls to business firms and consumers.

Exhibit 10–6 provides the range of costs for each.

The different cost range between inbound and outbound calls should be explained. In the case of inbound calls, the initiator is always a prospect or customer; the caller phones at a time of his or her convenience with a view of getting further information or negotiating an order. In the case of outbound calls, the initiator is always the marketer. The call might be made at an inconvenient time for the prospect, and the caller might have to generate awareness about a new product or service. Consequently, outbound calls are usually of longer duration, and often require more experienced, higher-paid personnel.

The range of costs, whether for inbound or outbound, depends a great deal on the telemarketing application and the complexity involved for each application. Exhibit 10–7 indicates where ranges of costs are most likely to fall, on average, by application.

Developing Work Sheets

Knowing the average range of costs for inbound and outbound calls is key, but it is just a start. The operation of an in-house telemarketing center requires a full range of personnel. Also, it is subject to taxes, fringe benefit costs, incentive costs, equip-

---

EXHIBIT 10–6

Per-Call Costs for Inbound and Outbound Calls

Category	Range of Cost
Inbound	
Business	$2.50–7.00
Consumer	1.50–3.00
Outbound	
Business	$6.00–16.00
Consumer	1.15–4.00

EXHIBIT 10–7

Range of Costs by Application

Application	Low Range	Mid Range	High Range
Order processing	X		
Order increase		X	
Customer service		X	
Sales support		X	
Account management			X
Sales			X
Sales promotion	X		

ment costs, and collateral materials costs. To get a true picture of all monthly costs, work sheets are advised.

Two work sheets are provided (Exhibits 10–8 and 10–9): one for inbound and one for outbound. It is important to note that the term *phone hour* means workstation time, *not* connect time.

It is easy to see how work sheets lead to capturing all the numbers. The key numbers to explore are:

1. Cost per phone hour

2. Cost per call

3. Cost per order (or response)

A review of the computations for Exhibit 10–8 (inbound) shows a significant difference in cost, for example, when phone representatives are able to handle 15 incoming calls per phone hour as contrasted to 12 calls per phone hour. The cost per order drops dramatically if the representative is able to close six orders per phone hour as contrasted to one order per phone hour.

In Exhibit 10–9 (outbound) similar significant differences are to be noted in costs at different levels relating to total dialings per phone hour, total decision-maker contacts per phone hour, and total orders per phone hour. Such computations provide a realistic approach to determine break-even point.

These two work sheets relate to the sale of products or services, but the same type of arithmetic can help predict likely costs for literature requests, product information, customer service calls, sales support, full account management, or sales promotion. The calls handled or made per phone hour might vary by application, but the principles are the same.

EXHIBIT 10–8

Monthly Expense Statement, Inbound: 9:00 A.M. to 5:00 P.M.

Direct Expenses	Cost	Cost/Phone Hour
Labor		
Manager (¹/₃ time)[a]	$ 1,250	$ 1.01
Supervisor (full time)[b]	2,750	2.23
Representatives[c] (10 @ 123.5 hours/month)[d]	16,000	12.96
Administrator (full time)[e]	1,213	0.98
Incentives (reps only)	2,000	1.62
Tax and benefits[f]	7,730	6.25
Subtotal	$ 30,943	$ 25.05
Phone		
Equipment and service[g]	$ 1,146	$ 0.93
WATS line[h]	7,770	6.29
MTS (Message Toll Service) line	—	—
Subtotal	$ 8,919	$ 7.22
Automation		
Depreciation[i]	$ 2,500	$ 2.02
Maintenance[j]	750	0.61
Subtotal	$ 3,250	$ 2.63
Other		
Lists	—	—
Mail/catalogs (F/S & result of requests)	$ 2,470	$ 2.00
Postage	1,235	1.00
Miscellaneous	1,000	.81
Subtotal	$ 4,705	$ 3.81
Total direct expenses	$47,814	$ 38,72
G&A (15%)	7,172	5.81
Total	$ 54,986	$ 44.53

[a] $45,000/year × ¹/₃ allocation = $1,250/month
[b] $33,000/year × full allocation = $2,750/month
[c] $9.23/hour × 40 hours/week × 52 weeks ÷ 12 months = $1,600/month
[d] 6.5 phone hours/day × 19 days/month = 123.5 phone hours/month
[e] ($7.00/hour × 40 hours/week × 52 weeks) ÷ 12 months = $1,213/month
[f] 33.3% of wages (including contest incentives)
[g] $50,000 depreciated over 5 years ÷ $3,750 annual maintenance
[h] Average 40 min. (60%) per labor hour. WATS connect time: 40 min. × $0.15/min. avg.
cost ÷ access charges for 10 lines
[i] $6,000 per work station for 15 stations (additional for growth) depreciated over three years
[j] 10% of total purchase cost

Note: The average number of calls handled per rep. phone hour is 12 @ 3.1 min. each
(as high as 15 per phone hour during peaks).

- 12 calls/hour = $3.71/call
- 15 calls/hour = $2.97/call
- 1 order/rep phone hour = $44.52/order
- 6 orders/rep phone hour = $7.42/order

EXHIBIT 10-9

Monthly Expense Statement, Outbound: 9:00 A.M. to 5:00 P.M.

Direct Expense	Cost	Cost/Phone Hour
Labor		
Manager (1/3 time)[a]	$ 1,500	$ 1.21
Supervisor (full time)[b]	3,000	2.43
Representatives[c] (10 @ 123.5 hours/month)[d]	18,000	14.57
Administrator (2 full time)[e]	2,426	1.96
Commissions[f]	12,529	10.14
Tax and benefits[g]	12,473	10.10
Subtotal	$49,928	$40.41
Phone		
Equipment and service	$ 350	$ 0.28
WATS line[h]	4,991	4.04
MTS (Message Toll Service) line[i]	1,112	.90
Subtotal	$ 6,103	$ 4.94
Automation		
Depreciation[j]	$ 3,542	$ 2.87
Maintenance[k]	1,063	0.86
Subtotal	$ 4,605	$ 3.73
Other		
Lists	$ 3,088	$ 2.50
Mail/catalogs	617	.50
Postage	358	.29
Miscellaneous	1,235	1.00
Subtotal	$ 5,298	$ 4.29
Total expenses	$65,924	$53,39
G&A (15%)	9,890	8.00
Total	$75,824	$61.39

[a] $54,000/year × 1/3 allocation = $1,500/month
[b] $36,000/year × full allocation = $3,000/month
[c] $10.38/hour × 40 hours/week × 52 weeks ÷ 12 months = $1,799/month
[d] 6.5 phone hours/day × 19 days/month = 123.5 phone hours/month
[e] ($7.00/hour × 40 hours/week × 52 weeks) ÷ 12 months = $1,213/month
[f] Reps, 40% of total remuneration; supervisor, 15% of total remuneration
[g] 33.3% of wages
[h] 23 min. per labor hour. WATS connect time: 25 min. × $9.15/min. ÷ access charges for 10 lines
[i] 5 min. per labor hour. Connect time: 5 min. × $0.18/min.
[j] $8,500 per work station for 15 stations (additional for growth) depreciated over three years
[k] 10% of total purchase cost

- 12 (TDs)/hour = $5.12/dial
- 15 (TDs)/hour = $4.09dial
- 5 (DMCs)/hour = $12.28/DMC
- 6 (DMCs)/hour = $10.23/DMC
- 1 order/rep phone hour = $61.39/order
- 2 orders/rep phone hour = $30.67/order

Privacy and Regulation

The high volume of calls to consumers has made many people very sensitive to receiving calls at home. Federal regulators have passed legislation in an effort to "police" the industry, resulting in continued high standards for those wishing to be in business. The Telephone Consumer Protection Act of 1991 and the Federal Trade Commission ruling of 1995 had the most impact on telemarketers during the 1990s. Additional regulation is anticipated.

Because of these two laws, marketers now maintain "do not call" lists of customers who ask not to receive phone calls. The Direct Marketing Association also maintains the Telephone Preference Service, a nationwide list that companies may license in order to purge their lists of "do not calls."

CASE STUDY: **Airborne Freight Corporation**

Adapted from Acxiom Case-in-Point, Vol. 3, Issue 2: March/April 1997

BACKGROUND

Airborne Express is the third largest airfreight carrier. One of its points of difference is the use of mass customized teleservices. This point of difference is important, since Airborne competes with industry leaders Federal Express and United Parcel Service in a commodity market characterized by low-price and volume services. Airborne has carved out a $2.4 billion niche by providing customized service to a smaller base of extremely loyal customers.

CHALLENGE

Develop and implement a mass customization strategy to make each customer feel that he or she is Airborne's most important customer.

SOLUTION

Information technology is a key enabler of this strategy. Employees are empowered to solve customer problems using systems that let them find, use, and update customer information when and where they

need it, on any of the million shipping transactions processed daily.

Airborne's call center automation (CCA) system marries management information systems and computer telephony to deliver more customer data to every customer service representative (CSR). The goal is to enable CSRs to treat every caller like they know them personally.

Information about specific transactions is provided to this relational database from a legacy operational system called FOCUS (Freight On-line Customer System), which provides global tracking and internal Airborne electronic communication facilities. The combination of transaction data, contact history, and customer profiling presented by CCA enables representatives to make service decisions appropriate to the revenue value of each incoming caller.

Customers are served by 1,200 U.S. service representatives in 21 centers driven by a teleservices information technology systems that permits Airborne and its customers to handle the bulk of their transactions electronically.

One-fifth of Airborne's customers are smaller businesses, which also expect top-notch service even though they ship less frequently. Airborne markets to them via direct mail, telemarketing, and independent channels, and services their needs through the same customer service organization that manages large accounts.

To serve both large and small customers with service that sets it apart from its big-name competitors, Airborne relies upon rich customer data resources to segment its service offerings. The goal of the new CCA is to give customers a level of service that makes them feel they are the most important customer the company has ever had, no matter what their size. That requires sophisticated behind-the-scenes profiling to understand the relative importance of each customer to the company's profitability, and to match service handling to customer needs.

For example, computations of call frequency from each account helped the company to determine a call routing strategy that puts callers into a center dedicated to their account or their region. The call-processing server automatically identifies the incoming caller using automatic numbering identification (ANI) and routes the call to the appropriate call center. Accounts requiring special priority—such as a medical laboratory or a major corporate account—are given preferred priority status and special routing, in some cases to a dedicated service team. And wherever the call ends up, the representative is fully informed by a complete transaction history and account profile at the instant the call hits the desk.

Each center is designated to serve certain accounts and regions. A few are also designated as backup centers to which the system sends overflow call volume from other regions. In every call center, the CCA delivers the appropriate subset of up-to-the-minute customer transaction history and profiling information. Airborne's CSRs have instant, on-screen reference to key information about incoming callers, including name, location, customer account number, service contract arrangements, transaction and contact history, and other crucial information needed to service that account.

Each call is also logged into the system, flowing back through as a transaction update to the FOCUS system so that freight stations, delivery drivers, and salespeople have access to it anywhere in the world.

Airborne is a company that partners with its customers to personalize products and services. Its employees are adaptable, flexible, and individually empowered to respond to nearly any situation.

Airborne does no advertising, relying instead upon direct communications with its half-million customers via direct mail, telemarketing, its 300-person direct sales force, and an elite national account team. Airborne listens to customer needs aided by in-depth knowledge from its database.

RESULTS

Airborne's mass customization strategy has helped the company prosper despite heavy price and promotional pressures from its competitors. Since the mid-1980s the company's revenues have grown by 10 percent annually.

Airborne's use of customer profiling, segmentation, and call center information technology is what drives its success. Airborne stands out as an innovator in this arena.

These lists are a boon to legitimate marketers because they prevent wasting time and money on customers who would certainly not respond to an offer. Unfortunately, many local telemarketing operations do not participate in the Telephone Preference Service and continue to call people on the list. And all teleservices companies are alarmed at the rate at which "do not call" lists are growing.

 PILOT PROJECT You are the marketing director of an envelope company. You have a customer base of 100,000 small business firms, all secured by direct mail. You have decided to test the efficiency of telemarketing.

Your assignment is to develop a telemarketing test plan. In developing this plan, please answer the following questions:

1. What data, or measure, will you use to estimate when inventories might be depleted for each customer?

2. What information might you request from each customer in the process of making your calls?

3. What special offers might you make in an effort to get repeat business by phone?

Key Points

▶ Both outbound and inbound telemarketing are live, interactive events well-suited to promoting the interactive business models now emerging on the Internet. Both can be used alone or in combination with other media.

▶ Outbound business-to-business calling is the fastest growing segment of the teleservice industry as companies seek new methods of contacting prospects and existing customers in a more cost-effective manner.

▶ Lead-generation calls let companies prospect by phone and deploy salespeople in following up on "hot" leads. However, care should be given to manage the lead flow, because a good telephone lead-generation program may produce more leads than the sales force can handle in a timely fashion.

▶ A successful outbound program depends upon four basic elements: List or Target Audience, Offer Being Communicated, Telephone Sales Representative, and Script or Message to Be Communicated. Of these four, the list is the most important.

▶ Outbound business-to-business calling involves account management rather than direct sales. These calls seek to develop a rapport with the decision maker and periodically make calls where no sale is attempted.

▶ Investing in the TSR selection process is more effective than investing in training programs. Finding a way to hire people who will stay longer in this high-turnover field more than pays for the investment.

▶ Outbound calls generally use a call guide to develop a genuine rapport and initiate a conversation with a prospect. In regulated industries, verbatim scripts are used because creative material has to be approved both by the client's legal staff as well as government offices.

▶ Two sets of numbers are key to estimating telemarketing costs: cost per call for handling *inbound* calls from business firms and consumers, and cost per decision-maker contact in making *outbound* calls to business firms and consumers. Outbound calls are usually of longer duration, and often require more experienced, higher-paid personnel.

▶ The Telephone Consumer Protection Act of 1991 and the Federal Trade Commission ruling of 1995 require marketers to confine calling to certain hours and to maintain "do not call" lists of customers who ask not to receive phone calls.

INTERNET DIRECT MARKETING

OVERVIEW OF
INTERNET DIRECT
MARKETING

The Internet has revolutionized business on- and off-line. Its long global reach, real-time immediacy, detailed knowledge sharing, and capacity to enable information-based dialogue with users—in short, its potential—has transfixed businesses both large and small.

Yet with less than a decade of experience, we have come to understand the power of the Internet, but not its rules of engagement. The thoughtful use of the tools and techniques of direct marketing appear to be a key driver of success on the Net. Organizations that offer customers convenience, service, selection, solid guarantees, and good customer service—all part of a successful mail order business—have achieved success.

Companies ignored these rules at their peril. Companies that spent no time worrying about their order transaction infrastructure, reliable fulfillment, or building customer relationships, more than likely have already failed. Their corpses litter the dot-com landscape. For many, simply applying the direct marketing disciplines as presented in this book could have changed their direction for the better.

Most, but not all, of the rules of direct marketing are directly applicable to the Internet. Price testing, a strategy common in direct mail and cataloging, is quite difficult on the Internet. Buyers and users get together in chat rooms or community areas created to enhance dialogue among organizations and their customers. Customers, prospects, and users talk and compare experiences in these areas. They can and do compare prices and incentives as well as other marketing practices, something that is rare in the off-line world. The challenge for marketers is to learn from these experiences, then adapt and evolve the tools and techniques of direct marketing to meet the requirements of the Internet.

Internet Applications

Organizations use the Internet as an advertising medium, a sales and marketing channel, even a distribution medium. A theater may sell tickets on-line for pickup later that day. An airline may sell tickets on-line and deliver them electronically, eliminating the need for a paper ticket. It can alert a passenger to a delay or schedule change with wireless technology, a real convenience for frequent fliers.

Websites such as CNET and ZDNET lose money on news gathering activities. Few have been able to make subscription models work. They hope to make it back through advertising and by selling archived content, products, and services. Software companies, resellers, and application service providers can sell and deliver software on-line. Auction sites earn fees on transactions, successfully competing against newspaper classified sections.

E-business applies information and Internet technology to business conducted among buyers, sellers, and other trading partners. It can improve performance, create value, and establish customer relationships. E-business includes three key components:

E-communications, through which organizations deliver messages to prospects and customers, including banners, buttons, E-mail communication, and other forms of on-line advertising

E-commerce, which comprises a variety of on-line commercial enterprises that include selling, logistics, data sharing, etc.

E-care, which includes customer contact, service, and fulfillment, and is quickly becoming one of the most important areas of E-business

In this chapter we will discuss the application of acquisition and relationship building tools and the techniques of direct marketing to E-business.

Fast Growth, Empowered Buyers

The Internet has grown faster than any other medium.

It took radio nearly 38 years to reach 50 million users. Television took 13 years. Cable, whose growth came at a point when television was starting to reach saturation levels in households, took 10 years to grow to 50 million users. The Internet took just five years to reach an estimated 50 million users. While there are more U.S. households today than there were 20, 30, or 50 years ago, this growth is still remarkable.

According to a report by *eMarketer* (eMarketer.com), there were 130.6 million worldwide on-line users at the end of 1999, up 35 million people from the previous year. By 2003, *eMarketer* predicts that the number of active Internet users in the world will reach 350 million, a 267 percent increase from the 95.4 million people who were actively using the Internet at the end of 1998.

Global growth is now outstripping U.S. growth. The number of people on-line in South America will rise from 4.1 million in 1999 to 26.6 million in 2002, a

550 percent increase. But while growth in new Internet users has been phenomenal, particularly in regions like Europe and Asia, Internet users represent only 2.2 percent of the world's 5.9 billion residents.

These millions of users are not the customers of yesterday. Buyers recognize that they don't have to play by the rules anymore. In fact, in this environment they *set* the rules.

"The world is changing from marketers finding customers to one in which customers find marketers," says Michael Zeisser, McKinsey & Company. Customers can quickly search the Web for products that meet their expectations and find products and services they can customize to fit their needs, wants, lifestyles, and how they want to do business. Often buyers, not sellers, set the prices paid. And if a buyer doesn't like a product, a price, or customer service, another "store" is a mere click away. A far cry from the old days, when comparing prices or service meant visiting multiple stores!

Researchers who have tracked the behavior of Internet users have discovered that the number one on-line activity is *not* buying. It's shopping. Empowered buyers use the Web to browse, compare, and learn. They are often impatient, and will click from site to site quickly if they encounter hard-to-load graphics or purchasing procedures that are unwieldy and confusing.

Privacy—A Growing Concern

For many people, the Internet is a source of concern as well as amazement. Users are discovering, to their dismay, that E-mail, chat rooms, and bulletin boards are not completely private communications vehicles. If comments posted on a news group discussing a delicate subject matter may be retrieved years later from a cache Web page, who knows what will happen to personal financial information volunteered to an on-line mortgage company?

Users will trade personal data for on-line convenience and service, but they want to know how a company will keep it from falling into the wrong hands. Prominently posted privacy policies like the one shown in Exhibit 11–1 can help reassure website visitors that their information will be safe. Today's best privacy policies share four traits:

1. *Notice and disclosure.* They explain how information is gathered and how it will be used.

2. *Choice and consent.* They let users decide whether their personal information may be used, or whether they want to receive E-mail solicitations.

3. *Data quality and access.* They explain how data is updated and give users access to make sure captured data is accurate. Some let users update their own information.

4. *Data security.* They explain measures taken to safeguard personal information.

EXHIBIT 11–1

Drkoop.com Privacy Center

All sites need clear privacy policies. Drkoop.com assures its members that the highly personal information they enter will remain private and cannot be accessed without the member's permission.

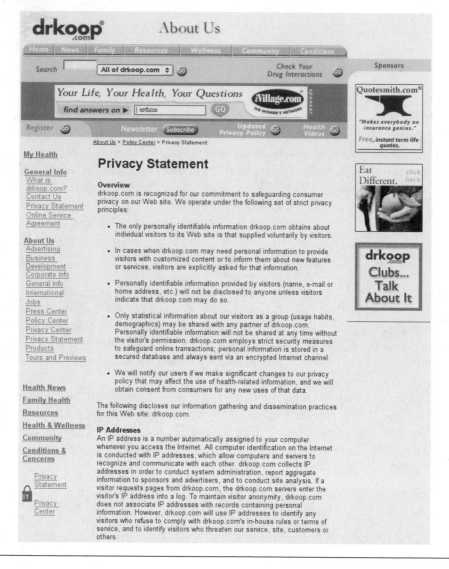

Direct Marketing and the Internet: A Perfect Marriage

A shakeout has already thinned the ranks of E-businesses with highly inflated stock values and great publicity, but no positive cash flow. Among those remaining are companies making a profit, with roots in direct marketing, and that know how to apply its tools and techniques.

Direct marketers have succeeded because they applied the profitable direct business model to the Web. Instead of seeing what would sell on-line and then creating a business model around it, they approached the Web like a test. They determined up front how much to invest, how much sales revenue would be needed, and how much the enterprise would cost. Applying this discipline enabled them to avoid the pitfalls that trapped businesses without direct marketing expertise.

Fulfillment is another reason for their on-line success. Direct marketers know how to pack, pick, and ship 100 to 10,000 boxes a day with shipping partners who are equal to the challenge. Their fulfillment systems are flexible, ready to gear up for the holiday season and scale back for summer—not true for E-tailers or dot-coms whose systems have disintegrated under holiday demand.

Direct marketers also know how to forecast demand and purchase inventory. They know how to judge the results of on-line efforts on some kind of a cost-per-metric basis. But most important, they know how to attract prospects and convert them to customers. They know how to capture and use customer information to fine-tune communications—while respecting a customer's wish for privacy. In contrast, many dot-coms, like traditional marketers, do not effectively use information from their databases.

Converting browsers to buyers requires powerful direct marketing strategies. In this environment, customer-centric strategies are critical. Fortunately, direct marketers have decades of experience fine-tuning strategies that center on the customer.

The Benefits of E-Commerce

Electronic commerce (E-commerce) is the electronic link from businesses to their suppliers, distributors, manufacturers, and customers that facilitates, creates, or supports transactions and interactions.

E-commerce is more than selling on-line. Business activities, enabled by technology, link organizations to their prospects and customers for communication and collaboration. This enhances an organization's ability to gain instant feedback and improve its business processes in real time.

E-commerce also extends to end-users, channel partners, vendors, and other intermediaries. It enables a free exchange of information, services, and interactions among individuals and organizations that are a part of a company's value chain. Because the Internet is not constrained by borders or boundaries, it enables organizations to become part of, or create, a global marketplace for their products and services.

The benefits of the Internet are legion.

Cuts Costs and Saves Time

In *The McKinsey Quarterly*, T. Michael Nevens noted that the Internet's single most significant effect is to cut the cost of interaction—the searching, coordinating, and monitoring that people and companies must do when they exchange goods, services, or ideas. The cost of searching for a mortgage, executing a bank transaction, and obtaining customer support, for example, drops by 80 percent or more when these activities are handled electronically.

Time can be saved in sourcing products. Buyers can be freed to work on tasks with long-term strategic value to the organization. Organizations can see improvements in supply-chain management and procurement.

Other benefits and savings include:

- Reduced overall operating costs

- Lower prices paid

- Optimized supply base

- Greater control over spending and inventory

- More efficient use of personnel through instantaneous communications and outsourcing

- Savings in order handling and processing through reduced transaction costs

- Enhanced marketing and customer service

Nevens observes that in just three years, E-commerce auto site Autobytel had sales equal to the second largest auto dealer in the United States. While the information that consumers gained on the site was important in their purchase decision, the real incentive was the savings—customers were able to purchase at a fixed amount above dealer invoice.

Cars are sold on the Autobytel site at a 6 percent margin (rather than the more common 10 percent) for dealers. The reason is clear. Before the Internet, geography limited customers to a small number of dealers within their sales area. On the Internet, customers can easily and cheaply compare the prices and options offered by any number of dealers.

Autobytel and its on-line rivals are successfully assuming the sales and service role of auto dealerships. Dealers' service and maintenance functions remain largely unchanged, but the dealers' role as a marketing channel is being replaced as their role is transformed into sales fulfillment. Auto manufacturers such as Ford, General Motors, and BMW have plans to compete as well.

Offers Value-Added Products and Services

The Web enables companies to offer value-added products and services. This includes enhancing and delivering old information in new forms or creating new kinds of information delivered when, where, and how customers want it through Internet appliances, portable Web devices, and a host of new gadgets.

Extends a Company's Reach

Because they operate 24 hours a day, seven days a week, without much supervision, E-commerce sites can extend a company's reach beyond working hours and without regard to location.

Using the Internet to connect offices of the same or different companies is easier to set up, maintain, and manage than an Electronic Data Interchange (EDI) system, a private network that connects far-flung computer networks but requires network interface software, applications software, and dedicated phone lines. The resulting cost savings can be enormous.

An intranet system—a private Web network set up within one organization—enables enterprisewide collaboration and coordination. Typically, intranets allow authorized users to gain access from inside as well as outside their offices.

A company may set up a password-protected system for customers, often with a website that has customized pricing and content. This is called an extranet system. While Internet, intranet, and extranet systems run over the same Internet backbone, they are distinguished by how they are used and accessed.

On-line Business Models

On the Internet, businesses are transforming themselves by using inventive new ways to generate revenue, and often contravening long-held beliefs. There are advertising-funded sites that lose money on product sales, but hope to make it back on advertising. Content sites like Wall Street Journal Online implement subscription models with varying degrees of success. Some sites charge transaction fees for bringing buyers and sellers together.

Affiliate programs offer commissions to sites that allow links to direct their customers to the affiliate's website. Amazon.com has thousands of such affiliates, which has contributed greatly to their success. Some on-line marketers create websites for their customers, extending the reach of their own marketing efforts, while earning commissions and profits on each sale.

In more traditional approaches, sellers offer their products to buyers. The growth of the pure Internet businesses, called dot-coms, has been well documented. Traditional "bricks-and-mortar" businesses have become "clicks-and-mortar" businesses by combining traditional and Web-based strategies to implement multichannel E-business strategies. Michael Killen, chairman of Killen and Associates, predicts that more than three-quarters of Global 2000 companies will implement a multichannel E-business strategy by 2005.

There are three multichannel E-business strategies:

1. *Clicks and mortar:* on-line outposts for traditional "bricks-and-mortar" companies like Sears or Schwab, set up to move some or all of their business to the Internet.

2. *Clicks and mail order:* websites set up by companies that understand direct-to-consumer marketing and are familiar with customer service, fulfillment, and other important back-end activities. Lands' End and Hanna Andersson are good examples of this category of E-commerce.

3. *Clicks, bricks, and mail order:* an emerging trend among companies that see the Internet as just another sales channel, this category includes companies that engage in retail, mail order, and on-line activities. Eddie Bauer is a good example. Buy an article on-line or from an Eddie Bauer, and you can return it to the retail store—an option not offered by many clicks-and-mortar enterprises, who would not accept a store return.

Companies that pursue these strategies will grow while reducing the cost of sales, distribution, and service, due to improvements in customer-contact center workload, marketing materials production, inventory management, and order processing.

Clicks and Mail Order: How Direct Marketers Use the Web

A 1999 survey of Direct Marketing Association (DMA) member companies found that 95 percent use the Internet for sales and marketing applications, up from 83 percent in 1998. More than half (52 percent) of the members make use of on-line services, up from 43 percent in 1998; and 51 percent use electronic data interchange (EDI), up from 45 percent in 1998. Thirty-nine percent are using E-commerce technology in marketing their products and services. Two-thirds of the companies surveyed said their websites were targeted at businesses, and 44 percent target consumers. This new model can be called "clicks and mail order." (See Exhibit 11–2.)

DMA members are beginning to go global. More than half (51 percent) of the companies surveyed reported domestic transactions only, with 46 percent indicating both domestic and international customers. About 5 percent of electronic con-

EXHIBIT 11-2

Direct Marketers' Use of the Web

A year 2000 study by the DMA showed that 96 percent of Its members had websites, but only 42 percent accepted orders on-line. Here's how respondents use their sites.

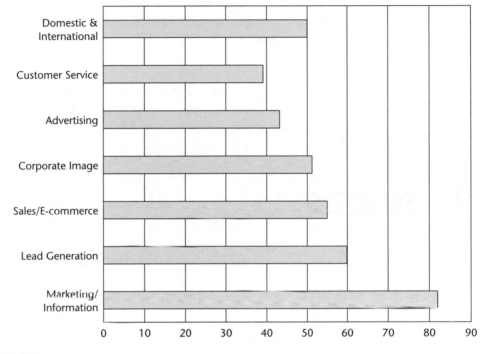

©2000, The DMA

sumer transactions and 10 percent of business-to-business transactions are from international customers. The top international markets cited by the respondents were Canada, the United Kingdom, Europe, and Japan.

One-third of DMA members responded that they advertise on other sites with banner ads. Two-thirds pay for the ads, while the remainder trade or barter banner ads. This is up from 61 percent in 1998 and 47 percent in 1997, reflecting the maturation of banner ads as a medium. Fifteen percent of the direct marketing companies surveyed accept banner ads on their site, and 74 percent are compensated for them.

Forty-three percent of the respondents told the DMA that electronic transactions are conducted at their websites. Most important, nearly half say they are making a profit from on-line transactions. This is in sharp contrast to what is generally believed about E-commerce.

Consumer E-Commerce Growth

Consumer marketing on-line is just in its earliest stage. According to a report from eStats, consumer E-commerce revenue is estimated to grow from $4.5 billion in 1998 to $26 billion in 2002 (see Exhibit 11–3).

Studies show that per session time on-line doubles with a similar increase in modem speed. Broadband communications such as cable modems and DSL promise to bring faster access to major markets, although Internet penetration in rural America will be slower.

In addition to books, toys, music, and brokerage accounts, consumer E-commerce will continue to grow in financial services, insurance, travel, entertainment, and sports. Even groceries are a growing on-line category. It will be some time before Internet E-commerce is a substantial threat to established consumer marketing channels.

EXHIBIT 11–3

E-Commerce Growth

U.S. On-line Shopping Forecasts

Legend:
- Forrester Research
- Jupiter Communications
- International Data Corp.
- Yankee Group

	1998	1999	2000	2001	2002	2003	2004
Forrester	N/A	$20.3	$38.8	$64.2	$101.1	$143.8	$184.5
Jupiter	$7.8	$14.9	$23.1	$34.6	$53.0	$78.0	N/A
IDC	$12.4	$24.2	$35.8	$48.1	$60.6	$75.0	N/A
Yankee	$11.5	$24.2	$36.6	$57.2	$86.6	$86.6	N/A

Sources: Companies listed.

Business-to-Business E-Commerce Growth

The greatest growth in E-commerce is in business-to-business. It is estimated by eStats that business-to-business E-commerce revenue will grow from $15.9 billion in 1998 to $268 billion in 2002. This growth is coming from companies that are migrating their customers to the Web as well as from new business models that appear every day (see Exhibit 11–4).

Customer Migration

Many organizations have created on-line success by employing a customer migration strategy. Instead of seeking new customers on the Web, they sought to move current customers onto the Web by providing another point of contact. By selling on-line to their customer base, they created a new, more efficient way for customers to do business with them.

Cisco Systems, a marketer of routers and computer networking products, was an early adopter of the customer migration strategy. It processes nearly 1,000 on-line orders per day and generates more than $11 million a day, or $4 billion annually, with its E-commerce site—accounting for 60 percent of its 1999 revenues.

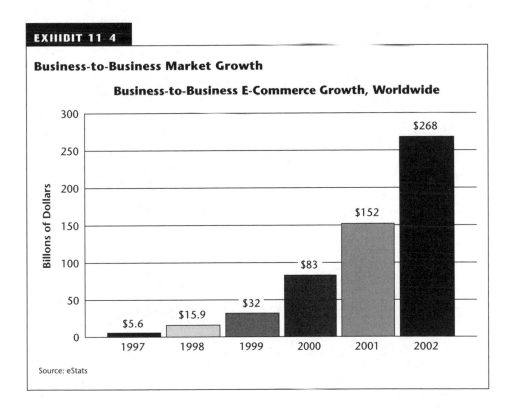

EXHIBIT 11-4

Business-to-Business Market Growth

Business-to-Business E-Commerce Growth, Worldwide

Source: eStats

Cisco was able to reduce customer service reps' time by 40 percent, allowing its reps to focus on relationship building rather than service problems. By enabling customers to configure their own orders, Cisco reduced configuration errors from 20 percent to near zero (see Exhibit 11–5).

Cisco is in one of the most lucrative categories on-line—computer products, one of the top on-line E-commerce categories since the first products were sold on the Internet. Cisco has taken advantage of knowledgeable business customers that were easy to migrate from other channels to the World Wide Web.

Reducing the cost of hiring, training, and retaining telephone customer service agents; reducing errors and speeding up business processes; and allowing customers to do business or ask questions at any hour of day— these are the significant benefits to be gained from a customer migration strategy.

Infomediaries

Business-to-business infomediaries, also called exchanges, bring hundreds or even thousands of buyers and sellers together and enable trade among them. In a typical system, specifications and needs are on the infomediaries' websites. Suppliers scan

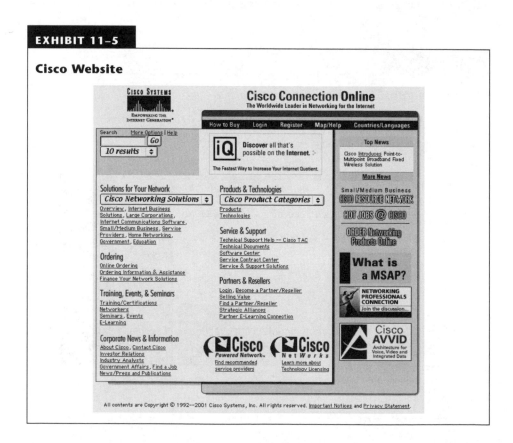

EXHIBIT 11–5

Cisco Website

them and then post bids in reply. Some infomediaries aggregate purchasing requests to achieve volume discounts. This is like outsourcing much of the work to the marketplace, reducing costs even more.

Infomediaries vary as much as the Internet. W.W. Grainger created Grainger.com for industrial supplies. IMXExchange.com was created as a place for mortgage brokers to find loans for their customers. GoFish.com was created to net new buyers for seafood companies. Plasticsnet brings plastics processors and suppliers together (see Exhibit 11–6). TPN Register, a joint venture of General Electric and Thomas Publishing, was originally created for GE, but includes 11,000 members that do $15 billion in purchases annually through the system.

Infomediaries earn a profit on each transaction at their website. According to Forrester Research, trade driven by business-to-businesses infomediaries will grow from $290 million in 1998 to $20 billion by 2002.

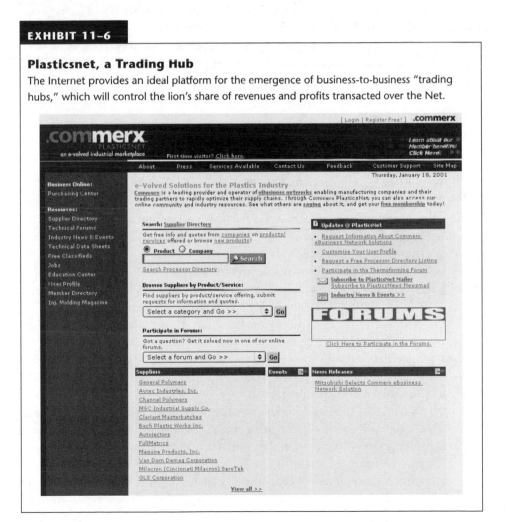

EXHIBIT 11–6

Plasticsnet, a Trading Hub

The Internet provides an ideal platform for the emergence of business-to-business "trading hubs," which will control the lion's share of revenues and profits transacted over the Net.

Procurement

Procurement is an area where the savings from E-commerce can easily be seen. More than 60 percent of office products, janitorial supplies, shipping materials, and other frequently repurchased products are bought without long-term contracts or preferred customer pricing in small-dollar purchases averaging $50 to $100 or less per order.

Traditionally, orders are placed by a purchasing agent who creates a purchase order that is called in or faxed to a sales rep at the vendor company. The sales person inputs the order and sends it to a warehouse, where the order is picked, packed for shipping, and put into an area for deliveries. Many Maintenance, Repair, and Operating supplies (MRO) vendor organizations have their own delivery fleets, and the order will typically be delivered the next day. Labor costs can account for as much as $125 per transaction, while the average order total is often much less.

The same order entered by a user into an E-commerce system will have a comparable labor cost as low as $1.50. Rather than using a freight company, the order will be shipped out via UPS at additional savings. Office Depot is an example of an organization that benefited from this use of E-commerce (see Exhibit 11–7).

E-Communications

The Internet may be the ultimate direct marketing message delivery medium. It can be used to deliver customized, targeted messages to users. Messages can be delivered when prospects or customers have the greatest interest in a brand or product category; for example, when they are in the process of making a purchase decision. Personalized messages on websites can constantly change and adapt to user behavior. Messages can be part of a relationship marketing program, linking ongoing customized campaigns to prospects and customers.

As the Internet has grown, more communications dollars have gone to it. According to the 1999 "eAdvertisingReport" by *eMarketer*, Web-based ad spending in 1997 of $650 million accounted for less than 0.34 percent of total ad spending in America. In 1998, ad spending on-line more than doubled to $1.5 billion, representing 0.74 percent of the total. In 1999, Web ad spending was at $2.61 billion, or 1.2 percent of the U.S. total of $216.6 billion. The "eAdvertising Report" projects that by the year 2002, Web ad spending will reach $8.9 billion and take 3.4 percent of the total media spending.

As an advertising medium, the Internet is still small when compared with television, newspapers, direct mail, and other media. However, it is likely that as on-line ad spending grows, these ad dollars will likely come from traditional media. This trend is under way.

E-communications enables individually addressable media channels that can help to build brands, but in a more customized way than traditional awareness-

EXHIBIT 11–7

OfficeDepot.com

Office Depot has created a synergy between its retail, teleservices, and Web businesses. Large customers take advantage of customized websites.

building media. These highly tailored messages can be inexpensively delivered to individual consumers—to acquire them as new customers, inform them, gain their loyalty. And it does this by getting them to respond in a way that can be measured.

Many traditional marketers use Internet media to build one-to-one relationships with prospects and customers on the Web, targeting their message to individual users based on geography, content, purchasing behaviors, and demographic or firmographic information. While that doesn't necessarily guarantee better communications, it has the potential to make advertising more effective and rewarding for both users and Web marketers.

Internet direct marketing can be used to help build consumer and business-to-business brands like television, radio, print, and out of home. Like direct mail, it can deliver or make available vast amounts of information relevant to prospects and customers. It can be used for traffic building for an on-line retailer or mall. It can be used to enable transactions like a visit to a retail store, the mail response to a catalog, or to contact a stockbroker.

E-Care: On-line Customer Service

E-care is Internet direct marketing used for customer service, helping users to learn order status, get additional instructions, and improve customer satisfaction.

An integral part of E-commerce, E-care brings companies closer to their customers by serving them the way they want to be served. The field has evolved quickly from the days when companies felt that posting a list of Frequently Asked Questions (FAQs) was sufficient to handle customer concerns. Today, the key is to offer real-time communications that give customers instant information about products and services, inventory levels, shipments, and returns.

E-care seeks to make these tasks as simple as possible for customers. To simplify the task of contacting the company, it may offer a variety of communications channels—voice, E-mail, or instant chat. To make it easy for customers to get the information they need, it seeks to develop clear policies, strong guarantees, and easy-to-follow on-line instructions on every step of the ordering and return process. Even some of the best E-commerce companies still can't seem to clearly explain how to return products!

A New Frontier: Wireless Internet Applications

An area poised for growth is wireless Internet, another application of the Internet to E-commerce, E-communications, and E-care.

Airlines are using wireless communications to alert customers of cancellations. Consumers are using wireless for entertainment, travel, and restaurant reservations. Other uses include banking, stock transactions, downloading music, tracking deliveries, and accessing information such as news or weather.

Wireless communications to cell phones, personal digital assistants (PDAs), pagers, and other devices promise a new avenue for precisely targeted and timed marketing messages. Marketers must pay wireless providers to get their content, such as news and sports scores, on the menus of users' cell phones. Advertising is one way to help pay the bill. Ovum (ovum.com), a research and consulting company, predicts "wireless advertising" will explode to $1.2 billion in 2003 and $16 billion in 2005.

Most "wireless advertising" today is in the form of highly targeted, time-sensitive, text-based ad messages. Consumers use wireless to gain information and complete transactions because they need something specific, and they need it now. While opt-in ads can be used to help build brand awareness, it's not clear if the wireless platform can offer much more than support for such efforts.

One of the strengths of wireless is also its greatest drawback: it can reach users anywhere there is service. Using location-finding technologies that are a required feature of future cell phones, a marketer with a database of consumer preferences and wireless E-mail addresses would be able to alert a consumer in the vicinity of its store about relevant product offerings or discounts. The transaction might not be completed on-line, but the message would advance consumers toward a purchase decision.

Not everyone is enthusiastic about this idea. Imagine a chorus of wireless devices beeping in restaurants or theaters with all manner of sales alerts. Imagine living 500 yards from Nordstrom and having a device that beeps constantly. Even the most wired consumer might be turned off! Privacy concerns with proximity tracking may be an issue as well.

Small screen sizes, difficulties in keying in information, slow access speeds, and lack of a single standard limit the market for wireless. Most of the early growth in wireless Internet usage has been outside of the United States, in Europe and Asia, where there is already high cell phone penetration. Cell phone penetration is 50 percent in Sweden and 85 percent in Finland. According Martha L. Stone, an adjunct professor at Northwestern University, the number of Japanese wireless phone subscribers (60 million) has surpassed fixed-line clients (58 million) in Japan. Every day, about 25,000 new Japanese mobile-phone clients, many of whom are teenagers, sign up for the service.

Ironically, one reason the United States lags in wireless is the higher home computer usage. U.S. Internet usage via home computer is 35 percent; in Japan it's only 14 percent. But the main difference is that in Europe and Japan a single cellular standard known as Global System for Mobile Communications (GSM) is in use.

In the United States there are at least four incompatible, competing cellular standards. None allows users to access content on the wired Web. Web content and ads must be adapted for browsers using each standard. This will change in 2002 or 2003 as third generation (3G) wireless protocols, which promise high-speed access and compatibility with Internet phones worldwide, begin deployment. Until then, tests of specific commerce (e.g., travel, financial, etc.) and marketing applications are likely to remain limited.

CASE STUDY: Dell Computer

EXHIBIT 11-8

Dell Direct Response Ad

Dell direct response ads feature current models and popular configurations. Pricing for the featured models as well as upgrades are shown to give prospective buyers an idea of cost. This makes the sales process smoother, as many questions are answered in the ads.

BACKGROUND

Since its founding, Dell Computers has built its success on a unique direct-to-customers strategy. Its products are built to order and sold direct to customers by phone, mail, and the Internet. The integrated company promotion strategy includes brand-building advertising, direct response ads, catalogs, and on-line/Web promotion.

Prospecting is done with multipage, direct response ads promoting the latest models (see Exhibit 11–8). Buyers have the option of calling Dell's toll-free number or going to Dell's website to complete their purchase or gain additional information.

Direct response ads run in computer publications targeted at computer users, buyers, and technology savvy consumers. In addition, Dell places image building ads in business publications, newspapers, and television (see Exhibit 11–9). This multimedia strategy has been adopted globally by Dell to sell products worldwide.

CASE STUDY: **Dell Computer** *(continued)*

EXHIBIT 11-10 *(continued)*

Customers are segmented into key buyer groups: Consumers, Small Business (less than 400 employees), Large Business, Small Office/Home Office, Education (K-12 & higher education), and Government. Computer systems are preconfigured for customers, although they may be customized, depending on customers' preferences. Catalogs are mailed regularly to customers in each buyer segment (see Exhibit 11–10).

Dell has learned that one key to improved profits is getting closer to customers. Selling direct allows many such opportunities. Michael Dell likes to say that the direct business is different combinations of "face-to-face, ear-to-ear, and keyboard-to-keyboard" communications. It's not good enough to partner with customers one-way; Dell tries to take every opportunity to forecast, learn, and respond to customer needs. Dell has learned that it is better to do this before a customer service call, rather than after.

An early adapter to E-commerce, Dell's first website was active in 1996. The site started small,

CASE STUDY: Dell Computer *(continued)*

EXHIBIT 11-9

Dell Awareness-Building Ads

Awareness building is part of Dell's overall Integrated Marketing Communications strategy. Ads are used to build credibility for Dell among prospects who have heard of Dell but may not realize its breadth, size, and commitment in relation to competitors in the computer business.

Everybody doing business directly—
To me that's the power of the Internet.

My name is Michael Dell. I like to think of myself as an innovator who started a company, Dell Computer, around an idea that everybody should be doing business directly with one another—one-to-one, with no barriers.

Today, the Internet is making that even more true, by enabling us all to establish direct relationships with our customers.

That's certainly true here. Once we start a relationship with you, we'll help you determine how best to integrate the Internet into your business.

At Dell, being direct is a philosophy of creating value for our customers. And it's our reason for being.

1-877-430-3355

Visit www.dell.com/innovator to learn more about how our new enterprise products, software, technology consulting and team of professionals can help make the Internet work for your business.

New Dell PowerEdge® 8450 Server

 Dell offers a complete line of Intel-based Systems. Simplify your e-business with robust Dell PowerEdge servers based on the Pentium-III Xeon™ processor, including the Dell PowerEdge® 8450 Server. This monster can accommodate up to eight Pentium III Xeon processors, up to ten 64-bit PCI slots and is expandable to 32GB RAM.

BE DIRECT™
DELL
www.dell.com

offering product information and limited ordering, and giving users an opportunity for feedback. Neither Dell nor its customers were absolutely certain how they wanted to use the Web. Dell used customer knowledge and suggestions to fine-tune its efforts. It made dozens of changes and completed three major updates. Dell's objective was to build a website that offered greater convenience and utility to customers than they could get by calling the company's toll-free number (see Exhibit 11–11).

The website contains more than 5,000 unique microsites, customized for each of Dell's largest customers. These sites, known as Premier pages, are password protected so that only users from the targeted organization can gain access. Once in their microsite, users find preconfigured systems with purchasing options that have been preapproved with the senior buyers in their organization.

Dell's sales reps have noticed a significant change. They have become sales consultants, helping cus-

---

CASE STUDY: Dell Computer *(continued)*

---

tomers develop technology migration strategies, recommending financing options, and understanding their customers' businesses well enough to recommend a variety of technology options.

When Dell introduced its website, its on-line business quickly grew into a $1 million-a-week business. Then it grew to $1 million a day. By 1999 the company sold $14 million in products over the Web each day, 25 percent of Dell's overall business. The firm expects to do 50 percent of its business on-line within a few years.

CHALLENGE

Many of Dell's customers are computer-savvy corporate Web users. Having proven the viability of its direct sales model in the traditional business marketplace, it was logical that Dell could migrate that strategy to the Web. However, Dell has not been as

successful capturing a share of the consumer market. Most of its on-line sales numbers represent orders made by companies that already have a relationship with the manufacturer.

SOLUTION AND RESULTS

To broaden its consumer E-commerce strategy, Dell launched Gigabuys.com. Dell is hoping that this new site will attract consumers to order not only its own PCs, but also a range of peripherals and software. Dell called the new site a "logical extension" of the company's existing on-line sales strategy.

Gigabuys.com offers an estimated 40,000 computer-related products and services with a number of leading brand names. Among the consumer-oriented selection of products available at the site are digital cameras, personal digital assistants, scanners,

---

EXHIBIT 11–10

Dell Catalogs

Dell mails catalogs to customers based on its customer segmentation. This strategy allows Dell to offer the most popular products in each category, and continues to reinforce that it stays close to its customers.

CASE STUDY: **Dell Computer** *(continued)*

and games, as well as businesses-related products such as routers and network interface cards.

Shoppers are able to search for products by category, manufacturer, product model, features, and price. The site also features customer product reviews and alternative product recommendations.

Customized features at Gigabuys.com include Dell.com's "customer kit," which identifies appropriate software and hardware upgrades for Dell systems according to system model. Shoppers on Dell.com can use the same shopping cart for both sites. Dell also announced it would offer customized versions of the superstore content to its corporate customers.

A leader in changing the habits of business market buyers, Dell, with Gigabuys.com, is striving to change the habits of consumers as well.

SOURCES

"Competitors Follow Dell's Lead in Making Computers on Demand," Minneapolis Star Tribune

Michael Dell and Catherine Fredman, Direct from Dell *(Harper Business, 1999)*

Bill Gates, Business at the Speed of Thought *(Warner Books, 1999)*

Newsbytes News Network, March 3, Matt Hines

EXHIBIT 11–11

Dell.com Home Page

Segmentation is carried over into Dell's easy-to-use and -navigate website, reported to generate $30 million a day. The "Ask Dudley" feature allows customers to ask and secure answers to technical questions. Note the prominence of the toll-free phone number.

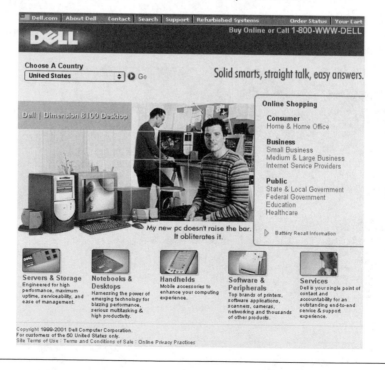

PILOT PROJECT Like other clicks and mail order companies, Dell has used traditional channels and the Internet to build its organization by forging direct links to end customers. This strategy, known as disintermediation, is one way to harness the power of the Internet.

For most companies, total disintermediation will never be possible. Because their reliance on channel partners will likely continue, they will need to evolve into customer-centric organizations with networked sales, marketing, and customer services processes. They will use the Internet to increase the loyalty of their channel partners and their end customers while gaining a deeper understanding of those customers.

1. Based on your knowledge of the growth of E-commerce, do you think that Dell could benefit from a strategy of intermediation (that is, adding channel partners to its direct customer contact)? If you believe the answer is yes, explain what kinds of channel partners Dell might seek. If you believe the answer is no, explain why you believe Dell will continue to be successful with its direct strategy.

2. Creating loyal customers is important no matter what strategy Dell pursues. Identify at least six pieces of customer information that Dell may want to collect from its customers. Should it capture this information from prospects as well as customers who visit its site? Why?

3. Outline the elements of a customer relationship management (CRM) program for Dell's E-commerce customers. Identify the objective, strategy, and tactics of the program. Would you only use Internet Direct Marketing tactics for a CRM program targeted at customers who purchased from the website? Why?

Key Points

▶ Direct marketers are well-positioned for success on the Internet because they already know how to forecast demand and purchase inventory, attract and convert prospects to customers, fulfill orders, and measure on-line results and use information from a database effectively.

▶ As the Internet empowers customers to search, compare, and customize products, and even set prices, marketers must build their businesses around customer-centric strategies.

▶ Today's best privacy policies explain how information is gathered, updated, used, and safeguarded, and lets users decide whether their personal information may be used and whether they want to receive E-mail solicitations.

▶ The three multichannel E-business strategies are "clicks-and-mortar" (on-line outposts for traditional "bricks-and-mortar" companies); "clicks and mail order" (sites set up by companies that understand direct-to-consumer marketing); and "clicks, bricks, and mail order" (companies that include the Internet as one among many sales channels).

- E-communications can build one-to-one relationships with prospects and customers on the Web and target messages to individual users based on geography, content, purchasing behaviors, and demographic or firmographic information.

- E-care—Internet direct marketing used for customer service—brings companies closer to their customers by serving them the way they want to be served. The best companies offer real-time communications in a variety of channels (voice, E-mail, or instant chat) that give customers instant information about products and services, inventory levels, shipments, and returns.

E-COMMUNICATIONS

The Internet may be the ultimate direct marketing message delivery medium. Its low cost of entry, pinpoint targeting, and measurement capability allow highly tailored messages to be inexpensively delivered to individual consumers, often at the moment of purchase decision.

But E-communications is not without controversy. While consumers like the convenience of ordering on-line from a company like Lands' End, they have mixed feelings when Lands' End contacts them by E-mail. As a careful marketer, Lands' End obtains permission from consumers before contacting them—called "opt in"—but many less scrupulous marketers contact consumers at will without ever asking permission.

This chapter examines how to get the most from three E-communications techniques: banner ads, meta- and microsites, and E-mail. Carefully adapted, many have proven to be successful.

Using E-Communications to Build Customer Perceptions

Building perceptions of on-line brands is a challenge. Brands are typically built on awareness, a created desire to be part of a larger group, and emotional decisions. The Internet works with one-to-one, dialogue-enabling activities and rational, considered decisions. That's where the synergy between brand building and direct communications is important.

Wendy Riches is president of D'arcy Direct and a former president of direct marketing and E-commerce at Hasbro, Inc. She is also the former chairman CEO of Ogilvy & Mather Direct, North America. In an article for *The DMA Insider* magazine, Riches said, "Generally the quickest way to build perceptions of the brand among a large audience is through advertising in mass media, supplemented by the strategic use of public relations." She continued, "Direct marketing (including Internet direct marketing) meanwhile is a wonderful vehicle for building trust in a brand . . . [and] for driving repeat purchase, up-selling, cross-selling across brand portfolios, and building loyalty."

Traditional brand advertising builds on a common communications platform and consistent messaging across every point of contact. Direct marketing's role is to reinforce the brand message(s) and to turn positive perceptions into actions. Exhibit 12–1 shows the role of direct marketing and brand advertising in the process of building an on-line brand.

On-line brand marketers have many tools at their disposal. Banner linking and affiliate marketing have helped generate thousands of orders from affiliate sites that link to Amazon.com as their bookseller. Sponsorships play a role in building on-line brands. They don't always generate direct responses. Their value is in enhancing credibility by sponsoring a website, the content area of a portal site, or some category that relates to an organization's target market.

Off-line advertising is also important. It may seem paradoxical that with so much communications flexibility, few businesses have been grown on-line without the help of off-line media. The growth of dot-coms has come, in part, from their use of television, radio, print, billboards, and direct mail to help build awareness of

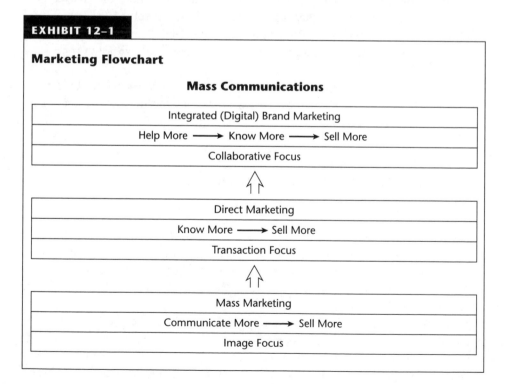

EXHIBIT 12–1

Marketing Flowchart

Mass Communications

| Integrated (Digital) Brand Marketing |
| Help More ⟶ Know More ⟶ Sell More |
| Collaborative Focus |

⇧

| Direct Marketing |
| Know More ⟶ Sell More |
| Transaction Focus |

⇧

| Mass Marketing |
| Communicate More ⟶ Sell More |
| Image Focus |

their brands. Top on-line brands such as AOL, Amazon.com, Yahoo!, and Ameri-Trade owe a large portion of their growth to their off-line advertising campaigns, in part because the Internet has not yet reached critical mass.

Banner Ads

Although the Internet is the only medium in history that wasn't created by advertising, advertising has played a role since 1994, when *Wired* magazine launched HotWired, the first advertising-supported website. Banner ads for AT&T, IBM, and Zima asked readers to respond by clicking on the banner.

This was a bold experiment for HotWired and its first advertisers, and no one was certain how "Netizens" would respond. Prodigy, a commercial on-line service launched in 1990 with advertising support, was the lone example of on-line advertising. The "gated village" charged subscribers to go on-line for Prodigy's proprietary content as well as for E-mail privileges. Other on-line services had not come around to the idea of advertising either. CompuServe was a subscription-only service; even AOL did not consider accepting paid advertising until 1995.

One of the early adopters was Zima, a clear-malt beer brand. Zima wanted to find a way to advertise to its young, college-age target market in a channel that fit the brand's cool image. Zima built a website that incorporated the essence of its brand. To build traffic for the brand, Zima paid HotWired for a banner ad it hoped would drive people to its website. It worked. With the excitement of being among the first to test-drive the next new thing, users came in droves to try it out.

Today banner ads account for two-thirds of on-line ad revenues and are one of the most important tools used in Internet direct marketing. However, click-through rates (CTRs) have been declining as the novelty of banners ads has worn off and the clutter of on-line promotion has increased. As few as one out of every 100 banner ads is clicked on.

Traditional advertisers hoped that banner ads on the Internet could be used as a branding medium to build awareness or create an image for their products and services. They quickly learned that the small size of banner ads was a significant drawback.

There are many different size banner ads (see Exhibit 12–2). The typical ad banner is 468×60 pixels, equaling a total of 28,080 square pixels. (*Pixel* is an abbreviation of "picture element," a single point in a graphic image.) The most commonly accepted default screen size is 640×480 pixels, a total of 307,020 square pixels. This means that a typical Web page is 91 percent editorial and 9 percent advertising. The advertising-to-editorial ratio of consumer magazines is in the 50-50 range. Local television is closer to 60 percent programming and 40 percent advertising.

A number of different kinds of banners have evolved. These include static, animated, and interactive banners.

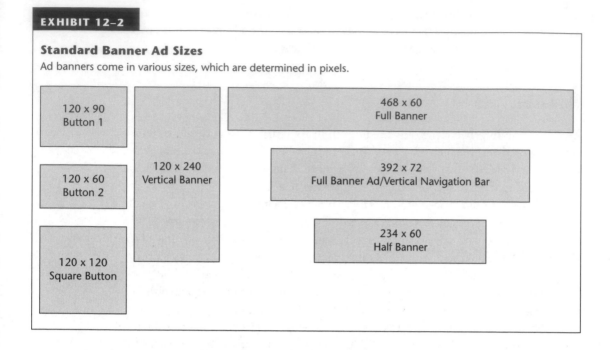

EXHIBIT 12-2

Standard Banner Ad Sizes

Ad banners come in various sizes, which are determined in pixels.

120 x 90
Button 1

120 x 60
Button 2

120 x 120
Square Button

120 x 240
Vertical Banner

468 x 60
Full Banner

392 x 72
Full Banner Ad/Vertical Navigation Bar

234 x 60
Half Banner

Static Banner Ads

Static banners—that is, fixed images on a page—are easy to create and have a small file size. They can easily be downloaded by practically any user, unlike large-file banners, whose significant download times are too slow for computer users whose modems have dial-in speeds of 56 kbs or less. Impatient users may click away from the banner before it fully loads.

The downside to static banner ads is that they look unexciting and generate significantly lower response rates than animated and interactive banners. However, static banners are often created for button- and microbutton-size banner ads (120 × 90 pixels or less), where space is limited and general acceptance by websites is important.

Animated Banners Ads

Animated banners use multiple frames to give the impression of movement, deliver graphic impact, and provide more room for copy to deliver the advertiser's message. They nearly always pull a higher CTR than static banners.

Animated banners usually include at least three frames with copy and graphics. The first frame acts like the teaser copy on an outer envelope—to gain attention and interest. The next frame continues the copy or graphic platform. The last frame pays off on the copy and has a call to action (e.g., "Click here"). Additional frames may be used to create the illusion or deliver a longer message.

All animations use additional bandwidth. While many sites allow continuous looping of the banner, large sites often restrict it (e.g., Yahoo! allows only four seconds of animation). To maximize your efforts, you need to be familiar with the media plan to know where each ad is running.

Most animated banners use small, easy-to-create GIF files, although graphics programs like Flash as well as sound files are sometimes embedded in banners. Additional programs can make them large and unwieldy. Also, not all websites can serve banners with additional programs embedded, nor can all browsers view them. This means that two versions of the banner must be created, adding cost and complexity to the program. However, server software can identify which browser software and plug-in programs a user is running, and then load the compatible version of the ad.

Interactive Banner Ads

Interactive banner ads allow users to fill out forms, answer surveys, play games, or place orders within the banner. This kind of banner has gained acceptance by users, websites that accept ads, and banner advertisers. It allows the user to click and act upon the banner without leaving the website—an ingenious solution to one of the inherent drawbacks of banner ads.

Simple but effective interactive banners can be created in HTML using a drop-down menu or table. These are relatively small files. They do require some additional work by Web servers, but can be easily accessed through slower dial-in connections.

Banners that have a higher level of interactive capability use rich media. These are larger files that require higher bandwidth connections to be activated. However, they can deliver a banner ad that has greater brand building and direct marketing capabilities. For example, using Java script, a games program may be activated with the banner, or an order for a product or service could be executed (see Exhibit 12–3).

EXHIBIT 12–3

Java-Based Game Banner on 3M Site

Java-based ads allow more interaction than traditional banners. This game banner for 3M's enhanced mouse-pad surface gains user attention and ultimately gets customers to click and learn more about the product.

As DSL, cable modems, and other high-bandwidth alternatives grow more common, interactive banner ads will gain greater acceptance. Today they often require users to have additional plug-in programs on their browsers, such as for RealNetworks Inc., Shockwave, Flash, etc. They are accepted by only a handful of ad sites, and require additional technology and programming by banner ad creators and ad servers. This means that such ads might not load while a user is at a website, or may not serve properly. It is a must to create a second ad that can be served to users who aren't able to download the interactive ad banner.

Banner Ad Success Borrows from Direct Response

Banners are more like direct response ads than image and awareness ads. Like other direct response ads, they can be tested to learn which ads pull best and which don't pull at all. Testing has demonstrated that some banner ads work better on certain websites than on others, and that small adjustments in copy, color, or offer can greatly increase CTRs. Because response—and therefore test results—are almost instantaneous, some marketers test as many as 100 ads a month against the control.

Unlike traditional direct marketing ads, banner ads have a high burnout rate. According to Double Click, a banner ad network, users are more likely to click onto a banner ad one of the first times that they see it. Half of on-line users report that they go to the same websites on an ongoing basis and don't really surf the Web. A carefully targeted banner ad campaign may get stale quickly, as users see the same banner ads many times.

Marketers usually create a series of three or more ads that are rotated on a server. Frequent site visitors have a chance of seeing a different ad when they visit. Pushing the reload or refresh button on a browser will cause a different ad to be served. Unlike the long lead times in print advertising (ad materials must be submitted a month or more in advance of publication), banner ads that don't get optimal CTRs or that have worn out can be replaced the same day. This greatly reduces the time for testing; banner campaigns make such tests virtually real time.

Creating Responsive Banner Ads

Creating responsive banner ads, like creating effective television, print, or direct mail ads, follows good direct marketing creative practice. Testing has confirmed that the following guidelines lead to banner ads that get the highest number of clicks:

Keep it simple. Too much text, too many graphics, too many colors, overload users and discourage them from clicking through.

Show people. Banner ads that depict people users can identify with get higher CTRs.

Use clear qualifying language. The better the copy describes what a site is about, the better qualified the person clicking through will be.

Use a strong call to action. The call-to-click should define the main action(s) prospects are expected to take.

Create a sense of urgency. Ask users to click now; no one can click on a banner once it's gone.

Use the words "Click here" on the banner. Simple as this sounds, banner ads with "Click here" consistently pull better than banner ads without.

Use color carefully. Look at the sites where the banner ad will run and choose colors that will complement the campaign objective on those sites.

Use movement. It draws attention to the ad on an otherwise static page.

Think of a banner ad as teaser copy for a website. Create a metapage or a unique "splash page" for transition.

Use high production values. The cleaner and more professional a banner ad looks, the more credibility it conveys, and the higher the CTR will be.

Test, test, test. Test new banner ads, new offers, new calls to action, new approaches, and rich media.

Creating Meta- and Microsites for Response

When used for Internet direct marketing, a banner ad needs to take the user to a meta- or microsite where the call to action can be responded to. A microsite created specifically for response to the banner may look like a home page or other page within the website, and may include a response form or a survey to complete.

Whether a response form seeks a magazine subscription, a lead, or information for a survey, everything possible must be done to get the response. Forgetting on-line concerns about privacy may encourage some to give you incorrect E-mail addresses or phony names. Leaving doubt as to how information will be used or whether there is a privacy policy will reduce response. (Chapter 11 discusses the issue of privacy and the Internet.)

Here's a short list of do's to get the greatest response:

- Ask only for the information that you need to collect

- Explain why you are collecting the information

- Explain how you will use the information

- Promise not to rent or resell the user's E-mail addresses

- Include a link to your privacy policy

- Create a thank-you page

- Confirm receipt of the user's information

Planning Banner Ad Campaign Objectives

Planning banner ad campaigns follows good direct marketing practice. Before developing the campaign, it's imperative to determine its end goal. Quantify the goal by specifying how many sales, leads, members, subscriber, downloads, completed surveys, etc., are expected for the program. How the campaign is executed, measured, targeted, and created will all depend on these factors.

Start with a quantified objective, such as a certain number of CTRs. Banner ad campaigns are often likened to traffic building. One goal of the banner ad is to drive the highest number of qualified CTRs. However, banner campaigns will ultimately be judged on how well they reach a marketer's final goal.

Changes in copy, call to action, animation, interactivity, color, the offer, banner size, and media placement can all impact how many people click through and how qualified they are. Banner ad media weight (i.e., total impressions) will impact the number of CTRs, as will technology issues (e.g., too many hits for the site server or Internet Service Provider to manage).

While many marketers may also have a branding goal as a direct response objective, one of these objectives must take precedence. Most campaigns are judged on a cost-per-action basis. The accountability offered by the Web lends itself perfectly to this objective.

Media Planning and Testing

To target banner ads, seek affinities between the ad's message and a website's audience. Do your best to match site demographics/psychographics with those of your target audience. Geography, content, and brand are also issues to consider when planning a campaign. Geography may seem like a surprising criterion for a medium that spans the globe, but a local restaurant chain, a regional auto dealer, and other companies seeking to promote a particular location will want to select sites with regional appeal.

An organization's Web log files are a good starting point for determining where to test banner ads. Log files maintain records of every "hit" on a website and may be accessed through your own server. Use them to discover the domains and sites where visitors came from and how long they stayed. They show domains and sites where existing traffic is already coming. It makes sense that the best of these would be good sites to place an organization's banner ads.

Choosing sites may not be easy. Start by testing sites that best reach the target audience and offer a lower CPM. After learning which sites perform the best, the test can be expanded to include the winners as well as additional sites from categories that performed well.

If some additional budget is available, testing new or even broader categories may be appropriate. This allows for a continued effort to accomplish quantified goals, while continuing to reveal what works and what doesn't.

Web Ad Networks

Web ad networks offer a number of advantages to marketers. They simplify Web media planning and buying by aggregating small, medium, or large websites. They offer advertisers a way to gain a reasonable amount of unduplicated reach from visitors to many different websites with the convenience of a single media buy.

While aggregation offers a benefit for people too busy to track down and review media kits for hundreds or thousands of small websites, it also has its downside. Although it is possible to specify or exclude certain broad categories of sites, it is difficult to request specific sites. Aggregators will try to place your ad on sites with compatible demographics and regionality, but buys are run-of-network or run-of-category. Most networks do not distribute impressions equally throughout all the websites within their network. Many sell "remnant inventory" from sites that may not have been able to sell their inventory individually.

Ad networks do offer the ability to test categories of sites at a significantly lower cost than testing just one or two sites. This allows advertisers to get their message in front of a lot of individuals, in different environments, with minimal financial exposure.

Upon completion of an ad network test, the results can show which sites or categories of sites performed best against the objective. The planner or buyer can then work with the network and negotiate a new buy that is more targeted, based on the actual test results. Networks also allow a banner ad campaign to be adjusted while the program is still in test. On short notice—even the same day— the schedule can be adjusted to replace banner ads in underperforming websites or categories.

For example, ad network Flycast routinely makes recommendations to optimize a campaign halfway through the term of the schedule. ValueClick, which charges on a cost-per-click basis (a small sum of money for a unique click to an advertiser's site), will continue to improve the efficiency of a buy on its network based on an advertiser's objective and target.

Not all ad networks are the same. DoubleClick and 24/7, two leading Web ad networks, have top websites that may be better choices for banner campaigns whose goals are brand building or awareness. BURST!, a network that aggregates medium and smaller sites, is best used where the greater reach using different categories and channels is a benefit. Ad network L90 has pioneered "Beyond the Banner" advertising for its group of premium websites. These programs link banner ad campaigns to sponsorships, cobranded microsites and jump pages, content integration, rich media, sweepstakes, and other promotional tools. Such programs are likely better where branding matters more than response.

Ad networks play an important role. They allow marketers to increase their reach across many different websites and categories. They have become an essential ingredient in on-line media planning. Their ability to aggregate websites and to test and implement changes means they should be considered in any Internet direct marketing banner ad campaign.

Ad Measurements

As this edition goes to press, there are a variety of on-line measurement standards. On-line advertising expenditures and audiences may be measured by number of ads served (i.e., impressions), number of ads clicked through (banner ads actually clicked on by a user), and dollar volume (a traditional ad spending metric).

Some organizations measure usage at the ad server, while others sign up consumer panels that agree to have their behavior monitored. Jupiter Media Metrix (mediametrix.com), Internet Advertising Bureau (iab.net), and Nielsen NetRatings (netratings.com) all provide slightly different views of demographics, session time, or other metrics.

A website's server also captures valuable information on its log files about every visitor to the site. Information to be harvested from the website's server includes:

- Time and date of each request

- What pages, files, etc. were requested

- The Internet Protocol (IP) address of the requesting computer

- The browser and version used by the visitor (e.g., Netscape 4.7, Explorer 5.0, etc.)

- The computer operating system used by the visitor (PC, Macintosh, etc.)

- The referring URL (e.g., where a visitor has clicked onto a link)

No matter which method of measurement is used, the Internet's real-time immediacy means that results are reported quickly. The response curve to banner ads is so steep that it's possible to gauge the performance of a banner ad an hour or two after it appears.

Using E-Mail in Internet Direct Marketing

E-mail is one of the most effective yet controversial tools in the Internet direct marketing arsenal. Airlines, on-line travel agents, E-commerce sites, and a host of

---

The Benefits of Internet Direct Mail

Internet Direct Mail . . .

- Reaches its target in seconds, not days or weeks.

- Begins to get responses seconds after it is sent. With 90 percent of the responses in just four days later, results can be tabulated and analyzed faster.

- Can reach customers and prospects in 160 countries irrespective of political borders, time zones, currencies, or postal systems.

- Is simple to produce. There's no need to involve designers, Web developers, or Web programmers unless the campaign will incorporate sophisticated graphics.

- Costs less and can be more profitable. Printing and mailing 100,000 pieces can cost $60,000 to $80,000. Internet direct mail costs pennies per prospect—and can yield a profit even with a 1 percent response rate.

- Works as well or better than regular direct mail. Targeted E-mail results in a sale 5 to 15 percent of the time, compared to 0.5 to 2 percent for banner ads. Response rates are higher, not lower, than conventional direct mail.

Source: *Internet Direct Mail: The Complete Guide to Successful E-Mail Marketing Campaigns* by Stevan Roberts, Michelle Feit, and Robert Bly

---

others have successfully implemented E-mail programs that generate significant results.

One of the drivers of this is growth in the number of E-mail boxes. According to a study by Messaging Online, the number of electronic mailboxes jumped 125 million in 1999, for a total of 435 million—a 66 percent growth rate in just a year. Worldwide, there are 200 million E-mail users, very few of whom, the study suggests, have only one mailbox. The typical person has a mailbox at work, one on a Web mail service, or one on an ISP E-mail account. In the United States that's 2.5 mailboxes per user; the 165 million mailboxes outside the United States, the study estimates, are used by approximately 90 million, or 1.8 each. While corporate E-mail accounts dominated for a long time, the study noted that the work/home E-mail split has shifted from 80/20 in the early 1990s to 40/60 in 1999.

E-mail is the natural evolution from direct mail. There are virtually no postage or printing costs, and development time can be lightning fast. E-mail can be the highest ROI form of direct marketing currently available. A complete E-mail campaign (list rental, creative development, fulfillment, etc.) can be conducted for pennies per contact and generate high response rates: CTRs of 10 to 20 percent.

There are two ways to get lists for E-mail programs. You can use rental "opt in" lists of users who have given permission to use their names in this way, or you can create a unique database of visitors to a website. Using a website's own database is the safest and most responsive way to do on-line E-mail programs.

Rented Opt-In Lists

Many firms offer lists that have been compiled from places within the Internet. However, before you use such lists, gain a good understanding of how the names were compiled. Virtually every on-line list claims to be opt-in, but it is easy for companies to use software that sifts the Internet, compiling names without users' knowledge. Mailing such names will create an avalanche of response by users who are offended.

The best protection is to work with a reputable on-line list broker or permission list marketers that use opt-in lists—no bulk Unsolicited Commercial E-mail (UCE), or spam. Companies such as PostMaster Direct, WebPromote, and YesMail all have lists where users have voluntarily signed up ("opted in") to receive commercial E-mail about topics and products that interest them (see Exhibit 12–4).

The precise definition of "opt-in" is unclear. Recent litigation forced YesMail to agree that the only true opt-in is double opt-in, in which a user gives permission and then confirms that permission by responding to an E-mail from the website that says, in effect, "Unless you respond to this E-mail, you are not opted in."

EXHIBIT 12–4

Category Registration at Chooseyourmail.com

This site allows users to register to receive permission E-mails by category or website and to specify how many E-mails a week they would like to receive and for how long.

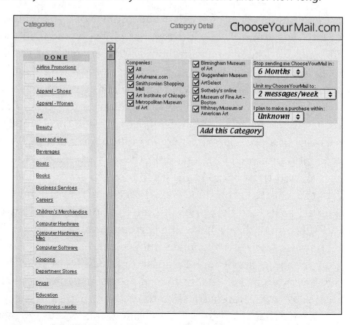

Creating an On-line Database

Creating an on-line database is the best way to ensure that the names mailed have indeed given their permission. Database names will also be the most responsive.

To build an on-line list, clearly inform customers or visitors to a website how you intend to use their submitted E-mail address. Many companies default any E-mail addresses they receive at their site into their outbound marketing lists. It remains imperative to give users a way to turn off this default. Better yet, leave the default off and provide the user a value reason to turn it on when they sign up. The list will be smaller, but better qualified.

If you have already collected E-mail addresses but aren't certain you have gained the user's permission, send users a simple, short statement E-mail of your intentions. Ask them to reply if they wish to not receive ads or to opt out at this point.

Seth Godin, author of *Permission Marketing: Turning Strangers into Friends, and Friends into Customers*, notes that users and customers don't give permission forever. Godin recommends that marketers regularly communicate with the names on their permission databases to renew that permission, and continue to build a long-term relationship.

Avoid Spam at All Costs

The postal direct marketing world operates on the principle of opt-out. *Opt-out* means that marketers can target anyone they wish and the person must contact the mailers to "opt out" of future mailings. Opt-out works in postal marketing because the economics dictate that marketers will target and limit their outbound mail. It is simply unprofitable to mass mail untargeted, low-response names.

However, in E-mail the economics logically dictate the opposite. With virtually no incremental variable cost, mass E-mailing 10,000 costs nearly the same as E-mailing 10 million. Marketers who use maximum outbound, untargeted, opt-out E-mail are known as "spammers" and their messages are called *spam*, a name given to parallel what happens to the luncheon meat when it meets with a fan—it shoots out indiscriminately.

Spamming first surfaced in 1994, when an immigration law firm called Canter & Siegel used E-mail to offer foreign nationals help in acquiring green cards they needed to gain employment in the United States. Canter & Siegel posted its "ad" to more than 7,000 Usenet groups, where users with a specific interest come together to have on-line chats. This action violated a number of rules of "Netiquette." Posting an unrelated message is frowned upon, and most of the discussion groups had nothing to do with the topic of immigration. Posting a commercial message is forbidden. And posting a message to hundreds or thousands of users who have not given their permission is enraging.

Retribution was quick. Canter & Siegel received thousands of angry E-mails (known as "flames") from Netizens. A concerted effort was made to overload the servers of Canter & Siegel's Internet Service Provider (ISP), interrupting service to other users. It was reported that 30,000 E-mails were sent to Canter & Siegel's ISP in less than a day. The ISP's server crashed 15 times under the load. Canter & Siegel's ISP cancelled its account.

Canter & Siegel earned wide press coverage and some business from its post, and boldly promised to continue its efforts. Under similar E-mail pressure from Netizens, Canter & Siegel's Internet access was cancelled by at least two more ISPs. Eventually, the firm found it more profitable to write a book and counsel others on what it had learned about commercial E-mail rather than to continue its own efforts.

Spamming continues—even though the negative public reaction from a spam campaign may irreparably damage a company's reputation and hamper its ability to conduct any future effective marketing on the net. Even though ISPs will terminate the Internet connection of any marketer caught using spam techniques—and some aggressively seek damages from spammers in court. And even though spam is illegal in many states and most likely will become illegal on the federal level soon.

The industry has also worked hard to self-police to prevent spamming. One such effort is the Spam Recycling Center (SRC), which collects, catalogs, and forwards unsolicited commercial E-mail to the Federal Trade Commission and spam-filter developers to help create better antispam software. In its first year of operation, the SRC collected more than 1.75 million unique spams.

The DMA has implemented a number of efforts for its members marketing on-line. It created a Privacy Promise, which its members marketing to consumers on-line must agree to follow. The DMA has put teeth into it, requiring member compliance. DMA Consumer Marketer's Promise:

I certify that my company:

Provides customers with notice of their ability to opt out of information rental, sale, or exchange.

Honors customer opt-out requests not to have their contact information transferred to others for marketing purposes.

Honors consumer requests for in-house-suppress to stop receiving solicitations from our company.

Uses the DMA Preference Service suppression files, which now exist for mail and telephone lists.

In addition, the DMA has created an E-Mail Preference Service (E-MPS), a nationwide opt-out database that E-mail marketers can use—for $100 a year—to purge from E-mail prospect lists people who don't want to receive unsolicited, commercial E-mail.

Only time will tell the efficacy of such programs. However, they are only a start in balancing consumer and marketing issues.

Creating Effective E-Mail Promotions

In general, writing E-mails is similar to writing direct mail, but there are inherent differences between E-mail and traditional communications. For example, an informal or conversational writing style seems to work better than formal writing. Most people scan interactive communications. With formal writing you need to read every word, which slows you down.

Use wide margins without wraps or breaks. Limit line length to 55 to 60 characters per line. This is consistent with good readability.

- Make sure it is clear to readers that their name was selected because it appeared on an opt-in mailing list. You will want to offer users a way to link or respond with the opportunity to renew their opt-in status, or to opt out. This is one of the most important aspects of maintaining good relations with your users. It also consistently improves results.

- Keep in mind that E-mail has a very steep response curve. Whereas in traditional direct marketing customers may respond over a number of weeks, on-line customers respond very quickly—or not at all.

CASE STUDY: Autobytel.com Open Road Banner Ad Campaign

Adapted with permission from (Channel Seven, Inc.'s) Ad/Insight

BACKGROUND

Autobytel.com is one of the most recognized websites on the Internet. It was launched in 1985 to empower consumers to purchase new or preowned vehicles, while offering a range of services from insurance to repairs.

CHALLENGE

Autobytel wanted to integrate its off-line traffic-driving and branding campaign with a coinciding on-line strategy.

SOLUTION

A sweepstakes promotion seemed like a great way to inspire consumers to go on-line, familiarize themselves with Autobytel.com, and build a more extensive customer database in the process. And so the Open Road Sweepstakes Promotion was created. Its objectives were to build Autobytel.com's database for future promotions, to generate qualified leads, and to drive traffic to the Autobytel.com website in a number of ways. The goal was to generate 1.4 million opt-in users.

Target Audience

Besides targeting consumers who were in the market for a vehicle or related services, Autobytel.com wanted to stimulate brand awareness among people who are not currently in a car-buyer mind-set, but who would be in the market in the future.

Campaign Strategy

Autobytel's agency, Webstakes.com, used a proprietary opt-in system called idialog™, which segments prospects as they respond to

CASE STUDY: Autobytel.com Open Road Banner Ad Campaign (continued)

the campaign. Each successive action by a respondent is dependent upon the previous choice of action, or in this case the answer to the previous question. Each time a respondent opted in for a chance to win a particular prize, they were served up another, even more targeted question, like, "Do you plan to buy a car within the next six months?" or, "Would you enter a sweepstakes to win a Mustang through Autobytel.com?"

Media

On-line media included banner ads promoting the Open Road Sweepstakes and an E-mail campaign to opt in names with an automobile purchase affinity. A fully integrated TV and print campaign was also developed to build awareness of Autobytel.com.

According to Autobytel.com's senior vice president of marketing, Anne Benvenuto, the main purpose for the off-line campaign was to position the company as one that puts consumers in control of the auto buying process. The sweepstakes was instrumental in "communicating this revolutionary role of empowerment . . . The key message [was] freedom and control."

Media Buying Strategy and Placements

A cross-promotional campaign for Autobytel.com used approximately 70 percent interactive media and 30 percent traditional media. In addition, the sweepstakes was a sponsorship with Webstakes.com. This added additional media weight at the Webstakes.com website.

On-line. Ads were placed on more than 100 sites, including high-profile portals and search engine home pages (e.g., Excite, AltaVista, etc.). Autobytel.com banners and tile ads were placed within Webstakes.com's Auto section, and Webstakes.com ads appeared on 9,000 sites. E-mail promotions and Autobytel.com's newsletter were sent to the existing customer base and opt-in database.

Off-line Media. TV spots ran on the three primary networks. In order to gain the attention of proactive people who strive for empowerment through access of specified information and news channels, the television media buying strategy focused heavily on cable. "We look at it as if we're using special, selective environments," said Benvenuto.

Microsite. Autobytel.com developed a broadband microsite, enabling total integration of all components. Clicks onto the banners and E-mail were directed to the microsite, rather than Autobytel's main website. The microsite was linked to the main site so users could execute new and used car searches with just a few clicks.

Creative Strategy

On-line banners and tile ads linked to the Open Road Campaign page on Webstakes.com, where a large image displayed a Ford Mustang speeding down the road and a woman relaxing happily with her laptop. The copy read: "Enter to win a Ragtop/Laptop and more." Consumers were asked to: "Enter your E-mail address so we can contact you if you win."

The TV spot, developed by Grey Advertising, contained shots that mirrored the on-line ads: the same woman accessed the Autobytel.com site on her laptop, ordered a Ford Mustang, and drove off into the sunset.

Results

Both Webstakes.com and Autobytel.com said they were pleased with the results. Webstakes.com sources noted it usually sees 30 to 40 percent CTRs since consumers are highly incentivized and targeted through use of the idialog system, and felt the Autobytel.com sweepstakes would be its most successful.

Autobytel.com was also pleased with the numbers, claiming that the company's ownership services rose during the first two weeks of the campaign. In addition, there was an overwhelming response from the existing customer base and opt-in database generated through Autobytel.com's newsletter and other E-mail promotions.

PILOT PROJECT   You're the media planner for a new website targeted at professional women. You've been asked to put together a banner ad campaign that will reach these women and drive traffic into the website.

Your client is a start-up without a marketing department. They have no idea how to budget or even where to look for media opportunities. They'd like to test a number of websites to get a feel for how well their program works.

Please help them by putting together a banner plan that includes your specific website recommendations, cost per thousand impressions, estimated number of impressions, length of campaign, and total budget. Use resources available on the Web to create your plan (e.g., the SRDS Online Interactive Advertising Source).

Key Points

▶ Although static, animated, and interactive banner ads account for two-thirds of on-line ad revenues, click-through rates (CTRs) are declining. As few as one out of every 100 banner ads is clicked on.

▶ Test banner ads to learn which ones pull best and which don't pull at all. Some sites work better than others, and small adjustments in copy, color, or offer can greatly increase CTRs. Test results will be almost instantaneous.

▶ Keep banner ads simple. Show people, use clear qualifying language, create a sense of urgency, and include a strong call to action. Ads with "Click here" consistently pull better than banner ads without.

▶ Establish a goal for a banner ad campaign by specifying how many sales, leads, members, subscribers, downloads, completed surveys, etc., are expected for the program. One goal is to drive the highest number of qualified CTRs. Banner ad media weight (i.e., total impressions) will impact the number of CTRs, as will technology issues (e.g., too many hits for the site server or Internet Service Provider ISP to manage).

▶ Target banner ads by seeking affinities between the ad's message and a website's audience. Match site demographics/psychographics with those of the target audience.

▶ Ad networks allow marketers to increase their reach across many different websites and categories by aggregating websites and quickly testing and implementing changes.

▶ E-mail promotions have virtually no postage or printing costs, and development time can be lightning fast. A complete E-mail campaign (list rental, creative development, fulfillment, etc.) can be conducted for pennies per contact and generate high response rates: CTRs of 10 to 20 percent.

▶ There are two sources of lists for E-mail programs: "opt-in" lists of users who have given permission to use their names in this way, and a website's own database—the safest and most responsive way to do on-line E-mail programs.

E-COMMERCE

There are many kinds of E-commerce sites on the Internet. Rob Jackson, database and E-commerce consultant and coauthor of *Strategic Database Marketing*, notes that not all companies need a fully implemented E-commerce site. There is often a pattern in how different organizations implement on-line strategies (see Exhibit 13–1).

Product-oriented organizations start at the first stage, Brochureware. These firms don't usually invest much of their small marketing budgets on websites. Their site is a one-way communication that focuses on products and services; it may include a few pages about the organization and its mission.

Sales-oriented organizations get to stage two. These organizations may have a small marketing budget relative to sales. Their website focuses on their products and services, with information on how and where a prospect can buy them. Additional pages may have a dealer locator, maps showing retail stores, and maybe special Internet pricing or sales. There is no ability for dialogue, interaction, or completion of an order on-line.

Stage three E-commerce sites are usually created by data-driven companies that recognize the need to use their website to communicate with customers, capture information, and enable on-line purchases. These firms allow for commerce at their sites, but don't link their on-line sites with their off-line systems. Users who register will be recognized whenever they visit the site. Stage three sites may integrate off-line sales and marketing efforts with their on-line activities. They take orders on-line, have a Frequently Asked Questions section (FAQ) to improve service, and allow E-mail communications for product or service queries. Most E-commerce sites fall into this category.

Stage four E-commerce sites are well implemented. On-line and off-line databases may be linked. Users who register can personalize their profile so that on each visit they can get directly to the information they are seeking. Customer dialogues are not only enabled but encouraged. Vast product databases are linked to allow for

E-Marketing Evolution Flowchart

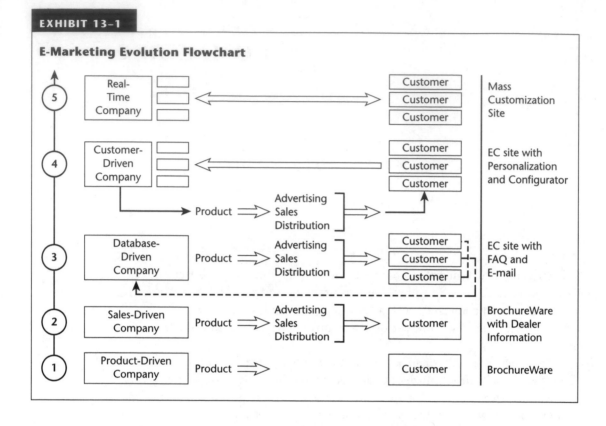

products to be configured to order, such as an automobile manufacturer's website. Outpost.com is an example of a stage four E-commerce site.

Stage five E-commerce sites are fully implemented and cost millions of dollars to create and maintain. They include everything in stage four, but have systems that customize the experience for users. These customer-centric E-commerce websites can help build customer relationships by allowing customers to personalize and individualize their association. They may also recognize an organization's customers who previously purchased from other channels. They offer choices for customer services, such as real-time keyboard chat or on-line voice operators. Such sites actually learn user preferences using collaborative filtering and rule-based software. CDNOW and Amazon.com are examples of E-commerce sites at stage five.

This chapter will assist you in developing a stage three, four, or five site by providing a method for evaluating and redesigning your business practices for the Web.

Channel Conflicts Exist

Channel conflicts can and do exist as the result of implementing an E-commerce strategy. Businesses-to-business marketers often find their Web presence a challenge to their sales force, their distributors, or other channel partners. Channel conflicts exist in consumer categories as well.

Jeans manufacturer Levi Strauss & Co. bowed to pressure and stopped selling direct to consumers when retailers threatened to stop carrying their brands. Home Depot, the leading home improvement products chain, has a policy of not carrying the products of manufacturers that sell direct. A shopping center in St. Louis attempted to ban retailers from promoting their websites within stores in the mall, fearing a loss of business and revenue (most shopping centers earn a percent of sales from stores in addition to rent).

Yet many marketers find that selling across multiple channels is imperative in today's customer-centric marketplace. Some buyers will only buy products through retail channels. Others prefer catalogs. As home computer penetration continues to grow, and more products and services are offered on-line, more consumers are becoming comfortable purchasing this way. What's most important for an organization is to learn how its customers would like to buy from them, and then to meet that need.

Redesigning Customer Business Processes for E-Commerce

How does an organization choose the right on-line business model? To make the most of this or any opportunity, an organization must pinpoint its core strengths. Then it must turn on the creative juices to come up with new revenue streams, utilizing those core strengths.

Most organizations developing E-commerce initiatives have a carefully crafted objectives statement that promises the investment in E-business will improve customer satisfaction, improve customer loyalty, and help them to gain a greater share of market/customers. These are fine objectives for any organization in today's highly competitive marketplace. But this is only a start at developing a successful on-line business model.

To achieve these goals requires translating an organization's business processes into processes that are Web-centric; that is, fast, easy to use, and stripped down. Revenues may come, but profits may not be so forthcoming. To understand these processes, organizations need to look at every aspect from a customer's point of view.

Customers no longer surf endlessly for information. They go on-line for a purpose. They want quick access to information, fast answers to their questions, and a purchase process that is easy and thorough. Many E-commerce sites fall flat in these areas. Some even fail at the ordering stage.

According to a report by Anderson Consulting, at least 80 percent of shopping carts were abandoned during the 1999 holiday season. Reports put this number at 60 percent during other times of the year. One organization waited until the last screen ("Press here to complete the order") before revealing shipping and handling costs. The shopping cart abandonment rate was staggering. By moving the shipping and handling costs to a screen with the complete order, they cut their shopping cart abandonment rate in half.

Many organizations find that they must change their existing thinking to streamline their systems for E-commerce. Before processes can be streamlined, E-commerce teams must learn how things really work within their organization.

To accomplish this, you need to gain an understanding of how interactions are triggered within your organization. Map out your organization's business processes as you believe they work. Identify the gaps in these processes and the work-arounds. Learn about the routine adjustments to the standard processes that ensure that orders are filled, billing problems solved, and delivery expedited.

In many ways an E-business launch resembles a catalog launch. To find ways to apply the tools and techniques of catalog marketing to the Internet, review Chapter 15.

Explore On-line Customer Relationship Management

Start by considering the customer relationship management elements within your organization. Determine if you will be able to link your customer profile data to on-line responses and transactions. Identify actionable pieces of information that can be used to launch applications within your systems to make the process more rewarding for your customers. This will require linking your on-line database with data gathered in sales, customer service, and marketing departments.

Example: AA.com captures profile information on-line and relates it to its AAdvantage Frequent Flier database. Using this profile, AA E-mails special offers based on a customer's home airport, where they like to travel, etc. Customers can purchase electronic tickets or electronic upgrade certificates at the website, which go into AA's general reservations system and can be accessed by a telephone sales rep or an agent at the airport. No matter how the customer chooses to communicate with the company, American Airlines staff can access the records and manage the relationship.

Generate a Set of Business Rules

Every organization has a set of business rules to guide its interactions with customers. Some of these rules of engagement are implicit, while others are explicit. They cover myriad areas. Combined with customer profiles, you can target the right information, offers, products, and pricing to the right customers.

Identify the business rules your company follows. Look at discount policies (If Customer X, then discount prices 15 percent); credit terms (Do not ship until credit card is approved, or, Ship net 30 to D&B rated firms); customer options (Customer requests hold order until complete to reduce shipping costs); and special promotions (Waive freight charges on orders until June 30).

Identify Business Events

Business events are the necessary steps in dealing with customer processes. Common business events include placing an order, checking credit, checking inventory, shipping products, invoicing customers, collecting payment, etc. Each event will trigger interaction among your customers and the software applications within your E-commerce site. You need to ensure that information and tasks flow smoothly from one system to another for each event.

For example, what happens when customers order a product that is out of stock? Do you want customers to see the current inventory status when they go to the site, or will you advise them after they have ordered that it is out of stock? Will you charge customers for out of stock products when they are ordered or when they ship? Will customers get an order confirmation, and will the confirmation tell them when the product will be in stock? Will you contact them and/or offer them an opportunity to cancel the order after x number of days? What do government regulations require, and are you in compliance or better than compliance?

Build a Business Object Dictionary

Every organization has a language unto itself. *Customer*, *account*, *order*, and *product* often mean different things to different organizations. In order to design electronic applications for customers to interact with, technical staff must have agreed-upon descriptions of these words or business objects. For example, a "customer" can be someone who purchased a product or service within a week, a month, or a year . . . inquiries, prospects, or people who have visited a store or website might be customers, or end-users or the purchasing agents who place the orders.

Business objects are elements that have an agreed-upon definition and create a common language within the organization. It would be difficult to design an E-commerce strategy without knowing those definitions up front.

The Buyer/Seller Model

To implement E-commerce, an organization's business processes must be transformed to accommodate E-business. Even direct marketing organizations have found it necessary to rethink their processes to fit this real-time form of marketing.

Walid Mougayar, president of CYBERManagement, developed the Buyer/Seller Model shown in Exhibit 13–2. It identifies the processes that any organization selling products through traditional or electronic channels must consider. It relates the sell-side processes with the customer buying processes, to help close the loop.

The balance of this section follows Mougayar's outline and discusses the seller processes that should be considered as an organization implements an E-commerce strategy.

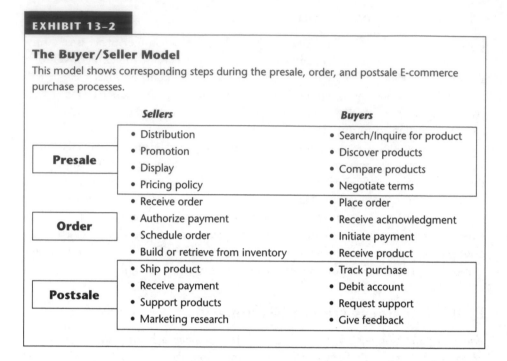

EXHIBIT 13–2

The Buyer/Seller Model

This model shows corresponding steps during the presale, order, and postsale E-commerce purchase processes.

	Sellers	Buyers
Presale	• Distribution • Promotion • Display • Pricing policy	• Search/Inquire for product • Discover products • Compare products • Negotiate terms
Order	• Receive order • Authorize payment • Schedule order • Build or retrieve from inventory	• Place order • Receive acknowledgment • Initiate payment • Receive product
Postsale	• Ship product • Receive payment • Support products • Marketing research	• Track purchase • Debit account • Request support • Give feedback

Distribution

Before you launch an E-commerce site, consider the steps in the purchase decision process that customers in your category go through. Focusing on your customers will yield insights that may help you clarify the kind and amount of content on your website.

If you learn that customers have a void in their information not filled by other marketers, you may wish to fill that void with content on your site. If they gain significant information through word of mouth or from information shared with others in their field, you may consider creating a community area to facilitate dialogue among peers.

If your customers purchase your products through established intermediaries such as distributors, as is common in the B2B marketplace, you may wish to create private intranets for them. These websites can be transparent, so customers purchasing products on the distributors' website will see the distributors' logo, pricing, and order process instead of your company's.

The same thing can be done for an organization's largest customers, if their purchases are great enough. Such personalized websites are common for procurement products—office supplies; Maintenance, Repair, and Operating supplies (MRO)—where the average order is less than $150. Computer products firms like Cisco and Dell have thousands of customer websites.

Another point to consider is the peaks and valleys of your business. Many times, an E-commerce site can help open up new markets to fill in these peaks and valleys, or migrate customers to a more cost- and time-efficient method of buying and selling. Many E-tailers find that a large portion of their business occurs over the annual holiday period. Every system in your E-commerce business must be prepared for the inevitable peaks caused by this shopping period. Businesses without robust, scalable systems may find themselves with dissatisfied customers or no customers at all.

Promotion

Getting users to a website, keeping them there as long as possible, and getting them to come back—these are the goals for most Web marketers.

E-commerce sites use banner ads, E-mail programs, search engines, portals, and a host of other strategies to help customers and prospects discover them on-line. Chapter 12 discusses many of these tactics.

Affiliate programs allow companies to expand their on-line presence by placing links for websites and even individual products on affiliated sites across the Web. Affiliate programs offer credibility and status to fledgling websites and can generate revenue for a website that is not fully enabled for E-commerce. A commission on each sale is paid to the affiliate, so there is little up-front cost for either organization. Commissions vary, but range from 5 to 20 percent of sales. Amazon.com pays 5 percent for a purchase linked to its general website and 15 percent for specific product page links, such as from an affiliated author's website to his or her book page at Amazon.

Word of mouth or viral marketing programs create a "buzz" for a product or service by urging customers or prospects to E-mail friends about an organization or offering incentives for users to talk about the website in chat rooms or other places where potential users lurk. More like public relations than targeted marketing, viral marketing programs are effective, but giving users incentives to share information via E-mail is controversial because it may be perceived as spam.

Promotion has been one of the greatest factors in the growth of Web businesses. Some companies have spent huge sums building their brands both on-line and off-line. On-line marketers will likely continue to use a mix of media in the future. Off-line media will be used to create awareness, build, and promote brands. A mix of on-line and off-line media, applying the tools and techniques of direct marketing, will be used to drive traffic to their websites.

Display

The on-line user interface—the E-commerce website itself—is a key element in the mix. Other chapters describe optimum characteristics for the site, such as frequent updates and design changes, graphics that are fast and easy to load, layout that allows fast click-throughs and similar customer friendly design.

Extensive use of graphics slows the processes of accessing, loading, and ordering from Web pages. On-line users want choices, the option to view even more models than might normally be in stock, so they can compare features, benefits, and prices against those on other sites. Many on-line customers report that their on-line shopping experiences are often unsatisfying. They can't find what they want because of poor layout, they can't purchase the product because the site isn't commerce enabled or the product is out of stock. The process of buying is too long and painful on too many sites. The self-service nature of the Internet means that customers are only willing to spend so much time searching. They are empowered on-line, and know that competitors are only a click away.

Jakob Neilsen, the Web's leading usability expert, believes that basic principles of good design are simple. If pages don't load quickly, customers won't wait. If customers can't find what they want, they won't buy. If pages are confusing or hard to read, customers will look elsewhere. Exhibit 13–3 lists Neilsen's Top Ten Mistakes in Web Design, a list direct marketers should take to heart.

Marketers need to focus more on usability than on design. E-commerce sites need to maintain brand and image consistency with an organization's other marketing efforts. Testing for usability is one way to learn how well customers can move around your website. Such testing is often done in rooms with an observer watching the user's keystrokes. If a user makes two or three keystroke errors while trying to navigate a task on a website, it is considered an error in design, not typing.

Some of the most visited sites on the Web are the plainest. Yahoo!, Netscape, Dell, and Cisco all see millions of dollars in revenue a day pass through their websites. Yet all of their sites are devoid of fancy splash pages, heavy graphics, the need

---

EXHIBIT 13–3

Nielsen's Top Ten Mistakes in Web Design

1. Use of frame
2. Gratuitous use of bleeding edge technology
3. Scrolling text, marquees, and constantly running animations
4. Complex URLs
5. Orphan pages
6. Long scrolling pages
7. Lack of navigation support
8. Nonstandard link colors
9. Outdated information
10. Overly long download times

for new browser plug-ins at each visit, or other techniques that deter usability. There seems to be a lesson there for E-commerce marketers.

Pricing Policy

In the past, a well-conceived pricing strategy was based on a combination of factors that considered cost, competition, and demand. Today, pricing is tempered with the reality that customers have a perceived value for a product, and often refuse to pay more for it. In addition to known name brands, many companies produce private label and generic products that are indistinguishable to consumers. Yet other products are used so often as loss leaders that consumers expect lower prices. This has led to seemingly irrational pricing policies for some organizations.

On the Internet, many E-commerce sites have taken to selling products below cost. They see this as a cost of doing business, to create a critical mass of customers who become loyal, so that over the long run the company becomes profitable. Of course, many such companies may run out of money before they ever see such profits. On the Internet, it is easy to find some company willing to offer a product at a lower cost.

Shopping agents or shopping bots make this easier. These programs search the Internet, scouring websites for the lowest price. There are now almost as many shopping bots as there are E-commerce sites, with names like DealTime, jango, Mysimon, and StoreRunner (see Exhibit 13–4). However, there are no unbiased comparison shopping sites. Many have arrangements with merchants to display those retailers' goods in a search. Some profit from these activities. To learn more about agent technology, go to botspot.com, a website devoted to intelligent agent technology.

Receive the Order

The on-line ordering process requires some type of shopping cart application. Many firms offer such software. The marketer still has a number of decisions to make regarding how to present information to customers. By and large, all the customer wants to do is to complete his or her order as simply and quickly as possible. With nearly 60 percent of shopping carts abandoned, customers may not be finding this part of the experience as they would like it.

To ensure that information all fits on a standard screen, some marketers have broken up their order forms into pieces. Most capture a customer's name, address, phone information, and E-mail address on the first form. A second form captures purchased products in the shopping cart or lists products on a wish list, allowing for deletions or changes. A third form captures credit information. Then all the information is shown with a tally of the order. Some firms only tally shipping and

EXHIBIT 13-4

Botspot.com

This site is devoted to "bots," software agents used to search the Web. Shopping bots that allow price comparisons get much of the attention, but this site offers links to many other types.

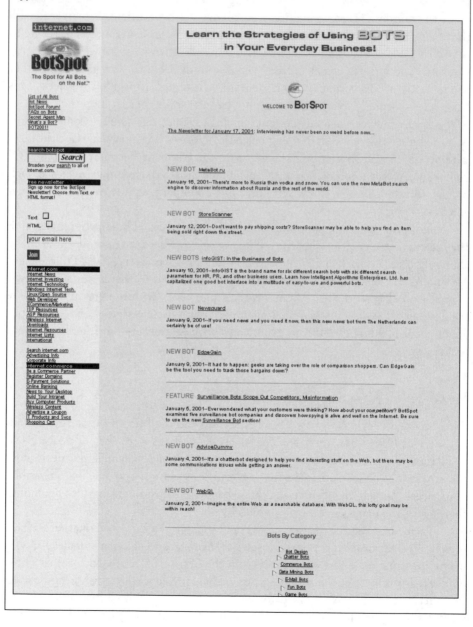

handling costs at the end of a transaction, not when subtotaling product purchases. These and many other reasons may have to do with the order abandonment rates.

Authorize Payment

Many of the largest websites handle ordering and payment authorization in real time. Other sites do this as an off-line process. Sites that have heavy traffic often use an outside firm for credit card clearing. Because these firms manage this process for many websites, they often can save money by offering lower merchant discount rates (the 1 to 4 percent of each transaction paid by the merchants to the credit card firm). This process is usually transparent to the customer.

Once the credit card is cleared, customers can have their order acknowledged. Order acknowledgments are usually sent as E-mail, confirming the order number, products purchased, total debited to their credit card, and a shipping date. Firms that handle credit processing off-line, or that do not have their inventory systems on-line, may take hours or days to acknowledge an order. Best practice in this category is for this acknowledgment to be sent moments after the order is confirmed in the shopping cart. This affords customers a feeling of confidence about the company behind the website.

Schedule Order

Fulfillment of the order is no different for E-commerce companies than for other direct marketing companies. Some organizations handle this process automatically, while others must manually send the completed order to the fulfillment center. Scheduling when the order will be picked is based on inventory and shipping times.

Large firms may have more than one warehouse or fulfillment center, due to geographical or timing considerations, such as when trucks going to different locations leave. This is often a far more complex task than is apparent to the consumer.

In the early days, start-ups such as Amazon.com may have taken orders without having inventory. They only kept best-sellers in stock, and ordered other books from a wholesaler each day. This is no longer true. This version of the "built on demand" meant a delay while Amazon.com waited for a book wholesaler to deliver ordered books to them. A virtual business may seem like a good idea, but it is not sustainable when selling products. Amazon.com has eight warehouses around the United States to get deliveries to its customers quicker.

Build or Retrieve from Inventory

This part of the fulfillment process is key. Building the product specified or picking/packing the right products is no simple feat. Imagine having to coordinate this for 25,000 orders a day! Many products do not lend themselves to totally automated systems. Most firms still have people involved in many stages of the operation.

Computer printouts tell where in the warehouse everything on an order is located, so the order can be assembled efficiently.

Often, picked products are put directly into shipping boxes. Computer software usually dictates the size box based on the products to be shipped. Once all the products are picked and the box is at the end of the line, it's checked one more time, packing materials are put into the box, it is sealed and labeled for shipment, then forwarded to the staging area.

Staging areas, where product ready for shipment is held, are sections of a warehouse or loading platform designated by geography and the method of shipping chosen. For instance, products going to the East Coast by overnight air express may be in a red section, while those going within the state by motor freight or ground transport may be in a green section. Shipments going by U.S. mail may all be assembled in a blue area. Color coding helps workers be more accurate in assembling shipments.

Many firms use fulfillment centers managed by others to complete the fulfillment process. Large shippers such as UPS and FedEx have entered this business. These firms fulfill thousands of orders in their centers. They can achieve greater efficiency than companies not accustomed to customer expectations of real-time fulfillment. They are an option to be considered for both start-ups and growing firms.

Ship Product

There are many choices for shipping products. UPS and FedEx have the lion's share of E-commerce shipping business. Speed and the capability for consumers to track their orders are the chief reasons these organizations are a favorite of E-businesses and consumers alike. However, there are many firms that offer similar services to E-commerce companies. The U.S. Postal Service offers tracking with proof of delivery for Express Mail, and tracking for Priority Mail, but not for standard shipments. The USPS reputation is not one of delivery reliability, which is an issue for consumers.

Companies with customers outside of the United States may also want to consider shippers that can accommodate domestic as well as foreign deliveries. Late order pickup is another need for some businesses. Outpost.com, a computer product seller, promises next day shipping on orders placed before midnight EST on weekdays. It was able to accomplish this through a special arrangement negotiated with its key shipper. However, many buyers have shipper preferences. It is best to offer a variety of shipping options to complement these preferences.

Receive Payment

Offer a variety of options for payment, and line up a reliable partner to verify and clear credit card payments. Take care to institute a system that can detect fraud. Credit card companies are holding E-commerce companies responsible for some of the bad debt created by on-line fraud. Take all steps necessary to avoid being a victim.

Micropayment systems or "electronic wallets" that handle small dollar-amount payments have not gained yet acceptance among consumers but are worth watching.

Support Products

Supporting products is one part of the E-care process, examined next in this chapter.

Market Research

Customer feedback is essential to gaining good customer insight, and the Internet is the perfect channel for companies to learn more about their customers. On-line surveys, targeted E-mail surveys, and questions at websites can help companies gain knowledge about customers as well as prospects.

Some firms rate customer experiences. At the end of an order, a screen comes up asking if the customer is willing to share answers about his or her experience. Such instant feedback is a terrific way to gain real-time insight into customer concerns. Firms such as Nielsen/NetRatings can provide the timely, actionable Internet audience information and analysis required for strategic decision-making.

Feedback from customers and prospects can help an organization gain a greater share of customers, as well as learn about issues they might not have known existed. It enables an E-business to quickly recognize and adapt to changing conditions and develop on-line business strategies based on deep customer insights. Even fledgling E-commerce firms can afford this kind of feedback. The truth is, companies can't afford not to.

E-Care: The Care and Feeding of On-line Customers

On the Internet, customers, not content, are king. Effective E-commerce sites are created with the idea of improving the customer relationship.

Repurposed content from catalogs, brochures, or annual reports seldom communicates information in a way that on-line customers are looking for. Customers don't care that a company's retail, catalog, and E-commerce may be separate divisions, they want an integrated customer experience. Anything that becomes a barrier to finding products and information—heavy graphics, poor site layout, incomplete content, etc.—is disabling to customers. Because the Internet is so collaborative, creating confidence and trust is a must with customers.

All of these functions are part of E-care, one of the fastest growing costs to E-commerce companies, and an area that has changed tremendously since the debut of the Internet.

In the early days of E-commerce, the focus was on enabling transactions. E-commerce sites often looked like electronic catalogs, with grand designs, large product pictures, and short product descriptions. Customer service consisted of a Frequently Asked Questions section. Usually buried in the FAQ was the telephone number for the customer service department, along with a notice that its hours were 9 A.M. to 5 P.M., weekdays.

The next step in customer service was for companies to develop large knowledge bases that could be accessed on-line by customers. IBM and Microsoft have many such knowledge bases for their products and services. Dell added a knowledge base, Ask Dudley, created by Ask Jeeves (askjeeves.com), which builds highly interactive automated-search and natural-language questions with answers created by people, not agent technology. This provides a unique knowledge base that can be queried by customers asking questions (see Exhibit 13–5).

During the 1999 holiday season, it became obvious that customers were fed up with the apparent lack of concern that E-commerce sites had regarding customer service. Many firms began to offer customer service via real-time chat. The firms learned that one customer service agent could help six or more customers at once

---

EXHIBIT 13-5

Ask Dudley Knowledge Base
Ask Dudley is a natural-language search tool that offers Dell's on-line customers the ability to ask questions in plain English.

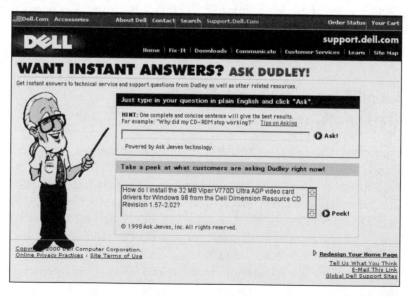

due to the lag in typing. Firms like Lands' End went a step further, offering live operator voice support while a user was on-line.

Internet consultant Kelly Mooney, of Resource Marketing, Inc., has created a best practice shopping audit of what makes customers click. Here is Mooney's E-care checklist:

Customer Service
Prebuying help: Assist customers with live operators if necessary
Postbuying acknowledgment: Most customers wait for an E-mail
Guarantee: Customer expects this in all forms of direct marketing
Privacy disclosure: Nothing is more important in building trust

Personalization
Customized pages: From home pages to the whole experience
Wish lists: Customers see this as a value-added service
One click ordering: Speeds up the ordering experience
Shipping and handling information stored: Convenience is key

Gift Giving
Offer ideas and save dates: This becomes a value-added benefit
Gift-wrapping alternatives: Choice is key for customers
Personalized gift cards: Personalization technology simplifies this

Browsing and Buying
Navigation: Customers want things to be two or three clicks away
Visual merchandising: Balance access with design
Product availability: Customers want to know before they order

Promotions
Purchase incentives: Rebates and points programs are all the rage
Contest/sweeps: As popular on-line as off-line
Loyalty programs: Most customers want to come back, honest!

Community
Access to unique brand content: Community is more than chat
Games/interactivity: Customers look for involvement
Sneak previews: Customers want something they can't get elsewhere

Delivery of a variety of E-care services is essential for customer conversion and retention. One of the things the Internet does well is connect people with information. Organizations that can offer a combination of automated technology and human intelligence have the best chance for success in the future. E-commerce companies that fail to provide a more personal, relevant E-care experience for their online customers risk losing those customers to companies that do. Companies that offer customers requesting support a variety of E-care services will see the investments in these services translated into a combination of higher conversion rates, lower support costs, valuable customer intelligence, and increased customer loyalty.

CASE STUDY: Barnes & Noble

Adapted from Wired *magazine, 7.06, Barnes & Noble's Epiphany*

BACKGROUND

Len Riggio built Barnes & Noble from a single 100-year-old bookstore in New York City to a powerful chain of book superstores by pursuing a signature marketing strategy: lure customers with deeply discounted best-sellers, then get them to buy lots of full-price titles.

Riggio believed independent bookstores were too small to be efficient. When customers couldn't find the books they wanted, they would wait weeks for special orders. Assembling a warehouse full of books would solve the problem, but readers didn't want to shop in a warehouse. They wanted to feel edified by their shopping experience.

Barnes & Noble added sofas and coffee bars in their stores, creating an image that is one part books and two parts social scene. This strategy attracted traditional readers and a new market: the 53 percent of Americans who purchase books in supermarkets, mail order clubs, or discount chains like Wal-Mart.

The rapid expansion of Barnes & Noble superstores, their product breadth and discount policy, squeezed out many independents. Barnes & Noble grew to 1,000-plus outlets. But the 1995 launch of Amazon.com cast a pall on Barnes & Noble's future.

Amazon.com seemed to go against everything that worked for Barnes & Noble. Consumers wanted to shop at "destinations"—large, comfortable places that felt like public squares. E-commerce, by contrast, was about the absence of destinations. There were no books to flip through, no shelf-side serendipities, no cute girls or guys to meet, no cappuccinos! Worst of all, Barnes & Noble's time-tested retail expertise is worth roughly $4 billion to investors, while still-unprofitable Amazon quickly became valued by the market at close to $20 billion.

CHALLENGE

In early 1996, a year after Amazon was actually ringing up sales, Len Riggio's brother Steve recommended that they look into the Web. They confronted a dilemma: selling books on-line could cannibalize the company's off-line business. Stores were located in prime real estate. They depended on high volume to turn a profit. But it seemed better to cannibalize themselves than to be cannibalized.

And so Barnes & Noble gathered a group of young, tech-oriented employees to create an E-commerce site, barnesandnoble.com, to apply its retail book-selling expertise to the Internet. Confident that once they were on-line, Barnes & Noble would crush Amazon, the team devoted a year to preparing the site launch. Barnes & Noble certainly seemed to have two advantages: an excellent distribution system, and deep pockets that would permit Barnes & Noble to outlast and outdiscount Amazon.

RESULTS

While Barnes & Noble was planning, Amazon.com was selling books. Jeff Bezos, the founder of Seattle-based Amazon.com, was doing electronically what Barnes & Noble had done in superstores: making a vast and potentially alienating landscape feel comfortable. Amazon scanned book covers and posted them on the site and encouraged customers to post their own reviews, creating the feel of a vibrant fellowship of readers. See Exhibits 13–6 and 13–7 to compare the page for the same book on barnesandnoble.com and Amazon.com.

A year later barnesandnoble.com debuted on American Online as AOL's exclusive book retailer. But the site's design was woefully lacking. Unlike Amazon, it provided no way for readers to post reviews, click-through paths were sloppy, and the team had doubts that the company was prepared to handle customer service issues. Within two years of launch, the site was completely redesigned to incorporate a number of technological advances. The look was clean, click-through paths were efficient, and soon there was accommodation for readers' reviews. But the redesigned site failed to differentiate itself from its primary competitor (see Exhibits 13–8 and 13–9).

CASE STUDY: **Barnes & Noble** *(continued)*

EXHIBIT 13-6

Barnesandnoble.com Product Page

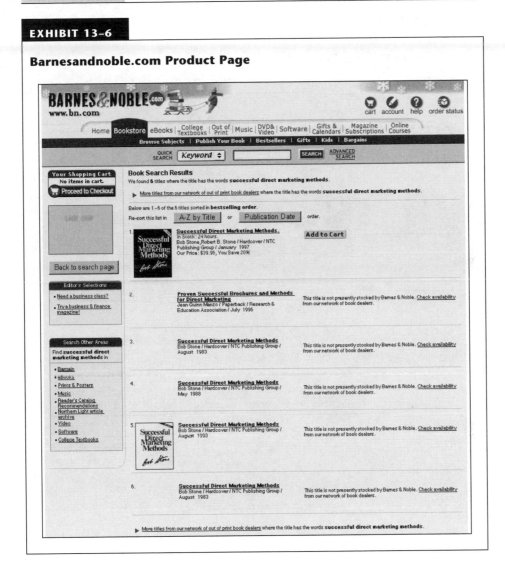

There was another issue. Amazon was deeply discounting its books, eschewing profits for "eyeballs" in order to build its brand—the very same strategy Barnes & Noble had implemented in building its superstores. Barnesandnoble.com needed to match those discounts. It thought about using the retail network to drive customers to the site. Most states' laws would conclude that this created "nexus," and would require customers to pay sales tax, even for books ordered on-line. Amazon's customers paid sales tax only in Washington and Nevada, where the company's headquarters and warehouses were located.

Steve Riggio faced a choice: use the superstores' marketing muscle and charge sales tax, but discount

CASE STUDY: **Barnes & Noble** *(continued)*

EXHIBIT 13-7

Amazon.com Product Page

Amazon.com product page showing search results for "successful direct marketing methods."

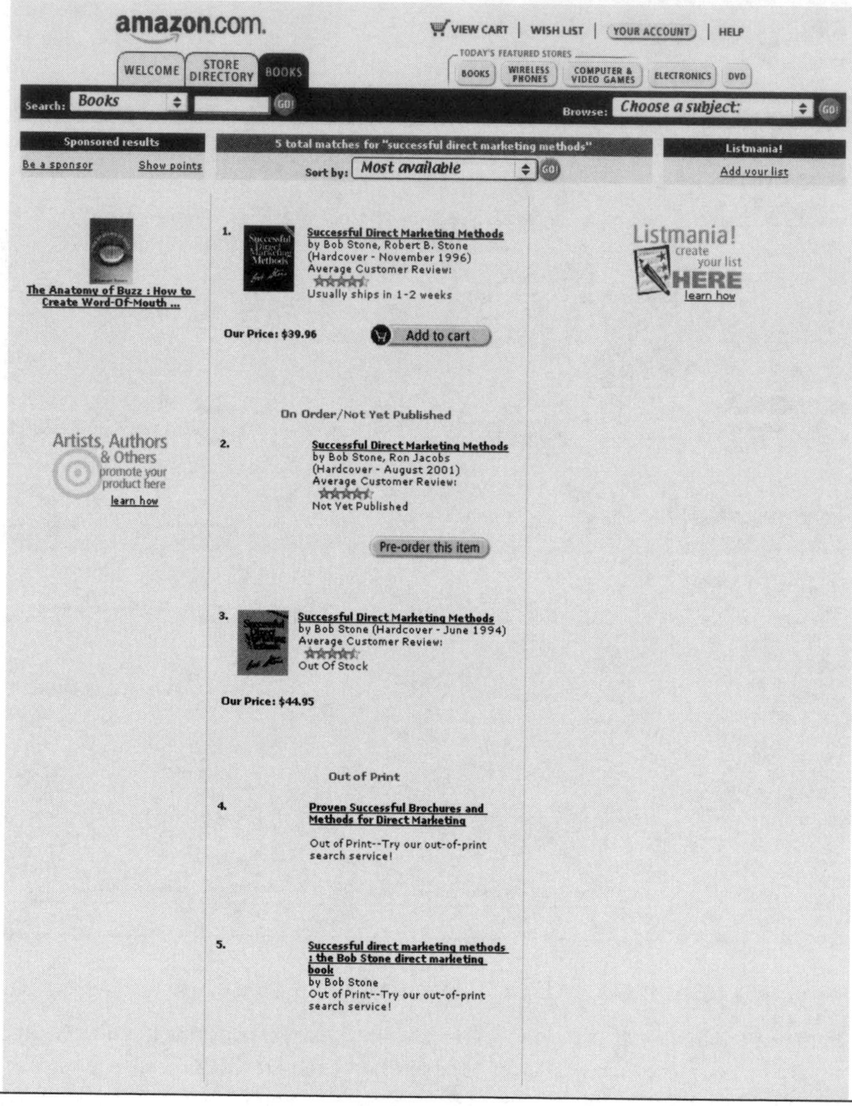

CASE STUDY: **Barnes & Noble** *(continued)*

EXHIBIT 13-8

Redesigned Barnesandnoble.com Home Page

the books even further to match Amazon's end prices; or forgo using the superstores entirely, and save a bit of the margin on each book sold. He chose the latter strategy. Barnesandnoble.com had to scrap the innovative on-line strategies it was planning—selling gift certificates redeemable in stores, placing search terminals in the stores, and allowing on-line customers to return books at their local Barnes & Noble. A clear advantage was lost.

More Obstacles

New difficulties ensued after the site's debut. In May 1997, Barnes & Noble Inc., which calls itself the "World's largest bookseller," sued Amazon for claim-

CASE STUDY: Barnes & Noble *(continued)*

EXHIBIT 13–9

Amazon.com Home Page

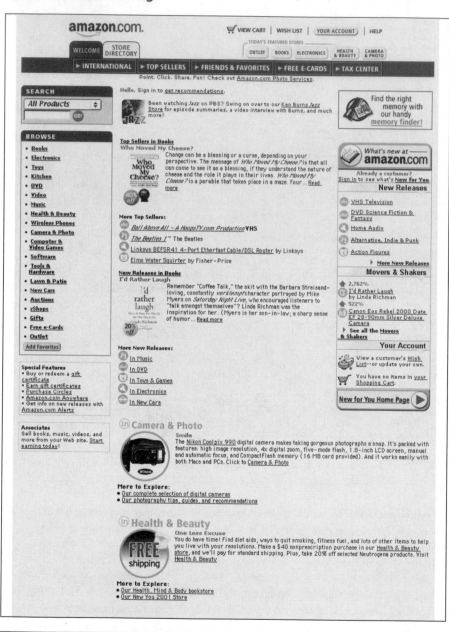

ing it was "Earth's biggest bookstore." Amazon countersued. The case was settled with the slogans intact, but it reinforced the view of Barnes & Noble as an old, tired, unhip giant—exactly the wrong image to project to the burgeoning Web audience. "Suing Amazon," one dismayed barnesandnoble.com employee says, "just wasn't cool."

In July 1997, barnesandnoble.com's exclusive arrangement with America Online eroded when the service provider struck a deal that made Amazon.com its sole bookseller on the public AOL.com (barnesandnoble.com continued to be the only bookseller within AOL's proprietary Marketplace). With its small market share, barnesandnoble.com had little choice but to secure the key portal space at any price: The Riggios paid a whopping $40 million to continue being AOL's bookseller for the next four years.

During the 1997 holiday sales season, Amazon sold upward of $20 million; barnesandnoble.com's take was a disappointing $5.6 million. By the end of 1998 the Riggios had thrown roughly $100 million at the on-line operation. The large expenditures meant there was a chance the Riggios' unprofitable business could shave enough off the margins of the profitable company to harm them both.

SOLUTION

In 1998 the Riggios partnered with Bertelsmann, a German publishing company; each invested $100 million to spin off barnesandnoble.com and take it public. Equally important, the joint venture company got a new CEO with substantial on-line marketing experience—Jonathan Bulkeley, the former head of AOL U.K. Then barnesandnoble.com hired a president with E-commerce experience to head up the new company.

Barnesandnoble.com remains committed. Its new strategy is to plan for a time when printed books cease to exist. Instead of being printed on paper and delivered to stores, barnesandnoble.com is betting that books will be stored digitally and downloaded from the Internet onto personal computers as electronic books or dashed off on home printers, or reproduced in small, highly efficient print runs by high-speed presses or on demand right in the bookstore.

In this vision of bookselling's future, students won't have paper textbooks anymore; they'll access texts over the Web, paying usage fees by the chapter. The sales exec who needs to learn about a potential client he's meeting the next day will just download the text onto an E-book and read it on the red-eye. A professor who needs 20 copies of an out-of-print book will place an order over the Web to have the books printed and delivered overnight.

Because Amazon, the dread enemy, is expanding to sell everything from flowers to pharmaceuticals, some think a narrow concentration on the evolution of the book will be Barnes & Noble's salvation.

"One of the irrefutable laws of brands is, once you expand the brand, you lose the niche," says Scott Heiferman, CEO of the on-line marketing firm i-traffic. "As Amazon becomes the place to sell anything online, it presents an opportunity for barnesandnoble.com to own books."

Steve Riggio puts the company's strategy in even more sweeping terms: "We intend to be the dominant portal for the delivery of information."

PILOT PROJECT Barnesandnoble.com now faces many of the issues that established companies face when developing an E-commerce strategy. What issues did barnesandnoble.com consider as it launched its E-tail experience? What other strategies could it have employed? How will its new strategy position it against its competitors? Compare the current barnesandnoble.com shopping experience with that of Amazon.com from the perspectives of usability and customer satisfaction.

Key Points

▶ Stage one E-commerce sites are one-way communications that focus on products and services. Stage two sites add information on how and where a prospect can buy products and services. Stage three sites allow for commerce, but don't link on-line sites with off-line systems. Users who register, however, will be recognized whenever they visit. Stage four E-commerce sites link on-line and off-line databases and enable and encourage customer dialogues. Vast product databases are linked to allow for products to be configured to order. Fully implemented stage five sites, which cost millions of dollars to create and maintain, include everything in stage four, but have systems that customize the experience for users.

▶ While a Web presence may trigger channel conflict among sales forces, distributors, and other channel partners, it is imperative to sell through channels that customers would like to buy from.

▶ To achieve its business goals on-line, an organization must translate its business processes into fast, easy-to-use processes that are Web-centric. To do so, it should examine every aspect of these processes from a customer's point of view, and understand how interactions are triggered within the organization.

▶ Identify the business rules your company follows and the business events common to your business: placing an order, checking credit, checking inventory, shipping products, invoicing customers, collecting payment, etc. Each event will trigger interaction among your customers and the software applications within your E-commerce site. You need to ensure that information and tasks flow smoothly from one system to another for each event.

▶ Know exactly what *customer*, *account*, *order*, and *product* mean to your organization. These business objects have an agreed-upon definition and create a common language within the organization. It is difficult to design an E-commerce strategy without knowing those definitions up front.

MANAGING THE
CREATIVE PROCESS

CREATING DIRECT
MAIL ADVERTISING

Before radio, television, telemarketing, the fax, E-mail, and the Web there was direct mail. With the introduction of each new medium have come dire predictions about the future of direct mail. Many have relegated "snail mail" to a minor role, at best, in the foreseeable future. Surprise, surprise. Direct mail is as strong or stronger than ever.

In addition to being a powerful medium for creating new customer bases, direct mail can serve as the ideal medium to maintain customer bases created by all the "new" media plus the customers first acquired by mail.

Direct mail is not restricted to 60 seconds (radio), 60 seconds (TV), the 7×10 inch page (magazines), one color (the fax and E-mail), or a screen (the Web). You can use large, lavishly illustrated brochures. You can have any number of inserts. Any colors you want. You can use pop-ups, foldouts, swatches, or even enclose a computer diskette. What you can do is limited only by your imagination, or budget.

Direct mail can be as simple as a postcard or as complex as a sweepstakes mailing. Self-mailers, which do not have an outer envelope, are another option. These mailers vary from a single sheet of paper folded once for mailing to wonderfully complex pieces with multiple sheets and preformed reply envelopes. In between is the classic mailing package, which consists of an outside mailing envelope, a letter, circular/brochure, and a response form with or without a business reply form.

Which format should you choose for your mailing piece? That depends. It depends on your budget. It depends on who you're trying to reach. Do you want a package that will stand out on the businessperson's desk? Or is it something designed for leisurely reading by the consumer at home? If you're not sure, you should use the classic format with a separate outer envelope and a separate letter. Most direct mail today uses this format, and although it is more expensive than a self-mailer, it will usually pull better.

One further caution on formats: postal regulations, which govern the mail-ability of any given piece, change regularly. You should check the layout of your mailing piece with your local post office before you produce it. There are few things in life more disheartening than a phone call that begins: "This is the post office, and we're holding your mailing because . . . "

The Letter Is King of the Package

The letter has long reigned as the most important component of the mailing package. Even though a letter may be mailed to thousands, it has an aura that creates the feeling of a personal message from one person to another. It must be said, however, that the quality of the message can range from "horrible" to "superb."

Put simply, the assignment of the letter writer is to make appeals that will satisfy one or more human wants of the prospect.

Translating Selling Points into Benefits

Before you write any copy, it is very important to dig out every selling point you can, and translate each selling point into a customer benefit. The more benefits prospects perceive (i.e., the more benefits you can point out to them), the more likely they will buy. Suppose you're writing copy to sell a portable countertop dishwasher, for example. Some of the selling points for this merchandise are listed below, and alongside each is the benefit the selling point makes possible:

Selling Point	Benefit
1. A 10-minute operating cycle	Does a load of dishes in 10 minutes; gets you out of the kitchen faster
2. Measures 18 inches in diameter	Is small enough to fit on a countertop; doesn't take up valuable floor space
3. Has a transparent plastic top	Lets you watch the washing cycle; you know when the dishes are done
4. Has a universal hose coupling	Fits any standard kitchen faucet; attaches and detaches in seconds

Copy Appeals and Basic Human Wants

With your benefits down on paper, you now have to decide on the appeals that will do the best selling job. Creative people refer to this in different ways. Some talk about how you "position" the product in the prospect's mind. Others refer to "coming up with the big idea" behind the copy. What is it about your offer and benefit story that is most appealing? When you stop to think about it, people respond to any given proposition for one of two reasons: to gain something they do not have, or to avoid losing something they now possess.

EXHIBIT 14-1

Two Categories of Human Wants

The Desire to Gain	The Desire to Avoid Loss
To make money	To avoid criticism
To save time	To keep possessions
To avoid effort	To avoid physical pain
To achieve comfort	To avoid loss of reputation
To have health	To avoid loss of money
To be popular	To avoid trouble
To experience pleasure	
To be clean	
To be praised	
To be in style	
To gratify curiosity	
To satisfy an appetite	
To have beautiful possessions	
To attract romantic partners	
To be an individual	
To emulate others	
To take advantage of opportunities	

Exhibit 14–1 shows how basic human wants can be divided into these two categories. Professional copywriters carefully sift and weigh the list of basic human wants to determine the main appeal of their proposition.

Eleven Guidelines to Good Copy

Does your proposition help people feel important? People like to keep up with the Joneses. People like to be made to feel that they are a part of a select group. A tremendous number of people are susceptible to snob appeal. Perhaps you can offer a terrific bargain by mail, and capitalize on the appeal of saving money. The desire to "get it wholesale" is very strong.

Don Kanter, long a V.P. with Stone & Adler, offers these guidelines as checkpoints for good, professional copy:

1. Does the writer know the product? Has he or she dug out every selling point and benefit?

2. Does the writer know his or her market? Is he or she aiming the copy at the most likely prospects rather than at the world in general?

3. Is the writer talking to the prospect in language the prospect will understand?

4. Does the writer make a promise to the prospect, then prove that he or she can deliver what was promised?

5. Does the writer get to the point at once? Does he or she make that all-important promise right away?

6. Is the copy, especially the headlines and lead paragraphs, germane, and specific to the selling proposition?

7. Is the copy concise? There is a great temptation to overwrite, especially in direct mail.

8. Is the copy logical and clear? Does it flow from point to point?

9. Is the copy enthusiastic? Does the writer obviously believe in what he or she is selling?

10. Is the copy complete? Are all the questions answered, especially obvious ones like size and color?

11. Is the copy designed to sell? Or is it designed to impress the reader with the writer's ability? If somebody says "that's a great mailing," you've got the wrong reaction. What you want to hear is, "That's a great product (or service). I'd love to have it."

Writing Letters to Formula

These guidelines establish a major point: no one should just "sit down to write a letter." Notes, even random notes, are essential. Appeals. Benefits. Selling points. Market facts. Offers. Free gifts, if any. Possible leads. Testimonials. Guarantees. Problems to overcome.

From this hodgepodge of notes and random ideas, a persuasive letter must emerge. The question is: How do you do that? One way is to give yourself a route to follow by using a formula.

The AIDA formula is perhaps the best known:

Attract	ATTENTION
Develop	INTEREST
Create	DESIRE
Get	ACTION

This is a good route to follow, but some explanations are in order. "Attract attention" refers to the lead and/or the first paragraph of the letter. Passive attention won't cut it; instead, an instant desire to learn more must occur.

EXAMPLE: THE LOWEST PRICE ON A COMPUTER THIS YEAR . . . AND NO INTEREST TO PAY FOR 24 MONTHS!

A lead of this type predictably will grab attention, and heighten the interest in learning more. Another method for attracting attention is to use a "Johnson box" right at the top of the letterhead (and before the salutation) which tells the whole story in capsulized form (see Exhibit 14–2).

The rest of the AIDA formula follows quite logically (see Exhibit 14–3 for a package that applies the AIDA formula). Attracting attention leads to a heightened interest to learn more about the product or services. Interest leads to a desire to possess. The final step—getting action—is the moment of truth.

EXHIBIT 14–2

Direct Mail Letter Using Johnson Box

```
* * * * * * * * * * * * * * * * * * * * * * * * * * * * * * * * * *
*                                                                 *
*        This November, you're invited to take an exciting look   *
*               at what computers can do for you...               *
*                                                                 *
*    ...at the landmark course that will give you--as it's given  *
* thousands of executives--the confidence and know-how you need to: *
*                                                                 *
*    * Clear up the mystery and confusion of data processing!     *
*    * Make your computer work harder for you!                    *
*    * Tell your systems people what you want--instead of the     *
*      other way around!                                          *
*    * Make computers your partner in management                  *
*                                                                 *
* * * * * * * * * * * * * * * * * * * * * * * * * * * * * * * * * *


Dear Executive:

    If you're baffled by computers...buffaloed when systems people
use words like "byte" and "nanosecond"...if you're tired of the data
processing department telling you what can be done, because you
don't know enough to give the orders...

...it's time you took the American Management Associations' course
that's cured thousands of "computer phobia"...

            FUNDAMENTALS OF DATA PROCESSING
            FOR THE NON-DATA PROCESSING EXECUTIVE

        Not for programmers or DP professionals...
        this 3-day course is one of the few computer
        seminars just for you, the data processing
        user! One at which you'll take a fascinating
        look at what computers can do for you...and
        learn how to utilize them to become a more
        effective manager...

        ...And this November, you can attend any of
        12 sessions in 10 major cities across the
        country--including a city near you!

    Thousands of managers and executives have attended this landmark
course and, without hesitation, many have called it "the best course
they've ever taken." Here's what just a few of the recent attendees
had to say:

    "I got terrific ideas and concepts that I can implement and

                                              (inside...)
```

American Management Associations · 135 West 50th Street · New York, N.Y. 10020 · (212)586-8100

EXHIBIT 14-3

Application of AIDA Formula

Shown here is the front of the teaser envelope and letter. Brochure cover and reservation certificate appear on the next page.

KCDMA
Kansas City Direct Marketing Association
P.O. Box 419264 / Kansas City, MO 64141-6264
816-561-5323 / Fax: 816-561-1991 / www.KCDMA

********************AUTO**MIXED AADC 640
Mr Bob Stone
Bob Stone Inc
3029 Iroquois Rd
Wilmette IL 60091-1106

Dear Bob,

Chemistry was fun when we were kids … mixing and stirring up potentially explosive combinations of various elements.

Today, it may not be all that different. If you're like me, you're working with marketing elements to boost response rates, get the message out and change behavior. In other words, getting the formula just right.

But just because yesterday's campaign was successful doesn't guarantee that tomorrow's will get the same response. You have to know what media works best for you, and what you can do to create the energy that gets your customers to buy. Every element in your media mix must work together if you're going to keep your customers satisfied and coming back for more.

And that's what KCDMA's Direct Marketing Conference 1999 is all about. On October 6 and 7, find out how to combine and integrate your media to fuel record-breaking results.

On Wednesday, start with **The Basic Institute** and discover beyond-the-basics formulas and more. Even if you've been in direct marketing for years, you'll find the day a refreshing way to recharge and reenergize your marketing efforts. Then, on Thursday, join the innovators in our industry for **DM Day**. You'll hear five powerhouse presentations about how integrating your efforts can send your responses into orbit.

Take a few minutes to review the enclosed brochure, then send in your Reservation Certificate to enroll today. Make sure you can create the right chemistry to get the results you deserve.

Sincerely,

Pam Linwood, PDM, President
Kansas City Direct Marketing Association

P.S.   You can't afford to experiment with your customers. Plan now to attend KCDMA's Direct Marketing Conference '99, and learn to apply the formulas that will generate record-breaking results. Register before September 17, and you'll get Ernan Roman's classic book *Integrated Direct Marketing*. Don't wait, because this offer will dissolve soon!

EXHIBIT 14–3   *(continued)*

KCDMA Direct Marketing Conference 1999

Wednesday, October 6: The Basic Institute
Thursday, October 7: DM Day

Does Your
Direct Marketing
Chemistry Kit
Have All the Right Elements???

Two full days of breakthrough ideas and secret formulas
to make sure your marketing mix maximizes results!

Presented by

kansascity.com
your home on the net

and   STAR DIRECT

RESERVATION CERTIFICATE

KCDMA's Direct Marketing Conference 1999
Wednesday, October 6 and Thursday, October 7
Harrah's Convention Center and Hotel

To Register, mail this form in the enclosed envelope
Or fax this form to (816) 561-1991

Mr Bob Stone
Bob Stone Inc
3029 Iroquois Rd
Wilmette IL 60091-1106

Questions? Call (816) 561-5323.

Registration Deadline: October 1, 1999. For registrations received after
October 1, 1999, add $20 per person.

EARLY REGISTRATION BONUS GIFT! Register before Sept. 17, 1999, and get a
complimentary copy of Bron Bonan's book, *Integrated Direct Marketing* (Retail value $45).

*Non-Members: All non-member tuitions (except luncheon only) include
Free KCDMA membership through March, 2000!

DMA1

○**YES!** I want to discover the secret formulas
and get explosive results from my marketing
mix. Register me for ...

	Member	Non-Member
○ DM Conference, Oct. 6&7	$290	$370*
○ DM Day, Oct. 7 only	$195	$245*
○ Basic Institute, Oct. 6 only	$130	$170*
○ AMBIT Awards Banquet, Oct. 6	$50	$50
○ Luncheon, Oct. 7 (subject to availability)	$45	$45

Total Enclosed $ _____

My Phone Number (____) _____

My Fax Number (____) _____

My E-Mail Address _____

○ Check enclosed

○ MasterCard ○ Discover ○ VISA ○ American Express

Card # _____

Expiration Date _____

Name on Card _____

Signature _____

The copywriter's mission at this point is to overcome human inertia, to get positive action NOW! This may be accomplished in a number of ways, such as setting a deadline date, offering a free gift for prompt action, or forgiving shipping and handling charges if an order is received before a certain date.

The Seven-Step Formula for Winning Letters

Many years ago Bob Stone came up with a letter-writing formula that he believed to be a few steps beyond the AIDA formula because it follows a more detailed route. Used wisely, Stone believes, it should not stifle creativity. All seven steps are illustrated in the promotion for *The Kiplinger Letter* shown in Exhibit 14–4.

1. *Promise your most important benefit in your headline or first paragraph.* You simply can't go wrong by leading off with the most important benefit to the reader. Some writers believe in the slow buildup. But most experienced writers favor making the important point first. Many writers use the "Johnson box": short, terse copy that summarizes the main benefits, positioned in a box above the salutation.

2. *Immediately enlarge on your most important benefit.* This step is crucial. Many writers come up with a great lead, then fail to follow through. Or they catch attention with their heading, but then take two or three paragraphs to warm up to their subject. The reader's attention is gone! Try hard to elaborate on your most important benefit right away, and you'll build up interest fast.

3. *Tell readers specifically what they are going to get.* It's amazing how many letters lack details on such basic product features as size, color, weight, and sales terms. Perhaps the writer is so close to the proposition that he or she assumes the readers know all about it. A dangerous assumption! When you tell readers what they are going to get, don't overlook the intangibles that go along with your product or service. For example, they are getting smart appearance in addition to a pair of slacks, knowledge in addition to a 340-page book.

4. *Back up your statements with proof and endorsements.* Most prospects are somewhat skeptical about advertising. They know it sometimes gets overly enthusiastic about a product, so they accept it with a grain of salt. If you can back up your own statements with third-party testimonials or a list of satisfied users, everything you say becomes more believable.

5. *Tell readers what they might lose if they don't act.* As noted, people respond affirmatively either to gain something they do not possess or to avoid losing something they already have. Here's a good spot in your letter to overcome human inertia—imply what could be lost if action is postponed. People don't like to be left out. A skillful writer can use this human trait as a powerful influence in his or her message.

6. *Rephrase your prominent benefits in your closing offer.* As a good salesperson does, sum up the benefits to the prospect in your closing offer. This is the proper pre-

lude to asking for action. This is where you can intensify the prospect's desire to have the product. The stronger the benefits you can persuade the reader to recall, the easier it will be for him or her to justify an affirmative decision.

7. *Incite action.* Now. This is the spot where you win or lose the battle with inertia. Experienced advertisers know that once a letter is put aside or tossed into a file, they're out of luck. So wind up with a call for action and a logical reason for acting now. Too many letters close with a statement like "supplies are limited." That argument lacks credibility. Today's consumer knows you probably have a warehouse full of merchandise. So make your reason a believable one. For example: "It could be many months before we go back to press on this book." Or: "Orders are shipped on a first-come basis. The sooner yours is received, the sooner you can be enjoying your new widget."

Should you write to formula or break the rules? Perhaps the best answer is this: if you are a neophyte, write to formula. It will keep you on track. If you are a professional commanding $50,000 or more for writing a letter, set your own rules. You've earned the right!

The Problem-Solving Strategic Approach

Not everyone writes to formulas. A somewhat different approach to putting a direct mail package together is to employ a problem-solution strategic approach.

Under this approach, the creative people review the problems to be faced and then come up with strategic solutions for each of the problems. Expressed as a formula, it would read: Problems ÷ Strategies = Solutions.

Bob Stone used this to great effect when he created a direct mail package to help sell a certificate program in direct marketing at the University of Missouri–Kansas City (UMKC).

In preparing to write the sales letter, Bob first listed seven problems he needed to address in his copy. Then he devised strategies to deal with each one in the six-page proposal letter presented in Exhibit 14–5. Let's look at how his letter addressed and solved three problems that focused on the relationship between Bob Stone and the reader.

Problem: Will a professional direct marketer accept the word of a college administrator over a professional colleague?

Strategic solution: Write the letter printed on his personal letterhead and use the salutation "Dear Colleague."

Problem: If Bob asked the prospect to return the enrollment form to UMKC, he might break the colleague-to-colleague relationship.

Strategic solution: Have the applicant return the enrollment form to Bob.

EXHIBIT 14-4

The Kiplinger Letter

STANLEY R. MAYES *ASSISTANT TO THE PRESIDENT*

THE KIPLINGER WASHINGTON EDITORS, INC.
1729 H STREET, NORTHWEST, WASHINGTON, D. C. 20006   TELEPHONE: 887-6400

THE KIPLINGER WASHINGTON LETTER   THE KIPLINGER TAX LETTER
THE KIPLINGER AGRICULTURAL LETTER   THE KIPLINGER FLORIDA LETTER
THE KIPLINGER CALIFORNIA LETTER   THE KIPLINGER TEXAS LETTER
CHANGING TIMES MAGAZINE

More Growth and Inflation Ahead...
and what YOU can do about it.

The next few years will see business climb to the highest
level this country has ever known. And with it...inflation.

This combination may be hard for you to accept under today's
conditions. But the fact remains that those who do prepare for both
inflation AND growth ahead will reap big dividends for their foresight,
and avoid the blunders others will make.

You'll get the information you need for this type
of planning in the Kiplinger Washington Letter...
and the enclosed form will bring you the next 26
issues of this helpful service on a "Try-out" basis.
The fee: Less than 81¢ per week...only $21 for the
6 months just ahead...and tax deductible for business
or investment purposes.

During the depression, in 1935, the Kiplinger Letter warned
of inflation and told what to do about it. Those who heeded its advice
were ready when prices began to rise.

Again, in January of 1946, the Letter renounced the widely-
held view that a severe post-war depression was inevitable. Instead
it predicted shortages, rising wages and prices, a high level of
business. And again, those who heeded its advice were able to avoid
losses, to cash in on the surging economy of the late '40s, early '50s
and mid '60s. It then kept its clients prepared for the swings of the
'70s, keeping them a step ahead each time.

Now Kiplinger not only foresees expansion ahead, but also
continuing inflation, and in his weekly Letter to clients he points
out profit opportunities in the future...and also dangers.

The Kiplinger Letter not only keeps you informed of present
trends and developments, but also gives you advance notice on the
short & long-range business outlook...inflation forecasts...energy
predictions...housing...federal legislative prospects...politics...
investment trends & pointers...tax outlook & advice...labor, wage
settlement prospects...upcoming gov't rules & regulations...ANYTHING
that will have an effect on you, your business, your personal finances,
your family.

To take advantage of this opportunity to try the Letter and
benefit from its keen judgments and helpful advice during the fast-

(Over, please)

EXHIBIT 14-4 *(continued)*

changing months ahead...fill in and return the enclosed form along
with your $21 payment. And do it with this guarantee: That you may
cancel the service and get a prompt refund of the unused part of
your payment any time you feel it is not worth far more to you than
it costs.

      I'll start your service as soon as I hear from you, and
you'll have each weekly issue on your desk every Monday morning
thereafter.

      Sincerely,

      Stanley Mayes
      Assistant to the President

SAM:kga

P. S.   More than half of all new subscribers sign up for a full year
at $42. In appreciation, we'll send you FREE five special Kiplinger
Reports on receipt of your payment when you take a full year's service,
too. Details are spelled out on the enclosed slip. Same money-back
guarantee and tax deductibility apply.

EXHIBIT 14–5

Certification Program Proposal Letter

BOB STONE

1630 SHERIDAN ROAD #8G • WILMETTE, ILLINOIS 60091

Dear Colleague:

If you accept this proposal it will cost your firm $4,500. Not an insignificant sum. And there's more. If you accept this proposal you or your designate will commit to a series of 14-hour days on a college campus.

So much for the agony: Now for the ecstasy!

If you accept this proposal you or your designate will be one of 35 nationwide who will be eligible to receive certification as a **PROFESSIONAL DIRECT MARKETER (PDM)**. This certification will come from the University of Missouri-Kansas City -- the first university in the nation to establish a Direct Marketing Center.

The significance of being certified probably won't strike home at first. For the opportunity never existed till now. But, to put certification into perspective, it's comparable to an accountant studying for CPA certification. Or, an insurance executive going back to college to become a chartered life underwriter (CLU).

CPA, CLU, PDM. Each certification tells the world the possessor is at the top of a chosen profession.

But you might rightly point out, "I've been to college. That's behind me. And I am a professional." Right on all counts! That's precisely why I'm writing you.

Take college background. If your experience is anything like mine, your major was in marketing. And what did marketing texts teach us about direct marketing? Nothing. Oh, there may have been a page or two about "sales letter writing." Maybe.

Contrast our college background and that of some of your people with collegiate marketing curriculums today. Over 160 colleges and universities teaching one or more courses in direct marketing. Graduate programs at UMKC, Northwestern University, University of Cincinnati, and others. Hundreds are entering the direct marketing

EXHIBIT 14–5   *(continued)*

2

profession with foreknowledge we never had.

The first day on the job these "kids" sit down with an incredible body of knowledge. Databases. Market segmentation. Socio-economic influences. Positioning. Pricing models. Operations research. Life-time value. Theories of productivity. Statistical theory. Quantitative methods. Consumer behavior. --- And more.

All these students are computer smart. Their PC's are to them what our slide rules were to us.

As one who has had the privilege of teaching Direct Marketing at both UMKC and Northwestern University, I've seen the advantages of a combination of academic theory and practical skills. They're inseparable. I've learned, without doubt, that <u>degree of skills is in direct ratio to acquired knowledge.</u>

The bottom line is that after only a few years I'm maintaining a lively correspondence with former students. The letterheads upon which they write speak volumes. **L. L. Bean, Hewlett-Packard, Spiegel, Allstate, Mayo Clinic, AT&T**. Their acquired knowledge has paid off. Big.

But what about the professionals? You. Me. Our brethren?

What are our avenues of continuing education? Chances are, like me, you've attended one-day, two-day seminars. You may even have enrolled in continuing education programs over several weeks. Most of these programs are excellent.

But the lasting impact might be compared to taking a cortisone shot to relieve a current problem as contrasted to a life-long infusion of healthy knowledge. The difference : night and day.

Now, for the first time, college education is available for the professional. End result: **certification**.

Actually there is strong precedent to recommend the UMKC Professional Direct Marketing Certification Program. It's in exactly the same mode as programs conducted at Harvard, Stanford and Northwestern's Kellogg School. America's major corporations send

EXHIBIT 14–5   *(continued)*

Certification Program Proposal Letter

3

their brightest to the on-campus
management programs of these
distinguished universities.

What the Chief Executive Officers of these leading
corporations have learned is that the brightest of
people become even brighter and more productive when
academic knowledge is melded with practical skills. As
one educator put it to me - "An astronaut can have all
the technical skills needed, but he can't fly to the
moon if he doesn't have the knowledge of the physicist."

So it is with direct marketing. A copywriter, for
example, can't become a true wordsmith unless he or she
clearly understands consumer behavior. No way. The
need for knowledge to implement experience is doubly
important for the professional direct marketing manager.

The advantage of the professional: <u>Experience</u>

As bright as these college kids are today, we have
an advantage that no <u>magna cum laude</u> can come close to
matching - <u>**experience.**</u> That's why UMKC has developed a
concentrated program that will lead to certification in
three weeks of on-campus time with several week
intervals between each of the three weeks. To catch up
with professionals, college students would have to attend
two classes a week for 15 consecutive weeks over several
semesters!

Here are the specific dates for on-campus course work:

    Week One: **October 30 thru November 3, 1989
                      (Mon.-Fri.)**

    Week Two: **February 26 thru March 2, 1990
                      (Mon.-Fri.)**

    Week Three: **April 30 thru May 4, 1990
                      (Mon.-Fri.)**

Classes will begin each day at 8:00 a.m. and
conclude at 10:00 p.m. (Remember, I warned you about
those 14-hour days!) But the pros get a break on
Fridays: classes conclude at 4:00 p.m.

Over the three one-week periods participants will
be graded on three examinations. Plus -- they will be
evaluated by their peers for excellence in team
assignments. A minimum of 85 percent attendance is

EXHIBIT 14–5   *(continued)*

4

<u>mandatory.</u>

There are just two other requirements:

1) To be eligible you or your designate must have two or more years experience as a direct marketer and 2) the enrollee must have completed a degree at an accredited college or university. (Special consideration will be given to applicants not fulfilling the college degree requirement provided they have a minimum of seven years of work experience.) That's it.

A word about UMKC.

University of Missouri-Kansas City School of Business - world renowned - is enshrined in a beautiful tree-lined campus in the cultural center of Kansas City, Missouri.   The number of UMKC students and faculty who have moved on to become Fulbright scholars is legend.

Classes in the Professional Certification in Direct Marketing program will be held in the magnificent new $8 million Henry W. Bloch School of Business and Public Administration. State-of-the-art in every way, including satellite communication.

Knowing that the 35 students in residence will all be mature professionals, the administration of UMKC has made some important concessions.

- **Housing.** PDM students won't be subjected to bare-bones college dormitories. Instead they will be housed at the Residence Inn Kitchenette Apartments, just a few blocks off campus. (The group can have their own "beer busts" - if they're up to it!)

- **Breakfast** will be provided with housing. Casual lunches will be provided at the Henry Bloch School.

- **PDM** students will have full access to the famed UMKC library, housing what many believe to be the most complete library of direct marketing books, tapes, videocassettes in the world.

- **And** for exercise buffs, UMKC will provide a <u>free</u> membership in the new multi-million dollar Swinney Recreation Center. The center is just across from the Bloch School.

EXHIBIT 14–5   *(continued)*

Certification Program Proposal Letter

5

About the Curriculum.

The curriculum will enhance all aspects of the direct marketing discipline. Strategy. System. Planning. Communication. Evaluation. There will be independent research, field study and team project development during the intervening time prior to Week Two and Week Three.

For a detailed outline of the on-campus curriculum, see separate sheet enclosed. It's all one could dream of – and more. I <u>guarantee</u> it.

About the faculty.

The UMKC faculty is the priceless ingredient that makes the Professional Direct Marketing certification program possible. The faculty is distinguished.

Among the faculty members who will instruct is **William B. Eddy**, Interim Dean of the business school. Then there's **Richard A. Hamilton**, Associate Professor of Direct Marketing, along with professors of finance, of quantitative analysis, of business operations, of organizational behavior, of operations management. A core of **49** professors in all. And most with a Ph.D. after their names.

This group will be reinforced by direct marketing professionals with extensive teaching experience. **Martin Baier**, for one, who pioneered the Direct Marketing Center at UMKC. And I will complete the faculty by teaching various aspects of direct marketing. (I'm thrilled to be asked.)

Why I am so excited.

Excited really isn't a strong enough word to describe how I feel about the Professional Direct Marketing Program. **Enthralled** comes closer. Enthralled that for the first time in our exciting history full-scale college education is available to professionals. Enthralled that for the first time in history certification (PDM) is available.

Because I believe so strongly in what this program will do for our profession, I made an unusual request of the UMKC administration. I asked if I could be personally responsible for 17 of the 35 students to be accepted nationwide. To my complete delight the response was, **"permission granted!"**

EXHIBIT 14–5   *(continued)*

6

The bottom line is - I <u>want your firm to be one of</u> <u>the 17 accepted.</u>

A challenge to you or your designate.

Because of your experience and stature you may choose to forego the college experience in deference to a designate of your choice. This would be the person in your organization who you single out to be capable of a quantum leap in knowledge and skills.

There is just one thing. To be accepted, your designate must meet both the academic and experience requirements set forth. And this person must be personally sponsored by you.

How to lock-up an enrollment.

$500 will lock-up an enrollment. (But as the S&L's put it - "Certain restrictions apply.") After 35 applications are received, additional applications will be put on a waiting list. Unfortunately there will be no exceptions to the maximum class size of 35.

Because I am personally responsible for 17 of the 35 applications, I want to maintain tight control. To accomplish this, I've enclosed a stamped envelope addressed to me at my study at home. I'd appreciate having your decision as quickly as possible.

I'll put your application through the moment I receive it. For sure. Sending the application in <u>guarantees</u> a once-in-a-lifetime experience that will pay off for decades to come!

Sincerely,

Bob Stone

Bob Stone

P.S. Let me give you my unlisted phone number. It is: 1-312-251-xxxx. You can reserve by phone, if you wish.

> *Because I am personally responsible for 17 of the 35 applications, I want to maintain tight control. To accomplish this, I've enclosed a stamped envelope addressed to me at my study at home. I'd appreciate your decision as quickly as possible.*

Problem: There is a need to speed up the response process and play on the one-on-one relationship Bob tried to establish.

Strategic solution: Use a postscript to give the prospect an opportunity to contact me directly and engage in a personal conversation.

> *P.S.: Let me give you my unlisted phone number. It is:*
> *1–847–251–XXXX.*

Results

This package—six-page letter, application form, and reply envelope—was mailed to Direct Marketing Association members at a cost of one dollar each. It produced some remarkable results:

1. Although originally the class was limited to 35 students, response was so strong that the class was expanded to 42 students.

2. Total revenue came to $168,000; promotion cost came to $3,500.

3. This package outpulled by five to one the traditional package, which consisted of a two-page letter, circular, application form, and reply envelope.

4. All but three of those who responded to this package called the unlisted number to make their reservation.

Letter Length, Appearance, and the Postscript

"Do people read long copy?" The answer is "Yes!" People will read something for as long as it interests them. An uninteresting one-page letter can be too long. A skillfully woven four-pager can hold the reader until the end. Thus, a letter should be long enough to cover the subject adequately and short enough to retain interest. Don't be afraid of long copy. If you have something to say and can say it well, it will probably do better than short copy. After all, the longer you hold a prospect's interest, the more sales points you can get across and the more likely you are to win an order.

Regardless of letter length, it should always look attractive and be easy to read. The pros keep paragraphs down to six or seven lines. They use subheads and indented paragraphs to break up long copy. They emphasize pertinent thoughts, knowing that many readers will scan indented paragraphs before they decide whether to read a letter clear through. They use underscoring, CAPITAL LET-

TERS, and a second ink color to make key words and sentences stand out. And they skillfully use leader dots and dashes to break up long sentences.

Finally, it usually pays to tack on a postscript. The P.S. is one of the most effective parts of any letter. Many prospects will glance through a letter. The eye will pick up an indented paragraph here, stop on an underlined statement there, and finally come to rest on the P.S. If you can express an important idea in the P.S., the reader might go back and read the whole letter. This makes the P.S. worthy of your best efforts. Use it to restate a key benefit. Or to offer an added inducement, like a free gift. Even when somebody has read the rest of the letter, the P.S. can make the difference between whether or not the prospect places an order. Use the P.S. to close on a strong note, to sign off with the strongest appeal you have.

Versioned and Personalized Copy

Instead of sending exactly the same letter to all your prospects, it is possible to create a number of versions for each major segment of your market. Then rather than talking about all the advantages and benefits of the product, you could simply zero in on those that fit each market segment. Sounds like a logical idea that should increase response—but it isn't always effective. Test it for yourself. If your product story should be substantially different for certain audience segments—and you can identify and select them on the lists you're using—develop special versions of your regular copy and give the technique a try.

One type of versioned copy that generally does pay off is special copy slanted to your previous buyers. Customers like to think a firm remembers them and will give them special treatment. In going back to your satisfied buyers, there's less need to resell your company. You can concentrate on the product or the service being offered.

Personalized letters usually outpull nonpersonalized ones, but not always. Also, they have to outpull by enough to pay for the extra cost of personalization. When you use personalization, use all the information you can. But don't scatter the person's name indiscriminately throughout the letter. A good rule to follow is to write a personalized letter as you would write a letter to any person you know fairly well.

Other Elements of the Classic Mailing Package

The Outer Envelope

The outer envelope, or carrier envelope, has one job: to get itself opened. To accomplish this, the envelope can use several techniques:

- It can dazzle recipients with color, with graphics, and with promises of important benefits if they will only open it.

- It can impress recipients with its simplicity and lead them to believe that the contents must be very important.

- It can tease recipients and so excite their curiosity that they simply must open it.

To help accomplish its purpose, the traditional paper envelope can have extra cutouts or "windows," or it can be made of transparent polyethylene or foil. Whatever it's made of and whatever it says, the outer envelope sets the tone of your mailing. It must harmonize with the materials inside.

The Brochure

As noted, most mailing packages require a good brochure or circular in addition to a letter. It can be a small, two-color affair or a beautiful, giant circular that's almost as big as a tablecloth. But the job it has to do is the same, and it deserves your best creative effort. One way or another your circular has to do a complete selling job. To give yourself every chance for success, review the appearance, content, and preparation of your circular. Exhibit 14–6 is a handy checklist for this purpose.

EXHIBIT 14–6

Brochure Checklist

Appearance
1. Is the circular designed for the market you are trying to reach?
2. Is the presentation suited to the product or service you are offering?
3. Is the circular consistent with the rest of the mailing package?

Content
4. Is there a big idea behind your circular?
5. Do your headlines stick to the key offer?
6. Is your product or service dramatized to its best advantage by format and/or presentation?
7. Do you show broadly adaptable examples of your product or service in use?
8. Does your entire presentation follow a logical sequence and tell a complete story—including price, offer, and guarantee?

Preparation
9. Can the circular be cut out of standard-size paper stock?
10. Is the quality of paper stock in keeping with the presentation?
11. Is color employed judiciously to show the product or service in its best light?

The Publisher's or Lift Letter

The second letter, or "publisher's letter," has become almost a must in direct mail today. Repeated testing indicates that such a letter boosts response 10 percent or more. The letter is either folded or in a separate sealed envelope that warns sternly: "Open this letter only if you have decided not to respond to this offer." Of course, everybody opens it immediately. This gives you the chance to do a little extra selling, primarily in reassuring the prospects that they really have nothing to lose and everything to gain in accepting your offer.

The Order Form

If Ernest Hemingway had been a direct response writer, he probably would have dubbed the order form "the moment of truth." Many prospects make a final decision on whether to respond after reading it. Some even read the order form before anything else in the envelope, because they know it's the easiest way to find out what's being offered at what price. The best advice on order forms comes from Henry Cowen, a direct marketing specialist:

> *There are direct mail manuals around that recommend simple, easy-to-read order forms, but my experience indicates the mailer is far better off with a busy, rather jumbled appearance and plenty of copy. Formal and legal-looking forms that appear valuable, too valuable to throw away, are good.*

The key words in Cowen's statement are "too valuable to throw away." The order form or reply form that appears valuable induces readership. It impels the reader to do something with it, to take advantage of the offer. High on the list of devices and techniques that make order forms look valuable are certificate borders, safety paper backgrounds, simulated rubber stamps, eagles, blue handwriting, seals, serial numbers, receipt stubs, and so on. And sheet size alone can greatly add to the valuable appearance of a response form. (Many of these techniques are on the order forms shown in Chapter 5, "The Offer.")

Above all, don't call your reply device an order form. Call it a Reservation Certificate, Free-Gift Check, Trial Membership Application, or some other benefit heading. It automatically seems more valuable to the reader.

Getting back more inquiry and order forms starts with making them appear too valuable to throw away. But to put frosting on the cake, add the dimension of personal involvement. Give readers something to do with the order form. Ask them to put a token in a "Yes" or "No" slot. Get them to affix a gummed stamp. Have them tear off a stub that has your guarantee on it. Once you have prodded the prospect into action, there is a good chance you will receive an order.

Finally, the order form should restate your offer and benefits. If a prospect loses the letter or circular, a good order form should be able to stand alone and do a complete selling job. And if it's designed to be mailed back on its own (without an envelope), it's usually worthwhile to prepay the postage.

Gift Slips and Other Enclosures

In addition to the letter, brochure, and order form, one of the most common enclosures is a free gift slip. If you have a free gift offer, you'll normally get much better results by putting that offer on a separate slip rather than building it into your circular.

If you insert an extra enclosure, make sure it stands out from the rest of the mailing and gets attention. You can often accomplish this by printing the enclosure on a colored stock and making it a different size from the other mailing components. Most free gifts, for example, can be adequately played up on a small slip that's 3½ × 8½ or 5½ × 8½ inches.

Another enclosure that's often used is a business reply envelope. This isn't essential if the order form can be designed as a self-mailer. But if you have an offer that the reader might consider to be of a private nature, an envelope is usually better. Buying a self-improvement book, for example. Or applying for an insurance policy, where the application asks some personal questions. Also, the extra expense of a reply envelope is often justified if you want to encourage more cash-with-order replies.

How to Improve a Good Mailing Package

So far we've been talking about how to create a new mailing package. Let's suppose you've done that and you want to make it better. Or you've got a successful mailing package you've been using for a couple of years (your control) and you want to beat it. How do you go about it? One of the best ways is to come up with an entirely different appeal for your letter. For instance, suppose you're selling an income tax guide and your present letter is built around saving money. That's probably a tough appeal to beat.

But to develop a new approach, you might write a letter around a negative appeal, something people want to avoid. Experience has proved that a negative appeal is often stronger than a positive one. Yet it's frequently overlooked by copywriters. An appropriate negative copy appeal for our example might be something like: "How to avoid costly mistakes that can get you in trouble with the Internal Revenue Service." Or: "Are you taking advantage of these six commonly overlooked tax deductions?"

Another good technique is to change the type of lead on your letter. If you're using a news lead, try one built around the narrative approach. Or develop a provocative question as the lead. Usually a new lead will require you to rewrite the first few paragraphs of copy to fit the lead, but then you can often pick up the rest of the letter from your control copy.

A creative professional with a well-organized approach for coming up with new ideas is Sol Blumenfeld. He uses the additive approach, the extractive approach, and the innovative approach, among others.

The additive approach adds something to a control package that can increase its efficiency in such a way as to justify the extra cost involved. Usually, this entails using inserts. Inserts that can be used to heighten response include testimonial slips, extra discounts, a free gift for cash with order, and a news flash or bulletin. Stamps or tokens may be built into the response device. And, if you have a logical reason to justify it, add an expiration date to your offer.

The extractive approach requires a careful review of your existing mailing package copy. You often can find a potential winning lead buried somewhere in the body copy.

Unlike the extractive approach, the innovative approach is designed to produce completely new ideas. If you are testing three or four new copy approaches, at least one of them should represent a potential breakthrough, something that's highly original, perhaps even a little wild. Let yourself go, and you may produce real breakthroughs this way: dramatic new formats, exciting copy approaches, and offers that will really shellac the old control!

When you create your own direct mail, consider the checklist in Exhibit 14–7. Remember that these are guidelines, not rigid rules, and that "X will usually outpull Y" means every so often X will *not* outpull Y.

Classic Mailing Packages Get Results

Proof that the classic direct mail package continues to perform in a multimedia environment can be found in stories from two organizations: the Light Opera Works and the Dreyfus Service Organization.

Light Opera Works

Thousands of struggling theater groups and performing arts groups in the United States face a common problem: the comparatively modest prices they charge for tickets is not sufficient to cover the total costs of producing plays, musicals, and operas.

Light Opera Works of Evanston, Illinois, is no exception. Its ticket sales cover only about 65 percent of its total costs. How does the organization raise the difference? Through professional fund-raising.

Light Opera Works is fortunate to have a very generous patron—G. Todd Hunt, president of his own direct marketing agency, the Hunt Company. His pro bono efforts have helped make Light Opera Works a thriving group.

EXHIBIT 14–7

Checklist for Direct Mail Packages

Mailing Format

- The letter ranks first in importance.
- The most effective mailing package consists of outside envelope, letter, circular, response form, and business reply envelope.

Letters

- Form letters using indented paragraphs usually outpull those in which paragraphs are not indented.
- Underlining important phrases and sentences usually increases results slightly.
- A letter with a separate circular generally does better than a combination letter and circular.
- A form letter with an effective running headline ordinarily does as well as a filled-in letter.
- Authentic testimonials in a sales letter ordinarily increase the pull.
- A two-page letter ordinarily outpulls a one-page letter.

Circulars

- A circular that deals specifically with the proposition presented in the letter is more effective than a circular of an institutional character.
- A combination of art and photography usually produces a better circular than one employing either art or photography alone.
- A circular usually proves to be ineffective in selling news magazines and news services.
- In selling big-ticket products, deluxe, large-size, color circulars virtually always warrant the extra cost over circulars 11" × 17" or smaller.

Outside Envelopes

- Illustrated envelopes increase response if their message is tied into the offer.
- Variety in types and sizes of envelopes pays, especially in a series of mailings.

Reply Forms

- Reply cards with receipt stubs usually increase response over cards with no stub.
- "Busy" order or request forms that look important usually produce a larger response than neat, clean-looking forms.
- Postage-free business reply cards generally bring more responses than those to which the respondent must affix postage.

Reply Envelopes

- A reply envelope increases cash-with-order response.
- A reply envelope increases responses to collection letters.

Color

- Two-color letters usually outpull one-color letters.
- An order or reply form printed in colored ink or on colored stock usually outpulls one printed in black ink on white stock.
- A two-color circular generally proves to be more effective than a one-color circular.
- Full color is warranted in the promotion of such items as food products, apparel, furniture, and other merchandise if the quality of color reproduction is good.

EXHIBIT 14–7   *(continued)*

Postage
- Third-class mail ordinarily pulls as well as first-class mail.
- Postage-metered envelopes usually pull better than affixing postage stamps (and you can meter third-class postage).
- A "designed" printed permit on the envelope usually does as well as postage metered mail.

According to Todd, fund-raising for Light Opera Works is closely tied in with ticket sales. That's because people who are most likely to contribute are those who attend the productions (ticket buyers). And the most committed ticket buyers are the *subscribers*, who purchase the entire four-show season package in advance. Therefore, most fund-raising energy and budget is directed at this target.

The most important effort is the renewal package, which urges existing subscribers to renew their season tickets for another year. It also emphasizes the need for additional contributions above and beyond the ticket price (see Exhibit 14–8).

The second most effective appeal is the preseason appeal. This is sent to subscribers two weeks before the season's opening production. Copy on the reply card is tailored to three segments:

1. Subscribers who have already given at least once in the current year.

2. Subscribers who have given in past years but who have not yet contributed in the current year.

3. Subscribers who have never given.

The mailing consists of an outer envelope, a reply card (with suggested amounts tailored to each person's contribution history), a letter from the general manager, a lift note to encourage response with a drawing for tickets to a popular musical in Chicago, and a reply envelope. (Exhibit 14–9 presents the letter and reply card.)

These fund-raising efforts are obviously professional. But were they successful? Yes. Total contributions from direct mail were $28,108. Expenses were $7,478. Therefore the contribution/expense ratio was 376 percent.

For 15 years Light Opera Works relied almost exclusively on direct mail campaigns like these to raise funds from its subscribers. As the company grew, its success created the need for even higher levels of fund-raising. So the company decided to hire a development consultant to personally nurture and solicit its best targets, people who give $100 or more to the direct mail appeals.

Direct mail now serves a dual purpose—not only to generate contributions, but also to create a growing pool of ripe prospects for the development consultant.

Personal solicitation efforts to the $100-plus donors, originally obtained via direct mail, generated additional net gifts of $119,000.

EXHIBIT 14–8

Light Opera Works Renewal Package

Check Priority Box 1 or 2:

☐ **1.** I want my **same seats and series** for 1999, as shown below (no changes):

Series	How Many	Section	Cahn Seats*	Total	Early Bird Price (ends 12/31/98)
SA-2	2	C	B801 B802	~~$298.00~~	$266

Thanks for your contribution this year. May we count on → your $150 gift now?	Processing Fee	$	3.50
	Tax deductible contribution .... *(Subscriptions cover only part of our costs)*	$	
	Total Order	$	

*You will receive comparable seating for *She Loves Me* at Second Stage (McGaw YMCA Child Care Center Auditorium).

☐ **2.** I want to **make changes** as marked below:

Series	How Many	Section	Price Each (Early Bird Price ends 12/31/98)	Total
			$	$

Thanks for your contribution this year. May we count on → your $150 gift now?	Processing Fee	$	3.50
	Tax deductible contribution .... *($75 or more gets seating priority as available)*	$	
	Total Order	$	

☐ Check (payable to LIGHT OPERA WORKS) ☐ AmEx ☐ MasterCard ☐ VISA ☐ Discover

Card # _____ Expires _____

Mail in the enclosed envelope to: LIGHT OPERA WORKS, 927 Noyes St, Evanston, IL 60201-2799

▲ Tear off and mail top portion. Keep bottom portion for your records.

Cahn Auditorium (Mainstage) above. You will receive comparable seating for *She Loves Me* at Second Stage (McGaw YMCA Child Care Center in Evanston).

Section	Value— 4 Shows	You Pay	Early Bird (ends 12/31/98)
A	$183.00	~~$149~~	$133
B	$139.00	~~$119~~	$99
C	$183.00	~~$149~~	$133
D	$118.00	~~$99~~	$88
E	$88.00	~~$69~~	$58

Age 21 and younger 1/2 price

Questions? (847) 869-6300

SUBSCRIBER RENEWAL for '99

Early Bird Savings offer ends Dec. 31, 1998! Mail now.

Please exchange my *Mikado* tickets to the performance I've checked below (if desired):
☐ New Year's Eve (Friday, Dec. 31, 1999 at 8 pm)
☐ Monday, Dec. 27, '99 at 2 pm   ☐ Wednesday, Dec. 29, '99 at 2 pm

You may request a specific date for *She Loves Me* if you wish: _____
Or we will give you best available seats for an appropriate date in your series. You may exchange later if necessary.

Home Phone: 773/248-5020

Business Phone: 773/248-5790 ext. 0

E-mail address (if you have one): CgoLnPk@aol.com
(Print E-mail address clearly with proper capital and small letters)

Mr. G. Todd Hunt
2626 Lakeview, #1312
Chicago IL 60614

Please mark any corrections to your address/phone/e-mail above.

Series	Time	Helen	Rose-Marie	She Loves Me*	Mikado**
SA-1	8 pm	Sat. June 5	Sat. Aug. 21	Sat, Oct. 9, 16, 23 or 30	Thu. Dec. 30
SU-1	2 pm	Sun. June 6	Sun. Aug. 22	Sun, Oct. 10, 17, 24 or 31	Sun. Dec. 26
FR-2	8 pm	Fri. June 11	Fri. Aug. 27	Fri. Oct. 8, 15, 22 or 29	Fri. Dec. 31 (New Year's Eve)
SA-2	8 pm	Sat. June 12	Sat. Aug. 28	Sat, Oct. 9, 16, 23 or 30	Sat. Jan. 1
SU-2	2 pm	Sun. June 13	Sun. Aug. 29	Sun, Oct. 10, 17, 24 or 31	Sun. Jan. 2

* We will assign you best available seats for *She Loves Me* for one of the dates listed in your series. Or you may request a specific date. Note *She Loves Me* matinees at 3 pm.

** *Mikado* also Monday Dec. 27 at 2 pm and Wednesday, Dec. 29 at 2 pm

EXHIBIT 14–8 *(continued)*

Light Opera Works Renewal Package *(continued)*

Use the pink form enclosed to renew your season tickets. And do it *now*, because your Early Bird Savings are valid only through December 31!

December 1998

Dear Subscriber,

Three big shows and one romantic jewel of a musical!

That's what's in store for you next year at LIGHT OPERA WORKS:

> Beautiful Helen of Troy (La Belle Hélène) by Jacques Offenbach in June

> Rose-Marie by Rudolf Friml in August

And one of our most asked-for shows in a glorious new production:

> The Mikado by Gilbert and Sullivan in December 1999 (next year at this time)

And the jewel of a musical? She Loves Me, from the creators of "Fiddler on the Roof," at our "Second Stage" in October at the McGaw YMCA Child Care Center Auditorium. Read about it in the colorful brochure enclosed.

I know you'll want to guarantee your seats for this fabulous lineup, so we've included your pink renewal form.

> If you want your same series and Cahn seats as listed on the form, just check Box 1.

> To make changes, check Box 2 and tell us what you'd like.

And you'll get the special Early Bird price when you renew before December 31!

With the hustle and bustle of the holidays practically upon us, why not mail your renewal now while it's on your mind.

And remember...

> Ticket sales alone do not cover the full cost of our music theater productions. So please add a generous contribution to your renewal.

Thank you so much for your continued support. Because of you, LIGHT OPERA WORKS has flourished and will do so for many years to come.

Sincerely,

Bridget McDonough

Bridget McDonough
General Manager

P.S.   This Early Bird Savings offer ends December 31, so act now.

> And remember, kids age 21 and younger are half-price (subscriptions and single tickets). What better way to introduce the young people in your life to the joys of music theater!

LIGHT OPERA WORKS
Illinois' Music Theater
A not-for-profit organization

927 Noyes Street • Evanston, Illinois 60201-2799 • Subscription Office (847) 869-6300 • FAX 6388
E-mail: postmaster@light-opera-works.org • Web site: http://www.light-opera-works.org

LIGHT OPERA WORKS
ILLINOIS' MUSIC THEATER

EXHIBIT 14–9

Light Opera Works Preseason Appeal Letter

ILLINOIS' MUSIC THEATER

Thank you for being part of our 19th Season!
Here's my report on the year ahead —

Wednesday, May 19

Dear Valued Subscriber,

I wish you could have seen the look on the poor gentleman's face when I answered his question "What's <u>Beautiful Helen of Troy</u> about?"

I bumped into one of our subscribers at Dominick's last Saturday when he posed that query about our upcoming season opener.

    "Well," I began, "It's basically about sex and lies in high places."

Seeing his expression I quickly added, "But it's by Offenbach and it's more than a hundred years old -- so you won't be offended!"

He sighed with relief.

I explained how the show premiered in Paris in 1864 as "La Belle Hélène." Critics were appalled at the burlesque treatment of the revered Greek gods -- and of course audiences loved it!

<u>Beautiful Helen of Troy</u>, our English version, opens the 19th season of LIGHT OPERA WORKS on June 5. It's a wild, toe-tapping parody of love and power that is not at all outdated.

    I'm writing to thank you for being part of our subscriber family and to answer some of the questions you have sent and e-mailed me in recent weeks.

But first I want to tell you about the outstanding director we've signed to helm <u>Beautiful Helen of Troy</u> -- Peter Amster.

Peter is an old friend of LIGHT OPERA WORKS, having directed <u>Die Fledermaus</u> (1986), <u>Lady in the Dark</u> (1989) and <u>H.M.S. Pinafore</u> (1997).

He's also serving as choreographer (just yesterday

LIGHT OPERA WORKS
Illinois' Music Theater
A not-for-profit organization

927 Noyes Street • Evanston, Illinois 60201-2799 • (847) 869-6300 • FAX 6388
E-mail: postmaster@light-opera-works.org • Web site: http://www.light-opera-works.org

EXHIBIT 14–9   *(continued)*

2

he showed me a little preview of the routines he's cooked up for
this wacky show). Believe me when I say you will <u>not</u> be bored!

Now, on to some of your questions.

**I think <u>Rose-Marie</u> has the best melodies ever written.
Is that why you're bringing it back in August?**

Of course! Who can resist "Only a Kiss," "Rose-Marie" and the
hauntingly beautiful "Indian Love Call"? And we have an extra
treat for you -- the LIGHT OPERA WORKS debut of David Perkovich,
one of Chicago's most acclaimed directors.

You may have seen his work at the Illinois Theatre Center,
Interplay and Candlelight Dinner Playhouse. David has forgone
the performing script usually offered by the leasing house;
choosing instead to revisit the original 1924 libretto. His
goal is to make this <u>Rose-Marie</u> as authentic as possible.

**We really enjoyed <u>The Fantasticks</u> last year in the new
LIGHT OPERA WORKS Second Stage. How did that work out?**

A big fat hit! Subscribers enjoyed it, critics enjoyed it, and
everyone fell in love with the intimate theatre space. In fact,
the Organic Theatre of Chicago will be the second performing arts
tenant at the McGaw YMCA Child Care Center Auditorium this fall
(alternating with LIGHT OPERA WORKS, of course).

We plan to continue using this cozy theater for our Second Stage,
producing smaller works that don't feel quite at home on the
larger stage of Cahn Auditorium. <u>She Loves Me</u> is our next
Second Stage show in October and November.

**We've subscribed for years and have learned that, even
if we're not familiar with a certain show, we're going
to enjoy it. LIGHT OPERA WORKS never steers us wrong.**

Thank you. There's always economic pressure to do "name" shows
that will sell tickets. While we love the old chestnuts as much
as the next person, we realize we have an obligation to offer
our subscribers lesser known works from time to time.
Your support enables us to do that without breaking the bank.
And what fun it is to discover those "forgotten" gems! Which
leads to the next question...

**<u>She Loves Me</u> sounds interesting in your season brochure.
What's the show like?**

In a word -- enchanting. If you saw the Tom Hanks/Meg Ryan movie

EXHIBIT 14-9   *(continued)*

Light Opera Works Preseason Appeal Letter

3

"You've Got Mail," it's based on the same story. Two co-workers who can't stand each other by day are actually secret pen pals by night. The score is by Bock and Harnick, who wrote "Fiddler on the Roof" and other great shows of the 50s and 60s. It's one of my all-time favorite musicals and I know you will love it too.

To direct, we've lured back Ronn Toebaas (<u>The Fantasticks</u>). Ronn is perfect for this beguiling show, which had two previous movie incarnations -- "The Shop Around the Corner" with Jimmy Stewart and "In the Good Old Summertime" with Judy Garland.

<u>The Mikado</u> is my favorite Gilbert and Sullivan. Thank you for scheduling it at New Year's!

Yes, we wanted to close out this century with a classic from the previous century. Ko-Ko, Yum-Yum, Katisha and those Three Little Maids from School will be on hand to delight us. And Ronn Toebaas will do double duty this season by directing "The Mikado."

It's not really news anymore, but we truly appreciate the renovation of Cahn Auditorium. The lobby, elevator and especially the washrooms are just great.

I'm glad you enjoy them, but don't thank us -- thank our landlord, Northwestern University. They certainly did a nice job throughout the theater.

But isn't LIGHT OPERA WORKS <u>part</u> of Northwestern?

I feel like a broken record, but there are still some folks who think we're affiliated with Northwestern. We are not. We are an independent organization that rents Cahn Auditorium. We receive no funding from the University.

Nor are we part of Evanston YMCA. We rent the McGaw YMCA Child Care Center Auditorium for our Second Stage, and receive no funding from that organization.

How is the financial health of LIGHT OPERA WORKS?

We're doing well as we enter our 19th season, thanks largely to our loyal subscribers and contributors.

Fiscal responsibility is important in any business, and at LIGHT OPERA WORKS our business is producing first-rate music theater.

Budgeting is a tedious but necessary process. To maintain a balanced budget, I examine expenses and income at monthly staff and board meetings, anticipating additional funding needs in some

EXHIBIT 14–9   (continued)

4

areas and savings in others.

Honestly, it's a challenge. That's the reality of a business where earned income (ticket sales) does not cover all our costs.

<u>In fact, sold-out houses cover only about 3 dollars out of every 5 it costs to put on the shows you see.</u>

Although this ratio ranks us among the most fiscally sound arts organizations in America, <u>we depend on those remaining 2 dollars out of every 5 from friends like you</u>!

You, perhaps more than anyone, understand the economics of mounting large-scale music theater works.

And you are among our group of special friends who respond generously when we ask for needed funds.

Now, as we open <u>Beautiful Helen of Troy</u>, I'm hoping we can count on you for an extra special "kick-off" gift -- to help launch our 19th season in style.

please be as generous as you can - our shows cost a lot to produce

I promise your gift will be used wisely, with not a single penny wasted. At LIGHT OPERA WORKS we don't have big expense accounts or fancy offices. We put every dollar we can up on the stage.

So please <u>mail the blue card with your gift now</u>.

And enjoy <u>Beautiful Helen of Troy</u> June 5 through 13. Thank you for your continued support.

Sincerely,

Bridget McDonough
General Manager

P.S. When you mail your contribution before the end of June,
     you'll be entered in a drawing for two tickets to <u>Fosse</u>,
     opening in September at the restored Oriental Theatre
     in Chicago! Please respond now.

EXHIBIT 14–9   *(continued)*

Light Opera Works Preseason Appeal Letter

> **YES,** I want to support LIGHT OPERA WORKS with a tax-deductible **19th Season "Kick-Off" contribution** of:
>
> ☐$120   ☐$160   ☐$225 $_____
>
> *See other side for your benefits under each category of giving.*
>
> ☐ Check enclosed, payable to LIGHT OPERA WORKS
> ☐ VISA ☐ MasterCard ☐ Discover ☐ Am Express
> Card # _____ Expires_____
>
> Mr. Howard Bonk
> 360 E Dingle Lane
> Apt. 1607
> Chicago IL 60601
>
> Signature _____
> **I understand my gift will enter me in the drawing for tickets to *Fosse* at the Oriental Theatre/Ford Center in Chicago.**
> ☐ Enclosed is a Matching Gift form from my employer.
> *Mail this card now in the enclosed envelope to:*
> LIGHT OPERA WORKS, 927 Noyes, Evanston, IL 60201-2799
>
> *Please mark any corrections to your name/address above.*

In summation, Mr. Hunt attributed the success to:

1. Isolating a small segment of most likely givers.

2. Mailing repeated solicitations.

3. Personally nurturing the best givers to generate additional higher gifts.

4. Positioning Light Opera Works as a successful, well-managed business. Contributors are asked to "buy in" to this success, rather than "give to charity."

Dreyfus Triple Advantage Variable Annuity Mailing

Three times the Dreyfus Service Corporation had attempted to market its "Triple Advantage" Variable Annuity to affluent consumers through the mail. Each time, it was unsuccessful. Dreyfus suspected that this product was too complex, and potential investors were confused or ignorant about its benefits.

Nevertheless, it decided to promote the product by mail one final time, and engaged Kobs Gregory Passavant (KGP), a Chicago-based direct marketing agency, to spearhead the effort. According to Senior Vice President and Creative Director Alan Fonorow, KGP's thinking began with two assumptions: (1) the product is extremely complex, and (2) the mailing should generate leads, and not attempt to get immediate sales. So, not surprisingly, the strategy that emerged can be summed up in a single word: *simplicity*.

Prior mailings had equally emphasized the triple advantages of tax deferral, choice of investment options, and the investor's flexibility in how the money is paid out after retirement. This new effort was primarily focused on tax deferral.

The envelope offered to reveal a "mystery investment," and the letter directed prospects to a brochure that summarized the hypothetical story of two people who invested $100,000 25 years ago. Today, the person whose investment was tax-deferred is $300,000 wealthier than the other!

This dramatic point was driven home by designing the brochure to look like a book jacket with sleeves. Its title was "The Mystery of the $300,000 Windfall." Text was divided into simple "chapters," each involving a brief story about a typical person who would benefit from a Dreyfus annuity. An investor's quiz, styled to resemble a bookmark, both involved and qualified prospects (see Exhibit 14–10).

This mailing generated a response well over 5 percent, which is quite good for a specialized investment product like this one. It also converted well, and led to new accounts that averaged an initial balance 20 times greater than the typical new Dreyfus account.

Dreyfus KGP Package

Shown here is the outside mailing envelope, front of a paneled brochure, and a Quick Quiz card.

EXHIBIT 14–10 *(continued)*

Dreyfus KGP Package

Front side of two-page letter.

Service Corporation
144 Glenn Curtiss Boulevard
Uniondale, NY 11553

002 002 *******AUTO**3-DIGIT 015
Sample A. Sample
123 Sample Ave.
Anytown, MA 99999-9999

Dear Sample A. Sample,

Could you benefit from an investment vehicle that may help reduce your annual tax bite, build a solid nest egg, and secure a steady income for your retirement?

You've already shown an interest in exploring sound financial planning when you asked about Dreyfus Mutual Funds. I'd like to suggest investigating another potentially valuable investment that provides the power of Dreyfus money management with advantages that may surprise you. Let me give you some clues:

- The power of its tax-deferred status can help you make the most of your savings.[1]
- You choose among 15 quality investment portfolios to help beat inflation.
- You can choose a flow of income for your retirement for as long as you live.

And, based on the hypothetical example in the enclosed brochure, it's possible you could earn $300,000 more than if you put your hard-earned money in an ordinary, taxable investment. You wouldn't pay taxes until you begin withdrawals.

Intrigued? It's really no mystery. It's the Dreyfus/Transamerica Triple Advantage® Variable Annuity.[2]

Investing in a variable annuity now lets you set aside money to grow, without the burden of being taxed year after year. You don't pay a penny of taxes on your earnings — until you withdraw them. And by the time you retire and begin distributions, you may be in a much lower tax bracket.

Actually, tax deferral is just one of three distinct advantages of our Triple Advantage Variable Annuity:

over, please ...

[1]Tax deferral is only available for individuals and is not available for corporations and most trusts. A sales charge on each premium may be imposed on withdrawals. Withdrawals will be subject to income taxes and if made prior to age 59 1/2 may be subject to an additional 10% penalty tax.

[2]Annuity contracts issued by Transamerica Occidental Life Insurance Company, Certificate Form GNC-33, Individual Contract Form 1-502.

EXHIBIT 14–10   (continued)

Dreyfus KGP Package

Back page of two-page letter and personalized response card.

1 <u>The tax advantage.</u> Just like an IRA or 401(k), your earnings grow faster when taxes are deferred. Better yet, you can make unlimited contributions to your annuity every year.[3]

2 <u>The investment advantage.</u> Choose from 15 Dreyfus investment portfolios. Tell us which ones you want your money in and at what percentages. You can even lock in the percentages, so if one grows disproportionately, your portfolio automatically re-balances the way you want it. You can also change your investment combinations up to 18 times a year without charge, completely tax-free.

3 <u>The annuity advantage.</u> You can choose how you want your money paid out, and also protect your family against any loss of principal if you should die before the pay-out phase begins.

Want to find out more? To get our fact-packed Tax-Deferred Investment Kit, just call 1-800-337-9339x5506 or mail the Free Kit card in the enclosed postpaid envelope. If you prefer to meet face-to-face with a Dreyfus representative, contact your local Dreyfus Financial Center for an appointment.

You won't be obligated, and it could mean you and your family may be able to live much more comfortably when you're ready to retire.

Sincerely,

Wilson Santos
Executive Vice President
Dreyfus Service Corporation

P.S.   Your Free Kit is filled with information about tax advantages and the specific investment choices available, including stock/growth, total return, bond, and money market portfolios. Just call toll free 1-800-337-9339x5506 or mail your Free Kit card today.

[3]Contribution limits may apply for certain qualified plans. Policies in excess of $1,000,000 require prior approval by Transamerica.

©1997, Dreyfus Service Corporation. Transamerica Securities Sales Corporation, Distributor.

D970309

FREE Tax-Deferred Annuity Kit

☐ **YES!** I want the whole story of how I can save for retirement and take the mystery out of retirement planning. Please send my FREE Kit, with complete information about the Dreyfus/Transamerica Triple Advantage Variable Annuity including details on 15 professionally-managed investment choices, all sales charges, fees and expenses. I will read the Prospectus carefully before I invest or send any money. I understand there is absolutely no obligation.

Sample A. Sample
123 Sample Ave.
Anytown, MA 99999-9999

(   )
Daytime Phone

(   )
Evening Phone

Please correct address at left if necessary, and fill in your telephone numbers.

Return this card in the enclosed prepaid envelope today.   Or call 1-800-337-9339x5506

D970309

CASE STUDY: Illinois Lottery Birthday Program

BACKGROUND AND CHALLENGE

The Illinois Lottery is a very nontraditional direct marketer. The product has a mass appeal with a tendency to gravitate to a very particular segment of the population. Recent lottery research indicated individuals involved with the lottery tended to be older, and had longtime experience playing lottery games. The young adult, new family segment of the population couldn't relate to the lottery's message, but the thought of the lottery as a form of entertainment, or even worth their time—let alone their money—did not even register on their radar screen.

The new general advertising for the Illinois Lottery, however, used a very hip "dancing illustrations" and a hot salsa-mambo music track to liven up its general image and promote the new Instant Games.

The challenge was clear: to attract new, younger players.

SOLUTION

According to Bill Foulas, Managing Director of Foote, Cone, and Belding Direct, FCB Direct proposed that the lottery embark on a direct marketing program that would allow it to directly acquire new players, and actually track their redemption rate. For the first time the Illinois Lottery would be able to know how successful its efforts were to acquire new players. In order to distinguish between new and existing players, the database gurus needed to bump up prospect lists against known players/winners and to take into account the average broad demographic of the current lottery profile.

The first program FCB Direct tested was called "Birthday."

The Birthday Program had the difficult task of reaching new players at the younger end of the audience spectrum. FCB Direct selected individuals from the ages of 21 to 29, ensuring the audience was of legal age to play the lottery, purposefully using broad criteria to extract the names they needed. (Honing

the lists to a tighter level by income level and other selects was possible but avoided, so that efforts would reflect an offering to the general population and not target any specific gender, race, or income level.)

Given the broad scope of the audience and the previous poor receptivity of the younger audience to the lottery, FCB Direct used a test quantity of 100,000. It felt this quality would accurately represent the audience and give enough responses to gain some learning for future use.

Creatively, FCB Direct decided that the best way to reach this younger audience was with a message that would get their attention—a combination of attention-getting, involving creative they could relate to, and message timing that they simply could not ignore. That said, the perfect message and timing combined to be a "birthday card" received on or around the birthday of prospective lottery players (actually the month of their birthday).

The execution was designed to look like a real birthday card—from the lavender envelope and live stamp to the handwritten laser front and "Pot-Of-Gold Greetings" logo on the back of the envelope. Once inside, the recipient did indeed get a birthday card along with a "birthday present." (See Exhibit 14–11.)

The card design was intentionally linked to the general advertising's illustrative style and color scheme. The integrated timing of the two efforts and the weight of the general television advertising could do nothing but boost the redemption rates of the direct marketing program. The message was clearly a birthday message along with a marketing promotion for the current "Lucky Checks" games (see Exhibit 14–12).

Tied to the Lucky Checks promotion was the "birthday present"—a scratch-off coupon. Designed to function like a Lottery Instant Game with the scratch and win involvement, this coupon not only got the prospect to take action but actually simulated the game-playing experience and put the

CASE STUDY: **Illinois Lottery Birthday Program** *(continued)*

EXHIBIT 14–11

Illinois Lottery

Center spread of birthday card with scratch-off

EXHIBIT 14–12

Illinois Lottery

Marketing Promotion for Lucky Checks

prospect in that euphoric winning state of mind from the get-go.

Of course, since it was a coupon, everyone who scratched the "birthday cake" was a winner—a free Lucky Checks game ticket. Not a bad birthday present when you consider it offered a chance to win thousands of dollars.

As mentioned earlier, each coupon was individually bar-coded to reflect the program, the month, the offer, and the individual's name. This permitted FCB Direct to get an instant read on results, add these results to the marketing database, and also take advantage of already existing operational infrastructure with the lottery's distribution channels. Also, an expiration date was lasered on the coupon for 30 days after the month of the recipient's birthday. In short, the coupon could be redeemed in exactly the same manner that a normal winning lottery ticket would be redeemed, and as a result prospects also found themselves at the point of purchase, and easily able to get their "real" ticket (and hopefully more).

RESULTS

Considering that the objective was to make inroads and establish some semblance of a relationship with the younger audience, it worked pretty darn well, gaining a 25 percent response rate! Better yet, that response rate has held pretty consistent from month to month (mailings happen every month according to the birthday month file), which means that this audience is responding to the message in a consistent, predictable, and actionable manner.

PILOT PROJECT Earlier, this chapter presented formulas as a route to follow in the construction of a mailing package. This pilot project introduces an evaluation index to be applied after the mailing package has been put together. The copyrighted Depth-Evaluation Index was created by James R. Rosenfield, chairman of Rosenfield & Associates of San Diego, California. Jim has spent more than 30 years learning about direct marketing. He has keynoted marketing conferences all over the world, taught hundreds of seminars, and has published more than 400 articles, as well as a book. He has counseled scores of companies, including AT&T, MasterCard International, Citibank, General Motors, American Airlines, and IBM.

For this exercise, Jim Rosenfield has selected a Book-of-the-Month Club mailing package (see Exhibit 14–13). Here is the critique in Jim's own words.

Book-of-the-Month Club is one of the great concepts in the history of marketing. It leverages a hoary mail order advantage, famously phrased by direct marketing pioneer Lester Wunderman as "adding a service to a product"—an advantage that translates directly into the Internet and E-commerce. But it goes far beyond that, in its ingenuity at exploiting human inertia via the negative option, which turns a sale into an annuity.

Based on an often-mailed control package, Book-of-the-Month Club (BOMC) seems to be sticking to the negative option like a barnacle, and along with using their heritage, they're invoking it. "FOUNDED 1926" proudly appears in several places, including on a personalized bookplate, "our way of saying 'Welcome to the Club.'"

At the same time, there's a nicely contemporary gesture of corporate responsibility on the inside front cover of the brochure/booklet: "Book-of-the-Month Club supports local public libraries . . . A portion of every purchase . . . is donated to this important cause."

The outer envelope pretty much tells the whole story: "FREE GIFT! (DETAILS INSIDE). You have been selected to receive 4 books for $1 at savings of up to $198. Which 4 would you like? Please respond by July 28, 1999 . . ." The time limit might be a cliché, but it's a cliché abandoned at one's peril.

Note BOMC's use of the numeral 4, rather than the word "four." Small numerals are in the right hemisphere of the brain communications, but the word "four" is left hemisphere. One never-to-be-ignored direct mail principle: when there's a choice, always use speedy right-hemisphere icons rather than more ponderous left-hemisphere communications.

Icons and Surfaces

An effective direct mail package has to place compelling right-hemisphere icons on key surfaces that relate to the eye: (1) front of outer envelope, (2) back of outer envelope, (3) above salutation of letter, (4) first line, first paragraph of letter, (5) P.S., (6)

EXHIBIT 14–13

Book-of-the-Month Club Package

Outside envelope and two-page letter

You have been selected to receive 4 books for $1 at savings of up to $198.

Which 4 would you like?

Please respond by July 28, 1999

BULK RATE
U.S. Postage
PAID
Book-of-the-
Month Club, Inc.

FREE GIFT!
(DETAILS INSIDE)

```
******************** 3-DIGIT 920
478023 881700 FRM05C 42001
J M ROSENFIELD
```

I invite you to take 4 books of your choice now.

Dear Reader,

As editor in chief of Book-of-the-Month Club, I would like to invite you to enjoy all the benefits of membership. But first, let me stress that this is no ordinary invitation.

It is my pleasure to extend to you a special offer reserved for a select group of people like you, who are well read and well informed.

We want to make it easy for you to share the Club benefits that are now more valuable than at any other time in our history. You'll enjoy even bigger savings on the finest books published.

The values of membership start right away. You can select 4 quality books for just $1—at savings of up to $198 off publishers' prices. Plus, we'll send you the Book-of-the-Month Club attaché, FREE, just for trying the Club!

Then, as a member, you save on each and every book you buy. Our New and Noteworthy books are up to 30% off the publisher's price, and some hardcovers are priced as low as $5.95.

And, as part of our generous new Dividend program, you can use the Credits you earn to purchase any book we offer. That can mean savings from 50% to 75%, and even free books.

When you qualify as a Preferred Member, you'll enjoy additional savings, exclusive benefits, and even more free books.

As a member, you can browse through a wide range of titles—everything from best-selling novels, children's books, reference books, and cookbooks to histories, biographies, self-help books, art books, even exclusive editions. Shop at your leisure from your favorite armchair, with your *Book-of-the-Month Club Views*.

If you see a book you'd like to read, let us know, and we'll deliver it to you. Rather not order in a particular month? That's fine, too. Just let us know by the date specified on the Reply Form enclosed with each *Views*.

Naturally I feel this is a wonderful opportunity. But the decision is up to you.

All you have to do is indicate the 4 books you want for $1, plus shipping and handling. Then buy just 2 more books within the next year. Why not fill in your Reply Form today?

I know you'll be glad you did.

Sincerely,

Greg Tobin

Greg Tobin
Editor in Chief

P.S. In addition to receiving your attaché FREE, you can begin your savings right now. I invite you to select a 5th book for only $4.95, plus shipping and handling. You can save up to an extra $36, and have just 1 more book to buy within the next year. See your Reply Form for details.

(over, please)

BOM0599/A

Printed in U.S.A.   © 1999 BOMC

EXHIBIT 14–13   *(continued)*

Book-of-the-Month Club Package

Order form, front of 30-page brochure with a selection of more than 200 books, front of lift note, and gift slip offering free brochure

front of brochure, (7) back of brochure, (8) response device. (The BOMC mailing is a variant of the classic package.)

There are seven icons on the outer envelope, enough to get those right-hemispheres humming nicely: The words "You" and "FREE," the name showing through the window, the monetary units ("$1, $198"), and the number of books you get ("receive 4 books," "Which 4 would you like?"). If BOMC wanted to achieve perfection, they would make the savings amount look larger: "$198.00" rather than "$198."

One negative: "You have been selected" has a dreadful subtext in the early 21st century. It implies passivity, hints at the diminution of the individual, and suggests privacy invasion.

The back of the outer envelope is not used at all, a definite oversight. There are only two predictable things people do with direct mail: they first look at the name, and address, then turn the envelope over to open it. The back of the envelope has high visibility and should generally be used to echo copy from the front. Reason: new copy might hinder the unconscious opening process.

Inside, there's a letter, a lift note, a premium slip, response device, and a brochure. Everything is good, but nothing is impeccable.

Impeccability Shortfalls

In a perfect direct mail world, the letter would not have a period after its headline. Even worse, the first page ends with a period, which is dreadful practice.

Never do this—always break in the middle of a sentence, with words along the lines of "over, please." A period is an irresistible "stop sign" for the right hemisphere!

Like so many direct mail letters, the BOMC letter would be improved by eliminating the first paragraph, which consists of "windup," nonfunctional verbosity preceding the pitch. Better to start with the second paragraph, which begins to state the offer.

The letter is unpersonalized, addressed to "Dear Reader." It's better to personalize the letter, but cost efficiencies probably dictate confining personalization to the response device and "Welcome to the Club" bookplate. Short lines—85 characters are maximum these days—enhance readability, as do indented paragraphs, which provide "hooks" for the eye. No paragraph is longer than five lines, maximum length for the postliterate 21st century.

The lift note is fine, bearing the excellent "FOUNDED 1926" and merchandising the offer. The back is blank, though. Why no message? Direct mail, like nature, abhors a vacuum, and the response device should have corrective language: "If your name or anything else is wrong, please change it."

The 16-page brochure/booklet also has the "FOUNDED 1926" message. Save for BOMC's insistence on putting periods at the end of headlines, it's a little masterpiece of its type, involving and eminently scannable.

Tactile Involvement and Specificity

Creatively, 21st century direct mail stands on four legs, two of which—icons and surfaces—have already been discussed. The other two relate to the hand and the left hemisphere of the brain: tactile involvement and specificity.

Tactile techniques—tokens or decals, design principles such as interruptive folds—have historically improved direct mail performance, for a variety of reasons. Most obviously, tactile involvement prolongs the time spent with a direct mail package. The BOMC package is a little weak here. Only the booklet gets the hand involved. The lift letter, for example, would benefit from a short fold, which invites the hand to get into action.

You can't create behavior without being specific about product and offer. But specificity works better now than ever before. Today's overloaded consumer seems to find comfort in bite-sized, systematic, presentations of information. "Enumerated specificity" can be particularly powerful: "7 Reasons to Join Book-of-the-Month Club Now!" Keep the numbers small and use uneven numbers—7, 11—to subliminally echo the rough edges of reality.

The Depth-Evaluation Index© Verdict

The BOMC package is excellent, but would be improved by a more systematic application of some of the principles discussed. My Depth-Evaluation Index© is based on a scale of 1 to 10 (1 = dreadful, 10 = terrific). BOMC gets an 8. Here's how things sum up, and why this excellent control package doesn't get a 10:

1. *Copy:* 8. The letter suffers from a weak opening, and icons should be used more systematically.

2. *Design:* 8. Not enough tactile involvement.

3. *Topography:* 8. Three surfaces—the back of the outer envelope, the back of the premium slip, and the back of the lift letter—are unused, which will cost BOMC a few basis points in response rate.

4. *Scannability:* 8. The lack of systematic attention to icons and surfaces compromises things a bit.

5. *Offer/Call-to-Action:* 10. BOMC is a master of offer structure.

6. *Clarity:* 8. In truth, negative option offers are usually a little opaque on purpose.

7. *Logic:* 10. Adding a service to a product is wonderfully logical.

8. *Involvement:* 8. Again, needs more icons, more tactile involvement.

9. *Honesty/Integrity/Believability:* 9. Compromised a bit by the overt flattery that opens the letter.

10. *Attention to Detail:* 9. Again, icons not used systematically enough.

Net Index: 8

Your Project

Apply the Depth-Evaluation Index to your last mailing package, or to a competitor's mailing package.

Key Points

▶ Whether to use a simple self-mailer, an elaborate self-mailer, or the classic mailing package (outside mailing envelope, letter, circular/brochure, and response form) depends upon your budget and your target market.

▶ Copy should include appeals that will satisfy one or more human wants of the prospect. Translate selling points into customer benefits. The more benefits you can point out for prospects, the more likely they will buy.

▶ Understand the product and the market. Talk to the prospect in language he or she will understand, and quickly get to the point or make a promise and prove that you can deliver what was promised.

▶ Selling copy, especially the headlines and lead paragraphs, should be concise, logical, clear, enthusiastic, complete, and germane and specific to the offer. While experienced writers may set their own rules, neophytes should use a formula such as AIDA or the problem-solution approach.

▶ Regardless of length, letters should look attractive and be easy to read. Keep paragraphs to six or seven lines. Use subheads, indented paragraphs, and leader dots and dashes to break up long copy. Use underscoring, capital letters, and a second ink color to make key words and sentences stand out. Add a postscript restating the offer to attract prospects' attention. Personalized letters usually, but not always, outpull nonpersonalized ones.

▶ Involve readers in inquiry and order forms by asking them to put a token in a "Yes" or "No" slot, affix a gummed stamp, or tear off a stub showing your guarantee. Be sure the order form restates your offer and benefits.

▶ To improve a letter, look for entirely different appeals. Consider leading with a negative appeal, a news lead, a narrative lead, or a provocative question. Add something to a control package, or extract a potential winning lead buried somewhere in the body copy.

CREATING AND
MANAGING CATALOGS

As the new millennium begins, cataloging is moving from the paper age to the digital age. The Internet has been likened to a train approaching the railroad station. Today's catalogers have the option of getting aboard or being left in the station. Most are opting to climb aboard.

The catalog industry enjoyed unparalleled growth through most of the 1990s and is projected to continue to outperform the retail sector by roughly double in the future. For the foreseeable future the two media can be expected to grow and prosper together, primarily because of their different and yet complementary uses.

This chapter describes and explains the catalog process and the strategies used to build and manage a successful catalog company. It examines eight core competencies of winning catalogers and the strategies they employ in merchandising, positioning, branding, and offers of the catalog, creative execution, new customer acquisition, customer list communication, and using the customer database, catalog fulfillment, and analysis of results. The catalog process chart shown in Exhibit 15-1 identifies the core competencies of a winning catalog. Refer to this chart as you read the rest of this chapter.

Core Competency #1: Merchandising

Catalogs are a blend of merchandise and audience. Most catalogs are merchandise-driven; that is, they start from a merchandise point of view and address the purchaser of the product. Many of the pioneers in cataloging—people like Roger Horchow of the Horchow Collection, Chuck Williams of Williams Sonoma, Manny Fingerhut of Fingerhut—were merchandisers who started with a solid product concept and from that concept built a growing business.

EXHIBIT 15–1

The Catalog Process

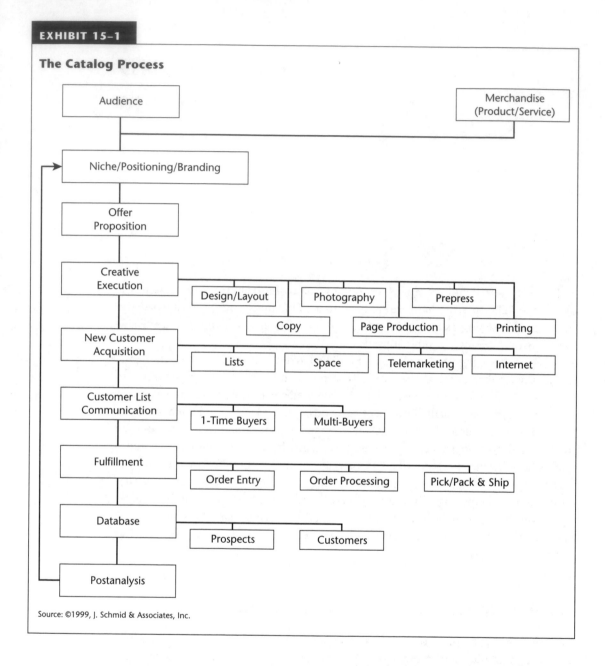

Source: ©1999, J. Schmid & Associates, Inc.

Even if a catalog is market- or audience-driven (that is, it starts with an audience that determines what products can be sold), merchandising is of vital importance. The familiar adage "Nothing comes before the product" means that if catalogers desire to build repeat buyers—a prime goal for profitability—they must start with and build a strong merchandising program that will continue to attract customers over time. Merchandising has been likened to the foundation of a building. Without a strong foundation, it is difficult to build a solid building or business.

Understanding the psychology of the catalog buyer is essential to catalog merchandising (see Exhibit 15–2). If the goal is to build repeat buyers, then understanding who those customers are and why they come back is paramount. Exhibit 15–2 also differentiates between frequent mail order buyers and "touch and feel shoppers" who prefer retail stores and who distrust catalog shopping. Internet shoppers can be equated to "frequent buyers," but they are even more driven by convenience and a confident outlook.

Know Thy Customer

"Know thy customer" is the first rule of catalog merchandising. A catalog product buyer must understand why and how people use the catalog. A classic mistake made by those who select products for catalogs is putting their own tastes and preferences first and paying little heed to what they know about the ultimate consumers.

EXHIBIT 15–2

The Psychology of the Catalog Buyer

Frequent Buyers	Infrequent Buyers
Convenience	
A quick and easy way to shop	Hassles in dealing with the PO
A comfortable alternative to retail shopping	Waiting for an order
A way to avoid crowds	Returning merchandise
Merchandise	
Unusual merchandise	Cannot see or feel merchandise
New products and styles	Hard to judge quality
Found merchandise that fits	Problems with fit, color, etc.
Consumer's Outlook	
Confident	Skeptical
In control	Afraid of losing control
Excited, anticipation	Fear of "rip-offs"
Dream fulfillment	
Value	
Lower prices on special promotions	Can shop around at retail
Added value from not having to drive to store	More sales at retail
Can comparison shop by using multiple catalogs	Can control bills
Brand	
Expertise in dealing with companies in direct mail selling uncommon brand names	Lack of expertise in buying unknown needs
Trust direct mail companies	Uncertain about the reputation of direct mail companies
Need	
Can wait for a number of products	Want immediate gratification at time of purchase
Order well in advance of special need	Waiting time is frustrating

How do you get to know your customers? Here are some techniques used by successful catalogs:

- A customer survey that rides along in the box to first-time customers

- Annual surveys to repeat buyers—by mail, phone, and even the Internet—that seek information on customers and what additional products they might like to see in the catalog

- Phone contact with customers through telemarketing representatives

- Regular dialogue between key people in the company and customers regarding how various aspects of the catalog might be improved, usually by taking phone call orders

- Customer focus groups

- Customer advisory boards

The key is to listen to what customers are saying in research surveys and phone conversations.

Build on Your Winners

Successful catalogers watch what their customers buy and listen to what they say. From a merchandise/sales standpoint, the worst catalog is the first catalog. With each successive mailing, a catalog should build on the merchandise categories and the price points that the customer is buying. Postanalysis of catalog sales results is essential.

One company that has listened to its customers is Lands' End (see Exhibit 15–3). This successful cataloger started in the retail business selling sailing gear. Over several decades it listened and watched as its customers bought more and more soft-sided luggage, sportswear, and nonsailing items. Its merchandise mix evolved into men's, women's, and children's clothing, soft goods, and luggage. Could it have experienced outstanding growth to a billion dollar plus public company had it not listened to its customers and built on its winning merchandise? Lands' End's newest thrust is Internet buying, and it promotes its website on its cover and inside the catalog.

Other Merchandise Strategies

What other merchandise strategies are smart catalogers using? Here are several that have proved successful.

Improve Product Quality While Reducing Cost. Customers are concerned about the value of products they buy through a catalog or the Internet. Value is a perceived price/quality relationship. Smart catalogers constantly try to improve product quality while improving their margins. Through importing, buying in

Lands' End Catalog Back Cover

Introducing the new Spring Slicker:
sheds water, breathes easy, feels light as a breeze for only $28.

Come spring, you don't want a slicker that weighs you down. You want a slicker like this: incredibly lightweight and easy to move in, unlike stiff, rubbery ones. It's coated nylon, plenty water-resistant if you get caught in a drizzle. And has covered pockets so nothing seeps in. Yet unlike most slickers like this, it's vented both back and front, so you breathe easy, don't get all clammy inside. Neat features include zip front with storm flap, adjustable cuffs, slash pockets, a visored drawcord hood that keeps water from getting in your eyes.

At our low price, why not buy a couple? Machine wash. Imported. *Colors below.*

Men's Regular S 34-36, M 38-40, L 42-44, XL 46-48.   6403-3K13   28.00

Women's Regular S 6-8, M 10-12, L 14-16, XL 18-20.   6403-4K19   28.00

Pearl Gray

Light Quartz
(Women's only)

Dusty Teal

Deep Cardinal

Dark Gray

1-800-356-4444 · We're open 24 hours a day · www.landsend.com

LANDS' END
DIRECT MERCHANTS

Lands' End Lane
Lands' End, Inc.
Dodgeville, WI 53595

OR CURRENT RESIDENT

REQUESTED IN-HOME FEB. 9-11

C 7375 6735 4   ECRLOT*C018
JACOBS AND CLEEVENGER   L00K1
401 N WABASH AVE STE 620
CHICAGO   IL 60611-5647

Bulk Rate
U.S. Postage
PAID
Lands' End, Inc.

EXHIBIT 15–3 *(continued)*

Lands' End Catalog Spread

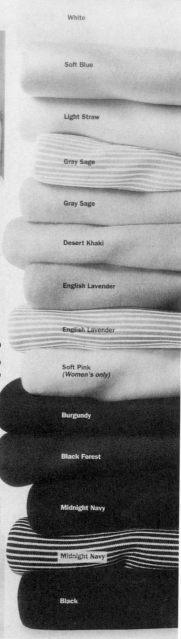

White

Soft Blue

Light Straw

Gray Sage

Gray Sage

Desert Khaki

English Lavender

English Lavender

Soft Pink
(Women's only)

Burgundy

Black Forest

Midnight Navy

Midnight Navy

Black

Here's a knit that may send happy shivers down your spine. It gives you the same kind of luxurious softness as that cashmere sweater you just tucked away for spring, because it's interlock knit of Peruvian pima cotton – one of the finest varieties in the world. So fine, it must be handpicked like fruit, lest its fragile fibers be damaged. *"Suave como el pelo de un angel,"* they say in Peru – "Soft as the hair of an angel."

Another plus: this polo is so nicely tailored, you won't think twice about wearing it on workdays as well as weekends, top button buttoned, almost like a knitted dress shirt.

It has a smoothly taped neck and shoulder seams. Longer three-button placket. Neat topstitching at shoulders and armholes. Straight bottom with side vents. And your choice of hemmed or banded short sleeves, or long sleeves with rib-knit cuffs.

Hard to believe we can bring you a polo this soft, this stylish starting at $24. Enjoy! Machine wash. Imported.

Men's Regular S 34-36, M 38-40, L 42-44, XL 46-48, 2XL 50-52.
Men's Tall M 38-40, L 42-44, XL 46-48, 2XL 50-52.
Women's Regular XS 4, S 6-8, M 10-12, L 14-16, XL 18-20.

Solid banded short sleeve: *Colors right.*
Men's Regular S-2XL.	3661-7K18	24.00
Men's Regular with pocket S-XL.	5136-8K15	24.00
Men's Tall M-2XL.	3661-8K13	27.00
Women's Regular XS-XL.	3661-9K19	24.00

Solid hemmed short sleeve: *Colors right.*
Men's Regular S-2XL.	6464-2K14	24.00
Men's Tall M-2XL.	6464-3K1X	27.00
Women's Regular XS-XL.	6464-4K15	24.00

Solid long sleeve: *White, Black Forest, Midnight Navy, Black. (Men's in White, Black only).*
Men's Regular S-2XL.	3709-2K18	28.00
Men's Tall M-2XL.	3709-3K13	31.00
Women's Regular XS-XL.	3709-4K19	28.00

New! Stripe short sleeve (with self collar, hemmed short sleeves): *Three colors right.*
Men's Regular M-XL.	6421-1K10	28.00
Women's Regular S-XL.	6421-2K16	28.00

New! Tonal Collar Polo (with rib-knit collar, hemmed short sleeves): *Four colors left.*
Men's Regular M-XL.	6420-9K1X	28.00
Women's Regular S-XL.	6421-0K15	28.00

Gray Sage

Sandalwood

English Lavender

Silver Birch

6

EXHIBIT 15–3 (continued)

Lands' End Catalog

In the shadow of the Andes, where cotton grows so fine it must be picked by hand, they knit a polo shirt

"Soft as the hair of an angel."

1-800-356-4444 · We're open 24 hours a day · **www.landsend.com**

larger quantities, and improving vendor relationships, a catalog's challenge is to buy better and at the same time give customers more for their money. Surely that will keep them coming back.

Strengthen New Product Development Efforts. During periods of recession, it is common for companies to cut back or discontinue new product development. New product development, however, is the lifeblood of the catalog. Winning catalogers keep it at the forefront of their minds and budgets at all times.

Strengthen Inventory Control Systems. One major difference between retailing and cataloging is exemplified by the statement, "Retailers sell what they buy and catalogers buy what they sell." Retailers buy merchandise for an entire season. If a woman comes into a shop to buy an advertised dress and finds her size is unavailable, the shop owners will try to sell her another dress in her size. They are "selling what they bought." A catalog, however, normally will commit for only 40 to 50 percent of its anticipated needs for a season. Then it will read the selling results early in the season and reorder ("buying what they are selling").

It is vital for catalogs to have reliable vendors who can back them up in merchandise and turn around reorders quickly. It is also crucial to have a buying and rebuying staff, as well as computer systems, that can help forecast product needs down to the last stockkeeping unit (SKU).

The final aspect of catalog inventory control is disposing of leftover merchandise at the end of a season. Items can be repeated in a future catalog or featured on special sales pages, in package inserts of remainder products, in a telephone special, or on the Internet. Outlet stores, annual warehouse sales, and special sales at large events like state fairs are also useful. Remainder merchants can also dispose of unsold merchandise. Most successful catalogs have fine-tuned their remainder systems so they minimize the markdown expense that haunts retail stores.

Core Competency #2: Positioning the Catalog

To set themselves apart from the competition, most catalogs seek to define a niche and develop a brand. A niche is both a unique identity and a special place in the market where there is a void not being met by the competition. A catalog can be unique or set apart from its competition by its merchandise, creative style or format, offers, and customer service.

"Brand development" is a relatively new term for catalogers. Branding has been the purview of manufacturers such as Procter & Gamble but seldom is given consideration by catalogers. Branding is having "top of mind" recognition when a customer thinks about a product. L.L. Bean has brand awareness and brand equity in the outdoor market. Dell and Gateway have brand strength in computers. Branding and positioning are very complementary creative components.

Defining the Catalog's Niche and Brand

What does a cataloger need to think about before beginning creative execution? Often, catalogers, particularly first-timers, jump right into the creative process without first thinking through some very basic issues:

1. Who is the company, the catalog? What product or service does it sell? Is there any brand awareness or strength?

2. To whom does it sell? Who are its primary customers, secondary customers, and even tertiary customers?

3. How is the catalog unique? What sets it apart from its competitors? Its products? Its service? Its offers? Its pricing?

4. Who is the competition? What are their niches? What are their strengths? Weaknesses? Do they have brand recognition? Do they have a serious void or weakness that can be exploited?

Differentiating the Catalog from the Competition

There are innumerable ways to set a catalog apart, but here are five variables to consider:

1. *Merchandise.* This is a vital area in which to be different. Perhaps it is acceptable to be No. 2 in the auto rental area, as Avis has shown, but to be No. 2 in a catalog niche, and not have a defined difference in product, can be financially disastrous.

2. *Pricing or use of credit.* A pricing method can help set a catalog apart. Current Inc.'s catalog uses a three-part pricing strategy that basically says to the customer: "The more items you buy, the better the price." Discounters such as Damark or Viking are also good at using pricing to help build a unique identity. Fingerhut sells only on credit (its own), and establishes a niche in doing so.

3. *Catalog format and creative presentation.* Besides merchandising, the catalog's creative format, design, and copy can make a tremendous difference in establishing its niche. Think of Patagonia and its unique in-use photography (all supplied by readers and customers); Gooseberry Patch's unique catalog size and illustrative art; and L.L. Bean's square shape, cover art, and catalog layout.

4. *Offer.* An offer, or proposition, is what the cataloger is willing to give to customers in return for their response. What catalog has a unique offer that sets it apart? Hammacher Schlemmer consistently offers a special in its catalog: "Buy two items and get a third free." Nordstrom offers free pickup on any return.

5. *Customer service/fulfillment.* Here is an ideal way to set a catalog apart: service so good that it is the envy of every competitor. It starts with the ability to accept orders by mail, phone, fax, or the Internet with well-trained people and a database system that allows real-time access to customers' records. Next is on-line inventory so customers know before finishing the order whether the size and color of the item

is in stock, and they can make a decision about alternatives. Then it's the delivery time of the product. Finally comes the handling of returns and inquiries. Without a doubt, customer service can set a catalog apart.

Core Competencies #3 and #4: New Customer Acquisition and Customer List Communication

It is critical for a catalog to build a buyer list—a group of people or companies that will keep coming back again and again to order.

When a new catalog starts, it has no buyers and probably no affinity names—names of potential buyers who have some relationship to the company or catalog. About 1.8 million people visit Hershey Chocolate World every year. Some sign up to receive a Hershey Chocolate catalog during the holiday season. Although these are not proven catalog buyers, they represent a list of prospects with which the company has had some relationship. There is a good chance that these prospects will be pleased to receive and order from a chocolate catalog.

If a company has no affinity names, it must rely on building its customer list from list rentals and other alternative media that can be targeted to its audience. It is not unusual for the buyer list to outperform an outside list or nonaffinity names many times over. This is why it usually takes a new catalog three years to break even and about five years to recapture its initial investment.

Front-End/Back-End Marketing

A concept well understood by veteran catalogers is front-end and back-end marketing (see Exhibit 15–4). Front-end marketing refers to prospecting or new customer acquisition. Few catalogers make money on prospecting; it is a cost-related activity. The objectives of front-end marketing are to acquire new first-time customers, or to acquire leads and inquiries that can be converted into first-time buyers, and to acquire the most names at the least cost. Smart catalogers measure precisely what it costs to acquire a new, first-time buyer and are tenacious about tracking where the name came from.

Back-end marketing refers to working the customer list. This is where the profitability of the catalog comes from. The objectives of back-end marketing are to convert first-time buyers into second-time buyers, to maximize the number of profitable mailings to this list each year, and to determine where the best long-term customers come from so that the catalog can change or modify its front-end media. A winning catalog carefully observes the growth of its buyer file, watching especially for buyers who have purchased more than twice. Large catalogers often divide the marketing functions by front end and back end. The small cataloger must understand and play both roles within the company.

EXHIBIT 15–4

Front-End/Back-End Concept of Marketing

Prospects = Costs

Customers = Profits

Objective   **How Results Are Measured**

Front-End Marketing

Acquire New, First-Time Customers   Cost per Customer
Acquire New Leads   Cost per Lead
Acquire New Inquiries   Cost per Name
Convert Leads and Inquiries to Customers   Cost of Conversion
Minimize Cost of Building the Customer File

Back-End Marketing

Convert First-Time Buyers into   Growth of Multibuyer File
   Second-Time Buyers
Maximize Number of Mailings to   Number of Customer Mailings
   Customer List Each Year
Make a Profit   Return on Investment
                                             Return on Sales
                                             Value of a Customer Over
                                                Three Years

The Customer Hierarchy

The cataloger has to understand the hierarchy of a customer (see Exhibit 15–5). Because the primary goal of a catalog is to get repeat orders from its customer list, a successful catalog must build trust, credibility, and confidence. In this process there are three distinct hurdles to be surmounted. The first is converting prospects to first-time buyers. Perhaps these first-time buyers should be called "tryers." They are cautious, have a low response rate, have a lower average order size, and expect the catalog to prove itself worthy before ordering again.

What message do buyers give when they purchase a second time? Generally, it's: "You're OK. I like your products and your service is acceptable." Average order value goes up. A higher response rate is the norm.

A further step is building the multibuyers into advocates who will recommend the catalog to others. They will peruse the catalog carefully and usually respond at many times the rate of first-time buyers. This phenomenon is what makes a successful, profitable catalog.

EXHIBIT 15–5

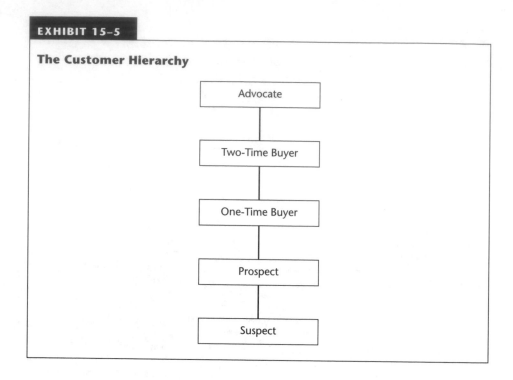

The Customer Hierarchy

Advocate

Two-Time Buyer

One-Time Buyer

Prospect

Suspect

New Customer Acquisition Strategies

Historically, catalogs have relied heavily on rented lists to develop their customer base. But this isn't the only method. Because of rising postal and mailing costs, catalogers are seeking alternative ways to obtain new buyers. Innovation is the name of the prospecting game. Here are 16 options, other than list rentals, that catalogs are using today:

1. The Internet. As a minimum, every catalog should have a website from which a potential customer can request a catalog. While the verdict is still out on lifetime value of Internet catalog requesters, this is an important medium for every cataloger.

2. Customer referrals. These are very good quality names. Ask "advocate" customers for names of friends, relatives, coworkers, and the like.

3. Space advertising. Many of today's large catalogs built their buyer lists through space advertising. There are many options: small space ads (one-sixth page) versus large space ads (full page), and the direct sales of a product versus generating a lead or inquiry.

4. Magazine catalog sections. Many consumer and some business magazines publish an annual or a biannual catalog lead-generation section.

5. Free-standing newspaper inserts (FSIs). These are usually applicable to more "downscale" marketers.

6. Package inserts. These ride along in the box shipment of another mailer, and can promote a catalog request or sell a winning product.

7. Co-op mailings. Carol Wright is an example.

8. Trade shows. These are especially effective for business catalogs.

9. Television.

10. Catalog of catalogs. Today there are several lead-generation publications, such as *Shop-at-Home Directory* and *The Best Catalogs in the World*, that exclusively promote catalogs.

11. Card decks.

12. Credit card or billing inserts.

13. Doctor's or dentist's office "take-ones."

14. Back panels of cereal boxes.

15. Public relations.

16. Gift recipients.

Winning catalogs use a variety of innovative strategies to acquire new customers. Consider the following list:

1. Source-coding every new customer acquisition effort, tracking results, and capturing original source codes on the customer database.

2. Seeking as much publicity as possible by creating events (e.g., marathon races sponsored by marketers of health-related products).

3. Measuring the cost of acquiring names by each type of medium and determining what the catalog can afford to spend for a new customer.

4. Developing customer referral programs such as those used by book clubs.

5. Carefully watching the seasonality of mailings and concentrating prospecting in the prime season.

6. Targeting, targeting, targeting mailings, especially when using list rentals.

7. Telephoning to prequalify names before mailing a business-to-business catalog, or sending a postcard before the catalog mails to prequalify the name.

8. Keeping names of old buyers and inquiries that are no longer mailed, putting them into merge/purge in order, and matching them against outside rental names (de-dupe).

9. Establishing and maintaining a detailed prospect database of inquiries, gift recipients, people who paid for a catalog and the like, and capturing original source codes and dates of inquiry.

10. Getting the catalog to the prospect who requests it as fast as possible and letting the prospect know that "this is the catalog you requested." (Maximum turnaround time should be no more than a week.)

11. Correlating back-end customer name value with front-end name source to maximize quality of names over quantity of names.

12. Watching the aging of buyers, inquiries, and catalog requests. (People who have not purchased in more than 12 months need a special message or incentive to remind them that they asked for the catalogs they receive.)

The Customer List: A Catalog's Most Important Asset

Even though few catalogs identify their customer list on the company's balance sheet, it is their most important asset. The buyers are their major source of revenue, through sales of merchandise or list rentals. To maximize the use of this asset, however, the list must be maintained and mailed.

List Maintenance. The use of the Postal Service's National Change of Address program (NCOA) during the merge/purge of the customer list with outside lists is well worth the cost and effort in ensuring better delivery. In addition, most catalogers will include a "return service" request for address correction by the USPS in at least one or two mailings a year. In this way they can update the names of people or companies that have moved, and eliminate catalogs being discarded for insufficient address.

Mailing the Customer List. Mailing catalogs is expensive. Also, too often companies tend to undermail their best customers. During the mid-1970s, for example, Fingerhut was mailing its customer list 20 times a year. By using simple segmentation techniques such as recency, frequency, monetary, and product category, the company was able to test and ultimately increase its mailings to 30 times a year. Most catalogers probably underutilize or undermail their customer list. One reason is that they tend to treat all customers alike.

Using the Customer List More Effectively. To more effectively and efficiently use the customer list, track buyers by source. A catalog fulfillment database system will let you track, measure, and segment the customer list and track its growth on a weekly or monthly basis.

Know who the best customers are. Survey them. Ask them for help. Research them. Talk to them on the phone. And when you discover your best customers—mail them more often and treat them like good friends.

Build a simple segmentation system to prioritize the buyer file. All customers are not created equal. Keep track of when and what customers buy, how they respond (phone/fax/mail/E-mail), how they pay (check/cash/credit card/purchase order), and how and why they return merchandise.

Maintain the list and keep it updated. Remember that 20 percent of the list changes each year. Rent the list for extra income.

Reactivate former-year buyers. It's easier and less expensive to approach a past customer than it is to obtain a new first-time buyer. After all, once you have a relationship with your customer, why give up on it?

Circulation Planning

Circulation, a familiar word to magazine publishers, is starting to mean more to catalogers. It means: When are you mailing which catalog, and to whom? At a recent catalog conference, a forum of small catalogers identified circulation as the most important marketing skill for profitable growth.

Core Competency #5: Creative Execution

The challenge in catalog creative execution is in differentiating the catalog from its competition. There are six aspects of the creative process:

1. Pagination

2. Design and layout

3. Color as a design element

4. Typography as a design element

5. Copy

6. Photography or illustrative art

Pagination

Many catalog experts think pagination, or planning the overall scheme of the catalog, is the most important aspect of the creative process. Pagination determines the catalog's organization (i.e., by product category, mixing product, product function, theme, color, or price). Pagination determines exactly what product goes where in the catalog and how much space each product will be given. It is the master plan for the catalog.

The most important thing to keep in mind in pagination is knowing who the customers are and how they will use the catalog. Sound pagination puts the best-selling products in the "hot spots" of the catalog, and thereby maximizes sales. Another consideration of pagination is the niche, or positioning, of the catalog. A catalog must provide the ambience that its audience expects. Pagination ensures that there is "flow" from page to page, and from product category to product category.

Design and Layout

If pagination is the master plan, then design and layout form the blueprint that will guide the creative construction process. Unlike many direct mail creative projects that are directed by the copywriter, the catalog is clearly design-driven.

Two critical areas of design are covers and page or spread layouts.

Catalog Covers. The front and back covers have the following roles:

- Attracting customers' attention

- Telling what the catalog is selling

- Reinforcing the catalog's niche

- Getting readers inside the catalog

- Offering a benefit

- Selling products

- Getting the catalog mailed

- Offering service information such as the telephone/fax/website, guarantee, and credibility information

Preliminary design of a new catalog concentrates a lot of effort on getting the right "feel" on the cover. Note in Exhibit 15–6 how Wolferman's cover illustrates the "bite off the page" feeling that is so important to selling English muffins and other food delicacies by mail.

Page or Spread Layouts. The second critical area of catalog design is page or spread layout. (Most professionals advocate spreads because the eyes tend to scan two facing pages.) Layout options break into five categories:

1. Grid layout

2. Free form (asymmetrical)

3. Single item per page

EXHIBIT 15–6

Cover of a Wolferman's Catalog

4. Art and copy separation

5. Product grouping

Because the layouts provide the blueprint for copy and photography, it is important that they reinforce the image of the company selling the products. Successful catalogers:

- Make the product the hero. The product is what's being sold, not the models, the props, or the backgrounds.

- Use "hot spots," such as front and back covers, inside front cover, inside back cover spreads, the center of a saddle-stitched catalog, the order form, and additional spreads in the front of the catalog (i.e., pages 4–5, 6–7), to effectively promote winning products—those with the best margins.

- Remember their customers and how they will use the catalog.

- Use a logical eye flow within a spread from the right-hand page to the left-hand page, and back again to the right-hand page.

- Use the telephone/fax number/website address and other information—such as testimonials, technical specifications, and the like—as part of the design of the catalog.

- Strive for consistency in layout from catalog to catalog so the customer will not be confused.

Color as a Design Element

People react differently to the use of color in catalogs. Red and yellow are strong colors that attract attention. Blue is seldom used with food. Research shows that people prefer the use of white, beige, or gray for backgrounds. Catalog readers like contrast between the product and the background. White space is clearly a design element. Too much of it and layouts appear to have gaping holes; too little, and readers are confused. Care in the use of color is especially important in page backgrounds, photo backgrounds, headlines, and screens for special sections.

Typography as a Design Element

Everyone learns to read black on white, left to right, left-justified columns, top to bottom, with short column length, reasonably sized type, and a serif typeface. Varying from these patterns affects readability and customer response. Attractive type helps readability and ease of catalog use. Unattractive type can actually turn off the reader, and result in lost sales. Catalogers must remember their catalog's positioning and target audience in selecting the appropriate type. Art directors should be careful not to overuse reverse type, overprint type on a busy photo, or use all capital letters, extended line length and type, or calligraphy that is difficult to read.

Catalog Copy: Your Salesperson

Saying that a catalog tends to be layout-driven does not imply that copy is unimportant! While the layout helps to attract and direct the reader's attention, it is the copy that closes the sale. Catalog copy must reinforce the catalog's niche or positioning; "grab" readers with headlines; inform, educate, entertain, and reassure the reader while building credibility and confidence. Of course, it must also describe the product and close the sale.

It is not unusual to have a number of writers working on catalog copy. It is therefore important for all of the writers to understand the positioning of the catalog, to know precisely who the target customer is, and to have agreed on a copy style. Many catalogs have even developed style manuals to achieve consistency. There are numerous copy styles from which to choose. The right one is selected with the customer in mind.

Photography or Illustrative Art

Photography, a key design element, helps attract readers' attention to the product. It also shows product features and color differences. Photography or artwork builds credibility for the product and romances the product. But, most important, the photo or illustrative art makes the product the hero.

The photographer, art director, and photo stylist together can make products come alive with effective use of propping, accessorizing, lighting, and level of contrast. Whatever the photo style or type of camera, and whether or not models are used, photography is a vital part of the catalog creative process. Illustrative art is also used in catalogs to promote greater understanding of hard-to-shoot subjects, to be different from other catalogs, or, sometimes, to effect a cost savings.

Core Competency #6: Catalog Fulfillment

Fulfillment, an essential element of a profitable catalog, closes the loop with the customer and is a "must have" function for catalogers. Order entry by phone, mail, Internet, and fax, as well as data entry and fulfillment systems; warehousing and pick, pack, and shipping; credit handling; return handling; customer communications— all have become essential to the fulfillment function. Today's customers demand quality service in every aspect of the catalog operation.

Core Competency #7: Catalog Database Strategies

The fulfillment function provides information about prospects and customers. Catalogers relish having information about their customers that will help them improve the response percentage, obtain a larger average order, and get customers to buy more frequently.

With today's improved computer hardware and software, the arduous task of maintaining critical customer purchase information and demographic data has become very manageable. There are fairly good generic Windows-based software packages available, and they are affordable! At the upper end of the catalog management systems are a number of expensive systems that can handle all a cataloger's needs, including Internet connectivity. There is no excuse for a catalog not to have a state-of-the-art fulfillment and database system to track customer activity.

Core Competency #8: Analysis— the Numbers Side of Catalogs

Closing the loop. Ensuring that every catalog is better than the last one. Making sure that catalog promotions are measurable. This is what analysis is all about. Analysis helps critique each mailing and therefore makes the next one better.

Most prosperous catalogs devote a lot of effort and staff time to the numbers side of the business. Here is a checklist of the typical analyses that catalogers perform:

1. List/source/media analysis

2. Merchandise analyses:
   - Price points
   - Square inch
   - Product category
   - Sales by catalog item, page, and spread

3. Inventory analyses:
   - Product returns
   - Cancellations
   - Back orders
   - Remainders/markdowns of merchandise

4. Analyses of tests such as offers, covers, seasonality, and lists

5. Mailing plan: actual results versus projection

6. Profit and loss: actual results versus plan

7. Lifetime value of customers

Cataloging and the Internet

The impact of the Internet on cataloging of every kind—business, consumer, and retail—has already been felt. Most smart direct marketers feel that the surface has barely been scratched.

Considering that statistics show that between 30 percent and 100 percent of on-line revenues are coming from new customers, the rush to the Internet is understandable. Websites are a boon for new and growing catalogers who place a high priority on building their customer lists, as well as for established catalogers seeking new business.

The huge top-level websites, of course, are building their brand and the accompanying share of mind, and they are investing millions of dollars in developing their sites and links to get potential customers to visit. Hardly a television commercial, radio spot, or even billboard is without a Web address today.

But the Internet levels the playing field among companies of all sizes. Smaller and new start-up companies can have a website by building and maintaining it themselves, and have much lower costs sustaining a Web presence than their big-company counterparts.

Paper and digital cataloging should be pursued hand in hand. If planned correctly, catalog photography can be used on-line. The printed catalog can promote the E-catalog, and the E-catalog can be used for intermediate communications with customers, and so on. For business, consumer, and retail catalogs, the Internet *must* be part of the marketing mix. Business-to-business Internet selling is maturing quite nicely, but consumer and retail-oriented catalogs need to ensure that the Internet is not delayed or forgotten.

The growth of Internet sales will come at the expense of traditional (off-line) marketing, and those companies (catalogers) that espouse the Internet as a complementary selling tool to the printed word are going to steal market share from those that remain traditional catalog (printed word) purists.

Being Passive Aggressive

To establish an on-line offering, catalogers must overcome the passive nature of the Internet as a communication medium. Where traditional catalogers are accustomed to mailing to prospects and customers based on targeted selections, E-catalogers are generally at the mercy of the surfer. In other words, your customers, or prospective customers, have to find you. Websites have been likened to retail stores. Unless you are in a high-traffic mall or advertise your store, there is little chance that prospective customers will ever find you.

Herein lies the primary difference between paper catalogs and on-line catalogs: paper catalogs are intrusive by nature, on-line catalogs are passive by nature. Once businesses understand this fundamental limitation of E-cataloging, they can become creative in ways that generate more traffic and, most important, more sales through the Web.

Three Factors of On-line Success

Success in on-line cataloging is a result of the marriage of technical elements (programming), graphics (creative), and marketing (direct marketing principles).

Each one plays a role in the success or failure of an on-line venture. For instance, a site that is too graphically intense may load slowly and discourage participation. Likewise, a site with too few graphics may be unappealing to visitors or fail to show products in a positive light. Finally, a beautifully crafted, highly engaging site is wasted if the ordering process is cumbersome and confusing.

Technical Skills

From a technical standpoint, companies must consider the target market's "lowest common denominator" with regard to things like browser version, monitor settings, plug-ins, and connection speeds. Using the newest available technologies makes for very exciting Web pages. But you may be alienating more people than you're impressing if your fancy technology exceeds the capabilities of your audience. While modems are getting faster, more than half of all users connected at 28.8 kbs or fewer in 1999—too slow for many of the new bells and whistles.

On the server side, two technical issues must be considered:

- Are the customer and product databases updated in real time or must orders be batch processed?

- Are customers given the ability to track orders throughout the order and shipping process?

Questions like these help you determine whether your E-catalog is making on-line ordering easier and more beneficial for your customers. Much-heralded Dell Computers (dell.com) lets customers track orders from the time the order is placed to the time it ships, and follows up each shipment with a confirmation E-mail that tells the customer his or her computer has left the building (see Exhibit 15–7).

Graphics Skills

Graphically, E-catalogers must again consider the technical capabilities of the customer's computer. Making sure that GIF images are optimized and reduced to a limited color palette vastly improves download times by making image files smaller. Large images can be saved in segments to improve download times, and no image needs to be displayed at a higher resolution than 72 pixels per inch (that's all that a monitor can interpret), unless you intend for it to be printed from the Internet for reuse.

With advances in monitors and scanners, image presentation is better than ever. However, presenting too many images or images that are very large makes downloading almost unbearably slow. A download that is too slow increases the likelihood that no one will stay at your site long enough to purchase. J.Crew.com is a good example of a site that is quite good from a graphic standpoint. J.Crew picks up photography from the printed catalog but keeps images a manageable size.

EXHIBIT 15–7

Dell Computers Web Page

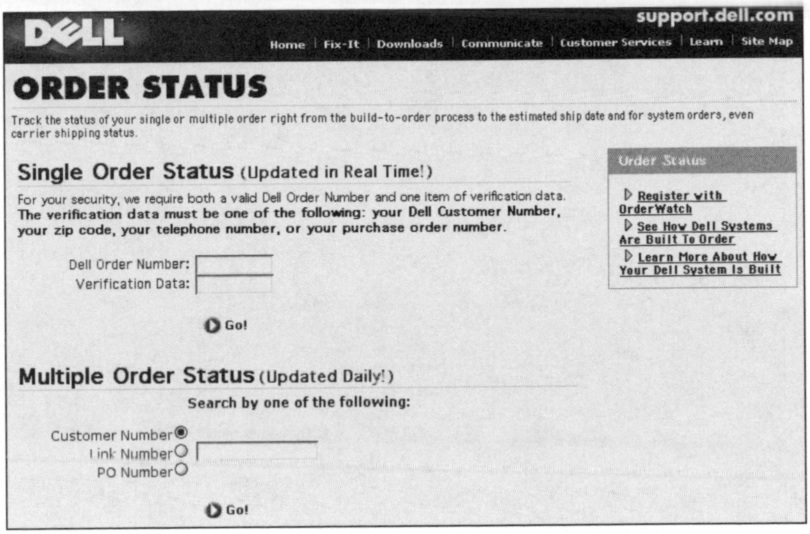

Marketing Skills

Marketing the on-line catalog may be the most difficult task of all. The million-dollar question always seems to be: How do we get more traffic to our site? The half-million-dollar question is: How do we keep them coming back? A number of strategies exist to answer both questions.

Generating first-time traffic to a site is crucial and not always easy. One way is to participate in on-line catalog portals such as CatalogCity.com, CatalogSite.com, CatalogSavings.com, or CatalogLink.com. These portals offer links to the E-catalog's site, and in some cases to product sales (see Exhibit 15–8). It is also a good idea to develop on-line alliances with vendors and clients where you reciprocate placement of links on each other's site. You should also register your site with the most applicable search engines and directories (there are literally hundreds to choose from).

Send targeted E-mail to available on-line mailing lists—making sure, of course, that the recipients on the list have opted in to the list; opt-out E-mail is not part of the DMA's Privacy Promise guidelines.

Include your website on every piece of marketing material that goes out the door—particularly to prospects. Paper catalogs should show their website address and toll-free telephone number on every page if they expect people to use it for ordering directly.

The ease with which shoppers can leave your site to go to another makes customer retention an integral part of building an on-line revenue stream. There are

EXHIBIT 15-8

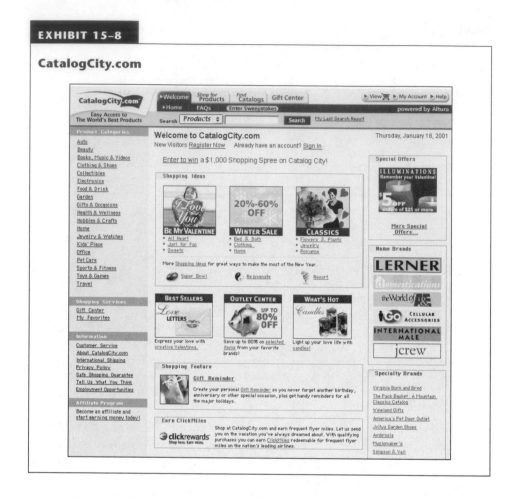

several key elements to keeping customers coming back, many of them common to traditional cataloging.

Get permission to communicate. Getting customers to opt in to an E-mail marketing program makes follow-up communication much easier. J.Crew, Victoria's Secret, and Cabella's do an excellent job of keeping the lines of communication open with customers through all seasons. Omaha Steaks (omahasteaks.com, see Exhibit 15–9) even puts out an electronic version of the Omaha Steaks Catalog via E-mail. The message itself can be a self-sufficient on-line ordering device.

Drive repeat purchases with special E-mailed offers or offers made in the paper catalog to encourage on-line sales. Electric Odyssey used a special cover burst to drive customers to electricodyssey.com for a two-dollar savings on on-line purchases (see Exhibit 15–10). When customers request a catalog from the Internet and opt in, promptly send out the paper catalog and follow it up with a special E-mail offer. In other words, reach these customers in the same manner they reached you.

EXHIBIT 15–9

Omahasteaks.com

Provide helpful customer service. Without a customer service representative to walk customers through the ordering process, your site needs to provide everything needed to order with comfort and ease. Remember the crucial element: a shopper/prospect should never be more than one click away from ordering.

Make purchasing easy by designing an order form that captures the necessary information succinctly. Don't forget to capture a source code if you're driving sales to the Web from the paper catalog.

Keep the site fresh. Some E-catalogs update their sites daily with on-line specials. Just as with paper catalogs, existing customers want to see what's new. Use icons and special bursts to point out those items. If you lack the staff for more frequent updates, be sure to refresh your content at least once a quarter.

The beauty of the Internet is that an organization can secure multiple addresses and operate transparently as two distinct organizations, not unlike catalogers that publish multiple titles. This chameleon quality means that catalogers can use the Web, among other things, as an avenue to liquidate inventory. A good

EXHIBIT 15–10

Electricodyssey.com

A cover burst helps direct customers from a paper catalog to its on-line version.

EXHIBIT 15–11

Andysgarage.com

example of this type of operation would be Andy's Garage (andysgarage.com), an on-line outlet for Fingerhut (see Exhibit 15–11).

The Future of Cataloging

Today, the most successful on-line catalogers are taking advantage of the economies that come from integrating the traditional catalog with the E-catalog. Whether sharing photography and copy elements or using one medium to generate sales and traffic for the other, it is undeniable that the two formats go hand in hand.

But the paper catalog will not go away, and the catalog process presented in this chapter will continue to be important. To survive and prosper, catalogs cannot do some of the tasks mentioned in the catalog process and leave others to chance. Winning catalogs—paper or electronic—must be able to perform every task well. That's the challenge and the opportunity.

CASE STUDY: Children's Memorial Hospital

Written by Carla Johnson, St. Mary's College, Notre Dame, Indiana, and Eve Caudill, Mendoza School of Business, University of Notre Dame, for the DePaul University Institute for Interactive and Direct Marketing's Case Writer's Workshop.

BACKGROUND

Children's Memorial Hospital in Chicago, one of the top ten pediatric hospitals in the United States, has been a leader in health care for children, pediatric research, medical education, and child advocacy for more than a century.

The Children's Holiday Card Collection, launched by the parent of a patient, features the artwork of young patients on cards that reflect the core values of the hospital—"treating the whole child." Since the collection's introduction in 1980, it has grown to become one of the hospital's most recognized programs, with all net proceeds funding programs that help young patients cope with the emotions of a hospital stay, grow intellectually, and remain stimulated and excited about life.

Although Children's has many household card buyers, it targeted its larger purchasers in the business-to-business holiday greeting card market.

Rapp Collins Worldwide took on Children's as a pro bono client in 1996 and launched a catalog featuring 22 card designs. Its direct mail and print campaign positioned the cards as more than just unique cards, but a gift a company could give to enhance the emotional well-being of a child while at Children's. Headlines played up the cause and the charm of the cards: "$1.33 a Card. Marked Down from Priceless," and "Ordering Your Company's Holiday Cards Should Be a Joy. Not a Job." These headlines appeared in childlike fonts along with bold, colorful pictures drawn by the children. Actual art class photography, patient success stories, the names and ages of each child artist, and heartwarming copy about hospital services were all communicated to prospective buyers.

To emphasize the quality of the cards, the 1996 catalog also included a bound-in card so the buyer could sample the product before ordering. To emphasize ease of ordering, Rapp Collins redesigned the order form, simplified instructions, and created a 1-800 number repeated throughout the catalog, on the order form, and in the print ads.

Catalogs were mailed in late September to 5,481 businesses and 2,714 households, 27 percent of whom were past customers and 73 percent of whom were prospects. Black-and-white print ads ran in *Chicago* magazine and *Crain's Chicago Business* in September and October.

The 1996 catalog generated a 3.75 percent average response rate, with 100 percent conversion to sales. It generated 50 percent higher sales than the 1995 catalog, with an average order increase of 300 percent—three times higher. The campaign resulted in a $35,000 donation to the hospital. A follow-up mailing thanking customers for their orders and asking for address correction and referrals generated a 60 percent response, with 25 percent of the respondents providing new prospect names.

Encouraged by its first-year results, Rapp Collins made 1997 the year of "testing": testing the effectiveness of print and co-op ride-alongs as a way to generate catalog requests, testing a much stronger corporate creative execution, testing a four-color ad with a catalog and sample offer, and testing an optional "additional donation" line on the order form. The catalog was mailed in early September to past customers and prospects from 12 lists. About 10,000 catalogs rode along in the October 6 issue of *Crain's Chicago Business*. Print ads ran in *USA Today*, *Crain's*, and *The Wall Street Journal*, and enjoyed regional and national runs in *Newsweek*, *Time*, *Forbes*, *Fortune*, and *Business Week*.

Dubbed the "Angel" campaign, the 1997 campaign featured an angel drawn by a young patient and the headline, "Be an Angel. Buy Our Cards." The catalog also had more pages so cards could be shown large enough to capture every detail.

The Holiday Card Campaign was another big success: a half-million holiday cards sold, nearly tripling the 1996 sales results. The hospital had to hire two more people to keep with the orders. In total, 430,675 cards were ordered, with an average sale of $290 and total sales of $631,398. The "additional donation" line on the order form resulted in an additional $19,000 in donations. The 1997 campaign won the Tempo Award.

CHALLENGE

In 1998, Rapp Collins realized that the competition was going on-line with information about their holiday cards and, in some cases, had begun to sell cards on the Internet. The key to continued success would be to effectively integrate the Web into the Holiday Card Program strategy and still target the business card buyer.

SOLUTION

Gold stars and a gold font set dramatically over a deep blue background gave the 1998 catalog cover, shown in Exhibit 15–12, an especially sophisticated look. The catalog, in a metallic blue envelope that also featured the gold stars and font, was mailed in August to "get the jump" on the competition. However, it had become too expensive to print and mail the number of catalogs that the growing mailing list demanded. The agency created a two-step process, sending a card to see if people were interested in receiving a catalog before sending one. The card mailings cost 24 cents apiece and brought in 498 accounts (sales) via 101,113 mailed. At a cost of a dollar each, 25,178 catalogs were mailed.

Rapp Collins also decided to create a website, although it was "very last-minute," according to Lydia Gaston, Rapp Collins Worldwide account supervisor. The website heavily featured the "star" motif of the 1998 campaign. A banner ad featuring this motif ran pro bono on the *Chicago Tribune* website.

Print ads included the website address beneath the 800 number. In addition, the Children's website address (childrensmemorial.org) was included in the catalog and in the two-step mailer and address update form. Clicking onto the Children's website became an alternative to a phone call as a way to obtain further information or to receive a catalog.

To access this information, the visitor would first download the Children's Memorial home page. By choosing the "How You Can Help" icon, the visitor was provided with several options to help the hospital, such as how to become a volunteer, provide financial support, give donations, or purchase holiday cards. Once chosen, the Holiday Card Collection Web page offered information on the holiday cards and the benefits from purchasing them, including qualities both intangible ("sure to bring a smile to your face") and tangible ("all cards are reproduced on high quality paper"). The campaign theme, "The holiday cards that brighten the life of a child," appeared on the home page in conjunction with the star graphic, integrating the campaign through the verbal and visual consistency with the print ads, banner ad, and catalog. The Web page, which could be accessed directly through cmhkids.com, let visitors browse through the cards, learn more about Children's Memorial, obtain order information, or contact the hospital.

A visitor wishing to see each Christmas card had two browsing options. First, card titles were contained in a menu list format and listed by name, including "The El Train" or "Good Dog," with the accompanying inside greeting. Visitors could download a specific card or cycle through the pictures of the cards one by one, by hitting the Previous or Next keys.

To order, the soon-to-be customer had three options: call the 800 number that appeared prominently throughout the Web pages; fax the order to an 800 number; or mail the order to a post office box address. A "Contact Us" option encouraged visitors to respond via Internet by requesting a free catalog or providing feedback in the form of a short questionnaire made up of questions such as: "Are there any other kinds of holiday cards you'd like to see in our collection?" and "How did you find out about this website?" and "Does it provide everything you need to make a decision to order?"

CASE STUDY: Children's Memorial Hospital *(continued)*

RESULTS

The Children's Memorial website generated 4,022 hits between the end of August 1998 and the beginning of January 1999. The numbers were expected to be higher, but the site had not been registered properly with search engines until late November. Of those who visited, 132 ordered catalogs. Sales from all channels were: 498 accounts via the two-step process, 980 accounts via catalogs, and 129 accounts via print media (although 22 percent of the orders were not trackable to a source).

The 1998 donation was approximately $10,500, down 27 percent from 1997 due to overhead investments, database system costs, and other factors, even though there was a 15.1 percent increase in the number of cards sold. In 1999, Rapp strengthened its efforts to drive buyers to the Holiday Card Program website by including the website address on print ads, mailers, and catalogs, and placing interactive banner ads on *Chicago Tribune Online* and elsewhere.

EXHIBIT 15–12

Cover of Children's Hospital Catalog

Brighten the life of a child.

1998 Holiday Card Collection
CHILDREN'S MEMORIAL HOSPITAL

PILOT PROJECT You have been asked by a leading brewery to do a feasibility study concerning a new gift catalog. There are two key audiences for the product that the catalog might promote.

The primary audience is young men and women, age 21 to 35, who consume more beer than the average American. This audience tends to be middle American, blue collar, and have a high school rather than a college education. The secondary audience is men and women, age 35 to 60, who are collectors of various beverage paraphernalia—beer glasses, steins, mugs, trays, and the like.

With this background, develop a feasibility plan and a strategic business plan that would include answers to the following questions:

1. What might be an appropriate name for the catalog?

2. How could this catalog be unique? What niche could this catalog fill to be successful?

3. Identify 20 items that might be appropriate for this catalog to promote.

4. What mailing lists should the catalog rent for an initial test?

5. What publications might be used to obtain catalog requests and inquiries?

6. What alternative media should the catalog test?

7. What is the role of the Internet in this catalog launch?

8. How would you treat the front cover of the catalog to maximize the appeal of the first catalog and attract the reader's attention?

Key Points

▶ Paper and digital catalogs should be pursued hand in hand. The printed catalog can promote the E-catalog, and the E-catalog can be used for intermediate communications with customers.

▶ Develop a distinct niche and a brand for the catalog—a place in the market where there is a void not met by the competition. Set your catalog apart from its competition by merchandise, creative style or format, offers, and customer service. Understanding your competition, its niches, and its strengths and weaknesses, will also facilitate positioning.

▶ Front-end marketing seeks to acquire new first-time customers, leads, and inquiries that can be converted into first-time buyers, and the most names at the least cost. Back-end marketing seeks to convert first-time buyers into second-time buyers, to maximize the number of profitable mailings to the list each year, and to determine where the best long-term customers come from so that the catalog can change or modify its front-end media. Front-end marketing costs money; back-end marketing yields profits—but both are essential functions.

▶ Maximize the value of your customer list by maintaining it and mailing it frequently. Don't underutilize or undermail! Track, measure, and segment the customer list to prioritize the buyer file. Test to find out how frequently you can mail.

▶ Sound pagination puts the best-selling products in the "hot spots" of the catalog and thereby maximizes sales. Pagination ensures that there is "flow" from page to page and from product category to product category.

▶ Reinforce the catalog's positioning and target market through design, use of color and photography, type, and copy. Catalog copy should "grab" readers with headlines, inform, educate, entertain, and reassure the reader while building credibility and confidence—plus describe the product and close the sale.

▶ The effective use of a database can provide customer information that helps catalogers improve the response percentage, obtain a larger average order, and get customers to buy more frequently.

▶ Analyses of list, source, media, merchandise, tests and offers, mailing plans, response, and profit help critique each mailing and therefore improve each subsequent issue.

▶ When developing an on-line catalog, consider the target market's "lowest common denominator" with regard to things like browser version, monitor settings, plug-ins, and connection speeds. Avoid large images that download slowly.

▶ Generate first-time traffic to a site by participating in on-line catalog portals that offer links to the E-catalog's site and product sales. Place links on the sites of vendors and clients. Register the site with the most applicable search engines and directories. Send targeted E-mail to available "opt in" on-line mailing lists, and include your website on every piece of marketing material.

▶ Retain customers by enrolling them in an E-mail marketing program that sends follow-up communications. Drive repeat purchases with special E-mailed offers or offers made in the paper catalog to encourage on-line sales.

CREATING PRINT
ADVERTISING

Knowing the "mechanics" of print advertising is essential to success, but no more so than knowing how to create winning ads. You may be running the "right" size ads at the "right" time in the "right" publication but still have advertising that is *least noted*. If that is the case, it is likely that the trouble lies in creative.

The competition your ad faces is every other ad in a given issue of a publication. It is not unusual to be one of 100 or more advertisers in a given magazine or newspaper. So you are competing for reading time with every reader of the magazine, not counting concurrent competition from TV, radio, and E-commerce. The job of the ad writer, put simply, is to stop the reader and engage his/her attention and interest.

Visualizing the Prospect

Every good magazine ad should attract the most attention from the likeliest prospects. Capable creators of direct response advertising visualize their prospects with varying degrees of precision when they sit down at the computer or drawing board.

Good direct response advertising makes its strongest appeal to its best prospects and then gathers in as many additional prospects as possible. And who are the prospects? They are the ones with the strongest desire for what you're selling. You must look for the common denominators. For instance, let's say you are selling a book on the American Revolution. Here are some of the relevant common denominators that would be shared by many people in your total audience:

1. An interest in the American Revolution in particular

2. An interest in American history in general

3. A patriotic interest in America

4. An interest in history

5. An interest in big, beautiful coffee-table books

6. An interest in impressing friends with historical lore

7. A love of bargains

8. An interest in seeing children in the family become adults with high achievement

Now, out of a total audience of 1,000, some readers would possess all eight denominators, some would possess some combination of six, some a different combination of six, some just one of the eight, and so on.

If you could know the secret hearts of all 1,000 individuals and rank them by their desire to buy, you would place at the very top of the list those who possessed all eight denominators, followed by those who possessed just seven, and so on down to the bottom of the scale, where you would place those who possessed none.

Obviously, you should make as many sales as possible among your hottest prospects first, for that is where your sales will be easiest. Then you want to reach down the scale to sell as many of the others as you can. By the time you get down to the people possessing only one of the denominators, you will probably find interest so faint that it would be almost impossible to make your sales effort pay unless it were fantastically appealing.

Obvious? Yes, to mail order professionals who learned the hard way. But to the novice it is not so obvious. In an eagerness to sell everybody, he or she might muff the easiest sales by using a curiosity-only appeal that conceals what is really being offered.

On the other hand, the veteran but uninspired pro might gather up all the easy sales lying on the surface but, through lack of creative imagination, fail to reach deeper into the market. For instance, let's say that of 1,000 readers, 50 possess all eight denominators. A crude omnibus appeal that could scoop up many of them would be something like: "At last! For every liberty-loving American family, especially those with children, whose friends are amazed by their understanding of American history, here is a big, beautiful book about the American Revolution you will display with pride. Yours for only one-fifth of what you'd expect to pay!" A terrible headline, but at least one that those possessing the denominators of interest would stop to look at and consider. You might get only 5 percent readership, but it will be the right 5 percent.

On the other hand, suppose you want to do something terribly creative to reach a wider market. So you do a beautiful advertising message headed "The Impossible Dream" in which you somehow work your way from that starting point to what it is you're selling. Again, you might get only 5 percent readership, but these readers will be scattered along the entire length of your scale of interest. Of the 50 people who stopped to read your message, only two or three will be prime prospects possessing all eight denominators. Many people really interested in books on the American Revolution, in inspiring their children with patriotic sentiments, and in acquiring big impressive books at big savings will have hurried past, unaware.

The point: don't let prime prospects get away. In mail order you can't afford to. Some people out there don't have to be sold; they already want what you have, and if you tell them that you have it, they will buy it. Alone they will not constitute enough of a market to make your selling effort pay, but without them you haven't got a chance. So, through your clarity and directness, you gather in these prime prospects; then through your creative imagination, you reach beyond them to awaken and excite mild prospects as well.

Writing the Headline

Once the prospect is clearly visualized, a good headline almost writes itself. For example, here is an effective and successful headline from an ad by Quadrangle/New York Times Book Company. It defines the prospect so simply and accurately that the interested reader feels an instant tug:

> *"For people who are almost (but not quite) satisfied with their houseplants . . . and can't figure out what they're doing wrong . . . "*

A very successful ad for the Washington School of Art, offering a correspondence course, resulted from bringing the psychographic profile of the prime prospect into sharp focus. The prospect was someone who had been drawing pictures better than the rest of us since the first grade. Such people are filled with a rare combination of pride in their talent and shame at their lack of perfection. And their goal is not necessarily fame or fortune, but simply to become a "real artist," a phrase that has different meanings for different people. The winning headline simply reached out to the right people and offered them the right benefit:

> *"If you can draw fairly well (but still not good enough), we'll turn you into a real artist."*

Of course, a good headline does not necessarily present an explicit definition of the prospect, but it is always implied. Here are some classic headlines and the prospects whom the writer undoubtedly visualized.

> *"Can a man or woman my age become a hotel executive?"*

The prospect is, probably, a middle-aged man or woman who needs, for whatever reason, an interesting, pleasant, not too technically demanding occupational skill such as hotel management and is eager for reassurance that you can teach an old dog new tricks. Note, however, how wide the net is cast. No one is excluded. Even people who worry they are too young to be a hotel executive can theoretically read themselves into this headline.

"Don't envy the plumber—be one"

The prospect is a poorly paid worker, probably blue-collar, who is looking for a way to improve his lot in life and who has looked with both indignation and envy at the plumber, who appears not much more skilled but earns several times as much per hour.

"How to stumble upon a fortune in gems"

The prospect is everybody, all of us, who all our lives have daydreamed of gaining sudden wealth without extreme sacrifice.

"Is your home picture-poor?"

The prospect is someone, probably a woman, with a home, who has a number of bare or inadequately decorated walls, and who feels not only a personal lack but also, perhaps more important, a vague underlying sense of social shame at this conspicuous cultural "poverty." Whether she appreciates it or not, she recognizes that art, books, and music are regarded as part of the "good life" and are supposed to add a certain richness to life.

"Become a 'nondegree' engineer"

This is really a modern version of "Don't envy the plumber." The prospect is an unskilled or semiskilled factory worker who looks with a mixture of resentment and grudging envy on the aristocracy in his midst, the college grads who earn much more, dress better, and enjoy special privileges because they are credentialed engineers. The prospect would like to enjoy at least some of their job status but is unwilling or unable to go to college and get an engineering degree.

"Are you tired of cooking with odds and ends?"

The prospect is that Everywoman or Everyman who has accumulated over the years an enameled pan here, an aluminum pot there, an iron skillet elsewhere, and to whom a matched set of anything represents neatness, order, and elegance.

"Can you call someone a failure at 30?"

The prospect is a young, white-collar worker, 25 to 32 years old, who is deeply concerned that life isn't turning out the way he or she dreamed and that he or she is on the verge of failing to "make it"—permanently.

Selecting Advantages and Benefits

Advantages belong to the product. Benefits belong to the consumer. If the product or service is unique or unfamiliar to the prospect, stressing benefits is important. But if it is simply a new, improved model in a highly competitive field where there already exists an established demand, the product advantage or advantages become important.

When laptop computers were first introduced, such benefits as weight and screen size and resolution were important attributes. But as the market became flooded with competing types and brands, and professionals began to use laptops instead of—rather than in addition to—a desktop computer, product advantages such as power and memory became more important.

There are two kinds of benefits: the immediate or obvious benefit, and the not-so-obvious ultimate benefit—the real potential meaning for the customer's life, or the product or service being sold. The ultimate benefit often proves to have a greater effect, for it reaches deeper into the prospect's feelings.

Victor Schwab, one of the great mail order pioneers, was fond of quoting Dr. Samuel Johnson's approach to auctioning off the contents of a brewery: "We are not here to sell boilers and vats, but the potentiality of growing rich beyond the dreams of avarice."

It pays to ask yourself over and over again, "What am I selling? Yes, I know it's a book or a steak knife, or a home study course in upholstering—but what am I really selling? What human values are at stake?"

For example, suppose you have the job of selling a correspondence course in advertising. Here is a list of ultimate benefits and the way they can be expressed in headlines for the course. Some of the headlines are patently absurd, but they illustrate the mind-stretching process involved in looking for the ultimate benefit in your product or service:

Health: Successful ad people are healthier and happier than you think— and now you can be one of them.

Money: What's your best chance of earning $150,000 a year by the time you are 30?

Security: You are always in demand when you can write advertising that sells.

Pride: Imagine your pride when you can coin a slogan repeated by 50 million people.

Approval: Did you write that ad? Why, I've seen it everywhere.

Enjoyment: Get more fun out of your daily job. Become a successful ad writer!

Excitement: Imagine working until 4:00 A.M.—and loving every minute of it!

Power: The heads of giant corporations will listen to your advice—when you've mastered the secrets of advertising that works. (Just a wee bit of exaggeration there, perhaps.)

Fulfillment: Are you wasting a natural talent for advertising?

Freedom: People who can get million-dollar advertising ideas don't have to worry about punching a time clock.

Identity: Join the top advertising professionals who keep the wheels of our economy turning.

Relaxation: How some people succeed in advertising without getting ulcers.

Escape: Hate going to work in the morning? Get a job you'll love—in advertising!

Curiosity: Now go behind the scenes of America's top advertising agencies and find out how multimillion-dollar campaigns are born!

Possessions: I took your course five years ago—today I own two homes, two cars, and a Chris-Craft.

Hunger: A really good ad person always knows where his or her next meal is coming from.

Classic Copy Structure

In a classic mail order copy argument, a good lead should be visualized as the first step in a straight path of feeling and logic from the headline or display theme to the concluding call for action. In that all-important first step, the readers should be able to see clearly where the path is taking them. Otherwise they might not want to go. (This is the huge error of ads that seek to pique your curiosity with something irrelevant and then make a tie-in to the real point. Who's got time for satisfying that much curiosity these days?)

The sections of a classic copy argument can be labeled *problem, promise of solution, explanation of promise, proof,* and *call to action.* However, if you're going to start with the problem, it seems like a good idea at least to hint right away at the forthcoming solution. Then the readers won't mind your not getting to the point right away, as long as they know where you're going. A generation ago, when the pace of life was slower, a brilliant copywriter could get away with spending the first third of his copy leisurely outlining the problem before finally getting around to the solution. But in these hectic times it's riskier.

Here is an ad seeking Duraclean dealers in which the problem lead contains the promise of solution:

- I found the easy way to escape from being a "wage slave."

- I kept my job while my customer list grew . . . then found myself in a high-profit business. Five years ago I wouldn't have believed that I could be where I am today.

- I was deeply in debt. My self-confidence had been shaken by a disastrous business setback. Having nobody behind me, I had floundered and failed for lack of experience, help, and guidance.

The copy could have started out simply, "Five years ago, I was deeply in debt," and so on. But the promise of happier days to come provides a carrot on a stick, drawing us down the garden path. You could argue that the headline had already announced the promise. But in most cases, good copy should be able to stand alone and make a complete argument even if all the display type were removed.

Here, from an ad for Isometric exercises, is an example of the flashback technique.

[*Starts with the promise*]

Imagine a six-second exercise that helps you keep fit better than 24 push-ups. Or another that's capable of doubling muscular strength in three weeks!

Both of these "quickie" exercises are part of a fantastically simple body-building method developed by Donald J. Salls, Alabama Doctor of Education, fitness expert, and coach. His own trim physique, his family's vigorous health, and the nail-hard brawn of his teams are dramatic proof of the results he gets—not to mention the steady stream of reports from housewives, athletes, even schoolchildren, who have discovered Dr. Salls's remarkable exercises.

[*Flashback to problem*]

Most Americans find exercise a tedious chore. Yet we all recognize the urgent personal and social needs for keeping our bodies strong, shapely, and healthy. What man wouldn't take secret pride in displaying a more muscular figure?

What woman doesn't long for a slimmer, more attractive figure? The endless time and trouble required to get such results has been a major, if not impossible, hurdle for so many of us. But now [*return to the promise*] doctors, trainers, and physical educators are beginning to recommend the easy, new approach to body fitness and contour control that Dr. Salls has distilled down to his wonderfully simple set of 10 exercises.

Of course, a really strong, exciting promise doesn't necessarily need a statement of the problem at all. If you're selling a "New Tree that Grows a Foot a Month," it could be argued that you don't actually have to spell out how frustrating it is to spend years waiting for ordinary trees to grow; this is well-known and implied.

Other Ways to Structure Copy

There are as many different ways to structure a piece of advertising copy as there are to build a house. But response advertising, whether in magazines or newspapers, has special requirements. The general advertiser is satisfied with making an impression, but the response advertiser must stimulate immediate action. Your copy must pile in your readers' minds argument after argument, sales point after sales point, until their resistance collapses under the sheer weight of your persuasiveness and they do what you ask.

One of the greatest faults in the copy of writers who are not wise in the ways of response is failure to apply this steadily increasing pressure. This may sound like old-fashioned "hard sell," but, ideally, the impression your copy makes should be just the opposite. The best copy, like the best salesperson, does not appear to be selling at all, but simply to be sharing information or proposals of mutual benefit to the buyer and seller.

Of course, in selling certain kinds of staple merchandise, copy structuring is not important. There the advertising can be compared to a painting in that the aim is to convey as much as possible at first glance and then convey more and more with each repeated look. You wouldn't sell a 35-piece electric drill set with a 1,000-word essay, but rather you would sell it by spreading out the set in glowing full-color illustrations richly studded with feature "call-outs." But where you are engaged in selling intangibles, an idea or ideas instead of familiar merchandise, the way you structure your copy can be vitally important.

In addition to the classic form mentioned above, here are some other ways to structure copy. With the "cluster of diamonds" technique, you assemble a great many precious details of what you are selling and present them to the reader in an appropriate setting. A good example is the "67 Reasons Why" subscription advertising of *U.S. News & World Report*, listing 67 capsule descriptions of typical recent news articles in the magazine. The "setting"—the surrounding copy containing general information and argumentation—is as important as the specific jewels in the cluster. Neither would be sufficiently attractive without the other.

The "string of pearls" technique is similar but not quite the same. Each "pearl" is a complete little gem of selling, and a number of them are simply strung together in almost any sequence to make a chain. The late David Ogilvy's "Surprising Amsterdam" series of ads was like this. Each surprising fact about Amsterdam was like a small-space ad for the city, but only when all these little ads are strung together do you feel compelled to get up from your easy chair and send for those KLM brochures. This technique is especially useful, by the way, when you have a vast subject like an encyclopedia to discuss. You have not one but many stories to tell. If you simply ramble on and on, most readers won't stay with you. So make a little list of stories you want to tell, write a tight little one-paragraph essay on each point, announce the subject of each essay in a boldface subhead, and then string them all together like pearls, with an appropriate beginning and ending.

The "fan dancers" technique is like a line of chorus girls equipped with Sally Rand fans. The dancers are always about to reveal their secret charms, but they never quite do. You've seen this kind of copy many times. One of the best examples is the circular received in answer to an irresistible classified ad in *Popular Mechanics*. The ad simply said: "505 odd, successful enterprises. Expect something odd." The circular described the entire contents of a book of money-making ideas in maddening fashion. Something like. "No. 14. Here's an idea that requires nothing but old coat hangers. A retired couple on a Kansas farm nets $240 weekly with this one."

With the "machine gun" technique, you simply spray facts and arguments in the general direction of the reader, in the hope that at least some of them will hit. This is called the no-structure structure, and it is the first refuge of the amateur. If you have a great product and manage to convey your enthusiasm for it through the sheer exuberance of your copy, you will succeed, not because of your technique, but despite it. And the higher the levels of taste and education of your readers, the less chance you will have.

Establishing the Uniqueness of Your Product or Service

What is the unique claim to fame of the product or service you are selling? This could be one of your strongest selling points. The word *only* is a great advertising word. If what you offer is "better" or "best," this is merely a claim in support of your argument that the reader should come to you for the product or services offered. But if what you are offering is the "only" one of its kind, then readers must come to you if they want the benefits that only you can offer.

Here are some ways in which you might be able to stake out a unique position in the marketplace for the product or service you are selling: "We're the largest." People respect bigness in a company or a sales total. They reason that if a product leads the others in its field, it must be good. Thus "No. 1 Best-Seller" is always a potent phrase, for it is not just an airy claim but a hard fact that proves some kind of merit.

But what if you're not the largest? Perhaps you can still establish a unique position, as in, "We're the largest of our kind." By simply defining your identity more sharply, you might still be able to claim some kind of size superiority. For example, there was the Trenton merchant who used to boast that he had "the largest clothing store in the world in a garage!"

A mail order photo finisher decided that one benefit it had to sell was the sheer bigness of its operation. It wasn't the biggest—that distinction belonged, of course, to Eastman Kodak. But it was second. And Eastman Kodak was involved in selling a lot of other things, too, such as film and cameras and chemicals. Its photo-finishing service was only one of many divisions. So the advertiser was able to fashion a unique claim: "America's Largest Independent Photo Finisher."

"We're the fastest-growing." If you're on the way to becoming the largest, that's about as impressive a proof of merit as being the largest. In fact, it can be even more impressive, because it adds the excitement of the underdog coming up fast. *U.S. News & World Report* used this to good effect during the 1950s while its circulation was growing from approximately 400,000 to about three times that figure: "America's Fastest-Growing Newsmagazine." More recently, the same claim has been used effectively for Internet service provider Juno.com.

"We offer a unique combination of advantages." It could be that no one claim you can make is unique, but that none of your competitors is able to equal your claim that you have all of a certain number of advantages.

In the early 1960s the Literary Guild began to compete in earnest with the Book-of-the-Month Club (BOMC). The Literary Guild started offering books that compared very favorably with those offered by BOMC. But the latter had a couple of unique claims that the Guild couldn't match—BOMC's distinguished board of judges, and its book dividend system, with a history of having distributed $375 million worth of books to members.

How to compete? The Guild couldn't claim the greatest savings; one of Doubleday's other clubs actually saved the subscriber more off the publisher's price. It couldn't claim that it had books offered by no other club; some of Doubleday's other clubs were offering some of the same books, and even BOMC would sometimes make special arrangements to offer a book being featured by the Guild.

But the Guild was able to feature a unique set of advantages that undoubtedly played a part in the success it has enjoyed: "Only the Literary Guild saves you 40–60 percent on books like these as soon as they are published." Other clubs could make either of these two claims, but only the Guild could claim both.

"We have a uniquely advantageous location." A classic of this was James Webb Young's great ad for "Old Jim Young's Mountain Grown Apples—Every Bite Crackles, and the Juice Runs Down Your Lips." In it, Jim Young, trader, tells how the natives snickered when his pappy bought himself an abandoned homestead in a little valley high up in the Jemes Mountains. But "Pappy" Young, one of the slickest farmers ever to come out of Madison Avenue, knew that "this little mountain valley is just a natural apple spot—as they say some hillsides are in France for certain wine grapes. The summer sun beats down into this valley all day, to color and ripen apples perfectly; but the cold mountain air drains down through it at night to make them crisp and firm. Then it turns out that the soil there is full of volcanic ash, and for some reason that seems to produce apples with a flavor that is really something."

Haband Ties used to make a big thing out of being located in Paterson, New Jersey, the silk center of the nation. Even though most of the company's ties and other apparel were made of synthetic fibers, somehow the idea of buying ties from the silk center made the reader feel he was buying ties at the very source. In the same way, maple syrup from Vermont should be a lot easier to sell than maple syrup from Arizona.

Finally, suppose you believe that you have something unique to sell but you hesitate to start an argument with your competitors by making a flat claim they might challenge. In that case, you can imply your uniqueness by the way in which you word the claim. "Here's one mouthwash that keeps your mouth sweet and fresh all day long" doesn't flatly claim that it's the only one. It simply says, "At least we've got this desirable quality, whether any other product does or not." *Newsweek* identified itself as "the news magazine that separates fact from opinion"—a powerful use of that innocent word *the* that devastates the competition.

CASE STUDY: *Prevention* **Magazine**

There are various ways to test print advertising in magazines and newspapers. A/B splits are available from most newspapers and magazines. The process is to test two different ads on an every-other-copy basis in one particular edition of a magazine or newspaper.

The two-ad test method can be expanded greatly by conducting "telescopic testing," which enables an advertiser to test different ads in as many regions as a magazine publishes. Testing validity is maintained by doing an A/B split in each region so that the A ad is the same in all regions but each B ad in a region is unique to that region (different from all other B ads being tested in other regions). Joan Throckmorton presents a most interesting case in the second edition of her fine book, *Winning Direct Response Advertising*.

BACKGROUND

Prevention wanted to expand circulation, especially among "mainstream Americans"—people not obsessively interested in health and nutrition—but still take advantage of growing interest in health and fitness.

CHALLENGE

Develop ads that would catch readers' interest and motivate them to clip the coupon and mail in their response.

SOLUTION

Five ads were developed, each using a headline with a play on words to pull the reader into the copy. All ads had text set in columns with line art illustrations. The basic hypothesis was different in each ad, and copy supported that hypothesis. Coupon placement was in the same location for each ad—lower right corner—and coupon appearance was different for each ad.

The five ads appeared in regional editions of *TV Guide*, *Parents*, and *Parade*. Regions were matched from one publication to another. Full-page, black-and-white ads were used in all publications. *Parents* and *Parade* were chosen because their regions complemented each other and provided a "match" to the regional editions offered by *TV Guide*.

RESULTS

Ad A, shown in Exhibit 16–1, outpulled the next best ad by two to one.

CASE STUDY: *Prevention* **Magazine** (continued)

EXHIBIT 16–1

Ad A ("Illness isn't natural") outpulled . . .

Illness isn't natural.

It isn't even inevitable.

And if you find it hard to believe, mail the coupon below and we'll send you a free copy of a book that may change your mind. And perhaps your life.

Sickness may seem like a natural part of life . . . until you consider just how much sickness we actually create for ourselves. By not taking good care. By doing things we shouldn't. Or avoiding things that could help.

Take cancer and heart disease, today's leading killers. Nature didn't create them, we did. And medical experts have already linked them to how we eat. To the extra stress and pounds we carry around. And to our habits.

In fact, many doctors now agree that many illnesses may be preventable. The serious stuff and the minor ailments.

What's more, the really modern physicians now say it's easy to look better, feel younger, and live longer, just by making some simple (and, we think, pleasant) adjustments in your lifestyle.

People want to know "Which ones? Is it going to hurt? Will these changes help my arthritis? Can I eat healthier and still love food? How much exercise do I really need? Is there truly a way to be rid of this heavy, half-sick feeling once and for all?"

And PREVENTION, America's best-kept health secret, says: in many cases, yes! For the past 40 years we've been helping millions to discover the path beyond mere relief. To a state of more positively robust and radiant health.

We take readers beyond the commonplace "low salt/high fiber" topics. (Good advice, but many PREVENTION readers have enjoyed those health benefits since the 1950s when we first reported on them.)

These days the pages of PREVENTION are filled with today's really exciting health discoveries. Like how to prevent a stroke, the nation's third biggest crippler. Ten ways, researchers say, you can now heal with vitamin C—not just colds and flu, but now wounds, nerves, periodontal disease, even high cholesterol. Plus repairs on simple, natural ways to relieve arthritis pain.

PREVENTION is buzzing with news of the vitamin that banishes depression and perks-up memory, according to a medical study. And meals that help bring high blood pressure down. Plus the foods so totally health-building, they're being called " the 25 best superfoods."

And there's much more, too, but you get the picture.

The bottom line is: all this illness just isn't necessary. Or natural. And there's plenty you can do to keep much of it off your doorstep.

Want proof? Mail the coupon below for a free copy of our book, "How To Live It Up and Live Longer," and see for yourself.

And while we're mailing your book, we'll also include a free inspection copy of the latest issue of PREVENTION with a money-saving opportunity to try our magazine on a "don't like it, don't buy it" subscription offer.

Naturally, you've got nothing to lose, subscribe or not. (Except some of your un-natural ills, pills, and doctors bills.)

FREE BOOK BONUS!

Mail the coupon today and receive a free copy of "How To Live It Up and Live Longer." In it you will discover little known ways to add perhaps 5 to 10 extra years to your life . . . find more energy . . . relieve stress . . . plus so much more. Send for your free copy right away.

How to Live It Up & Live Longer

free copy!

YES! Please send me my free copy of "How To Live It Up and Live Longer," enter my 12-month trial subscription to PREVENTION, and please bill me at the special rate of $12.97 for 12 monthly issues. If not satisfied, I'll mark "cancel" on the subscription bill, return it to you and owe nothing. The first issue—and the free book—are mine to keep without obligation.

NAME _____

ADDRESS _____ APT # ____

CITY _____

STATE _____ ZIP _____

Clip and mail to PREVENTION, Emmaus, PA 18049

Prevention.
THE MAGAZINE FOR BETTER HEALTH

THE NEW
NATURAL WAY TO
LOWER BLOOD
PRESSURE

PILOT PROJECT You are a copywriter by profession. You have just been employed by a direct response advertising agency. The agency has been appointed by a home study school offering a course in accounting. Your copy supervisor has asked you to come up with headlines designed to get inquiries. Develop one headline for each of these ultimate benefits:

CASE STUDY: *Prevention* **Magazine** (continued)

EXHIBIT 16-1 (continued)

Ad B ("How many of these medical myths . . . ") two-to-one.

279c

How many of these medical myths do you still subscribe to?

If you still believe in any of these medical myths, PREVENTION—America's most popular better health magazine—would like to offer you a second opinion. Because an ounce of information now could save you a ton of trouble later.

Illness is a natural part of growing older.

NOT SO. Sure, sickness does occur, but that doesn't mean it has to. In fact, the latest scientific thinking indicates that we create most of our health problems. By eating and doing what we shouldn't. And by ignoring things that could help. Research clearly shows that the majority of illness can be prevented or can be avoided altogether.

How?

For over 40 years, the pages of PREVENTION have been filled with medical reports that show people how to keep their health longer. These days, PREVENTION is reporting on the very newest health discoveries. Like what you can do to prevent stroke. How you can bring down high blood pressure without drugs. Plus a way of eating that offers the best-known protection against cancer. So if you're missing PREVENTION, you're missing a lot.

If I eat well enough, I won't need vitamins.

SORRY. Researchers have found that the foods we eat today are so processed that many won't even support laboratory life. In fact, experts blame our poor diet for many of today's serious health problems. This, they report, plus our extra stress, requires that we strengthen ourselves with vitamins to be optimally healthy.

But which vitamins do what? And how much do you need? And what are the best sources?

In PREVENTION magazine, you'll read about vitamins that give extra energy. The vitamin that banishes depression and perks up memory, according to a medical study. The vitamin shown to build a stronger heart. Plus ten ways to heal with vitamin C, many of them new. When it comes to vitamins, PREVENTION is the most reliable source of information in print today.

The doctor knows best.

NOT ANYMORE. As helpful as doctors are, they don't have all the answers. And the good ones will be the first to admit it. Nearly 20% of all hospital patients *get sick as a result of their medical treatment.* As high as 25% of all surgery may be unnecessary, it is estimated.

Who knows best?

You *should.* Because you just can't afford to depend on your doctor for health, no matter how good he or she may be.

That's why PREVENTION magazine brings you news of how to take better care of your health yourself, so you can have it longer. You'll see how to rate your physician—and important questions to ask. Plus a list of the most addictive and sickening prescription drugs. And how to tell if your x-rays, tests, and surgery are really necessary.

These days, it's easy to make a medical mistake. Or become one.

Take better care of yourself.

MAIL THE COUPON BELOW TODAY for a free examination of the latest issue of PREVENTION and see why nearly three million health-loving Americans subscribe to its natural advice.

FREE BOOK BONUS! Mail the coupon today and receive a free copy of "How to Live It Up and Live Longer." In it you will discover little-known ways to add perhaps 5 to 10 extra years to your life . . . find more energy . . . relieve stress . . . plus so much more. Send for your free copy right away.

FREE COPY! YES Please send me my free copy of "How to Live It Up and Live Longer," enter my 12-month trial subscription to PREVENTION magazine and please bill me at the special rate of $12.97 for 12 monthly issues. If not satisfied, I'll mark "cancel" on the subscription bill, return it to you and owe nothing. The first issue—and the free book—are mine to keep without obligation.

NAME _____

ADDRESS _____ APT # ____

CITY _____

STATE _____

Clip and Mail to PREVENTION® Emmaus, PA 18049

Health   Identity   Enjoyment

Security   Escape   Power

Approval   Possessions   Freedom

Excitement   Money   Relaxation

Fulfillment   Pride   Curiosity

Key Points

▶ Print ads must stop the reader and engage his or her attention and interest in order to stand out among the advertisers in a magazine or newspaper. While the general ad may rest after making an impression, the response ad must stimulate immediate action.

▶ Make your strongest appeal to your best prospects—people with the strongest desire for what you're selling. Use clarity and directness to gather in prime prospects; then use creative imagination to reach beyond them to awaken and excite mild prospects as well.

▶ If the product or service is unique or unfamiliar, stress benefits. If it is simply a new, improved model in a highly competitive field with established demand, stress product advantages.

▶ A good lead is the first step in a straight path of feeling and logic from the headline or display theme to the concluding call for action. Readers should be able to see clearly where the path is taking them.

▶ The sections of a classic copy argument can be labeled *problem, promise of solution, explanation of promise, proof,* and *call to action.* If you start with the problem, hint right away at the forthcoming solution.

▶ Other ways to structure copy include the "cluster of diamonds" technique, which assembles and presents details in an appropriate setting; the "string of pearls" technique, which strings together complete little gems of selling in a sequence; and the "fan dancers" technique, which teases readers with short product facts. Avoid the "machine gun" technique—simply spraying facts and arguments in the general direction of the reader, in the hope that at least some of them will hit.

▶ Establish the unique claim to fame of the product or service. Is it better? Best? Largest? Newest? Fastest growing? Use it to stake out a unique position in the marketplace for the product or service you are selling.

MARKETING TO BUSINESSES

BUSINESS-TO-BUSINESS DIRECT MARKETING

The opportunities in business-to-business direct marketing are great: to get qualified leads, to screen leads, to sell by telephone, to create catalogs and sales support material, and to conduct E-commerce. Business-to-business direct marketing uses the same tools as consumer direct marketing, but significant differences separate the two (see Exhibit 17–1). The major difference is an economic one.

The average order size of business-to-business direct marketing offers is large, and the lifetime value of a single customer can be enormous. For example, IBM sells $50,000 equipment using direct marketing techniques. With order sizes of this type, the lifetime value of a business-to-business customer can be extremely high. It is not uncommon for a single business-to-business customer to represent millions of dollars in lifetime value.

Although economic value is high, target market universes can be small. In some cases this involves fewer than a hundred companies. Therefore, the mass-marketing techniques that work so well in consumer direct marketing are often not applicable to business-to-business.

This means that businesses must invest far more in building and supporting a relationship with the customer—the loss of one customer can have a great economic impact on the business. As a result, direct marketing takes on new dimensions when used in business-to-business applications. No longer are its goals the capturing of an order or the acquisition of a new customer. Rather, the goals become increasing sales productivity while sustaining relationships with existing business customers. Instead of emphasizing new customer acquisition, we "cultivate" existing customers and use that information to broaden our customer base.

Through this we begin to build a spirit of community among our customers. We want to leverage our relationship with the customer to build a bond that translates into a lasting relationship based on mutual interests, mutual trust, and healthy

EXHIBIT 17-1

Consumer versus Business-to-Business Direct Marketing

Consumer Direct Marketing	Business-to-Business Direct Marketing
Individuals frequently buy for themselves	Individuals buy on behalf of an organization
Buying decision involves relatively few others	Decisions frequently involve multiple individuals
Single buyer groups	Multiple buyer groups
Informal buying process	Formal and informal buying process
Transaction-based	Relationship-based
Average order size is relatively small	Average order size tends to be large
Lifetime value is relatively low	Lifetime value can be very large
Easy to reach individuals	Difficult to reach individuals
Large target market universe	Small target market universes
Transaction-focused	Relationship process-focused

Source: Hunter Business Group, LLC

interdependence. We make the customer community economically desirable and stable through lowering selling costs for the seller and delivering higher product/service value to the customer.

Of course, this means that direct marketing processes look quite different in business-to-business marketing. For example, the functions or uses for direct marketing change. In business-to-business applications, direct marketing is used for such functions as reducing the number of face-to-face contacts with the customer, reaching marginal accounts that might not be profitable to contact through a face-to-face sales call, and building sustainable relationships with the customer at lower costs.

Also, the measurements or metrics used to evaluate results change. Rather than focusing on transaction- or campaign-based measurements, such as cost per thousand, number of calls per hour, response rates, etc., business-to-business direct marketing uses such qualitative measures as customer satisfaction, product penetration, account penetration, referrals, and loyalty.

Another difference is that we are dealing with individuals who represent economic value beyond themselves. They are the buyers, specifiers, approvers, etc., who influence or direct purchases for companies, institutions, or other organizations. As such, they are not spending their money—they're spending someone else's. As a result, this is a more complex buying process. Typically, more than one person is involved in a single buying decision; or there might be multiple buying groups within the same organization, buying the same type of product. With this complexity, it is difficult to find key buying influences and the purchasing patterns within an organization.

Value-Added Direct Marketing

In the early 1980s, Hunter Business Group, LLC, began using and refining a highly effective business-to-business direct marketing technique called value-added marketing. The differences between traditional and value-added marketing are shown in Exhibit 17–2.

In value-added marketing, Hunter starts with the premise that it is dealing with a market size of a single individual. This is the key—marketing to individuals, not to accounts or organizations. Individualized messages go to target markets. Each has a size of one.

Make that paradigm shift—from selling to accounts to selling to individuals who buy on behalf of others—and the rest of the elements fall into place. For example, if you're selling to individuals, you can ask what their needs are and store them in a database. You don't have to guess. You can then look for product or service applications that meet their specific business needs.

In this approach, businesses manage contacts with the customer through a centralized operation, called the customer center (CC) or market center. This gives them the ability to integrate direct marketing tools with field sales to provide the customer with a seamless flow of value-added information. That is, they ensure that every contact with the customer delivers value, as perceived by the customer.

A key concept here is to focus on retaining customers and building customer loyalties. Studies have shown that retaining existing customers is significantly less

EXHIBIT 17–2

Traditional versus Value-Added Direct Marketing

Traditional Marketing		Value-Added Marketing
Mass marketing	—	n = 1
Projected needs	—	Actual needs
Product driven	—	Customer driven
Account focus	—	Individual focus
Activity based	—	Application based
Acquisition focus	—	Retention focus
Events and activities	—	Systems and procedures
Projected results	—	Actual results
Independent contacts	—	Integrated contacts
Impersonal communication	—	Personal communication
Supports traditional sales channels	—	Supports all sales channels

Source: Hunter Business Group, LLC

expensive and more profitable than acquiring new customers. So, direct marketing tools must focus on retaining customers, not simply getting them to place an order. This requires another paradigm shift, away from the transaction-based traditional approach to one focused on building long-term relationships.

A strategy of retention can build customer loyalty. This has distinct advantages: loyal customers are less likely to defect and more likely to become your "champions" within their organization and industry. Only when we understand who our loyal customers are can we look at acquiring new customers. The reason is simple: we want new customers that look like and act like our best loyal customers. If we blindly pursue an acquisition strategy designed to replace lost customers, we are likely to get some new customers that look like the customers we just lost. That's not smart marketing.

The principles and techniques of value-added marketing produce three major benefits:

1. Improved sales force productivity and reduced sales costs to revenue of up to 15 percent

2. Increased customer loyalty, which leads to customer retention

3. Sales revenue growth and increased profitability

These are dramatic benefits in today's highly competitive business-to-business world. They can be accomplished through a four-stage process: (1) understanding the customer, (2) developing a value-added communication strategy, (3) using cultivation to build retention and loyalty, and (4) acquiring new customers based on existing customer experience.

Listening to the Customer's Voice

Value-added marketing is built around the premise that all contacts with the customer deliver value. It is through this value-based approach that businesses can build long-lasting and sustainable relationships with customers. The first step in this process is understanding what the customer values in the relationship. As Stephen Covey noted in *The Seven Habits of Highly Effective People*, we must "seek first to understand." To accomplish this, first listen to the voice of the customer. Try to understand why customers buy from you, what needs your products or services fulfill, how you stack up against the competition, and how you can use this information for competitive advantage. Exhibit 17–3 summarizes the steps to take.

One of the most difficult aspects in understanding why customers buy from you is identifying their needs. These fall into three categories: basic, unfulfilled, and future needs. Basic needs are those you need to satisfy in order to be considered by the customer. These are needs that every entrant into the market must meet

EXHIBIT 17–3

Understanding the Customer

Task	Description	Implemented by	Information Source
Customer needs assessment	Identify basic, unfulfilled, future, and at-risk needs	Marketing	Customer surveys
Attribute/feature analysis	Identify all attributes or features of your product or service	Marketing	Marketing
Competitive analysis	Compare attributes/features with competitors	Marketing	Competitive intelligence
External service values	Determine why customer buys product/service from you	Marketing	Attribute/feature and competitive analyses
Segment target markets	Group customers with common set of needs into target segments	Marketing	Database

Source: Hunter Business Group, LLC

or they become barriers to entry. If all competitors only satisfied basic needs, we would be dealing with a commodity-type product or service.

Unfulfilled needs are the path to competitive dominance. If you can uncover and meet needs that the competition is not meeting, it gives you a distinct advantage. At the same time, if you are not meeting unfulfilled needs, and the competition is, these become at-risk needs and can cause customer defections. By listening to the customer's voice, you can anticipate his or her future needs. This requires a means of continuously monitoring a customer's changing needs.

Businesses identify customer needs by determining external service values—the reasons customers buy a product or service, and buy from them.

Determining External Service Values or Brand Promise

The step-by-step process used to uncover external service values starts with an understanding of the products and services. First, identify all of the product's features or attributes. In some cases this can involve more than 100 attributes. Next, compare these attributes with those of competitive products or services. The result is a competitive analysis that helps to distinguish your product from competitive offerings and leads to defined external service values. Exhibit 17–4 shows a portion of a competitive attribute/feature analysis.

This type of analysis provides a clear picture of the competitive position. It shows a unique set of features or attributes that distinguishes your product from the competition. However, this is strictly an internal analysis and must be tested against market realities by asking customers what is important. This can be accomplished

EXHIBIT 17–4

Competitive Attribute/Feature Analysis

Feature	Our Company	Competitors A	B	C
Time to ship	Same day	2 days	5 days	Same day
Guarantee	Unlimited	60	120	90
Handling charge	No	No	Yes	No
Quote turnaround	8 hours	2 days	24 hours	N/A
Volume pricing	Yes	Yes	Yes	Yes
Accuracy of order fulfillment	100%	98%	95%	100%
Recycled packaging	No	No	No	No
Price guarantee	90 days	No	30 days	No
Toll-free number	Yes	Yes	Yes	Yes
Customizing	5–10 days	6 weeks	5 weeks	No

Source: Hunter Business Group, LLC

in several ways. The simplest is to call customers following receipt of the order and ask why they purchased. Then match that answer to the unique feature list.

A more systematic approach is to conduct periodic customer surveys. These surveys identify the key attributes/features and ask the customers to rate your unique value for that attribute compared to the competition's. Then ask them to rate each in importance in the buying decision. By multiplying the unique value by the level of importance in the purchasing decision, you have a quantitative measure of external service values. It's always good to go back and verify that this is why customers buy from you.

Another technique is to interview customers who defected or are no longer buying from you. By asking them why they are no longer buying, you can determine what external service values were not satisfied. This not only gives you valuable information about unfulfilled customer needs, but also can be an early warning system to help prevent additional defections.

A New Segmentation Tool

The external service value analysis enables you to group customers with like needs and reasons for buying. For example, when customers rank order in the attribute/feature list, they are building a basis for target market segmentation. If no-cost shipping and handling, order turnaround time, and volume discounts are important to a select group of customers, these customers represent an identifiable target segment. Segmentation is a critical early step in grouping your customers to allow for creation and execution of far more effective communications.

Contact Channels and Communication Strategies

Successful businesses manage communications with their internal and external customers at every possible point of contact, and they use the knowledge gained from those contacts to create value in the relationship. Contacts are information pathways. Whoever owns these vital pathways owns the relationship with the customer.

There are two main objectives in developing specific communication strategies and plans. First, direct marketing enables you to leverage the high cost of field sales. For example, the cost of a typical business-to-business sales call averages more than $400. Therefore, direct marketing techniques should, and can, be used to support and leverage the field sales process. Second, studies have shown that frequency of valued contacts is more important than contact media. Therefore, focus on the use of low-cost contact media if the same value-based communication can be made. Exhibit 17–5 summarizes the steps used in developing an effective contact plan and communication strategy.

First you need to know how, when, and about what customers contact you and you contact them. To do this, start by analyzing current contact practices. Identify

EXHIBIT 17-5

Contact Plan and Communication Strategies

Task	Description	Implemented by	Information Source
Contact analysis	Identify all contact points with customer by type and content	Marketing	Internal observation
Communication workshop	Identify customer contact preferences	Marketing	Customer
Grade customers	Determine which are most valuable customers (AA, A, B, C, D)	Marketing	Database
Customer contact matrix	Match customer contact preferences with contact media cost with economic value	Marketing	Database
Communication plan	Determine specific communication elements for contact matrix	Marketing	Marketing and sales
Develop offer	Base offer on external service values	Marketing	Database
Customer contact	Implement the communication plan	CIC	Database

Source: Hunter Business Group, LLC

every customer contact point within the organization, no matter how infrequent or at what location. Over a predetermined period, record all contacts with the customer. This is typically done using a contact log like the one shown in Exhibit 17–6. The contact log not only records the contact, but it also identifies the information content, the source of the contact (inbound or outbound), the contact owner, and the frequency of contact. You can then prepare a cumulative analysis that covers all contact points.

If you understand how customers want to receive certain types of information, and then proceed to deliver it to them in that manner, this adds value to the

EXHIBIT 17–6

Sample Contact Log

Department (Group)	Key Contact:		Approvals:	
	Time Period			
Activity	Phone	Mail	Electronic	
	In	Out	In	Out	In	Out
A. Sales/revenue generation						
1. Orders/applications						
2. Contracts/confirmations/modifications						
B. Requests/exchange of information						
1. Product information						
2. Pricing/bid requests						
3. Literature/material						
4. Account related						
5. Special programs						
6. Other: _____						
C. Problems/customer service						
1. Shipment/completion status						
2. Problems/complaints						
3. Account corrections/adjustments						
4. Service related						
D. Messages/transfers						
E. Prospect/lead identification (solicited)						
F. Invoices/payments/claims/purchase orders						
G. Misdirected contacts/referrals						
H. Other: _____						

Source: Hunter Business Group, LLC

relationship with the customer. This forms the base for the next step and helps in building the infrastructure for the customer center.

Customer Contact Preferences

After you understand current contact practices, and what the customer values, you need to ask customers about their contact preferences.

- What types of information does the customer consider important or value based?

- How does the customer want to be contacted on each occasion?

- When does the customer want contact?

- How frequently does the customer want to be contacted?

One way to gather this customer-specific information is to ask customers during the normal course of business. That is, during a phone call with the customer, the representative is prompted to ask specific questions related to communication preferences. A second way is to use a mail survey. Another technique is the customer communication workshop. Here, groups of customers, sales representatives, and product marketing representatives meet to:

- Review the cumulative contact log

- Have each group identify the top 10 to 12 contact items

- Have each group present their selections and state reasons for selecting the item

- Resolve differences between groups

This process has the customer, together with the business, define what contacts and what content are important, what contact medium the customer prefers, and how frequently the customer wants the information. From this process a contact model can be developed for communication planning. Exhibit 17–7 shows a sample contact model. For example, it shows that the customer is willing to have 12 notifications for program specials. They prefer to have this notification through E-mail, but consider mail, phone, and face-to-face notification acceptable.

Grading Customers

One mistake some companies make is to consider all customers equal for the purposes of direct marketing programs. This is highly ineffective—customers are not equal. They have different needs (market segment) and different economic potential/value (grade). Some require more contact than others; frequent contact is not

EXHIBIT 17–7

Value-Based Contact Model

Contacts	Frequency	E-Mail	Phone	Field	Mail
1. New-product announcements	4	P	A		A
2. Product application information	4	P	A	A	A
3. Product updates/new releases	4	P	A	A	
4. Case studies	4	P			A
a. Product application					
b. Results					
5. Industry research	1	P			A
6. Article reprints	6	P			A
7. Program specials	12	P	A	A	A
8. Industry trends	2	P			A
9. Product uses/performance assessment	4		A	P	

P = Preferred medium   A = Acceptable medium

Source: Hunter Business Group, LLC

economically justified for other customers. To avoid such mistakes, it is wise to grade customers on an economic basis and develop direct marketing programs that specifically address the needs of each economic grade of customers.

Most marketers are familiar with the 20/80 form of grading customers: 20 percent of your customers account for 80 percent of your sales volume. Taking this a step further, you can grade customers into five categories—AA, A, B, C, D—to allow for a closer match of economic value to contact mix and frequency. The criteria used can include past sales history, profitability, potential, or any other measure of customer value. Typically, active customers can then be divided as follows:

AA = Top 5 percent
A = 15 percent
B = 25 percent
C = 25 percent
D = 30 percent

Creating a Customer Contact Plan

Once you have the customer contact preferences and have graded customers, you can build a contact plan that economically leverages sales contact costs in a highly effective manner. In essence, the plan delivers value, as defined by the customer, with every contact. Because the financial aspect is essential, you first need to set a budget. This includes setting a total budget and a budget for each customer grade. Next, establish costs for each type of media. Then generate a mix of media that satisfies the objectives of leveraging higher-cost media and being effective. After these steps, a customer contact plan is developed. Media costs can vary dramatically from one medium to another. Exhibit 17–8 shows the range of typical media costs.

The next step is to develop a mix of contact media that best fits your objectives and meets your budgets. Be advised that as you build a contact plan you need to repeatedly adjust the mix until you reach the optimum plan.

Exhibit 17–9 shows a completed customer plan. This sample is derived from a base of 1,000 buyer groups. To illustrate what each item represents, let's use Grade B customers. First, this group represents customers with $20,000 to $40,000 in annual sales revenue. There are 250 customers in this category. According to the contact plan, this group is expected to generate about $7.5 million in sales revenue during the year. The plan is to invest approximately 13 percent of sales revenues, or $988,000, into communication and contact with customers. This translates to 50 mailings (about one per week), 25 phone calls (about one every two weeks), and eight face-to-face sales contacts (about one every six weeks) for each customer in this buyer group.

Marketing and Sales Communication Plan

Specific marketing communication and sales plans are now developed. First the 50 direct mail pieces must be developed: what each piece will consist of, its format, its content, and which external service values will be stressed. The customer's external service values are known, so they are the basis for message content. Remember, these contacts are defined by the customer to have value if mailed to them with this frequency.

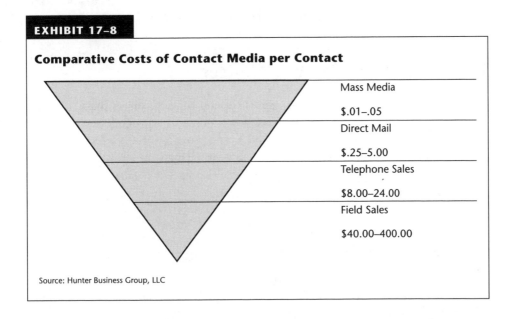

EXHIBIT 17–8

Comparative Costs of Contact Media per Contact

Mass Media
$.01–.05

Direct Mail
$.25–5.00

Telephone Sales
$8.00–24.00

Field Sales
$40.00–400.00

Source: Hunter Business Group, LLC

EXHIBIT 17–9

Customer Contact Plan Sample

Grade/Sales ($000)	1,000 = Buyer Groups	Mail Count	Phone Count	Field Count	Sales Cost ($000)	Percentages of Revenue
AA $60 +	50	75 3,750	50 2,500	20 1,000	$ 469	13.4%
A $40–60	150	75 11,250	40 6,000	15 2,250	1,076	14.4
B $20–40	250	50 12,500	25 6,250	8 2,000	988	13.2
C $10–20	250	25 6,250	12 3,000	4 1,000	491	13.1
D > $10	300	25 7,500	10 3,000	1 300	218	14.5
Total	1,000	41,250	20,750	6,550	$3,242	13.6%

Source: Hunter Business Group, LLC

To show how this works in practice, let's assume you have a monthly newsletter that you send to customers. You plan the newsletter so that each issue includes information related to your core external service values. Then you use the cover letter to call attention to specific pieces of information within the newsletter that meet the individual customer's external service values. This adds value to your communication with the customer and delivers 12 mail contacts throughout the year.

Building the Customer Center

Because value-added direct marketing uses the full range of direct marketing and sales tools, you need a means to manage and monitor the process: the customer center. All activities are coordinated and flow through the CC. Exhibit 17–10 shows the CC model. The CC's role involves acquiring customer information and then using that information for marketing activities. It is the central contact point for customers and the place from which all outgoing contacts with the customer are initiated.

Database Is the Heart of the CC

In direct marketing, the database is the heart of the process. It serves as the collective memory of all customer transactions and is the depository for customer

EXHIBIT 17–10

Customer Information Center

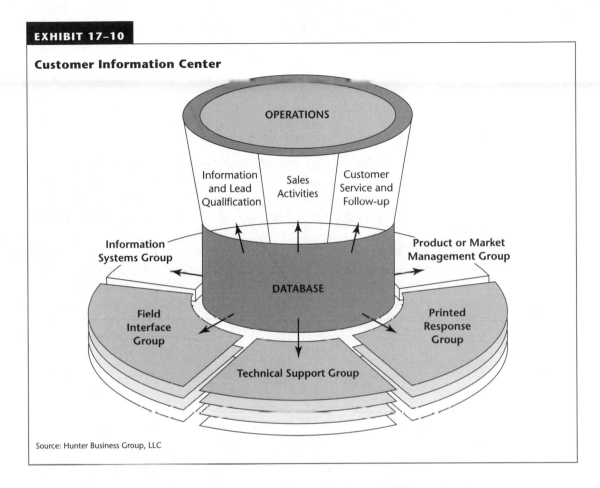

Source: Hunter Business Group, LLC

attribute information. Because all customer information is contained in the database, it must be accessible to anyone who has contact with the customer. Through this, the business can achieve seamless, synchronized interaction with the customer.

For example, a salesperson could access the customer's file before making a sales call. Then the salesperson could review all contacts since the last sales call, review all actions taken on behalf of the customer, and access any specific interest areas the customer has identified. Equipped with this information, the salesperson has a more productive sales call and adds value to the relationship. The database plays a critical role in many aspects of business-to-business direct marketing.

Target Market Segmentation. Use the customer attribute information for segmenting target markets.

Single Source for Customer Inquiries. Access to the database enables fast answers to customer inquiries and eliminates unnecessary transferring of customer calls.

Product Development. Record customers' changing needs to detect new product opportunities.

Analysis. Information stored in the database can be used for analysis, such as expense-to-revenue ratios to determine customer profitability.

Metrics. Database information facilitates a number of measurements, such as the effectiveness of lead-generation sources or loyalty of a customer.

Operations for Customer Interface

The operations portions of the CC is shown at the center of the model in Exhibit 17–10. This is the core set of functions that includes information and lead qualification, sales activities, customer service, and follow-up. Typically, a centralized group of telemarketers are the primary contact point for customers and field sales reps.

The CC phone reps input and extract data from the CC database during their dialogue with customers and sales reps. This high-frequency, two-way dialogue continually validates and refreshes the database at low cost. Each group of telemarketers performs a function defined by the marketing and sales communication plans.

Communication Management Group

This group plans and executes direct marketing campaigns. It controls the message being delivered to the customer. It designs campaigns and contact plans. A primary responsibility is to ensure that all communications with customers and prospective customers deliver value. The communications management group performs several important functions.

Design and Develop Direct Mail Pieces and Electronic Communications. Communications managers are responsible for creating and producing direct mail items, generating and acquiring lists, and mailing. They also produce all electronic communications.

Define Telemarketing Guides. In business-to-business direct marketing, scripts are rarely used for outbound calling. The length of a call becomes a minor issue in building dialogue with the customer because obtaining certain types of information requires lengthy conversations. The guides remind the telemarketing representative of the information needed.

Determine Measures. Develop methods to measure customer satisfaction, customer loyalty, profitability, lead sources, etc.

Develop Lead-Generation Programs. Create and execute electronic, advertising, direct mail, and telemarketing lead-generation programs. Define lead-qualification criteria.

Coordinate Program Training and Instruction. Provide training and instruction to keep telemarketing representatives current on product/service features and applications.

Print and Electronic Response Group

This group performs all mail room functions for printed material or personalized letters and responses. The group stocks, mails, and reorders literature supplies and other fulfillment material. They also manage electronic communications.

Technical Support Group

This group answers technically specific questions from customers, end-users, or channel distributors that cannot be answered by the telemarketing representative.

Field Interface Group

This group provides a central, personal contact for dealers, jobbers, franchisees, national accounts, sales reps, wholesalers, and retailers to interface with the CC. It supports sales and channel management functions to coordinate account planning activities among the customer, field sales reps, and telephone contacts.

Information Systems Group

This group interfaces with electronic communication networks and the centralized database. It maintains the internal network linking all functional groups with the database (e.g., inventory, order processing status, accounting). Obviously, the CC involves a highly integrated process. To be effective, the processes leading up to the CC must be completed. Completion of these processes enables businesses to better plan, design, and staff the CC. Too often companies make the mistake of starting with the CC and ignoring the other processes. This leads to underutilizing the inherent power of the CC and results in disappointment.

Cultivating Customers and Acquiring New Customers

The two major goals of direct marketing in a business-to-business environment are: (1) to increase sales productivity (while reducing sales costs), and (2) to build customer relationships. The CC is the tool used to accomplish these goals. The specific applications that lead to satisfying these goals are *cultivation* and *acquisition*.

The cultivation process is designed to build the customer relationship. Businesses must build a bond with the customer that leads to a long-term relationship that benefits both parties. Exhibit 17–11 summarizes the steps in this process.

An adage in business-to-business marketing is that your best source for new business is your current customers. Existing customers represent growth opportunities. The cultivation process takes advantage of this by actively searching out sales opportunities and by closely monitoring the relationship.

Increasing Sales Opportunities

After gaining a customer, businesses can use the CC and direct marketing to pursue penetration strategies. They should penetrate the account to search out additional sales opportunities and strengthen relationships. They pursue this at several levels: the individual, the buyer group, the location, and the organization. Exhibit 17–12 illustrates an account model and the penetration strategy.

1. At the individual level is the product penetration strategy. Businesses must ask customers what additional needs they have and what solutions might meet those needs.

2. At the buyer group level, they ask the customer to refer them to other people within the same department or function, at the same location. The idea is to find additional applications for the businesses' products or services.

EXHIBIT 17–11

Cultivation Process

Task	Description	Implemented by	Information Source
Product penetration	Determine which other products customer has application for	CIC	Database
Account penetration	Obtain customer referrals for others within buying group	CIC	Database
Location penetration	Obtain customer referrals for others within location and/or organization	CIC	Database
Complaint handling	Procedures for handling customer complaints	CIC	Marketing and database
Customer-at-risk	Determine which customers or target segments are at risk	CIC and marketing	Customer surveys and database
Measurements	Continuously monitor and measure the customer relationship	CIC and marketing	Database

Source: Hunter Business Group, LLC

EXHIBIT 17-12

Account Model with Penetration Strategies

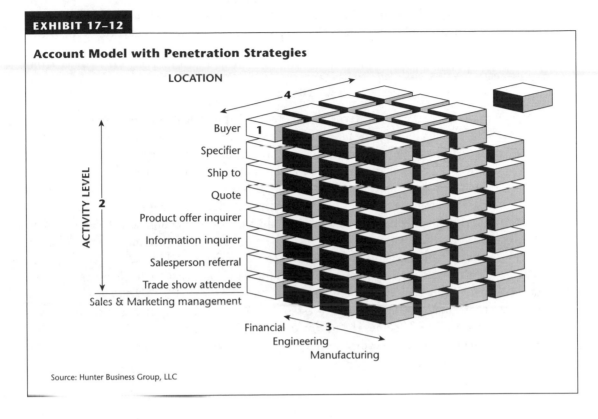

Source: Hunter Business Group, LLC

3. At the functional level, they find out whether the customer can lead them to other buyer groups within the customer's location. Here, the area sales manager introduces his company to people in finance, manufacturing, and engineering located in the same area.

4. Finally, they move to the account level and determine whether there are other locations or operations within the organization with similar applications. The same area sales manager now introduces them to other area sales managers within the company or with affiliates.

Combined, these efforts enable businesses to build a stronger bond with the customer. By referring them to others within the organization, the customer takes a proactive role in the relationship. By focusing on delighting the sales manager, an apostle is created, more loyal to the company and helpful in growing the business profitably.

Protecting Your Customer Base

Although expanding your customer base is important, so is protecting this base. This involves customer-at-risk detection. Detecting customers at risk requires an ongoing program of monitoring the state of your customer relationships. This is an early warning system that detects changing customer needs, etc., and permits corrective actions before customers defect.

Acquiring New Customers

Acquiring stable, long-term customers is only possible if you know and retain your current customers. The most profitable new or prospective customers will look like your best current customers. The customer information gathered by the CC will help you acquire new customers. Using the information in the CC's database, you can identify attributes among current customers that will help you identify potential customers. From these attributes you can build a target segment, identify the unfulfilled needs or external service values of that segment, and determine how to position the product or service in respect to competitive products or services.

The next step in this process is lead qualification. The CC is used to qualify leads before sending them to the sales force or other channel members. A communications plan is developed—similar to the one used with current customers—for those qualified leads that express a current interest and have a customer buyer profile. This becomes the qualified prospect list and is managed through the CC. The goal here is to advance the sales process so the prospect is converted into a buyer.

Assimilation

Finally, new customers need to be assimilated into the customer community. Assimilation is the process of absorbing customers into the culture of the company—an initial "bonding" with the customer by acquiring and sharing valuable information. Think of it as welcoming a new employee into a company. It is the building of a "community of customers."

Meeting the Challenges of Our Decade

Enter E-business as a new, low-cost, contact medium for business-to-business contacts. Fax, E-mail, and Internet-based communications fall into this category of electronic contacts, by far the fastest growing medium and the least understood in its impact on buying behavior. Its effect on buying behavior is even less studied when considered as a part of an integrated sales process.

Early E-business users have focused on the low cost of communication and the intimacy of private extranet corporate sites. Low-cost communications push the message to broad and deep penetration of the market. Corporate extranets focus special messages to select audiences. Both are highly successful within the same medium.

In general, E-commerce impact will be highest when supporting the usefulness of a search-and-acquisition process, logistics, and service processes.

As network bandwidth broadens and Internet-based technology continues to advance, more integration of media will take place on the Internet. For example, early research on business E-commerce offerings showed that potential customers often became confused or needed additional support while on-line and then abandoned the ordering process. New technology makes a phone button available on the terminal screen. When clicked, a phone operator viewing the same screen is connected to the prospective customer through the Internet.

Phone-assisted E-commerce will grow just as phone-assisted catalogs have proven successful in the business community. The addition of real-time, personal video-to-audio customer contact will continue to grow the importance of electronic media. Experts forecast $1.5 trillion in E-business-to-business sales by the year 2004.

The temptation is to revisit the marketing mania of the first Sears Roebuck catalogs, the advent of zip codes, and computer-managed mailing lists. These were times when the cost to get a customer contact dropped significantly. The result was an ever-increasing volume of contacts with less concern for relevance than for cost per contact. Those times are gone.

Unwanted contacts with a business-to-business customer not only are a waste of money but actually are a "vaccination" for the customer. Those continued pricks of valueless faxes, E-mails, mailings, and phone calls build up an immunization. It looks like unreturned phone calls and broken sales appointments. The result is customer and prospect alienation and poor economic results.

CASE STUDY: **Contract Office Products**

BACKGROUND AND CHALLENGE

Like many large, well-established companies, Contract Office Products (COP), a mature manufacturer of office products, generated a considerable number of inquiries, leads, and opportunities just because of its wide and ubiquitous presence. Although COP had been using a fulfillment company to respond to inquiries with product literature, there were no service standards in place and no qualification or follow-up of leads. Customers were complaining, prospects were unhappy, leads were not qualified, and opportunities were lost.

Faced with these problems, COP decided to tighten up its lead-management process.

SOLUTION

COP searched out and contracted with a firm to develop and manage a new process. The new process was designed to include:

- Inbound telephone reps for fielding inquiries, qualifying leads, and closing the loop on qualified leads
- Tight qualification criteria approved by the field sales reps
- A closed-loop tracking system implemented via fax and phone calls
- Summary reporting of lead status and results

The program ran under this configuration for a number of years and was considered successful since

---

CASE STUDY: **Contract Office Products** *(continued)*

---

it generated more than $6 million in revenue. This was about a million dollars per year of incremental revenue from a program that was implemented primarily for the purpose of reducing customer and prospect dissatisfaction.

However, like so many lead-management programs—especially for companies relying on independent dealer reps—the program did not accommodate customers; prospects with high potential to purchase but who did not fit the qualification criteria were lost. The qualification criteria agreed to by the field reps was naturally biased to their needs for hitting quarterly targets.

The criteria used included a time frame of less than three months. Prospects who met all other elements of the criteria such as budget, authority, needs, but not timing, were kicked out. Once kicked out, they usually disappeared because there was no process for tracking or nurturing them until the timing was right.

Fortunately, the inbound reps recognized the lost opportunities and informally added prospect cultivating to their list of responsibilities. The reps, using their own judgment, would each identify one or two leads per week that they felt would be worthy of further investment. During slow times of inbound activity, these reps would proactively nurture these leads through proactive, outbound calls.

Typically, the duration of the nurturing efforts would run from 2 to 60 days. In addition, the inbound telephone reps decided to recontact disqualified prospects who, in their view, had high potential. They did this via mail in hopes that the individual's interest would be rekindled.

RESULTS

The mailings to disqualified prospects yielded approximately five inbound calls per month. Over a period of nine months, these guerrilla tactics generated $1 million in sales, and additional opportunities estimated at another $1 million. The cost to generate the additional $2 million from prospect cultivating is approximately $1,200 per month—a $14,400 investment for $2 million in revenue.

This base lead-management program, run by two individuals on the phone, now generates more than $3.5 million in incremental revenue per year. If the outstanding cultivation leads close, that revenue will come close to $5.5 million; and this is without any corporate advertising or other lead-generation activity.

Few companies, especially large companies in mature industries, are not looking for ways to increase revenue and profit. For many, rising to this challenge leads them to search for a silver bullet or pursue the latest technology or a glitzy ad campaign. Often, as this case illustrates, there is a great deal to be gained by better managing the hundreds of little activities that, added together, could make a huge, positive bottom-line impact.

PILOT PROJECT   You work for a quality-focused printer with less than 10 percent market share. Your culture has been product- and technology-focused, but your vision statement is customer-focused. Your firm seems to replace technology leadership every quarter, and margins continue to erode.

The chief operation officer came up through manufacturing but is "street smart." Budgeting is next month, and he has asked for a "white paper" to show how direct marketing can help the company grow and prosper by focusing on the customer. He and the president have asked you to address the following questions that were raised at a recent executive marketing committee meeting:

1. What is special about integrated direct marketing?

2. What are the three to five key concepts the company must embrace to be successful in focusing on the customer?

3. How can you drive down sales costs and increase service levels?

4. Can you market or sell to individual customers even when you do a mailing?

5. What are the key steps you need to go through in building a pilot direct marketing program?

Key Points

▶ Large average order sizes, enormous lifetime values, and small target market universes dictate that the goal of business-to-business direct marketing is to increase sales productivity while "cultivating" relationships with existing business customers—the buyers, specifiers, approvers, etc., who influence or direct purchases for companies, institutions, or other organizations.

▶ To uncover and meet needs that the competition is not meeting, seek to understand why customers buy from you, what needs your products or services fulfill, and how your products' features or attributes compare with those of competitive products or services. Ask customers to rank order this attribute/feature list to find new opportunities and to begin to segment customers.

▶ Identify how and when customers want to receive certain types of information, and develop an effective contact plan and communication strategy that delivers it in that manner.

▶ Establish a contact center to manage all contacts with customers—ingoing and outgoing. It can acquire customer information for marketing activities and coordinate those activities.

▶ Develop strategies to penetrate existing accounts to search out additional sales opportunities and strengthen relationships.

▶ Use database information to identify attributes among current customers that will help you identify potential customers. From these attributes you can build a target segment, identify the unfulfilled needs or external service values of that segment, and determine how to position the product or service in respect to competitive products or services.

▶ Qualify leads before sending them to the sales force or other channel members. The goal is to advance the sales process so the prospect is converted into a buyer.

MANAGING A
LEAD-GENERATION
PROGRAM

Not long ago the "face" that a company had to its customers was the sales force. Salespeople represented the company in every way—in fact, to customers they *were* the company. The sales force answered questions, demonstrated the product, offered solutions to problems, and established loyal relationships.

The sales force is still a vitally important function of marketing and sales, but its job is different. Instead of "cold canvassing" to solicit interest, "appointment selling" is preferred when a face-to-face visit is needed to sell the product—usually one with a high-ticket price tag or a complex selling proposition. For other products and services, technology has made it easier for customers to make purchase decisions on their own without a salesperson's visit.

Lead-generation programs are a method devised to flow leads into the sales force and classify those leads so the sales force knows which lead is "hot," "warm," or "cool." Thus, they can prioritize their efforts and focus on closing more sales, more often.

But the constantly increasing costs of a sales visit (often in excess of $800) make them cost prohibitive for most companies. Once, it was inconceivable that high-tech or high-ticket items could be sold via traditional direct marketing channels. You needed a sales force to explain complicated products or stay with the prospect while he/she considered a high-ticket purchase. This took considerable time. The sales force needed a system where prospects were identified so they could focus on closing sales, not on cold calling.

But take a look at media today. You can get scads of information on new cars over the Internet, including specific dealer inventory and pricing. You can even tell the nearest dealer what color and/or options you want and how much you are willing to pay. You can respond to an infomercial to get a videotape that describes expensive exercise equipment. You can buy a computer manufactured to your unique needs from a catalog. Negotiate complicated telephone service agreements over the phone. Even buy a private jet from a direct mail package.

In these instances, the communication becomes a surrogate for a human sales force. If developed properly, the marketer will provide all sorts of information so the customer can make the decision on his/her own. Furthermore, every contact a consumer has through these vehicles, whether requested or not, serves to establish and build upon a relationship the customer has with the company. So, these communications not only sell products, but they support the brand image of the company and are inextricably linked to long-term customer loyalty.

Today, marketing and advertising are even more critical to the sales process. Everything moves faster than it did five years ago. Product information is required sooner and buying decisions are made more quickly. The faster information can be provided to a prospect, the better the sales opportunity for the company. In this environment, the rewards go not only to the smartest marketers, but also to the most relevant and responsive.

The Role of the Internet in Generating and Managing Leads

The Internet is fast becoming the medium of choice for marketers wishing to get a great deal of information to prospects in a short time frame. The Internet is in many ways a marketer's dream come true. Reams of product information can be supplied on a company's home page, to be searched and sorted in countless ways. In this case, the onus is on the marketer to ensure that the prospect finds the information he or she needs to make the purchase decision in a quick and easy manner.

"Cookies," or codes attached to the computer of the person searching the site, can track which site prospects have come from, which pages they viewed while on your site, how long they spend on each Web page, which product listings they examine, and which website they go to next when they leave your site. Although cookies cannot be tracked back to individual prospect names and addresses, this information is enormously helpful in determining how to map out the most customer-friendly environment and encourage repeat site visits.

Many companies that utilize lead-generation tactics in a digital environment require a prospect to register with the site before key information and/or benefits are offered. The registration process allows the marketer to gain valuable learning about the prospect, which can lead to more robust marketing programs down the road.

For advanced marketers, information gained through registration can drive the software to acknowledge prospects by name, and thus create a personalized environment where the prospects see only those things that are pertinent to their needs.

All extraneous information is out of their field of vision, and all possible sales tactics can be deployed to close the sale either directly over an E-commerce enabled site or via traditional distribution channels. The Internet is perhaps the closest possible communications parallel to the responsibilities and function of a human salesperson.

Today's Sales Force: People or Process

A sales organization can be a group of specially trained salespeople or, alternatively, a communications process driven by technology.

Many industries today utilize a human sales force or people organized into territories and sales districts with clearly articulated sales quotas. For industries that simply don't have the manpower or the budget to keep a sales force in operation, communications must fill the void, and alternative channels of distribution must be created. The Internet is a terrific example of communications creating alternative methods to distribute product literature, demonstrate benefits, and close the sale.

It is important to note that communications can never replace the sales force completely. There is no substitute for personal relationships between buyer and seller. However, communications (including those on the Internet) can augment, enrich, and support the traditional sales organization.

Before we get carried away with the possibilities, let's start at the very beginning and identify the various types of lead-generation programs.

Types of Lead-Generation Programs

There are three overall types of lead-generation programs. Although the principles that govern them are the same, the needs that dictate the programs differ.

Business-to-Business

The primary objective in business-to-business lead generation is to get qualified leads from prospects who, in effect, raise their hands and say, "I'd like more information about your proposition." The thrust of the promotion can be as simple as encouraging prospects to request literature, with an inducement to order by a variety of distribution channels. Telephone or E-mail follow-ups of those who request literature are often an integral part of the lead-generation program.

For the most complex propositions, the objective is to get a request for a salesperson to call so specific questions can be answered. However, since the cost of an industrial sales call has become prohibitive, direct mail, E-mail, and/or telephone follow-up is becoming the norm rather than the exception.

Business-to-Consumer

The feasibility of lead-generation programs for consumer products is almost always dictated by price point, complexity, and available channels of distribution. The unit of sale inherent in package goods, for example, obviates the practicality of a lead-generation program except in the case of a cents-off coupon co-op. (See Chapter 9, "Co-ops.")

However, lead-generation programs do make eminent sense for the likes of a lawn care service where the annual expenditure is in the area of $1,500. Or for mortgages or car insurance or appliances—each a considered purchase of magnitude for the consumer.

Many manufacturers have begun to sell major equipment directly to the consumer. Their objective is to get qualified leads and to complete the transaction via their website, mail, phone, or salesperson.

Public Relations

A third type of lead-generation program uses public relations as the medium for getting leads. Done right, PR is an extremely effective method of producing leads in both the consumer and business field. As a matter of fact, more often than not, editorial mention of a free booklet offer is likely to produce more leads than a space ad. The theory is that the reader puts more stock in third-party editorial endorsements than in advertising. The flip side of the coin is that conversion to orders is more likely from space ads than from editorial mentions.

Planning Successful Lead-Generation Programs

To develop a successful marketing program, you have to know what you're up against. Here are a few eye-opening facts from the Advertising Research Foundation.

- Up to 60 percent of all inquiries are made with a view to purchase within one year.

- Up to 25 percent of those with a purchase in view will have an "immediate need," and will purchase the product or service advertised from the company of which they inquired, or from a competitor.

- Up to 10 percent of those with a purchase in view will be "hot" leads.

- Up to 60 percent of the inquirers who contact you also contact your competitor.

- In 20 percent of all prospects' requests for information, the respondents never received any material.

- In 43 percent of those inquiries, the material was received too late to be of any use.

- Fifty-nine percent stated that they threw away one or more pieces of the response material because it provided no value.

This data suggests there is a substantial waste of communications expenditures, which results in a feeling of disenchantment by large numbers of people because of unresponsive companies. So how does one overcome these hurdles?

Successful implementation involves consideration of eight key steps:

1. Involving the Sales Force

2. Determining Objectives

3. Developing the Promotion Strategy

4. Developing the Creative Strategy

5. Developing the Media Strategy

6. Planning Capacity and Lead Flow

7. Developing the Fulfillment Strategy

8. Measuring Results

Essentially, these steps create a feedback loop to the very beginning so that actual results can be measured against objectives, modifications can be made, and the process can begin again.

Step One: Involving the Sales Force

If a company utilizes a lead-generation program to support a human sales force, it should involve the sales force in the planning process. No other source will be able to relate as well to the marketplace. The sales force is on the "firing line." Salespeople know the specific needs of their territory, who the competition is, and the spheres of influence among their prospect base.

Even the message in your communications can be influenced in both tone and content by the sales force. Front-end involvement is essential, but don't discount their ability to judge the effectiveness of the promotion. A feedback loop should be established for a qualitative assessment of positive and negative results.

Step Two: Determining Objectives

The need for objectives in a lead-generation program relates to the quality and quantity of leads, and the cost of generating them. An abundance of leads can be meaningless if an insufficient number convert to sales. Key questions are:

- What ratio of leads to sales (often called conversion percentage) is needed to make this program profitable?

- What is the maximum allowable expenditure for every qualified lead generated?

It is important to set these benchmarks at the beginning of the planning process and to use them as guideposts for the development of the program. It's extremely inefficient—and sometimes impossible—to change objectives in midstream.

Step Three: Developing the Promotion Strategy

Strategies should identify the steps required for accomplishing the program's objectives. They are the road map for getting from where you are to where you want to be. In addition, they should mesh with the strategies being applied by the sales force and other distribution channels. For example, if a computer manufacturer has identified the legal profession as a prime opportunity segment, the promotion strategy may be to develop a lead-generation program directed to the same target audience timed in conjunction with personal sales force contact. Qualified leads generated from the program will augment efforts of the sales force and result in a greater sales closing percentage than if the sales force had no support.

Step Four: Developing the Creative Strategy

The creative strategy for any lead-generation program *must* reflect the brand promise. The look and feel of all brand communications should be consistent with the overall image of the company in order to leverage the full benefits of an integrated campaign. This is not to say that all communications should slavishly adhere to precise elements of the current general advertising campaign. The intent is to represent the brand consistently, so that universal brand attributes and emotions are reinforced with every contact the consumer has with the brand.

Step Five: Developing the Media Strategy

The key question is, given the target market and the product offering, what media will most effectively accomplish the task? Whether it be direct mail, E-mail, Internet banners, print, or broadcast, consideration must be given to historical effectiveness, penetration, number of contacts or impressions required, and so on. Once the media strategy is developed, it is possible to project lead flow and to begin the capacity planning process.

Step Six: Planning Capacity and Lead Flow

Lead flow is not a faucet that can be turned on or off at will. It must be planned so leads come in at a rate equal to the sales force's capacity to handle them. Although there will be more on this subject later in this chapter, the key point to remember is that either too few leads or too many leads will work to the detriment of the program.

Step Seven: Developing the Fulfillment Strategy

Immediate response and rapid cycles of contact improve the chances of gaining and maintaining a customer. The sooner information can be delivered or fulfilled, the higher the odds of closing the sale. The smartest marketers will use lead-generation programs to preempt a customer inquiry, and send information and/or pertinent offers at the precise moment the customer is ready to receive them. This demonstrates the symbiotic relationship between lead generation and database marketing. (See Chapter 3, "The Impact of Databases.")

But how does one know what customers want and when they are ready to buy? The answer: leverage every contact with a customer to learn more about him or her. Asking the appropriate questions leads to highly profitable answers.

And, as simple as it sounds, one must know exactly what will happen to a lead once it's received. If there is to be a brochure, for example, ample quantities must be in stock before the initial communication occurs. Measurement systems must be in place for scheduling sales calls, referring leads to the field, recontact programs, and so forth. Failure to be ready to fulfill promptly can kill the best of promotions.

Step Eight: Measuring Results

It is imperative that the program be measurable and accountable. Success and failure factors need to be identified before the program is developed to ensure that results tracking and analysis are conducted properly once the program is in place.

So, how will your program be measured? Gross sales? Revenue? Cost per lead? Cost per order? Beyond these traditional measures, you'll need to ask yourself some additional questions:

- What constitutes a good/bad lead?

- How many leads are enough?

- Which is worse—no leads or too many?

- How will we track leads? Who will be responsible for them?

- How will we automate our processes for secure data flow?

- What is the best way to convert leads into profitable sales?

- How will we report our progress to management?

Other Ingredients of an Effective Lead-Management System

A good inquiry follow-up system should address the interaction problem often associated with the activities of the salespeople, the marketing manager, and the advertising manager.

Sales representatives in general loathe and avoid paperwork. They often resent any intrusion into their territory, and scorn measurement and control. A good lead-management system must be simple to use, easy to work with, and not looked upon by salespeople as a burden. Also, sales representatives typically do not supply the complete feedback necessary for proper evaluation. A smart system must be able to supply the necessary analysis without total reliance on the sales representative.

The Inquiry System Does Not Exist Without an Offer

Communications objectives should be inquiry-oriented. The creation of advertising that employs known response techniques should be the mission of agency and/or staff copywriters and art directors. The advertising produced should be measured against response-oriented goals.

The offer must be in line with program objectives, and with the company's operational ability to follow-up on responses. If the objective is to generate leads, make an offer that will generate only as many as you can effectively handle. Too many leads can be even more destructive to the program than not enough. Lead quantity is not as important as lead quality.

When testing a less expensive offer against your control offer, don't assume that a lower response rate is less effective. Include the costs for the offer, then review the total direct marketing costs per responder and per order. You might find that the less expensive offer produces a more valuable customer over time, thus producing a more profitable program.

Do Not Be Afraid to Mention the Price

As stated previously, lead-generation programs were initially developed for products and services with high price tags. Even if the price is prohibitive, it will immediately weed out those who cannot afford it. They are unqualified. You should spend the majority of your time talking to prospects who have the money, authority, need, and desire to purchase what you have to sell.

Ask the Prospect Some Leading Questions

The questions you ask will allow you to determine where the prospect falls in the purchase decision process. Use every available opportunity, but don't turn your qualification effort into market research. There's no need to overload a single contact with a customer or prospect by asking them lots of questions—too many questions can actually decrease response. Spread them out; use several contacts. This will not only improve the probability that you'll get answers to all your questions, it will also provide a reason to keep communicating. After all, don't forget the out-of-sight, out-of-mind rule. Stay in your prospect's field of vision at all times. Sample questions and their implications are shown in Exhibit 18–1.

Note that answers to these questions can provide important learning. Use all this data to build a rich database from which to develop ongoing marketing communications. Constantly add new data to the old; refresh worn-out data. If, in your database, you find a prospect who: (1) already has experience with your company, (2) is the decision maker in the buying process, and (3) has an immediate need, make sure you get to him/her quickly. You're about to close a sale!

EXHIBIT 18–1

Questions for Sales Prospects

Authority in the buying decision	How would you describe your involvement in the decision to purchase our product? • You make the decision. • You investigate and recommend. • The decision is made elsewhere in the company. (*Make sure to get the name of that person.*)
Monetary resources	How much are you willing to spend?
Potential sales volume	How many people in your company could benefit from our products? How will you put our product to use?
Predisposition to buy from you/customer loyalty	Have you purchased any of our products in the past? Which ones? Would you like to remain on our mailing list?
Immediacy of need/desire	Are you ready to buy now? In 3–6 months? 6–12 months? Over 12 months? Would you like a salesperson to call/visit?

Incorporate a Feedback Loop

Consider adding a device that poses some of the questions above into your fulfillment offering. This could be a bounce-back postcard or fax form, an E-mail (assuming you've already captured the prospect's E-mail address), or even a page within your website. A feedback loop will allow you to qualify the lead after the prospect has a chance to review the information requested.

Monitor the time from the shipment date of the fulfillment package. If the feedback device is not returned within a specified time, send another one. After three unsuccessful efforts, you can call it quits. Additional follow-up beyond this point is unproductive. Analyze and compile the data from the feedback device and the original inquiry to classify the lead as qualified or unqualified.

Understanding the Art of Communications

Hierarchy of Effects

Any purchase decision is an evolutionary process. The advertising industry has accepted a model developed by researchers Lavidge and Steiner to explain how advertising works (see Exhibit 18–2). Their model is based on a hierarchy of effects in the communication process that move the prospect from awareness to purchase.

Before purchasing action occurs, an evolution takes place. Mentally, the prospect moves through a series of steps, starting with awareness and ending in the purchasing action. Within these stages of involvement, different modes of com-

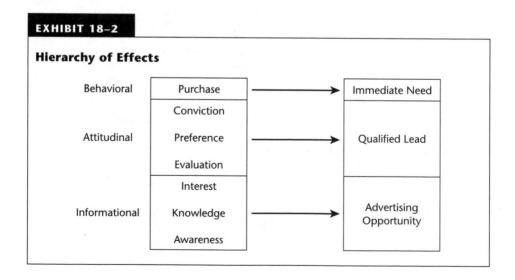

EXHIBIT 18–2

Hierarchy of Effects

Behavioral	Purchase	Immediate Need
	Conviction	
Attitudinal	Preference	Qualified Lead
	Evaluation	
	Interest	
Informational	Knowledge	Advertising Opportunity
	Awareness	

munication play different roles. Although responsibility overlaps, it's clear to see how direct marketing plays a significant role in the selling process.

General advertising is most effective in generating awareness, knowledge, and interest. Direct marketing's strength lies in encouraging evaluation, preference, conviction, and ultimately purchase. These steps often require more information, whether that is delivered in a one-on-one conversation (in person or on the telephone), a product demonstration, an information-rich brochure, or a home page on the Internet.

To increase efficiency and cut costs, marketers should insist that each mode of communication is accountable for what it does best. General advertising should be measured on its ability to generate awareness and consideration; direct marketing should be evaluated on its ability to move the prospect from consideration to purchase and beyond. An effective lead-management system assigns specific roles to both, and leverages the strengths inherent within each. Working seamlessly together, they comprise a communications program that's unbeatable.

Checks and Balances

Multimedia synergy (the combination of two or more forms of communication) can dramatically affect results and productivity. For example, if you are running television advertising in a market and simultaneously mail within that market, you will see lifts in response. But there's another benefit to integrated marketing programs: checks and balances.

Advertising is expensive. You need tools to measure and compare results in order to focus your resources on the most effective channels and activities. The lead-management system should provide reports of inquiries by medium, product, and sales territory. This is a valuable tool, not only for results analysis, but also for advertising planning.

Adjusting Quality and Quantity of Leads

All types of lead-generation programs can produce what are commonly referred to as "soft" or "hard" leads. Soft lead offers can be expected to produce a higher front-end response; hard lead offers can be expected to produce a lower front-end response but a higher closure percentage. Exhibit 18–3 presents ten lead softeners and ten lead hardeners.

Experience will dictate whether you want soft leads or hard leads. If salespeople close only one out of ten soft leads, for example, they may become discouraged and abandon the program. On the other hand, if salespeople close three out of ten soft leads versus five out of ten hard leads with twice as many leads to draw from, they (and management, too) might opt for the soft lead program.

EXHIBIT 18-3

Lead Softeners and Hardeners

Softeners:	Hardeners:
1. Tell less about the product.	1. Mention a price.
2. Add convenience for replies.	2. Mention a phone or sales call.
3. Give away something.	3. Tell a lot about the product.
4. Ask for less information.	4. Ask for a lot of information.
5. Highlight the offer.	5. Specify terms for the offer.
6. Make the ad "scream."	6. Ask for postage on the reply.
7. Don't ask for the phone number.	7. Bury the offer in the copy.
8. Increase the offer's value.	8. Tie the offer to a sales call.
9. Offer a contest or sweepstakes.	9. Change the offer's value.
10. Run in more general media.	10. Ask for money.

Capacity Planning

Capacity planning is a critical component of the up-front planning process, and key to managing the program on an ongoing basis. No matter how carefully planned, a program can change because of internal and external variables.

For instance, market conditions may change, postal deliveries might be slower or faster than anticipated, a computerized customer file might malfunction, a complex new product could take twice as much time to sell as anticipated. The possibilities are endless, but the point is simple: *plan your capacity to be flexible to change.* Exhibit 18–4 is a typical capacity planning chart for a direct mail program, indicating optimum lead flow for various sales districts.

Assuming a salesperson can average one cold prospect call a day, Exhibit 18–4 shows how many calls each office can make in a working month of 20 days. This information determines what quantity of mail is required at a 5 percent return to furnish leads for these calls, given that probably 20 percent of them will be qualified and the rest will be screened out prior to a sales call.

Thus, control can be exercised over mailings so that the two salespeople in Denver, for example, will not be suddenly swamped by scores of sales leads. In their district, 4,000 mailing pieces would be needed to furnish them with 40 qualified leads; as many as the two salespeople can follow up in one month. Zip code selectivity helps to target mailings within a district.

To keep a constant flow of leads moving to the field at an average of 3,500 a month would require 70,000 mailing pieces per month. A year's campaign (12 months multiplied by 70,000) requires 840,000 mailing pieces.

EXHIBIT 18–4

Capacity Planning Chart

District Offices	No. of Salespeople in Each	Total Qualified Calls Needed Each Month	Total Leads Required (at 20% Qualified)	Mailings Required (at 5% Return)
Indiana	10	200	1,000	20,000
Tennessee	14	280	1,400	28,000
Virginia	10	200	1,000	20,000
Michigan	10	200	1,000	20,000
Illinois	16	320	1,600	32,000
West Virginia	13	260	1,300	26,000
New Jersey	5	100	500	10,000
San Francisco	8	160	800	16,000
Maine	9	180	900	18,000
Seattle	9	180	900	18,000
New York City	10	200	1,000	20,000
Ohio	10	200	1,000	20,000
Texas	7	140	700	14,000
Utah	3	60	300	6,000
Connecticut	6	120	600	12,000
Pittsburgh	9	180	900	18,000
Philadelphia	11	220	1,100	22,000
Miami	3	60	300	6,000
Des Moines	7	140	700	14,000
Los Angeles	2	40	200	4,000
Denver	2	40	200	4,000
Atlanta	3	60	300	6,000
Totals	**177**	**3,540**	**17,700**	**354,000**

Lead-Flow Monitoring and Contingency Planning

As mentioned earlier in this chapter, the more quickly a lead is acted upon, the higher the likelihood of conversion. The theory behind this is that the interest is highest when a prospect first responds to an offer. The longer a lead sits, the "colder" the prospect becomes.

But as anyone who has worked with a lead-generation program will tell you, sometimes leads come in at a greater rate than anticipated. This will not cause a multitude of cold leads, but it could have impact on sales force morale, overhead costs, and so on. Whether too high or too low, it pays to have contingency systems in place.

Let's look at a typical lead flow planning model to see the normal distribution of leads from a direct mail program (see Exhibit 18–5). It has been proven that responses to direct mail programs will almost always follow this response curve, with 50 percent of total responses in the first four weeks, and the balance over the next six weeks. Lead distribution will vary depending on the medium utilized. Although lead generation will always be measured on a bell curve, specific response over time will vary; thus the height and width of the curve will vary.

Exhibit 18–6 is a series of these response waves, each representing mailings. The dotted line represents capacity; the maximum number of leads that can be handled effectively within a predetermined time period. At best, our planning will keep us within 90 to 110 percent of the dotted line. But what if some of the internal or external events mentioned earlier should change our response curve and create a shortfall? There are two basic systems that can be employed to effectively manage around this: in queue (or lead bank) and shelf contingency systems.

In Queue (Lead Bank) System

Many companies create a lead bank system, which is a purposeful manner of always operating above capacity. When a lead enters the sales center, it first enters the lead bank before being dispatched for follow-up. If there is always an extra week's worth

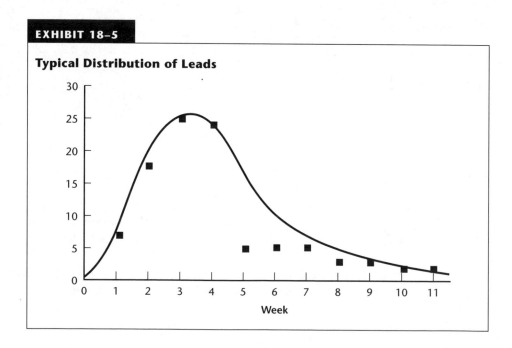

EXHIBIT 18–5

Typical Distribution of Leads

EXHIBIT 18-6

Response Waves from Successive Mailings

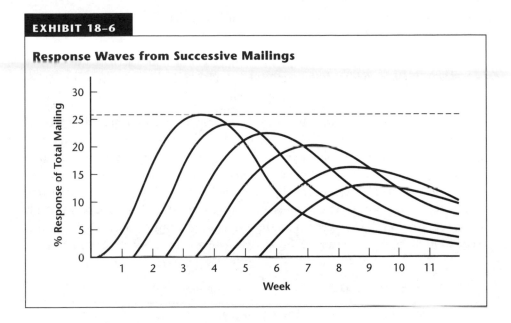

of leads and they are handled first in, first out, no leads are penalized or allowed to get cold. Naturally, the lead bank would be stocked with mail responses. You must handle Internet, E-mail, and telephone responses immediately.

If and when there is an underdelivery of leads, the lead bank is drawn down until additional leads can be driven into the center. Or the bank can be increased temporarily when an overdelivery occurs until the up-front solicitation can be decreased.

Shelf Contingency

It is always wise to have additional up-front communications "on the shelf," produced and ready to go in the event of an underdelivery of leads. If the lead-generation program utilizes direct mail, for example, two weeks of additional mail packages in reserve will ensure a timely response to an underdelivery problem; after normal capacity resumes, the shelf can be replenished.

Lead Classification and Scoring

It is no secret that in any lead-generation program lead quality varies a great deal. The 80/20 rule can be applied here. Generally speaking, 80 percent of total sales revenue will be driven by about 20 percent of all leads received. Given this, it makes sense to optimize time and effort with a good lead classification system. There are two good reasons for optimizing time and effort:

1. *Time is money.* It simply costs too much to have a salesperson call on unqualified prospects.

2. *Good leads get cold.* If salespeople are spending their time pursuing low-quality leads, high-quality leads will get cold. Each day a lead is not acted upon makes the likelihood of sales conversion less likely.

How can leads be qualified? The best way is to build screening devices into the upfront media selection. Lists in the business field, for example, can be selected by sales volume, number of employees, net worth, etc. It must be recognized, however, that while such selectivity can produce a better-qualified lead, it can also reduce the volume of leads generated, sometimes significantly. If a product or service tends to have more of a mass application, this may not be desirable. Not all leads are created equal. A classification system is needed to prioritize which ones to respond to first, assuming they have an immediate need and will close most quickly.

ABC Classification

ABC Classification is a one-dimensional approach to lead classification (see Exhibit 18–7). It's based on categorizing leads by likelihood of when that lead is expected to convert to a sale. When a salesperson is requested, or any other clues are given that the prospect is ready to buy, the lead is classified "A," and sent to the sales force for immediate follow-up. This "A" will be used for forecasting sales potential.

Leads that are analyzed as having a continuing interest are classified "B." They are qualified leads and need to be developed either through personal contact with a salesperson or by sending more information.

All other inquiries are classified "C." They are the emerging market, and a very responsive mailing list for future efforts. It is this group that represents the advertising opportunity. The goal here is to drive the group up the purchasing decision hierarchy through a combination of media. Keep an eye on this group. Too often, companies discard inquiry names if they are not immediately productive. This is a major error and a waste of excellent business potential.

Three-Dimensional Scoring

The previous model assumed that every lead generated by the system, if closed, would become a profitable customer. That's not always the case. Which would you rather have, a sale to a onetime customer, or a sale to a customer who would continue to buy from you over time? Of course, you want to close both sales, but it would be wise to focus your effort on the latter first. In order to factor other elements into the lead classification process, you need to evaluate those factors in three dimensions:

- *Speed of Action.* How quickly will the buying decision be made?

- *Closing Potential.* How well can we satisfy the consumer's need?

EXHIBIT 18–7

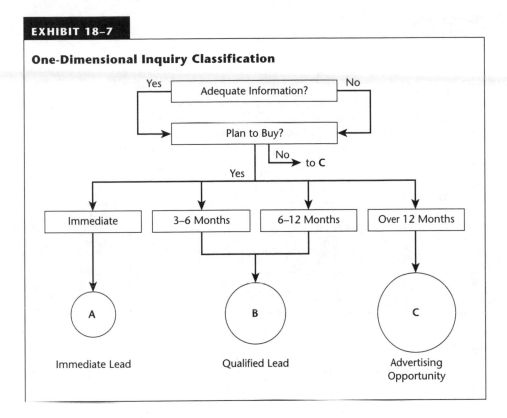

One-Dimensional Inquiry Classification

- *Account Value.* What is the total anticipated amount of the purchase, or the projected value of the customer to your company?

A three-dimensional model scores the relative value of leads compared to one another and provides learning that will allow you to develop the best communications plans (see Exhibit 18–8).

To rank the prospect on three dimensions, you need to assign values that will classify each component. For the purposes of illustration, let's assign the value 3 as "high," 2 as "medium," and 1 as "low." This allows a potential for 27 possible scores, where the best lead is classified a "333" and the poorest a "111." This model will help to determine the best next steps: determination of your allowable spending per lead, when to time the communications, and the basis for evaluation pre- and postcontact.

Inquiry Processing Cost Analysis

We've been looking at inquiry management effectiveness, but it's also very important to consider how much your company is spending to manage inquiries. There isn't any right amount to spend. You can spend too little as well as too much. If your

EXHIBIT 18–8

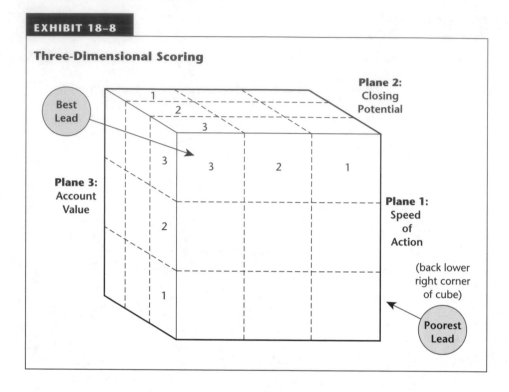

Three-Dimensional Scoring

company isn't spending enough to make full use of the inquiries generated, you aren't saving money on inquiry fulfillment, you're wasting money on advertising.

The real questions are what level of service you want to provide and how much that level should cost. Setting levels of service is always difficult, and it's particularly difficult in inquiry management. Wide fluctuations in inquiry volume (see Exhibit 18–9) caused by sudden surges in the number of calls can jeopardize the level of service.

If you are managing inquiries via a traditional sales center, you need to have enough people, machines, and other facilities to handle lead volumes. If you manage these resources to deliver a high level of service, you'll have unused capacity (and high cost) when volumes fall. But lower capacity can lead to poor response times when volumes are high, which in turn can waste advertising investment. The trick, of course, is to organize your operation so as to minimize fixed costs, so that costs will vary with volume.

The use of temporary labor and shared facilities can help, but more management time will be required to ensure that service is maintained. Another solution is to obtain inquiry management support from outside sources, which can level the peaks and valleys among many customers, providing universal cost effectiveness without adversely affecting service levels.

If you are managing inquiries via a website or other technologically driven channel, it is always best to have system capacity capable of handling at least three

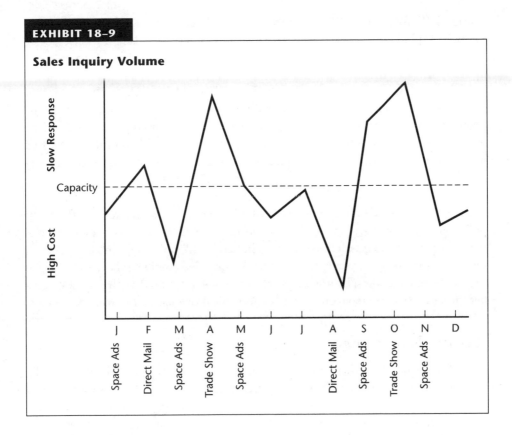

EXHIBIT 18-9

Sales Inquiry Volume

times the projected maximum lead volume. This will ensure consistency of service, even if actual results are much greater than you anticipate.

Tracking and Results Reporting

Tracking and results reporting are as important as management of leads in the sales center. These activities will result in quantification of the actual effort, relating the success of the program to its objectives, and making management aware of the program's return on investment.

Tracking

Which information an advertiser decides to track is largely a function of individual needs. However, the following data will be essential.

Number of Leads by Effort. Whether for a mailing, print ad, Internet banner, or broadcast spot, the number of leads resulting from each effort should be captured. This is usually handled by a specific code for each. For instance, a mailing with a split copy test is actually two mailings. Therefore, each response device should have a specific code so when it's received at the sales center, the proper mailing can be credited.

If telephone response is encouraged, as it should be, a unique phone number or extension should be given for each mailing, thus making it possible to credit the proper promotion effort. Internet banners can be coded by linking to a unique page within the website. Quite often these are "mirror pages" of the home page with a unique URL address, and are completely transparent to the prospect. By capturing information by code, the winning test promotions will emerge.

Quality of Lead/Conversion Information. The marketing effort that pulls the most responses isn't always the most successful, for it is conversion to sales that is the true measure of success. The comparison of two efforts in Exhibit 18–10 illustrates the point. As you can see, effort A would seemingly be more successful if responses were the sole measure. But when conversion is factored in, the greatest number of sales actually came from effort B; this is the more successful marketing tactic.

Results Reporting

There's little question that an efficient lead-generation program will increase the volume of sales and cut sales costs. But it is essential that results be measured and reported. Documentation of results is essential for three basic reasons: (1) to measure against original objectives of the lead-generation program, (2) to prove value to the sales force, and (3) to prove value to management.

Decision Support Tools

Information generated in any phase of a lead-generation program provides a database from which a wealth of useful information is available. Once the results of marketing efforts are summarized, they can be sorted in countless ways. The resulting

---

EXHIBIT 18-10

Comparison of Two Marketing Efforts

	No. Mailed	Percentage Response	No. of Responses	Percentage Conversion	No. of Sales
Package A	20,000	2%	400	6%	24
Package B	20,000	1	200	15	30

information can help provide accountability. It can also prove useful in researching and evaluating new markets. It can evaluate media effectiveness and provide insight into the value of various creative appeals.

Some information can be used to evaluate the effectiveness of sales follow-up activity, and even the equity of sales territory assignments. Once all these variables are understood, the learning can be leveraged into smarter program planning for future efforts.

Sample Reports for Sales Managers

The Purchase Potential Report. When leads are ranked by closing potential, it is possible to track current month activity against previous month activity, and to compare achievements against year-to-date objectives. This report also identifies the volume of potential sales, which is extremely useful for manufacturing planning. (See Exhibit 18–11.)

EXHIBIT 18–11

The Purchase Potential Report

National Potential for Lead Closing

Date: June
Page: 1

Name	Company	City	State	POT	PROD	TER	REG
R P Sloane	Honeywell	Phoenix	AZ	1	E2	RK	DW
A P Masino	Hansens Lab Inc.	Rochester	NY	1	V0	CD	PC
D Halpern	Easton Corp	Murray Hill	NH	1	U1	JX	PC
C A Chang	Wyeth Labs	Toledo	OH	1	I3	LL	HD
G Larson	A W Lyons	Raritan	NJ	1	L0	LC	PC
C K Kim	Ortho Pharm Corp	Spring House	PA	1	I9	JC	TM
J R Breco	Sherwin Williams	Philadelphia	PA	2	N8	CJ	TM
C T Kitchen	Kitchen Microtech	Morgantown	WV	2	L9	GC	HD
F Randa	Parker Corp	Des Plaines	IL	2	G1	GD	HD
S G Weber	Pennwalt Corp	Aurora	IL	2	V0	DC	TM
D Jung	General Grain	Cranbury	NJ	2	V0	JK	PC
R La Corte	Smith Kline & French	Pittsburgh	PA	2	V0	DC	TM
B Peppe	Univ Pittsburgh	Pittsburgh	PA	2	V0	DC	TM
E N Plosed	S C Johnson Co	Racine	WI	2	I3	GO	HD

The Product Inquiry Report. This report maintains a running record of inquiries by product line. Quite often there is a correlation between product inquiries and product sales volume. The report can also highlight those areas where more advertising is needed to increase the number of inquiries (see Exhibit 18–12).

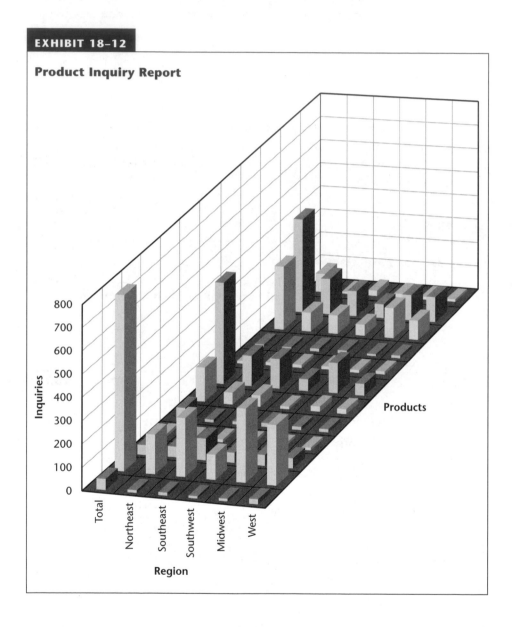

EXHIBIT 18–12

Product Inquiry Report

Sample Reports for Advertising Managers

The Daily Flash Report. This report identifies the daily status of each promotion. A bar chart records total inquiries for each day of the campaign. As time progresses, the bar chart forms a bell-shaped curve that can be used to identify the life of the promotion (see Exhibit 18–14).

The Media Effectiveness Report. This report lists the various media employed and identifies the total expenditure of the promotion. This report should also include measures of the percentage of qualified inquiries, the cost per qualified inquiry, and the projected revenue-to-expense ratio.

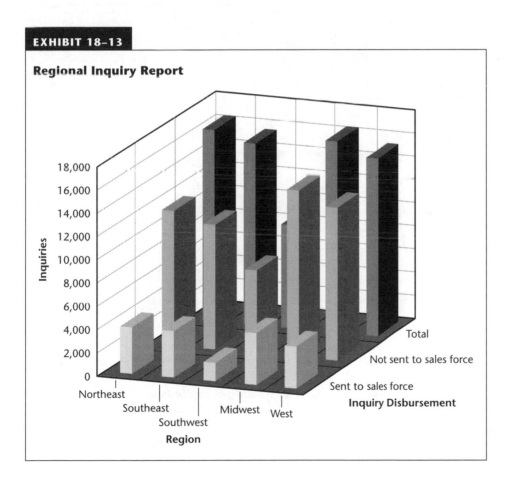

EXHIBIT 18–13

Regional Inquiry Report

EXHIBIT 18–14

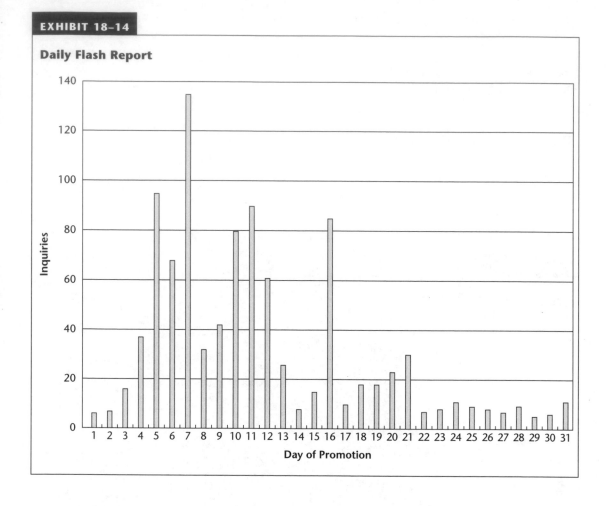

Daily Flash Report

CASE STUDY: **Allstate Insurance Company Life Campaign**

BACKGROUND

In support of the Allstate agency force, an integrated life insurance campaign was developed. This promotion included:

- An overall theme, "I want to be your agent for Life" (a double entendre)
- National and local advertising support utilizing the Life theme
- An agent-paid and company-subsidized targeted lead-generation mailing

The promotion was geared to increasing the number of Life sales in the Allstate agent's current book of business/customer base. Research has shown that Allstate's current customer base was virtually an untapped market in terms of cross-selling life insurance. Research also indicated that there was an increase in property and casualty insurance retention if there was Allstate life insurance present in a household.

SOLUTION

The objectives of the program were to:

- Promote Allstate's financial strength and rating in the life insurance business.

- Create awareness of Allstate's Life products and promote agents as the prospect/customer's primary source of contact for more information.
- Increase Life sales within agent's own customer base.
- Meet or exceed the Life Company's 1991 premium plan.
- Increase retention through cross-selling life insurance.

Strategies used to accomplish these objectives included:

- Developing a comprehensive communication plan integrating all marketing efforts.
- Increasing life insurance cross-line sales through lead-generation mailings and co-op advertising.
- Providing national advertising support for the Life Campaign.
- Creating employee awareness of the Life Campaign.

Target audience for the promotion was current customers with and without life insurance. Components of the program included a national advertising campaign (television, radio, print), local advertising (agent and company participation in cost), a lead-generation mailing program (agent and company participation in cost), sales support material, billing messages, employee awareness, and agent communication.

RESULTS

Life Company year-end premium plan was exceeded (102 percent) and promotion results were 40 percent over the prior year's. Putting together an integrated campaign calls for a sophisticated planning process. Here is how advertising support was orchestrated.

The advertising message was twofold: (1) Allstate agents can take care of their customers' life insurance needs and (2) a long-term relationship with an Allstate agent is important.

NATIONAL ADVERTISING

Television. Messages used the ongoing, distinctive campaign currently airing that included the highly successful combination of live action with animation and capitalized on one of Allstate's best recognized assets, the "Good Hands."

Advertising messages ran throughout the promotion period on programs that supported Allstate's objectives of product awareness and agent support.

Two 15-second executions were utilized that emphasized the "I want to be your agent for Life" message. These executions highlighted the lead lines (auto/home) as a transition into the life insurance sale.

Radio. National radio advertising via Paul Harvey supported the product message during the promotion period. Radio scripts focused on the life insurance product message and were aired where appropriate. National radio schedules were integrated with television air dates.

Print. Print ads featured the same look and message as the television messages. Print ads lent topspin to the promotion effort and provided merchandising consideration to agents. Print ads were featured in national magazine publications, and national print schedules were integrated with television and radio schedules.

LOCAL ADVERTISING

A portfolio of new Life Co-op advertising materials was developed for Allstate agents' individual use. It focused on the same theme as the national advertising message: "I want to be your agent for Life."

Television. Two 30-second Life Co-op television commercials were developed based on the national messages; they included a 15-second tag for agent personalization.

Radio. A 30-second live-read radio script was developed that could be personalized for each agent's use.

Print. Two versions of a Life print ad were developed that focused on the "I want to be your agent for Life" message and incorporated a new concept that allowed agents to personalize the ad with their signature.

Telephone (office support). Life product scripts for agent offices' use with customer-on-hold phone systems were developed.

With advertising support in place, the next step was to create lead-generation support for those Allstate agents involved in the total campaign.

MAILING/LEAD-GENERATION SUPPORT

Mailing Package. The letter emphasized the agent-customer relationship and made an effort to review the customer's current insurance portfolio to make certain existing coverage is keeping pace with current lifestyle.

Features included:

- Professionally written and designed mailing package
- Business card with the agent's name, address, and phone number
- "I want to be your agent for Life" theme printed on business card
- Multiline reply device offering various life products
- Business reply envelope

List selections were varied. Agents had the choice of mailing to several targeted lists:

- Auto customers with homeowners
- Auto customers with property
- Property customers
- Auto customers
- Life customers
- Customers without Life
- Other line customers

Special Offer. To encourage agents to order the lead-generation mailings, the company subsidized 50 percent of the mailing cost for letters sent to the agent's customers.

Follow-up. As with any lead-generation effort, follow-up is critical for success. Agents received an extensive follow-up list for each of their mailings that included the following:

- Customer name
- Customer address
- Customer phone number
- Description of mailing package
- Date that the mailing package was sent

SALES SUPPORT MATERIALS

Agents were provided with an array of product support materials, including brochures, counter cards, buttons and banners, letters, mailing kits, and postcards. The words "Your Allstate agent wants to be your agent for Life" were even printed on the policy-billing envelope.

INTERNAL SUPPORT

A comprehensive Administrative Guide, which gave a clear picture of what the Life Campaign was all about, was produced and distributed to field managers so they could review the program details with their agents.

The internal theme "Jazz up your Life" contained various award levels that were appropriately named for famous jazz musicians. To win one of the awards, an agent needed to sell a specified amount of life insurance.

Agent support was also provided through internal communications—desk-toppers and letters touting the theme "I want to be your agent for Life."

"Jump Start Your Market"—a starter kit consisting of actual samples and ordering information on all of the marketing materials available—was provided for all agents.

The Life Campaign was a remarkable program from the standpoint of planning and execution. Exhibit 18–15 presents representative executions. Exhibit 18–16 is one of two Life Co-op television commercials that included a 15-second tag for agent personalization.

CASE STUDY: Allstate Insurance Company Life Campaign *(continued)*

EXHIBIT 18-15

Ad Campaign Mailings

Lead-Generation Mailing

Co-op Mailing

Agent-Support Materials

Employee Awareness

CASE STUDY: **Allstate Insurance Company Life Campaign** *(continued)*

EXHIBIT 18–16

Life Co-Op Television Commercial

(MUSIC: UNDER THROUGHOUT)
1. (AVO): The Allstate agent . . .

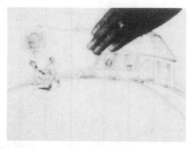

2. who helps insure your home . . .

3. (SFX: THUNDER)
(AVO): can give you a hand with a
plan for life insurance.

4. . . .

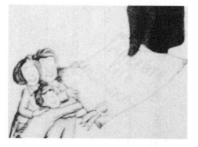

5. Life insurance, your Allstate agent
wants to be your agent for Life.

6. You're in Good Hands With
Allstate.

PILOT PROJECT You work for a firm that manufactures central air-conditioning systems for the home. A minimum sale comes to $5,000. All sales are handled through a sales force. The target market is home owners with a median income of $50,000.

Your firm has decided to test the viability of a lead-generation program to develop a marketing plan for management review.

In preparation for actually writing the marketing plan, answer the following questions:

1. What information will you need from the sales force?
   Examples might be: Who is the firm's competition? Who is the decision maker in the home? What are the major objections the sales force has to overcome?

2. What objectives will you set for the program?
   For example: How many leads per day will you propose to furnish each salesperson? How would you propose to screen leads so you could distinguish between high potential and low potential? What other objectives would you set?

3. What would be your strategies for obtaining highly qualified leads?
   One strategy, for example, might be an offer to conduct a free survey to determine the cost of central air-conditioning in a home. Another strategy might be a special promotion, aimed at customers in Milwaukee, asking them to provide names of friends whom they consider most likely to have an interest in central air-conditioning. What other strategies might you employ?

4. How will you implement your lead generation program?

   Here are some key questions you should answer in your marketing plan:

   • Will you ask your sales force to provide names of key prospects? How else will you involve the sales force?

   • What media strategies will you employ?
     1. Will you use newspapers? Which ones?
     2. Will you use magazines? Which ones?
     3. Will you use radio? Which stations?
     4. Will you use TV? Which stations?
     5. Will use you use cable TV? Which channels?
     6. Will you use the Internet? What kind of website?

Key Points

▶ The efficient handling and managing of leads is a major problem for many companies. A well-run lead-management system can be a solution and also become a valuable corporate asset.

▶ A well-run lead-management system helps advertising expenditures become more accountable; it integrates advertising and selling functions into a unified whole.

▶ The system can increase sales productivity by the elimination of unproductive follow-up calls; it is an aid in finding prospects ready to buy.

▶ The application of an inquiry system to the advertising and marketing functions can become a valuable management tool, one that is useful in assessing progress toward objectives.

▶ In summary, an inquiry management system works because it measures results—the ingredient most wanted in marketing activity today.

MARKETING
INTELLIGENCE

MODELING FOR
BUSINESS DECISION
SUPPORT

W hile no one can predict the future, marketers can reduce the risk of failure by using technology to combine product, market, and customer knowledge drawn from an organization's database. The outcome—expressed in a model—can help marketers support business strategy decisions.

"Modeling" means simplifying a complex situation and observing key components or relationships. The Wright brothers built model airplanes before they tested a full-scale one. Architects build models of proposed buildings. In a similar way, marketers build models to simplify and see clearly what is going on in their customer campaigns.

Modeling is a critical tool that helps marketers who have more data than they know what to do with. Using modeling, marketers can identify their "best" customers from a 10-million-name database and present their conclusions in visual, easy to understand graphs or charts. Of course, *best* has many definitions. For some organizations *best* means customers who have purchased the most recently, frequently, or spent the most money. Others define *best* as customers with the greatest propensity to buy, or those likely to produce the greatest profit. The definition depends on where an organization is in its growth phase, and whether it is trying to maximize profits or sales.

Modeling doesn't actually sift through all the names on a database. A statistically reliable sample of 10,000 names is enough to gain important knowledge about huge data sets. Modeling also doesn't automatically yield visual reports. Most models generate tabular information that can be challenging to read, and a statistician is still best qualified to interpret the complex mathematical relationships between variables. But a simple spreadsheet program can turn the information into a graph that marketing, finance, and other nontechnical management can understand.

Modeling is not the same as testing or data mining. Like traditional testing, modeling isolates causal variables to determine their impact. The essential elements are a controlled offer to a known selection of customers coupled with the capability of tracking the results. However, with traditional in-the-mail testing, a marketer must correctly anticipate the variable that has the greatest impact, and a relatively small number of variables can be tested at one time. In contrast, modeling permits marketers to test a large number of variables and discover, in the process, which has the greatest impact.

Modeling is directed. Before it begins, you need to define the variables that will be modeled and predetermine what you are looking for. Data mining is an open-ended exploratory process, giving marketers (the miners) access to data with dynamic, easy-to-use, graphical query tools. Skilled data miners can often find surprises in their data that lead to marketing breakthroughs, changes in the offer, product, or customer profile. Data mining is less directed, so considerable time can be spent without drawing significant conclusions.

The modeling process is not so much data mining as data *sluicing*. Sluicing is the process of washing river gravel through a machine that finds the gold. It is far more efficient and automated than the traditional panning for gold. Large amounts of data may be sifted through quickly until all that is left are shiny nuggets of information: the customers you've described as the precise ones you want to reach.

Because it allows marketers to define and pinpoint their "best" customers and prospects, modeling is an important first step in designing contact strategies that enhance the lifetime value of a customer.

The Purpose of Modeling: Looking Back in Order to Look Ahead

The starting point of all modeling is looking at past campaigns and their results. The clearest examples of modeling are analyzing who was contacted, who responded, and who didn't. Comparing characteristics between the two groups gives a marketer insight into what made the difference between responding and not responding—insight that can be applied to the next campaign.

To look back in time, modeling begins by making customers or prospects look like they did when mailed, then compares who responded, purchased, and so forth. By comparing the difference between responders and nonresponders, it is possible to identify the correlation between independent variables and the dependent variable. This ability to look into the past at many more variables makes modeling much more powerful than traditional segmentation methods.

While tomorrow may not be exactly like yesterday—seasonality, changes in the economy, politics, and events can all affect future response—generally, modeling suggests that similar things can be expected to work again. Look-alikes for the best customers today will likely work in the future. Modeling will never exactly predict the future, but it will give a clearer picture of the recent past, which, all things being equal, is the best that most marketers can hope for.

Customer and Prospect Modeling

Marketers most frequently use customer and prospect models. Customer models use purchase history, credit usage, and other behavior data to sort the customers from best to worst so that it is clear who most qualifies for a specific offer. If all customers are included in a mailing (or contacting), then the order in which you rank them makes little difference. When a very specific model for a single offering is built, only a small percentage of customers will be viable, and modeling can generate a tremendous payback.

While modeling began as a segmenting tool, it plays an increasingly important role in communications. Knowledge gained about certain customers can help marketers identify compelling reasons for the segment to buy—reasons that can be prominently featured in creative executions. A credit card company that discovered that its optimal customers used the card five times a month might develop a program to prompt customers who use the card three times a month to use it twice more. Modeling demonstrated to a membership organization the relationship between usage of key benefits and customer retention. Discovering that members who did not use benefits did not renew, it designed programs to stimulate usage of the benefits. Renewal rates rose because members who used the benefits were better able to understand the value proposition.

Unlike customer models, prospect models have no behavior variables. Prospect models are designed to find the worst neighborhoods and avoid mailing into them. There are several popular dependent variables. Most common are response rate per postal code, and revenue per piece per postal code. Presumably, the best mailing lists have already been identified. They would normally be mailed in their entirety. Middle performing lists might be reduced by 30 to 50 percent, and poor lists could be reduced by 50 to 90 percent. This elimination of the marginal zip codes allows many more lists to be used, dramatically improving the number of names available while maintaining overall performance.

Defining the Variables

The key to successful modeling is carefully defining the variables.

Variables are characteristics linked to customers. Key types of characteristics might include neighborhood factors (median income, age, dwelling value, or high school graduation rate), household factors (mortgage amount, income, type of car, presence of children, education level), behavior (how recently, frequently, and how much people have purchased, types of merchandise purchased), and contact (subject and frequency of offers sent).

Modeling uses two kinds of variables: independent and dependent. A model compares one *dependent variable* against any number of *independent variables*. The use of multiple variables is known as multivariate analysis.

The independent variables—what you already know about the customer, or what you can observe—are used to build a predictive model. The list of independent variables pretty much stays the same through all models.

The dependent variable is the key ingredient in the modeling process—really the defining characteristic of the model. It is the behavior being analyzed, the difference between two groups of customers. In other words, it is the factor you want to be able to predict or forecast.

Calculating the dependent variable can be very simple or complex. With a single price offer, there are two variables—response vs. no response. But some customers may buy more than others, some may return items, or some may cancel their service permanently. Some will be heavy users of customer service, others will not. All these events will affect individual customer profitability. Since as few as 10 percent of your customers generate 90 percent of your profits, it would be foolish to reduce their behavior to the simple response/nonresponse level.

Instead, the dependent variable should be calculated as carefully as possible for each person contacted. It should certainly include sales minus costs (order entry cost, cost of goods sold, and contact cost).

For example, geography is a variable that is often important in consumer marketing. Using a geodemographic mapping program, customer counts can be overlaid with median household income. If the customers appear concentrated in areas of high (or low) income, it would suggest a connection that could be further explored (and illustrated) by summing (and graphing) the total population vs. customers in high-, medium-, and low-income geographies.

Income could be the dependent variable for a marketer trying to determine a certain segment's propensity to buy. All other characteristics—age, number of children, home ownership, and so forth—would be independent. Successive models would run through these variables, testing income against different independent variables until it arrived at a result of statistical importance.

When it comes to variables, more is almost always better. Using modeling, marketers can refine model after model until they can pinpoint the exact set of characteristics or variables that have the greatest impact on the decision to buy. Modelers go through the process multiple times until they have a result they feel comfortable with.

Observation alone may not reveal why a variable is important—but if that variable is left out of the analysis, a key ingredient is missed. For example, AT&T observed that phone color was an important variable when assessing which businesses stayed with them after the breakup. No one knew why, but companies with black phones were the most likely to stay with AT&T.

Three behavior variables are consistently most important and form the foundation for customer segmentation, especially in combination with each other: RFM (Recency, Frequency, Monetary). But while RFM clearly and consistently identifies the best customers, it cannot break out people who have only ordered once, didn't spend much, and haven't been heard from in quite a while. By adding purchase activity, product category, or individual, neighborhood, and spending variables, modeling can move beyond simple RFM to find good in the bad and bad in the good. Descriptive categorical variables such as state of residence, sex, occupation, or even number and kind of pets, are also useful, and can be analyzed using cross tabulation, frequency distributions, or CHAID (Chi-squared Automatic Interactive Detector).

It is important to define the dependent variable carefully. A specific model will have far greater force than a general one. Asking the question, "Who is most likely to buy something?" will generate a weak model with recency likely at the top. All things being equal, people who have bought recently are most likely to buy next. If, however, you ask, "Who is most likely to buy from the fishing catalog?" (as opposed to hunting, camping, or boating), you will generate a very interesting model where recency may not even be found. The second model will have about ten times the power of the first. Gain—the difference between the top performing decile and the bottom—is important in modeling, which can be very expensive.

Logic, not modeling, tells marketers that customers who have bought most recently or spent the biggest dollar amounts are likely to buy again and spend more. But adding categorical data will reveal which customers are more likely to buy more of which product. The resulting gains chart doesn't just say "These people will buy more"; it says "These people are going to be X percent more likely to buy than those people."

Exhibit 19–1 is a picture of customers scored on Frequency. Five is given to the customers who accumulate 20 percent of the purchases—perhaps only 1 to 4 percent of all customers. Response percentage can be improved simply by eliminating the ones. But instead of eliminating these low frequency customers, a spending variable could be added. The big spenders (5 on the horizontal scale) would be mailed, and the high-frequency low spenders would not be (see Exhibit 19–2).

Collecting Variables

There are two basic techniques for connecting customer characteristics to those contacted: recording relevant behavior and dynamically generating variables.

The simplest way to collect variables is to just keep a record of the relevant behavior scores for each customer at the time they were mailed. This snapshot records RFM, product scores, demographic values, and anything else on hand at the time of the mailing. It can be somewhat cumbersome to keep precise track of all these snapshots for each customer, and it takes time. Suppose, for example, that other companies are successfully using the "werewolf" variable. Named for the werewolf that changes from man to beast only at the full moon, this variable notes the phase of the moon for specific events. You can't wait to try it. Alas, it's not one of the variables in your database. You won't be able to include it in your models until it gets into your snapshots several months to a year later.

The alternative method is to dynamically create all your behavior variables. Rarely will the variables coming off the order processing system be completely

EXHIBIT 19–1

Frequency Distribution

Part A uses a histogram, and Part B uses a bar graph to represent customers scored using a Frequency Distribution.

Part A

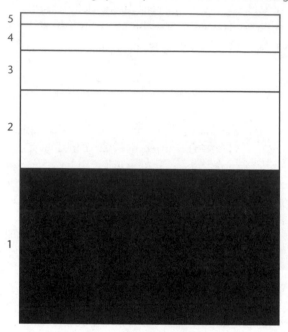

Part B

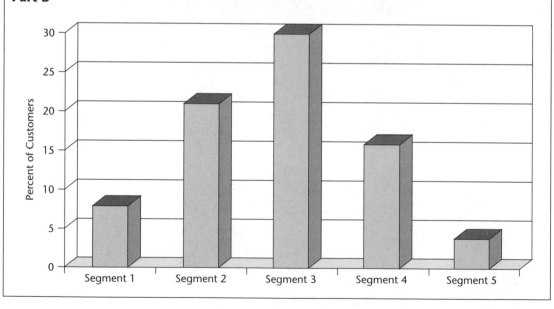

EXHIBIT 19–2

Modeling Chart Showing Dozens of Variables

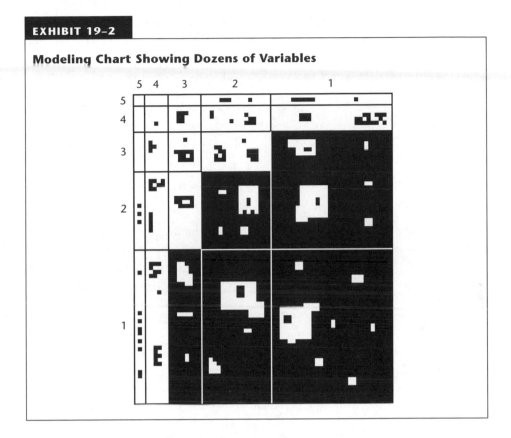

accurate, so it is in your best interest to recalculate them. Since the marketing database should be calculating variables, it is relatively simple to specify the date ranges for your recalculation. The data preparation would include building a sample database and recalculating all the behavior variable scores to what they would have been at the mail date. This technique effectively rolls the customer file back in time. Now you cannot only make your customers look like they did at the mail date, but you can also calculate the werewolf variable for your entire customer file . . . and use it immediately.

The key to regularly improving models is regularly improving the variables. As more creative data types are used, models will become better. There are an infinite number of variables for any event or object. Do not settle for two or three. Play the "what if" game.

A high-end menswear company had been modeling for several years, and was concerned that they were wearing out the modeling process. They had never used Standard Industrial Classifications (SIC—U.S. government numeric codes for types of businesses) but couldn't think of any interesting connection between business-to-business data and their customer base. "How about country clubs per capita?" came a voice from the back of the room. The census data had postal code area, population, and number of country clubs so CC/km (country clubs per kilometer) could also be built. It took a few days to generate, but sure enough, it turned up in the next sportswear model.

Neither sample size (as long as it's huge) nor which statistical technique is applied (as long as you are careful, and know what you're doing) are as important as the variables. Behind it all, the creativity will be in the variable creation. The variables drive the model.

Validation

Validation is one of the most important elements of modeling. To validate a model, construct a mailing that includes a "null set" of names that were not modeled. If they are drawn from the same universe but haven't been modeled, their response rate can be expected to be lower. Lower response rates from this segment validate the model. Equal or higher response rates indicate problems.

Validation reports look exactly like traditional list reports. Each model cell or decile has a name count; in addition, the number of orders, response rate, average order size, etc., can be generated. The best cells in the model should perform the best in the validation—if not, there will be an opportunity to retune the model before mailing. There are additional, more complex methods of validation, but regardless of statistical technique, validation must be part of the modeling process.

Useful Modeling Techniques

Marketers can model many things. Response modeling is very common. It involves determining which characteristics of a product or service need to be highlighted to make a prospect or customer buy. The cost of direct mail or an Internet marketing campaign is directly proportional to the number of prospects being targeted: each contact, whether by E-mail, direct mail, or telephone, increases costs.

Only prospects or customers who purchase the offered product or service contribute to revenue. The goal of most modeling is reducing the number contacted while at the same time increasing response rates. This reduces promotion costs while increasing profits.

Two useful techniques for response modeling are regression and CHAID.

Regression

Regression modeling, the most commonly used analytical technique, comes in a number of flavors: simple, multiple, multivariate, logit, logistic, and stepwise, to name a few. Regression models compare individual variables to the dependent variable. The one that best correlates is given the highest statistical weight in the model, the next best correlation a lower weight, etc. Because regression models tend to isolate a small number of really significant variables and eliminate or ignore less important variables, they are more easily understood by nonstatisticians. Their relatively simple output also makes it is easy to generate a scoring equation to apply the model to current customers.

A disadvantage is that this simplification can also eliminate important variables whose impact is more complex. Regression then requires relatively skilled people to prepare the data correctly. If you know what you are doing, regression will perform comparably to any other technique.

A cable television company developed a regression model that could help isolate the point in time when customers have a propensity to reduce or disconnect service. The company was able to segment by service level (e.g., basic, plus, premium) and pay-per-view usage. Direct mail and phone retention efforts were directed at subscribers weeks before this point in time. Customers with a higher propensity to disconnect were offered free movies and additional premium channels. Customers with a low propensity to disconnect were sent "love mailings" that reminded users of program benefits but without an incentive. This program significantly improved retention percentages, extending the lifetime value of each subscriber.

CHAID

Chi-squared Automatic Interactive Detector (CHAID) is another well-proven modeling technique. Instead of looking for correlations, CHAID estimates the probability of independence. The lower the probability, the more important the variable. As the name implies, the process is highly automatic. CHAID also evaluates all variables—as many as a thousand—and builds a tree with the most important variable at the top, less important variables under each cell. It is very easy to understand.

CHAID reports let nonstatistical users almost instantly gain considerable insight into important data relationships, which in turn triggers creative inspiration for creating new variables. A CHAID model evaluates complex interactions among predictive variables and results in an easy-to-understand tree diagram. The trunk of the tree represents the total database universe. The model automatically determines how to group the values of this predictor into a manageable number of categories.

Let's say that to build a model to identify your most profitable customers, you begin by analyzing 12 age categories. The CHAID model could collapse that to six or even four statistically significant groups. Within each age group, household size might be the next most important variable. The model could identify what household size generated the greatest profit. For example, single person households might not generate as much profit as households with two to four people.

You could then learn that within two- to four-person households, homes that owned sport utility vehicles had a higher profitability. At the next level, you could discover that households with two to four persons and a sport utility vehicle return an average profit three times that of similar-sized households with a luxury import car. However, the model might show that within the sport utility segment, a white-collar head of household would be twice as profitable as a blue-collar household. These facts are revealed graphically in the tree diagram.

Modeling: Expensive, Essential, and Not for Statisticians Only

Modeling is expensive, but essential. To be effective, a model must beat what a manager could have done with a little thought.

Exhibit 19–3 illustrates a substantial catalog test in which 1.2 million pieces were tested using two mailing methods: RFM and CHAID modeling. Both techniques selected most of the good names, and both eliminated most of the poorer names. However, the exact results differed substantially. Unique names were key coded separately; common names were randomly allocated back into each sample. This yielded an easy-to-understand comparison between the old and new method. The modeled panel generated $454,000 more profit from the same mailing quantity—well worth the investment.

It's surprising how few companies invest in statistical modeling despite its demonstrated effectiveness. One reason may be that many companies, especially business-to-business marketers, mail universes that appear to be too small to justify the cost of modeling. Smaller universes make the cost of modeling appear to be a higher percentage of creating the list.

Yet modeling is worth every dollar of its cost. It helps correct the leading problem in direct marketing: mailing people who don't want your mail and calling people who don't want your calls. Modeling brings an organization closer to the people who *do* want to receive your mail and calls. The high cost of modeling should not keep an organization from investing in a technique that will improve its profitability more than any other tool.

Another reason marketers avoid modeling is its perceived complexity. Marketers (and even more, senior managers) get nervous when faced with abstract neural algorithms. If they can't understand it, how can they tell if there is something wrong with it? Graphs and charts can make outcomes comprehensible by making the abstract more tangible.

While experts are important, effective modeling cannot be completely assigned to the "statistician." It takes more than one person to develop a modeling capability. Careful, methodical people are needed to load data, update the database,

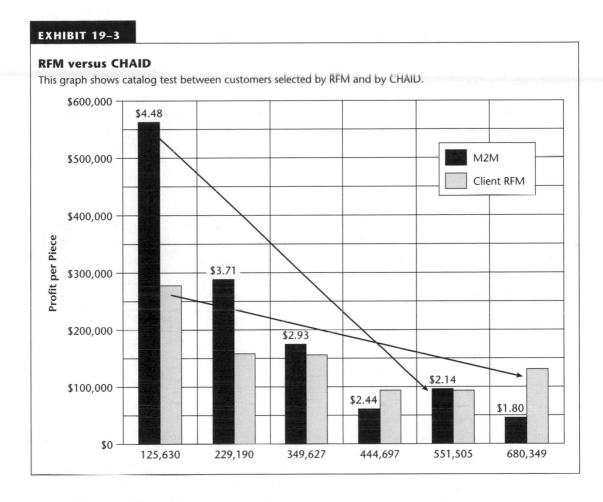

EXHIBIT 19–3

RFM versus CHAID

This graph shows catalog test between customers selected by RFM and by CHAID.

and pull names. Creative people are needed to build, validate, and analyze the results of the model and create new variables. These skills arc not combined in one single person.

Finally, modeling must be accountable to businesspeople who clearly understand the customers. It is not enough to just produce better mailings or campaigns; insight must be gained and communicated.

Modeling is neither as easy as flying by the seat of the pants nor as hard as self-administered brain surgery. Somewhere in between lies the art of turning data into money. Understand this if nothing else: careful analysis of marketing campaigns will certainly improve contact accuracy. Modeling is the direct marketing technology of the future. Ignore it at your peril!

CASE STUDY: Benefiting from Predictive Modeling with Databases

BACKGROUND

A travel company that offers package tours through mail order to older persons desires to increase its marketing effectiveness by segmenting its marketplace within the state of Florida.

CHALLENGE

The firm has developed, from census and proprietary data sources, a total of 103 demographic variables describing each of 35,000 geographic zip code areas. Test variables are expressed as either averages or frequency distributions.

Using these demographic independent variables in addition to age, the travel company wants to segment its marketplace in Florida.

SOLUTION

Several of these variables have been normalized. That is, they have been indexed to some larger area such as a Sectional Center (the first three digits of a five-digit code) or a state (such as Mississippi versus New York) in order to achieve environmental, as opposed to absolute, measurement. This means that the relative income level in a rural Mississippi zip code area is compared with the relative income level of an urban area in New York City, rather than compared in absolute dollars. A "high" dollar income level in the rural Mississippi area could be relatively "low" in New York City.

Variables have also been subjected to factor analysis in order to discover the typical lifestyle factors and the associated independent variables. The dependent variable is market penetration, defined in this instance as the response rate (total responses divided by the total number of pieces mailed) to the travel company's direct mail offer of tours to the older residents of Florida.

To maximize the number of observations and ensure statistical validity of both measurement and prediction, the response rate is calculated within clusters of zip code areas with common characteristics produced using cluster analysis. Ultimately, these clusters will be described as market segments in which

penetration levels can be correlated with their characteristics. At this stage, both environmental (indexed) measurement and interaction among the variables defining clusters are important considerations.

Calculation of penetration is simple. Within each cluster of zip code areas, the response rate is calculated as shown here:

ZIP CODE AREA CLUSTERS	TOTAL NO. OF PIECES MAILED	TOTAL NO. OF RESPONSES	PERCENTAGE OF RESPONSES
A	5,793	60	1.04%
B	2,735	33	1.21
C	6,731	136	2.02
D	4,341	118	2.74

From this table it is readily apparent that there is an increasing rate of response from A to B, from B to C, and from C to D. These differences can be explained by evaluating the independent variables entering in, and deemed significant through regression analysis shown in Exhibit 19–4. Regression analysis enables the transfer of these findings from a sample to the total population without first having mailed that total population. The linear regression equation (of the form: $Y = a+bX$) becomes a formula for predicting estimated response rates from zip code area clusters not yet solicited but having similar characteristics to those sampled.

Correlation analysis by the travel company identifies the strength of the relationship between cluster response rates (the dependent variable), and each of the 103 selected demographics (independent variables). Exhibit 19–4 reproduces a condensed printout of the stepwise multivariate regression analysis that follows the correlation analysis. From 27 available independent variables, each a surrogate of a demographic characteristic of zip code areas, 10 steps are taken. Eight variables remain at the conclusion of step 10. The reference numbers of these eight variables, together with their simple correlation coefficients, are shown at the bottom of Exhibit 19–4.

CASE STUDY: **Benefiting from Predictive Modeling with Databases** *(continued)*

EXHIBIT 19.4

Stepwise Multivariate Regression Analysis

STEP #1
  VARIABLE ENTERING   X-5
R = 0.583959   R SQ. =   0.341008
 F LEVEL =   23.8036
 STANDARD ERROR OF Y =   0.06341
 CONSTANT TERM =   0.27470726

VARIABLE NO.	COEFFICIENT	STD ERR OF COEFF
X-5	-0.28683022E-01	0.00594

STEP #2
  VARIABLE ENTERING   X-2
R = 0.717396   R SQ. =   0.514658
 F LEVEL =   16.1004
 STANDARD ERROR OF Y =   0.05504
 CONSTANT TERM =   0.25037676

VARIABLE NO.	COEFFICIENT	STD ERR OF COEFF
X-2	0.11710477	0.02951
X-5	-0.25006641E-01	0.00524

STEP #3
  VARIABLE ENTERING   X-16
R = 0.814453   R SQ. =   0.663334
 F LEVEL =   19.4310
 STANDARD ERROR OF Y =   0.04637
 CONSTANT TERM =   0.17120540

VARIABLE NO.	COEFFICIENT	STD ERR OF COEFF
X-2	0.12946498	0.02503
X-5	-0.21160301E-01	0.00450
X-16	0.10500204E-01	0.00241

STEP #4
  VARIABLE ENTERING   X-14
R = 0.831825   R SQ. =   0.691934
 F LEVEL =   3.9919
 STANDARD ERROR OF Y =   0.04488
 CONSTANT TERM =   0.11676645

VARIABLE NO.	COEFFICIENT	STD ERR OF COEFF
X-2	0.12659431	0.02427
X-5	-0.18140811E-01	0.00462
X-14	0.27103789E-01	0.01373
X-16	0.99606328E-02	0.00235

STEP #10
  VARIABLE ENTERING   X-22
R = 0.896520   R SQ. =   0.803748
 F LEVEL =   2.8542
 STANDARD ERROR OF Y =   0.03766
 CONSTANT TERM =   0.39812356

VARIABLE NO.	COEFFICIENT	STD ERR OF COEFF
X-2	0.13928533	0.02095
X-9	-0.20301903E-02	0.00064
X-10	-0.87198131E-02	0.00257
X-14	0.69082797E-01	0.01875
X-15	0.13623666E-01	0.00421
X-16	0.22368859E-01	0.00380
X-22	-0.15226589E-02	0.00091
X-23	-0.21373443E-02	0.00081

The resulting R^2 value of 0.803748 (the multiple coefficient of determination) indicates that 80 percent of the variance in response is explained by the presence or absence of these eight variables. The derived regression equation enables a rank ordering of predicted response rates attributable to each five-digit zip code area within each cluster.

Exhibit 19–5 shows the highest to the lowest, as well as the cumulative, predicted penetration percentages (response rates). It also shows both individual and cumulative base mailing list counts for each zip code area within each cluster. Note the variance of the actual response rate, shown for each zip code area in the third column, attributable to the small number mailed in each area. Exhibit 19–5 reveals that, from a total mailing quantity of 1,277,262 pieces, the overall average response rate is predicted to be 1.95 percent. The response rate from the top cluster (#39) is predicted at 4.49 percent (.0449 in exhibit); that from the bottom cluster (#30) is predicted at 0.76 percent (.0076 in exhibit). The ratio, top versus bottom, is very nearly 1:6. Note, too, that the response rate from the top cluster is 2.3 times the overall average of 1.95 percent; that from the bottom is 39 percent.

To attain an average response of 2.55 percent (31 percent better than average), the company should stop after cluster #10, with marginal response of 2.06 percent (.0206 in exhibit), mailing 511,276 pieces. Limiting mailing quantity to 242,935 pieces, about 20 percent of the list availability, average response would be 2.87 percent, an improvement of 47 percent over the 1.95 percent overall average.

From this analysis, the company decides how big a market segment is needed, then predicts what the overall response rate will be. It sets its minimum response rate requirement (average or marginal), then determines how many pieces it can mail. At this point, of primary importance to the travel company is a description of the profiles that exist in Florida. Just what influence might each of these exert on the response rate to a travel tour offer directed to older persons? Factor analysis produces these three explanatory lifestyle profiles, which are present in clusters with high response rates.

Rural Residers. Variables positively associated with this factor include rural farm and rural nonfarm types of areas; farm manager, and farm laborer occupations; housing in mobile homes and trailers; housing equipped with food freezers, lacking formal kitchens; East European ancestry. Negatively associated variables are access to public water and sewers; finance industry; multifamily dwelling units.

Social Class. "Lower half" variables positively associated with this factor include occupation as laborers, operatives, service workers, unemployed; poverty levels; divorced, separated, and widowed marital status; older housing; longer tenure of residence. "Upper half" variables, negatively associated, are high housing value; housing equipped with amenities such as air-conditioning and dishwashers; two or more autos; high income; high education levels; occupations in management, sales, professional, technical; finance industry.

Ancestry/heritage. Variables with positive association are native-born with English as mother tongue; foreign-born with countries of origin including the United Kingdom, Canada, Ireland, Austria, and Germany; housing in owner-occupied single-family units. Negatively associated variables include foreign-born; emigrated from Cuba; Spanish as mother tongue; multiple-family rental housing.

RESULTS

Because the overall response to this offer is double the break-even requirement for the acquisition of new customers, the travel company decides to validate its research. Six months after the first offer, the entire list is remailed, rank-ordered in quintiles of response as predicted from regression analysis. As expected, the overall response drops to about half that of the first effort. What is important, however, is that the relationship (response rate indices) of the quintiles are virtually the same for both efforts, as detailed in Exhibit 19–6.

CASE STUDY: **Benefiting from Predictive Modeling with Databases** (continued)

EXHIBIT 13-3

Rank Ordering of Zip Code Clusters According to Response Rate Predicted by Regression Analysis

Cluster	Zip #	Penetration Actual	Percentages Pred	Percentages Cum Pred	****Base Counts**** Zip Only	****Base Counts**** Cumulative
39	32009	.00	.0449	.0449	89	89
	32265	.00	.0449	.0449	4	93
	32560	.1070	.0449	.0449	93	186
	32563	.00	.0449	.0449	6	192
	32710	.00	.0449	.0449	37	229
	32732	.00	.0449	.0449	200	429
	32740	.00	.0449	.0449	42	471
	32766	.1500	.0449	.0449	200	671
	33070	.0460	.0449	.0449	651	1322
	33470	.00	.0449	.0449	132	1454
	33527	.00	.0449	.0449	716+	2170
	33534	.0590	.0449	.0449	505	2675
	33550	.00	.0449	.0449	194	2869
	33556	.0750	.0449	.0449	528	3397
	33569	.0480	.0449	.0449	1637	5034
	33584	.0390	.0449	.0449	1001	6035
	33586	.00	.0449	.0449	62	6097
	33592	.0770	.0449	.0449	518	6615
	33600	.0750	.0449	.0449	398	7013
	33943	.00	.0449	.0449	139	7152
3	32600	.0420	.0342	.0363	28855	36007
11	32301	.0560	.0327	.0360	3533	39540
	32304	.0230	.0327	.0358	2532	42072
	32500	.0360	.0327	.0355	4873	46945
	32570	.0120	.0327	.0354	2312	49257
	32601	.0330	.0327	.0350	7826	57083
	33030	.0120	.0327	.0348	5564	62647
13	32211	.0240	.0246	.0291	6134	222185
	32303	.0160	.0246	.0290	4243	226428
	32561	.0330	.0246	.0289	1203	227631
	32701	.0140	.0246	.0289	2038	229669
	32751	.0140	.0246	.0288	3379	233048
	32786	.00	.0246	.0288	229	233277
	32789	.0170	.0246	.0287	7543	240820
	33511	.0370	.0246	.0287	2115	242935
10	33900	.0210	.0206	.0255	53503	511276
37	33062	.0170	.0111	.0198	6834	1234153
	33140	.00	.0111	.0198	56	1234209
	33154	.0060	.0111	.0198	3120	1237329
	33160	.0130	.0111	.0197	16354	1253683
	33306	.0100	.0111	.0197	986	1254669
30	33064	.0210	.0076	.0196	8210	1262870
	33516	.00	.0076	.1095	11202	1274072
	33570	.0090	.0076	.0195	3190	1277262

CASE STUDY: **Benefiting from Predictive Modeling with Databases** (continued)

EXHIBIT 19-6

Response Rate Indices for Each Quintile

Rank Ordered Quintile	No. of Pieces Mailed	First Effort Response (%)	First Effort Index	Second Effort Response (%)	Secomd Effort Index
1	242,935	2.87%	147	1.36%	143
2	268,341	2.26	116	1.08	111
3	230,592	1.94	99	0.96	99
4	290,001	1.54	79	0.81	84
5	245,393	1.19	61	0.67	67

PILOT PROJECT   An important modeling application is predicting attrition or churn. Credit card companies need to identify customers least likely to renew before the annual fee cycle. Long distance and wireless phone companies want to identify customers who are most likely to switch, and to determine when they will switch.

You've been asked to help a wireless company develop an attrition model. This company has enjoyed a net customer growth rate of 40 percent annually. Its net revenue is $200 million annually and it has approximately 400,000 customers. The customer attrition (churn) rate is 2.5 percent per month, or 30 percent annually; however, only 60 percent of total attrition is voluntary.

How much net revenue does this company lose annually to total churn? How much is each reversible churn point worth to them? How many customers does it lose through voluntary churn? If the company was able to reduce total churn by five points per year (from 30 to 25 percent), how much additional revenue would it generate? What additional information would you need to create an attrition model for this company?

Key Points

▶ Modeling enables marketers to simplify and see clearly what is going on in their customer campaigns. Using modeling, marketers can identify their "best" customers from a 10-million-name database and present their conclusions in visual, easy-to-understand graphs or charts. Comparing customer characteristics provides insight into what made the difference between responding and not responding—an important first step in designing contact strategies that enhance the lifetime value of a customer.

▶ Modeling permits marketers to test a large number of variables and discover which has the greatest impact. Modeling compares one *dependent variable* (the behavior being analyzed—the factor you want to be able to predict or forecast) against any number of *independent variables* (what you know about the customer, or what you can observe). The use of multiple variables is known as multivariate analysis. The key to regularly improving models is regularly improving the variables.

▶ Because modeling can reduce the number of those contacted and increase response rates, it is worth every dollar of its cost. It helps correct the leading problem in direct marketing: mailing people who don't want your mail and calling people who don't want your calls. Modeling brings an organization closer to the people who *do* want to receive your mail and calls. Do not let the high cost of modeling keep you from investing in a technique that will improve your organization's profitability more than any other tool.

MATHEMATICS OF
DIRECT MARKETING

The mathematics of direct marketing is a high-tension web of interacting revenues and costs supported by three strands: sales, marketing cost, and contribution to marketing cost and profit. There is no single balance of the strands that is right for all direct marketing businesses, but similar threads exist in all direct marketing programs. Direct marketers need to learn the elements in general, quantify them for their specific situation, and then determine which can be tuned to create a stronger business (see Exhibit 20–1).

The unique ability to track and measure results of specific marketing decisions supports a high level of analysis. The belief that the future will be somewhat similar to the past supports reasonable forecasting of the probable results from marketing decisions. The availability of individual specific databases, computers, and statistics supports differential marketing investment at the customer level.

The challenge to the direct marketer is to identify, evaluate, and respond to the vast amount of available marketing information without drowning in the flow. The decision to spend marketing money is applied at the individual customer level, but in actuality, the marketer usually keeps the number of decisions within reason by identifying groups of customers with similar propensities to buy. The marketer never bets on an individual's buying behavior, but willingly bets on the combined buying behavior of sets of people, usually thousands at a time.

Single Transaction Costs and Contribution to Marketing Costs and Profit

A convenient starting point for understanding any direct marketing activity is to determine the amount of money from a single transaction that is available for marketing cost and profit after direct costs associated with the transaction are

EXHIBIT 20–1

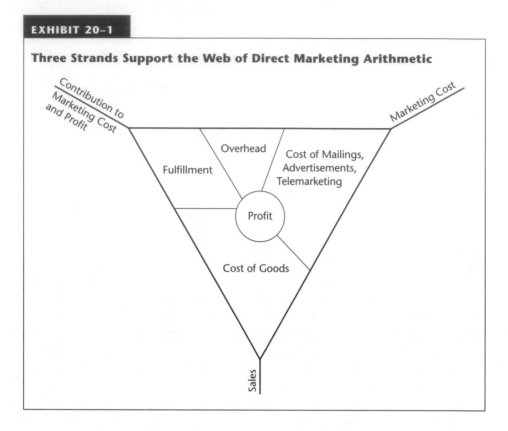

Three Strands Support the Web of Direct Marketing Arithmetic

subtracted. This entails working with averages, cost allocations, and the cost struc-ture of the full business. These direct costs are known before marketing decisions and are often relatively stable over long periods. If different marketing programs have different average transaction sizes and cost structures associated with them, then each must be analyzed separately.

At a very high level, the direct costs can be classified into three categories: merchandise or service, fulfillment, and direct overhead. The merchandise or ser-vice costs should include all expenses and staffing related to purchasing, making, transporting, and storing the product(s) or service(s) being sold. Fulfillment costs should include all costs and people related to processing, filling, and delivering an order. Such diverse items as customer service, bad debt, costs of returns and exchanges, and charges for payment by credit card are usually included in fulfillment. Direct overhead can include costs associated with computer services, finance/accounting, office space, and a charge for some management staff.

Exhibit 20–2 shows a very simple example of this idea. This company has two quite different offers, with average transaction sizes of $50 and $80. We chose to treat shipping and handling charges paid by the customer as an offset to fulfillment costs. Some companies list shipping and handling revenues as other income that would increase both the average order and the fulfillment costs but would not change the contribution to marketing costs and profit. However, all of the percentages would change. Notice in Exhibit 20–2 that the fulfillment cost of $6 is the same for both orders. If the nature of transactions in a given business is reasonably similar, fulfillment tends to be a constant cost per transaction.

As a reminder that this is a very high-level view, Exhibit 20–3 shows a possible breakdown of this $6 fulfillment cost. Even this list is simplified, but it shows that considerable analysis can be applied to determine reasonable values for each of the direct cost elements. Usually companies perform these analyses over a long time, as much as a year. If there is strong seasonality to the business, calculate separately for seasons.

EXHIBIT 20–2

Contribution to Marketing Cost and Profit

	Offer A	Offer B
Average transaction (goods only, no S&H)	$50.00	$80.00
Cost of goods	20.00 (40.0%)	36.00 (45.0%)
Fulfillment (after S&H revenue offset)	6.00 (12.0%)	6.00 (7.5%)
Overhead	5.00 (10.0%)	8.00 (10.0%)
Contribution to marketing cost and profit	$19.00 (38.0%)	$30.00 (37.5%)

EXHIBIT 20–3

Cost Detail for Fulfillment of Transaction During Fall Season

Cost Center	Assumptions	Cost per Transaction
Transaction processing	All transactions	$3.53
Inbound phone	70% of transactions at $3.50/call	2.45
Credit card discount	75% of transactions at 2.5%/transaction	1.65
Customer service	6% of transactions at $8/case	0.48
Returns and exchanges	3% of transactions at $15/case	0.45
Collections and bad debt	0.5% of transactions at $88/case	0.44
Pick and pack	All transactions	1.75
Postage	All transactions	2.91
Management	All transactions	0.09
S&H revenue	All transactions	– 7.75
Net cost per transaction		$6.00

It might seem strange to exclude all marketing costs from these calculations, but the goal is to understand the share of revenue committed to "fulfilling the promise" if a customer makes a purchase. These costs are relatively fixed, predictable, and stable. The revenue remaining after covering these direct costs can be applied to paying marketing costs and obtaining some profit. Exhibit 20–4 shows how this approach divides revenue into these direct costs and the contribution to marketing cost and profit.

Marketing Costs

In direct marketing, the costs of placing advertisements, making mailings, or selling by telephone are really selling expenses rather than advertising. The messages, delivered by the chosen media, are the salespeople of direct marketing. Referred to as marketing costs, they are highly controllable. Very importantly, they are committed to a given program before any sales are obtained.

When catalogs or other mailed materials are used, it is customary to express their costs on the basis of each thousand pieces mailed or otherwise distributed. When an advertisement is placed in a magazine or electronic medium, the cost of each advertising appearance or group of appearances is used. Telemarketers usually work with cost per completed call.

Often it is advisable to test variations in advertisements and/or mailing packages. Because variations are tested in small quantities, extra costs are incurred

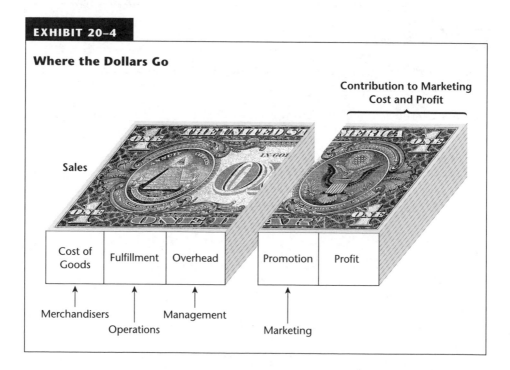

EXHIBIT 20–4

Where the Dollars Go

Contribution to Marketing Cost and Profit

Sales

| Cost of Goods | Fulfillment | Overhead | | Promotion | Profit |

Merchandisers   Operations   Management   Marketing

for printing and additional creative efforts. It would be misleading to include these onetime extra costs as part of the regular profitability calculation. It is generally preferable to include the added costs of creative and small printing quantities associated with testing as a budgeted part of overhead expense. Evaluation of potential profitability of a total direct marketing effort should be computed on the basis of marketing costs one expects to encounter in an ongoing larger-scale program of the size normally conducted in the business.

Exhibit 20–5 provides a simplified marketing cost worksheet for a cataloger, showing how direct marketers think in costs per thousand people contacted as well as total costs of the program. Some direct marketers choose to think in terms of 55 cents per name contacted instead of $550 per thousand contacts, but many prefer thinking in "units" of 1,000.

Several items are interesting to note: 600,000 names were processed to obtain 500,000 contacts; creative, testing, and the cost of the marketing department staff are carried as a lump sum, possibly a budget line item. Two sharply different promotion costs are computed to account for whether the name was owned or rented.

Response Rate

Once you know the promotion costs and the contribution to marketing costs and profit associated with each transaction, you can calculate the response rate required to achieve a given level of profitability. Think of the promotion costs as the money invested at the beginning of the program, and the contribution per transaction multiplied by the number of transactions as the return on that investment.

EXHIBIT 20–5

Marketing Cost Worksheet

	Quantity	Cost	Cost per 1,000
Catalog	500	$110,000	$220
Transaction form	500	16,000	32
List unduplication	600	4,200	7
Address/mail	500	12,000	24
Postage	500	115,000	230
Creative/testing/overhead		16,000	32
		$273,200	$545
House list preparation	150	750	5
Rented names	450	45,000	100
		$318,950	

Total cost per thousand house names, $550; rented names, $645

Using the current examples, one question for Offer B from Exhibit 20–6 might be how many net transactions contributing $30 each are needed to recover marketing costs of $550 per thousand? The answer, shown in Exhibit 20–6, is 550/30 or 18.33, a 1.83 percent net response with product sales of $1,467 per thousand contacted (18.33 × 80). For Offer A, how many completed transactions contributing $19 each are needed to recover marketing costs of $550 per thousand? The answer is 550/19 or 28.95, a 2.90 percent net response with product sales of $1,447 per thousand contacted (28.95 × 50).

However, these calculations merely find break-even, the sales needed to cover selling costs but make zero profit. If the goal were 10 percent pretax profit, we must set aside the target profit, and use the remainder of contribution to cover marketing cost. For the $80 transaction, a 10 percent profit target of $8 must be deducted from contribution. The questions would become how many transactions contributing $22 ($30–$8) or $14 ($19–$5) each are needed to recover marketing costs of $550 per thousand.

Note that these calculations are based on completed transactions or net revenue. If returns are 5 percent of gross orders, each of the preceding answers would need to be divided by 1–(5/95), or .947. Also, these sales per thousand are product revenues, which are less than the total revenue received when shipping and handling are included.

EXHIBIT 20–6

Break-Even to a Goal

	Offer A (Zero Profit)	Offer A (10% Profit)	Offer B (Zero Profit)	Offer B (10% Profit)
House transactions				
Response percentage	2.90%	3.93%	1.83%	2.50%
Average transaction	$50	$50	$80	$80
Sales per 1,000	1,447	1,964	1,467	2,000
Contribution per 1,000				
(38%, 37.5%)	550	746	550	750
Promotion cost per 1,000	550	550	550	550
Profit		196		200
Rental transactions				
Response percentage	3.39%	4.61%	2.15%	2.93%
Average transaction	$50	$50	$80	$80
Sales per 1,000	1,697	2,304	1,720	2,345
Contribution per 1,000				
(38 %, 37.5%)	645	875	645	880
Promotion cost per 1,000	645	645	645	645
Profit		230		235

Key Performance Indicators

There are two types of numbers: measures of heft and measures of rate. Measures of heft use a single measure such as contacts, orders, revenue, direct costs, marketing costs, or profit. Measures of rate are the quotient of two measures, often two heft measures: response percent means orders per hundred contacts or orders divided by contacts times 100, while average order size means dollars per order or total revenue divided by total orders.

Hefts provide the size of the endeavor and are treasured by finance, but rates provide comparisons to other marketing efforts and are treasured by marketers. However, return on marketing investment, ROMI, which is profit divided by marketing costs, is highly valued by all.

Unfortunately, there is no standardized list of direct marketing measures, and most players pride themselves on creating acronyms. One company has a "dictionary" of more than 75 measures—such as CPO, CPM, OPM—that it provides to new employees. The way to understand the key performance indicators of any business is to translate to words you understand; and remember that "per" means divide.

Setting the Marketing Investment

Long-Term or Lifetime Value of a Customer

In a typical direct marketing business, 40 to 60 percent of customers who buy once will purchase again. Some two-time buyers will buy a third time and so on. The first transaction should be the beginning of a long-term, repeat buying relationship for many customers. The greater the average value of new customers acquired, the more a company should be willing to spend to acquire those customers so as to reap future revenues and profits from the repurchases. This concept is known as the long-term or lifetime value of a customer (LTV).

The LTV of a new customer is the net present value of all future revenues minus all attributable costs that are associated with an average customer. Note that it is based on profits, not revenue. A discount factor is used to recognize that money earned in the future is worth less than money earned today. Some offspring of the LTV idea are the remaining value of an established customer and the value of a reactivated dormant customer. Also, some businesses are trying to estimate different LTVs for groups of customers such as inquirers or rented names or buyers with high-dollar first orders.

If profit or loss earned on the first purchase is excluded from the long-term value calculation, the net of the first transaction can be thought of as the acquisition investment. Future purchases begin to offset that investment and contribute to the long-term value.

Marketing contacts have the single greatest impact on LTV: too few contacts will lower LTV, but too many will lower it even faster.

LTV can be estimated by extrapolating current customer performance under "business as usual" assumptions. There are numerous approaches to estimating LTV, which probably suggests that there is no one "right" way. Most approaches eventually derive a table like the one shown in Exhibit 20–7. Notice how the same principles that have already been developed are used, except now the numbers represent multiple contacts over multiple years.

The LTV calculation is *based* on all activity from a group of new customers subsequent to their acquisition. Because fewer and fewer customers buy in each succeeding year, sales decline each year, even if remaining customers increase their purchases. In this example, the LTV is $8.73 per new customer if profits are discounted at 15 percent, or $7.05 if a 25 percent discount factor is used. If another year were added, the LTV would increase by less than $0.50. The combination of customer attrition and the effect of discounting make it meaningless in most businesses to carry out the calculation for more than five to seven years. That is why some prefer the description *long-term value* over *lifetime value*.

If a business can develop an estimated LTV for new customers, this can be used to establish how much to spend on acquiring them. Given the uncertainty of the future, and the ability to do "business as usual," many companies prefer to invest only 30 to 40 percent of the expected LTV in acquisition, or to apply a 25 to 30 percent hurdle rate as a discount. Either way, LTV is primarily used to help set an allowable cost or loss for acquiring customers and quantify the return on that

EXHIBIT 20–7

Six-Year Value of 1,000 New Buyers

	Year 1	Year 2	Year 3	Year 4	Year 5	Year 6
Purchase transactions	279	233	168	132	100	79
Average transaction size	$51.22	$51.35	$51.60	$51.75	$52.01	$52.06
Gross product sales	$14,296	$11,940	$8,659	$6,834	$5,200	$4,101
Returns	572	478	346	273	208	164
Net sales	13,724	11,462	8,313	6,561	4,992	3,937
Merchandise costs	6,213	5,189	3,763	2,970	2,260	1,783
Operating costs	1,381	1,153	836	660	502	396
Overhead	2,041	1,704	1,236	975	742	586
Contribution	4,089	3,416	2,477	1,956	1,488	1,172
Selling cost	2,687	2,608	1,799	1,495	1,146	911
List rental income	311	111	84	65	50	39
Cash flow	1,713	919	762	526	392	300
Discounted at 15 percent	1,490	695	501	301	195	130
Cumulative present value	1,490	2,184	2,685	2,986	3,181	3,311
Discounted at 25 percent	1,370	588	390	215	128	79
Cumulative present value	1,370	1,959	2,349	2,564	2,693	2,771

investment. It also can be used to estimate the value of a current house file and to set an appropriate level of ongoing marketing expense.

Customer Groups and Targeting Within Customer Groups

One key to successful contact planning is divide and conquer. That is, potential buyers should be separated into large groups with similar marketing potential. Each of these groups would be evaluated separately. For example, past buyers can be separated into onetime and multibuyers, and rental lists can be grouped by list categories. This supports marketing contact decisions at a finer level.

Buying potential within each group can be further differentiated using RFM or statistical models that estimate likelihood of purchase from a given contact. Based on historic buying rates and patterns, these estimates need to be adjusted for changes in the offer, the competition, or the economy.

The goal is to forecast buying levels and resulting profitability in order to identify which customers or potential customers to contact, given specific marketing goals. The aim is to create a hierarchy of expectations, establish profitability at each level, and find the "margin"—the weakest set of people who should be contacted. Exhibits 20–8 and 20–9 provide examples of estimated performance for representative groups, but they do NOT make the contact decision.

Contact Goals

The contact decision must be made relative to established business goals. These should vary by group and should provide not only desired performance on average, but also desired performance at the margin. The most difficult and most important

---

EXHIBIT 20–8

Historic Performance for Onetime Buyers

Recency of Last Purchase	Response Percentage	Sales per 1,000	Profit per Buyer at Promotion Costs of		
			$450/K	**$500/K**	**$550/K**
Less than 6 months	4.2%	$2,520	$9.09	$7.90	$6.70
6–12 months	3.5	1,995	5.95	4.52	3.10
12–24 months	2.4	1,248	– 1.59	3.67	– 5.76
24–36 months	1.8	900	– 8.50	– 11.28	– 14.06
36–48 months	1.2	564	– 21.99	– 26.16	– 30.32
48+ months	0.9	405	– 35.15	– 40.71	– 46.26

EXHIBIT 20–9

Historic Performance for Rental List 506

Select	Response Percentage	Sales per 1,000	Profit per Buyer at Promotion Costs of		
			$550/K	$600/K	$650/K
Buyers in the last 3 months	2.8%	$1,596	– $0.83	– $2.62	– $4.40
4–12-month multibuyers	3.5	1,995	3.10	1.67	0.24
12–24-month multibuyers	2.1	1,092	– 9.03	– 11.41	– 13.79
4–12-month single buyers	2.6	1,482	– 2.34	– 4.27	– 6.19
12–24-month single buyers	1.7	884	– 15.19	– 18.13	– 21.08

goals are those that state profitability of the weakest cells you elect to contact. If the worst cell contacted breaks even, the whole program will be profitable. However, even if the poorest cell contacted shows a loss, the whole program still could be highly profitable.

Depending on overall business needs, it is reasonable to set different marginal goals at different times. When near-term profit is crucial, the goals can be set very high. When volume, expansion, and growth are important, the marginal goals can be lowered as the business elects to invest in the future. This could entail acquiring new customers as well as reactivating stagnant customers, both at a short-term loss.

Exhibit 20–10 provides a simplified mail plan that uses the three key strands of promotion cost, purchase size, and single-order contribution to marketing cost and profit, plus marginal profit-per-buyer goals to establish minimal performance to meet the goals. Considering the interactions of these multiple elements, the required purchase rate from the "last" or marginal cells varies from barely 1 percent to more than 2.4 percent, while the sales per thousand varies within a much tighter band. Can you imagine some of the thinking that went into establishing these groups, and setting such varied goals? Can you believe that each group has been differentiated so that only those customers and prospects who might be expected to meet the minimal standards could be chosen for contact?

Continuous Revenue Relationships

All of the discussion so far assumes you have a good estimate of the revenue from an initial response. However, the fastest growing area within database marketing involves companies that establish an ongoing revenue stream from the first response. When someone chooses a long distance phone service provider, the revenue or "transaction size" will be the sum of a continuous revenue stream that extends over

EXHIBIT 20–10

A Sample Mail Plan

	Promotion Cost/K	Average Transaction	Contribution Percentage	Goals for Marginal Profit/Buyer	Required to Reach Marginal Goal Sales/K	Response
House file						
Big spenders	$400	$100	33%	– $5	$1,052	1.05%
Middlers	400	75	33	– 2	1,121	1.50
Pikers	400	50	33	0	1,212	2.42
Inquirers	400	60	33	– 3	1,053	1.75
External lists						
MO rental	525	75	33	– 5	1,324	1.76
Subscribers	475	60	33	– 4	1,197	2.00
Compiled	450	50	33	– 3	1,154	2.31

an unknown time frame. Insurance and investment companies, Internet access providers, banks, utilities, credit card companies, cable TV providers, and music or books or coffee continuities all have *continuous revenue* relationships rather than *single order* relationships: the initial join or enrollment creates a multiple payment revenue stream without the necessity of further marketing contacts.

Continuous revenue programs can be quantified using the principles established in this chapter, but estimating the average revenue and the contribution to marketing cost and profit becomes much more difficult. Retention and level of spending combine to set the revenue, with the unfortunate fact that often those who spend the most leave the soonest. Direct costs often are hard to quantify at the individual customer level, and that makes contribution to marketing cost and profit a soft number.

The dynamics of continuous revenue relationships are such that, while each payment may be small, on average the total revenue from one customer is high. This usually justifies spending much larger amounts to acquire the customer, including sweeteners and signing bonuses. This marketing investment is spent up front, but the revenue comes in over many months. If retention and/or revenue are overestimated, it is easy to make poor marketing judgments—but greater reward is definitely associated with the greater risk.

Inquiry Conversion Programs

Previous examples in this chapter have assumed that the first transaction is a purchase triggered by advertisements or direct contacts. Sometimes the difficulty in targeting possible buyers makes it more profitable to generate inquiries using various low-cost methods and then to convert those inquiries into buyers by using one or more mailings, telephone calls, and/or sales visits. This usually is advantageous when selling high-ticket items, when prospects need prequalification or cultivation, when personal contact is needed to close the sale, or when the same inquirers become good prospects for multiple additional offers.

Inquiries can be generated through any of the media available to the direct marketer. For example, if an advertisement costing $5,000 placed in a magazine produces 1,000 inquiries, the cost per inquiry would be $5. In addition, there will be a cost of perhaps $75 per thousand to process inquiries into a computer file. This processing should be done promptly, and the promotion activity taken immediately, because all studies have shown that the sooner the response to an inquiry is received, the higher the likelihood of response.

Varying the media, kinds of advertisements, appeals, and offers, will affect the cost of generating inquiries and possibly the rate at which they convert to buyers. Typically, the more highly qualified an inquiry, the more costly it will be to generate, but the higher the conversion rate will be. The thoughtful direct marketer will experiment continuously with various ways of producing inquiries and various means of converting them to fine-tune a program and to maximize profits.

The marketer has the right to repromote inquiries, and most companies find that an inquiry list will support repeated conversion contacts. There will be a fall-off in response to each successive effort, but it is profitable to continue making conversion contacts until the incremental cost of the last one is greater than the contribution it generates.

Exhibit 20–11 shows a typical set of inquiry conversion results when multiple contacts are used. The costs of acquiring the inquiry and making repeated conversion efforts are the marketing investment. As inquirers are converted to buyers, the quantity available for subsequent contacts goes down. The likelihood of response goes down very quickly as the best prospects are captured and removed from the group. The true measure of performance is the cumulative cost and profit associated with the series of contacts including acquisition costs. Did they go one contact too far here, should they go one more, or did they do it just right?

Engineering a Direct Marketing Business

Spreadsheet-based computer models can be used to simulate a direct marketing business quite accurately. Usually these use monthly time frames and spread both response and costs so the final model provides a reasonable set of expectations for cash flow. Many companies have found these extremely useful for long-term planning and identifying the profit sensitivity to key parameters.

In addition, these models can be used to assess the consequences of changes in strategy or policy. Exhibit 20–12 illustrates the impact on return on investment

EXHIBIT 20–11

Inquiry Conversion with Multiple Follow-up Contacts

	Inquiry Acquisition Cost	Contact #1	Contact #2	Contact #3	Contact #4	Total Program
Quantity mailed		$1,000	940	912	898	3,750
Response percentage		6.0%	3.0%	1.5%	0.6%	2.9%
Net transactions		60	28	14	5	107
Net sales		$9,000	$4,200	$2,100	$750	$16,050
Contribution		3,600	1,680	840	300	6,420
Selling cost	$5,075	400	376	365	359	6,575
Profit	– 5,075	3,200	1,304	475	– 59	– 155
Cumulative profit	– 5,075	– 1,875	– 571	– 96	– 155	
Cumulative profit per buyer		– 31.25	– 6.49	– 0.94	– 1.45	

of the pursuit of three different strategies to build a catalog mail order business. The model assumes the same amount of money is invested in each strategy. The strategies are to:

1. Mail more catalogs to rented lists to acquire more customers.

2. Expand the catalogs by adding more products and increasing the number of pages.

3. Create an extra catalog to be mailed to better customers during the fall season.

Over the five-year horizon for which results are simulated, the company in question would invest most advantageously in expanding its product line. Notice, however, that the customer acquisition strategy appears to be closing the gap quickly at the end of the period and might be expected to outperform the product line expansion strategy in the sixth or seventh year. Further study might indicate that this particular company could blend the two approaches by expanding the size of some of its catalogs and also increasing its customer acquisition.

This example underscores the fact that direct marketing is accountable marketing where the impact of specific marketing actions can be estimated, tested, and evaluated. If the marketer is willing, able, and persistent, the potential exists to understand the impact of decisions and make significant, measurable contributions to the profitability of the business. The web of interacting costs and profit drivers is remarkably resilient, rebounding from and adjusting to small pressures. Sharp blows or inordinate forces can cause great damage, but the web glistens in the morning dew and has singular attractive powers.

EXHIBIT 20–12

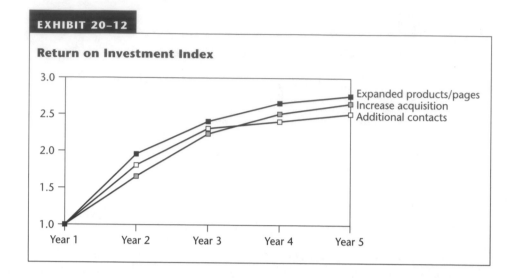

Return on Investment Index

CASE STUDY: **The Dressing Under Duress Society, or DUDS**

BACKGROUND

A space ad program with a circulation of 90,000 offered a Funky Furzy shirt for $17.95 plus $5.95 shipping and handling. The ad cost $8,000; a total of 1,412 shirts were sold. Each order was for one shirt, and no shirts were returned. The company uses shipping and handling as an offset to fulfillment and as a contribution to marketing cost and a profit of 34 percent.

CHALLENGE

Prepare a presentation for upper management that fully quantifies the results, explains what was learned by the effort, and suggests the future opportunities supported by your analysis.

SOLUTION

Many numbers can and should be calculated: total product sales, total revenue, and total profit. Others are quite uninformative, such as sales per thousand circulated or ad cost per thousand circulated.

The most important numbers are the acquisition of space ad buyer names at a profit of 44 cents each, and a ROMI of 7.7 percent over a very short time frame. You are challenged to derive these two numbers.

DUDS is able to acquire new buyers at a profit, at least in this one publication using this particular product. This is unusual in today's world, when new buyers are usually acquired at a loss. Any time it can be repeated with similar results, there are no reasons not to do so.

As for future opportunities, the results suggest a series of tests to expand this small program. The small circulation suggests a specialty media; so, there may be opportunities to seek new buyers at a profit in similar specialty media using the same product. Given natural wear-out of a product, it is important to test other products within the same publication to establish a group of profitable space ad products if possible. These other products should test the boundaries of price point as well as product type.

Finally, there is a need to promote these space ad buyers with other direct programs to see if they will become profitable repurchasers from other programs. This single, small, but successful program can serve as a springboard to a host of spin-offs where results may not be quite so rosy but the sheer quantity of programs will begin to create some business heft.

PILOT PROJECT

1. A test mailing of 15,000 pieces with a total promotion cost of $4,500 generated $13,500 net sales. The average order size was $50, and each order contributed $20 to promotion costs and profit after paying for the cost of goods, fulfillment, and an overhead allocation. Compute the following:

  a. Total orders
  b. Total contribution
  c. Total profit
  d. Profit as percentage of net sales
  e. Response percentage
  f. Orders/thousand
  g. Promotion cost/thousand
  h. Contribution/thousand
  i. Profit/thousand

2. A company has the following cost profile:

  Cost of goods   40.0 percent of net sales
  Operating expenses   11.6 percent of net sales
  Overhead expenses   14.4 percent of net sales

  • What is the contribution to promotion costs and profit?
  • Find the sales/thousand break-even if:
    (a) Promotion cost is $425 per thousand
    (b) Promotion cost is $425 per thousand and there is a targeted profit of 9 percent

3. A firm has two different methods by which it can generate average orders of $80 with a contribution to promotion costs and profit of $32.

  Complete the break-even analysis.

	MAGAZINE SPACE AD	SMALL CATALOG
Promotion cost/thousand		
Break-even:		
Orders/thousand		
Response percentage		
Sales/thousand		
Break-even given a 15 percent profit target:		
Orders/thousand		
Response percentage		
Sales/thousand		

Answers to Pilot Project

1a. 270
1b. $5,400
1c. $900
1d. 6.67%
1e. 1.80%
1f. 18
1g. $300
1h. $360
1i. $60
2. 34% of net sales
2a. $1,250
2b. $1,700

	MAGAZINE SPACE AD	SMALL CATALOG
Promotion cost/thousand	$12	$360
Break-even:		
Orders/thousand	0.375	11.25
Response percentage	0.0375%	1.125%
Sales/thousand	$30	$900
Break-even given a 15 percent profit target:		
Orders/thousand	0.6	18
Response percentage	0.06%	1.8%
Sales/thousand	48	$1,440

Key Point

▶ Direct marketing is accountable. The impact of specific marketing actions can be estimated, tested, and evaluated. By mastering the mathematical concepts in this chapter, a marketer can understand the impact of decisions and make significant, measurable contributions to the profitability of the business.

INNOVATION
THROUGH CREATIVITY
AND TESTING

Traditional direct marketers are often able to create, validate, and improve on their ideas using two very different processes. One process is subjective and relies upon a number of techniques designed to inspire ideation. The other technique is objective and used to validate these ideas. Applying these two processes—*creativity* and *testing*—over and over again, marketers are able to achieve refinement and success in their campaigns.

Talking about creativity and testing together may seem odd. One relies upon right-brain thinking and the other left-brain thinking. Both are necessary to successfully apply the tools and techniques of direct marketing.

Creativity focuses on generating novel and useful ideas that are the solutions to problems, opportunities, and challenges. It relies upon divergent thinking, the ability to imagine original, diverse, and elaborate ideas. Creativity also relies upon convergent thinking. This has to do with appropriateness, the ability to evaluate, critique, and choose the best idea from a selection of ideas.

Testing can be thought of as extension of convergent thinking. Testing is a basis for developing real-world performance measures of creative ideas. It is a way to learn how the market votes regarding a new idea. This direct linkage is one of the things that make the practice of direct marketing unique. Using the tools and techniques of direct marketing, creative ideas that might not otherwise be considered can be tested and proven in the marketplace. Testing is still the best way to find true breakthroughs.

The never-ending quest for a breakthrough is motivated by fantastic payoff potential. When it was introduced in the 1930s, "Book-of-the-Month Club" was a breakthrough concept leading to billions of dollars in book sales. Amazon.com chose to go where no bookseller had gone before . . . to the Internet. Its success is well documented. There are many, many more.

Creativity and Being Creative

Anyone can be creative. What hinders most people from coming up with creative ideas is a belief that they are not creative. There is no empirical evidence that people are born creative. It is more a state of being than a gift. "Being creative" means overcoming the obstacles to creativity that are within each of us.

Obstacles to creative thinking include fear of criticism, lack of confidence, and stress. Sometimes we may be too busy or have to deal with other issues. We may not allow enough time to relax and renew our mind and spirit. Or we may have conflicting goals and objectives that keep us from focusing on creative solutions. Exercises and tools to stimulate creativity can help, but ultimately creativity stems from a point of view about an individual's self and abilities. The iconoclastic behavior of people cited as creative is likely a reflection on how they focus on solutions to problems, release pressure, and have the confidence to be "themselves."

Any organization can also be creative, but many choose not to be. There are two reasons that organizations fail to generate new ideas: (1) the tendency to "play it safe" to protect the bottom line, and (2) not enough way-out testing to lead to creative new breakthroughs.

But how does one develop breakthrough ideas? Are there specific techniques that can be applied? Yes.

Brainstorming

Brainstorming, first popularized in the 1950s by Alex Osborne of BBD&O, continues to be an effective method of finding new creative solutions to difficult problems. Brainstorming is part of a three-phase process:

1. Before starting, create an agenda and carefully define problem(s) in writing.

2. Set quotas for ideas and a time limit for each section of the agenda.

3. Review the house rules with participants before each brainstorming session.

Let's look at some rules for brainstorming, and then consider a few examples of breakthroughs that have emerged from the process.

Selecting a Leader

Select a leader and have him or her take all responsibility for contact with reality. Everyone else in the brainstorming meeting is to "think wild." In a brainstorming meeting, the leader plays a low-key role. It's important to avoid influencing the participants. The duties of the leader are as follows:

- To see that detailed notes are taken on all ideas expressed

- To see that the agenda and time schedule are adhered to

- To admonish any critical thinkers in the group—no negative thinking is allowed during the brainstorming session

- To see that the group takes time to "build up" each idea

- To keep all participants involved and contributing

House Rules During Brainstorming

1. Suspend all critical judgment of your own—or other people's—ideas. Don't ask yourself if this is a good idea or a bad idea. Accept it and rack your brain for ways to improve the concept.

2. Welcome freewheeling, off-the-wall thinking. Wild, crazy, funny, far-out ideas are important. Why? Ideas that are the most way out often shock us into a totally new viewpoint of the problem.

3. Quantity, not quality, is the objective during the brainstorm session. This sounds contradictory—it's not. Remember that every member of the group has been briefed on the problem in advance. You have a carefully planned agenda of material to cover. Consequently, your group is well-directed toward the right problem. Therefore go for quantity in the idea session.

4. Build up each idea. Here's where most brainstorming sessions fail. They just collect ideas as fast as they come and let it go at that. The leaders should carefully slow the group down so they stop with each idea and help build it up. Enhance each idea, no matter how crazy or offbeat it seems.

It's the leader's responsibility to see that these four guidelines are adhered to in every meeting; but he or she should do this in a very low-key, informal manner. It is important that the leader not become a dominant authority figure in meetings.

When the session is over, then—and only then—use your normal, everyday judgment to logically select ideas with the most potential from all of the available alternatives.

Brainstorming Examples

Example 1. The problem: insurance companies are not allowed to give free gifts as incentives for applying for an insurance policy. How can we offer a free gift and stay within the law? Sounds like an impossible problem, right? Wrong. Brainstorming participants broke through with a positive solution, a blockbuster.

The breakthrough: the brainstorming idea that hit pay dirt was to offer the free gift to everyone, whether they apply for the policy or not.

The result: a 38 percent increase in applications.

Example 2. The problem: How can we avoid paying postage for sending prizes to "no" entrants in an "everybody wins" sweepstakes? (Possible savings in postage to the marketer if the problem could be solved was about $250,000.)

The breakthrough: we asked "no" entrants to provide a stamped, self-addressed envelope. We included a prize in the shipping carton for those who said "yes." (The USPS approved the requirement at the time.)

The result: this was the most successful sweepstakes contest the sponsor ever conducted. The sponsor also enjoyed savings of $250,000 in postage.

Example 3. The problem: we have 36 competitors selling to schools. They all promise "prompt shipment" of their pompoms. How can we dramatize the fact that we ship our pompoms in 24 hours and thus capture the bulk of the market?

The breakthrough: we inserted a Jiffy Order Card in the catalog, in addition to the regular order form, featuring guaranteed shipment within 24 hours.

The result: pompom sales increased 40 percent!

Example 4. The problem: as a leading agricultural chemical company, we manufacture both a corn herbicide and corn insecticide. Each product has its own positioning in the farm market and each product has a different share of market in various geographic areas across the nation. How can new users for each product be won over from the competition?

The breakthrough: we created a combination rebate program. Because the ratio of herbicide to insecticide remains relatively constant regardless of order size, we offered a rebate on both products when purchased at the same time.

The result: a significant number of farmers who had planned to purchase the two products from different manufacturers took advantage of the rebate offer and purchased both products from the sponsor, with an average order of $25,000.

Creative Stimulators

The degree of truly creative output is directly related to two factors: (1) clear and specific definitions of problems to be solved, and (2) the right "atmosphere" for developing creative solutions. There are many tools and tricks used to stimulate creative thought in addition to brainstorming.

SCAMPER is one such method. It was designed for finding creative solutions for new products, consumer advertising, and many other general uses. SCAMPER is an acronym for:

Substitute
Combine
Add or Adapt
Modify
Put to other uses
Eliminate
Reverse

Frank Daniels, a former creative director with Stone & Adler, used a version of SCAMPER as an effective system for stimulating creative people to think about solutions for marketing products/services direct. This version uses many of the same points as SCAMPER, but adds points that recognize the need to balance creative solutions with the need to stimulate an immediate response.

The examples that follow were applied to Lanier Worldwide, Inc., a major provider of office equipment including copiers, fax machines, and dictating equipment. Creativity was being stimulated for promoting a minirecorder, Lanier's Pocket Secretary. A key thought accompanies each of the stimulators as well as a series of questions designed to promote creative solutions.

S—Can We Substitute?

The major product benefit for a product is often so similar to major product benefits of competitive products that it is difficult for the consumer to perceive the difference. Substituting another theme, such as Avis did when the company changed its theme to "We Try Harder," can often establish a point of difference. These questions inspire participants to think in terms of substitution.

Key Thought. Substitute the familiar for another familiar theme for emphasis; substitute the unfamiliar for the familiar for emphasis.

- Can a well-known theme for another product be substituted for our theme, or can a well-known benefit for another product be substituted for our benefit?

- Can an incongruous situation be used to focus emphasis on our theme or benefits?

- Can a series of incongruous situations be found for every benefit we have? Can they be used in one ad? Can they form a continuity series of ads?

- What can be substituted for our product appeal that will emphasize the difference between us and our competitors?

- Can an obviously dissimilar object be substituted for the image of our product?

- Can a physical object be used to give more concrete representation of a product intangible?

- Is our product replacing a process rapidly becoming dated? Can we substitute the past for the present, or the future for the past or the present?

- Can we visualize our product where the competitor's product is normally expected to be?

- Can we visualize our product as the only one of its kind in the world, as if there were no substitutes for our product?

C—Can We Combine?

Combining two or more elements often results in new thought processes. The following questions are designed to encourage brainstorming participants to think in terms of combinations.

Key Thought. Combine appropriate parts of well-known things to emphasize the benefits of our product. "Think of owning a Rolls-Royce the size of a Volkswagen" (Lanier Pocket Secretary).

- What can be combined physically or conceptually to emphasize product benefits?

- Can the product be combined with another so that both benefit?

- Where in the product offer would a combination of thoughts be of most help?

- What opposites can be combined to show a difference from competitive products?

- What can we combine with our product to make it more fun to own, use, and look at?

- Can part of one of our benefits be combined with part of another to enhance both?

- Can newness be combined with tradition?

- Can a product benefit be combined with a specific audience need through visual devices? Copy devices?

- What can we combine from the advertising and sales program to the benefit of both? Can salespersons' efforts be combined into advertising?

- Can we demonstrate product advantages by using "misfit" combination demonstrations?

- Can we combine manufacturing information performance tests with advertising to demonstrate advantages?

A—Can We Add or Adapt

An axiom of selling is that the customer often unconsciously compares the added benefits of a competitor's product with those of your product. The product with the most added benefits traditionally sells better. These questions are designed to ferret out added benefits and adapt them for a particular product.

Key Thought. Look for ways to change the way that benefits are expressed by relating functional advantages of unrelated products or things. "We've taken all the best cassette recorder features and added one from the toaster" (pop-out delivery).

- What has been added to our product that's missing from others?

- Do we have a deficiency due to excess that can be turned into advantage?

- Is our product usable in many different ways aside from the intended use?

- Is our product instantly noticeable? Is it unusual in terms of size, shape, and color? What unrelated symbols can we use to emphasize this unique characteristic?

- Does our product make something easier? What have we added by taking this something away?

- Does our product make order out of chaos or meaningful chaos out of total chaos? What have we added by taking this something away?

- What does the purchase of our product add to the buyer's physical condition, mental condition, subconscious condition, present condition, and future condition?

- Where will the buyer be if he or she does not purchase? What will be missing from the buyer's life?

- Does our product give its full benefit to the buyer immediately, or does the buyer build up (add to) his or her well-being through continued possession?

M—Can We Modify: Are There Time Elements That Can Be Emphasized?

Saving time and having extra time are conventional human wants. This series of questions is designed to expand one's thinking toward making time a plus factor in the product offer.

Key Thought. Modify time factor(s) in present offer, present schedules, and present product positioning to motivate action.

- Does seasonal timing have an effect on individual benefits?

- Can present seasonal timing be reversed for special effect?

- Can limited offers be effective?

- Can early buyers be given special consideration?

- Can off-season offers be made?

- Are there better days, weeks, or months for our offers?

- Can we compress or extend present promotional sequencing?

- Can our price be keyed to selected times of the week, month, and year?

- Can we feature no-time-limit offers?

- Can we feature limited-time offers?

- Can we feature fast delivery or follow-up?

P—Can We Put to Other Uses?

Favorable associations are one way to show how products can be used in other ways. They are often the most effective way to emphasize product benefits. "Like sterling on silver," a classic example of a favorable association, is a comment that accrues to the benefit of the product being compared with other products.

Key Thought. Associate benefits with product usage and features, or lack thereof, to surprise and delight. Show and tell comfort and success as part of the product features and benefits.

- Form a link with unrelated things or situations to emphasize benefits.

- Can we link our product to another, already successful product to emphasize benefits?

- Can we appeal to popular history, literature, poetry, or art to emphasize benefits?

- What does the potential buyer associate with our product? How can we use this association to advantage?

- When does the potential buyer associate our product with potential use?

- Can associations be drawn with present or future events?

- Can associations be made with abstractions that can be expressed visually, musically, with words, and so forth?

- Can funny, corny, challenging associations be made?

- Can associations be made with suppliers of component parts?

- Is our product so unique that it needs no associations?

- Can our product be associated with many different situations?

E—Can We Eliminate or Simplify?

Taking away can often be as appealing as adding to. Less weight, less complexity, less fuss, less bother are fundamental appeals. These questions steer brainstorming participants in that direction.

Key Thought. Subtract from the obvious to focus attention on the benefits of our product or service. "We've weighed all the minirecorders and made ours lighter."

- What deficiencies does our product have competitively?

- What advantages do we have?

- What features are the newest? The most unusual?

- How can our product use/cost be minimized over time?

- Can a buyer use less of another product if he or she buys ours?

- Can the evidence of total lack of desire for our product be used to illustrate its benefits?

- Can the limitations of our benefits be used as an appeal?

- What does lack of our product in the buyer's living habits do to him or her?

- Does our product offer a chance to eliminate any common element in all competitive products?

- Does our product reduce or eliminate (subtract) anything in the process of performing its work?

- Will our product deflate (subtract from) a problem for the buyers?

Can the product be simplified? What is the simple way to describe and illustrate our major product benefit? As sophisticated as our world is today, the truism persists that people relate best to simple things. These questions urge participants to state benefits with dramatic simplicity.

Key Thought. Dramatize benefits individually or collectively with childishly simple examples, symbols, images.

- Which of our appeals is strongest over our competition? How can we simplify to illustrate?

- Is there a way to simplify all benefits for emphasis?

- Where is most of the confusion about our product in the buyer's mind?

- Can we illustrate by simplification?

- Is our appeal abstract? Can we substitute simple, real visualizations to emphasize?

- Could a familiar quotation or picture be used to make our appeal more understandable?

- Is our product complex? Can we break it up (literally) into more understandable pieces to emphasize benefits?

- Can we overlap one benefit with another to make product utility more understandable?

- Can we contrast an old way of doing something with the confusing part of our product to create understanding?

- Is product appeal rigidly directed at too small a segment of the market? Too broad a segment?

- Can we emphasize benefits by having an unskilled person or child make good use of the product in a completely out-of-context situation?

R—Can We Make a Reversal?

The ordinary can become extraordinary as usual situations are reversed. A man wearing a tennis skirt. A woman wearing a football helmet. A trained bear pushing a power mower. These questions are designed to motivate participants to think in terms of reversing usual situations.

Key Thought. Emphasize a benefit by completely reversing the usual situation.

- What are the diametrically opposed situations for each of our product benefits?

- For each copy point already established, make a complete reverse statement.

- How would a totally uninformed person describe our product?

- Can male- and female-oriented roles be reversed?

- Can art and copy be totally reversed to emphasize a point?

- How many incongruous product situations can be shown graphically? Verbally?

- Can we find humor in the complete reversal of anticipated product uses or benefits?

Test the Big Things

Testing is one of the most important direct marketing techniques. The notion that creative, media, mailing lists, offers, etc., can all be tested to reduce marketers' risk is one of the greatest attractions of direct marketing. With the growth of on-line marketing and the ability to do real-time testing, the need to understand when and what to test has never been greater.

Whether testable ideas come out of pure research, brainstorming, or self-developed creativity, the same picture applies: test the big things. Trivia testing (e.g., the tilt of a postage stamp, the effects of various colors, one graphic versus another, etc.) is passé. Breakthroughs are possible only when you test the big things. Here are six big areas from which breakthroughs emerge:

1. The products or services you offer

2. The media you use (lists, print, broadcast, the Internet)

3. The propositions you make

4. The copy platforms you use

5. The formats you use

6. The timing you choose

Five of the areas for testing appear on most published lists these days. But testing new products and new product features is rarely recommended. Yet everything starts with the product or service you offer.

Many direct marketers religiously test new ads, new mailing packages, new media, new copy approaches, new formats, and new timing schedules season after season with never a thought to testing new product features. Finally, the most imaginative of creative approaches fails to overcome the waning appeal of the same old product, so still another product bites the dust.

This need not happen. For example, consider the most commonplace of mail order items—the address label. Scores of firms offer them in black ink on standard white stock. Competition is keen. Prices all run about the same. From this variety of competitive styles, however, a few emerge with new product features: gold stock, colored ink, seasonal borders, and so forth. Tests are made to determine appeal. The new product features appeal to a bigger audience.

As we consider our products, we should all ask ourselves these questions:

- Do we have products or services that have become obsolete?

- Is there a way to improve upon on them?

- Is there a way to combine two ideas that already exist into something that hasn't already been thought of? (Gutenberg combined a die punch with a wine press, and ended up with the printing press.)

Projectable Mailing Sample Sizes

Some direct marketers live by probability tables that tell the mailer what the sample size must be at various response levels within a specified error limit, such as 5 or 10 percent. No one argues the statistical validity of probability tables. Although probability tables can't be relied on too heavily because it is impossible to construct a truly scientific sample, such tables, within limits, can be helpful. Exhibit 21–1 is based on a 95 percent confidence level at various limits of error.

Testing Components versus Testing Mailing Packages

In the endless search for breakthroughs, the question continually arises: In direct mail, should we test components or mailing packages? There are two schools of thought on this. The prevailing one is that the big breakthroughs come about through the testing of completely different mailing packages as opposed to testing individual components within a mailing package. Something can be learned from each procedure, of course. However, the more logical procedure is to first find the big difference in mailing packages and then follow with tests of individual components in the losing packages, which can often make the winning packages even better.

In package testing, one starts with a complete concept, and builds all components to fit the image of the concept. Consider the differences between two package concepts:

CONTENTS	PACKAGE ONE	PACKAGE TWO
Envelope	9 × 12 inch	No. 10
Letter	8 single-side pages, stapled, not personalized	4 double-side pages, personalized
Circular	None	4-page, illustrated
Order Form	8½ × 11 inch, perforated stub	8½ × 3½ inch

EXHIBIT 21-1

Test Sample Sizes Required for 95 Percent Confidence Level for Mailing Response Levels from 0.1 Percent to 4.0 Percent

R (Response)	Limits of Error (Expressed as Percentage Points)														
	.02	.04	.06	.08	.10	.12	.14	.16	.18	.20	.30	.40	.50	.60	.70
.1	95,929	23,982	10,659	5,995	3,837	2,665	1,957	1,499	1,184	959	426	240	153	106	78
.2	191,666	47,916	21,296	11,979	7,667	5,324	3,911	2,994	2,366	1,917	852	479	307	213	156
.3	287,211	71,803	31,912	17,951	11,488	7,978	5,861	4,487	3,546	2,872	1,276	718	459	319	234
.4	382,564	95,641	42,507	23,910	15,303	10,627	7,807	5,977	4,723	3,826	1,700	956	612	425	312
.5	477,724	119,431	53,080	29,858	19,109	13,270	9,749	7,464	5,987	4,777	2,123	1,194	764	531	390
.6	572,693	143,173	63,632	35,793	22,908	15,908	11,687	8,948	7,070	5,727	2,545	1,432	916	638	467
.7	667,470	166,867	74,163	41,717	26,699	18,541	13,622	10,429	8,240	6,675	2,966	1,669	1,068	744	545
.8	762,054	190,514	84,673	47,628	30,482	21,168	15,552	11,907	9,408	7,621	3,387	1,905	1,219	847	622
.9	856,447	214,112	95,160	53,528	34,258	23,790	17,478	13,382	10,573	8,564	3,806	2,141	1,370	952	699
1.0	950,648	237,662	105,628	59,415	38,026	26,407	19,401	14,854	11,736	9,506	4,225	2,376	1,521	1,056	776
1.1	1,044,656	261,164	116,072	65,291	41,786	29,018	21,319	16,322	12,897	10,446	4,643	2,611	1,671	1,160	853
1.2	1,138,472	284,618	126,496	71,155	45,539	31,624	23,234	17,788	14,055	11,385	5,050	2,846	1,821	1,265	929
1.3	1,232,097	308,024	136,899	77,006	49,284	34,225	25,145	19,254	15,211	12,321	5,476	3,080	1,971	1,368	1,006
1.4	1,325,529	331,382	147,280	82,845	53,021	36,820	27,051	20,711	16,364	13,255	5,891	3,314	2,121	1,472	1,082
1.5	1,418,769	354,692	157,640	88,673	56,751	39,410	28,954	22,168	17,515	14,188	6,305	3,547	2,270	1,576	1,158
1.6	1,511,818	377,954	167,980	94,489	60,473	41,595	30,853	23,622	18,664	15,118	6,719	3,780	2,419	1,680	1,234
1.7	1,604,674	401,168	178,297	100,292	64,187	44,574	32,748	25,073	19,811	16,047	7,132	4,012	2,567	1,783	1,310
1.8	1,697,338	424,334	188,592	106,083	67,894	47,148	34,639	26,521	20,955	16,973	7,543	4,243	2,716	1,886	1,385
1.9	1,789,810	447,452	198,868	111,863	71,592	49,717	36,526	27,966	22,096	17,898	7,955	4,474	2,863	1,988	1,461
2.0	1,882,090	470,523	209,121	117,631	75,284	52,280	38,410	29,407	23,235	18,821	8,365	4,705	3,011	2,091	1,536

EXHIBIT 21-1 *(continued)*

Test Sample Sizes Required for 95 Percent Confidence Level for Mailing Response Levels from 0.1 Percent to 4.0 Percent *(continued)*

R (Response)							Limits of Error (Expressed as Percentage Points)								
	.02	.04	.06	.08	.10	.12	.14	.16	.18	.20	.30	.40	.50	.60	.70
2.1	1,974,178	493,544	219,352	123,386	78,967	54,838	40,289	30,846	24,372	19,742	8,774	4,935	3,158	2,193	1,611
2.2	2,066,074	516,518	229,564	129,129	82,643	57,391	42,165	32,282	25,507	20,661	9,182	5,165	3,306	2,295	1,686
2.3	2,157,778	539,444	239,753	134,861	86,311	59,938	44,036	33,715	26,638	21,578	9,590	5,394	3,452	2,397	1,761
2.4	2,249,290	562,322	249,920	140,581	89,972	62,480	45,903	35,145	27,769	22,493	9,997	5,623	3,599	2,499	1,836
2.5	2,340,609	585,152	260,068	146,288	93,624	65,017	47,767	36,572	28,896	23,406	10,403	5,851	3,745	2,600	1,911
2.6	2,431,737	607,934	270,192	151,983	97,269	67,547	49,627	37,996	30,021	24,317	10,807	6,079	3,891	2,702	1,985
2.7	2,522,673	630,668	280,296	157,667	100,907	70,074	51,483	39,416	31,144	25,227	11,211	6,307	4,036	2,803	2,059
2.8	2,613,416	653,354	290,380	163,339	104,537	72,595	53,335	40,834	32,264	26,134	11,615	6,534	4,181	2,904	2,133
2.9	2,703,968	675,922	300,440	168,998	108,159	75,110	55,183	42,249	33,382	27,039	12,017	6,760	4,326	3,004	2,207
3.0	2,794,328	698,582	310,480	174,645	111,773	77,620	57,026	43,661	34,497	27,943	12,419	6,986	4,471	3,105	2,281
3.1	2,884,495	721,124	320,499	180,281	115,380	80,125	58,867	45,070	35,611	28,845	12,820	7,211	4,615	3,205	2,355
3.2	2,974,470	743,618	330,496	185,904	118,979	82,623	60,702	46,476	36,721	29,745	13,220	7,436	4,759	3,305	2,428
3.3	3,064,254	766,063	340,471	191,516	122,570	85,118	62,535	47,878	37,830	30,642	13,619	7,660	4,903	3,404	2,501
3.4	3,153,845	788,461	350,427	197,115	126,154	87,607	64,364	49,278	38,936	31,538	14,017	7,884	5,046	3,504	2,574
3.5	3,243,244	810,811	360,360	202,703	129,730	90,089	66,188	50,675	40,040	32,432	14,414	8,108	5,189	3,603	2,647
3.6	3,332,452	833,113	370,271	208,278	133,298	92,568	68,009	52,069	41,141	33,325	14,811	8,331	5,332	3,702	2,720
3.7	3,421,467	855,367	380,163	213,842	136,859	95,041	69,825	53,460	42,240	34,214	15,207	8,554	5,474	3,801	2,793
3.8	3,510,290	877,572	390,031	219,393	140,412	97,507	71,638	54,848	43,336	35,103	15,601	8,776	5,616	3,900	2,865
3.9	3,598,921	899,730	399,878	224,932	143,957	99,969	73,446	56,233	44,430	35,989	15,995	8,997	5,758	3,988	2,938
4.0	3,687,360	921,840	409,706	230,460	147,494	102,426	75,252	57,615	45,522	36,874	16,388	9,218	5,900	4,097	3,010

The differences between these two package concepts are considerable. Chances are great that there will be a substantial difference in response. Once the winning package evolves, component tests make excellent sense. Let us say the 9 × 12 inch package is the winner. A logical subsequent test would be to fold the same inserts into a 6 × 9 inch envelope. A reply envelope could be considered an additional test. Personalizing the first page of the eight-page letter could be still another test.

How to Test Print Advertising

For direct marketing practitioners who are multimedia users, testing print advertising is just as important as testing direct mail; and, as with direct mail, it is important that the tests be designed to produce valid results.

Gerald Schreck, as media director of Doubleday Advertising Company in New York, gave the following pointers on A/B split tests in an *Advertising Age* feature article.

The split helps determine the relative strengths of different ads. For example, run two ads, A and B, in a specific issue or edition of a publication so that two portions of the total run are equally divided and identical in circulation. The only difference is that Ad A will run in half of the issue and Ad B will run in the other half.

For measuring the strength of the ads, a split includes an offer requiring the reader to act by writing or sending in a coupon. Then you simply compare the responses with the individual ads. If done properly, this A/B split method can be accurate to two decimal points. There is also the advantage of real-world testing to find out what people actually do, not just what they say they do. And, because all factors are held equal, the difference in results can be attributed directly to your advertising (see Exhibit 21–2). Although the A/B split can't tell you why individuals respond to your ad, the technique can tell you what they responded to. A real bonus is that when you have completed your tests, you'll have a list of solid prospects.

EXHIBIT 21–2

Variations in the Uses of Splits

A/B Split	Clump Split	Flip-Flop Split
A	A	A
B	A	B
A	A	B
B	B	A
	B	
	B	

A/B Splits

In an ideal situation, an issue of a split-run publication will carry Ad A in every other copy and Ad B in the alternate copies.

Clump Splits

Most often, however, publications cannot produce an exact A/B split. They will promise a clump. That is, every lift of 50 copies, for instance, will be evenly split, or even every lift of 25 or 10. The clump can be very accurate when the test is done in large circulations.

Flip-Flops

For publications that offer no split at all, you can create your own. Take two comparable publications, X and Y. Run Ad A in X and Ad B in Y for the first phase. Then for the second phase, reverse the insertions: Ad B in X and Ad A in Y. Total the respective results for A and B and compare.

The Split That Is Not

We recently asked one magazine publisher if he ran splits. The production manager told us, "Oh, yes, we run a perfect split. Our circulation divides exactly—one-half east of the Mississippi and one-half west." Look out. That is not a valid split.

In the A/B split, how can you compare one run against another run of the same ad? Following are ideas for keying coupons or response copy:

- Dating. On your coupons, try JA320NA for January 3, 2000, in *Newsweek* for Ad A and JA320NB for the same insertion of Ad B.

- Department numbers. Use Dept. A for Ad A and Dept. B for Ad B in your company's address.

- Color of coupon. One color for Ad A, another for Ad B.

- Color of ink.

- Names. In Ad A ask readers to send correspondence to Mr. Anderson; for Ad B have them write to Mr. Brown.

- Telephone numbers.

- Shape of coupon.

- The obvious. Right on the coupon, use "For Readers of *Glamour*" in Ad A and "For *Glamour* Readers" in Ad B.

- Abbreviations. In your address, New York for Ad A, NY for Ad B.

- Typeface. In Coupon A, all caps for NAME and so forth, and in Coupon B, upper and lowercase for Name and so on.

The possibilities are virtually unlimited. All you need is a code that's in keeping with your ad and the publication, one you find easy to understand and use.

Insert Cards

Testing the use of insert cards with print ads can also yield important results. Sometimes the card can be turned into a full-page card insert. This is another way to simultaneously test multiple ads in magazines. Scores of magazines now accept such inserts. This allows for many different ways to test offers and creative.

Testing Hypotheses in Print Ads

It is important to remember that in testing ads in publications, you are looking for breakthroughs, not small differences. As Tom Collins, a pioneer in print ad testing, puts it: "We are not merely testing ads, we are testing hypotheses. Then when a hypothesis appears to have been proved by the results, it is often possible to construct other, even more successful ads, on the same hypothesis."

Test hypotheses tend to fall into four main categories:

1. What is the best price and offer?

2. Who is the best prospect?

3. What is the most appealing product advantage?

4. What is the most important ultimate benefit? (e.g., pride, admiration, safety, wealth, peace of mind)

Testing On-line

The growth of marketing on-line has added unique dimensions to testing. One of those dimensions is time. Marketers testing three banner ads, served in rotation, on high volume websites can sometimes learn within a day how well each ad is doing. They can track which ad had the greatest click-through rate (CTR), what site the ad was clicked on, and what action the user took as a result of clicking. This can be compared to ad server logs, allowing for volumes of response data to be created for broad on-line campaigns.

Marketers can learn if one ad pulls better against the others on one website, one category of websites (e.g., portals, search sites, etc.), or across the board. They can modify or change an ad or ads and test new ads on the fly. The low production costs for on-line promotion allows for significant variations in testing and real-time adjustments of programs to improve results.

Marketers using direct mail might have to wait weeks for results. Using print, the wait might be months. Television direct response marketers get fast input similar to on-line. However, the high cost of TV production makes it unlikely that a marketer would revise two or three spots that didn't do well, and retest them without further research into why they didn't work (e.g., Is it the creative, offer, spokesperson, product, etc.?).

On-line testing is maturing well beyond the banner ad. Organizations are testing customer migration strategies to move established customers from expensive traditional marketing processes to on-line processes. National Semiconductor saved millions of dollars by moving product sell sheets to its E-commerce site, rather than mailing out printed copies. More than 11,000 product sheets are downloaded every day on their website. With the potential savings of such magnitude, marketers will continue to test these methods.

Creativity and Testing, Not Creativity versus Testing

For all of its strengths, testing answers only one part of the equation. It tells a marketer "what" works, not "why" it works. To learn "why" different techniques work requires the use of research. This will be discussed further in the chapter on research.

Idea development and testing are soul mates. When thought of together, the options are endless. These options are applicable when marketing to consumers, businesses, across product/service categories, and across media. The two things to keep uppermost in mind are: (1) strive for breakthrough ideas, and (2) test the big things.

CASE STUDY: Yamaha Piano

Adapted from materials supplied by IBM for its Lotus Notes and Domino products

BACKGROUND AND CHALLENGE
Yamaha Piano had succeeded in capturing 40 percent of the global piano market. But just when it became market leader, the overall demand for pianos started declining by 10 percent a year.

Around the world, in living rooms, dens, and concert halls, there are some 40 million pianos. For the most part, the pianos just sit and gather dust.

Some American analysts would advise: "Get out of the piano business!" Instead, Yamaha used the technique of innovation—an important form of creativity in business—to create a new market for its pianos.

SOLUTION
Yamaha's marketers determined that one possible way to solve the problem was to add value to the millions of pianos already out there. In this exercise they remembered the old player piano—a pleasant idea with a not very pleasant sound.

Using sophisticated computer-driven technology known as "MIDI," Yamaha developed a player pro gram that can distinguish 92 degrees of speed and strength of key touch. With this technology, piano owners could record live performances by the pianists of their choice, or they could buy such recordings on computer disks. So now, for an expenditure of around $2,500, piano owners could retrofit their idle, untuned, dust-collecting pieces of oversized furni ture and have great artists play for them in the pri vacy of their homes.

Owners of 40 million mostly idle pianos became a vibrant market for $2,500 retrofitting sales. Computer-controlled reproducing systems have been a success for Yamaha. This very technology created a new interest in learning to play the piano. These sys tems are believed to be the only catalyst to enlarge the piano market.

Website Serves New Market

Most Yamaha Disklavier owners don't think of piano stores as a place to purchase music. Music stores don't typically carry Yamaha diskettes. Yamaha Artist Services faced this issue as it tried to find the best way to distribute music for its Disklavier digital acoustic piano. This music was only available on CDs recorded, produced, and distributed by Yamaha.

Since the introduction of the Disklavier, high-volume businesses and music professionals who are able to justify the significant cost of acquiring and maintaining a library of recordings have driven music sales. What Yamaha needed was a way to boost sales into the mainstream home market.

The answer was to create a website where this music was accessible to all who wanted it. The web-site, globaljukebox.com, added variety as well as a cost-effective solution to the distribution of Disklavier music. It is a "store" that is always open and acces sible to anybody, anywhere, having Internet access.

An added bonus is the exposure for music artists who deserve distribution but previously weren't avail-able through Yamaha's limited in-store service. "One of the things that is always on my mind is how to add

utility to the relationship that Yamaha has with pro fessionals," explains Eric Johnson, director of Artists Services, Yamaha. "My feeling was, if we could come up with a way of expanding the reach of a particu-lar artist's music to Disklavier customers, that would be added utility."

This added utility also includes a broader base from which to interpret decision-support data from customer interactions with the website. Yamaha has acquired the potential to collect complex data on its customers, down to the musical attributes that a par-ticular customer prefers.

Disklavier owners can go to the website and search for new music, say, in the key of G. When they find a piece by an artist that interests them, they can play a WAVE file to see if it's really what they're look-ing for. If they like it, they order it, download, and play it instantly. Another option is that the music can be played live on the Disklavier while being accom-panied by vocals downloaded from another field in the database, creating a mix of live piano and recorded CD-quality lyrics.

Yamaha's Internet catalog offers a number of search options. Users can search by artist, music style, description, and even by a phrase of a song.

RESULTS

The long-range success of Yamaha's Global Jukebox can be measured only by charting and analyzing activity at the website. MIDI sites generally require extensive support, receiving thousands of hits each day. Recognizing this, Yamaha plans to add new search capabilities gradually. So far, the system has proven efficient in its ability to allow complex searches of MIDI files for particular instruments because of an index-creating ability.

As traffic at the site expands, Yamaha expects to launch new search options and provide additional hardware to accommodate its growth. Although cur-rently running well on its current system, Yamaha plans to move to a larger server in the future to uti-lize the increased internal bandwidth without any changes to the application.

PILOT PROJECT This case demonstrates how creative ideas must constantly be updated as market conditions change or new opportunities arise.

Do your own brainstorming and think of ways for Yamaha to test new ways of driving traffic to its on-line Global Jukebox. Should it test promotion techniques, creative ideas, media, offers, etc.? Think of as many different ways of testing as possible. Then apply the concept of convergent thinking to evaluate, critique, and select the most appropriate ideas for Yamaha.

Key Points

▶ Direct marketers use the subjective process of creativity to generate novel and useful ideas, and the objective technique of testing to validate those ideas. Thus, creative ideas that might not otherwise be considered can be tested and proven in the marketplace.

▶ Creativity can be developed in all people and organizations using brainstorming and other creative stimulators. The degree of truly creative output is directly related to two factors: (1) clear and specific definitions of problems to be solved, and (2) the right "atmosphere" for developing creative solutions. Brainstorming addresses these factors.

▶ Avoid trivia testing (e.g., the tilt of a postage stamp, the effects of various colors, one graphic versus another, etc.) and test the big things: products or services, media, propositions, copy platforms, formats, timing, and new products.

▶ On-line testing provides results within a day—even hours. Marketers can learn if one ad pulls better against the others on one website, one category of websites (e.g., portals, search sites, etc.), or across the board. The low production costs for on-line promotion means they can modify or change ads and test new ads on the fly.

RESEARCH FOR DIRECT
MARKETERS

Over the years, the use of research in direct marketing has evolved as traditional and nontraditional direct marketing have converged, integrated marketing communications has grown, and marketers have sought to get closer to their customers.

Traditional users of direct marketing find themselves in a maturing marketplace in which the major competitors are experienced and sophisticated. Many market segments are glutted with products, services, and offers that are nearly indistinguishable from each other. Home, school, and office mailboxes are cluttered with similar catalogs and mailing pieces. Many have sought refuge from a barrage of unsolicited promotional phone calls with unlisted numbers, voice mail, and Caller ID.

Research can help marketers break through this clutter. It can help marketers better understand the needs and wants of their various customer groups and target them more discretely and relevantly. Research can help marketers develop new offers and refine their visual and message elements. This can lead to dramatic increases in response rates and enhance the marketer's image while making the sale.

Research can help marketers develop more effective prospecting programs by gaining an in-depth understanding of the types and numbers of "high-propensity prospects" available and translating these consumer segments into targetable groups that can be directly accessed. This could help reduce quantities mailed as well as mailing costs.

Research can provide strategic direction for growing traditional direct marketing businesses in terms of identifying new products and service categories with high growth potential, assessing the most dynamic segments within each category, and screening for the most viable products and services within each segment.

Research can help nontraditional direct marketers such as consumer goods manufacturers, retailers, telecom providers, and airlines identify the issues around direct distribution systems such as barriers to entry (channel conflicts, shopping habits, etc.) and key opportunities for success.

The nontraditional direct marketers can use direct mail to identify and test new positionings for a brand economically and discretely, without telling the media or competitors, and without disturbing their current franchise. They can develop targeted promotions to selected prospects and customers who provide specific measurable, projectable results. And, research can help them to develop mass customized communications that deliver discrete, measurable messages targeted to specific customer or prospect profiles.

Research and Testing: A Complementary Process

Since the inception of direct marketing, the primary method for assessing programs has been the "in-market" or "in-mail" test. The results produced by these tests are measurable, quantifiable, and predictable. They provide a quantified measurement of overt response in terms of "making the sale," "producing a qualified sales lead," or "stimulating someone to request further information."

By overlaying this overt behavior with geodemographic data, it has been possible to build statistical models that can define high-propensity response groups, providing far more precise methods for marketing and prospecting.

Frequently, research and testing are viewed as an either/or proposition. There are financial trade-offs in choosing whether to test or to use marketing research. Such reasoning, however, overlooks the fact that testing is an integral part of the total marketing research process and that marketing research and testing are, therefore, not separate issues.

The most important question concerning marketing research is: When should I spend money on marketing research? The answer is easy: spend money on marketing research before testing "the big things."

Direct marketers who complain that research has not worked frequently use it to evaluate subtactical issues. For example, they employ focus groups to respond to various offers or laundry lists of product attributes. As Exhibit 22–1 shows, this lower, subtactical level is where the test plan should be implemented, not researched. Overlay selections and specific offers should not be considered before a new target audience is defined and selected. Headlines and product attributes should not be evaluated without first developing a strong, relevant product positioning for the new target segment. Many research dollars are wasted on researching such subtactical issues.

Marketing research dollars are most effectively spent on evaluating strategic issues—evaluating the big things to be sure they are worth spending the time and money for testing. The use of marketing research in testing the big things serves two functions. First, it provides the basis for the financial go/no-go testing deci-

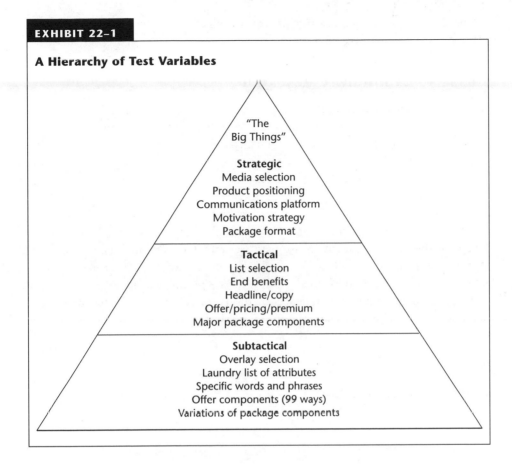

EXHIBIT 22-1

A Hierarchy of Test Variables

"The Big Things"

Strategic
Media selection
Product positioning
Communications platform
Motivation strategy
Package format

Tactical
List selection
End benefits
Headline/copy
Offer/pricing/premium
Major package components

Subtactical
Overlay selection
Laundry list of attributes
Specific words and phrases
Offer components (99 ways)
Variations of package components

sion. That is, the cost estimate of the research can be compared with the projected revenue and profits obtained if the test is successful.

Second, marketing research can serve as a valuable insurance policy against possible test failure if the strategic marketing variables to be tested turn out not to be "the big things." Thus the estimated cost of the research can be compared with the projected profit and time losses if the test is a failure.

The rest of this chapter demonstrates how marketing research has been, and can be, used to help develop and test the big things.

Testing and the Total Marketing Research Process

The testing process consists of four phases: (1) exploratory research, (2) pretesting, (3) testing, and (4) post-testing assessment. All phases of testing must be included in the marketing research process to achieve valid directions for the most effective utilization of resources (see Exhibit 22–2).

Phase 1: Exploratory Research

The exploratory phase of the testing process deals with defining and understanding the target audience as well as the marketplace in which you compete. The focal point of the exploratory phase is situation analysis, which deals with understanding the geodemographic characteristics of the target audience as well as its attitudes, habits, and needs—particularly those characteristics that are most influential on heavy, regular usage of your product or service.

The situation analysis should also cover the competition and market dynamics in terms of what attributes and benefits each competitive product or service brings to the market, and why consumers are attracted to them. The end result of this situation analysis should be points of maximum leverage on which a direct marketing program can be developed. Such leverage points usually center on special ways of segmenting a target audience, methods for reaching each specified target audience segment, and special ways of segmenting products or services.

EXHIBIT 22–2

The Total Marketing and Research Process

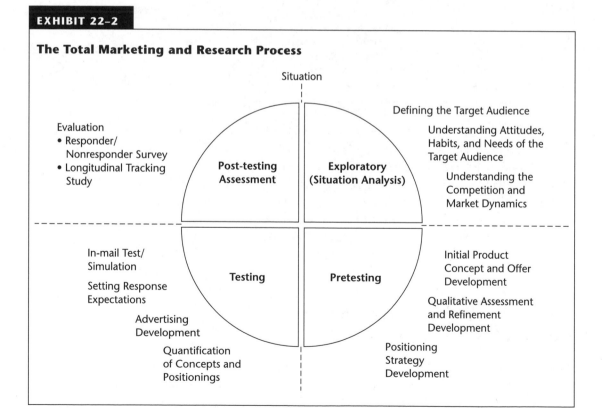

Phase 2: Pretesting

The pretesting phase consists of developing, assessing, and refining the marketing and creative products before in-market testing. Several issues should be addressed in this phase.

- Determine that your product or service is offering an attribute or benefit that the consumer really wants—that is, something that is preemptive, setting it apart from the competition.
- Develop and refine the creative and the offer. In this area, qualitative research such as focus groups or in-depth individual interviews can help determine whether the creative approach is communicating information about the product or service, and the offer, in a manner that is clear, believable, and relevant to consumers in the target audience.
- Research usually referred to as copy testing can be used to assess alternative creative executions, and offers. This research is usually quantitative in nature; that is, a survey is used to develop comparative profiles of the creative, and the offer. Such research is useful in two ways.

First, it helps to provide objective criteria for improving the creative or the offer, rather than giving them some subjective grade. Second, and even of greater importance, however, is that this research can reduce the number of alternatives to be tested, thus greatly reducing test costs and increasing the accuracy of reading back-end results. Research done in the pretest phase can often help to uncover variables or clarify issues that should be addressed in the testing phase.

Phase 3: Testing

One question asked by businesses new to direct marketing is: "When can we stop testing?" The answer, of course, is "Never." The testing process is dynamic and continuous (which is why the diagram in Exhibit 22–2 is a circle). The main objective in all testing is to learn, modify, and improve.

The testing phase brings together five key variables for assessment in the market, later called five testing.

1. The product or service

2. The medium or method of accessing the defined target audience

3. The time or season

4. The advertising/communication

5. The offer or promotion

The test plan consists of the combinations in which these variables will be tested as well as the determination of response expectations and financial objectives.

Although all of the elements of the test plan are crucial, the most important single variable in direct marketing is the medium, or the access to the consumer, because this access provides the strongest point of leverage for all other test variables. In fact, if the medium cannot provide access to qualified consumers in sufficient quantities, the rest of the elements in the direct marketing mix become almost irrelevant by comparison. That is why testing is so critical to finding the lists that will access high-propensity prospects in sufficient quantities.

An alternative method of testing is simulation, which can be used in conjunction with five testing. Simulation systems such as STAR (Simulator Testing Advertising Response—a system developed by Direct Marketing Research Associates and Erard Moore Associates)—predict response without running actual space advertising, package/statement inserts, or direct mail packages. Simulation can save time and costs by reducing the number of variables to be tested in-market, and often by eliminating the need to address variables or issues that are of little importance to the direct marketing mix.

Simulation uses a close facsimile of an actual ad or direct mail package mailed to a sample of consumers with a questionnaire and letter. Separate packages are mailed to test and control cells. Data from the questionnaires are combined with actual responses to the simulated mailing to develop a prediction of relative response performance.

Phase 4: Post-Testing Assessment

Post-testing assessment is potentially the area of greatest strength for direct marketing research. Assessment attempts both the analysis of test response and the development of diagnostic information in order to determine why the response rate was achieved and what can be done to achieve higher response rates.

The analysis of response rates is a measurement of overt behavior in terms of making a sale, a request for more information, or qualifying a sales lead. Marketing research can also provide diagnostic insights that can help to measure the quality of the response. For example, responder/nonresponder surveys can help pinpoint these issues:

- Incremental sales: the degree to which new consumers were attracted to the offer versus the sales' merely subsidizing current customers, particularly heavy or frequent buyers

- Competitive conquest: the degree to which competitive customers tried your product or service and were converted to regular customers

- Attitudinal shifts: the degree to which the brand image of your product or service was enhanced by direct advertising.

In addition, questionnaires, which can help provide much added value to both the consumer and the marketer, can be included in the mailing package.

The response to relevant questions about the product or service helps to establish a vital two-way communication, or dialogue, between the marketer and the consumer.

The dialogue can help establish a relationship with the consumer that can give the product or service a preemptive position in the mind of the consumer.

The information provided by consumers can be used to qualify or segment them, giving the marketer valuable insights into subsequent positioning of products or services, and more precisely targeting the appropriate message to the appropriate segment.

Primary and Secondary Research

Much of this chapter deals with the use of primary data, that is, research collected for a specific purpose. It is expensive to do primary research, but it is the only way to gain insight into the attitudes, behaviors, and drivers of an organization's own customers. Because it is so expensive, it is important to learn all you can about a market, a product category, customer groups, etc., before you attempt to do primary research. You can often do this with secondary data.

Marketers use a significant amount of secondary data, which is published, purchased, or syndicated research collected for some other purpose but that is relevant and can be applied to the needs of others. Secondary data is available from sources including federal, state, and local governments; trade associations; private research organizations; media providers; foundations; universities; and financial institutions. Much information can be found in the research section of a business or university library. Today, the Internet provides a key source for locating such data.

Many of the sources of secondary data are available on the World Wide Web. There are many search engines and directories that can lead to the information you are looking for. Some have specialized libraries of data that can help in your searches. Search engines such as Alta Vista (altavista.com), Google (google.com), Ask Jeeves (askjeeves.com), and Northern Light (www.northernlight.com) are important tools in beginning a search for information.

Learning good on-line search techniques is important to your success. Most search engines have a FAQ section and tutorials that help you learn the peculiarities of their systems. It is well worth spending the time and effort to learn to use the tools of the search engine that best fits your needs.

Organizations such as the Direct Marketing Association and the American Association of Advertising Agencies offer research services to members. Working with skilled researchers at such groups can be a real benefit to smaller organizations that can't afford full-time research staff.

While doing your own on-line searches may allow you to broaden and customize your search, it is still time-consuming. Having a professional do your research can yield more information and allow you more time to develop strategy, tactics, and meet your other responsibilities.

Direct Marketing Research for Consumer Products

In the past, direct marketers centered their research activities on analyzing consumers' geodemographic characteristics and purchase behaviors. Direct marketers used these approaches because these two variables are most readily linked with list and prospect selection. Attitudinal, psychographic, and lifestyle data have been much underutilized by direct marketers because these factors are not readily translated to list or prospect selection.

To realistically define, understand, reach, and communicate with target audiences, however, it is imperative that research deal with consumers on all four relevant levels:

1. Geodemographics

2. Psychographics and lifestyles

3. Attitudes

4. Purchase behavior

All four factors must be integrated to form pictures of "real" consumers: who they are and where they live (geodemographics); what their basic attitudes and values toward life are, and how these attitudes are translated into the way these persons live (psychographics and lifestyles); their perceptions, attitudes, and values with respect to various product and service categories (attitudes); and how these perceptions, attitudes, and values translate into selection-making in the marketplace (purchase behavior).

Positive Attribute Group

The Stone & Adler Study of Consumer Behavior and Attitudes Toward Direct Marketing was the first attempt to perform such an interdisciplinary synthesis. The study was designed, fielded, and analyzed with the help of Goldring & Company Inc. and the Home Testing Institute. Once the data were collected within each of the four levels, they were integrated through a software program called PAG (Positive Attribute Group).

PAG is a comprehensive analytical technique for determining the combination of purchase activities, demographics, psychographics and lifestyles, and attitudes toward direct marketing at work in the direct marketing environment. PAG enabled us to segment the direct marketing environment, and identify the four variables and their combinations that were active in each segment.

The PAG program subsequently produced six consumer clusters arrayed in an order (of importance) that breathed life into each of the clusters.

Cluster 1: Mailbox Gourmets. Mailbox Gourmets are the magical 26 percent of the population targeted by almost all direct marketers. In terms of psychographics and lifestyles, Mailbox Gourmets perceive themselves to be sophisticated. They want more of everything, especially travel. They are extremely active and involved, and perceive themselves as not having enough leisure time.

Mailbox Gourmets are affluent. Their demographics show them to be above average in education and income, and to be engaged in white-collar occupations. This cluster is also female-intensive. Although three-fourths are married, this percentage is slightly below marriage averages. The family structure is less traditional with more two-paycheck families or single professionals, particularly women.

It is not surprising that their attitudes toward direct marketing are extremely positive. They enjoy it, are comfortable with it, and perceive themselves to be experts when transacting by mail, phone, or Internet.

All of this information translates into direct marketing purchasing behavior that earns this cluster its name: they spend a lot (significantly more than any other cluster) and they buy often.

Cluster 2: Young Turks. In terms of psychographics and lifestyles, the Young Turks are very trendy, as one would expect. They also consider themselves to be—whether they are, in fact, or not—sophisticated and worldly. Demographically, this group accounts for 10 percent of the households, and forms a perfect yuppie profile: they are single, male-intensive, well-educated, and economically aspiring.

Although Young Turks are also very positive toward direct marketing, they tend to be cautious because they are emerging consumers. This makes them very "presentation sensitive." Because they are so active, they are more likely to order via an 800 number or Internet than any other cluster group. The Young Turks are the second highest group in terms of dollars spent and purchase frequency, but their expenditures are significantly less than those of the Mailbox Gourmets.

Cluster 3: Life Begins at 50. The Life-Begins-at-50 cluster comprises 7 percent of households and is completely middle-of-the-road in terms of psychographics and lifestyle. Demographics indicate that these older consumers are "empty nesters": Their children are grown, away at college, or married. As a group they are engaged in a mixture of blue- and white-collar occupations.

Like the Young Turks, the Life-Begins-at-50 cluster is also quite positive but cautious toward direct marketing. The cautiousness, in this case, is due to the fact that these people are the experienced "old pros" who have been shopping direct for 20 to 30 years. This experience has been transformed into a demanding attitude. They know what they want, and the marketer had better give it to them.

These data translate into direct marketing dollar expenditures and purchase frequencies just below those of the Young Turks, but the products this cluster is likely to buy are vastly different. The Life-Begins-at-50 cluster is more likely to buy higher-ticket items such as home furnishings or housewares. They are also more likely to buy vitamins and minerals and to belong to a book club. Young Turks, on the other hand, are more likely to purchase products related to self-indulgence such as electronic toys and sports equipment.

Cluster 4: Dear Occupant. Now we come to the great faceless, nameless masses that account for 14 percent of households—"Dear Occupant." Actually, they are the leftovers in the clustering process, and therefore represent those who were:

- Neither too positive nor too negative in their attitudes

- Neither affluent nor destitute

- Neither the lightest nor the heaviest buyers

As such, they are truly the mundane, the moderate, and the middle.

Cluster 5: Kitchen Patriots. When members of these households (23 percent of the total) are not out shopping at their favorite shopping mall or mass merchandiser, they are likely to be home reading the daily newspaper, a magazine, or their mail at the kitchen table.

In terms of lifestyles and psychographics, this cluster is the backbone of traditional American morality and values:

- They are extremely patriotic.

- Home, family, and community are extremely important to them.

- They have sufficient leisure time, which is one reason they shop so much; in fact, many of them have more time than money.

- Demographically, this group is blue-collar intensive, average in income and education, and indexes highest among those 55 years old and older.

Although the Kitchen Patriots' attitudes toward direct marketing are basically negative, they like to browse through their mail, including direct mail pieces, and catalogs. But because of their negative attitudes toward direct marketing, coupled with their propensity toward retail shopping, Kitchen Patriots tend to be nondirect marketing buyers or light, selective buyers at best.

Cluster 6: Above-It-Alls. Finally, we have the most negative, the proretail cluster, the "Above-It-Alls" that account for 20 percent of all households. They are nearly a carbon copy of the Mailbox Gourmet, with a major difference: they are antimailbox. In terms of lifestyles and psychographics, this cluster is career-oriented, active, and involved in fads and causes. It perceives itself as taking a leadership position and it is athletic.

Demographically, Above-It-Alls are somewhat more affluent than Mailbox Gourmets. They tend to be more traditional in household compositions. Wives are, more often than not, full-time homemakers—which, of course, gives them more time for retail shopping. This cluster also tends toward strictly suburban, unlike the Mailbox Gourmets, who are split between suburbs and cities. The Above-It-Alls' attitude toward direct marketing is basically negative. In fact, not only do Above-It-Alls like mail, in general, much less than any other group, but they also don't like to browse. In particular, they don't see direct marketing as a convenience. Not surprisingly, this cluster rates as nondirect marketing buyers or light, selective buyers at best. They want to see and touch the merchandise first, try it on, and obtain instant gratification both in purchasing and returning merchandise.

Using Attitudinal Research to Profile Target Audiences and Product Categories

Attitudinal research can be helpful in profiling target audiences and product categories. Such profiling is essential in two situations: new business development and expanding an established business.

For new business development, it is important to know who are the users within a category. Not only is it important to know who they are geodemographically for the purpose of list selection, but it is also important to know who they are attitudinally. Attitudinal understanding leads to meaningful positioning to the target audience. Thus the target audience can be communicated with in the most relevant, believable, and understandable manner.

For expanding an established business, profiling can provide an important perspective to the direct marketers by showing how high is up. Unfortunately, too many direct marketers are trapped by their house files; they don't have the necessary information to make the best strategic use of media when prospecting.

Profiling can provide these insights by allowing direct marketers to compare customers on their files against category users on a national basis. Thus, direct marketers can judge whether they are obtaining their fair share of the target audience pie. If they are not, they can fine-tune their demographics for media selection. Even more important, they can fine-tune their creative approach and offer so they have a better chance of being seen and read by their target audience prospect.

A marketer's first step in profiling and segmentation is to perform a buyer concentration analysis from its customer file, as shown in Exhibit 22–3. Such a buyer concentration study will segment the file into groups of heavy or frequent buyers, medium buyers, and light or infrequent buyers.

The second step consists of overlaying the buyer segments with attitudinal and lifestyle data, and then developing a second level of segmentation, as shown in Exhibit 22–4. This segmentation is accomplished by selecting a sample of names from the house file and administering a survey questionnaire containing attitudinal and lifestyle questions. By combining the answers to these questions with the geodemographic and purchase behavior data already on file, PAG clusters can then be developed. At this stage, two analyses are critical: (1) the percentage of the customer file that comprises each of the six clusters, and (2) the percentage of light, medium, and heavy buyers that comprise each of the six clusters.

The third step consists of developing a profile comparing your customer file and a nationally representative sample of consumers (i.e., a consumer database). This comparison allows you to determine whether you are getting your fair share of the following consumer segments:

- Affluent/upscale consumers

- Younger or emerging consumers entering the marketplace

- Transitional consumers who are changing their lifestyles and their purchasing habits.

For example, the comparative profile shown in Exhibit 22–5 points to a possible problem with the highest-propensity direct marketing consumers who are significantly underrepresented in the customer file. There could be similar problems if the buyer concentration analysis shows that a disproportionate number of Mailbox Gourmets, Young Turks, and Life-Begins-at-50 consumers are merely medium and light buyers.

EXHIBIT 22–3

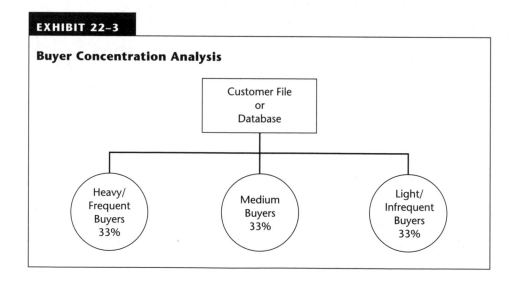

Buyer Concentration Analysis

Customer File or Database

Heavy/ Frequent Buyers 33%

Medium Buyers 33%

Light/ Infrequent Buyers 33%

Attitudinal and Lifestyle Overlay

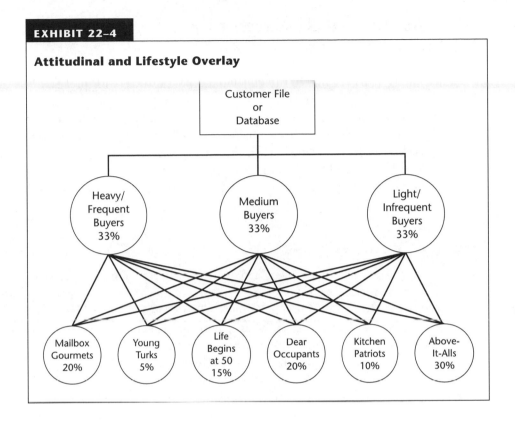

Comparative Consumer Profile

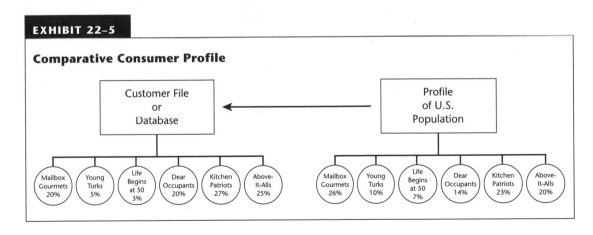

Using Attitudinal Research for Customer Segmentation

Attitudinal research also facilitates the segmentation of customers for precise file selection and developing highly targeted products, services, and creative appeals.

The use of national consumer databases can bring additional strategic marketing insights to your business when applied across a variety of product and service categories, as well as segments within these categories. (See Chapter 3 for a discussion on databases, and Chapter 19 for more about modeling.) Let us review some examples of such applications in three diverse categories: insurance, credit cards, and clothing catalogs.

Insurance Profiles

The Stone & Adler Study of Behavior and Attitudes Toward Direct Marketing examined both the incidences of insurance inquiries and insurance purchases (by mail or phone) during a preceding 12-month period. The total incidences of inquiries were higher than expected, at 25.9 percent. When the incidences of inquiries were analyzed by individual consumer clusters, it was observed that inquiries were relatively flat across all six clusters (see Exhibit 22–6).

Thus, inquiries were not skewed toward those clusters that were direct mail responsive. In other words, of the total inquiries, the extremely direct-marketing-positive Mailbox Gourmets accounted for 26 percent of the inquiries, while the extremely direct-marketing-negative Above-It-Alls accounted for 20 percent of the inquiries, which is directly proportional to their representation in the general pop-

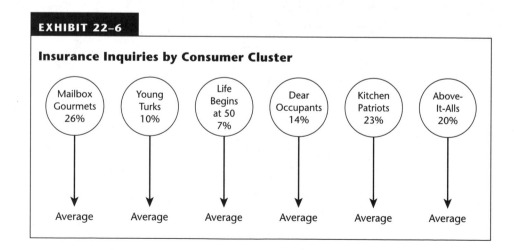

EXHIBIT 22–6

Insurance Inquiries by Consumer Cluster

Mailbox Gourmets 26%	Young Turks 10%	Life Begins at 50 7%	Dear Occupants 14%	Kitchen Patriots 23%	Above-It-Alls 20%
Average	Average	Average	Average	Average	Average

ulation. If the inquiries were indexed by cluster, therefore, each cluster would index at 100.

The incidence of insurance conversions by mail or phone totaled approximately 44 percent of the conversions, or 11 percent of the total sample (Exhibit 22–7). When the incidences of conversions were analyzed by individual consumer clusters, the same pattern emerged for conversions as for inquiries.

Conversions were also relatively flat across all six clusters. That is, conversions were not skewed toward those clusters that were the most direct mail responsive in other categories. Again, conversions were proportionate to each cluster's representation in the total U.S. population. All clusters would therefore index at or near 100.

The conclusion drawn was that insurance was one of the least direct marketing responsive of all the 26 product and service categories surveyed in the Stone & Adler study. However, the potential direct marketing audience for insurance is much larger than many other categories, because it has a less negative bias toward direct marketing.

But to take advantage of such an opportunity, direct marketers must strategically use research data of the type shown above to:

- Define the highest propensity consumer segments for each type of insurance product

- Understand the needs for each type of insurance product from the perspective of each consumer segment

- Communicate the positioning, offer, and benefits of each insurance product in a manner that is understandable, relevant, and believable to the targeted consumer segments

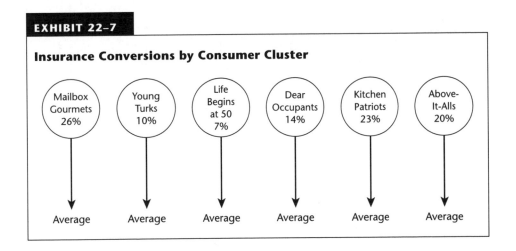

EXHIBIT 22–7

Insurance Conversions by Consumer Cluster

Mailbox Gourmets 26%	Young Turks 10%	Life Begins at 50 7%	Dear Occupants 14%	Kitchen Patriots 23%	Above-It-Alls 20%
Average	Average	Average	Average	Average	Average

Credit Card Acquisition Profiles

Credit card acquisition in the Stone & Adler study included only new credit cards from new credit card sources that were obtained within the past 12 months. Acquisition did not include any credit cards that had expired, and for which the company sent a new one. Acquisitions were based on either a solicitation received in the mail or a coupon sent in from a newspaper or magazine ad.

Acquisition profiles were developed for the four major categories of cards:

1. Bank cards such as Visa and MasterCard

2. Travel and entertainment cards such as American Express or Diners Club

3. Department store cards such as those from Sears, JCPenney, Wards, Neiman Marcus, Saks Fifth Avenue, and local department stores

4. Gasoline cards such as Amoco, Shell, and Texaco

The total incidence of bank card acquisition was 20 percent. As you can see in Exhibit 22–8, the incidence by cluster was heavily skewed toward the clusters that are the most positive toward direct marketing.

EXHIBIT 22–8

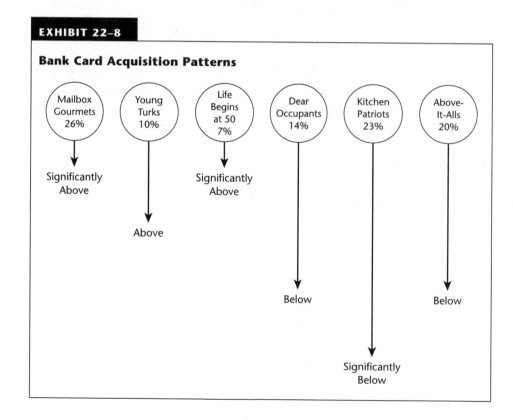

Bank Card Acquisition Patterns

The total incidence of travel and entertainment card acquisition was 5 percent, which was the lowest of all four credit card market segments, and a good indication of the maturity that this segment is displaying. Again, acquisition of travel and entertainment cards, for the most part, is skewed toward the most direct-marketing-positive clusters (see Exhibit 22–9).

The total incidence of department store card acquisition was 23 percent. This percentage was the highest of all four credit card segments. The same skewed pattern that we observed in bank and travel and entertainment cards persists, except that it is even more accentuated (see Exhibit 22–10).

The gasoline credit card segment also showed a degree of maturity similar to that of travel and entertainment cards, with an incidence of acquisition at 12 percent. The skewing of acquisition toward positive direct marketing clusters is the least pronounced in this market segment (see Exhibit 22–11).

In summary, when above-average acquisition patterns are observed across all four credit card segments, clearly the most positive direct marketing clusters demonstrate the highest propensity to obtain credit cards (see Exhibit 22–12).

What are the implications of credit card acquisition being so heavily skewed toward positive direct marketing consumers? First, there is a general need for

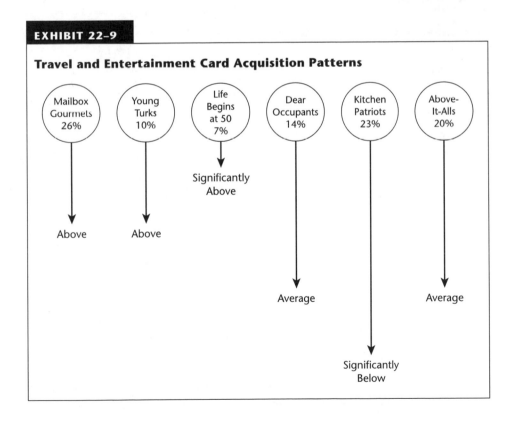

EXHIBIT 22–9

Travel and Entertainment Card Acquisition Patterns

- Mailbox Gourmets 26% → Above
- Young Turks 10% → Above
- Life Begins at 50 7% → Significantly Above
- Dear Occupants 14% → Average
- Kitchen Patriots 23% → Significantly Below
- Above-It-Alls 20% → Average

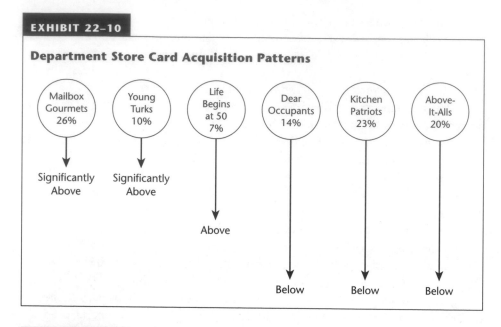

EXHIBIT 22–10

Department Store Card Acquisition Patterns

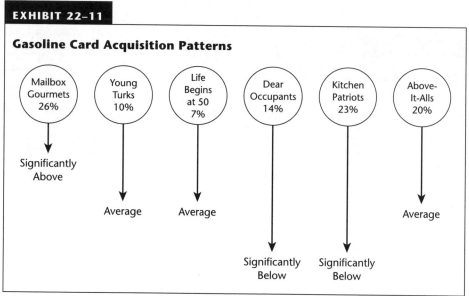

EXHIBIT 22–11

Gasoline Card Acquisition Patterns

credit. Clearly, there is a new need for total credit in the form of multiple cards, not merely one card. But who are these high-propensity credit card acquirers? Supplementary work in this area shows that there are identifiable, targetable groups such as emerging and transitional consumers.

Emerging consumers can be found in the Young Turks cluster and among the younger Mailbox Gourmets. Demographically, these are recent college or techni-

---

EXHIBIT 22-12

Above-Average Acquisition Patterns

	Mailbox Gourmets 26%	Young Turks 10%	Life Begins at 50 7%	Dear Occupants 14%	Kitchen Patriots 23%	Above-It-Alls 20%
Bank cards	X	X	X			
T-and-E cards	X	X	X			
Department store cards	X	X	X			
Gasoline cards	X					

---

cal school graduates, young aspiring professionals, newlyweds, and new parents. Transitional consumers can be most readily found in the Life-Begins-at-50 cluster and among the older Mailbox Gourmets. These people are undergoing major lifestyle changes such as divorce, remarriage, or a midlife career change, all of which affect credit needs.

Catalog Clothing Buyer Profiles

Respondents to the Stone & Adler study were asked whether they had purchased any clothing within the past three months either at retail outlets or through mail order (where "you sent in a mail order form or phoned in your order, and the item was delivered to your home, office, or elsewhere"). At 74 percent, the total incidence of purchasing clothing from all sources, both retail and direct, was the highest of all 26 categories measured in the Stone & Adler study.

As can be seen in Exhibit 22–13, the Mailbox Gourmets and Young Turks, the two most positive direct marketing clusters, demonstrated the highest incidence; the Kitchen Patriots and Above-It-Alls, the most negative direct marketing groups, showed the lowest incidence.

When we isolate catalog clothing purchases, a somewhat different pattern emerges (Exhibit 22–14). The incidence of purchase among Mailbox Gourmets registers significantly above average at 52 percent on an index of 200. Conversely, the incidence among Young Turks slips below average at 8 percent; the incidence among Kitchen Patriots slips to under one-half of their representation in the sample of 11 percent; while purchase incidence of Above-It-Alls registers a mere 5 percent, or one-quarter of their representation in the sample. Several strategic implications can be drawn from these data.

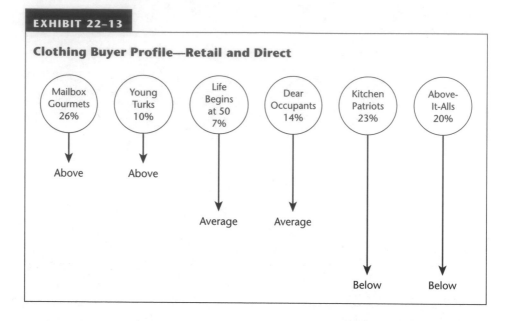

EXHIBIT 22-13

Clothing Buyer Profile—Retail and Direct

• Mailbox Gourmets are conspicuous consumers in the clothing category. They buy more at both retail and catalog. Unfortunately, the growing mailbox clutter is also centering on this group because Mailbox Gourmets are on everyone's mailing list. Research should be used, therefore, to develop intrusive catalogs and mass media advertising to break through the clutter and to develop unique types or lines of merchandise that will continue to attract the loyalty of Mailbox Gourmets.

• Although the Life-Begins-at-50 cluster exhibited the second highest propensity to buy clothing from catalogs, their purchases tend to be concentrated on a much narrower range of merchandise than the Mailbox Gourmets. Research should be used, therefore, to develop creative messages that motivate this cluster to try products they have not purchased by mail before and to select the merchandise with the highest propensity to generate trial.

• The underperformance by the Young Turks represents a major lost opportunity to clothing catalog marketers, particularly in terms of an extremely high net present value. Research could help by directing catalog marketers on the best ways of communicating with the Young Turks and reassuring them about the key issues of styling and fit.

• Although the Kitchen Patriots and Above-It-Alls do not represent a major opportunity for direct mail clothing sales, they should not be summarily dismissed by direct marketers. Since direct mail, particularly catalogs, is used by both of these groups as reference materials for retail shopping, direct marketing can be used effectively among both groups as a targeted advertising vehicle to increase retail traffic.

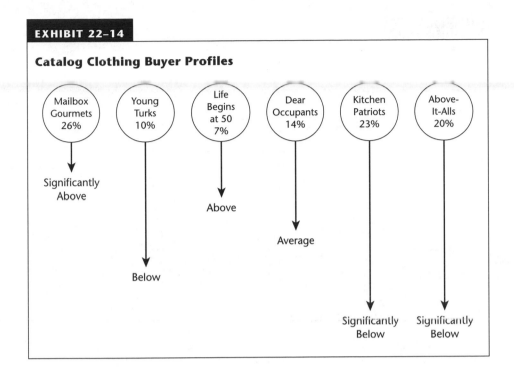

EXHIBIT 22–14

Catalog Clothing Buyer Profiles

| Mailbox Gourmets 26% | Young Turks 10% | Life Begins at 50 7% | Dear Occupants 14% | Kitchen Patriots 23% | Above-It-Alls 20% |

- Significantly Above
- Above
- Average
- Below
- Significantly Below
- Significantly Below

Research for Business-to-Business Applications

Many people ask whether the principles of marketing and research are the same for business-to-business products and services as they are for consumer products and services. After all, this line of reasoning goes, the people making purchases for businesses are the same consumers who buy television sets, automobiles, and toothpaste, aren't they? Not exactly.

When John Q. Consumer begins buying products for a business, the situation becomes much more complicated than it is for consumer products. In a business environment, he is part of a much larger, more complex institutional hierarchy. Thus, responsibility for the purchase decision, as well as the ultimate consumption of the products or services, is a much more involved process.

For example, regardless of the organization of the business, the target audience within a business will normally have at least three hierarchical levels (see Exhibit 22–15). The purchaser is the person responsible for recommending and making the purchase, whether he or she is the purchasing agent, office manager, or director of human resources. The gatekeeper is a CEO or chief financial officer from whom the purchaser must often obtain approval. The end-user is often a department manager in the production, accounting, or marketing department whose department will actually be using the products or services purchased. In fact, either the gatekeeper or end-user can originate the purchasing process as well as influence it.

EXHIBIT 22–15

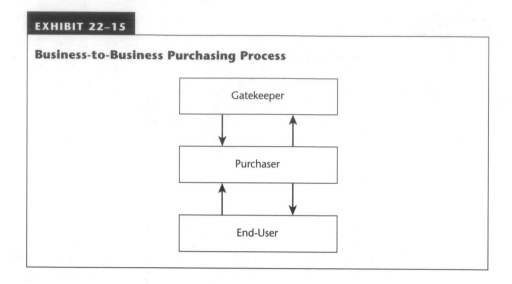

Business-to-Business Purchasing Process

Finding Qualified Prospects

To make matters even more difficult, there are problems with finding qualified prospects on each of these three levels. First, not everyone contacted is in the market for your products or services. At one extreme are prospects who are simply not interested in your product or service category or in the particular brand you are selling. Others who are interested in the category might have recently purchased and made long-term commitments, and will not be available for an extended time.

At the other extreme are a group of prospects called active considerers. Not even all of these prospects are available, because they must first be converted from prospects to serious shoppers.

Thus, direct marketers often approach business-to-business marketing problems by merely testing and retesting rather than carefully defining and thoroughly understanding each level of prospect audience being targeted. You can readily see why the odds of success are so often slight. Profiling, covered in Chapter 4, fills the gap.

Primary Research for Marketing and Creative Development

Sometimes there is insufficient information available for profiling, particularly when a new market or segment is being entered. Such situations call for the marketer to obtain primary information directly from prospects in the form of qualitative information (focus groups or in-depth personal interviews), and/or quantitative data (surveys).

The need for research relating to a new marketing venture arose when a large computer manufacturer asked Jacobs & Clevenger to develop qualified leads for marketing data-warehouse software. This software only ran on this company's minicomputers. While the company was a leader in the field and had a large installed user base, not all of the users were prospects for this product. A software partner of the computer manufacturer that would be responsible for servicing and maintaining the software had created the software.

Because this was a new marketing venture for the company, research was needed to provide a basic understanding of the attitudes toward, and the decision-making process involved in, selecting this software solution.

- How is the need for data-warehousing software arrived at? How is the purchase process initiated?

- Who is involved in the decision-making process?

- What criteria are used in the decision-making process?

- What information sources are used in the decision-making process?

- Research was also needed to understand what the effect of the computer manufacturer as an entrant in this market would have on key prospects.

Because the proposed target audience for this system were the Fortune 1,000 companies, the research process began with focus groups consisting of key decision makers for software systems selected from a sample of the manufacturer's installed base. A wide variety of industry groups were included.

To begin with, the exercise of finding the real key decision makers in the sample corporations became a survey unto itself. Often, three to five contacts had to be made before a decision maker was reached.

Because data warehouses are enterprise-level software applications, this decision was made at a very high level within the corporation. Jacobs & Clevenger quickly learned that there were multiple decision makers and influencers in every company.

This knowledge had major implications for the ultimate targeting, because the actual titles of the decision makers varied. In many large corporations, the Chief Executive Officer (CEO) was involved in the decision process. Because financial data would be stored on the data warehouse, the Chief Financial Officer (CFO) of the organizations was involved. And because this was a software product, the Chief Information Officer (CIO) was involved in the decision.

Research showed that traditional titles such as President, Controller, or Manager of Information Technology did little to reveal who the final decision maker was. In many firms, titles were unique, causing even more difficulty in identifying the decision makers and influencers. This was consistent with other projects that the agency had worked on.

Decision-Making Process

Regardless of the decision maker's title, however, he or she formed one level within a three-level purchase process decision matrix (see Exhibit 22–16).

The purchase process centered on the manager/director of information technology (IT) as the functional leader, the technical expert. Research showed that data warehouse software was considered a major purchase because it affected nearly every department within a firm. It was clear that the final decision would change in each organization. Research revealed there was no way to predict if the CEO, CFO, or CIO was the originator of the purchasing process.

However, each decision maker or influencer came at the process from a different perspective. The CIO wondered how the new software would integrate with the organization's other software, as well as how much time it would take to support and maintain the new software. The CEO's or president's involvement in the decision-making process tended to revolve around the issues of teamwork and process improvement in the operating efficiencies of the whole organization. The CFO was interested in cost savings provided by the data warehouse, as well as the initial cost of the software, installation, and maintenance.

The Marketing Environment

The introduction of this new software came at the beginning of the data warehouse evolution. The category was not well-known. Demand had not been created for this new product category.

Prospects were uncertain of their need for this type of software. They needed to understand what a data warehouse could do to solve the problems that they might be having. Therefore, the emphasis for most target prospects was on

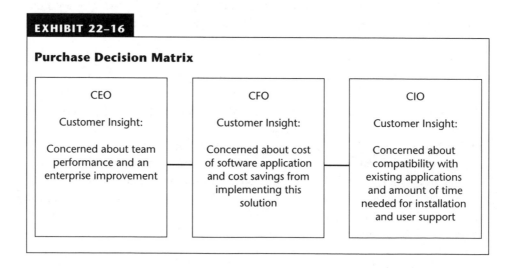

EXHIBIT 22–16

Purchase Decision Matrix

CEO	CFO	CIO
Customer Insight:	Customer Insight:	Customer Insight:
Concerned about team performance and an enterprise improvement	Concerned about cost of software application and cost savings from implementing this solution	Concerned about compatibility with existing applications and amount of time needed for installation and user support

educating them to the concept, as much as solving a problem they were not certain they had.

The procedures for purchasing software appeared to be ritualized and formal. Many corporations have ongoing software investigation committees. Purchases are often made based on an "approved vendor list" consisting of large, well-known companies such as IBM or Microsoft. (This company was on the approved vendor lists of most companies, but thought of as a computer hardware company, not a software solutions provider.) These decisions are of such high visibility that key decision makers tend to be relatively conservative in terms of not looking to be "the first" to try a new product or software application. One decision maker put it simply: "I have no desire to be on the bleeding edge."

Major Criteria for Software Selection

A major requirement when purchasing new software is system compatibility. Companies have invested a significant amount of money in their hardware and software; new products must be able to integrate with a minimum of conflict. This was true of the new data-warehouse software.

New software systems often require faster processing, more memory, and additional storage. This is one reason computer hardware manufacturers began offering software solutions; but it does conflict with a concern of prospects. It is a discussion point that must be addressed as part of the overall decision-making process. Decision makers expect to factor it into their final decision. It can often be a deal breaker when the costs are too high.

Most software applications have user interfaces. They are purchased to be used by managers and support workers rather than for data-processing staff. New software must require a minimum of training and support; data from the new software must be compatible with standard word processing, spreadsheet, and presentation software.

Sources of Information in Decision-Making

When looking for information on new software solutions, key decision makers tended to rely on the following sources:

- Word of mouth from peers in the field and other technical people at work, which are viewed as the most important source of information

- Marketing representatives and their companies' literature

- Seminars

- Trade publications

- The Internet

- Direct mail

A variety of other information was developed from the study:

- Reactions to concept statements describing the proposed software application and its features

- A gap analysis of buyer expectations versus what the product delivered

- Key user benefits as described by prospects

- A competitive analysis to determine features offered by competitive products

- A propensity-to-buy analysis based on this company versus competitors offering such software

Conclusions and Implications

The conclusions and implications on which the subsequent campaign strategy was developed revolved around five issues:

1. Educating users on a new category of products (data warehouses)

2. Credibility, or the ability to convince prospects that the computer hardware manufacturer understood their business category and had the high level of experience and technical expertise to offer sophisticated software solutions

3. Complexity of the decision-making process with multiple levels of target audiences, each having its own needs and points of view

4. Conservatism on the part of key decision makers because of the high visibility of the decision and the concomitant need for risk reduction through vendor approval lists

5. Compatibility with current systems in terms of both hardware and software

The Future of Research in Direct Marketing

The future of research will be dictated by the problems that it is asked to address. For example, as traditional marketing categories continue to mature, and competitors face increasing clutter, the problem of identifying, understanding, and reaching the highest-propensity prospects looms larger and larger.

Hence the major problem common to both traditional and nontraditional direct marketers is identifying and understanding key target audience segments. This is particularly true in terms of focusing on points of greatest strategic leverage and developing techniques to gain direct access to these segments. The problem is shared and must be jointly solved by research and media working in tandem.

As long as the disciplines of research and media are treated as separate functions, they will not be able to participate in the consumer insights and delivery process needed to address the problems of both traditional and nontraditional direct marketers.

As you can see by the integrated process shown in Exhibit 22–17, the process begins with research defining who the target audience is and why it behaves the way it does.

The primary purpose of this chapter has been to show the value of research and the types of research that can identify target markets and lead to well-executed direct response advertising. Conducting the actual research is best left to professional researchers. For the direct marketer, knowing what should be researched is imperative.

EXHIBIT 22–17

Consumer Insights and Delivery Process

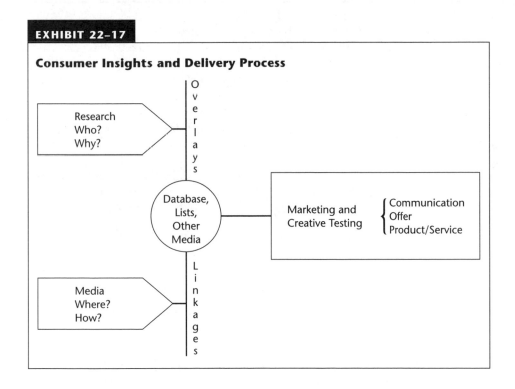

CASE STUDY: *Latina Style* Magazine

BACKGROUND

Launching a new magazine is a risky business. A new magazine needs to find a niche among an avalanche of established publications, all vying for readers and advertising dollars.

Anna Maria Arias had a dream. She wanted to start a magazine that would address the needs of Latinas (Hispanic women). The traditional media had long perpetuated a stereotype of Hispanic women as sexy sirens or as little gang members à la *West Side Story*.

Arias researched the market. She learned that U.S. Hispanics comprised about 10 percent of the U.S. population, or nearly 29 million—more than the population of Canada.

Annual growth of the Hispanic market exceeds 2 percent a year. This is higher than U.S. population growth at the peak of the baby boom era. The U.S. Bureau of the Census estimates that by 2010 there will be 41 million U.S. Hispanics. That year, Hispanics are projected to become the second largest race/ethnic group, surpassing African Americans. By 2050, Hispanics could make up 25 percent of the U.S. population, according to the Census Bureau.

CHALLENGE

Find revenue sources to enable publication of the magazine. A secondary challenge was to show depth and breadth of a market for a magazine for professional Latinas.

SOLUTION

Using research, Arias identified an underserved market: a segment of 3 million educated, affluent Latina professionals that had not been targeted by traditional media.

Armed with her market research and a dream, Arias went to advertisers to learn if they were interested in reaching this heretofore neglected market through *Latina Style* magazine. Advertisers like Nissan and Nordstrom were persuaded immediately. They knew that advertising in this publication would indicate they were interested in this market segment's business.

The use of research was instrumental in the launch of *Latina Style*. Without a clear understanding of the market, its potential, and its opportunities, few new products or services can be successfully launched.

RESULTS

Latina Style was launched as an English-language lifestyle magazine for the Latina professional, Latina business owner, and Latina college student. Its editorial highlights career opportunities; home and family issues; music, book, and movie reviews; travel tips; investment guidance; food and drink recipes; health advice . . . in short, all things that impact the quality of life of today's professional and upcoming Hispanic women.

The publication has a national controlled circulation of 150,000 and a readership of over half a million. It is projected to earn $100,000 on revenues of $1 million.

PILOT PROJECT   Suppose that your company acquired a product line in a category totally unfamiliar to you. No information exists about who uses such products or why. Consumer attitudes toward the line and competitive products are unknown.

Your assignment is to prepare a research plan that will provide the basic information necessary to market this product line. This plan should include a statement of research objectives for each project item, and the specific type of technique best suited to meet the objectives.

Key Points

▶ Research and testing are not an either/or proposition. Testing is an integral part of the total marketing research process.

▶ Marketing research dollars are most effectively spent on evaluating strategic issues—evaluating the big things to be sure they are worth spending the time and money for testing. Doing so provides the basis for the financial go/no-go testing decision, and serves as a valuable insurance policy against possible test failure if the strategic marketing variables to be tested turn out not to be "the big things."

▶ The four phases of the testing process must be included in the marketing research process to achieve valid directions for the most effective utilization of resources: (1) exploratory research, (2) pretesting, (3) testing, and (4) post-testing assessment.

▶ Secondary data can be obtained from federal, state, and local governments; trade associations; private research organizations; media providers; foundations, universities, and financial institutions; and the World Wide Web. However, on-line searches are time-consuming. Having a professional do your research can yield more information and allow you more time to develop strategy, tactics, and your other responsibilities.

▶ To realistically define, understand, reach, and communicate with target audiences, research must deal with consumers on all four relevant levels: geo-demographics, psychographics and lifestyles, attitudes, and purchase behavior.

▶ Attitudinal research can be helpful in profiling target audiences and product categories, especially in new business development and when expanding an established business. Attitudinal research also facilitates the segmentation of customers for precise file selection and developing highly targeted products, services, and creative appeals.

▶ Direct marketers should approach business-to-business marketing problems by carefully defining and thoroughly understanding each level of prospect audience being targeted, not by merely testing and retesting.

▶ In a new business-to-business marketing venture, research can provide a basic understanding of the attitudes toward, and the decision-making process involved in, selecting a particular product or solution.

APPENDIX: CAREERS IN
DIRECT MARKETING

By Laurie Spar, Vice President, Industry Academic Relations
Direct Marketing Educational Foundation

According to the 1999 DMA study "Economic Impact: U.S. Direct Marketing Today," direct and interactive marketing has now penetrated U.S. companies in 53 major industries.

All businesses are becoming aware of the advantages and opportunities. The ability to form ongoing relationships with 20 percent of a customer base that will provide 80 percent of the revenues is a big motivator in the acceptance of this method of marketing and channel of distribution. Virtually any kind of organization, from entrepreneurs and small businesses to Fortune 500 and 1,000 companies, can use direct marketing to sell products and services, raise funds, generate inquiries, call attention to issues, elect candidates, build store traffic, build brands, and generate leads for salespeople.

Changes in demographics, advances in technology, the popularity of the Internet, the advent of E-commerce, and increases in bandwidth are causing businesses to rethink their business practices. Career opportunities are vast. The rapid growth of direct marketing has led to a shortage of qualified talent. The individual possessing a basic knowledge of "direct" techniques stands a chance to enjoy a great career. To quote a motto from the Direct Marketing Association: "The future is an exciting place to be!"

For someone considering direct marketing as a career, there are two basic entry paths to consider: with a user or with a supplier.

A user either integrates direct marketing into its total advertising and marketing programs or engages in direct marketing as the sole method of fund-raising and/or selling products and/or services.

A supplier—most often a direct marketing agency—creates direct marketing programs for its clients. The agency or freelance person deals with a number of suppliers in the course of fulfilling assignments.

Employment opportunities in the user category break into two broad classifications: consumer and business-to-business. Marketing volume reaching the consumer can be huge. It is not unusual for a book club, insurance company, or tape club to mail in the millions. These companies expand their reach beyond direct mail with TV, radio, space, the Internet, and E-mail.

While on the surface the consumer route appears to offer the best opportunities, business-to-business direct marketing is really a "sleeper." In comparison to the unit-of-sale in the consumer field, B-to-B wins hands down. As a matter of fact, business-to-business direct marketing reached $696.1 billion in sales in 1999.

So, deciding which way to go—consumer or B-to-B—is a nice problem to have. You can win either way.

The constant emphasis on testing new ideas, offers, premiums, lists, etc., and the ability to measure the return on investment (ROI) makes direct marketing accountable and therefore different from general marketing and advertising. There's a constant opportunity to learn, along with an opportunity for advancement. It's fun, and it's never dull!

Careers in Direct Response Advertising Agencies

Job titles and departments in direct response agencies are similar to those in general advertising agencies, but the opportunity for advancement *can be* more rapid in direct. Trends in integrated marketing and advertising (where direct is often used in tandem with sales promotion, public relations, and media advertising) make the individual with the knowledge of direct response advertising much more valuable.

Depending upon background, interests, and goals, an individual can choose a direct response agency career in traffic, account management/client services, media, creative, or production. With increased sophistication, many agencies now have research, database, and interactive departments. Many agencies are "full service" agencies with additional departments to service client needs in teleservice, list consulting, website development, and letter-shop services.

Traffic. Traffic is an excellent entry-level, foot-in-the-door position, providing opportunities to advance into other areas. The traffic coordinator is responsible for coordinating the component parts of a total advertising project with each of the agency's departments.

Account Executives. Account executives are responsible for liaison with the client, involvement in marketing strategy, and coordinating with various other departments involved in the creation of the advertising and its implementation.

While a background in marketing, market segmentation, business, advertising, or communications is not necessarily a prerequisite, it is extremely helpful and frequently preferred.

Account Supervisors. Account supervisors oversee the effective day-to-day account planning, administrative, and client service support. The supervisor actively participates and develops marketing strategies and program development, acting as liaison between the agency and the client and supervising the communications between the account group members and other agency departments. The supervisor proactively develops new ideas and insights for client business; initiates and effectively participates in discussions, brainstorming, and planning meetings; and must anticipate, recognize, and solve problems through research and analysis.

A master's degree is frequently helpful for management positions, along with at least six years of experience at a direct marketing agency or corporation.

Copywriters. Unlike general advertising, which seeks to create awareness (often through clever, creative ads), direct response advertising must sell. The copywriter must have a thorough knowledge of the target audience . . . what it wants, why it buys, and how it reacts.

Direct marketing copywriters are really *salespeople* who must have a thorough knowledge of the product or service. They must tell what the product or service *can do* (benefits) for the customer, rather than *what it is* (features). The copy, along with the proper offer and media, is what does the selling.

Artists and Layout Artists. Those with artistic talents can find jobs as artists, desktop designers, and product photographers, working closely with the copywriters in developing the creative concept and "marrying" the copy to the graphics. Talent—as demonstrated by a portfolio and ultimately through experience—is positively required as evidence of ability.

Media Planners, Buyers, and Analysts. Some agencies handle all direct response media (mail, print, broadcast, electronic, and telephone), while others specialize. A background in media, communications, and sometimes liberal arts is desirable. Media personnel are responsible for the selection and purchase of lists, print space, and TV/radio time, as well as analysis of the results.

Production. Production personnel are responsible for purchasing print materials that are used in direct mail, catalogs, space advertisements, inserts, co-op mailings, etc. They should be familiar with printing techniques and processes (such as inkjet, impact, offset, Web, gravure, digital) so they know what is feasible and cost effective to use.

Researchers. In direct marketing research, customer acquisitions, purchase and repurchase patterns, and promotions (by product, list, and creative) are analyzed. The research assistant can help to determine the profitability of tests, conduct feasibility studies, help develop mathematical models, coordinate focus group surveys, and develop demographic and psychographic information. Research assistants can advance to managers and directors. In order to advance, an MBA degree may be required.

Careers in the List Field

List brokers. The list broker serves the list owner and the mailer (user), helping the marketer to select lists that will work best for the particular product or offer. The broker helps in the planning of the mailings, the analysis of the response, and the forecasting for future mailings, and is often involved in the clients' marketing strategy. Brokers are measured by their clients on the success of their recommendations. The more sophisticated list brokers engage in regression analysis and modeling on behalf of their clients. Entry level jobs are at the administration assistant level or that of assistant account manager (or executive), and lead to senior account manager and vice president/account supervisor. Client contact is part of the job. Account executives (AE) must be ambitious and eager to learn about new lists, pay attention to detail, and have good oral and written communication skills.

The Internet has opened a whole new category of lists for brokers: E-mail. E-mail "addresses" are growing by leaps and bounds. There are two categories of E-mail addresses: opt-in and opt-out. Opt-in addresses are individuals who have granted permission to be reached via their E-mail address. Opt-out addresses are not to be used by other marketers.

List Managers. During the past decade there has been a trend toward list management, whereby a given list broker takes over the complete management of a list for rental purposes. Under the arrangement, the list manager performs most of the clerical functions relating to orders secured by other list brokers. The commission for list management is usually 10 percent.

List Compilers. Compilers capture data from a variety of commercial and public sources such as directories and voter and automobile registration lists. The very large compilers have databases with marketing-oriented information on millions of individuals and households. Compilers must have experience in developing sources for names and a methodology for producing lists with a high degree of accuracy.

Careers in Database Marketing

A database marketer must be well-grounded in marketing and marketing communications in order to understand the value of data and the kind of data that should be collected to enhance a client's overall marketing plan. She or he should understand how the database can help the company address that situation, solve a problem, and create new business opportunities.

A basic understanding of computer hardware and database software is essential, along with an understanding of relational databases. The sought-after database marketer will know what data to collect and be able to think creatively ("outside the box") to propose the best marketing solutions to specific marketing problems.

Regardless of how technical the job, communication and listening skills are essential. The database marketer has to "translate" the needs of the marketing department to the MIS department or the service bureau.

Service Bureaus. Service bureaus perform sophisticated data processing and data conversion tasks such as merge/purge, personalized computer letters, postal presorting, model development and analysis, and list rental fulfillment, which require the services of individuals with a computer and technical background. In addition, they need sales personnel to sell their services to brokers and managers.

Careers in Catalog Marketing

You have only to open your mailbox (or your PC) to realize the number of catalogs and hence the number of job opportunities. Some mail order companies create their own marketing strategies, develop and rent lists, do their own testing, and so forth, while others work with catalog agencies. The individual seeking a job with a particular catalog company will have to do corporate research to determine whether to apply to the company or its agency.

Jobs in mail order companies can include titles like telephone order takers and processors; copywriter; artist; production manager; list manager; pickers and packers; warehouse managers; operations manager; marketing director; catalog circulation director; customer acquisitions and retention manager/director; customer service representative; database manager/directors; inventory director/manager.

Fulfillment. The "fulfillment" functions of the catalog/mail order business present some excellent entry-level training opportunities for newcomers who want to learn the catalog business.

Customer Service Representatives. Since customer service is critical to the success of *all* businesses, job candidates with such experience will be a step ahead of their competition, and the experience will prove invaluable throughout *any* business career.

Merchandise Buyers. A career as a merchandise buyer for a catalog is similar to a retail buyer. Buyers must have a good eye for merchandise and a sense of what their *customers* want. They should like to shop and to travel, and they must be good negotiators. Courses in merchandising are helpful and may be required by some companies. Catalog companies that design their own merchandise seek individuals with design degrees.

Entering the field as an assistant merchandise manager or buyer is a good start. In this capacity, the individual performs detailed functions for the buyers and gains hands-on experience in selecting merchandise, writing orders, receiving, delivery, and follow-up. Other entry level possibilities include sample room administrators and assistant catalog coordinators.

Circulation Managers. The catalog circulation manager, like the magazine circulation manager, is responsible for acquiring and retaining customers. (Also see "Careers in Customer Acquisition and Retention.") Nowadays, circulation staff must be involved with the lifetime value of a customer (utilizing the internal database), as this determines how much the company can profitably spend on customers.

The Newest Direct Medium: The Internet

The Internet is not a separate business, but rather an additional medium in a direct marketer's media tool chest. With many companies developing websites for marketing, sales, information, public relations, and brand and relationship management, there is an increasing need for agencies and clients to have the capability to develop and analyze the composition of E-mail lists.

Careers in Telemarketing

Telemarketing, often the subject of negative publicity, does have many advantages. As a matter of fact, in deference to a major function—customer relations—a new term is gaining favor. It is "teleservices."

One way to explore telemarketing opportunities is to look at a telemarketing sales continuum as a means of identifying applications (see Exhibit A–1). Another way to look at telemarketing is to explore some of the job titles.

Account Executives. A telemarketing account executive organizes and manages the client's program within the agency, coordinates scriptwriting, testing, list preparation, and client reports. Good communication, organizational, and analytical skills are required.

Creative/Writers. Scriptwriters are the creative people of the telemarketing agency. Different copy skills are required in telemarketing because the script must be written to be *heard*, anticipating questions and preparing responses in advance to prospect's questions. Journalism and creative writing are helpful backgrounds for this line of work.

Center Managers. Some direct marketing companies do their own telemarketing in-house; others utilize telemarketing agencies that have "call centers." It is the telemarketing center manager's responsibility to supervise the making or receiving of calls based on the client's marketing strategy, lists, and script requirements. The center manager must recruit, train, schedule, and motivate the center's "communicators."

Trainers. Telemarketing trainers instruct the communicators about the products or services. In addition, they teach listening skills and sales techniques. They

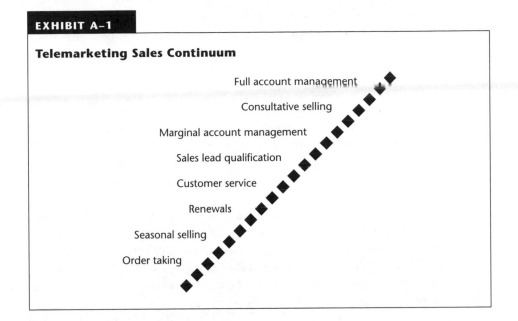

EXHIBIT A–1

Telemarketing Sales Continuum

Full account management

Consultative selling

Marginal account management

Sales lead qualification

Customer service

Renewals

Seasonal selling

Order taking

may monitor the communicators during the sales call, making sure all goes according to the script and making any necessary adjustments.

Telephone Representatives/Communicators. Communicators often work part-time and come from all walks of life . . . students, homemakers, actors, etc. For this reason, a communicator is a good entry-level job and provides excellent training and advancement opportunities.

Careers in Customer Acquisitions and Retention

Many business segments such as magazine and newsletter publishers (acquiring and retaining subscribers), fund-raisers (donors), trade associations (members), book and record clubs (members), or mail order catalogs, must devote significant portions of their marketing and advertising budgets to acquire and keep customers. Called "circulation," the art of acquiring and keeping customers is a direct-marketing-driven business. All media are used, including direct mail, telemarketing, direct response TV, home shopping, and DR print ads and on-line technologies.

An individual who has worked in the circulation department can make career changes to any of the previously mentioned business segments. They all have to reach the right audience and depend upon repeat business. Circulation is a very numbers-driven business, since testing and analysis of media, creative, offers, price, etc., are required.

In addition to marketing and advertising majors, journalism majors may want to consider the business side of publishing (advertising and circulation marketing).

Careers with Suppliers

Printers. Printers are considered suppliers to the direct marketing field and must have an understanding of the printing techniques so they can sell the services of their company to mailers. The printer with knowledge of ways to save the client money on paper and postage costs is in great demand and can be very successful.

Generally, larger printing companies have formal training programs and hire entry-level candidates.

People with printing backgrounds fill technical or operational positions. Such people often cross over to sales and, since they know the services firsthand, can become an asset to the sales force. Ad agency print buyers can frequently switch to sales, as they have a good understanding of the product.

Letter Shops. Letter shops perform a critical function for the mailers, and hence represent good opportunities for sales positions, as well as mechanical or clerical jobs. Letter shops, which can be independently owned and operated, or part of full-service direct response agencies, represent the final link in the direct mail process.

Your First Job

While many employers prefer candidates with some experience, entry-level opportunities are nevertheless numerous. Course work, internships, and outside reading may help fill the experience gap. And, while there are obviously many basic skills inherent to direct marketing (such as facility for numbers), employers seek candidates with leadership *potential*, strong initiative, good oral and written communication skills, and excellent computer skills.

They look for individuals who have good interpersonal skills (teamwork), who are flexible and dedicated and who have drive, *passion*, ambition, and enthusiasm. *Every* employer, regardless of the business, seeks those skills—regardless of the level!

Advancing in Your Career: What Skills Will Be Needed?

Since direct and interactive marketing play such an important role in all business, it's important for the newcomer to know what will be expected on the path to career advancement and success.

Leaders in tomorrow's business world must be global-minded, embrace technology by recognizing and harnessing its potential, and focus on the customer. Leaders will have to be creative as well as analytical, to determine new business opportunities by examining their databases and listening to their customers. Direct marketing leaders will have to have broad management skills, think strategically, and have the ability to integrate all elements of direct marketing into a company's business strategy.

How Do I Get Started?

Individuals with academic and, ideally, professional training in direct marketing in the form of internships, will have an advantage over their competition and a head start on a challenging and rewarding career.

If you're interested in pursuing jobs in this field, you should read books on the various aspects of direct response. Be familiar with its "lingo" and be acquainted with its techniques.

Read the trade press, do research on the Internet, keep up with who's doing what, with mergers and acquisitions, with promotions and career changes. Make lists of people and companies. Build your personal database. Do your homework!

Contact "prospects" for copies of their promotional materials and annual reports. Visit corporate websites. Interview for information. Visit the DMA websites (the-dma.org) to learn about facts and statistics, trends, news, publications, and resources. Visit often!

Several colleges and universities have degree, diploma, and certificate programs in direct and interactive marketing. The Direct Marketing Educational Foundation lists these schools on its website (the-dma.org/dmef), and further information can be obtained directly from the schools and their websites.

The directory, *The Direct Marketing Market Place* (National Register Publications), lists hundreds of companies in the direct marketing field by business category. Included are key contacts, addresses and phone numbers, and brief corporate descriptions.

The Direct Marketing Association's very extensive reference Library and Resource Center is available by appointment (212-768-7277; extension 1930). It's free of charge to full-time students with ID for on-site visits. (For others, there's a fee for onetime use.) The library contains a wealth of direct marketing information, including all books dealing with the subject, trade press, a database of articles, portfolios of DMA's award-winning ECHO campaigns, and much, much more.

Full-time students (with ID) can now join the Direct Marketing Association for a nominal annual fee. Among the many benefits is on-line access to DMA's library. Detailed information about membership benefits can be found on their website (the-dma.org/dmef).

Join local direct marketing organizations. There are over 40 of these (a list can be found on the DMA website) scattered throughout the country. Most of these groups have local Direct Marketing "Days" that offer wonderful networking and educational opportunities. Some also have student memberships and college programs.

Internships help you gain actual work experience in direct marketing . . . a chance to turn theory into practice. The Direct Marketing Educational Foundation and some of the local clubs sponsor internship programs. DMEF publishes a directory of summer positions. The directory is also available on-line (the-dma.org/dmef).

Full-time students interested in gaining hands-on experience might want to enter the Leonard J. Raymond Collegiate ECHO Awards Competition. Student teams act as direct response agencies, plan the marketing and creative strategies, devise the campaign, construct the budget, and project the results for an annual major corporate sponsor.

Valuable prizes aimed at furthering direct response education (including attendance at a DMA Annual Conference or a local Direct Marketing "Days" or reference books) are available for winning teams and faculty advisers. Honorable mention certificates are awarded for creativity, marketing, budgeting, and most innovative campaign concept.

Full-time juniors, seniors, and graduate students can apply for DMEF's four-day "Collegiate Institutes." These competitive seminars include the basics of direct marketing and direct response advertising and are taught by leading practitioners.

Along with other academic programs, DMEF also provides general career information and various resources for faculty members. For more information about the programs of the Direct Marketing Educational Foundation, contact DMEF at 1120 Avenue of the Americas, New York, NY 10036-6700 (phone: 212-768-7277; ext. 1329), or visit the website (the-dma.org/dmef).

Where Are the Jobs and How Can I Find Out About Them?

Although New York, Chicago, and Los Angeles are often referred to as direct marketing centers, jobs can be found in increasing numbers throughout the United States and abroad. Consult local classifieds and/or trade press advertisements and listings in club/association newsletters.

Several executive recruiters deal with direct response positions, but rarely at the entry level. Entry level applicants will have to take the initiative by reading local and trade publications, reviewing classified sections, consulting websites and reading annual reports, networking, making contacts with college alumni working in direct marketing, joining local organizations, etc.

Job Banks/On-line Resources

The DMA has a *Service Locator* on its website, a directory of DMA member service companies that can be a great resource for developing a prospect database.

Direct Careers Job Bank (the-dma.org). Although many jobs require experience, there are entry-level openings from time to time. Students can gain a good idea of job titles and required skills. Job seekers must register (free) to post their résumé. Corporate names are not identified, but information is contained on geographic location, required experience, and salary information (if available).

Direct Marketing Website (directmarketingcareers.com). This site links employers and job seekers in the direct marketing field. Most listings require experience, but there may be entry-level opportunities, too. The site also lists internship opportunities. Its *Additional Services* page lists links to other sites that can help with important information like cost-of-living comparisons, real estate needs, résumé preparation, and much more. If you're a "passive" job seeker, you can sign up to receive automatic E-mails informing you whenever new jobs are posted that could be a fit for you.

The Association for Interactive Media (AIM) (interactivehq.org/) lists job resources and contains over two dozen links to job banks. The site also contains a free E-mail newsletter.

A Word About Salaries

Dozens of variables for each job function make it practically impossible to quote typical salaries. Salaries depend upon the location of the company, its size, the job responsibilities, benefits, and so forth. Job seekers would be advised to consult local classifieds to determine the "going rate" or range for a particular job title.

Entry level salaries in direct marketing are competitive with salaries in other areas of marketing and advertising, but due to direct marketing's testability, measurability, and accountability, opportunities for advancement are much greater. While salary is an important consideration, it should never be the sole deciding factor. Responsibilities, educational and learning opportunities, and promise for future advancement are equal if not more important considerations.

Marketing Yourself

The various techniques you have learned throughout this book will help you with the most important job—that of marketing yourself. Just as you would do research before marketing a product, you must do research about your own goals, likes and dislikes, and strengths and weaknesses, and research prospective employers.

The information you glean from directories, annual reports, trade publications, and through personal contacts, will serve to make up your own personal database of prospects. The research will help you target your résumé to your best prospects.

The job hunter who uses direct marketing techniques in developing a personal marketing plan, creating the résumé and cover letter, and doing follow-up, can be much more successful in the job search. Similar to the way you want your prospect to act immediately and buy your product or service, you want that employer to act . . . by calling you for an interview and then by hiring you.

Remember that your résumé is your ad: your cover letter is your sales pitch; your interview is your sales call; and your thank-you letter is your follow-up. Don't do anything that you wouldn't do in marketing a product or service.

The cover letter and résumé won't get you the job, but they can lose it for you if you do not proof carefully, confirm titles of individuals to whom you are writing, and specify the job you want. Remember to keep your résumé benefit-oriented, telling what you can do for the company, stressing accomplishments rather than responsibilities. List only relevant information . . . information that will help you get the job you are seeking.

GLOSSARY

ABC (Audit Bureau of Circulations) Audits and certifies magazine circulation.

Action devices Items and techniques used in direct mail to encourage positive response (e.g., tokens, scent strips).

Active buyer Customers whose latest purchase was made within the last 12 months. *See also* **Buyer** *and* **Actives**.

Active member Customer who is fulfilling the original commitment or who has fulfilled that commitment and has made one or more purchases in the last 12 months.

Active subscriber Customer who has committed for regular delivery of magazines, books, or goods or services for a period of time still in effect.

Actives Customers who have made purchases within a prescribed time, usually one year; subscribers whose subscriptions have not expired.

Acquisition cost The cost of creating or acquiring a new customer. The maximum allowable cost of a customer is usually based on their lifetime value, less the organization's profit goal.

Additions New names, either of individuals or companies, added to a mailing list.

Address Correction Requested Endorsement printed in the upper left-hand corner of the address portion of the mailing piece (below the return address), which authorizes the U.S. Postal Service, for a fee, to provide the known new address of a person no longer at the address on the mailing piece.

ad hoc report A summary of computer information conceived after the master files have been created, usually produced by an after-the-fact reporting system designed for the purpose.

ADI (Area of Dominant Influence) Geographic division of markets by Arbitron, based on preponderance of television viewing.

Advertising schedule List of advertisements booked by media showing details of sizes, timing, and costs.

Affinity Relationships among customers and their purchases, lifestyles, etc. (e.g., People who travel internationally are often prospects for fine dining, wine, or luxury goods.)

Against the grain Folding paper at right angles to the grain of the paper; a sheet of paper will fold easily along the grain but will possibly crack when folded against the grain.

AIDA Most popular formula for the preparation of direct mail copy. The letters stand for (get) Attention, (arouse) Interest, (stimulate) Desire, (ask for) Action.

Airbrush Small pressure-gun shaped like a pencil that sprays paint by means of compressed air. Used to obtain tone or graduated tonal effects in artwork.

Airtime Jargon term denoting the amount of actual transmission time available for an advertisement on television and radio.

Algorithm A sequence of instructions that describes how to solve a particular problem.

American Standard Code of Information Interchange (ASCII) Widely used computer code adopted by the American Standards Association for transmission of information.

ANOVA (Analysis of Variance) In research, the results of testing the impact of a variable upon the desired response. If more than one independent variable is tested, the approach is called a "two-way ANOVA."

Art paper Paper coated with a mineral substance to produce a glossy surface.

Artwork Finished layout consisting of drawings, photographs, lettering, and copy.

Assigned mailing dates Dates by which the list user has to mail a specific list; no other date is acceptable without approval of the list owner.

Assumptive close Closing technique in which the salesperson offers the product or service with the assumption that the target has made the decision to buy.

Asterisk bills State laws that require telephone companies to advise subscribers that they can have an asterisk placed in front of their names if they do not want to receive telemarketing calls.

Attrition Model A model that predicts which customers are most likely to leave. Usually expressed as a percentage of likelihood.

Attrition Rate The percentage of customers who are no longer active from one purchase period to the next.

Audience Total number of individuals reached by a promotion or advertisement.

Audit Printed report of the counts involved in a particular list or file.

Automatic call distributor (ACD) Equipment that automatically manages and controls incoming calls, sends calls to the telephone representative who has been idle the longest, answers and queues calls during busy periods, and plays recorded messages for waiting callers. It automatically sends overflow calls to a second group and provides management reports on the call activity. It can stand alone or be integrated with a PBX.

Automatic dialing recorded message player (ADRMP) Machine that dials preprogrammed telephone numbers, automatically plays a prerecorded message (normally a sales pitch), then records responses.

Automatic interaction detection (AID) Program for segmenting a list from a heterogeneous to a homogeneous market.

Automatic redial Telephone feature that permits the last number dialed to be automatically dialed again at the push of one button.

Automatic route selection (ARS) Switching system that chooses the least costly path from available owned or leased circuits.

Backbone Back of a bound book connecting the two covers; also known as the *spine*.

Back-end Activities necessary to complete a mail order transaction once an order has been received; measurements of buyers' performance after they have ordered the first item in a series offering.

Bangtail Promotional envelope with a second flap that is perforated and designed for use as an order blank.

Banker envelope Envelope with the flap on the long edge.

Banner A graphic image, usually 469 by 60 pixels displaying an ad with a clickable link.

Batch Grouping of orders.

Batch processing Technique of executing a set of orders/selections in batches as opposed to executing each order/selection as it is received; batches can be created by computer programming or manually by date.

Benefits Features of a product or service. Benefits are what sell the product or services.

Bill enclosure Promotional piece or notice enclosed with a bill, invoice, or statement.

Bindery Place where final trimming, stitching/stapling, order-form insertion, and any necessary off-press folding is done.

Binding Finishing process that glues, staples, or stitches the pages of a catalog to the cover.

Bingo cards Reply card inserted in a publication and used by readers to request literature and samples from companies whose products and services are either advertised in the publication or mentioned in its editorial columns and feature articles.

Bleed Extension of the printed image to the trim edge of a sheet or page.

Block A subset of a *block group* that includes about 14 households.

Block group A subset of a census tract, usually no smaller than 600 people. In rural areas, is called an "enumeration district."

Body type Types used for the main body of the text as distinct from its headings.

Boiler room/bucket shop Term to describe outbound phone rooms where facilities are less than ideal for the telephone sales representative and sometimes for the activity itself. High turnover of representatives and low overhead for the owners are trademarks of this kind of operation.

Boldface type Type that is heavier than standard text type, often used for headlines and paragraph lead-ins, and to emphasize letters, words, or sentences.

Bond paper Grade of writing or printing paper used when strength, durability, and permanence are essential.

Book Catalog.

Booklet Usually, a small flyer-type promotional piece.

Boom In broadcasting, a semirigid, tubelike apparatus that extends from the headset and positions the microphone close to the user's mouth.

Bounce-back Offer enclosed with a mailing sent to a customer in fulfillment of an order.

Brand A name, term, design, symbol, or other feature that identifies one seller's good or service from others. A brand may identify one item, a family of items, or all items of a seller.

Brand image A group of characteristics or associated relationships that a consumer attributes to or identifies with a specific brand.

BRC or BRE Business Reply Card or Business Reply Envelopes are pre-addressed and have postage paid by the advertiser.

Bringing up the color Color correcting; intensifying color on press or in separations.

Broadcast media Direct response source that includes radio, television, and cable television.

Broadside Single sheet of paper, printed on one or two sides, folded for mailing or direct distribution, and opening into a single, large advertisement.

Brochure Strictly defined, a high-quality pamphlet, with specially planned layout, typography, and illustrations; also used loosely to describe any promotional pamphlet or booklet.

Broker Agent authorized to buy or sell for an organization or another individual.

Bromide Photographic print made from a negative, or a positive used as a proof.

Bulk Thickness of paper.

Bulk mail *See* **Standard Mail.**

Burnout Exhaustion and lack of motivation often experienced by telephone sales representatives working long shifts without proper training or compensation.

Burst To separate continuous-form paper into discrete sheets.

Business list Any compilation of individuals or companies based on a business-associated interest, inquiry, membership, subscription, or purchase.

Business-to-business Any business activities directed toward corporate or industrial decision makers, decision influencers, or buyers.

Business-to-business telemarketing Telemarketing to industry.

Buyer One who orders merchandise, books, records, information, or services.

C/A Change of address.

Call In telemarketing, this term encompasses uncompleted and completed connections, busys, temporarily disconnected, disconnected–no referral, disconnected but referred, and no-answers; does not include status of results such as sale/no-sale/follow-up.

Call-back Any contact required to follow up an activity.

Call center An organization's inbound telephone center.

Call forcing Call distribution feature that automatically directs a waiting call to an available agent. The agent receives an audible tone burst that signals the call coming through. A button need not be pressed to receive this call.

Call guide Informal roster of points to be covered during a telephone sales presentation that allows for personalization.

Call management Process of selecting and managing the optimum mix of equipment, network services, and labor to achieve maximum productivity from a teleservices center.

Call management system Equipment that gives detailed information on telephone activity and cost.

Call objective Clear reason for the call; the best calls are those that tend to have only one objective.

Call objective guideline Worksheet that allows preparation for the specific objective; often used in training and for new product introductions.

Call queuing Placing incoming calls in a waiting line for access to an operator station.

Case Complete and measurable telephone sales cycle from beginning to end (e.g., 100 names on a list equals 100 cases).

Cash buyer Buyer who encloses payment with order.

Cash on delivery (COD) Expression meaning that a customer pays for an order when it is received.

Cash with order Requirement made by some list owners for full payment at the time an order is placed for the list.

CASS (Coding Accuracy Support System) Offered by the Postal Service to mailers, service bureaus, and software vendors to improve the accuracy of delivery points codes, zip +4 codes, 5-digit zip codes, and carrier route information on mail pieces.

Catalog Book or booklet displaying photos of merchandise with descriptive details and prices.

Catalog buyer Person who has bought products or services from a catalog.

Catalog request Order for the catalog itself. The catalog might be free, there could be a nominal charge for postage and handling, or there could be a more substantial charge that is often refunded or credited on the first order.

Cell size Smallest unit or segment quantity of an individual variant within a test program.

Census tract Area within a zip code group

denoting households with uniform social and economic characteristics.

CHAD Change of address; also called *C/A*.

Charge buyer Person who has charged merchandise ordered by mail; or a person who has paid for merchandise only after it has been delivered.

Cheshire label Specially prepared paper (rolls, fanfold, or accordion fold) used to reproduce names and addresses to be mechanically affixed to mailing pieces.

Chromalins One method of proofing a color separation. Four separate, extremely thin plastic sheets (one for each color) are overlaid, producing a color reproduction of the separations.

Churning The practice of customers switching to another supplier based on special discount offers. Cellular telephone and credit card customers often have high churn rates.

Circulars General term for printed advertising in any form, including printed matter sent out by direct mail.

Cleaning lists *See* **List hygiene.**

Click The action of a user pressing the mouse button.

Click-through The action of a user clicking on an ad banner or HTML link that results in a new Web page being loaded.

Clustering Grouping households on a list according to geographic, demographic, or psychographic characteristics. A number of clustering systems are available from companies such as Claritas, Donnelly Marketing, CACI, etc.

Cluster selection Selection routine based on taking a group of names in a series (e.g., a cluster selection on an nth name basis might be the first 10 out of every 100 or the first 125 out of 175; a cluster selection using limited zip codes might be the first 200 names in each of the specified zip codes).

COAM Customer owned and maintained equipment.

Coding (1) System for ascertaining from replies the mailing list or other source from which an address was obtained, (2) structure of letters and numbers used to classify characteristics of an address on a list.

Cold calls Sales calls to an audience unfamiliar to the caller.

Cold lists Lists that have no actual or arranged affinity with the advertiser (i.e., they have not bought from, belonged to, or inquired of the advertiser itself or of any particular affinity group).

Collate (1) To assemble individual elements of a mailing in sequence for inserting into a mailing envelope; (2) program that combines two or more ordered files to produce a single ordered file; also the act of combining such files. *See also* **Merge/purge.**

Collation Orderly assembly of sheets or signatures during the bindery process.

Color print Printed reproduction of a transparency or negative, inexpensive but not of top quality; also called a *"C" print*.

Commercial envelope Oblong envelope with a top flap.

Communicator call report (CCR) List identifying for each telephone sales representative what calls were handled during a shift, the date, the contact name, and all information pertaining to the details of each call made.

Compiled list Names and addresses derived from directories, newspapers, public records, retail sales slips, trade show registrations, and the like, to identify groups of people with something in common.

Compiler Organization that develops lists of names and addresses from directories, newspapers, public records, registrations, and other sources, identifying groups of people, companies, or institutions with something in common.

Completed cancel Person who has completed a specific commitment to buy products or services before canceling.

Completed contact Any contact that finalizes a preplanned portion of a sales cycle.

Comprehensive Complete and detailed layout for a printed piece; also called *comp* or *compare*.

Computer letter Computer-printed message providing personalized, fill-in information from a source file in predesignated positions; full-printed letter with personalized insertions.

Computer personalization Printing of letters or other promotional pieces by a computer using names, addresses, special phrases, or other information based on data appearing in one or more computer records; the objective is to use the information in the computer record to tailor the promotional message to a specific individual.

Computer record All of the information about an individual, a company, or a transaction stored on a specific magnetic tape or disk.

Computer service bureau Facility providing general or specific data-processing.

Consultative selling Personalized method of sales that identifies a customer's needs and then sells a product or service to meet those needs.

Consumer list List of names (usually with home address) compiled or resulting from a common inquiry or buying activity indicating a general buying interest.

Consumer location system Market identification system containing information derived from Target Group Index and ACORN.

Contact Any conversation with a decision maker or any communication that advances a case toward completion.

Contact-to-closed-case ratio Number of completed contacts required to complete a case (e.g., contact mail contact would be a two-contact-to-closed-case ratio).

Continuity program Products or services bought as a series of small purchases, rather than all at one time, generally based on a common theme and shipped at regular or specific time intervals.

Contributor list Names and addresses of persons who have given to a specific funding effort. *See also* **Donor list**.

Control Last successful mailing package without any changes that allows a true measurement of the performance of each of the variants on test; generally used to test against new variants.

Controlled circulation Distribution at no charge of a publication to individuals or companies on the basis of their titles or occupations; typically, recipients are asked from time to time to verify the information that qualifies them to receive the publication.

Controlled duplication Method by which names and addresses from two or more lists are matched (usually by computer) in order to eliminate or limit extra mailings to the same name and address.

Conversion (1) Process of reformatting or changing from one data-processing system to another; (2) securing specific action such as a purchase or contribution from a name on a mailing list or as a result of an inquiry.

Conversion rate Percentage of potential customers who, through a direct mail solicitation, become buyers.

Co-op mailing Mailing of two or more offers included in the same envelope or other carrier, with each participating mailer sharing the mailing cost based on some predetermined formula.

Copy Written material intended for inclusion in the various components of a mailing package or advertisement.

Copy date Date by which advertising material ready for printing must reach a publishing house for inclusion in a particular issue.

Cost per inquiry (CPI) Simple arithmetical formula derived by dividing the total cost of a mailing or an advertisement by the number of inquiries received.

Cost per order (CPO) Similar to cost per inquiry but based on actual orders rather than inquiries.

Cost per thousand (CPM) Common rate for list rentals when fee is based on every 1,000 names rented to telemarketers.

Coupon Part of an advertising promotion piece intended to be filled in by the inquirer or customer and returned to the advertiser; it often entitles the bearer to a discount on an item at time of purchase.

Coupon clipper Person who has given evidence of responding to free or nominal-cost offers out of curiosity, with little or no serious interest or buying intent.

Creative Preprinting aspects of catalog preparation: design, layout, copy writing, and photography; used as a noun in the catalog business.

Crop To trim part of a photo or copy.

Cross-selling Encouraging existing customers to purchase products or services from other categories, departments, or divisions.

CTO Contribution to overhead (profit).

Cyberspace This is a coined word from the novel *Neuromancer* by William Gibson. The word referred to a computer network that people plugged their brains into. Today the word is used to refer to the Internet or BBS services such as CompuServe.

Databank Information resources of an organization or business.

Database Collection of data to support the requirements and requests for information of a specific group of users.

Database definition The clear understanding between telemarketing management and database management about what will be captured and displayed from the database.

Data capture/entry Any method of collecting and recording information.

Data processing Organization of data for the purpose of producing desired information; involves recording, classifying, sorting, summarizing, calculating, disseminating, and storing data.

Data sheet Leaflet containing factual information about a product or service.

Deadbeat Person who has ordered a product or service and, without just cause, hasn't paid for it.

Decile The portion of a frequency distribution that contains one-tenth of the total sample.

Decoy Unique name especially inserted in a mailing list for verifying list usage.

De-dupe *See* **Duplication elimination**.

Delinquent Person who has fallen behind or has stopped scheduled payment for a product or service.

Delivery Method of oral presentation used (e.g., businesslike, informal, formal).

Delivery date Date a list user or designated representative of the list user receives a specific list order from the list owner.

Demographics Description of the vital statistics of an audience or population; includes personal characteristics, name, title, occupation, address, phone number, etc.

Direct mail Printed matter usually carrying a sales message or announcement designed to elicit a response from a carefully selected consumer or business market.

Direct mail advertising Any promotional effort using the Postal Service, or other direct delivery service, for distribution of the advertising message.

Direct Marketing Association (DMA) Organization representing special interests of those in the business of direct marketing.

Direct response Advertising through any medium inviting direct response by any measurable means (mail, telephone, walk-in, etc.).

DMA Mail Preference Service Service provided by the Direct Marketing Association that allows consumers to request that their names be added to or deleted from mailing lists.

Donor list List of persons who have given money to one or more charitable organizations. *See also* **Contributor list**.

Doubling day Point in time established by previous experience by which 50 percent of all returns to a mailing will normally have been received.

Drop closing Process of completing a sale by initially offering top-of-the-line items or services and then adjusting the offer to a lower range of prices.

Drop date *See* **Final date**.

Drop out Deletion of type from all four colors, resulting in "white" type.

Drop ship Fulfillment function whereby the manufacturer of the product does the actual shipping of the item to the customer.

Dummy (1) Mock-up giving a preview of a printed piece, showing placement of the material to be printed; (2) fictitious name with a mailable address inserted into a mailing list to verify usage of that list.

Dummy name Fictitious name and address inserted into a mailing list to verify usage of that list; also known as a *sleeper*.

Duplicate Two or more identical name-and-address records.

Duplication elimination Specific kind of controlled duplication providing that no matter how many times a name and address is on a list or how many lists contain that name and address, it will be accepted for mailing only once by that mailer; also known as *dupe elimination* or *de-duping*.

800 service Inbound long-distance service that is free to the caller and paid for by the recipient.

E-mail Short for *electronic mail*, the transmission of messages over computer networks. The messages can be entered from a keyboard, PDA, mobile telephone, or electronic files stored on a disk.

Enamel Coated paper that has a glossy finish.

Enhancement Using compiled and proprietary data to upgrade information contained in a list or database. Often referred to as *"appending" data*.

Envelope stuffer Any advertising or promotional material enclosed with business letters, statements, or invoices.

Ergonomics Study of the problems of people adjusting to their environment, especially seeking to adapt work or working conditions to suit the workers.

Exchange Arrangement whereby two mailers exchange equal numbers of mailing list names.

Exhibition list List of people who have registered as attendees at trade or consumer exhibitions.

Expiration Subscription that is not renewed.

Expiration date Date on which a subscription expires.

Expire Former customer who is no longer an active buyer.

File maintenance Activity of keeping a file up to date by adding, changing, or deleting data. *See also* **List maintenance** and **Update**.

Fill-in Name, address, or words added to a preprinted letter.

Film positive Photographic print on transparent film taken from artwork for use by the printer.

Final date Targeted date for mail to be in the hands of those to whom it is addressed.

Finished size Overall dimensions of a piece of printed matter after folding and other procedures have been completed.

First-class letter contract Post office service for mailers that consist of at least 5,000 identical items, can sort into towns, and require first-class service; offers discounts of up to 12 percent.

First-time buyer Person who buys a product or service from a specific company for the first time.

Fixed field Way of laying out, or formatting, list information in a computer file that puts every piece of data in a specific position relative to every other piece of data. If a piece of data is missing from an individual record, or if its assigned space is not completely used, that space is not filled. Any piece of data exceeding its assigned space limitation must be abbreviated or contracted.

Fixed lists Cost per sale including all other costs except promotions.

Flag Computerized means of identifying data added to a file; usage of a list segment by a given mailer.

Flat Paper industry's term for unprinted paper adopted by the direct mail industry to refer either to unprinted paper or, more particularly, to printed paper prior to folding.

Flat charge Fixed cost for the sum total of a rental list; usually applies to smaller lists.

Flat file A computer readable file that contains no information in any field about the order in which to read records. Also known as a *sequential file*.

Flight A given mailing, particularly when multiple drops are to be made on different days to reduce the number arriving at one company at one time.

Focus Group A moderated session, where a group of prospects or customers are assembled to discuss a product or service. The results are qualitative, but useful in learning what consumers think about a product, a company, or an advertising message.

Folio Page number as it appears on a printed page.

Follow-up contact Any contact required to finalize a previous commitment or to close a transaction.

Follow-up system Part of an automated telemarketing system that keeps track of calls that should be recycled into the outgoing program and rescheduled at a later time; its purpose is to trap information and release it to communicators at the appropriate time.

Foreign mail Lists of householders and businesses outside the United States.

Format Size, style, type page, margins, printing requirements, and the like that are characteristic of a publication.

Former buyer Person who has bought one or more times from a company but has made no purchase in the last 12 months.

Fortune 1,000 Thousand largest industrial companies in the United States, as published by *Fortune* magazine; almost all have sales volumes per year of over $1 billion.

Fortune 300 *Fortune* magazine's selection of the 50 largest companies in 6 classifications: banking, retailing, wholesaling, insurance, construction, and utilities.

Four-line address Typical individual-name list with at-business addresses that require a minimum of four lines: name of individual; name of company; local address; and city, state, and zip code.

Four-up, three-up, two-up Number of similar items printed on one sheet of paper (e.g., four-up indicates the sheet will be guillotined to print four finished articles). Also called *four-to-view*, *three-to-view*, etc.

Freelancer Independent artist, writer, or photographer who is not on staff but works on a per-project or hourly rate as the need arises.

Free-ride *See* **Envelope stuffer** and **Piggy-back**.

Free-standing insert (FSI) Promotional piece loosely inserted or nested in a newspaper or magazine.

Frequency Number of times an individual has ordered within a specific period of time. *See also* **Monetary value** and **Recency**.

Friend of a friend Name of someone thought to be interested in a specific advertiser's product or service; submitted by a third party.

Front-end Activities necessary, or the measurement of direct marketing activities, to obtain an order.

Fulfillment Process of supplying goods after an order has been received.

Fund-raising list List of individuals or companies based on a known contribution to one or more fund-raising appeals.

Galley listing or **sheet list** Printout of list data on sheets, usually in zip code or alphabetic order.

Galleys Proofs of typesetting in column width taken before page make-up.

Gathering Assembly of folded signatures into correct sequence.

Genderization Program run to add gender to mailing lists (based on first names where available).

Geocoding The process of assigning geographic designations to name and address records.

Geodemographics Census data appended to a household file once it has been geocoded. This includes variables such as income, education, home type, etc. Derived from census data reported for the neighborhood of the household.

Geographics Any method of subdividing a list based on geographic or political subdivisions (zip codes, sectional centers, cities, counties, states, regions).

Gift buyer One who buys a product or service for another.

Giftees List of individuals sent gifts or magazines by mail, by friends, donors, or business firms. Giftees are not truly mail order buyers; rather they are mail order recipients and beneficiaries.

Gimmick Attention-getting device, usually dimensional, attached to a direct mail printed piece.

Governments Often-overlooked source of lists (e.g., lists of cars, homes, dogs, bankers, hairdressers, plumbers, veterinarians, buyers, subscribers, inquirers, TV stations, ham operators, and CBs).

Grid test Means of testing more than one variable at the same time; a useful method for testing different offers by different packages over a group of prospect lists.

Groundwood pulp Paper that contains wood pulp.

Groups Number of individuals having a unifying relationship, (e.g., club, association, membership, church, fraternal order, political group, sporting group, collector group, travel group, singing group).

Guarantee Pledge of satisfaction made by the seller to the buyer and specifying the terms by which the seller will make good his pledge.

Gummed label *See* **Label, gummed**.

Half-life Formula for estimating the total response to be expected from a direct response effort shortly after the first responses are received; makes valid continuation decisions possible based on statistically valid partial data.

Halftone Photograph or other tonal illustration reproduced by lines of small dots.

Handling charge Fixed charge added per segment for special list requests; also shows up as part of shipping and handling charges for transportation of labels, cards, sheets, or tape.

Hard copy Printout on a sheet list or galley of all data available on a magnetic source such as a tape, hard disk, or floppy disk.

Head of family From telephone or car data, the name and sex of the individual on the registration file.

Headline Primary wording utilized to induce a direct marketing recipient to read and react.

Heat transfer Form of label that transfers reverse carbon images on the back of a sheet of mailing pieces by means of heat and pressure.

High-Potential/Immediate Need Any case that requires immediate contact by the outside sales force.

High school student list Several compilers provide lists of high school juniors and seniors with their home addresses; original data, usually printed phone rosters, are not available for all schools or localities.

High-ticket buyer Buyer who has purchased expensive items by mail.

Hit Name appearing on two or more mailing lists.

Home office For major businesses, the executive or home office location as differentiated from the location of branch offices or plants.

Homogenization Unfortunate and misleading combination of responses from various sources; often the use of a single "average" response for a mailing made to customers and prospects alike.

Hot line Most recent buyers on a list that undergoes periodic updating. (Those who have just purchased by mail are the most likely buyers of other products and services by mail.)

Hot-line list The most recent names available on a specific list, but no older than three months; use of the term *hot-line* should be modified weekly, monthly, etc.

Households (HH) Homes selectable on a demographic basis; householders (consumers) can be selectable on a psychographic basis.

House list Any list of names owned by a company as a result of compilation, inquiry or buyer action or acquisition, that is used to promote that company's products or services.

House list duplicate Duplication of name-and-address records between the list user's own lists and any list being mailed by the list user on a one-time use arrangement.

HTML (Hypertext Markup Language) The standard set of formatting codes that are inserted into a text file to be published on the World Wide Web. These codes affect how the text in the file will be displayed when viewed.

Hypertext Text that includes hot links to other text or files, which allows the reader to easily access information by merely moving to and clicking on the hotlinked word, phrase, or image.

In-house Related to services or products that can be furnished by the advertiser (e.g., in house lists, in-house print).

In-house telemarketing Telemarketing done within a company as a primary or supplementary method of marketing and selling that company's own products.

Inactive buyer Buyer who has not placed an order or responded during a specified period.

Inbound calls Calls that come into a tele-marketing center.

Inbound telesales A department within a telemarketing operation devoted to the handling of incoming calls.

Income Perhaps the most important demographic selection factor on consumer files. Major compiled files provide surprisingly accurate individual family incomes up to about $40,000. Incomes can be selected in $1,000 increments; counts are available by income ranges for every zip code.

Incoming specialist Trained professional telephone specialist skilled at handling incoming order requests and cross-selling or up-selling to close a sale.

Indexing Creation of a standard, say, 100 percent of recovery of promotion cost, to allow comparison between mailings of different sizes.

Indicia The required indication in the area usually reserved for the postage stamp designating the type of mailing.

Individual Most mailings are made to individuals, although all occupant or resident mail is, in effect, to an address only. A portion of business mail is addressed to the establishment (by name and address) only, or to a title and not to an individual.

Influentials In business mail order, those executives who have decision-making power on what and when to buy; those who exercise clout in their business classification or community; in consumer mail, those individuals (executive, professionals, educators, clergy, etc.) who make a difference in their localities or workplaces.

Initial source code Code for the source that brought the name to the customer file for the first time.

Ink-jet Computer-generated ink printer that applies ink through a small orifice to form characters; often used for purposes of personalization.

Input data Original data, usually in hard copy form, to be converted and added to a given file. Also, taped lists made ready for a merge/purge or for a databank.

Inquiry (1) Request for literature or other information about a product or service; (2) response in the form of an inquiry for more information or for a copy of a catalog.

Inset Leaflet or other printed material bound in with the pages of a publication rather than inserted loose.

Insert Leaflet or other printed material inserted loose in a publication or mailing package.

Installment buyer Person who orders goods or services and pays for them in two or more periodic payments after their delivery.

Insurance lists Lists of people who have inquired about or purchased various forms of insurance; lists of insurance agents, brokers, adjustors, executives.

Intelpost Royal Mail electronic transmission service for copy, artwork, and other urgent documents.

International 800 service Telephone service allowing toll-free calls to another country.

Internet A large network of networks and computers, all of which use the Internet protocol. The Internet was first developed by the U.S. Department of Defense in the 1960s and 1970s.

Intralist duplication Duplication of name and address records within a given list.

Italic Sloping version of a typeface, usually used for emphasis.

Item In the selection process for a mail order list, term denoting the type of goods or service purchased; in input terms, it is a part of a record to be converted.

JPEG (Joint Photographic Experts Group) An image file format commonly used for ad banners.

Julian dating Three-digit numerical system for date-stamping a transaction by day: January 1 is 001, December 31 is 365.

Key code Means of identifying a given promotional effort so that responses can be identified and tracked.

Key code (generic) Form of hierarchical coding by which promotional vehicles can be analyzed within type of media—newspapers, magazines, Sunday supplements, freestanding stuffers, mailing-lists, radio promotion, TV promotion, takeovers, and so on.

Key code (key) Group of letters and/or numbers, colors, or other markings, used to measure the specific effectiveness of media, lists, advertisements, offers, etc., or any parts thereof.

Keystroke Means of converting hard copy to machine-readable form through a keyboard or similar means.

Key verifying For 100 percent accuracy, having two operators at the data-entry stage enter the same data.

Kill To delete a record from a file.

Label Slip of paper containing the name and address of the recipient that is applied to a mailing for delivery.

Label, gummed Perforated label form on paper stock that must be individually separated and moistened before being applied with hand pressure to the mailing piece.

Label, one-up Conventional pressure-sensitive labels for computer addressing are four-across horizontal; one-up labels are in a vertical strip with center holes for machine affixing.

Label, peel-off (pressure-sensitive) Self-adhesive label form that can be peeled off its backing form and pressed onto a mailing piece.

Laid paper Paper having parallel lines watermarked at equal distances, giving a ribbed effect.

Laser letters Letters printed by a high-speed computerized imaging method. Lasers can print two letters side by side, each of 35 or 40 lines, in one second.

Late charge Charge imposed by some list owners for list rental fees not paid within a specific period.

Layout (1) Artist's sketch showing relative positioning of illustrations, headlines, and copy; (2) positioning of subject matter on a press sheet for most efficient production.

Lead generation Mailing used to invite inquiries for sales follow-up.

Lead qualification Determination, by telemarketing, of customer's level of interest in and willingness and ability to buy a product or service.

Length of line The computer, which has the capacity to print 132 characters across a 14½″ sheet, has forced discipline in the choice of line length. In four-across cheshiring, the longest line cannot be more than 30 characters; for five-across this limit is 23 characters. Capable data processors, utilizing all 8 lines available on a 1″-deep label, can provide two full lines, if need be, for the title line.

Length of residence Major compilers who utilize telephone or car registration data maintain the number of years (up to 16) a given family has been at the same address, thereby providing another selection factor available from these stratified lists.

Letterhead Printing on a letter that identifies the sender.

Lettershop Business organization that handles the mechanical details of mailings such as addressing, imprinting, and collating; most offer some printing facilities, and many offer some degree of creative direct mail services.

Lifestyle selectivity Selectivity based on the lifestyle habits of segments of the population as revealed through lists indicating what people need, what they buy, what they own, what they join, and what they support; major lists based on consumer surveys provide data on hobbies, ownership, and interests.

Lifetime value (LTV) In direct mail and marketing, the total profit or loss estimated or realized from a customer over the active life of that customer's record.

Lift letter Separate piece added to conventional solo mailings asking the reader to consider the offer just once more.

List acquisition (1) Lease or purchase of lists from external services; (2) use of internal corporate lists.

List affinity Correlation of a mailing offer to selected mailing list availabilities.

List bank Names held in inventory for future use.

List broker Specialist who makes all necessary arrangements for one company to use the list(s) of another company. A broker's services include research, selection, recommendation, and subsequent evaluation.

List building Process of collecting and utilizing list data and transaction data for list purposes.

List bulletin Announcement of a new list or of a change in a list previously announced.

List buyer Technically, one who actually buys mailing lists; in practice, one who orders mailing lists for one-time use. *See* **List user** and **Mailer**.

List card Conventional 5″ × 8″ card used to provide essential data about a given list.

List catalog Directory of lists with counts prepared and distributed, usually free, by list managers and list compilers.

List cleaning List updating or the process of correcting a mailing list.

List compilation Business of creating lists from printed records.

List compiler One who develops lists of names and addresses from directories, newspapers, public records, sales slips, trade show registrations, and other sources for identifying groups of people or companies having something in common.

List count Number of names and addresses on a given segment of a mailing list; a count provided before printing tapes or labels; the universe of names available by segment or classification.

List criteria Factors on a mailing list that differentiate one segment from another; can be demographic, psychographic, or physical in nature.

List, customer-compiled In prior years, list typed and prepared to customer order. Today, virtually all lists are precompiled on tape for any selection the user orders.

List, mailing Names and addresses of individuals and/or companies having in common a specific interest, characteristic, or activity.

List databank *See* **Databank**.

List enhancement Addition of data pertaining to each individual record that increases the value of a list.

List exchange Barter arrangement between two companies for the use of a mailing list; may be list for list, list for space, or list for comparable value other than money.

List hygiene Correcting names, addresses, and zip codes on house or rented mailing lists. This also reduces duplicates and corrects spelling, punctuation, and other addressing errors.

List key *See* **Key code**.

List maintenance Any manual, mechanical, or electronic system for keeping name-and-address records (with or without other data) up-to-date at any specific point(s) in time.

List management system Database system that manages customer and prospect lists, used to merge and purge duplicates between in-house lists and those obtained from outside sources and to select names for direct mail promotions and outgoing telemarketing programs.

List manager Person who, as an employee of a list owner or as an outside agent, is responsible for the use, by others, of a specific mailing list(s), and who oversees list maintenance, list promotion and marketing, list clearance and record keeping, and collecting for use of the list by others.

List manager, in-house Independent manager serving multiple lists. Some large list owners opt to manage the list rental activity through full-time in-house employees.

List monitoring *See* **Monitoring**.

List owner Person who, by promotional activity or compilation, has developed a list of names having something in common; or one who has purchased (as opposed to rented, reproduced, or used on a onetime basis) such a list from the list developer.

List performance Response logged to a mailed list or list segment.

List protection Safeguarding of a list through review of mailing and mailer, insertion of list seeds, and obtaining of a guarantee of onetime use only.

List ranking Arranging list items in descending order on the basis of logged response and/or logged dollars of sales.

List rental Arrangement whereby a list owner furnishes names to a mailer and receives a royalty from the mailer.

List rental history Report showing tests and continuations by users of a given list.

List royalty Payment to a list owner for use of a list on a onetime basis.

List sample Group of names selected from a list in order to evaluate the responsiveness of that list.

List selection Process of segregating smaller groups within a list, i.e., creating a list within a list. Also called *list segmentation*.

List sequence Order in which names and addresses appear in a list: by zip code, alphabetically, chronologically, etc.

List sort Process of putting a list in a specific sequence.

List source Original source used to generate names on a mailing list.

List test Part of a list selected to try to determine the effectiveness of the entire list. *See* **List sample**.

List user Company that uses names and addresses on someone else's lists as prospects for its product or service.

Load up Process of offering a buyer the opportunity of buying an entire series at one time after the customer has purchased the first item in that series.

Logotype (logo) Symbol or statement used consistently to identify a company or product.

Look-up service Service organization that adds telephone numbers to lists.

Machine-coated paper Paper coated on one or both sides during manufacture.

Machine-readable data Imprinted alphanumeric data, including name and address, that can be read and convened to magnetic form by an optical character reader.

Magalog Mail-order catalog that includes paid advertisements and, in some cases, brief editorials, making it similar to a magazine in format.

Magnetic tape Film for storing electronically recorded data, often in list format to allow computerized matching with other lists for purposes of appending phone numbers or eliminating duplications.

Magnetic tape charge Charge made for the tape reel on which a list is furnished and which usually is not returnable for credit.

Mail count Amount of mail deposited with the Postal Service on a given date as reported on the certification form.

Mail date Drop date planned for a mailing, usually as agreed upon by the mailing list owner and the list user.

Mailer (1) Direct mail advertiser who promotes a product or service using outside lists or house lists or both; (2) printed direct mail advertising piece; (3) folding carton, wrapper, or tube used to protect materials in the mails.

Mailgram Combination telegram-letter, with the telegram transmitted to a postal facility close to the addressee and then delivered as first-class mail.

Mailing house Direct mail service establishment that affixes labels, sorts, bags, and ties the mail, and delivers it in qualified zip code strings to the Postal Service for certification.

Mailing List/Users and Suppliers Association Association founded in 1983, specifically targeted to mailing list uses and abuses.

Mailing machine Machine that attaches labels to mailing pieces and otherwise prepares such pieces for deposit in the postal system.

Mailing package The complete direct mail unit as it arrives in the consumer's mailbox.

Mail monitoring Means of determining length of time required for individual pieces of mail to reach their destinations; also utilized to verify content and ascertain any unauthorized use.

Mail order Method of conducting business wherein merchandise or services are promoted directly to the user, orders are received by mail or telephone, and merchandise is mailed to the purchaser.

Mail order buyer Person who orders and pays for a product or service through the mail.

Mail Preference Service (MPS) Service of the Direct Marketing Association for consumers who wish to have their names removed from national commercial mailing lists.

Make-up Positioning of type and illustrations to conform to a layout; in lithography usually called a paste-up.

Makeready In letterpress, the building up of the press form so that heavy and light areas print with the correct impression.

Management information system (MIS) System, automated or manual, that provides sales support information for the sales representative to enhance sales activity and for management to evaluate sales performance.

Manual telephone sales center Completely paper-driven telephone sales center.

Marginal list test Test that almost, but not quite, qualifies for a continuation.

Market Total of all individuals or organizations that represent potential buyers.

Market identification Establishment of criteria to predetermine specific markets that will be primary targets of a telemarketing project.

Market penetration Proportion of buyers on a list to the total list or to the total area. For business lists, penetration is usually analyzed by two-digit or four-digit Standard Industrial Classification codes.

Marketing mix Various marketing elements and strategies that must be used together to achieve maximum effectiveness.

Markup Details of the size and style of type to be used; also known as type specification.

Marriage mail Form of co-op in which the offers of two or more disparate mailers are combined in one folder or envelope for delivery to the same address.

Master file File that is of a permanent nature,

or regarded in a particular job as authoritative, or one that contains all subfiles.

Match To cause the typing of addresses, salutations, or inserts into letters to agree with other copy that is already imprinted.

Match code Code determined by either the creator or the user of a file for matching records contained in another file.

Matched city pairs For testing purposes when individual markets must be utilized, a means to do A in City Y but not B, while doing both A and B in City X, with the premise that the two cities are reasonably matched as to size, income spread, and lifestyles.

Matte finish Dull paper finish that has no gloss.

Maximum cost per order Lifetime value of each major cell of customers on a customer file; helps set a limit on the price to pay for a new customer.

Mean The sum of the values of the items divided by the number of items. Also known as arithmetic average. Frequently used as a measure of location for a frequency or probability distribution.

Mechanical Finished artwork ready for printing production; generally includes matter pasted in position.

Mechanical addressing systems System in which small lists are filed on cards or plates and addressing is done by mechanical means.

Media Plural of *medium*; the means of transmitting information or an advertising message (direct mail package, inserts, magazines, posters, television, etc.).

Media data form Established format for presenting comparative data on publications.

Media insert Insert, either loose or bound, generally in business and consumer publications.

Median The value of the middle item when all the items are arranged in either ascending or descending order of magnitude. Frequently used as a measure of location for a frequency or probability distribution.

Median demographic data Data based on medians rather than on individuals (e.g., a census age is the median for a group of householders).

Medium Channel or system of communication (e.g, specific magazine, newspaper, TV station, or mailing list).

Member get member A promotion where existing members are offered a gift for enrolling new members.

Merge To combine two or more lists into a single list using the same sequential order, and then to sort them together, usually by zip code.

Merge/purge To combine two or more lists for list enhancement, suppression, or duplication elimination by a computerized matching process.

Military lists Lists of persons in military service.

Minicatalog New prospecting device consisting of a fanfolded set of minipages $3'' \times 5''$ used as cardvertisers, billing stuffers, and package inserts; also utilized by some mailers as a bounce-back.

Minimum (1) Minimum billing applied to list rentals involving a small number of names; (2) minimum billing for given mailing and/or computerized sources.

Minimum order requirement Stipulation, irrespective of the quantity ordered, that payment of a given number of dollars will be expected.

Mobility rate Annual rate at which families move or businesses fail, change names, or are absorbed each year.

Mode The mode is the score in a population that occurs most frequently. The mode is not the frequency of the most numerous score. It is the value of that score itself.

Model A symbolic representation of reality. In

quantitative forecasting methods, a specific model is used to represent the basic pattern contained in the data. This may be a regression model, which is causal in nature, or a time-series model.

Modeling Process involving the use of spreadsheets via a computer that provides reasonable answers to "what-if" scenarios.

Modem The hardware that translates between digital and analog codes enabling a digital computer to talk through an analog phone line.

Monetary value Total expenditures by a customer during a specific time, generally 12 months.

Monitoring Listening in on a telephone conversation from extensions, usually for training of telephone sales representatives; also known as *service observing*.

Mono In printing, printed in a single color.

MPS *See* **Mail Preference Service**.

MSA (Metropolitan Statistical Area) Areas that contain a city of 50,000+ population or an area of 50,000 people within a larger city.

Multibuyers Identification through a merge/purge of all records found on two or more lists.

Multifamily *See* **Multiple dwelling**.

Multimedia The presentation of text, graphical images, moving images (animation, video clips), and sound in a single package, to create an effect greater than the sum of the parts.

Multiple buyer Person who has bought two or more times (not one who has bought two or more items at one time only); also known as *multibuyer* or *repeat buyer*.

Multiple contact case Situation in which more than one contact with a prospect or customer is needed to complete or close a sale.

Multiple dwelling Housing unit for three or more families at the same address.

Multiple regression Statistical technique that measures the relationship between responses to a mailing with census demographics and list characteristics of one or more selected mailing lists; used to determine the best types of people/areas to mail to, and to analyze customers or subscribers.

Multiple regression analysis Statistical procedure that studies multiple independent variables simultaneously to identify a pattern or patterns that can lead to an increase in response.

Multiple SICs On major files of large businesses, the augmentation of the primary Standard Industrial Classification with up to three more four-digit SICs. Business merge/purges often disclose multiple SIC alignments unavailable on any single list source.

Name Single entry on a mailing list.

Name acquisition Technique of soliciting a response to obtain names and addresses for a mailing list.

Name drain Loss, mainly by large businesses, of the names and addresses of prospective customers who write to them or visit their stores.

National Change of Address (NCOA) Service of the U.S. Postal Service that provides national data on changes of address.

Negative Photographic image on film in which black values in the original subject are transparent, white values are opaque, light grays are dark, and dark grays are light.

Negative option Buying plan in which a customer or club member agrees to accept and pay for products or services announced in advance at regular intervals unless the individual notifies the company, within a reasonable time after announcement, not to ship the merchandise.

Nesting Placing one enclosure within another before insertion into a mailing envelope.

Net name arrangement Agreement, at the

time of ordering or before, whereby a list owner agrees to accept adjusted payment for less than the total names shipped to the list user. Such arrangements can be for a percentage of names shipped or names actually mailed or for only those names actually mailed.

Net names Actual number of names on a given list mailed after a merge/purge; the concept of paying only for such names.

Net-net names Agreement made by a renter with a list owner to pay only for names that survive such screens as income, credit, house list duplicates, prior-list suppress names, and zip suppress programs; the surviving portion can be quite small.

Net unique name file Resultant one-per-record unique unduplicated list, one of the chief outputs of a merge/purge operation.

Neural network An information processing model that emulates the densely interconnected, parallel structure of the human brain processes. Good for pattern recognition and classification, able to make generalized decisions regarding imprecise input data and capable of learning. Used to solve problems too complex for traditional methodologies.

New case Telephone contact yet to be made.

New connects New names added to the connected lines of telephone, gas, and electric utilities.

New households New connects by local phone companies; data on new names from one telephone book to another are over one year old.

Newspaper lists List data on engagements, births, deaths, and news-making items and changes published in newspapers.

Nine-digit zip code Postal Service system designed to provide an automated means of utilizing an extended zip code to sort mail down to small contiguous areas within a carrier route.

Nixie Mailing piece returned to a mailer (under proper authorization) by the Postal Service because of an incorrect, or undeliverable, name and address.

Nonprofit rate Preferential Postal Service rate extended to organizations that are not maintained for profit.

No-pay Person who has not paid for goods or services ordered. Also known as an *uncollectable*, a *deadbeat*, or a *delinquent*.

North/south labels Mailing labels that read from top to bottom and that can be affixed with Cheshire equipment.

Novelty format Attention-getting direct mail format.

nth name or interval Statistical means of a given number of names equally selected over the full universe of the list segment being sampled. The nth number interval is derived by dividing the total names in the list by the sample number desired.

nth name selection Method of selecting a portion of a mailing list for test mailings (e.g., every fifth, tenth, twentieth name).

Objective case Each telemarketing project has a specific objective for each case (e.g., make a sale, reactivate an account, arrange for an appointment).

Occupant list Mailing list that contain only addresses (no names of individuals and/or companies).

OCR *See* **Optical Character Reader**.

Offer The terms promoting a specific product or service.

Offices Compilations of businesses with telephones providing offices of professionals and of multiple professionals per office, where desired, brought together by their common telephone number.

Offset litho Method of transferring the printing image from flat plate to paper via a covered cylinder.

One-off *See* **Onetime use of a list**.

One-shot mailing Offer designed to make the sale in a single transaction.

One-stage mailing Mailing designed to take orders directly without any follow-up process.

Onetime buyer Buyer who has not ordered a second time from a given company.

Onetime use of a list Intrinsic part of the normal list usage, list reproduction, or list exchange agreement in which it is understood that the mailer will not use the names on the list more than once without specific prior approval of the list owner.

One-year contract Form of lease in which the renter is granted unlimited use for one year of a given set of compiled records; usually treated as a "sale for one year."

On-line availability Linkup system in which an operator at a remote terminal can obtain list information from a data bank or database at another location.

Opacity Property of a sheet of paper that minimizes the show-through of printing from the reverse side or from the next sheet.

Open account Customer record that at a specific time reflects an unpaid balance for goods and services ordered without delinquency.

Operations review Annual or semiannual review of the entire telephone sales center and strategic plan of a company.

Opportunity seeker Class of mail-order buyer or prospect that seeks a new and different way to make an income; ranges from people who look for ways to work at home to expensive franchises.

Optical character reader (OCR) Electronic scanning device that can read characters, either typed with a special OCR font or computer created, and convert these characters to magnetic form.

Optical scanner Input device that optically reads a line of printed characters and converts each character to its electronic equivalent for processing.

"Or Current Resident" Line added by computer to a three-line consumer list in an attempt to obtain greater deliverability and readership in case of a change in residential occupants.

Order blank envelope Order form printed on one side of a sheet, with a mailing address on the reverse; the recipient simply fills in the order and folds and seals the form like an envelope.

Order card Reply card used to initiate an order by mail.

Order entry procedure Process of capturing the name, address, item, dollars, and key for a transaction, and connecting it to electronic data, which then trigger creation of a picking document, a billing document, and usually the effect of that transaction upon inventory and inventory control.

Order form Printed form on which a customer can provide information to initiate an order by mail.

Order margin Sum represented by the difference between all costs (except promotion) and the selling price (after returns).

Origination All the work needed to prepare a promotional package (e.g., copy, design, photography, typesetting, color separation).

Outbound calls Calls that are placed by the telemarketing center. *See also* **Inbound calls**.

Outbound telesales Proactive approach to a given market by a planned program to develop leads and/or sales.

Outside list manager *See* **List manager**.

Overlay In artwork, a transparent or translucent covering over the copy where color breaks, instructions, or corrections are marked.

Overprinting Double printing; printing over an area that already has been printed.

Owners Owners of mail order response lists and operators of mail response companies who "own" the customer and inquiry lists that they offer on the list rental market. All such proprietary lists must be "cleared" by such owners or their agents to be rented for onetime mailing by others.

Package insert Any promotional piece included in merchandise packages that advertises goods or services available from the same or different sellers.

Package test Test of part or all of the elements of one mailing piece against another.

Page proofs Proofs taken after make-up into pages, prior to printing.

Paid cancel Person who completes a basic buying commitment before canceling that commitment. *See also* **Completed cancel**.

Paid circulation Distribution of a publication to individuals or organizations that have paid for a subscription.

Paid during service Method of paying for magazine subscriptions in installments, usually weekly or monthly, and usually collected personally by the original salesperson or a representative of the publisher.

Panel Group of people having similar interests that is used for research purposes.

Para sales force Sales team that works as a supplement to another sales team either on the telephone or in the field.

Pareto's rule Also known as the 80/20 rule. It was named after Vilfredo Pareto, an Italian economist and sociologist. In the late 19th century, he studied the distribution of wealth in Europe and found that 80 percent of the wealth was held by 20 percent of the population.

Pass (1) One run of the paper through the printing press; (2) to clear a page for a subscription.

Pass-along effect Additional readership acquired as executives forward particularly interesting mail to their associates. Business catalog makers seek to harness this effect by printing a group of germane titles on the cover as a suggested routing for such pass-along readership.

Passing a file Process of reading a file sequentially by computer to select and/or copy specific data.

Past buyer *See* **Former buyer**.

Paste-up Process by which an artist puts together type copy and photographs into final artwork ready for photographic reproduction.

Payment, method of Record or tag showing how a customer paid for a purchase (by check or credit card or money order); available as a selection factor on a number of response lists.

Payment rate Percentage of respondents who buy on credit or take a trial on credit and who then pay.

Peel-off label Self-adhesive label attached to a backing sheet that is attached to a mailing piece. The label is intended to be removed from the mailing piece and attached to an order blank or card.

Peg count Tally of the number of calls made or received over a set period.

Pending case Case in which an initial contact has been made and the communicator is waiting for a response or additional information.

Penetration Relationship of the number of individuals or families on a particular list (by state, zip code, SIC code, etc.) compared to the total number possible.

Penetration analysis Study made of the "share of market" held by a given mailer within various universes by classification or other demographic characteristics; for business mailers, the chief means to ascertain which markets by SIC and number of employees are most successfully penetrated in order to prospect more efficiently.

Perceptual mapping A research technique that uses graph coordinates to analyze the relationships among a group of products, positioning, etc., to identify market gaps and opportunities.

Performance evaluation Weekly or monthly review of a salesperson's performance by first-line supervision.

Periodical Publication issued at specific intervals.

Peripheral listing Creation of a variant kind of audience from that specified (e.g., addressing to the parents of College Student or High School Student X, titling to Mrs. X from a list of doctors by name and address at home, addressing a child by name to attract the eye of the parent, or inviting the new neighbors to view a new car at a given address).

Personalization Adding the name of the recipient to a mailing piece, or the use of a computer to input data about the psychographics of the customer being addressed.

Phone list Mailing list compiled from names listed in telephone directories.

Photosetting Production of type matter in positive form on bromide or film by the use of electromechanical equipment that is usually computer-assisted.

Pick-up and delivery charges Charges relating to collection or delivery of outside lists or components involved in the mailing process.

Piece rate Third-class mail breaks into two main rate categories—third-class bulk rate (for discounts) and third-class piece rate. For the price of a first-class stamp, a piece weighing up to 3-1/2 ounces may be placed in the mail stream without any prior sortation, a charge that is currently over 40 per-

cent greater than the unit charge for third-class bulk mail.

Piggy-back Offer that hitches a free ride with another offer.

Pigment Powdered substance used to give color, body, or opacity to printing inks.

Pilot Trial program designed to test the feasibility of a possible telemarketing program.

Platemaking Process by which artwork is converted into letterpress or off-set plates for printing.

Pocket envelope Envelope with the flap on its short side.

Point Measure used to describe type sizes.

Political lists Mailing lists that break into two main categories: voter registration files mailed primarily during political campaigns and fund-raising files of donors to various political causes.

Poly bag Transparent polyethylene bag used as envelopes for mailings.

Pop-up Printed piece containing a paper construction pasted inside a fold that, when the fold is opened, "pops up" to form a three-dimensional illustration.

Positive Photographic image on film that corresponds to the original copy; the reverse of a negative.

Positive option Method of distributing products and services incorporating the same advance notice techniques as a negative option but requiring a specific order each time from the member or subscriber, generally more costly and less predictable than negative option.

Postage refund Sum returned to a mailer by an owner or manager for nondeliverables exceeding a stipulated guarantee.

Postcard Single sheet self-mailer on card stock.

Postcard mailers Booklet containing business reply cards that are individually perforated for selective return to order products or obtain information.

Post-paid impression (PPI) *See* **Printed postage impression**.

Precall planning Preparation before a sales call to promote maximum effectiveness.

Preclearance Act of getting clearance on a rental before sending in the order.

Predictive modeling A statistical process that estimates the value of a dependent variable, given data values of predictor variables. Used to predetermine response rates of mail offers based on historical response data.

Premium Item offered to a potential buyer, free or at a nominal price, as an inducement to purchase or obtain for trial a product or service offered via mail order.

Premium buyer Person who buys a product or service in order to get another product or service (usually free or at a special price), or person who responds to an offer of a special premium on the package or label (or sometimes in the advertising) of another product.

Preprint Advertising insert printed in advance for a newspaper or magazine.

Prerecorded message Taped message often recorded by a celebrity or authority figure that is played to inbound callers or included in an outbound call.

Presort To prepare mail for direct delivery to post offices or to carriers at post offices. Over half of all for-profit third-class bulk mail is now mailed at carrier-route presort discount rates.

Press date Date on which a publication goes to print.

Prestructured marketing Marketing using computer software that provides a highly efficient system for annual fund-raising and capital drives, special events, and membership development by providing detailed information on specific target groups.

Price lining Setting of prices by a seller in accordance with certain price points believed to be attractive to buyers.

Printed postage impression (PPI) System enabling producers of bulk mailings to preprint "Postage Paid" on their envelopes, a wide range of designs is available allowing compatibility of style with other print detail on the envelope.

Printer's error Error in printed copy that is the fault of the typesetter and corrected at the printer's expense.

Printout Copy on a sheet of a list, or of some selected data on a list such as matched pairs indicating duplication from a merge/purge, or an array of largest buyers or donors.

Priority For a continuation, method of arranging the tested lists and list segments in descending order on the basis of number of responses or number of dollars of sales per thousand pieces mailed; for political mail, a special next-day delivery service offered by the Postal Service.

Prior list suppress Utilization of prior data to remove matching data from a new run and thus reduce the payment for the list data as used.

Private mail Mail handled by special arrangement outside the Postal Service.

Proactive telemarketing Seller-initiated or outbound calling.

Probability The degree of plausibility, based on available data, of a given event to occur. Expressed as a number from 0 through 1 (impossible = 0; certain = 1).

Process colors Black and three primary colors—magenta (red), cyan (blue), and yellow—into which full-color artwork is separated before printing.

Product information cards Business reply cards bound in a booklet for selective return to order products or obtain information;

also sometimes mailed loose in the form of a pack of cards.

Professional lists Direct marketing lists that break down into some 30 categories, from architects to veterinarians. For example, a new list on the market based on a classified list of doctors (MDs) with phones has verified addresses and phone numbers of over 100,000 of some 190,000 physicians in private practice.

Profiling To build a picture of a target customer by utilizing information from various sources.

Projected roll-out response Based on tests results, the response anticipated from a large continuation or program.

Prompt Form of sales presentation by a professional telesalesperson that is comprised of predetermined but unscripted steps in the telephone call that will be presented in every closed case.

Proof Impression taken from types, blocks, or plates for checking for errors and making amendments prior to printing.

Prospect Name on a mailing list considered to be that of a potential buyer for a given product or service who has not previously made such a purchase.

Prospecting Using mailings to get leads for further sales contacts rather than to make direct sales.

Protected mailing period Period of time, usually one or two weeks prior to and one or two weeks after the mail date for a large quantity of names, in which the list owner guarantees no competitor will be given access to the list.

Pseudocarrier routes The Postal Service Carrier Route (CRIS) tape lists millions of bits of data delineating 160,000 individual carrier routes. Major consumer compilers break up the areas not serviced by individual carriers into 240,000 extra pseudocarrier routes for marketing penetration selection or omission.

Psychograhics Characteristics or qualities used to denote the lifestyle or attitude of customers and prospective customers.

Publisher's letter Letter enclosed in a mailing package to stress a specific selling point.

Pull Proportion of response by mail or phone to a given promotional activity.

Purge Process of eliminating duplicates and/or unwanted names and addresses from one or more lists.

Pyramiding Method of testing mailing lists that starts with small numbers and, based on positive indications, follows with increasingly large numbers of the balance of the list until the entire list is mailed.

Qualification sortation Third-class bulk mail sorted to meet Postal Service qualifications for three different mail streams.

Qualified lead Potential customers that have been determined to need, want, and be able to purchase a specific product or service.

Qualitative In research, relates to or involves quality or kind. Considered not projectable.

Quantitative In research, relates to or involves the measurement of quantity or amount. Often used to describe projectable data.

Quantity pricing Pricing, usually by compilers, offering price breaks for varying list quantities rented over a period of a year.

Queue A function of an automatic call distributor that holds all (incoming) calls in the order in which they arrive until the next available agent takes the first in line, moving the next call up in sequence.

Questionnaire Printed form presented to a specific audience to solicit answers to specific questions.

Query A question structured in a database language to sort, group, or select records from a table or multiple tables.

Quintile The portion of a frequency distribution containing one-fifth of the total sample.

Quotation Price presented to a prospective mailer before running a list order requiring special processing.

Random access Access mode in which records are obtained from or placed into a mass storage file in a nonsequential manner so that any record can be rapidly accessed.

Random sampling A statistical sampling method involving selection, in such a way that every unit within that population has the same probability of being selected as any other unit.

Rate card Issued by the publishers of magazines, journals, and newspapers detailing advertising costs, advertisement sizes, and the mechanical details of production.

Rating points Method of measurement of TV or radio audience size.

Reactive telemarketing Customer-initiated buying by telephone (inbound calling).

Readership Number of people who read a publication as opposed to the number of people who receive it.

Rebate *See* **Bulk rebate**.

Recency Latest purchase or other activity recorded for an individual or company on a specific customer list. *See also* **Frequency** and **Monetary value**.

Record Data elements that are grouped together and treated as one unit, typically stored in a table. Each element is identified by a unique field name.

Record layout Description covering the entire record length to denote where on a tape each part (or field) of the record appears, such as name, local address, city, state, zip code, and other relevant data.

Record length Number of characters occupied by each record on a file.

Referral name *See* **Friend of a friend**.

Reformatting Changing a magnetic tape format from one arrangement to another, more usable format; also called *conversion*.

Refund (1) For a list, return of part of payment due to shortage in count or excessive nondeliverables (over the guarantee); (2) for a product sold by mail, a return of the purchase price if an item is returned in good condition.

Registration list List constructed from state or local political-division registration data.

Regression analysis Statistical means to improve the predictability of response based on an analysis of multiple stratified relationships within a file.

Relational database A storage format in which data items can be stored in separate files but linked together to form different relations, thus giving great flexibility.

Renewal Subscription that has been renewed prior to or at expiration time or within six months thereafter.

Rental *See* **List rental**.

Repeat buyer *See* **Multiple buyer**.

Repeat mailing Mailing of the same or very similar packages to the addresses on a list for the second time.

Reply card Sender-addressed card included in a mailing on which the recipient can indicate a response to the offer.

Reply-O-Letter One of a number of patented direct mail formats for facilitating replies from prospects, featuring a die-cut opening on the face of the letter and a pocket on the reverse; an addressed reply card is inserted in the pocket and the name and address shows through the die-cut opening.

Reprint Special repeat printing of an individual article or advertisement from a publication.

Repro High-quality reproduction proof, usually intended to be used as artwork for printing.

Reproduction right Authorization by a list owner for a specific mailer to use that list on a onetime basis.

Request for proposal (RFP) Pro-forma device for outlining specific purchasing requirements that can be responded to in kind by vendors.

Response Incoming telephone contacts generated by media.

Response curve Anticipated incoming contact volume charting its peak and its decline, based on hours, days, weeks, or months.

Response rate Gross or net response received as a percentage of total promotions mailed or contacts made.

Return envelopes Addressed reply envelopes, either stamped or unstamped—as distinguished from business reply envelopes that carry a postage payment guarantee—included with a mailing.

Return postage guaranteed Legend imprinted on the address face of envelopes or other mailing pieces when the mailer wishes the Postal Service to return undeliverable third-class bulk mail. A charge equivalent to the single-piece, third-class rate is made for each piece returned. *See also* **List cleaning**.

Returns Responses to a direct mail program.

Reverse To change printing areas so that the parts usually black or shaded are reversed and appear white or gray.

RFM Acronym for recency-frequency-monetary value ratio, a formula used to evaluate the sales potential of names on a mailing list.

ROP *See* **Run of Paper**.

Roll-out Main or largest mailing in a direct mail campaign sent to the remaining names on the list after tests to sample portions of the list have shown positive results.

Rough Rough sketch or preliminary outline of a leaflet or advertisement; also known as a *comp*.

Royalty Sum paid per unit mailed or sold for the use of a list, an imprimatur, a patent, or the like.

Running charge Price a list owner charges for names run or passed but not used by a specific mailer.

Run of Paper (ROP) (1) Term applied to color printing on regular paper and presses, as distinct from separate sections printed on special color presses; also called *run of press*. (2) Term sometimes used to describe an advertisement positioned by publisher's choice—in other than a preferred position—for which a special charge is made.

Run-on price Price from a supplier for continuing to produce (generally print or envelopes) once an initial run is in process; includes only materials and ongoing charges, and not origination or machine makeready.

Saddle stitching Stapling a publication from the back to the center.

Sale Formal agreement to buy, make an appointment, or any other definition of a sale as determined by the objective of a specific case.

Sales conversion rate Number of sales in relation to number of calls initiated or received.

Sales message Description of the features and benefits of a product or service.

Sales presentation Structured anatomy of an offer describing how the product or service works.

Salting Deliberate placing of decoy or dummy names in a list for the purpose of tracing list usage and delivery. *See also* **Decoy** and **Dummy**.

Salting via seeds, dummies, or decoys Adding names with special characteristics to a list for protection and identification purposes.

Sample package (mailing piece) Example of the package to be mailed by the list user to a particular list. Such a mailing piece is submitted to the list owner for approval prior to commitment for onetime use of that list.

Scented ink Printing ink to which a fragrance has been added.

Score Impressing of an indent or a mark in the paper to make folding easier.

Scoring The process of using the correlation derived from a model to project and forecast the potential propensity of lifestyles and penetrations.

Scratch and sniff *See* **Scented ink**.

Screen (1) Use of an outside list (based on credit, income, deliverability, zip code selection) to suppress records on a list to be mailed; (2) halftone process in plate-making that reduces the density of color in an illustration.

Screen printing Method of printing from stencils placed on a fine mesh tightly stretched on a frame, through which ink or paint is forced.

Script Prepared text presentation used by sales personnel as a tool to convey a sales message in its entirety.

Seasonality Selection of time of year; the influence of seasonal timing on response rates.

Second class Second-class mail in the postal rate system; covers periodicals.

Sectional center (SCF or SCF center) Postal Service distribution unit comprising different post offices whose zip codes start with the same first three digits.

Sectional center facility (SCF) Geographic area designated by the first three digits of a zip code.

Seed Dummy or decoy name inserted into a mailing list.

Seeding Planting of dummy names in a mailing list to check usage, delivery, or unauthorized reuse.

Segment Portion of a list or file selected on the basis of a special set of characteristics.

Segmentation Process of separating characteristic groups within a list for target marketing.

Selection Process of segregating or selecting specific records from a list according to specific criteria.

Selection charge Fee above the basic cost of a list for a given selection.

Selection criteria Characteristics that identify segments or subgroups within a list.

Self-cover Cover printed on the same paper as the test pages.

Self-mailer Direct mail piece mailed without an envelope.

Self-standing stuffers Promotional printed pieces delivered as part of a daily or Sunday newspaper.

Senior citizen lists Lists of older individuals past a specific age, available for over age 50, 55, 60, or 65.

Separations Color separations either prepared by an artist using separate overlays for each color or achieved photographically by use of filters.

Sequence Arrangement of items according to a specified set of rules or instructions.

Series rate Special rate offered by publications and other media for a series of advertisements as opposed to a single insertion.

Set-up charge Flat charge assessed on some lists in addition to the cost per thousand.

Sheet fed Relating to a printing technique whereby paper is fed into the printing press in single sheets, as opposed to paper on a roll.

SIC (Standard Industrial Classification) Classification of businesses, as defined by the U.S. Department of Commerce.

SIC count Count of the number of records available by two-, three-, four-, or five-digit Industrial Standard Classification.

Signature In book, magazine, and catalog production, name given to a large printed sheet after it has been folded to the required size; a number of signatures makes up a publication.

Significant difference In mathematical terms, difference between tests of two or more variables, which is similar differentiation. The significant difference varies with the confidence level desired. Most direct mail penetration utilizes a 95 percent confidence level, wherein 95 times out of 100 the results found in the test will come close to duplicating on a retest or combination.

Single-family household Private home, housing only one household, as distinct from multiple-family residences.

Singles (1) One- or single-person household; (2) list of unmarried adults, usually for social linking.

Single-step *See* **One-stage mailing**.

Solo mailing Mailing promoting a single product or a limited group of related products, and usually consisting of a letter, brochure, and reply device enclosed in an envelope.

Sorting (1) Computerized process of changing the given sequence of a list to a different sequence; (2) interfilling two or more lists.

Source count Number of names and addresses, in any given list, for the media (or list sources) from which the names and addresses were derived.

Space ads Mail order ads in newspapers, magazines, and self-standing stuffers; one of the major media utilized for prospecting for new customers.

Space buyer Media buyer (usually in an advertising agency) who places print mail order advertising.

Space-sold record Any record on a house file (customers, inquirers, catalog requests) that has been generated through advertising space placed in publications.

Special position Designated location in a publication ordered by the advertiser for his advertisement, usually at extra cost.

Specific list source Original source material for a compiled file.

Specific order decoy Seed or dummy inserted in the output of a list order for that order only. The specific seed, which identifies the order, is usually in addition to list protection decoys in the same list.

Specifier Individual who can specify or purchase a product or service, particularly at larger businesses; in many cases, this is not the individual who enters the order.

Spine *See* **Backbone**.

Split run Printing of two or more variants of a promotional ad run on an nth or A/B split through the entire printing; use of geographic segments of a publication for testing of variants.

Split test Two or more samples from the same list, each considered to be representative of the entire list and used for package tests or to test the homogeneity of the list.

Spot color Use of one additional color in printing.

SRDS (Standard Rate & Data Service) Prints a rates and data book covering basic information on over 20,000 mailing lists.

Standard Deviation The standard deviation is one of several indices of variability that statisticians use to characterize the dispersion among the measures in a given population. Numerically, the standard deviation is the square root of the variance.

Standard Industrial Classification (SIC) Classification of businesses as defined by the U.S. Department of Commerce, used to segment telephone calling lists and direct marketing mailing lists.

Standard Mail Standard Mail, formerly

known as Bulk Mail, is the most economical method of sending printed material through the postal system. Standard Mail is only for domestic addresses. Each mailing must be identical in size, weight, envelope, and content. It may not contain subject matter considered to be First-Class Mail content. Each mailing must contain a minimum of 200 pieces. The mailer receives increased discounts for greater levels of presorting.

State count Number of names and addresses, in a given list, for each state.

Statement stuffer Small printed piece designed to be inserted in an envelope carrying a customer's statement of account.

Step up Use of special premiums to get mail order buyers to increase their unit of purchase.

Stock art Art sold for use by a number of advertisers.

Stock cut Printing engravings kept in stock by the printer or publisher.

Stock format Direct mail format with preprinted illustrations and/or headings to which an advertiser adds its own copy.

Stopper Advertising slang for a striking headline or illustration intended to attract immediate attention.

Storage Data-processing term indicating the volume of name-and-address and attached data that can be stored for future use on a given computer system.

Student lists Lists of college or high school students. For college students, both home and school addresses are available; for high school students, home addresses for junior and seniors are available.

Stuffers Printed advertising enclosures placed in other media (e.g., newspapers, merchandise packages, and mailings for other products).

Subblock Along with enumeration districts, the smallest geographic segment of the country for which the U.S. Census Bureau provides demographic data.

Subscriber Individual who has paid to receive a periodical.

Success model Set of logical steps followed by successful salespeople to sell a product or service and used as a training example for new salespeople.

Suppression Utilization of data on one or more files to remove any duplication of specific names before a mailing.

Suppression of previous usage Utilization of the previous usage or match codes of the records used as a suppress file. Unduplication can also be ensured through fifth-digit pulls, first-digit-of-name pulls, or actual tagging of each prior record used.

Suppression of subscribers Utilization of the subscriber file to suppress a publication's current readers from rental lists prior to mailing.

Surname selection Ethnic selection based on surnames; a method for selection of such easily identifiable groups as Irish, Italian, Jewish, and Spanish. Specialists have extended this type of coding to groups such as German, English, Scots, and Scandinavian.

Suspect (1) Prospect somewhat more likely to order than a cold prospect; (2) in some two-step operations, a name given the initial inquirer when only one in X can be expected to convert.

Swatching Attaching samples of material to a printed piece.

Sweepstakes list (sweeps) List of responders, most of them nonbuyers, to a sweepstakes offer.

Syndicated mailing Mailing prepared for distribution by firms other than the manufacturer or syndicator.

Syndication (1) Selling or distributing mailing lists; (2) offering for sale the findings of a research company.

Syndicator Operation that makes available prepared direct mail promotions for specific products or services to a list owner for mailing to its own list; most syndicators also offer product fulfillment services.

Tabloid Preprinted advertising insert of four or more pages, usually about half the size of a regular newspaper page, designed for insertion into a newspaper.

Tagging (1) Process of adding information to a list; (2) transfer of data or control information for usage and unduplication.

Take-one Leaflet displayed at point of sale or in areas where potential consumers congregate (e.g., credit card recruitment leaflets, display and dispenser units at hotels and restaurants).

Tape Magnetic tape, the principal means of recording, storing, and retrieving data for computerized mailing list operations.

Tape conversion Conversion of hard-copy data to magnetic tape.

Tape format (layout) Location of each field, character by character, of each record on a list on tape.

Tape record All the information about an individual or company contained on a specific magnetic tape.

Tape reel Medium on which data for computer addressing or merge/purge are handled.

Target Person to whom a sales call is directed.

Target group index (TGI) Analysis of purchasing habits among consumers covering 4,500 brands/services in over 500 product fields.

Target market Most likely group determined to have the highest potential for buying a product or service.

Tear sheet Printed page cut from a publication; sometimes used in place of a complete voucher copy as evidence of publication. *See also* **Voucher copy**.

Teaser Advertisement or promotion planned to excite curiosity about a later advertisement or promotion.

Telco Telephone-operating company.

Telecommunication Any electrical transmission of voice or data from sender to receiver(s), including telegraphy, telephony, data transmission, and video-telephony.

Telecommuting Practice of employees working in their homes while linked to their office by telephone and, in most cases, a computer, sometimes referred to as *telework*.

Telecomputer Nontechnical term for an Automatic Dialing Recorded Message Player (ADRMP), a machine that automatically dials, plays a prerecorded message, and records responses.

Telemarketing Use of the telephone as an interactive medium for promotion or promotion response; the contemporary term is *teleservices*.

Telemarketing-insensitive medium Any medium used to advertise a product or service that does not properly highlight a telephone number.

Telemarketing service bureau One who sells the service of conducting telemarketing calls; also called *telemarketing agency*.

Telephone household Household with a listed phone number. (Random access calling can ring unlisted and nonpublished numbers.)

Telephone list List of consumers or establishments compiled with phone numbers from published phone directories.

Telephone list appending Adding of telephone numbers to mailing lists.

Telephone marketing Any activity in direct marketing involving the telephone (e.g., list, building or telephone follow-up to a lead-generation program).

Telephone Preference Service (TPS) Program of the Direct Marketing Association that allows consumers who do not want telemarketing calls to have their names removed from most telemarketers' lists with only one request.

Telephone sales Implementation of the telemarketing plan.

Telephone sales representative (TSR) Person who markets and sells by telephone; also known as a *telemarketer* or *agent*.

Telephone sales supervisor (TSS) Person who oversees the performance of TSRs.

Telephone sales techniques Formalized methods that structure the entire sales process.

Telephone service center *See* **TSC**.

Teleprospecting Cold canvassing of telephone households or telephone nonhouseholds by personal phone calls (not to be confused with telemarketing, which pertains to calls made to customers or inquirers).

Teleprospecting list List of prospects with phones used for telephonic (cold calling) prospecting.

Telesales Function dedicated to receiving or making outgoing contact by telephone.

Test Period of time in which a minimum of 100 cases are completed for analysis and management decisions about whether a particular project or program is viable.

Test campaign Mailings of test pieces to a number of outside lists to establish a bank for continuation mailings; must not be to only one list, which is a "continuous series of one experiment."

Testing Preliminary mailing or distribution intended as a preview or pilot before a major campaign. Test mailings are used to determine probable acceptance of a product or service and are usually made to specially selected lists.

Test market Trial market for a new product or service offer.

Test panel List of the parts or samples in a split test.

Test quantity Test mailing to a sufficiently large number of names from a list to enable the mailer to evaluate the responsiveness of the list.

Test tape Selection of representative records within a mailing list that enables a list user or service bureau to prepare for reformatting or converting the list to a more efficient form for the user.

Text Body matter of a page or book as distinguished from the headings.

TGI *See* **Target group index**.

Third-class mail Bulk mail. The U.S. Postal Service delivery of direct-mail promotions weighing less than one pound.

Third-party endorsement In a mailing made for the joint benefit of an outside mailer and a company over the company's customer file, the imprimatur of the company (e.g., *Britannica* mailing the *Farm Journal* list with an offer ostensibly from the publication to its subscribers).

Third-party unit Service bureau that makes calls for hire; also known as a contract unit.

Three-digit zip First three digits of a five-digit zip code denoting a given sectional center facility of the Postal Service.

Three-line address For consumer mail, a conventional home or household address of an individual; for business mail, the name and address of an establishment without the name of an individual.

Three-up *See* **Four-up**.

Throwaway Advertisement or promotional piece intended for widespread free distribution. Generally printed on inexpensive paper stock, it is most often distributed by hand to passersby or house to house.

Tie-in Cooperative mailing effort involving two or more advertisers.

Till forbid Order for service that is to

continue until specifically canceled by the buyer; also known as *TF*.

Time Media buyer (usually at a specialized agency for direct response electronic) who "buys" time periods and spots for direct response radio or TV promotion.

Time zone sequencing Preparation of national telemarketing lists according to time zones so calls can be made at the most productive times.

Tint Light color, usually used for backgrounds.

Tip-on Item glued to a printed piece.

Title Designation before (prefix) or after (suffix) a name to accurately identify an individual (prefixes: Mr., Mrs., Dr., Sister, etc.; suffixes: M.D., Jr., President, Sales, etc.).

Title addressing Utilizing the title or function at a business; adding a title to a business address rather than addressing to a specific person by name.

Token Involvement device, often consisting of a perforated portion of an order card designed to be removed from its original position and placed in another designated area on the order card, to signify a desire to purchase the product or service offered.

Town marker Symbol used to identify the end of a mailing list's geographic unit; originated for towns but now used for zip codes and sectional centers.

Track record Accounting of what a given list or list segment has done for given mailers in the past.

Trademark The legal term for a brand. If used for the firm as a whole, the preferred term is *trade name*.

Trade show registrants (1) Persons who stopped at a given trade show booth and signed up to receive additional information or a sales call; (2) persons assigned by their companies to operate a trade show booth or booths.

Traffic Number of calls made or received per hour, day, or month on a single line or trunk of a telephone system.

Traffic builder Direct mail piece intended primarily to attract recipients to the mailer's place of business.

Transparency Positive color film such as a slide.

Trial buyer Person who buys a short-term supply of a product, or who buys the product with the understanding that it may be examined, used, or tested for a specified time before they need to decide whether to pay for it or return it.

Trials Individuals who ordered a short-term subscription to a magazine, newsletter, or continuity program. In list rental, trials are not equal to those who convert to customer status.

Trial subscriber Person who orders a service or publication on a conditional basis, which may relate to delaying payment, the right to cancel, a shorter than normal term, or a special introductory price.

Truncation Dropping the end of words or names to fit an address line into 30 characters for four-across Cheshire addressing.

TSC (Telephone Sales Center) The department that is responsible for making and receiving telemarketing sales contacts.

Turnover rate Number of times within a year that a list is or can be rented.

Two-stage sell Process that involves two mailings or approaches—the first inviting an inquiry and the second converting the inquiry to a sale.

Typeface All printing type of a specific design.

Type specification *See* **Markup**.

Uncollectible One who hasn't paid for goods and services at the end of a normal series of collection efforts.

Undeliverable Mailing piece returned as not being deliverable; also known as a *nixie*.

Unique zip code Five-digit zip code assigned by the Postal Service to a company or organization to expedite delivery of its large volume of incoming letter mail. With the advent of zip+4, a large number of businesses and institutions now have their own unique zip code.

Unit of sale Average dollar amount spent by customers on a mailing list.

Universe Total numbers of individuals that might be included on a mailing list; all of those fitting a single set of specifications.

Update Addition of recent transactions and current information to the master (main) list to reflect the current status of each record on the list.

Up front Securing payment for a product offered by mail order before the product is sent.

UPS (United Parcel Service) A major supplier of small-package delivery.

Up-scale list Generic description of a list of affluents; can be mail-responsive or compiled.

Up-selling Promotion of more expensive products or services over the product originally discussed.

URL (Universal Resource Locator) The unique address for each page on the web. It points to the IP address and domain where the resource is located.

Usage history Record of the utilization of a given list by mailers, managers, or brokers.

U.S. Business Universe Database containing the names and addresses of virtually every business, institution, and office of a professional in the United States.

User Firm that uses telemarketing in its overall marketing program, whether it is executed in-house or by a telemarketing service vendor.

Usenet Usenet forums, called "newsgroups", are bulletin-board like forums centered around every conceivable topic of human interest and endeavor. They are always open to the public (except for the few commercial newsgroups), enabling anyone to read or post.

Utilities One of the major groupings of business lists, public service industries (such as water, power, light), often included with mining, contracting, manufacturing, and transportation as part of the industrial complex.

Validation mailing Second modest mailing to confirm initial test results prior to making a large continuation or rollout.

Variable field Way of laying out list information for formatting that assigns a specific sequence to the data, but not specific positions.

Variable-length record Means of packing characters on a name and address record so as to eliminate blank spaces. For most rental work such lists must then be reformatted to fixed fields in which each field, whether filled or unfilled, occupies the same numerical positions on a tape.

Variables (criteria) Identifiable and selectable characteristics that can be tested for mailing purposes.

Variance A summary statistic (parameter) for a sample population that is the average of squared deviations from the mean.

Vendor Supplier of any facet of direct response advertising: lists, creative, printing, marketing, computerization, merge/purge, fulfillment.

Verification Process of determining the validity of an order by sending a questionnaire to the customer.

Volume discount Scheduled discount for volume buyers of a given compiled list.

Voters registration list List utilized to add

multiple family members as well as age data to compiled consumer files.

Voucher copy Free copy of a publication sent to an advertiser or organization as evidence that an advertisement has been published.

Wallet flap envelope Special business reply envelope that utilizes the inside of a large flap to serve as the order form.

Warranty list List of buyers who mail in warranty cards identifying the particular product and its type, with or without additional demographic data.

Web browsers Graphical interface to content on the World Wide Web (e.g., Netscape, Mosaic).

Weighting (1) For evaluation of customer lists, a means of applying values to the RFUISM data for each cell (for larger lists this is better done by a computer regression analysis); (2) for merge/purge, a means of applying a form of mathematical analysis to each component for unduplicating.

White mail Incoming mail that is not on a form sent out by the advertiser; all mail other than orders and payments.

Wholesaler (reseller) Merchandiser of lists compiled or owned by others, usually working with compiled lists mainly covering a local area; differentiated from a broker by type of list and coverage.

Window envelope Envelope with a die-cut portion on the front that permits viewing the address printed on an enclosure; the die-cut window may or may not be covered with a transparent material.

Wing mailer Label-affixing device that uses strips of paper on which addresses have been printed.

With the grain When folding paper, parallel to the grain.

Word processor Computer software utilized to produce individualized letters; also use-

ful in updating and expanding smaller mailing lists.

Working women In direct mail, a relatively new selection factor. Lists may be either compiled (e.g., women executives of S&P major companies) or mail order responsive (e.g., paid subscribers to *Working Woman* magazine).

Workstation (1) Area where telephone reps perform their jobs; (2) integrated voice/data terminal.

Yield (1) Count anticipated from a computer inquiry; (2) responses received from a promotional effort; (3) mailable totals from a merge/purge.

Yuppies Young, upwardly mobile professional people.

Zip code (Zone Improvement Plan) Registered trademark of the Postal Service; a five- or nine-digit code identifying regions in the United States.

Zip code count In a list, the number of names and addresses within each zip code.

Zip code omission Loss of a zip code on a given mailing list.

Zip+4 Designation by the Postal Service for the nine-digit zip-coding structure.

Zip code sequence Arrangement of names and addresses on a list according to the numeric progression of the zip code in each record. This form of list formatting is mandatory for mailing at bulk third-class mail rates, based on the Postal Service sorting requirement.

Zip code string Merging of multiple selections into one zip code string to avoid minimums.

Z Score Also called a *standard score*. The z score for an item, indicates how far and in what direction that item deviates from its distribution's mean, expressed in units of its distribution's standard deviation.

INDEX

For More Information

Please visit our companion website at www.sdmm.com.
You will find links to complimentary articles, training aids,
resources, tools, and updated material.